T0191535

Lecture Notes in Computer Science 12181

Founding Editors

Gerhard Goos
  Karlsruhe Institute of Technology, Karlsruhe, Germany
Juris Hartmanis
  Cornell University, Ithaca, NY, USA

Editorial Board Members

Elisa Bertino
  Purdue University, West Lafayette, IN, USA
Wen Gao
  Peking University, Beijing, China
Bernhard Steffen ⓘ
  TU Dortmund University, Dortmund, Germany
Gerhard Woeginger ⓘ
  RWTH Aachen, Aachen, Germany
Moti Yung
  Columbia University, New York, NY, USA

More information about this series at http://www.springer.com/series/7409

Masaaki Kurosu (Ed.)

Human-Computer Interaction

Design and User Experience

Thematic Area, HCI 2020
Held as Part of the 22nd International Conference, HCII 2020
Copenhagen, Denmark, July 19–24, 2020
Proceedings, Part I

 Springer

Editor
Masaaki Kurosu
The Open University of Japan
Chiba, Japan

ISSN 0302-9743 ISSN 1611-3349 (electronic)
Lecture Notes in Computer Science
ISBN 978-3-030-49058-4 ISBN 978-3-030-49059-1 (eBook)
https://doi.org/10.1007/978-3-030-49059-1

LNCS Sublibrary: SL3 – Information Systems and Applications, incl. Internet/Web, and HCI

© Springer Nature Switzerland AG 2020
This work is subject to copyright. All rights are reserved by the Publisher, whether the whole or part of the material is concerned, specifically the rights of translation, reprinting, reuse of illustrations, recitation, broadcasting, reproduction on microfilms or in any other physical way, and transmission or information storage and retrieval, electronic adaptation, computer software, or by similar or dissimilar methodology now known or hereafter developed.
The use of general descriptive names, registered names, trademarks, service marks, etc. in this publication does not imply, even in the absence of a specific statement, that such names are exempt from the relevant protective laws and regulations and therefore free for general use.
The publisher, the authors and the editors are safe to assume that the advice and information in this book are believed to be true and accurate at the date of publication. Neither the publisher nor the authors or the editors give a warranty, express or implied, with respect to the material contained herein or for any errors or omissions that may have been made. The publisher remains neutral with regard to jurisdictional claims in published maps and institutional affiliations.

This Springer imprint is published by the registered company Springer Nature Switzerland AG
The registered company address is: Gewerbestrasse 11, 6330 Cham, Switzerland

Foreword

The 22nd International Conference on Human-Computer Interaction, HCI International 2020 (HCII 2020), was planned to be held at the AC Bella Sky Hotel and Bella Center, Copenhagen, Denmark, during July 19–24, 2020. Due to the COVID-19 coronavirus pandemic and the resolution of the Danish government not to allow events larger than 500 people to be hosted until September 1, 2020, HCII 2020 had to be held virtually. It incorporated the 21 thematic areas and affiliated conferences listed on the following page.

A total of 6,326 individuals from academia, research institutes, industry, and governmental agencies from 97 countries submitted contributions, and 1,439 papers and 238 posters were included in the conference proceedings. These contributions address the latest research and development efforts and highlight the human aspects of design and use of computing systems. The contributions thoroughly cover the entire field of human-computer interaction, addressing major advances in knowledge and effective use of computers in a variety of application areas. The volumes constituting the full set of the conference proceedings are listed in the following pages.

The HCI International (HCII) conference also offers the option of "late-breaking work" which applies both for papers and posters and the corresponding volume(s) of the proceedings will be published just after the conference. Full papers will be included in the "HCII 2020 - Late Breaking Papers" volume of the proceedings to be published in the Springer LNCS series, while poster extended abstracts will be included as short papers in the "HCII 2020 - Late Breaking Posters" volume to be published in the Springer CCIS series.

I would like to thank the program board chairs and the members of the program boards of all thematic areas and affiliated conferences for their contribution to the highest scientific quality and the overall success of the HCI International 2020 conference.

This conference would not have been possible without the continuous and unwavering support and advice of the founder, Conference General Chair Emeritus and Conference Scientific Advisor Prof. Gavriel Salvendy. For his outstanding efforts, I would like to express my appreciation to the communications chair and editor of HCI International News, Dr. Abbas Moallem.

July 2020   Constantine Stephanidis

HCI International 2020 Thematic Areas and Affiliated Conferences

Thematic areas:

- HCI 2020: Human-Computer Interaction
- HIMI 2020: Human Interface and the Management of Information

Affiliated conferences:

- EPCE: 17th International Conference on Engineering Psychology and Cognitive Ergonomics
- UAHCI: 14th International Conference on Universal Access in Human-Computer Interaction
- VAMR: 12th International Conference on Virtual, Augmented and Mixed Reality
- CCD: 12th International Conference on Cross-Cultural Design
- SCSM: 12th International Conference on Social Computing and Social Media
- AC: 14th International Conference on Augmented Cognition
- DHM: 11th International Conference on Digital Human Modeling and Applications in Health, Safety, Ergonomics and Risk Management
- DUXU: 9th International Conference on Design, User Experience and Usability
- DAPI: 8th International Conference on Distributed, Ambient and Pervasive Interactions
- HCIBGO: 7th International Conference on HCI in Business, Government and Organizations
- LCT: 7th International Conference on Learning and Collaboration Technologies
- ITAP: 6th International Conference on Human Aspects of IT for the Aged Population
- HCI-CPT: Second International Conference on HCI for Cybersecurity, Privacy and Trust
- HCI-Games: Second International Conference on HCI in Games
- MobiTAS: Second International Conference on HCI in Mobility, Transport and Automotive Systems
- AIS: Second International Conference on Adaptive Instructional Systems
- C&C: 8th International Conference on Culture and Computing
- MOBILE: First International Conference on Design, Operation and Evaluation of Mobile Communications
- AI-HCI: First International Conference on Artificial Intelligence in HCI

Conference Proceedings Volumes Full List

38. CCIS 1224, HCI International 2020 Posters - Part I, edited by Constantine Stephanidis and Margherita Antona
39. CCIS 1225, HCI International 2020 Posters - Part II, edited by Constantine Stephanidis and Margherita Antona
40. CCIS 1226, HCI International 2020 Posters - Part III, edited by Constantine Stephanidis and Margherita Antona

http://2020.hci.international/proceedings

Human-Computer Interaction Thematic Area (HCI 2020)

Program Board Chair: Masaaki Kurosu, The Open University of Japan, Japan

- Salah Uddin Ahmed, Norway
- Zohreh Baniasadi, Luxembourg
- Valdecir Becker, Brazil
- Nimish Biloria, Australia
- Scott Cadzow, UK
- Maurizio Caon, Switzerland
- Zhigang Chen, P.R. China
- Ulla Geisel, Germany
- Tor-Morten Groenli, Norway
- Jonathan Gurary, USA
- Kristy Hamilton, USA
- Yu-Hsiu Hung, Taiwan
- Yi Ji, P.R. China
- Lawrence Lam, USA
- Alexandros Liapis, Greece
- Bingjie Liu, USA
- Hiroshi Noborio, Japan
- Denise Pilar, Brazil
- Farzana Rahman, USA
- Manuel Rudolph, Germany
- Emmanuelle Savarit, UK
- Damian Schofield, USA
- Vinícius Segura, Brazil
- Charlotte Wiberg, Sweden

The full list with the Program Board Chairs and the members of the Program Boards of all thematic areas and affiliated conferences is available online at:

http://www.hci.international/board-members-2020.php

HCI International 2021

The 23rd International Conference on Human-Computer Interaction, HCI International 2021 (HCII 2021), will be held jointly with the affiliated conferences in Washington DC, USA, at the Washington Hilton Hotel, July 24–29, 2021. It will cover a broad spectrum of themes related to Human-Computer Interaction (HCI), including theoretical issues, methods, tools, processes, and case studies in HCI design, as well as novel interaction techniques, interfaces, and applications. The proceedings will be published by Springer. More information will be available on the conference website: http://2021.hci.international/.

General Chair
Prof. Constantine Stephanidis
University of Crete and ICS-FORTH
Heraklion, Crete, Greece
Email: general_chair@hcii2021.org

http://2021.hci.international/

Contents – Part I

Understanding Users

Usability, User Experience and Quality

Images, Visualization and Aesthetics in HCI

Contents – Part II

Speech, Voice, Conversation and Emotions

Multimodal Interaction

Human Robot Interaction

Contents – Part III

Learning, Culture and Creativity

Human Values, Ethics, Transparency and Trust

HCI in Complex Environments

Design Theory, Methods and Practice in HCI

Applying Designing Lines to Develop Audiovisual Systems

Valdecir Becker[✉], Daniel Gambaro, Rafael M. Toscano,
Helder Bruno A. M. de Souza, Thayná dos S. Gomes,
Maria C. D. Silva, and Ed Porto Bezerra

Audiovisual Design Research Group, Informatics Center,
Federal University of Paraíba, João Pessoa, PB, Brazil
audiovisualdesign@lavid.ufpb.br

Abstract. This article describes the use of Designing Lines for the development of an audiovisual system. The Designing Lines comprise a set of recommendations for developing strategies related to content, identity, motivation and experience, focusing on each of the four roles of Audiovisual Design model. To test the concept of the Lines, an application was developed for a TV newscast, including a web portal for viewing the data collected from the interaction of individuals. In conclusion, this research points out that the Designing Lines are important elements for the Producer to plan and execute content adapted to the demands of individuals.

Keywords: Audiovisual Design · Designing Lines · Audiovisual systems

1 Introduction

This paper describes what are "Designing Lines" and their uses for development and production of audiovisual content. Designing Lines are a part of Audiovisual Design (AD), a theoretical-methodological model to assess the creation and analysis of audiovisual systems, converging elements from Human-Computer Interaction (HCI) and Media Studies. As the audiovisual industry continuously presents more integration with software development, the AD model becomes necessary due to its capability of addressing the converging chain of creation, production and consumption [1]. Content, under such perspective, is defined as the textual, aural and visual components, aligned with the graphical interfaces that allow interactions. A complex audiovisual system is a configuration that includes the content, the hardware and software that support the interfaces, as well as the infrastructure for storage, recovery and transmission.

There are four Designing Lines: Line of Content, Line of Identity, Line of Motivation and Line of Experience. These lines hold general orientations, serving as foci for creators and producers when conceiving the different elements of an audiovisual system. The AD also indicates that there are four main roles to be performed by people in contact with the audiovisual system, each one representing a level of activity, from passive fruition to creation of derivative pieces: 1) Audience, 2) Synthesizer, 3) Modifier and 4) Producer. People in each role may reach an elevated level when they

© Springer Nature Switzerland AG 2020
M. Kurosu (Ed.): HCII 2020, LNCS 12181, pp. 3–19, 2020.
https://doi.org/10.1007/978-3-030-49059-1_1

explore advanced or hidden features of the content: they are called 'Players'. The Lines, thus, shall help creators and developers to consider the diverse expectations, uses and competences of individuals who have access to the content, considering that these elements may vary according to each different role.

Two sets of knowledges are presented as tools to analyze how the roles are performed and the application of Designing Lines in content development: from a consumption perspective, it is called Configuration of Fruition; and from the perspective of creation and development of workpieces, it is called Configuration of Design. Although the first approach will be briefly mentioned, this paper will focus mainly in the second one. In summary, the Configuration of Design starts from the strategies of the Producer, i.e., the individual or group responsible for designing the content and configuring the audiovisual system. From the analysis of data about audience, behavior and market, the Producer defines the work's scopes. Regarding the Audience, the focus resides on the individuality and on private fruition; for the Synthesizer, the creation of identity is fundamental; and for the Modifier and the elevated role Player, the experience resulting from the interaction is the most important aspect. Each focus has correspondence with a different Line of Design. Therefore, the Producer's connections with Audience occurs primarily through the Line of Identity; Synthesizer, through the Line of Motivation; Modifier, through the Line of Experience. The connections, however, are not exclusive, and most times there occur a combination of strategies to guide the design of the content.

To illustrate the use of Designing Lines in the development of an audiovisual system, it will be presented and analyzed the case of the 'JPB1' mobile application. JBP1 is a TV newscast, and the app must engage viewership and promote the program, preferably through the change of roles between Audience, Synthesizer and Producer. The Designing Lines help to conceive elements to the application, so to provide experiences with 'catch-up' and exclusive in-app content besides the live broadcast of the newscast.

2 The Audiovisual Design Model

The Audiovisual Design is a theoretical-methodological model that covers the entire ecology from the development to the fruition of complex audiovisual systems, comprising the content, the expectations and strategies for its fruition, the relationship of individuals with the workpieces, and the different software platforms used for production, distribution and interaction. The Model's premise is that software and interaction interfaces play an important part in the production, distribution and fruition of audiovisual works.

Fruition is understood as the entire process, or relationship, involving audiovisual content, beginning with the selection of content and continuing with the use or interaction, the consumption or enjoyment, appropriation, modification, and evaluation. Also, fruition is mediated by interaction interfaces. Software is more and more determinant of the availability of media products, their distribution models and the decisions regarding their consumption. The curation is divided between humans and machine [2], with possible predominance of algorithms in some contexts. On the one hand, software provides a better adjustment of content to individuals. On the other hand, there is a risk of limiting access due to filters placed between the delivery mechanisms and the point of access [3, 4].

A similar perspective may be applied to the development of software for video repositories, social media or any other application that uses audiovisual content. Software like these have a straight connection to audiovisual elements. Films, music concerts, TV shows, texts and memes can motivate the audience to seek and learn how to use software, hence the interfaces mediate one's good experience. Good interfaces make it easy for individuals to interact and engage, while bad graphical designs with deficient implementations can compromise the enjoyment of the workpieces. For that reason, Audiovisual Design sustains that an audiovisual system is more than simply the audio or video content, it must include the hardware and software that supports interfaces, storage, recovery and transmission networks.

The AD model indicates that individuals can perform four different roles when they engage with complex audiovisual systems. A first-level role is called *Audience*, i.e., all people who watch and interact with the content in a non-sophisticated way, that is, the traditional fruition when someone passively watches or listens to audiovisual works, mainly receiving the content. From the moment the individuals identify with the content or part of it, and start to comment and share data online about it – mainly in social media, they are acting as the second-level role *Synthesizers*. These are individuals with more activity, whose interactions are basically commentary and simple online sharing of information. As the engagement increases, then emerges the motivation to interfere with the work, modifying and appropriating part of it. This third-level role is called *Modifier*, and requires some competences related to software usage such as programming and sound and video editing. People in this level alter the original content, by means of participation, changes or recreation of narrative elements. The most complex level of fruition of audiovisual systems is occupied by the role of *Producer*. Further then possessing competences required to perform the other roles, Producers – acting alone or in teams – are responsible for the creation, production and distribution of the workpieces, including the design of content, development of strategies for the act of fruition undertaken by the other roles, and the provision of all tools required to viewing and interaction. In summary, the Producer configures the audiovisual system, choosing the storage, recovery and transmission infrastructures that better corresponds to the content's purpose. Finally, there can be non-predicted uses and interactions undertaken by individuals in any role, in many cases subverting the original intentions placed on of a workpiece: these activities are performed by people acting as the elevated role *Player*.

Figure 1 shows how Audiovisual Design converges two knowledge areas for a complete comprehension of production and fruition of audiovisual content. The first one is called Configuration of Fruition and contemplates theories and concepts of media studies to understand the relationship of individuals with the workpieces. From an analysis of how individuals perceive value in the content and the manner they interact with it, it is possible to detail how they alternate between roles. The individual configures the best way to enjoy the content and the interfaces, using the tools and affordances available from the audiovisual system. The Configuration of Fruition allows analyzing, during the act of fruition, how individuals receive the content, physically and psychologically, how they interpret the information, how they are affected in short and long term by it, and how they insert information to feedback the audiovisual system. This Configuration algo includes analyses of behavior and of the development of abilities and competences that stimulate the complete fruition of audiovisual workpieces.

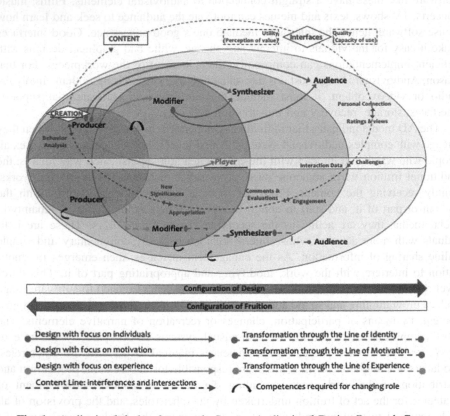

Fig. 1. Audiovisual design framework. Source: Audiovisual Design Research Group.

The second knowledge set, named Configuration of Design, is based on theories and methods of HCI, aiming at the appropriate design of content. This configuration aims at the individuals' good fruition experience, thus taking as central elements the processes of creation, development, production, transmission and implementation of audiovisual elements and interaction artefacts. The Configuration of Design also includes the processes of and methods for creation of audiovisual works, especially scripting, production and output technics for different media and platforms.

The relation between the two Configurations is analyzable from the perspective of utility and quality of the product. Utility comes mainly from the perception of value regarding the content, and can be divided in two approaches, referring to intrinsic and extrinsic values of the works. The intrinsic value is expressed by the truly audiovisual elements of the workpieces, including the script, the narrative, environment, soundtrack, artists, among others. In summary, all audiovisual components of the workpiece. The extrinsic value, on its turn, is related to elements external to the work, such as the underlying characteristics of the product, e.g., whether it is meant for TV, cinema, digital, online, sound media etc. For instance, the value of TV as background and Cinema as arts: in this case, value is found in how the product is presented instead of in its content.

In contrast, quality derives from the capacity of people to use interfaces and perceive their affordances. Usability represents a crucial point in quality, one that may be expressed as the capacity of use adapted to different audience profiles. Utility and quality together lead to a satisfying experience of fruition. The Producer, who, according to Audiovisual Design, has the competences of software development, holds the obligation to ensure that utility and quality are correctly perceived by individuals.

Therefore, the creation and development of products start from the Configuration of Design. Conversely, the analysis of concluded workpieces departs from the Configuration of Fruition. As a response to the first Configuration, the Audiovisual Design model seeks to provide essential tools for the development of audiovisual systems that meets the specificities of each role performed by individuals. These tools include the Designing Lines, media affordances and triggers. To examine concluded works, AD provides resources to investigate identity, motivation and experience from the individuals' point of view.

3 The Concept of Designing Lines

The Designing Lines are general orientations for creators, producers and developers to conceive the different elements of an audiovisual system, considering the different roles performed by individuals, as well as the competences required in each level to alternate between roles. Thus, each Line is composed by theoretical and conceptual sets, oriented to the four roles and their elevated instances, being useful to structure the entire experience of fruition that may be expected by the individuals: a concern under the Configuration of Design.

The Designing Lines help the producer or developer of content to draw up strategies to comply with Configurations of Fruition, focusing on specific results that varies in accordance to the individuals' behaviors, expectations and demands. Different uses, interactions, markets and available technologies must be considered on the side of fruition, and so they must be incorporated in the designing process.

Once, according to the AD model, interaction is mediated by interfaces, *media affordances* become a key concept [5]. Affordances are perceived through indicative elements, present both in traditional media and audiovisual systems, that direct to meanings and means of fruition. When the producer desires that individuals change roles during the fruition, then it is required a correct perception of affordances, associated with the environment designed for fruition.

Authors [5] summarized the sources of media affordances as: a) Physical, affordances materialized in elements that can be actively manipulated, with clear potential uses, composed by technologies used for fruition of content; b) Graphical, affordances present in interactional graphical interfaces implemented by software, in part responsible for the mediation between content and individuals; c) Symbolic, affordances originated in the storytelling or inserted amid the audiovisual elements, mainly when physical affordances are more subtle; the resulting cognitive and sensory perceptions depend upon social, cultural, aesthetic and narrative elements besides the technology and the available interface.

Media affordances are hence connected to *Interaction Triggers*, i.e., elements planned by the Producer that, during the fruition, invite the individuals to perform an action (to view, to spread, to participate, to pay attention etc.). From the moment an individual perceives value in an element and identify the available affordances, this trigger leads to an action. For instance, a 'share' button inserted in the content indicates to the individual [using the audiovisual system] that a new interaction mode is available (a new affordance). This button, then, is an Interaction Trigger, since it influences a given behavior that leads to greater engagement of the individual with the audiovisual system.

Interaction Triggers take the form of sound and visual elements, interface and interaction features, or even a 'call for action' inserted in the narrative (e.g., an invitation hidden in a conversation between two characters during a movie). The AD model presents two types of triggers: Trigger of Action and Trigger of Inertia. The first one stimulates the perception of value or of utility regarding the audiovisual system, to increase engagement. For example, a person can leave the Audience level while watching a TV show to become a Synthesizer that share impressions about the content on the internet. Put differently, this is a movement of the individual that, encouraged by the trigger, change roles from the right to the left in the AD framework (Fig. 1).

The Trigger of Inertia, instead, stimulates the individual to receive the content by means of greater attention, analysis or interpretation. This trigger stimulates inertia or a relaxation during interaction, securing more passivity during fruition. Considering the AD model (Fig. 1), Triggers of Inertia enables changing roles from the left to the right. As example, a sudden audio vignette during the same TV show may call the attention of the individual, who momentaneous leaves the role of Synthesizer to act as Audience watching the program.

3.1 The Line of Content

Before continuing, it is worth remembering that, according to the Audiovisual Design (AD), content are the audiovisual elements (visual and sound elements combined) plus interfaces responsible for interaction in the proposed audiovisual system. As a result, the Line of Content is inscribed in the entire flux of activities envisaged by the AD model, substantiating the scheme of sets represented by Fig. 1. Interaction occurs by means of interfaces after the perception of utility and quality.

Initially, the Line of Content corresponds to the producer's intention to communicate something. This Line defines the components of the workpiece that allow the perceptions of utility and quality. Since content comprises the interfaces, it is a qualitative aspect whether the possibilities of action (affordances) are evident to individuals as *triggers*. The utility of the workpiece is perceived through interpretation and analysis of static elements, such as texts and pictures, and dynamic ones, such as sounds and moving images.

Following the Line of Content, the Producer shall create and produce elements to every portion of an audiovisual system, considering the roles performed by individuals and the competences required to alternate between them. To people performing the role of Audience, the content must provide personal connection and substantiate the creation of identity; in return, it shall be possible to generate behavior analyses, which shall help the Producer to evolve the system. Regarding the Synthesizer, the conception of the content must incorporate strategies to promote the engagement of individuals, thus generating commentaries and evaluations of the workpieces. For the Modifier level, the Line of Content supports strategies to allow the appropriation of the content and attribution of new meanings through modifications and recreation. As example, the Producer makes available part of the content in a free access format, to allow manipulation through pre-defined software tools, perhaps allowing adjustments in the story.

The Producer, once responsible for the creation of the workpiece, closes the cycle of fruition by evaluating data about behaviors related to each piece of the audiovisual system. The analysis might present four core elements: the technical operation of interaction artefacts; the alternance of roles and the corresponding knowledge of triggers; the perception of value and utility; and the development of strategies to evolve the work (including new audiovisual elements or the incorporation of interaction resources). The Producer may, then, identify demands originated during the fruition and solve them by planning new affordances and implementing Interaction Triggers. The nature of each demand corresponds to each role performed by individuals and the related Configuration of Fruition. Regarding the development of media affordances and Interaction Triggers, the Producer must have sufficient knowledge about the technologies to support the content, especially the available interaction artefacts and the audiovisual language (narrative, interactive and fruition) that will be part of the system.

3.2   The Line of Identity

The Line of Identity was described by Becker, Gambaro and Ramos [6] as responsible for generating identification of individuals with audiovisual workpieces. It is a core element to the audience recognition and, consequently, to the commercial success of the products, irrespective of whether it is entertainment, journalistic, instructional or technical.

The definition originated from the observation of how the audiovisual language endorses ties with spectators, establishing a medium as a mediator of reality both through factual journalistic coverage and the reconstruction of reality as perceived through drama productions [7]. Narrative aspects such as characters, situations, locations or even the whole story universe enable individuals to perceive value in the content and to feel they belong to, or are represented by, the workpiece. In the case of instructional products, further then these elements, the content contextualization, the use of visual assets and resources for learning, and the availability of information are also elements that may stimulate the identification with the workpiece.

Although this approach is more common when TV is observed because the medium creates affective ties with viewers through its show formats, we may extend it to cinema and video productions, which represent a significant part of all audiovisual content available today. Throughout history, social changes were incorporated in fictional narratives [8], proposing a synthesis of the reality. Taking the Brazilian TV as an example, drama scripts have been elaborated so the audience assimilate the narrative, developing a psychological and emotional involvement [9]. Viewers recognize themselves (their realities, even if romanticized) on what they are watching, and that endorses the legitimacy of the audiovisual drama. As part of the same movement, the current audiovisual fiction also reflects the weakening of shared identities and the strengthening of individualities, sustaining the idea of an emancipated subject [10] whose identity reflects the fragmentation of all aspects of the quotidian life [11]. The contemporary subject come up with consumption strategies to try creating a coherent self and the sensation of a historically conquered autonomy [12, 13]. The audiovisual productions become, then, an important element to support and promote an idealized identity.

The process of identification relates to two facts regarding the use of audiovisual information and communication technologies: the expansion of communication possibilities and the expression of the self. First, technologies increase the communication reach with ubiquitous systems of information transmission, storage and recovery. If access was constrained by physical aspects of time and space, now it is independent from locality and from the specific moment when content was made available. Second, technologies allow people to self-expression, potentialized through a renewed visibility [14] on an online universe, sometimes acting as sources of information. Media unidirectionality, when a few producing companies generated material for a dispersed audience, gave space for environments dominated by collaboration, customization and decentralized production, as described in the AD model. From the moment the individuals recognize themselves as potential creators and value generators, they construct *selves as a source* of communication. Sundar [15] points that *self as a source* is central for the success of computer-mediated communication forms. When the system allows the self to serve as the source of messages, the communication becomes truly interpersonal.

In summary, as a result of the process, people identify with the audiovisual workpieces that come to represent their construed selves. This performance that are effective from the screens confirms an affective relationship with the content, first generating the engagement to uphold and propagate the work, and later the appropriation of parts of it (or even of the entire work) under illimited possibilities for modifications. Sundar named this process 'agency', or the sensation of being relevant to online interactions [15].

3.3   The Line of Motivation

From the process of identification there is a natural change in the relationship of individuals with the content. The mediation of reality, which generates a first step for identification, gradually rises a purpose, or a desire, to be closer to some elements of the workpiece. This perception of value derived from the Line of Content leads to engagement. This process is based on motivation, described here as the activator or awakener of behaviors, in general oriented to satisfy a necessity or to fulfil a desire.

Thus, we are referring to an inner state of the individual, resulting from varied perceptions about the content that are responses to identity and to some related demands.

The origins of motivation, or motivational factors, can be internal or external [16]. In the first case it is called intrinsic motivation, described as the human inclination to assimilation, domination, spontaneous curiosity and exploration, all of which are essential to social and cognitive development. It also contemplates values and pleasures associated to personal and individual activities.

External factors are extrinsic motivations. In this case, the focus is an external objective that carries some type of gratification. That is, the individual tries to reach an external goal. Motivations of this type may vary with relative autonomy, implicating in personal efforts when the individual faces possible alternatives and the fulfilment of regulations and social practices to achieve the goal. In this case, the Line of Motivation also embraces the notion of community among individuals, encouraging relationships to allow exchange of information about the work.

In summary, the perceptions of utility and quality carried out through the Line of Content generate intrinsic motivations. Especially the perception of value about the content, notwithstanding whether informative or entertainment, generate mental states important for personal satisfaction. The consciousness and comprehension of the world represented in the audiovisual content can be considered a state of mind, leading to some action.

Thus, following the Line of Motivation, it is possible to predict an increase in the individuals' activity level, derived from the promptness in using the original product to communicate something about themselves, for example, through social media. Engagement is increased when one associates with elements from the workpiece, bringing pleasure in any kind of *participation*. The engagement becomes an extrinsic motivation, then, when the individuals identified with the content develop emotional commitment to the action afforded by the content. Subsequently, a kind of complicity arises, through which individuals agree to experience the same meanings in terms of content and, in exchange, receive an infinitude of new possibilities of action and emotion.

The relationship, both with the content and with the Producer, also includes trust, power and status of the individual who assume any of the other roles. Their networked activities with other people or with/directed to the Producer feeds a reputation level [17] that, at the same time, also becomes one among other factors that motivate sharing. So, Producers must understand the individuals' participation as important and desirable. From this moment on, the Line of Motivation mix with the Line of Identity, because the actions depend upon representation of the *selves* projected by the individuals, as well as their intentions of agency. Both Identity and Motivation Lines sustain a complementary relationship that allows individuals to alternate roles between Synthesizers and Modifiers.

3.4   The Line of Experience

The Line of Experience condenses the characteristics of the other Lines (identity, engagement, motivation) and sums up elements for creation, appropriation, revision, remediation and participation. By incorporating complex activities in the circuit of production, it enables individuals as Modifiers, coproducers or autonomous producers. Motivation and engagement reach the highest levels in this Line, allowing the individuals a stronger and deeper emotional and psychological relationship with the content. The construction of the self is consolidated, and agency becomes a core feature to lend credibility to new productions or modified ones.

It is important to highlight that Experience may be analyzed according to time, considering short-term and long-term fruition. While in short-term fruition a sense of well-being and satisfaction with the process are essential, in long-term fruition consolidation of competences is preponderant to the immersion of individuals in the processes of creation and production.

The described characteristics can be found in every activity performed by individuals in any role affected by the Line of Experience, regardless whether it is professional or amateur, for- or non-profit. To summarize this description, this text will now focus on professional for-profit productions, being the amateur non-profit productions a suggestion for future works to continue the current investigation.

The Line of Experience presupposes contributions to an existing work. Some modification made by the public can add value, thus serving to improve the perceived utility of the audiovisual system, even when directed to a niche of public. Whilst for the roles of Audience and Synthesizer utility is intrinsically perceived in the content and is related to the formation of identity and motivations, Modifiers and Producers combine commercial and/or eudaimonic elements to perceive value.

In the specific case of professional activities, the Line of Experience conducts the individuals to a mental immersion on the creation, or recreation, of workpieces. During production or modification of works, the creative and technical process requires understanding and analysis of demands, desires and needs from the other roles performed by individuals, including full knowledge of abilities and competences required and available for a complete fruition. Besides, motivation and identification with works during production or modification are directly related to professional activities. It doesn't matter whether the workpiece has or doesn't have a commercial purpose, motivation relies on financial aspects and potential monetary gains. The identity will, later, reinforce the consumer's credibility regarding how the content was generated.

On the other hand, on amateur production or modification, satisfaction and personal well-being are more relevant than eventual monetary gain. On the simplest examples of amateur production, when the distribution occurs inside restricted, private circuits of known people, normally the focus is not on the workpiece, but on the process of production or modification. For example, a person mashes up personal photos with scenes of a favorite movie and a preferred song to pay a tribute to a family member; the symbology and the event are more important than the nature of the song or movie. In this example, the personal satisfaction and the sensation of relevance overcomes any other motivation.

4   Analysis of the Use of Designing Lines in the Development of 'JPB1' Mobile Application

To validate the theory of Designing Lines, the concepts were applied in the development of a mobile app for a TV News program, Jornal da Paraíba First Edition (JPB1), broadcast by TV Cabo Branco, a regional station that tops the audience ranking in the Paraíba Estate, Northeast Region of Brazil. The app became necessary when the newscast production team wanted to obtain more information about its audience. Data provided by Kantar IBOPE, the company responsible for audience research in Brazil, are collected through notes made by the viewers themselves, then they are registered and made available only twice a year. Moreover, data are restricted to quantitative information about the viewership of the newscast, showing only the basic composition of the audience: gender, age and social class.

Since it is a regional newscast, the main demand is for local news and current affairs that matters to people living in the area. Furthermore, being a live transmission, it is important to know in real time whether the audience is enjoying the programming. The agenda definition and duration of segments may vary according to the reaction of the audience during the newscast.

Given this background, the AD research team started to format the Line of Content. From the premise that individuals shall perceive utility and quality to interact with the app, it was decided that it should be interesting during the show's broadcast as well as throughout the day. So, the live broadcast is vital. An individual may watch the newscast on free-to-air TV or via mobile app, with options to 'like' or discuss each news, segment or reportage. Every broadcast news is available for latter visualization.

To comply with the requirements for localization and more details on information, an initial subscription was created: name, gender, age, neighborhood and social class (Fig. 2a), to start to know the newscast audience's characteristics and their georeferencing data.

The acquired data were used to start the formatting of the Line of Identity. Journalism, more specifically TV journalism, usually generates automatic identification of individuals through news coverage. The concept of noticeability criteria [18], commonly used for selection of facts to become news, considers elements regarding identification of the public with the reported matter, mainly for value attribution and geographical proximity. A news should be released if the facts are considered interesting, meaningful and relevant enough for the public.

Therefore, the content that is shown in the newscast already generates identity. However, it was noticed that this form of identification, present on television, may not be immediately transferred to the app users. At this point, it became clear a demand for an additional motivation for using the application. This additional demand is fulfilled with backstage videos and teasers of novelties to be introduced in the JPB1. The backstage videos show how people act in the newsroom, pranks with reporters, presenters and other team members, and behind-the-scenes of news coverage and feature series. It also includes material such as unpublished interviews or entire investigations that didn't make to the TV program due to time constraints. The app also makes available all reportages presented on JPB1 (Fig. 3a).

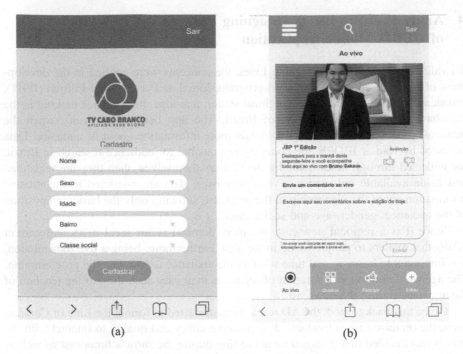

Fig. 2. (a) Page of access to JPB1 App; (b) Main page of JPB1 App. Source: screen capture of prototype of JPB1 app, made on Aug 15, 2019.

This example of expansion of content in the app still? corresponds to the Line of Identity, leaving the realms of representation through identification with the news to another type of identification: a personal bound with the team that generates the information. This increasing connection between audience and the audiovisual system, formed by the mobile application and the newscast, generates an intersection with the Line of Motivation (which, in this example, derives from the Line of Identity).

Following the Line of Motivation, the app promotes sending comments about any content related to JPB1 during the transmission. The message may or may not be displayed during the newscast, a decision to be taken by the production team. When it is displayed, it increases the identification of the individual with the program and boosts engagement and motivation to expression of the *self*, leading to agency. The sensation of being praised, listened to and respected (eudaimonic) is crucial for a long-lasting engagement with the show.

The maximum expression of this engagement with JPB First Edition is the possibility to send suggestions of topics and material produced by the public to segments of the show. These items compose the Line of Experience. In the first case, people are invited (Trigger of Action) to send general suggestions of topics (through video, text and audio), or specific themes for a chosen segment. The individual can record details about the suggested topic, narrate a fact, take pictures of something interesting and send them to the production team. Moreover, they can send messages to family members, friends, public people etc., which are read or displayed on air (Fig. 3a and b). As well,

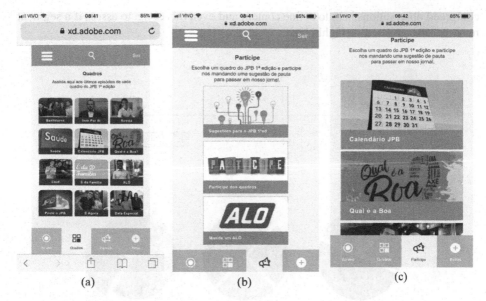

(a)   (b)   (c)

Fig. 3. (a) The audience can watch again the reportages exhibited in segments of JPB; (b) Channels the JPB1's audience can use to participate in the program during all day; (c) Suggestions can be sent directly to segments of JPB1. Source: screen capture of prototype of JPB1 app, made on Aug 15, 2019.

the segment Chef JPB once a week presents recipes of typical dishes from the region, and then invites the audience to make the dish at home, record a video with the result and send it to the producers.

A relevant factor in the formatting of the Designing Lines is the perception of quality in the app, or the capacity of the individual to fully use its resources. The newscast's audience profile varies in terms of age, social condition and education. To conform with such profile, the graphic design and the information architecture favor the simplicity and functionality of the interfaces. After login, if the newscast is on air, the user is directed to the Live page (Fig. 2b); if not, then the individual will see a page with the 'last edition' videos (Fig. 2b).

The bottom of the app show four icons to make the navigation easer. The first one is the 'Live' section, which is also the main page (Fig. 2b). The second one is the Segments (Fig. 3a), giving access to content displayed on segments of JPB1 (Chef JPB, Qual é a Boa?, É da Família, Calendário JPB and Saúde), besides videos informing about the backstage, what's new and factual information. The third icon shows the Take Part (Fig. 3a and b), encouraging the individuals to produce content. The fourth icon shows exclusive material in the app, being called Extra.

There is a web-based portal where the production team can access statistic data about the profile of JPB1's audience, generating daily, weekly and monthly reports (Fig. 4). Besides the total amount of interactions, this monitoring can provide more detailed data, concerning specific segments of the newscast (Fig. 5a and b). These continued observations help to define content and even more, e.g. to assess if a segment must be discontinued or highlighted.

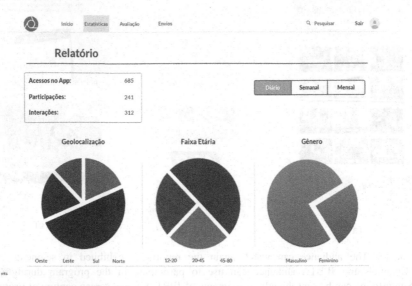

Fig. 4. Screen showing statistic data about JPB1's audience. Source: screen capture of computer desktop made on Sep. 20, 2019.

To analyze the mobile application's functionalities and usability, two tests were conducted with users. The first test, with the audience, selected 47 viewers to participate in a usability test followed by a feedback form about quality and perception of value. Since the objective of our group is to stimulate, facilitate and increase the engagement of JPB1's audience with the newscast, participants were chosen among people who watches the show, frequently or not. Everyone answered that the app is interesting, bring novelties, is easy to use and stimulate the participation in the TV program. 19 users suggested improvements, such as allow to download material and individual feedback to each commentary or suggestion of topic sent to the production team.

For the second test, five members of the newscast team, among management, edition and production, were chosen to experiment with the portal. They confirmed the relevance of the information, the simple usage and an improvement in the knowledge about the audience.

Fig. 5. (a) Detailed information about JPB1's audience participation; (b) Detailed information about JPB1's audience interaction activities. Source: screen capture of prototype of JPB1 app, made on Aug 15, 2019.

5 Conclusion

This paper detailed the theory of Designing Lines, described as general orientations for creator, producers and developers to conceive different elements in an audiovisual system, considering roles assumed by individuals during the fruition of content and the required competences for them to alternate between roles. It is a key concept inside the framework of the Audiovisual Design model, integrating elements from Human-Computer Interaction and Media Studies to develop complex audiovisual systems.

From a theoretical and conceptual analysis of Roles and Lines, the Audiovisual Design was fully applied in the development of a mobile application for the TV newscast JPB1. The objective is to engage the public who watches the newscast, thus providing detailed information about its composition and behavior. The app allows the viewer to perform any of the four roles described in the AD model: Audience, Synthesizer, Modifier and Producer. The most expressive role – also the focus of JPB1's journalism team – is the Synthesizer, who can compile, classify, comment, recommend and share the pieces of content they enjoy, thus bounding to, and creating identity with, the newscast.

The relationship of the program's production team with the roles rely on the four Designing Lines: Content, Identity, Motivation and Experience. The Line of Content focus on the audiovisual system, that is, the journalistic content of JPB1, exclusive behind-the-scenes videos and other content present in the app, interfaces for interaction and participation, and the software and hardware connecting all these parts. The content available through the app is used by individuals to alternate between roles.

Taking as example a video posted on the application from the segment Chef JPB, which provides culinary recipes, a viewer may only view the content (Audience). But, if through the Line of Identity (e.g., the exhibition of the recipe may bring memories of the childhood, or it can strength the bounds with the sense of belonging to a place) she is motivated to "like" the recipe, comment on the post about this connection, or share it with friends, this individual becomes a Synthesizer.

Moreover, if the recipe motivates the viewer to make her on version of the dish, she may record it and send the video to JPB1's newsroom via the app's social media (this tool, although foreseen as a proposal for future developments of the app, is not yet implemented), or even post it on her own social media profile tagging the program. In every case, the individual will be performing an action implemented through the Line of Motivation.

And nothing prevents the individuals to take the Line of Experience and, using their knowledge of interactive resources and other required software, modify a content originally published in JPB1's app, so they can republish it on the same tool or in any other available, following the communication model described by Jenkins, Green and Ford [19] as *spreadable*. JPB1's app case study proves that the alternance between roles is a pertinent feature, and that Designing Lines are an important tool for content production.

Some limitations were identified during this research. First, the Line of Motivation was treated only as a concept, without the required theoretical exploration. It is of utmost importance to incorporate theories and analyze a real process that indicates how the content can generate intrinsic and extrinsic motivation, beyond the persuasion needed for engagement. Second, during the description of the Line of Experience to make this text clearer, it was decided to focus on the analysis of professional for-profit activities, being amateur non-profit activities a suggestion for future research, together with the development of the Line of Motivation.

Finally, as a third point to be further investigated, arises the question whether a given Line always derives from another. In the given example of JPB1's mobile app, the Line of Motivation derives from the Identity, since it is a strengthening of bounds through additional content on the app that incites engagement and the change of role from Audience to Synthesizer. However, there is a possibility this is an exclusive case, and the three lines more easily only intersect with each other instead of being derivatives. Further investigations are required to determine how frequent occurs intersections or derivations of processes as evolutions of the Lines.

References

1. Becker, V., Gambaro, D., Ramos, T.S.: Audiovisual design and the convergence between HCI and audience studies. In: Kurosu, M. (ed.) HCI 2017. LNCS, vol. 10271, pp. 3–22. Springer, Cham (2017). https://doi.org/10.1007/978-3-319-58071-5_1
2. Martel, F.: Smart: o que você não sabe sobre a internet. Editora José Olympio, Rio De Janeiro (2015)
3. Pariser, E.: O filtro invisível: o que a internet está escondendo de você. Zahar, Rio De Janeiro (2012)
4. Van Dijck, J., Poell, T.: Understanding social media logic. Media Commun. 1(1), 2–14 (2013). https://doi.org/10.17645/mac.v1i1.70
5. Becker, V., Gambaro, D., Saraiva Ramos, T., Moura Toscano, R.: Audiovisual design: introducing 'media affordances' as a relevant concept for the development of a new communication model. In: Abásolo, M.J., Abreu, J., Almeida, P., Silva, T. (eds.) jAUTI 2017. CCIS, vol. 813, pp. 17–31. Springer, Cham (2018). https://doi.org/10.1007/978-3-319-90170-1_2
6. Gambaro, D., Ramos, T.S., Becker, V.: TV drama, representation and engagement. In: Abásolo, M.J., Silva, T., González, N.D. (eds.) jAUTI 2018. CCIS, vol. 1004, pp. 43–59. Springer, Cham (2019). https://doi.org/10.1007/978-3-030-23862-9_4
7. Machado, A.: A televisão levada a sério. Editora Senac, São Paulo (2019)
8. de Lopes, M.I.V.: Telenovela as a communicative resource. Matrizes 3, 21 (2011). https://doi.org/10.11606/issn.1982-8160.v3i1p21-47
9. Bucci, E.: Brasil em tempo de TV. Editora Boitempo, São Paulo (1996)
10. Harvey, D.: Condição pós-moderna. Editora Loyola, São Paulo (2011)
11. Hall, S.: A identidade cultural na pós-modernidade. Editora TupyKurumin, Rio De Janeiro (2006)
12. Ortiz, R.: A moderna tradição brasileira: cultura brasileira e industria cultural. Editora Brasiliense, São Paulo (1994)
13. Elliott, A., du Gay, P.: Identity in Question. SAGE Publications Ltd., London (2009)
14. Thompson, J.B.: The new visibility. Matrizes 1, 15 (2008). https://doi.org/10.11606/issn.1982-8160.v1i2p15-38
15. Sundar, S.S.: Self as source: agency and customization in interactive media. In: Konijn, E.A., Utz, S., Tanis, M., Barnes, S.B. (eds.) Mediated Interpersonal Communication, pp. 72–88. Routledge, New York (2008)
16. Deci, E.L., Ryan, R.M.: The "what" and "why" of goal pursuits: human needs and the self-determination of behavior. Psychol. Inq. 11, 227–268 (2000). https://doi.org/10.1207/S15327965PLI1104_01
17. Jenkins, H.: Convergence Culture: Where Old and New Media Collide. NYU Press, New York (2008)
18. Traquina, N.: Teorias do jornalismo. Editora Insular, Florianópolis (2005)
19. Jenkis, H., Ford, S., Green, J.: Spredable Media: Creating Value and Meaning in a Networked Culture. NYU Press, New York (2018)

"Boundaries Do Not Sit Still" from Interaction to Agential Intra-action in HCI

Claude Draude[(⊠)]

Faculty of Electrical Engineering and Computer Science,
University of Kassel, Kassel, Germany
claude.draude@uni-kassel.de

Abstract. We live in a world that is increasingly shaped through computational technology. The expansion and pervasiveness of computing brings along opportunities and challenges for the field of HCI. New application domains evolve and technological advances pose novel interaction possibilities. But with computing's shaping power comes also the need for increased responsibility and attention to the societal, political and ecological impact of technology. In this conceptual paper, new materialist thinking is employed to locate these societal etc. aspects as inextricably enmeshed within computing research and development. New materialism is a multi-vocal, cross-disciplinary field of doing-thinking. In contrast to Western dichotomic tradition, a monistic, post-anthropocentric perspective is provided and matter as an active agent in world-making is acknowledged. Central to this paper is the questioning of the human and computer dichotomy at the core of the field of HCI. For this, a material-semiotic perspective on human-computer interaction is elaborated upon. Furthermore, the paradigm of interaction is revisited and reworked as a conception of agential intra-action, a term coined by physicist Karen Barad. From this interrogation of dichotomies and the notion of intra-action follow further conceptual shifts that are discussed as productive for the future of HCI, namely responsibility as specification of ethical agency and performativity in contrast to representationalism.

Keywords: HCI methods and theories · Philosophy of computing · Computing and humanities · New materialism · Posthumanism · Epistemology

1 Introduction

In computing, the way we think, structure and conceptualize is very closely related to the way we construct and build technology. Reinvestigating key principles or assumptions that constitute computing and its sub-fields gains even more significance in a world that is increasingly transformed through digitalization. In 1948, Alan Turing cautioned humanity against intelligent machinery being allowed to "roam the countryside" [2]. Contrary to this, the expansion and pervasiveness of computing technology throughout the last decades have been enormous. Today, the machines not just roam the countryside; they influence the majority of life domains.

Karen Barad [1].

© Springer Nature Switzerland AG 2020
M. Kurosu (Ed.): HCII 2020, LNCS 12181, pp. 20–32, 2020.
https://doi.org/10.1007/978-3-030-49059-1_2

Historically, the evolution from early large machines to desktop computers as work tools to today's leisure devices and digital infrastructures led to qualitative and functional shifts in interaction and usage scenarios. With these developments the image of computer users changed considerably from a few experts/programmers to the diversity of everyday users – calling for interaction technology that is usable for all in a variety of contexts [3, 4].

Assessing the future impact of technologies is never trivial and the challenge increases with complexity and ubiquity. To give just two examples: First, the invention of the World Wide Web in 1989 by Tim Berners-Lee altered the way people could interact with the Internet and, more importantly, how they could connect to each other and access and distribute information and goods. Web technologies, social media, digital platforms have enabled new business and work models – which oscillate between innovative potential and problematic effect, e.g. when it comes to workers' rights [5, 6]. Furthermore, the role of digital information distribution in the shaping of public opinion and political discourse has been widely discussed [7]. Second and interrelated, in the past decade, artificial intelligence has gained new momentum, in particular through the rise of machine learning (ML) and algorithmic decision-making (ADM). The use of ML/ADM in the public sector has received criticism for amplifying societal inequalities, e.g. in social services [8, 9] or in criminal sentencing [10], while also promising benefits in other areas such as diagnostics or treatment plans in medicine [11]. Machine learning's role in the climate crisis is viewed controversially. Though helpful in assessing the future impact of carbon emission, ML technology itself requires large amounts of energy [12].

Hence, profound societal, political, economic and environmental effects make clear that developers and engineers not just design technology, they shape the world. Or, expressed more strongly, computing cannot be separated from societal settings – making research and development processes inherently sociotechnical [13–16]. Viewing social questions as an integral part of computing, however, continues to be a challenge for a discipline with roots in mathematics, formal logic and electrical engineering. Traditionally, those fields achieve their scientific validity through abstraction from social contexts, not from their integration [17–19]. Following this, computer science education mostly is not equipped to account for the social impact of digital technology. Yet, changes in computer science curricula are discussed [20]. It is also important to note that topics like computing and society, ethics, technological impact assessment or value orientation play a role of growing interest in computing [21–23].

Human-computer interaction with its focus on the interplay of human and technological matters, has always been prominent in providing connecting points to sociocultural, political or philosophical thought. A significant body of work in HCI is devoted to those interconnections – the carving out of grand challenges for HCI demonstrates this [24, 25]. In the face of the challenges of our accelerated sociotechnical world, this paper turns to new materialism and critical posthumanism as a means to rethink human-machine relations and come up with ideas for future research conceptualizations.

2 Beyond Dichotomies: Rethinking HCI – Introducing New Materialism

Central to the argument of this paper is the finding that the dichotomic structures that guide Western research and development since the Enlightenment are neither sufficient to account for the complexities, concomitances and entanglements of contemporary reality nor for shaping a sustainable future. To extrapolate what this means for computing and for HCI, this section rethinks the dichotomy between human and machine which is a foundational one for the field. Before proceeding with new materialism, a material-semiotic perspective on human-computer interaction is introduced as a conceptual connecting point.

2.1 A Material-Semiotic Perspective on Human-Computer Interaction

Most commonly, good interaction design is understood in its ability to mediate between the formalized, rule-oriented operations of the computer and the multeity of the human world. The human-computer interface can be described as transfer site between both. Prominently, Donald Norman and Stephen Draper have stated that the prevailing question at the interface is whether to "move the system closer to the user" or to "move the user closer to the system" [26]. This idea of a gap between user and system, which is reflected in the naming of the field of HCI, transports a Cartesian understanding of human-computer interaction: "For Descartes, mind-body interaction took place at the pineal gland. Today human computer interaction takes place at the interface. (...) The German term for interface is 'Schnittstelle', which literally translates to 'location of the cut [27].'"

The triad of human, computer and the modelling of interaction between the two entities in actual research and development practices is much more multifaceted and never as clear cut. This is reflected in the richness of the field of HCI and its ability to integrate a variety of disciplinary approaches [28]. Already early definitions of the field seek to expand the triad and include a broader understanding of context in HCI: "Human-computer interaction is a discipline concerned with the design, evaluation and implementation of interactive computing systems for human use and with the study of major phenomena surrounding them [29]." In their HCI curriculum suggestions, Thomas T. Hewett et al. also account for shifts in understandings of what is considered characteristic for the human and what for the computer/technology side. This becomes even more of a pressing topic in the light of current developments. Human and computing agency in ML/ADM systems, for example, can be described as hybrid agency [30].

For understanding what is called a material-semiotic perspective, the special character of the computer is commented on first. The computer has been termed a "symbolic machine" [31] or a "semiotic machine" [32], a view which expresses its uniqueness as a universal tool to process symbols. These, of course, are stored as numbers in the computer and ultimately manipulate the on/off binary electrical signals. Famously, when filing for the patent of the Z3 engineer Konrad Zuse referred to the device as "fleischgewordene Mathematik" (incarnate mathematics) [33]. Following this, mathematics stands for a world of abstraction that comes alive through computational processes. In the very early days of computing, before the existence of software, this 'incarnation' of mathematics was far more tangible because of programming structures being materialized as hardware. The Z3 electromechanical computer is an example for this.

In the history of computing respectively human-computer interaction the perception of the material grounding of computing recedes into the background [34, 35]. The success of graphical user interfaces demonstrates how the realization of an interface that everyday users can relate to, simultaneously 'hides' the underlying computational operations and distances the users from gaining access to and understanding underlying technological structures. In a way, usability for all comes at the price of deepening the gap between basic computing operations and the interaction possibilities humans are offered.

With his notion of human-computer interaction as "signs and signals interfacing", Frieder Nake closely interlinks the material and the semiotic dimension of computing [36]. Because of the computer's unique character, everything is subjected to a three-step of semiotizing, formalizing and algorithmizing to become processible. Furthermore and with reference to Charles S. Peirce, Nake formulates the concept of the "algorithmic sign" [37]. Most interesting is that, in contrast to common concepts of signs as dyadic (the representation and the object or meaning it refers to), the algorithmic sign is triadic. By introducing an interpretant as third-dimension, the production of meaning becomes an active part of the sign itself. To illustrate the relational character, Nake gives the example of a computer screen icon: The folder we see on the screen is not already a sign itself but a part of sign-production. When interacting with a computer, we learn to relate the manipulation of the folder icon to actions we want to achieve. We also either relate certain graphics on the screen, such as folder or trash basket, to everyday physical objects or we learn what they are supposed to stand for [37].

For the argument of this paper, it is important to note the interplay of materiality and semiotics throughout the process of human-computer interaction. Taking up the folder example: The icon on the screen has its own materiality of light points. It is also a product of graphic or interface design work and it references a specific office work place culture. Hence, it must be seen in the context of culture, corporate structures, regulations and standards (e.g. accessibility), electronics etc. It connects different material and meaning-making qualities and can be viewed as a networked activity rather than as a fixed entity. On the computer's side, of course, the important process ultimately is signal manipulation. This perspective also makes it clear that computers process data, not information. The semantic dimension comes through interpretations from humans. This distinction is made to draw attention to different qualities of computers and humans. Still, focusing on a clear cut between human and computer is insufficient in describing the complex, interwoven, multi-level transformations that actually take place [38–40].

To sum up, the notion that human-computer interaction is always simultaneously material and semiotic allows to transgress common dichotomic concepts and to rethink HCI as a relational, networked activity of matter and meaning intermeshing. Central to this argument is the notion of computing as "technological semiotics" [36, 41, 42]. This view provides an alternative framing, more specifically tied to the uniqueness of the computer, than, for example, concepts of cognitive engineering that have been influential in HCI [43].

2.2 Introducing New Materialism

Terms like new materialism, feminist (new) materialism, critical posthumanism describe a multi-vocal field which has evolved since the paradigmatic shift of the 'material turn' in the 1980s and 1990s. New materialism is cross-disciplinary, spanning from the arts and design to the humanities and the social and natural sciences. New materialist thinking has been developed in disciplines as diverse as philosophy of science [44], cultural theory [45, 46], physics [1, 47], biology and anthropology [48], psychology [49] or political science [50].

Beyond theory-building, new materialist thought has informed applied fields such as universal design and disability studies [51], education [52], fashion design [53] or politics [54]. In information systems research and organizational studies the concept of sociomateriality follows new materialist/posthumanist thought [55, 56]. Furthermore, computing practices and effects of digitalization have been examined through the lens of "materialist informatics" [57–59]. Still, in computing new materialism has not received much attention so far, with notable exceptions [60, 61]. Human-computer interaction, in its engagement with various forms of materiality and modalities and its need to integrate both human and non-human processes and contexts, promises to be a productive field for connecting new materialism [62, 63].

With divergent roots such as in material philosophy, history of science, feminist and postcolonial studies, one common denominator of new materialism is a critique of Western Cartesian, positivist thinking. Instead, new materialism offers a post-anthropocentric, monist perspective, acknowledges matter as an active agent in world-making and calls for accountability of scientific knowledge production. New materialism is mostly positioned in distinction to Euro-Western thought. Acknowledging this, scholars such as Juanita Sundberg [64] and Zoe Todd [65] have pointed out that perspectives new materialism and critical posthumanism provide comply with indigenous knowledge and First Nation conceptualizations of knowing-being.

In new materialism matter and meaning are never to be conceptualized separately which is in continuation with the material-semiotic perspective explored in Sect. 2.1. This challenges conceptions of modern science. Bruno Latour has vividly expressed that the impossibility of dissecting our embodied and embedded existence and experiences clashes with academic organization and political infrastructure: "Press the most innocent aerosol button and you'll be heading for the Antarctic, and from there to the University of California at Irvine, the mountain ranges of Lyon, the chemistry of inert gases, and then maybe to the United Nations, but this fragile thread will be broken into as many segments as there are pure disciplines. By all means, they seem to say let us not mix up knowledge, interest, justice and power. Let us not mix up heaven and earth, the global stage and the local scene, the human and the nonhuman [66]."

Key figures in new materialist/feminist new materialist thinking, like physicist Karen Barad and biologist/history of science scholar Donna Haraway, take up the challenge of thinking matter and meaning as co-productive and account for socio-cultural-political-technical-ecological entanglements. Among others, their work is central to the suggested reformulation of HCI in the following section.

3 Reconfiguring HCI Through New Materialism

If we take the proposed transgressing of traditional boundaries, such as between meaning and matter or between human and technology, seriously, what does this mean for human-computer interaction? The following section takes up threads from new materialism to interrogate, and possibly innovate, key assumptions of HCI. Conceptual shifts suggested are from interaction to intra-action, from ethics to response-abilities and from representation to performativity. While all these shifts are connected to each other or rather *through* each other, the understanding of intra-action is the basic premise.

3.1 Agential Realism: From Interaction to Intra-action

With a background in theoretical physics, Karen Barad's work has been influential in opening up dialogues between the sciences and the humanities. Taking up the philosophical work of quantum physicist Niels Bohr, Barad stresses the active role of matter or even "how matter comes to matter" and provides an understanding of non-human agency. It is important to note that her concept of agential realism does not attribute agency to already existing entities but instead allows to grasp how differences (such as those between of what are in effect perceived as entities) come into existence [47].

Central for this is the reconfiguring of interaction to intra-action. 'Inter', derived from Latin, means 'between', 'among' or 'in the midst of'. Hence, interaction locates agency between pre-existing entities. Those entities, like the human and computer, are thought of as independent from each other. 'Intra', in contrast, means 'within'. Intra-action finds that both, the ability to act as well as relevant actors and objects emerge as such from within the networked activity itself. Agency then is not an intrinsic quality of an independent entity encountering another independent entity but something which is realized through relational settings [1].

This rather abstract concept becomes clearer when we think of how the human becomes configured as a user in technologically mediated interactions. Human to human interaction, when using video conference systems or engaging in social media, not just changes on a functional level, it also changes qualitatively. Work meetings, where people are physically present, are different from meetings where telepresence systems are used. A new materialist perspective takes those differences seriously by simultaneously drawing attention to meaning and matter. Therefore, the perspective that a telepresence set-up is mirroring a face to face meeting negates the materiality of the technology and of human embodiment alike. Accepting the transformative power of different materialities, forms of embodiments, surroundings/locations, technological devices, software, hardware etc. opens up a creative leeway to rethink what is relevant in specific settings of human-computer intra-action.

The finding that intra-action allows to traverse traditional dichotomies (like society-technology, human-computer, nature-culture) does not mean that boundaries or dichotomic structures are non-existent. Barad's notion of agential realism, however, opens up the possibility to ask how and where these differences come into existence, how power relations come into play and eventually how boundaries could be relocated or even dissolved. To describe boundary-making activities Barad introduces the concept of agential cuts: "It is through specific agential intra-actions that the boundaries and properties of 'individuals' within the phenomenon become determinate and particular material articulations of the world become meaningful. A specific intra-action enacts an 'agential cut' (in contrast to the Cartesian cut—an inherent distinction—between subject and object), effecting a separation between 'subject' and 'object' within the phenomenon. In particular, agential cuts enact a resolution within the phenomenon of some inherent ontological indeterminacies to the exclusion of others [67]."

3.2   Becoming with: Further Renderings of New Materialism into HCI

"Becoming with" is a term with which Donna Haraway describes "becoming worldly" [68] as relational practices and shared agency across species. She states: "If we appreciate the foolishness of human exceptionalism then we know that becoming is always becoming with, in a contact zone where the outcome, where who is in the world, is at stake [68]." In a world that is increasingly transformed through digitalization this also means becoming with technologies. Agential realism highlights that we are always partaking in world-making. Below, the possibilities of ethical agency and the performativity of digitalization are discussed against this background.

Beyond Ethics, Towards Responsibility and Response-Abilities. In compliance with the notion of agential realism, Barad has coined the term "ethico-onto-epistemology" to grasp the co-construction of knowing, being, thinking and mattering [1]. Inherent to new materialism and critical posthumanism is an understanding of ethical and political agency as relational [44]. In the following paragraphs, responsibility respectively response-ability is explored as a specific way of conceptualizing relational ethics.

An intra-active perspective on computing views responsibility and accountability as interwoven with the fabric of sociotechnical construction. Responsibility is not something which a person or a corporation can choose to have or not to have "but rather an incarnate relation that precedes the intentionality of consciousness" [67]. Therefore, the responsibilities that come with, for example, the environmental impact of computing emerge from within the field [69].

Highlighted in feminist new materialism is the capacity to respond. Hence, responsibility is expressed as "response-ability" or "response-abilities" [70]. This entails paying attention to, enabling and cultivating different ways to be able to respond [71]. With agency as something that emerges within intra-actions, a sensitivity towards other-than-human responses is also fostered. This resonates with ubiquitous, embedded, 'intelligent' systems research. Internet of Things, smart homes and smart cities demonstrate the multiplicity of possible agents that affect and might be affected. Weather conditions, built environment, public/private transportation, humans (with all their different affordances), animals, landscapes/nature, power grids, technological infrastructures etc. all have to be accounted for.

Beyond this, the design of interactive technology as such is concerned with what kind of possibilities of immediate response (interactions, feedback, modalities) are realized in a system. New materialism draws attention to the active role of matter which corresponds with tangible interaction scenarios and understanding (digital) materiality more comprehensively [72]. How and which modalities and interaction choices are supported in a specific system depends on anticipated users and their affordances, the existing sociotechnical set-up, participating stakeholders, standards and regulations, conventions, used metaphors and scenarios etc. Thus, response-ability in human-computer interaction cross-cuts actual technological solutions, sociotechnical contexts and regulatory practices. This transgressing and all-encompassing approach certainly can appear overwhelming. Response-ability, however, does not mean accounting for everything at all times. Rather, it can be thought of as an exercise in attention and awareness. New materialism advocates to give space for positions that might otherwise be overlooked and draws attention to inequal power relations. This might comprise humans who are not users or non-human life who/which will be affected by the technology, its usage or production cycle. It might also include paying closer attention to which materials are chosen, the form factor of a product or changing usage contexts.

Beyond Representation, Towards Performativity. New materialism's questioning of the validity of the Cartesian disposition also challenges the predominance of representationalism. The Cartesian perspective distinguishes between description and reality, where descriptions are considered adequate if they mirror reality. What is described is regarded as independent from the description/representation and, importantly, from how the description was attained. The observer is also configured as independent and because of this, objective [47]. This is an idealistic concept and proves to be problematic when put into practice. Representationalism masks the sociocultural embeddedness of both subject and object of observation. Furthermore, it advocates universalism and is in danger of providing weak or false objectivity [73].

In contrast to representationalism, Barad introduces posthumanist "performativity (…) as iterative intra-activity. On an agential realist account of technoscientific practices, the 'knower' does not stand in a relation of absolute externality to the natural world being investigated—there is no such exterior observational point. It is therefore not absolute exteriority that is the condition of possibility for objectivity but rather agential separability—exteriority within phenomena. 'We' are not outside observers of the world. Nor are we simply located at particular places in the world; rather, we are part of the world in its ongoing intra-activity" [47].

Posthumanist performativity corresponds with the material-semiotic perspective on human-computer interaction explained earlier (see Sect. 2.1). The simple example of an icon on the computer screen ties together different materializations and meanings, invokes a specific context (e.g. 1980s office work), renders actions possible or impossible, may not be meaningful or accessible to some, has its own materiality etc. Therefore, understanding computing as taking parts from the world or characteristics from humans and mirror them in technological systems is not a realistic account of what is happening at the human-computer interface.

Furthermore and like responsibility, performativity exceeds the boundaries of what is typically perceived as human-computer interaction. Current debates on facial recognition technology's usage in public places are a fitting example for performative boundary work: through intra-action within discourses on public safety; regulatory practices; different technologies and different ways of being human (as data set, as biometric measurement, as a potentially high-risk person, as detected/non-detected by a camera); a variety of situations, places, environments; classification and categorizations etc. a sociotechnical setting of facial recognition emerges as meaningful, albeit contested, materialization.

4 Concluding Remarks

The aim of this contribution was to start a productive exchange between new materialism and computing, in particular, human-computer interaction. HCI is an interdisciplinary, ever growing field with no clear-cut demarcations. New materialism/critical posthumanism cuts across disciplines and is as divergent in roots as it is in its current positioning in-between the sciences, the humanities and the arts and design. The openness of HCI and the field's rich history of integrating societal aspects makes HCI a fitting ally for integrating such new schools of thought into computing.

In this paper, new materialism served as an epistemological basis to interrogate and possibly innovate key principles or assumptions of HCI. To provide connecting points between new materialism and HCI, this paper also made basic assumptions: The first one stems from acknowledging the relevance of computational technology in world-making and the intertwining of social, political, ecological, economic and technological development. Hence, a sociotechnical perspective is followed, meaning research and development in computing must be held accountable for effects that are beyond what is usually considered technological.

Second, building on traditions that view computing as 'technological semiotics' helps establishing a material-semiotic perspective on human-computer interaction. The notion of thinking materiality and meaning/semantics as concurrent and not in dichotomic separation is foundational for the subsequent reconfiguring of HCI key assumptions, such as the human-computer dichotomy or the interaction paradigm. Employing a material-semiotic perspective substantiates the claim of transgressing the human-computer (also the social world-technology) boundary from within the field of computing/HCI. With a clear cut between the social and the technological world dissolved, responsibility and accountability have to be viewed as an integral part of computing. With new materialism this responsibility is understood more comprehensively than in current notions of ethics. Materiality is considered as an active, vital part and not as a passive resource. This also calls for attention towards social and ecological sustainability, posing questions such as where material resources for computing come from and how and what kind of people or environments are affected by their extraction/usage. Furthermore, new materialism addresses other-than human and hybrid ways of being in the world and the power imbalances that come with these. This expands the human-centeredness of HCI and supports a systemic approach.

New materialism matches HCI in tying together fundamental research and application orientation. As pointed out in Sect. 3.2, responsibility/response-ability comprises both dimensions: realizing a wider range of interaction choices and also being able to respond to grander societal questions. This is in consistency with current debates of ML/ADM technology and social acceptability. In the field of 'explainable

AI' (XAI), societal, ethical, regulatory, legal aspects, user affordances, corporate interests and technological conditions form a suspenseful sociotechnical network. Modelling the inter/intra-actions in a way that human users gain insight into how recommendations are made, what their impact are, which data was used and what will happen with their own data, what kind of interventions from the users' side are possible etc., while still providing a usable, accessible interface for all, poses many unanswered question for future research.

This contribution is a first attempt to transform computing through a new materialist reconfiguring of some of HCI's key assumptions. More extensive research and further translational work is certainly needed. Beneficial for future research would be the development of a framework for new materialism and HCI, as well as a more comprehensive elaboration of the conceptual shifts proposed in this paper. This could be done through reviewing existing research and development in human-computer interaction through the diffractive lens of new materialism. Moreover, the proposed shifts could inspire and be explored in experimental settings for future developments in HCI.

References

1. Barad, K.: Meeting the Universe Halfway. Quantum Physics and the Entanglement of Matter and Meaning. Duke University Press, Durham (2007)
2. Turing, A.: Intelligent Machinery. Report for National Physical Laboratories, London (1948). http://www.turingarchive.org/browse.php/C/11. Accessed 15 Jan 2020
3. Stephanidis, C. (ed.): User Interfaces for All. Concepts, Methods, and Tools. Human Factors and Ergonomics. Lawrence Erlbaum Assoc, Mahwah (2001)
4. Stephanidis, C.: The Universal Access Handbook. Human Factors and Ergonomics. CRC Press, Boca Raton (2009)
5. Meil, P., Kirov, V. (eds.): Policy Implications of Virtual Work. Dynamics of Virtual Work. Springer, Cham (2017). https://doi.org/10.1007/978-3-319-52057-5
6. Bates, O., Kirman, B.: Sustainable platform cooperativism: towards social and environmental justice in the future of the gig-economy. In: Limits (2019)
7. Neudert, L.M., Marchal, N.: Polarisation and the use of technology in political campaigns and communication. EPRS—European Parliamentary Research Service. European Union, Brussels (2019)
8. Eubanks, V.: Automating Inequality. How High-Tech Tools Profile, Police, and Punish the Poor. St. Martin's Press, New York (2017)
9. Pilkington, E.: Digital Dystopia: How Algorithms Punish the Poor. Automating Poverty Series. The Guardian, 14 October 2019 (2019). https://www.theguardian.com/technology/2019/oct/14/automating-poverty-algorithms-punish-poor. Accessed 10 Jan 2020
10. Angwin, J., Larson, J., Mattu, S., Kirchner, L.: Machine bias. There's software used across the country to predict future criminals. And it's biased against blacks (2016). https://www.propublica.org/article/machine-bias-risk-assessments-in-criminal-sentencing. Accessed 05 Jan 2020
11. Le, D.H., Stacey, J.: Machine learning in cancer diagnostics. EBioMedicine 45, 1–2 (2019)
12. Ekin, A.: AI can help us fight climate change. But it has an energy problem, too (2019). https://horizon-magazine.eu/article/ai-can-help-us-fight-climate-change-it-has-energy-problem-too.html. Accessed 06 Jan 2020

13. MacKenzie, D.A., Wajcman, J. (eds.): The Social Shaping of Technology. How the Refrigerator Got its Hum. Open University Press, Milton Keynes (1994)
14. Agre, P., Schuler, D. (eds.): Reinventing Technology, Rediscovering Community. Critical Explorations of Computing as a Social Practice. Ablex Publishing, Greenwich (1997)
15. Bijker, W.E., Law, J. (eds.): Shaping Technology/Building Society. Studies in Sociotechnical Change. MIT Press, Cambridge (1992)
16. Akrich, M.: The de-scription of technical objects. In: Bijker, W.E., Law, J. (eds.) Shaping Technology/Building Society. Studies in Sociotechnical Change, pp. 205–224. MIT Press, Cambridge (1992)
17. Harding, S.G.: Whose Science? Whose Knowledge? Thinking from Women's Lives. Cornell University Press, Ithaca (1992)
18. Harding, S.G.: Science and Social Inequality. Feminist and Postcolonial Issues. Race and Gender in Science Studies. University of Illinois Press, Urbana (2006)
19. Rheinberger, H.-J.: On Historicizing Epistemology. An Essay. Cultural Memory in the Present. Stanford University Press, Stanford (2010)
20. Grosz, B.J., et al.: Embedded EthiCS. Commun. ACM **62**(8), 54–61 (2019)
21. Zweig, K., Neuser, W., Pipek, V., Rohde, M., Scholtes, I. (eds.): Socioinformatics - The Social Impact of Interactions Between Humans and IT, 2014th edn. Springer, Cham (2014). https://doi.org/10.1007/978-3-319-09378-9
22. Kaczmarczyk, L.C.: Computers and Society: Computing for Good. CRC Press Inc., Boca Raton (2011)
23. Stahl, B.C., Timmermans, J., Mittelstadt, B.D.: The ethics of computing. ACM Comput. Surv. **48**(4), 1–38 (2016)
24. Stephanidis, C., et al.: Seven HCI grand challenges. Int. J. Hum.–Comput. Interact. **35**(14), 1229–1269 (2019)
25. Shneiderman, B., Plaisant, C., Cohen, M., Jacobs, S., Elmqvist, N., Diakopoulos, N.: Grand challenges for HCI researchers. Interactions **23**(5), 24–25 (2016)
26. Norman, D.A., Draper, S.W.: User Centered System Design. New Perspectives on Human-Computer Interaction. L. Erlbaum Associates Inc., Hillsdale (1986)
27. Scherffig, L.: It's in Your Eyes. Gaze Based Image Retrieval in Context. ZKM—Institute for Basic Research, Karlsruhe, Diebner (2005)
28. Carroll, J.M.: Human computer interaction. Brief intro, Chap. 2. In: Soegaard, M., Friis Dam, R. (eds.) The Encyclopedia of Human-Computer Interaction. Online textbook, 2nd edn.. Interaction Design Foundation, Denmark (2014)
29. Hewett, T.T., et al.: ACM SIGCHI Curricula for Human-Computer Interaction, New York, NY, USA. Technical report (1992)
30. Moradi, M., Moradi, M., Bayat, F., Toosi, A.N.: Collective hybrid intelligence: towards a conceptual framework. Int. J. Crowd Sci. **3**, 198–220 (2019)
31. Krämer, S.: Symbolische Maschinen. Die Idee der Formalisierung im geschichtlichen Abriß. Wiss.Buchgesellschaft, Darmstadt (1988)
32. Nadin, M.: Semiotic machine. Publ. J. Semiot. **1**, 57–75 (2007)
33. Zuse, K.: Der Computer – Mein Lebenswerk. Springer, Berlin (1993). https://doi.org/10.1007/978-3-642-12096-1
34. Schelhowe, H.: Das Medium aus der Maschine. Zur Metarmorphose des Computers. Campus-Verl, Frankfurt/Main (1997)
35. Norman, D.A.: The Invisible Computer. Why Good Products can Fail, the Personal Computer is So Complex, and Information Appliances are the Solution. MIT Press, Cambridge (1999)
36. Nake, F.: Human-computer interaction: signs and signals interfacing. Lang. Des. **2**, 193–205 (1994)

37. Nake, F.: Das algorithmische Zeichen. In: Bauknecht, W., Brauer, W., Mück, T. (eds.) Informatik 2001. Tagungsband der GI/OCG Jahrestagung. Informatik 2001, Wien, pp. 736–743 (2001)

38. Draude, C.: Computing Bodies. Springer, Wiesbaden (2017). https://doi.org/10.1007/978-3-658-18660-9

39. Manovich, L.: The Language of New Media. MIT Press, Cambridge (2002)

40. Kittler, F.A., Johnston, J. (eds.): Literature, Media, Information Systems. Essays. Critical Voices in Art, Theory and Culture. Gordon & Breach, Amsterdam (1997)

41. Nadin, M.: Interface design and evaluation – semiotic implications. In: Hartson, H.R., Hix, D. (eds.) Advances in Human-Computer Interaction, II, pp. 45–100. Ablex Publishing, Norwood (1988)

42. Andersen, P.B.: A Theory of Computer Semiotics. Semiotic Approaches to Construction and Assessment of Computer Systems. Cambridge Series on Human-Computer Interaction, vol. 3. Cambridge University Press, Cambridge (1990)

43. Norman, D.A.: Cognitive engineering—cognitive science. In: Carroll, J.M. (ed.) Interfacing Thought. Cognitive Aspects of Human-Computer Interaction. A Bradford book, pp. 325–336. MIT Press, Cambridge (1987)

44. Braidotti, R.: The Posthuman, 1st edn. Wiley, New York (2013)

45. van der Tuin, I., Dolphijn, R.: The transversality of new materialism. Women: Cult. Rev. 21 (2), 153–171 (2010)

46. van der Tuin, I., Dolphijn, R. (eds.): New Materialism: Interviews & Cartographies. Open Humanities Press, Ann Arbor (2012)

47. Barad, K.: Posthumanist performativity: toward an understanding of how matter comes to matter. Signs: J. Women Cult. Soc. 28, 801–831 (2003)

48. Myers, N.: Rendering Life Molecular. Models, Modelers, and Excitable Matter. Experimental Futures. Duke University Press, Durham (2015)

49. Cano Abadía, M.: New materialisms: re-thinking humanity within an interdisciplinary framework. Special Issue of InterCultural Philosophy – Phenomenological Anthropology, Psychiatry, and Psychotherapy in Theory and Practice, pp. 168–183 (2018)

50. Bennett, J.: Vibrant Matter: A Political Ecology of Things. Duke University Press, Durham (2010)

51. Hamraie, A.: Universal design research as a new materialist practice. Disabil. Stud. Q. 32(4) (2012). https://doi.org/10.18061/dsq.v32i4

52. Hinton, P., Treusch, P. (eds.): Teaching with Feminist Materialisms. ATGENDER, Utrecht (2015)

53. Smelik, A.: New materialism: a theoretical framework for fashion in the age of technological innovation. Int. J. Fashion Stud. 5, 33–54 (2018)

54. Coole, D., Frost, S. (eds.): New Materialisms. Ontology, Agency, and Politics. Duke University Press, Durham (2010)

55. Niemimaa, M.: Sociomateriality and information systems research. SIGMIS Database 47(4), 45–59 (2016)

56. Shotter, J.: Reflections on sociomateriality and dialogicality in organization studies: from "inter-" to "intra-thinking"… in performing practices. In: Carlile, P.R. (ed.) How Matter Matters. Objects, Artifacts, and Materiality in Organization Studies. Perspectives on Process Organization Studies, 1st edn., vol. 3, pp. 32–57. Oxford University Press, Oxford (2014)

57. Hayles, K.N.: The materiality of informatics. Issues Integr. Stud. 10, 121–144 (1992)

58. Colman, F.: Digital feminicity: predication and measurement, materialist informatics and images. Artnodes 14, 1–17 (2015)

59. Nakamura, L.: Prospects for a Materialist Informatics: An Interview with Donna Haraway. Electronic Book Review (2003)

60. Rose, E.J., Walton, R.: Factors to actors. In: Gossett, K., Mallory, A., Armfield, D.M. (eds.) Proceedings of the 33rd Annual International Conference on the Design of Communication. The 33rd Annual International Conference, Limerick, Ireland, 16 July 2015–17 July 2015, pp. 1–10. ACM, New York (2015)

61. Pihkala, S., Karasti, H.: Politics of mattering in the practices of participatory design. In: Huybrechts, L., Teli, M. (eds.) Proceedings of the 15th Participatory Design Conference Short Papers, Situated Actions, Workshops and Tutorial. The 15th Participatory Design Conference, Hasselt and Genk, Belgium, 20–24 August 2018, vol. 2, pp. 1–5. ACM (2018)

62. Klumbyte, G., Draude, C., Britton, L.: Re-imagining HCI: new materialist philosophy and figurations as tool for design. standing on the shoulders of giants: exploring the intersection of philosophy and HCI. In: CHI 2019 Workshop, 4 May 2019, Glasgow (2019). https://authentic.sice.indiana.edu/philosophy-hci-workshop/papers/P33-Klumbyte_Draude_Britton.pdf. Accessed 05 Jan 2020

63. Britton, L., Klumbyte, G., Draude, C.: Doing thinking: revisiting computing with artistic research and technofeminism. Digital Creativity **30**, 313–328 (2019)

64. Sundberg, J.: Decolonizing posthumanist geographies. cultural geographies **21**, 33–47 (2014)

65. Todd, Z.: An indigenous feminist's take on the ontological turn: 'ontology' is just another word for colonialism. J. Hist. Sociol. **29**, 4–22 (2016)

66. Latour, B.: We Have Never Been Modern. Harvester Wheatsheaf, New York (1993)

67. Barad, K.: "Intra-actions" (Interview of Karen Barad by Adam Kleinmann). Mousse, pp. 76–81 (2012)

68. Haraway, D.J.: When Species Meet. Posthumanities, vol. 3. University of Minnesota Press, Minneapolis (2008)

69. Chien, A.A.: Owning computing's environmental impact. Commun. ACM **62**(3), 5 (2019)

70. Haraway, D.J.: Staying with the Trouble. Making Kin in the Chthulucene. Experimental Futures. Duke University Press, Durham (2016)

71. Schrader, A.: Responding to pfiesteria piscicida (the Fish Killer): phantomatic ontologies, indeterminacy, and responsibility in toxic microbiology. Soc. Stud. Sci. **40**, 275–306 (2010)

72. Jung, H., Stolterman, E.: Digital form and materiality. In: Pederson, T., Malmbord, L., Malmborg, L. (eds.) NordiCHI 2012, Making Sense Through Design: Proceedings of the 7th Nordic Conference on Human-Computer Interaction, Copenhagen, Denmark, 14–17 October 2012, p. 645. ACM (2012)

73. Haraway, D.: Situated Knowledges: The Science Question in Feminism and the Privilege of Partial Perspective. Feminist Studies (1988)

Contextual Research

Why We Need to Research in Context to Deliver Great Products

Sabrina Duda[1]([✉]), Carolyn Warburton[2], and Nissa Black[1]

[1] Valtech, London, UK
sabrina@smiling.club, nissa.black@valtech.com
[2] Valtech, Manchester, UK
carolyn.warburton@valtech.com

Abstract. This paper is part of a panel about user research methods and how they are applied to the benefit of products. The method of contextual research is discussed, and three case studies from the public sector are illustrating how contextual research has been driving product development. Contextual research is part of field study methods and used when exploring the context of usage of a product or service, or the cultural context. It is applied when users' tasks are involving other people or processes which need to be observed to fully understand users' needs and goals. The concept of contextual research has been developed by Holtzblatt and Beyer and for the first time completely described in 1995. The case studies from the Ministry of Justice, from Greater Manchester Transport, and the Blue Badge project are showing why this method is so important for successful product development. Especially when designing services which are involving various user groups interacting with each other, combining offline and online tasks, or when developing B2B tools embedded in processes in the office, research in context is necessary.

Keywords: Contextual inquiry · Contextual research · Contextual design · User research · User experience

1 What Is Contextual Research?

Susan Farrell [2] describes several examples of field studies: user tests in the field, customer visits, direct observation, ethnographic research, and contextual inquiry which is a combination of several field-study activities. All these approaches differ in how much the researcher interacts with the participant; it can range from just observing the user to a co-discovery session when researcher and user are both sharing ideas.

Contextual research is a combination of observation and conversation with the user while the user is performing tasks at work or at home. Users are not interrupted during their tasks, but still insights are derived by asking additional questions.

The Book of Knowledge from UPA, 2010 defines it as following: "Contextual inquiry is a semi-structured interview method to obtain information about the context of use, where users are first asked a set of standard questions and then observed and questioned while they work in their own environments" [1].

© Springer Nature Switzerland AG 2020
M. Kurosu (Ed.): HCII 2020, LNCS 12181, pp. 33–49, 2020.
https://doi.org/10.1007/978-3-030-49059-1_3

Contextual research is uncovering latent needs and desires and core values. Usually it is analyzed with affinity sorting.

Contextual inquiry is part of the contextual design process, developed by Karen Holtzblatt and Hugh Beyer [4]. This approach is so much more than just a method; it is a certain view of the world about how to treat each other and how to work together.

Teamwork and Immersion: The core of Holtzblatt and Beyer's contextual design approach is effective teamwork: "Contextual design creates a new team culture and way of working – committed to using data about people's real lives to drive requirements and design" [4]. "No one person is enough to make a great product – but a well-functioning team can be."

The team should be immersed in the world of the user and needs to internalize the user in order to design user centered. That is why the team is involved in the research, either by taking directly part or via interpretation sessions where the interviews are analyzed as a team to achieve a shared understanding of the user. "Hearing about the user is one thing; understanding and embodying knowledge about the user at a gut level is another. Because people are people, just telling them information about the user doesn't really communicate – not at the level necessary for design" [4].

2 How to Conduct Contextual Inquiry

The contextual interview is a one-on-one interview which lasts about 1.5–2 h with a user in context.

The basic concept of contextual inquiry is quite simple: "[…] go to the user, watch them to do activities you care about, and talk with them about what they're doing right then" [4]. However, it is a sophisticated technique which requires an experienced interviewer and is embedded in a cross-functional team.

Contextual inquiry is based on a relationship and partnership with the user, respect for the user and the team members. It is a shared inquiry and discovery of interviewer and user. Therefore, it is by nature subjective; it is influenced by the interviewer's point of view, his experiences, and personality. But only in that way the best possible insights can be achieved, including uncovering users' emotions and needs: the interviewer should "probe emotional energy and find its origins and motivations" [4]. Since the whole team is involved in the research and roles can be shared, either for the research itself, or at least for the interpretation of the interviews, the team members will contribute with different point of views and perspectives, and thus arrive at well-rounded conclusions regarding the design. "Some data gathering methods ask for total objectivity from the interviewer; we don't think that's possible and use the interviewer's subjectivity instead" [4].

The interviewer has an "[…] attitude of inquiry, attention to detail, and humility" [4] and the "[…] user is the only true expert on their own activities" [4]. "[…] interviewers can learn by immersion in the world of the user, discovering what's important from the people who know best" [4]. It is much more than empathizing with the user; it is putting yourself into users' shoes and experiencing their emotions. This is only possible by being subjective and establishing a real relationship with the user. "So where the target activity is happening, observe it, sense the user's feeling, and talk about it, all while it happens" [4].

A guideline for all contextual inquiries is: Be concrete, focus on describing a specific task or event, and avoid all generalizations and summaries: "Don't allow the user to summarize, abstract, or report [...]" [4]. Sticking to a concrete task makes it easier for the user to describe it and also to memorize past events; the current task will trigger past experiences (retrospective accounts). It is important that the user talks through all steps, and the interviewer pays attention to emotions and motivations when the user performs the task.

The interviewer and the user should try to find the right interpretations for the facts that were discovered. The interviewer is creating hypotheses about the user's motives and is sharing them with the user to validate them. "When we go out into the field, we are not first collecting the facts of what people are doing – we must come back with an accurate interpretation of those facts. We must collect meaning" [4]. "It's the interpretation which drives the design decision" [4].

The interviewer should take notes himself. "Take notes by hand the whole time. Don't depend on a recording or a second person to catch everything" [4]. The interviewer is in close contact with the user and therefore catches emotional responses and tiny reactions better than a second person taking notes or a recording of the session.

The Four Principles of Contextual Inquiry

- **Focus:** You need to discuss with your team which parts of a process or which tasks are most relevant, so that you know on what to focus in the research.
- **Context:** You are visiting the user at the place where he performs a certain task (office, at home, on the move).
- **Partnership:** The interviewer and the user are in a partnership - like master and apprentice: the user is the expert and has the leading role because he shows the interviewer his tasks and explains them, the interviewer is learning about the task and context, observing and probing.
- **Interpretation:** Both interviewer and user are developing a shared understanding about the user's tasks, the interviewer is sharing his interpretations and the user confirms or corrects them. Having the correct interpretation of observed facts is important for making the right product decision.

The Structure of the Contextual Inquiry

- **Introduction:** Welcome and explanation, getting to know the user and getting an overview about his (work) day & life.
- **Transition:** Explaining how the contextual interview will work.
- **Contextual interview:** Observing & asking questions & suggesting interpretations. Eliciting retrospective accounts. Looking for emotional energy.
- **The wrap up:** Interviewer shares with the user final summary and interpretation of what he has learned for validation.

3 How to Analyze Contextual Inquiries

In qualitative research, especially contextual research, vast amounts of data are collected. Analyzing them time efficient and making sure the team gets actionable insights from the research fast is a challenge. "Capturing the data is not the major problem for product teams – having a shared understanding of the world of the user is" [4].

Holtzblatt & Beyer have a very good solution for that, the team analysis: "Together, the team generates a richer understanding of the user than one person alone would have been able to provide" [4]. They are suggesting interpretation sessions with the interviewer and between 2 and 5 team members. The interviewer talks through the events of a single interview, using his handwritten notes and memory. The team interviews the interviewer about the user session. One team member writes down the issues, the interpretations, and any design ideas. Thus, the team is actively involved in creating the insights and feeling ownership. In that way the problem of lacking buy-in for research results is avoided. The interpretation session should take place within 24–48 h after the interview, so that the memory is still fresh, and it is lasting about 2 h, the same length as the interview session. Interviews and interpretation sessions are taking turns, so each new interview can be adapted, if necessary.

A quick overview of how to conduct contextual research gives 'Contextual Interviews and How to Handle Them' from the Interaction Design Foundation (2019) [5] and an article from the UK government 'Contextual research and observation' (2017) [3].

In order to learn in detail how to apply contextual inquiry 'Principles of Contextual Inquiry' in Holtzblatt & Beyer Contextual Design [4] is highly recommended.

4 Benefits of Contextual Research

We need context to test our assumptions about how valuable a product or concept is for the user. Observing users in context gives more reliable and valid information about what they are doing, how they are doing it, and why they are doing it (use cases and scenarios).

A lab situation is artificial and often misses out on relevant aspects of using a product. Regarding services, it is often inevitable to research in context to explore all different steps and touch points of a service. Just asking users how they use a product or let them describe things they did in the past or plan to do in the future won't give reliable results. Even making users perform certain tasks in a lab usability test is already a limitation which could result in missing crucial aspects of product usage.

Context knowledge is also needed to create personas and user journeys. Impediments are in most cases not permanent, but dependent on the situation (see Fig. 1) and therefore temporary. With contextual research we can discover all relevant situational information.

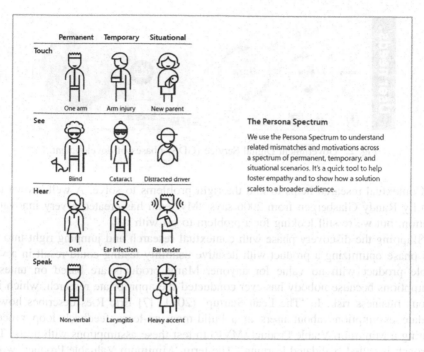

The Persona Spectrum

We use the Persona Spectrum to understand related mismatches and motivations across a spectrum of permanent, temporary, and situational scenarios. It's a quick tool to help foster empathy and to show how a solution scales to a broader audience.

Fig. 1. Microsoft Inclusive Design Toolkit.

5 When to Conduct Contextual Research

Contextual research is most useful during discovery phase, at the beginning of product development when you need to understand the potential customers and the market to find business opportunities.

Discovery projects are often starting without any product or service at all; it is necessary to go to workplaces or homes of users to gather information about context and needs. Based on this initial exploratory research, user needs and pain points are extracted, and assumptions and hypotheses are created about how the user needs can be met. Research in discovery starts very broad; later this converges, and the focus is defined. In alpha phase prototypes are created and iteratively tested with users. In beta phase, the product or service will be rolled out with a small segment of users to collect more quantitative feedback. Figure 2 shows an overview of the different phases in digital service development for the UK Government.

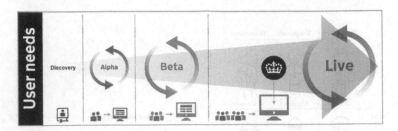

Fig. 2. Government Digital Service (GDS) phases of development.

Contextual research helps to find the right problems to solve. A well-known cartoon by Randy Glasbergen from 2006 says "My team has created a very innovative solution, but we're still looking for a problem to go with it."

Skipping the discovery phase with contextual research and jumping right into the beta phase optimizing a product with iterative usability testing could result in a very usable product with no value for anyone. Many products are based on untested assumptions because nobody has ever conducted the appropriate research, which is a serious business risk. In 'The Lean Startup' (2011) [7] Eric Ries describes how to validate assumptions about users in a build-measure-learn feedback loop process, creating a Minimum Viable Product (MVP) to test these assumptions with users. This approach is called 'validated learning'. The term 'Minimum Valuable Product' would be even more appropriate; emphasizing that it is about the value a product has for the user. A short overview about this approach is on the lean startup website [9]. Figure 3 shows the different phases of software development and what questions to ask about your users.

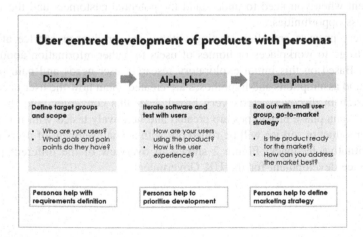

Fig. 3. User centered development

6   Challenges of Contextual Research

Despite all the benefits, there are challenges of conducting contextual research. In many cases it means more effort for recruiting, and higher incentives, to find people willing to let you observe their activities. Sometimes there are legal issues, because especially in B2B it is not always allowed to observe at the workplace (for confidentiality reasons, or because it would be too disruptive). Another example is election time in the UK when research activities with the public are restricted, in order not to influence any election outcomes. Sometimes home visits are not feasible. When working for the Ministry of Justice (MOJ), we were advised not to do home visits, because some of the appellants could be potentially violent.

Ross, J. (2012) is writing in his blog 'Why Are Contextual Inquiries So Difficult?' about the difficulties with this method and how to overcome them, based on his own experiences with clients, which is worth reading [8].

7   Examples of User Research with Contextual Research

7.1   HM Courts and Tribunal Service (HMCTS) Project

We were part of the Ministry of Justice (MOJ) reform program and were working on improving the appeals process for the Social Security and Child Support Tribunal (SSCS). People are appealing to HMCTS when their benefits are cut.

One of the challenges of the project were the many different user groups - appellants (citizens), judiciary, representatives, appointees, family and friends, admin staff (DWP and HMCTS) - and the fact that the main user group, the appellants, were vulnerable. Another challenge was the long and complicated appeals process (see Fig. 4).

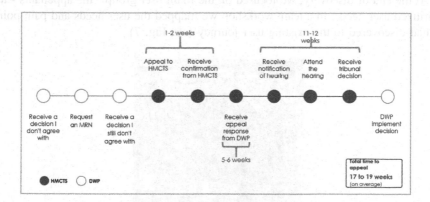

Fig. 4. Appeals process.

In discovery phase we did interviews with all user groups: appellants, representatives, judges, DWP, HMRC. We did contextual research in tribunals and call center listening. We visited two tribunals and attended hearings in London Fox Court and

Liverpool. We spoke to judges, medical experts, disability experts. Observing staff at a tribunal revealed that the work is mainly paper based; all appellant files, some are hundreds of pages long, are in paper format (see Fig. 5 and Fig. 6).

Fig. 5. Admin at work in tribunal.

Fig. 6. Appellant files.

At the end of discovery, we focused on the main user group - the appellants - and prioritized user needs. In a team workshop we mapped the user needs and pain points we had discovered to the existing user journey (see Fig. 7).

Fig. 7. User journey mapping with pain points.

We focused on the main pain points of our appellants and defined our alpha goal: "Remove confusion by making the appellant (and/or representant) understand the process and where they are in it."

We created a prototype giving status updates (see Fig. 8) about the appeals process in various formats (online, email, text) to address the most pressing user need we had identified in discovery: "I need to understand the process and where I am within it, so that I am not confused and know what to do next."

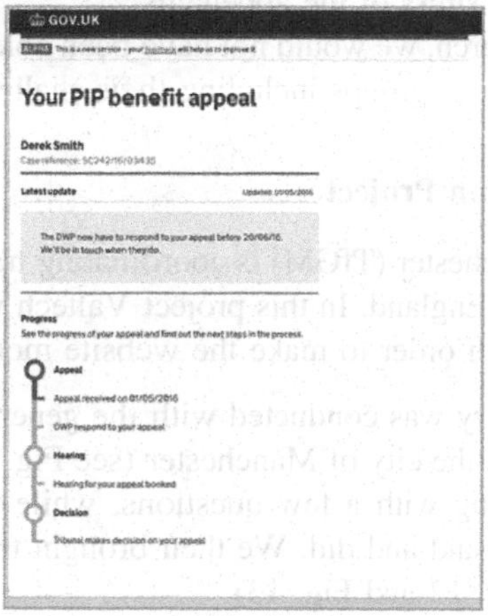

Fig. 8. Status information system.

Another major pain point we had identified in discovery was that appellants are very anxious about the hearing. They don't know who will be in the hearing, what will be happening in the hearing, how the room looks like. We created a page in our prototype (see Fig. 9) describing what to expect at the hearing to reduce anxiety to address the user need: "As an appellant, I want to know what the hearing involves, so that I am less anxious."

Fig. 9. What to expect at the hearing.

In alpha, we iterated on the prototype in 2-weekly sprints. User testing took place in different places in the UK every other week (London, Birmingham, Glasgow, Norwich). In addition, we continued with discovery and visited judges, representatives of welfare organizations, and Citizens Advice Bureaus to speak to people in their work environment.

Results. We successfully passed GDS alpha assessment for the service. User testing showed great appreciation of the status information system and the information on the web pages helped ease the stress of the appellants.

Without contextual research, we would not have been able to explore the whole user journey with all involved user groups including their challenges and emotions.

7.2 Public Transportation Project

Transport for Greater Manchester (TfGM) is coordinating transport services in Greater Manchester in North West England. In this project Valtech was researching how users are using public transport in order to make the website more inclusive [12].

Method. Contextual enquiry was conducted with the general public as they travel on public transport throughout the city of Manchester (see Fig. 10). Researchers went out in pairs, with one prompting with a few questions, while the other researcher made notes on what participants said and did. We then brought the results back to the team for affinity sorting (see Fig. 12 and Fig. 13).

Fig. 10. Manchester trams.

We talked with people on buses and trams, at stops and railway stations (see Fig. 11). People often don't want to engage, and so we approached them with a bright smile and the promise they'd be helping other local people, and most were willing to chat for a short time, around 10 min on average. We spoke with 130 people, selecting people with different age profiles, ethnicity and physical ability, to ensure we reached a cross section of the population.

Fig. 11. Interviewing user in context.

Fig. 12. Findings from user research.

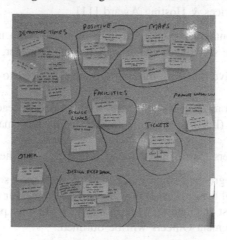

Fig. 13. Affinity sorting.

Results. We observed people on the move to find out what they were travelling for and see which devices and information they use to decide how best to travel. By focusing on people while they were on the move, we were able to find out how they accessed information, where things were going wrong, and learned how they respond to frustrations they were experiencing.

Contextual research taught us about problems they encounter, such as avoiding getting wet when it's bad weather, avoiding steps, and knowing about available facilities. We found that travelers with disabilities needed to know the layout of the station before they got there, an insight that could have been lost in the noise with other methods.

We were able to discover what people do if their travel is disrupted, while real disruptions were going on. We also saw some of the limitations of commonly used apps. The findings from this research proved most effective in helping us to design a better transport website for Greater Manchester that is inclusive for all (see Fig. 14).

Fig. 14. Website.

7.3 Blue Badge Digital Transformation Project

Blue Badge is a disabled parking permit. The Blue Badge is displayed when parking and is permitting the owner to park in a special reserved area. Valtech has won several awards for this project, three awards at the UK Digital Experience Awards 2019 [10], and the Managed Services & Hosting Award [11].

Method. We used contextual enquiry to help us make more informed design decisions. The Blue Badge service has many audiences to consider. The users include:

- Applicants who have difficulty moving around and need to park closer to where they need to go.
- Organizations such as charities that help disabled people lead a better life.
- Local Authorities (LAs) are administration teams that manage and administer applications.
- Enforcement Officers (part of LAs) inspecting badges on the streets.

We visited all user groups at their place of work or homes, so that we could gain a richer understanding of these users. We wanted to see how their environments affected their experience whilst interacting with the service. In this paper, the method for applicants and Enforcement Officers will be outlined.

Applicants. It is obvious that the main user group who requires the service has difficulty moving around. More so than ever, getting out of the building was an important decision we made as a team to ensure that we were meeting the user's accessibility needs. It also ensured a more realistic setting for them to apply with all the artefacts required and their own devices (see Fig. 15).

Fig. 15. Applicant at home.

Enforcement Officers. A few user interviews had taken place prior to the contextual enquiry. Assumptions surfaced from this research that needed backing up e.g. Enforcement Officers need a QR code to check badge details (see Fig. 16). It became clear that the team needed to get a feel for their day to day work on the streets. A very small camera (GoPro) was strapped to the researcher's body to maximize evidence capture for team playbacks (see Fig. 17).

Fig. 16. Enforcement Officer at work.

Fig. 17. User researcher with GoPro camera.

Result

Applicants. There are many insights to cover, however here we will focus on one.

We discovered users who are automatically eligible for a Blue Badge had problems with their DWP letters. These particular users are in receipt of certain DWP benefits and score a specific number of points for various measures of mobility one can be assessed on, such as "moving around". They need to be able to share this letter with the Local Authority to show they are eligible for a badge.

The majority of users found it difficult to find the correct letter and page. By visiting users in their homes and seeing how they interact with DWP correspondence, we discovered a few things that users were having problems with:

- DWP letters and benefits change format quite regularly, so users struggle to keep up with these changes.
- The letters are double sided and in thick wads. Users spend a lot of time sifting through the pages to try and find the information LAs need to make a decision.
- There's different scoring for different parts of certain benefits, so trying to differentiate these can be difficult.
- Users receive these letters once a year, and many users don't know where their letters are.
- Users expect government services to be unified. They expect the system to access the information from DWP and thus share with the LA to avoid the need to share the letter altogether.
- Users we visited with low digital skills struggle with uploading these letters.

Visiting the users in their homes meant we had increased empathy as we observed the problems they were facing in real time. The rich evidence we were able to gather took us to DWP to see how we could improve the user journey. Not only were users having issues with the actual letters, but we knew from quantitative feedback and analytics that uploading is difficult for a high proportion of users, so removing this action altogether would improve the journey significantly.

Here is one of the design improvements we made to the user journey to help solve the problems the users were facing regarding their DWP letters. The latest iteration is demonstrated in the image below (see Fig. 18). During the eligibility check, the user is prompted to get their letter before starting their application. This is to ensure they are prepared before starting the application process, as it may take them some time to find their letter. By using illustrations, we point out which part of their DWP letter they need to check to see if they are eligible.

Fig. 18. Blue Badge service design – gov.uk website.

Enforcement Officers. There were many findings from doing a contextual enquiry with Enforcement Officers. We will take you through one of them.

As mentioned previously, there was a team held assumption that Enforcement Officers would find a QR code useful to check badge details. Enforcement Officers use mobile phone devices to check badge details on the street. Therefore, we believed a QR code would reduce the time and effort needed to bring up badge details when on the move. We visited Enforcement Officers around the country and observed this solution wasn't appropriate. This was because:

- Blue Badges aren't always displayed on the dashboard in clear view. Sometimes they're placed quite far away from the dashboard. The type of vehicle can affect this placement, and other items may block parts of the badge. A badge number doesn't take up a lot of space on the badge, so it is less likely to get covered.
- They were worried about damaging windscreens and scratching cars with their devices or coats when leaning over the bonnet.
- There are different types of Enforcement Officers. Some are undercover and check badges away from the vehicle. They memorize the badge number and search for the owner on the system inconspicuously. They demonstrated that having a QR code to scan badges would make their job more obvious, and this may deter people from coming back to their car.

Based on these facts we agreed as a team that Enforcement Officers didn't need a QR code to do their job effectively. Contextual enquiry ensured that as a design team we were being outcome focused rather than solution focused (Fig. 19).

Fig. 19. Enforcement Officer checking Blue Badge details from his car.

8 Summary and Conclusions

Contextual research methods are a crucial part of successful product development. They will probably become even more relevant in the future as methods for product development are evolving and users are much more online and on the move which requires appropriate research methods.

We observe more and more specialization regarding research methods. Online remote methods have been improving a lot over the past few years, and are offering surveys, click tests, AB testing, unmoderated remote testing. On the other hand, qualitative methods are as popular as ever and their value is appreciated which is reflected in a surge in positions for qualitative user researchers. There is a need for experienced people with good interviewing and observation skills; especially for contextual research.

User research is much more common practice now than it was 20 years ago. Nonetheless, in many cases user needs are not shaping the company strategy. For becoming a truly user centered company, the whole organization needs to change its processes, ways of working, and its vision and values. Holtzblatt and Beyer are convinced: "But a truly user-centered organization is still a rare thing" [4]. "So we have come a long way, but the organizational change mission of our work […] is not over" [4].

References

1. Book of Knowledge, Usability Professionals Association (2010). http://www.usabilitybok.org/contextual-inquiry. Accessed 31 Jan 2020
2. Farrell, S.: Field studies (2016). https://www.nngroup.com/articles/field-studies/. Accessed 31 Jan 2020
3. Gov.uk website, Contextual research and observation (2017). https://www.gov.uk/service-manual/user-research/contextual-research-and-observation. Accessed 31 Jan 2020
4. Holtzblatt, K., Beyer, H.: Contextual Design: Design for Life, 2nd edn. Morgan Kaufman, Cambridge (2017)
5. Interaction Design Foundation Website: Contextual Interviews and How to Handle Them (2019). https://www.interaction-design.org/literature/article/contextual-interviews-and-how-to-handle-them. Accessed 31 Jan 2020

6. Microsoft Inclusive Design Toolkit. https://download.microsoft.com/download/b/0/d/b0d4bf87–09ce-4417-8f28-d60703d672ed/inclusive_toolkit_manual_final.pdf. Accessed 31 Jan 2020

7. Ries, E.: The Lean Startup. Portfolio Penguin, Penguin Random House (2011)

8. Ross, J.: Why are contextual inquiries so difficult? UX Matters (2012). https://www.uxmatters.com/mt/archives/2012/06/why-are-contextual-inquiries-so-difficult.php. Accessed 31 Jan 2020

9. The Lean Startup: Methodology. http://theleanstartup.com/principles. Accessed 31 Jan 2020

10. Valtech website. https://www.valtech.com/en-gb/insights/the-blue-badge-digital-service-has-won-three-awards-at-the-uk-digital-experience-awards-2019/. Accessed 31 Jan 2020

11. Valtech website. https://www.valtech.com/en-gb/insights/valtech-wins-managed-services-award/. Accessed 31 Jan 2020

12. Valtech website. https://www.valtech.com/en-gb/work/tfgm/. Accessed 31 Jan 2020

Development of an Assessment Model for the Human Centered Design Processes Specified in ISO 9241-220

Rüdiger Heimgärtner[(✉)]

Intercultural User Interface Consulting (IUIC), 93152 Undorf, Germany
ruediger.heimgaertner@iuic.de

Abstract. Process assessment is a disciplined project-oriented evaluation of an organizational unit's processes with respect to a process assessment model. The human centered design (HCD) process assessment model (PAM) is intended for use when performing conformational assessments of the process capability on the development of interactive systems. It was developed in accordance with the requirements of ISO/IEC 33020 combined with content from ISO 15504-5 and DIN SPEC 92412 relating to the process reference HCD processes specified in ISO 9241-220. If processes beyond the scope of ISO 9241-220 are needed, appropriate processes may be added based on the business needs of the organization. The derived HCD processes reference model (PRM) from the HCD processes specified in ISO 9241-220 together with the HCD-PAM must be applied when performing an HCD process assessment. The developed HCD-PAM contains a set of indicators to be considered when interpreting the intent of the HCD-PRM. These indicators may also be used when implementing a process improvement program subsequent to an assessment within an organization. In this paper, the structure and the content of the HCD-PAM applying the HCD-PRM is explained and exemplified by a practical example of assessing the HCD.3.4.2 process.

Keywords: Capability · Maturity · Process assessment model · Process reference model · Human centered design · User centered design · ISO · UX · Standards · User experience · ISO 9241-220 · Human centered design processes · IUIC · IUID · PAM · PRM · Processes · Models · HCD · SPICE

1 Introduction

Experience from various fields of technology shows that it is possible for a development process recognized as mature to produce products of higher quality. Process assessments and improvement are an everyday business. Each project team member must know the current process and its optimization potential. Self-assessments can be used for continuous process improvement. Each project team member can subsequently recognize what is important for successful projects and what is also asked in assessments. Therefore, time is saved sustainably, and productivity is increased in projects.

© Springer Nature Switzerland AG 2020
M. Kurosu (Ed.): HCII 2020, LNCS 12181, pp. 50–70, 2020.
https://doi.org/10.1007/978-3-030-49059-1_4

However, assessing processes is a complex endeavor and comprises those integrative parts necessary to obtain valid objective and comparable results. In this paper, the structure and content of a process assessment model (PAM) is explained and exemplified to yield an impression of how to determine the capability of the human centered design (HCD) processes.

The term "process" can be understood at three levels of abstraction (cf. Fig. 1). Note that these levels of abstraction are not meant to define a strict black-or-white split, nor is it the aim to provide a scientific classification schema – the message here is to understand that, in practice, when it comes to the term "process" there are different abstraction levels, and that a PAM resides at the highest.

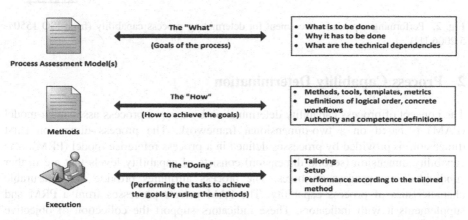

Fig. 1. Possible levels of abstraction for the term "process" (from ISO 15504-5:2006 [1])

Capturing experience acquired during product development (i.e. at the DOING level) in order to share this experience with others means creating a HOW level. However, a HOW is always specific to a context such as a company, an organizational unit, or a product line. For example, the HOW of a project, organizational unit, or company A is potentially not applicable to a project, organizational unit, or company B. However, both might be expected to adhere to the principles represented by PAM indicators for process outcomes and process attribute achievements. These indicators are at the WHAT level while deciding on solutions for concrete templates, proceedings, and tooling, etc. is left to the HOW level. Figure 2 shows the main steps necessary to come from the DOING and HOW level to ratings of these levels on the WHAT level during an assessment. In the following sections, these steps are explained in detail.

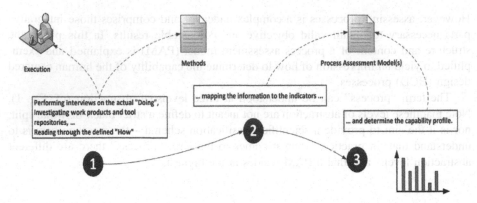

Fig. 2. Performing a process assessment for determining process capability (from ISO 15504-5:2006 [1]).

2 Process Capability Determination

The concept of process capability determination by using a process assessment model (PAM) is based on a two-dimensional framework. The process dimension (first dimension) is provided by processes defined in a process reference model (PRM). The capability dimension (second dimension) consists of capability levels that are further subdivided into process attributes. The process attributes provide the measurable characteristics of process capability. The PAM selects processes from a PRM and supplements it with indicators. These indicators support the collection of objective evidence which enable an assessor to assign ratings for processes according to the capability dimension. This relationship is shown in Fig. 3.

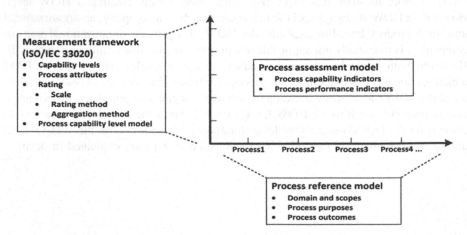

Fig. 3. Process assessment model relationship according to ISO 15504-5:2006 [1].

2.1 Process Reference Model

Processes are grouped by process category and at a second level into process groups according to the type of activity they address. In general, there are at least three process categories: primary life cycle processes, organizational life cycle processes and supporting life cycle processes. Each process is described in terms of a purpose statement. The purpose statement contains the unique functional objectives of the process when performed in an environment. For each purpose statement a list of specific outcomes is mapped, as a list of expected positive results of the process performance. For the process dimension, the HCD PRM provides the set of processes shown in Table 1 in ISO 9241-220:2019-03 [2], whereas HCP.3 is divided into further process groups according to the structured main HCD activities described in ISO 9241-210 [3] and taken into account in ISO 9241-220:2019-03 [2] as shown in Fig. 4.

Table 1. HCD processes according to ISO 9241-220:2019-03 [2].

Unique identifier	Process name	Primary audiences
HCP.1	Ensure enterprise focus on human-centred quality	Executive responsible for human-centred quality
HCP.1.1	Incorporate human-centred quality in business strategy	Ensures: executive management
HCP.1.2	Institutionalize human-centred quality	
HCP.2	Enable human-centred design across projects and systems	Those responsible for (HCD) processes used by the organization
HCP.2.1	Integration of human-centred quality	Ensures project, product and usability managemaent
HCP.2.2	Resources of human-centred quality	
HCP.2.3	Authorization and control of human-centred quality	
HCP.3	Executive human-centred design within a project	Technical leadership responsible for human-centred design
HCP.3.1	Plan and manage human-centred designor the project	Ensures: project and product management
HCP.3.1.1	Establish human-centred quality objectives	
HCP.3.1.2	Manage threats and opportunities that can arise from use of the interactive system	
HCP.3.1.3	Define extent of human-centred in the project	
HCP.3.1.4	Plan each HCD process activity	
HCP.3.1.5	Manage HCD process activities within the project	
HCP.3.2	Identify the context of use	
HCP.3.2.1	Identify the intended user population and differentiate group of users	
HCP.3.2.2	Identify other aspects of the context o use and reported issuses	
HCP.3.3	Establish the user requirements	
HCP.3.3.1	Identify the user needs	

(continued)

Table 1. (*continued*)

Unique identifier	Process name	Primary audiences
	Specify the user requirements	
HCP.3.3.3	Negotiate the user requirements in the context of a project	
HCP.3.4	Design solution that meets user requirements	
HCP.3.4.1	Specify the user-system interaction	
HCP.3.4.2	Produce and refine user interface design solution	
HCP.3.5	User-centred evaluation	
HCP.3.5.1	Plan for evaluation throughout the project	
HCP.3.5.2	Plan each evaluation(what to evaluate and how)	
HCP.3.5.3	Carry out the each evaluation	
HCP.4	Introduction, operation and end of life of a system	Technical leadership responsible for HCD
HCP.4.1	Introducing the system	
HCP.4.2	Human-centred quality in operation	Ensures: service and support management
HCP.4.3	Human-centred quality during upgrades	
HCP.4.4	Human-centred quality at the end of life of a system	

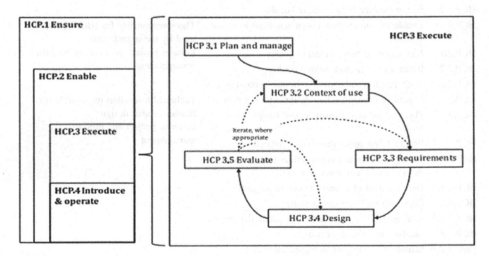

Fig. 4. Relationships between the HCD processes (including the sub-processes in HCP.3) from ISO 9241-220:2019-03 [2].

Organizational and Supporting Life Cycle Processes Category. The organizational life cycle processes category consists of processes that develop process, product, and resource assets which, when used by projects in the organization, will help the organization achieve its business goals. The organizational life cycle processes category consists of the following groups:

- the HCD.1 ensure process group;
- the HCD.2 enable process group.

The management processes may be used by anyone who manages any type of HCD project or process within the life cycle belonging to the supporting life cycle process category.

Primary Life Cycle Processes Category. The primary life cycle processes category consists of processes that may be used by the customer when acquiring products from a supplier, and by the supplier when responding and delivering products to the customer including the engineering processes needed for specification, design, development, integration and testing. The primary life cycle processes category consists of the following groups:

- the HCP.3 Execute process group;
- the HCP.4 Introduce & operate process group.

The HCP.3 Execute process group consists of processes addressing the elicitation and management of customer and internal requirements, the definition of the system architecture and the integration and testing on the system level.

3 Measurement Framework

The measurement framework provides the necessary requirements and rules for the capability dimension. It defines a schema which enables an assessor to determine the capability level of a given process. These capability levels are defined as part of the measurement framework. To enable the rating, the measurement framework provides process attributes defining a measurable property of process capability. Each process attribute is assigned to a specific capability level. The extent of achievement of a certain process attribute is represented by means of a rating based on a defined rating scale. The rules from which an assessor can derive a final capability level for a given process are represented by a process capability level model. The HCD PAM uses the measurement framework defined in ISO/IEC 33020:2015 [4]. Section 3.1 and 3.2 elucidate the concepts to handle the process capability level model presented in Sect. 3.3.

3.1 Process Capability Levels and Process Attributes

Process capability levels and process attributes are identical to those defined in ISO/IEC 33020:2015 [4]. Rough descriptions of the capability levels and the corresponding process attributes can be found in Sect. 5 in the paper at hand. Process attributes are features of a process that can be evaluated on a scale of achievement, providing a measure of the capability of the process. They are applicable to all processes. A capability level is a set of process attribute(s) that work together to provide a major enhancement in the capability to perform a process. Each attribute addresses a specific aspect of the capability level. The levels constitute a rational way of progressing through the improvement of the capability of any process. According to ISO/IEC 33020:2015 [4] there are six capability levels (Table 2), incorporating nine process attributes (PA) (Table 3).

Table 2. Process capability levels according to ISO/IEC 33020:2015 [4].

Level 0: Incomplete process	The process is not implemented, or ails to achieve its purpose
Level 1: Performed process	The implemented process achieves its process purpose
Level 2: Managed process	The previously described performed process is now implemented in a managed fashion (planned, monitored and adjusted) and its work products are appropriately established, controlled and maintained
Level 3: Established process	The previously described managed process is now implemented using a defined process the = at is capable o achieving its process outcomes
Level 4: Predictable process	The previously described established process now operates predictively within defined limits to achieve its process outcomes. Quantitative management needs are identified, measurement data are collected and analyzed to identify assignable causes o variation Corrective action is taken to address assignable causes of variation
Level 5: Innovating process	The previously described predictable process is now continually improved to respond to organizational change

Table 3. Process capability levels according to ISO/IEC 33020:2015 [4].

Attribute ID	Process attributes
Level 0: Incomplete process	
Level 1: Performed process	
PA 1.1	Process performance process attribute
Level 2: Managed process	
PA 2.1	Performance management process attribute
PA 2.2	Work product management process attribute
Level 3: Established process	
PA 3.1	Process definition process attribute
PA 3.2	Process deployment process attribute
Level 4: Predictable process	
PA 4.1	Quantitative analysis process attribute
PA 4.2	Quantitative control process attribute
Level 5: Innovating process	
PA 5.1	Process innovation process attribute
PA 5.2	Process innovation implementation process attribute

3.2   Process Attribute Rating

To support the rating of process attributes, the ISO/IEC 33020:2015 [4] measurement framework provides a defined rating scale with an option for refinement, different rating methods and different aggregation methods depending on the class of the assessment (e.g. required for organizational maturity assessments). Within this process measurement framework, a process attribute is a measurable property of process capability. A process attribute rating is a judgement of the degree of achievement of the process attribute for the assessed process. The rating scale is defined by ISO/IEC 33020:2015 [4] as shown in Table 4.

Table 4. Rating scale according to ISO/IEC 33020:2015 [4].

N	Not achieved	There is little or no evidence of achievement of the defined process
P	Partially achieved	There is some evidence of an approach to, and some achievement of, the defined process attribute in the assesses process. Some aspects of achievement of the process attribute may be unpredictable
L	Largely achieved	There is evidence of a systematic approach to, and significant achievement of, the defined process attribute in the assessed process. Some weakness related to this process, attribute may exist in the assessed process
F	Fully achieved	There is evidence of a complete and systematic approach to, and full achievement of, the defined process attribute in the assessed process. No significant weakness related to this process attribute exist in the assessed process

The ordinal scale defined above shall be understood in terms of percentage achievement of a process attribute. The corresponding percentages are indicated in Table 5.

Table 5. Rating scale percentage values according to ISO/IEC 33020:2015 [4].

N	Not achieved	0 to $\leq 15\%$ achievement
P	Partially achieved	$>15\%$ to $\leq 50\%$ achievement
L	Largely achieved	$>50\%$ to $\leq 85\%$ achievement
F	Fully achieved	$>85\%$ to $\leq 100\%$ achievement

The ordinal scale may be further refined for the measures 'partially' (P) and 'largely' (L) as defined in Table 6.

Table 6. Refinement of rating scale according to ISO/IEC 33020:2015 [4].

P–	Partially achieved	There is some evidence of an approach to, and some achievement of, the defined process attribute in the assessed process. Many aspects of achievement of the process attribute may be unpredictable
P+	Partially achieved	There is some evidence of an approach to, and some achievement of, the defined process attribute in the assessed process. Some aspects of achievement of the process attribute may be unpredictable
L–	Largely achieved	There is evidence of a systematic approach to, and significant achievement of, the defined process attribute in the assessed process. Many weakness related to this process attribute may exist in the assessed process
L+	Largely achieved	There is evidence of a systematic approach to, and significant achievement of, the defined process attribute in the assessed process. Some weakness related to this process attribute may exist in the assessed process

The corresponding percentages are indicated in Table 7.

Table 7. Refined rating scale percentage values according to ISO/IEC 33020:2015 [4].

P–	Partially achieved –	0 to ≤ 32.5% achievement
P+	Partially achieved +	>32.5% to ≤ 50% achievement
L–	Largely achieved –	>50% to ≤ 67.5% achievement
L+	Largely achieved +	>67.5% to ≤ 85% achievement

The rating and aggregation method in ISO/IEC 33020:2015 [4] provides the following definitions. A process outcome is the observable result of successful achievement of the process purpose. A process attribute outcome is the observable result of achievement of a specified process attribute. Process outcomes and process attribute outcomes may be characterized as an intermediate step to providing a process attribute rating. When performing rating, the rating method employed shall be specified relevant to the class of assessment. The use of rating method may vary according to the class, scope and context of an assessment. The lead assessor shall decide which (if any) rating method to use. The selected rating method(s) shall be specified in the assessment input and referenced in the assessment report. Further information can be taken from ISO/IEC 33020:2015 [4].

3.3 Process Capability Level Model

The process capability level achieved by a process shall be derived from the process attribute ratings for that process according to the process capability level model shown in Table 8. The process capability level model defines the rules about how the achievement of each level depends on the rating of the process attributes for the assessed and all lower levels. Generally, the achievement of a given level requires the predominant achievement (at least 'largely' achieved) of the corresponding process attributes and the full achievement of any lower lying process attribute.

Table 8. Process capability level model according to ISO/IEC 33020:2015 [4].

Scale	Process attribute	Rating
Level 1	**PA 1.1: Process performance**	**Largely**
Level 2	PA 1.1: Process performance	Fully
	PA 2.1: Performance management	**Largely**
	PA 2.2: Work Product management	**Largely**
Level 3	PA 1.1: Process performance	Fully
	PA 2.1: Performance management	Fully
	PA 2.2: Work Product management	Fully
	PA 3.1: Process definition	**Largely**
	PA 3.2: Process deployment	**Largely**
Level 4	PA 1.1: Process performance	Fully
	PA 2.1: Performance management	Fully
	PA 2.2: Work Product management	Fully
	PA 3.1: Process definition	Fully
	PA 3.2: Process deployment	Fully
	PA 4.1: Quantitative analysis	**Largely**
	PA 4.2: Quantitative control	**Largely**
Level 5	PA 1.1: Process performance	Fully
	PA 2.1: Performance management	Fully
	PA 2.2: Work product management	Fully
	PA 3.1: Process definition	Fully
	PA 3.2: Process deployment	Fully
	PA 4.1: Quantitative analysis	Fully
	PA 4.2: Quantitative control	Fully
	PA 5.1: Process innovation	**Largely**
	PA 5.2: Process innovation implementation	**Largely**

4   Process Assessment Model

An process assessment model (PAM) offers indicators in order to identify whether the process outcomes and the process attribute outcomes (achievements) are present or absent in the instantiated processes of projects and organizational units. These indicators provide guidance for assessors in accumulating the necessary objective evidence to support judgments of capability. They are not intended to be regarded as a mandatory set of checklists to be followed. In order to judge the presence or absence of process outcomes and process achievements an assessment delivers objective evidence. All such evidence comes from the examination of work products and the repository content of the assessed processes, and from testimony provided by the performers and managers of the assessed processes. This evidence is mapped to the PAM indicators to allow the establishment of a correspondence to the relevant process outcomes and process attribute achievements. There are two types of indicators. Process performance indicators, which apply exclusively to capability level 1, provide an indication of the extent of fulfillment of the process outcomes. Process capability indicators, which apply to capability levels 2 to 5, provide an indication of the extent of fulfillment of the process attribute achievements. Assessment indicators are used to confirm that certain practices were performed, as shown by evidence collected during an assessment. All such evidence comes either from the examination of work products of the processes assessed, or from statements made by the performers and managers of the processes. The existence of base practices and work products provide evidence of the performance of the processes associated with them. Similarly, the existence of process capability indicators provides evidence of process capability. The evidence obtained should be recorded in a form that clearly relates to an associated indicator, in order that support for the assessor's judgment can be confirmed or verified as required by ISO/IEC 33002:2015 [5].

4.1   Process Performance Indicators

Types of process performance indicators are base practices (BP) and work products (WP). Both BPs and WPs relate to one or more process outcomes. Consequently, BPs and WPs are always process-specific and not generic. BPs represent activity-oriented indicators. WPs represent result-oriented indicators. Both BP and WP are used for judging objective evidence that an assessor is to collect, and accumulate, in the performance of an assessment. In that respect BPs and WPs are alternative indicator sets the assessor can use. A PAM offers a set of work product characteristics (WPC) for each WP. These are meant to offer a good practice and state-of-the-art knowledge guide for the assessor. Therefore, WP and WPC are supposed to be a quickly accessible information source during an assessment. In that respect WPs and WPCs only represent an example structure. They are neither a "strict must" nor are they normative for organizations. Instead, the actual structure, form and content of concrete work products and documents for the implemented processes must be defined by the project and organization, respectively. The project and/or organization ensures that the work products are appropriate for the intended purpose and needs, and in relation to the development goals.

4.2   Process Capability Indicators

Types of process capability indicators are generic practice (GP) and generic resource (GR). Both GPs and GRs relate to one or more PA achievements. In contrast to process performance indicators, however, they are of generic type, i.e. they apply to any process. The difference between GP and GR is that the former represents activity-oriented indicators while the latter represent infrastructure-oriented indicators for judging objective evidence. An assessor must collect and accumulate evidence supporting process capability indicators during an assessment.

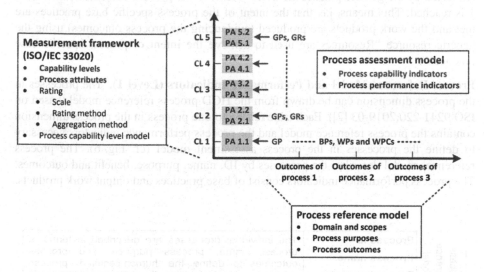

Fig. 5. Relationship between assessment indicators and process capability.

5 Process Capability Levels and Process Attributes

Process capability indicators are the means of achieving the capabilities addressed by the considered process attributes. Evidence of process capability indicators supports the judgment of the degree of achievement of the process attributes (cf. Fig. 5). The capability dimension of the PAM consists of six capability levels matching the capability levels defined in ISO/IEC 33020:2015 [4]. The process capability indicators for the 9 process attributes included in the capability dimension for process capability level 1 to 5 are described in Sect. 5.3. The generic practices address the characteristics from each process attribute. The generic resources relate to the process attribute. Process capability level 0 does not include any type of indicators, as it reflects a non-implemented process or a process which fails to partially achieve any of its outcomes.

5.1 Process Capability Level 0: Incomplete Process

The process is not implemented or fails to achieve its process purpose. At this level there is little or no evidence of any systematic achievement of the process purpose.

5.2   Process Capability Level 1: Performed Process

The implemented process achieves its process purpose. The following process attribute demonstrates the achievement of a performed process representing process capability level 1. The process performance process attribute for level 1 is a measure of the extent to which the process purpose is achieved. If the process achieves its defined outcomes requested by the generic practice GP 1.1.1 "Achieve the process outcomes", then level 1 is reached. This means, i.e. that the intent of the process specific base practices are met and the work products are produced (evidencing the process outcomes) using the generic resource "Resources are used to achieve the intent of process specific base practices".

Process Reference Model and Performance Indicators (Level 1). The processes in the process dimension can be drawn from the HCD process reference model (based on ISO 9241-220:2019-03 [2]). Each table related to one process in the process dimension contains the process reference model and the process performance indicators necessary to define the processes in the process assessment model (cf. Fig. 6). The process references model describes the processes by ID, name, purpose, benefit and outcomes. The process performance indicators consist of base practices and output work products.

Process reference model	Process ID Process name Process purpose Process benefit Process outcomes	The individual processes are described in terms of process name, process purpose, and process outcomes to define the human-centered process reference model. Additionally a process identifier is provided.
Process performance indicators	Base practices	A set of base practices for the process providing a definition of the tasks and activities needed to accomplish the process purpose and fulfill the process outcomes
	Output work products	A number of output work products associated with each process NOTE: Refer to Annex B for the characteristics associated with each work product.

Fig. 6. Template for the process description.

As an example of a process description, Table 9 shows the HCD process HCP.3.4.2 according to ISO 9241-220:2019-03 [2].

Table 9. HCD process description HCP.3.4.2 according to ISO 9241-220:2019-03 [2] where the activities have been turned into base practices of the PAM

Process ID	HCP.3.4.2
Process name	Produce and refine user interface design solutions
Process purpose	To produce and iteratively evaluate user interface design solutions from a user perspective to ensure that user requirements have been met NOTE 1 For an existing or procured system, if any gaps in meeting the human-centered quality objectives are identified, this process can be used to decide how it can be configured or customized to produce the optimal user interface design
Process benefit	User interfaces are designed that satisfy the user requirements and take account of the human-centered quality objectives. The iterative design of the user interface supports early identification and economical resolution of defects or other issues that cause human-centered quality problems
Process outcomes	a) The potential benefits of innovative solutions for the user interface design have been considered b) User interface technology is selected that supports the identified user-system interaction c) A user interface design solution is available that enables completion of one or more tasks by the intended range of users d) The user's interaction with the user interface design solution has been evaluated for acceptable human-centered quality before technical implementation e) Decisions are made on how to deal with identified problems related to the human centered quality for the redesign of the interactive system and/or, when necessary, alternatives such as training, help, or user support are to be provided f) Necessary corrective actions are initiated if the user interface design solution does not sufficiently meet the user requirements g) The development team has a basis for the technical implementation of the system (whether a new release of an existing system, a customization of a procured system or components, or development of a new system)
Base practices	**HCP.3.4.2.BP1: Explore the potential benefits of using an innovative solution** (the use of creative design and/or new technologies). [a] **HCP.3.4.2.BP2: Select the appropriate user interface technology for the system to support the identified user-system interaction, in conjunction with other project stakeholders.** [b] **HCP.3.4.2.BP3: Create an interface design solution that implements one or more user's requirements that support tasks defined in the context of use description.** [c] **HCP.3.4.2.BP4: If providing accessibility, decide whether to use a single design for all approaches or whether to support individualization to specific user needs.** [c] **HCP.3.4.2.BP5: Identify appropriate interaction styles** (dialogue techniques). [c]

(continued)

Table 9. (*continued*)

Process ID	HCP.3.4.2
	HCP.3.4.2.BP6: Derive the necessary interaction objects, the sequence and timing (dynamics) of the interaction and the navigation structure. [c]
	HCP.3.4.2.BP7: Design the information architecture to allow efficient access to interaction objects. [c]
	HCP.3.4.2.BP8: Identify and apply appropriate guidance for the design of the user interface and interaction of both hardware and software of the user interface according to the target platform. [c]
	HCP.3.4.2.BP9: Construct testable user interface design alternatives with a level of detail and realism that is appropriate to the issues that need to be investigated. [c]
	NOTE 2 The user interface design solution can be a prototype that is as simple as a sketch or static mock-up or as complicated as a fully functioning interactive system with more or less complete functionality
	HCP.3.4.2.BP10: Evaluate design with users in order to identify previously unidentified context information, identify emergent needs, and refine the user requirements, to identify design improvements and to ensure that any required objectives for human-centered quality have been achieved. (HCP 3.5) [d]
	HCP.3.4.2.BP11: Iteratively. adapt the concept based on the findings of user-centered evaluation until an acceptable cost-effective solution is obtained. [e, f]
	i) Take account of the costs and benefits of proposed changes when deciding what will be modified
	ii) Decide (using HCP.3.5) if the user interface design solution sufficiently meets the user requirements
	HCP.3.4.2.BP12: Communicate the acceptable solution to the development team, based on the user requirements and tasks to be supported by the solution. [g]
	NOTE 3 For a ready-to-use system (where the design is not under control of the project), evaluate the system (HCP 3.5) to determine whether it adequately meets then requirements established in HCP.3.4.1
Output work product	CIF.8 user interface specification (a, b, c, d, g)
	2.09 architectural design description (c, e, g)
	8.17 system interface requirements (b)
	Technological possibilities are in 8.17 system interface requirements
	Refinement includes development of low-fidelity prototypes

Output Work Products (Level 1). Work product characteristics (WPC) can be used when reviewing potential outputs such as work products of process implementation. The characteristics are provided as guidance for the attributes to look for, in a sample work product (WP) and to provide objective evidence supporting the assessment of a process. A documented process and assessor judgment are needed to ensure that the process context (application domain, business purpose, development methodology, size of the organization, etc.) is considered when using this information. WPs and their characteristics should be considered as a starting point for considering whether, given the context, they contribute to the intended purpose of the process, and not as a checklist of what every organization must have.

5.3 Process Reference Model and Performance Indicators (Level 2–5)

In contrast to level 1, the performance indicators on level 2–5, represented by generic practices and resources, relate to all process in the process reference model.

Process Capability Level 2: Managed Process. If the performed process is implemented in a managed fashion (planned, monitored and adjusted) and its work products are appropriately established, controlled and maintained, then it is called a "managed process". The performance management process attribute (PA 2.1) and the work product management process attribute (PA 2.2), together with the previously defined performance process attribute (PA 1.1), demonstrate the achievement of a managed process representing process capability level 2.

The performance management process attribute (PA 2.1) is a measure of the extent to which the performance of the process is managed:

a) Objectives for the performance of the process are identified;
b) Performance of the process is planned;
c) Performance of the process is monitored;
d) Performance of the process is adjusted to meet plans;
e) Responsibilities and authorities for performing the process are defined, assigned and communicated;
f) Personnel performing the process are prepared for executing their responsibilities;
g) Resources and information necessary for performing the process are identified, made available, allocated and used;
h) Interfaces between the involved parties are managed to ensure both effective communication and clear assignment of responsibility.

The work product management process attribute (PA 2.2) is a measure of the extent to which the work products produced by the process are appropriately managed:

a) Requirements for the work products of the process are defined;
b) Requirements for documentation and control of the work products are defined;
c) Work products are appropriately identified, documented, and controlled;
d) Work products are reviewed in accordance with planned arrangements and adjusted as necessary to meet requirements.

Process Capability Level 3: Established Process. The managed process is implemented using a defined process that can achieve its process outcomes. The process definition process attribute (PA 3.1) and the process deployment process attribute (PA 3.2), together with the process attributes for the performed (PA 1.1) and the managed process (PA 2.1 and PA 2.2), demonstrate the achievement of an established process representing process capability level 3.

The process definition process attribute (PA 3.1) is a measure of the extent to which a standard process is maintained to support the deployment of the defined process:

a) A standard process, including appropriate tailoring guidelines, is defined and maintained, which describes the fundamental elements that must be incorporated into a defined process;
b) The sequence and interaction of the standard process with other processes is determined.
c) Required competencies and roles for performing the process are identified as part of the standard process;
d) Required infrastructure and the work environment for performing the process are identified as part of the standard process;
e) Suitable methods and measures for monitoring the effectiveness and suitability of the process are determined.

The process deployment process attribute (PA 3.2) is a measure of the extent to which the standard process is deployed as a defined process to achieve its process outcomes:

a) A defined process is deployed based upon an appropriately selected and/or tailored standard process;
b) Required roles, responsibilities and authorities for performing the defined process are assigned and communicated;
c) Personnel performing the defined process are competent based on appropriate education, training, and experience;
d) Required resources and information necessary for performing the defined process are made available, allocated and used;
e) Required infrastructure and the work environment for performing the defined process are made available, managed and maintained;
f) Appropriate data are collected and analyzed as a basis for understanding the behavior of the process, to demonstrate the suitability and effectiveness of the process, and to evaluate where continual improvement of the process can be made.

Process Capability Level 4: Predictable Process. The established process operates predictively within defined limits to achieve its process outcomes. Quantitative management needs are identified, measurement data are collected and analyzed to identify assignable causes of variation. Corrective action is taken to address assignable causes of variation. The quantitative analysis process attribute (PA 4.1) as well as the quantitative control process attribute (PA 4.2), together with the process attributes for the performed (PA 1.1), managed (PA 2.1 and PA 2.2) and established (PA 3.1 and PA 3.2) process, demonstrate the achievement of a predictable process representing process capability level 4.

The quantitative analysis process attribute (PA 4.1) is a measure of the extent to which information needs are defined, relationships between process elements are identified and data are collected:

a) The process is aligned with quantitative business goals;
b) Process information needs in support of relevant defined quantitative business goals are established;
c) Process measurement objectives are derived from process information needs;
d) Measurable relationships between process elements that contribute to the process performance are identified;
e) Quantitative objectives for process performance in support of relevant business goals are established;
f) Appropriate measures and frequency of measurement are identified and defined in line with process measurement objectives and quantitative objectives for process performance;
g) Results of measurement are collected, validated and reported in order to monitor the extent to which the quantitative objectives for process performance are met.

The quantitative control process attribute (PA 4.2) is a measure of the extent to which objective data are used to manage process performance that is predictable:

a) Techniques for analyzing the collected data are selected;
b) Assignable causes of process variation are determined through analysis of the collected data;
c) Distributions that characterize the performance of the process are established;
d) Corrective actions are taken to address assignable causes of variation;
e) Separate distributions are established (as necessary) for analyzing the process under the influence of assignable causes of variation.

Process Capability Level 5: Innovating Process. The predictable process is continually improved to respond to change aligned with organizational goals. The process innovation process attribute (PA 5.1) as well as the process innovation implementation process attribute (PA 5.2), together with the process attributes for the performed (PA 1.1), managed (PA 2.1 and PA 2.2), established (PA 3.1 and PA 3.2) and predicted (PA 4.1 and PA 4.2) process, demonstrate the achievement of an 'innovating process' representing process capability level 5.

The process innovation process attribute (PA 5.1) is a measure of the extent to which changes to the process are identified from investigations of innovative approaches to the definition and deployment of the process:

a) Process innovation objectives are defined that support the relevant business goals;
b) Appropriate data are analyzed to identify opportunities for innovation;
c) Innovation opportunities derived from new technologies and process concepts are identified;
d) An implementation strategy is established to achieve the process innovation objectives.

The process innovation process implementation attribute (PA 5.2) is a measure of the extent to which changes to the definition, management and performance of the process achieves the relevant process innovation objectives:

a) Impact of all proposed changes is assessed with respect to the objectives of the defined process and standard process;
b) Implementation of all agreed changes is managed to ensure that any disruption to the process performance is understood and acted upon;
c) Effectiveness of process change based on actual performance is evaluated against the defined product requirements and process objectives.

6   Exemplifying a Process Assessment Rating

The assessment procedure contains at least the following steps:

- Explain process purpose and benefit and most important requirements of the process to the audience,
- Interview the audience regarding process life based on purpose, base practices and work products and collect documented evidences,
- Rate the evidence according to the rating scale,
- Accumulate the ratings for one process (e.g. HCP.3.4.2) to an overall rating considering:
  - Achievement of process purpose,
  - Achievement of all base practices,
  - Achievement of work products.

As an example, the summary of the results of the rating up to level 2 could appear as presented in Table 10. Depending on the rating, the HCD processes of the executing process group (HCP.3) are ratings up to level 2 in this figure addressing the performance process attribute (level 1) and the management process attributes (level 2). The only process that reached level 2 in this example is HCP.3.4.2 (Produce and refine user interface design solutions) indicating that all base practices are achieved and the work products of this process (such as system interface requirement, architectural design description and user interface specification) are available and reviewed, and the process is managed in a proper way. Other processes such as HCP.3.1.1 (Establish human-centered quality objectives) were not performed and managed properly and the work products are mostly missing.

Table 10. Example rating of the HCP.3 process group from ISO 9241-220:2019-03 [2].

HCP.3 Execute BP / GP Rating	HCP.3.1.1	HCP.3.1.2	HCP.3.1.3	HCP.3.1.4	HCP.3.1.5	HCP.3.2.1	HCP.3.2.2	HCP.3.3.1	HCP.3.3.2	HCP.3.3.3	HCP.3.4.1	HCP.3.4.2	HCP.3.5.1	HCP.3.5.2	HCP.3.5.3
BP1	P	P		L	L	P	P	P			L	P		P	P
BP2	P	P		L	P	P	P	P			P	P		P	P
BP3			P	P	L				P		L		P		
BP4	P	P	P	L	L	P	P	P	P	P	L	P		P	P
BP5	P	P	P		P	P	P	P	P	P	P	P		P	P
BP6	P	P			P		P				P	P			
BP7		P	P	L		P	P				P	P	L	P	P
BP8					P				P						
BP9		P					P				L		P		
BP10															
BP11				P											
BP12										P					
BP13										P					
BP14															
GP2.1.1				P	P				P	P	P	L	P	P	
GP2.1.2		P		P	P		P	P			P	L	P		
GP2.1.3	P		P		P						P				P
GP2.1.4	P		P		P	P			P		L			P	P
GP2.1.5	P		P		P				P		P		P		P
GP2.1.6	L		L	P	L		L	P	L	P		P	L		
GP2.1.7	P	L	P	L	P	P	P	L	P	P	L	P	P	P
GP2.2.1	P	P	P	P	P	P	P	P	P	P	P	P	P	P	P
GP2.2.2	L		L	P	P		L	P	P	P		P	P		
GP2.2.3	L		L	P	P		L	P	P	P		P	P		
GP2.2.4	P		P								P				P
Process Attributes Rating
PA1.1	P			P	P					L	P		P		P
PA2.1				P	P				P		P	L	P	P	
PA2.2	P			P	P				P	P	P	L	P	P	
Capability
Level	0	0	0	1	0	0	0	0	0	1	0	2	0	0	0

7 Discussion

With a seamless HCD development process, mistakes and unproductivity can be prevented and product quality rises with high quality process output contributing to a high-quality interactive product. Behind such experiences a causal relationship between process and product quality is assumed, which consists in the fact that a more mature process with a lower probability of error produces higher quality products than a less mature process. Since quality cannot be achieved without a sustainable focus on user requirements, usability engineering is also referred to as a human-centric development process. Requirements for a human-centered development process are defined in DIN EN ISO 9241-210:2011-01 [3]. The aim of usability engineering is to do everything necessary in a development process to steer it towards an optimal quality of use of the final product. Following a PRM like that derived from ISO 9241-220:2019-03 [2] ensures the involvement of users as requirement donors and as evaluators of a) the achieved quality of use, b) the application of suitable usability engineering methods, c) the documentation of design decisions with relevance for the quality of use, d) the establishment of a quality management system for the quality of use and e) setting up process roles with suitably qualified personnel (cf. DIN SPEC 92412:2015-11 [6]).

8 Conclusion

The presented PAM for the development process of interactive products serves to assess the process quality in development projects based on objective indicators for process capability and thereby to achieve quality of use referring to the HCD processes defined in ISO 9241-220:2019-03 [2]. Even if this HCD-PAM is still in a development state and, hence, must be improved and worked out in detail in accordance with all other relevant standards, the principles of this HCD-PAM have been confirmed for years by assessments in the automotive industry regarding software engineering processes. The presented HCD-PAM can be applied in conjunction with the process reference model (PRM) for human centered design (HCD) processes derived from the processes in ISO 9241-220:2019-03 [2] to a similar benefit. The refinement and application of the suggested HCD-PAM will show if it can be used to prove that the process has the capability of justifying trust in the HCD processes by all stakeholders.

References

1. ISO/IEC 15504-5:2006: Information Technology – Process assessment – Part 5: An exemplar Process Assessment Model
2. ISO 9241-220:2019-03: Ergonomics of human-system interaction - Part 220: Processes for enabling, executing and assessing human-centred design within organizations
3. DIN EN ISO 9241-210:2011-01: Ergonomics of human-system interaction – Part 210: Human-centred design for interactive systems
4. ISO/IEC 33020:2015: Information technology – Process assessment – Process measurement framework for assessment of process capability
5. ISO/IEC 33002:2015: Information technology – Process assessment – Requirements for performing process assessment
6. DIN SPEC 92412:2015-11: Ergonomics of human-system interaction - Auditing procedure for the development of interactive products based on DIN EN ISO 9241-210

Modeling and Runtime Generation of Situation-Aware Adaptations

Christian Herdin[1(✉)] and Christian Märtin[2(✉)]

[1] Department of Computer Science, University of Rostock,
Albert-Einstein-Str. 22, 18059 Rostock, Germany
Christian.Herdin@uni-rostock.de
[2] Faculty of Computer Science, Augsburg University of Applied Sciences,
An der Hochschule 1, 86161 Augsburg, Germany
Christian.Maertin@hs-augsburg.de

Abstract. SitAdapt 2.0 is an architecture and runtime system for building adaptive interactive applications. The system is integrated into the PaMGIS framework for pattern- and model-based user interface construction and generation. This paper focuses on the situation-rule-based adaptation process and discusses the interplay of the SitAdapt 2.0 components in order to support different categories of adaptations. As the system observes the user during sessions and collects visual, bio-physical, and emotional data about the user that may vary over time, SitAdapt 2.0, in contrast to other adaptive system environments, is able to create situation-aware adaptations in real time that reflect the user's changing physical, cognitive, and emotional state. The operation of the system is demonstrated with an example from an adaptive travel-booking application.

Keywords: Adaptive user interface · Situation analytics · Situation awareness · Model-based user interface development · Situation-aware adaptations

1 Introduction and Related Work

Situation- and context-aware computing has an established tradition in the area of distributed mobile computing [14] and interactive systems [6]. Challenging new application domains range from sport and fitness apps, driver assistance systems, E-commerce, digital marketing and other business applications to computer-based learning environments. Such applications require a new type of software engineering support, as was postulated in [3]. We are presenting the SitAdapt 2.0 modeling and design approach for such situation-aware software systems that has been refined over years in an evolutionary process [13].

The current implementation of our approach is mainly directed towards web applications and deals with the construction of user-centered interactive software that is able to dynamically adapt to the situations of users, and to guide them to meeting their objectives and successfully finishing their tasks. The main focus of this paper lies on the adaptation process and the detailed modeling of situation-aware adaptations.

© Springer Nature Switzerland AG 2020
M. Kurosu (Ed.): HCII 2020, LNCS 12181, pp. 71–81, 2020.
https://doi.org/10.1007/978-3-030-49059-1_5

1.1   Different Types of Adaptations

The PaMGIS framework [5] that is used by the SitAdapt 2.0 system offers development
and runtime support for multiple-adaptive migratory user interfaces and can react to
context changes in the user's environment as well as situational changes that include
the user's behavior and emotional state in real-time. In general, three different categories of adaptations were distinguished in the field of user interfaces [1, 15]:

- Adaptable user interfaces. The user customizes the user interface to his or her
  personal preferences.
- Semi-automated adaptive user interfaces. The user interface provides recommendations for adaptations. The user has to decide, whether he or she wants to accept
  the recommendation or not.
- Automated adaptive user interfaces. The user interface automatically reacts to
  changes in the context-of-use.

By adding the concept of situations that include and exploit the variability of the
cognitive and emotional states of the user to the adaptation modeling process, a new
category of individual adaptations is made possible. With SitAdapt 2.0, such situation-
aware adaptations can be modeled by the developer and generated at runtime.

The SitAdapt 2.0 runtime system allows to adapt the user interface in different
ways:

- Changes in content. The system can adapt button labels and offer help texts or a chat
  windows to the different types of users. In the e-commerce domain, specific
  advertising and offers, as well as additional elements or popups such as a voucher
  can be presented to the user, if the evaluation of the situation recommends such
  adaptations. Different users can also be offered different content. For example, more
  or less detailed text information or product images or more or less detailed content
  presentation by adding or removing content attributes, like, e.g., comments for a
  product.
- Changes in design. SitAdapt 2.0 can adapt colors, images and the contrast settings
  of a program or website or change text layout and font size and type. The sequence
  or layout of the website elements can be changed for different users.
- Changes of media and interaction object types. Such changes modify the way of
  information presentation. Different types of charts (mosaic or a bar charts), personalized areas or functions (areas with functions frequently used by the individual), etc., can be chosen by situation-aware adaptations. Other possibilities for
  adaptations can be the replacement of a form with a wizard or the change of the
  input media from text to language.

Depending on the adaptation rules and the available data about the user and in the
recorded situation profile, the SitAdapt 2.0 system can modify the user interface at
different times:

- Before the first display of the user interface,
- while interacting with the user interface, or,
- when the user accesses the interface again, at a later time.

1.2   Adaptive User Interface Approaches

Some related approaches for adaptive user interfaces either focus on adaptation or migration to other devices and platforms, or also cover user-related context-adaptations. Two interesting related approaches are the SUPPLE and Adapt-UI systems that are discussed in the following paragraphs.

SUPPLE has been developed at the University of Washington in Seattle. The first publication is from 2004 [9]. This approach evaluates functional interface specifications as well as device and user models [9]. The generation and adaptation of user interfaces is treated on the basis of solutions to decision-theoretic optimization problems.

SUPPLE searches for optimal renditions considering any relevant device constraints and minimizing the user's effort required to carry out the necessary user interface actions [9].

SUPPLE adapts the user interface to the individual work style [11] as well as to the habits of the user, for example an extra individual area for frequently used functions of a pocket calculator [7]. The necessary generation and adjustment of the surface happens at runtime [11]. SUPPLE++ is a variant of the SUPPLE system and supports automatic customization for visually impaired users with limited motor skills [8]. SUPPLE++ was developed in 2007 [10]. SUPPLE needs three input sources for the creation of adaptive user interfaces. An interface specification (I), a device specification (D), and a user model represented by user traces (T) [8].

Within SUPPLE a functional interface specification is defined as a set of interface elements and a set of interface constraints. The elements are specified in terms of their data types which can be either primitive or complex. The data types that can be either primitive or complex. The constraints are expressed as functions mapping renderings to a Boolean value and allow, for instance, to map certain elements to the same widget. The device model comprises the available widgets, device-related constraints, and two device-specific functions for evaluating the adequacy of the widgets to be used.

One function measures the appropriateness of the widgets for interacting with the variables of the given types while the other calculates the user's effort required for navigating through the user interface. The user model is defined by means of user traces, which are a type of logs of user actions, recorded at runtime. SUPPLE is aimed at finding the most appropriate rendering for each individual abstract interface element. This is achieved by means of a branch-and bound algorithm for minimizing a cost function, which is composed of the previously mentioned functions and information from the device and the user models [9]. The cost function consists of more than 40 concerted parameters and cannot easily be determined manually. Therefore, a tool named ARNAULD has been developed in order to facilitate this process [12]. SUPPLE++ primarily utilizes even more complex cost functions in order to consider the motor and visual impairments of handicapped users. In analogy to ARNAULD, SUPPLE++ is supported by the tool named Activity Modeler [7].

Adapt-UI [16], like SitAdapt 2.0, offers runtime-adaptation of the user interface. The system focuses on context-of-use adaptations when migrating to other devices and platforms, but also manages some user-related aspects. The system includes models of the user interface, the context, and the possible adaptations. Context-changes are triggered with adaptation rules. Such rules can show or hide pre-modeled UI elements, change navigation paths in pre-modeled ways, and react to a few simple user-related aspects that can be provided by a face detection library.

2 The PaMGIS Framework

The PaMGIS (Pattern-Based Modeling and Generation of Interactive Systems) framework architecture (Fig. 1) combines a situation analytics platform with pattern- and model-based user interface construction tools in order to build runtime-adaptive interactive applications with enhanced user experience and task-accomplishment characteristics [5]. The framework uses the ontological domain- and context models as proposed by the CAMELEON reference framework (CRF). The CRF [2], is the most common standard architecture for the model-driven construction of interactive systems. The CRF framework also includes structural guidelines for adapting the target software in predefined ways, mainly for responding to the requirements of different platforms and for migrating an application from a device to another device.

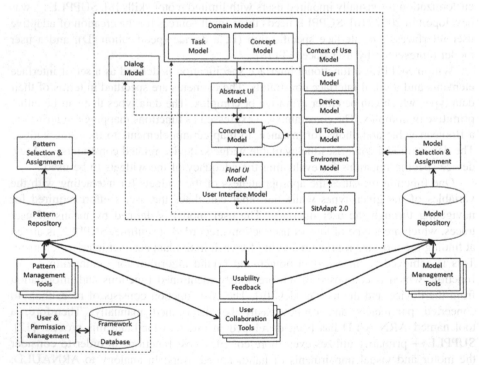

Fig. 1. Overview of the PaMGIS models and their interrelations

2.1 PaMGIS Models

The abstract user interface model (AUI) is generated from the information contained in the domain model of the application that includes both, a task model and a concept model. The AUI mainly includes the specifications of the abstract user interface objects.

In the domain model and the originally rendered AUI the user interface is still independent of the usage context.

After the completion of AUI modeling, the AUI model can be transformed into a concrete user interface model (CUI). The information of the context model and the structure of the dialog model are exploited by this process. For defining the dynamic aspects of the user interface, PaMGIS uses a dialog model. The dialog model is based on dialog graphs that were originally introduced by the TADEUS system [4].

In the next step the final user interface model (FUI) is generated automatically from the CUI model. Depending on the target implementation language, the FUI must either be compiled, or can be executed directly by an interpreter (Execute UI). The specification of the models is done in conformity with the Extensible Markup Language (XML) [5].

2.2 SitAdapt 2.0 Components

SitAdapt 2.0 (Fig. 2) is an integrated software system for enabling situation-aware real-time adaptations for web and mobile applications. The Interpreter is included in the PaMGIS framework (Fig. 1).

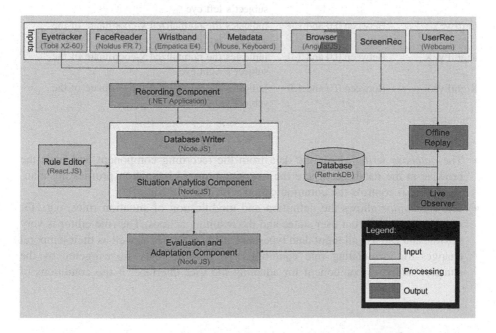

Fig. 2. Overview of the SitAdapt 2.0 system architecture and components

SitAdapt 2.0 consists of the following parts:

- The *data interfaces* use the different APIs of the devices (eye-tracker, wristband, facial expression recognition software interface, metadata from the application) to collect data about the user. SitAdapt 2.0 uses two different data types for generation and adaptation of the user interface received from the different input devices (Fig. 2). Atomic data types as constant attribute values (e.g., *age* = 30, or *glasses* = *true*) and temporal data types. Temporal data management makes it possible, to document and analyze changes in the recorded data by time-stamping these data. This allows to reconstruct; which value was valid at what time. For instance, *blood pressure* or *eye positions*. With the aid of the SitAdapt 2.0 rule editor (Fig. 2), these atomic and temporal data can be used to create rules, that have an effect on the adaptation of the user interface.
- The recording component synchronizes the different input records with a timestamp. In Table 1, for instance, the attribute value ranges are listed that can be received from the eye tracking system API.

Table 1. Data input from the eye tracking system

Attribute	Possible values	Description
LeftPupil diameter	Between circa 2.0 and 8.0	Describes the dilation of the subject's left pupil in mm
RightPupil diameter	Between circa 2.0 and 8.0	Describes the dilation of the subject's right pupil in mm
LeftEyeX	Between 0.0 and 1.0	Indicates the normalized x-coordinate of the subject's left eye
LeftEyeY	Between 0.0 and 1.0	Indicates the normalized y-coordinate of the subject's left eye
RightEyeX	Between 0.0 and 1.0	Indicates the normalized x-coordinate of the subject's right eye
RightEyeY	Between 0.0 and 1.0	Indicates the normalized y-coordinate of the subject's right eye

- The *database writer* stores the data from the recording component and from the browser in the database, where the raw situations and situation profiles are managed. It also controls the communication with the rule editor.
- The *rule editor* allows the definition and modification of situation rules, e.g., for specifying the different user states and the resulting actions. The rule editor is very flexible and can use all input data types and attribute values as well as their temporal changes for formulating rule conditions. At runtime rules are triggered by the situation analytics component for adapting the user interface, if the conditions of

one or more rules apply. However, situation rules can also activate HCI-patterns in the pattern repository. These patterns come with different levels of abstraction. They may contain concrete templates for generating interaction objects or information that describes, how low-level user interface attributes can be modified.

- The *situation analytics component* analyzes and assesses situations by exploiting the observed data. Situation rules are triggered by the situation analytics component when the rule conditions are satisfied. Situation rules interact with the situation profiles stored in the SitAdapt 2.0 database. The rule actions either directly trigger simple adaptations or interact with the PaMGIS resources as described above.

- The *evaluation and decision component* uses the data that are provided by the situation analytics component to decide whether an adaptation of the user interface is currently meaningful and necessary. For this purpose, the component evaluates one or more applicable situation rules and has to solve possible conflicts between the rules. Whether an adaptation is meaningful depends on the predefined purpose of the situation-aware target application. Such goals can be detected, if one or more situations in the situation profile trigger an application dependent or domain independent situation rule. Situation rules are related to patterns. They define behavioral and context-related situational patterns. If the decision component decides that a complex adaptation is necessary, it has to provide the artifacts from the PaMGIS pattern and model repositories to allow for the modification of the target application by the adaptation component.

- The *adaptation component* generates the necessary modifications of the interactive target user application.

2.3   SitAdapt 2.0 at Work

For the SitAdapt 2.0 system implementation, we developed a prototypical travel-booking application website to highlight and evaluate some of the system's capabilities. The application features elements typical for e-commerce applications, including the ability to enter query parameters, viewing and selecting query results, viewing product details, registering, logging in, modifying a selected product, and a payment process. Having the ability to collect information about a user's physical, physiological and emotional properties allows application designers, e.g., to help the user to fill out forms (Fig. 3).

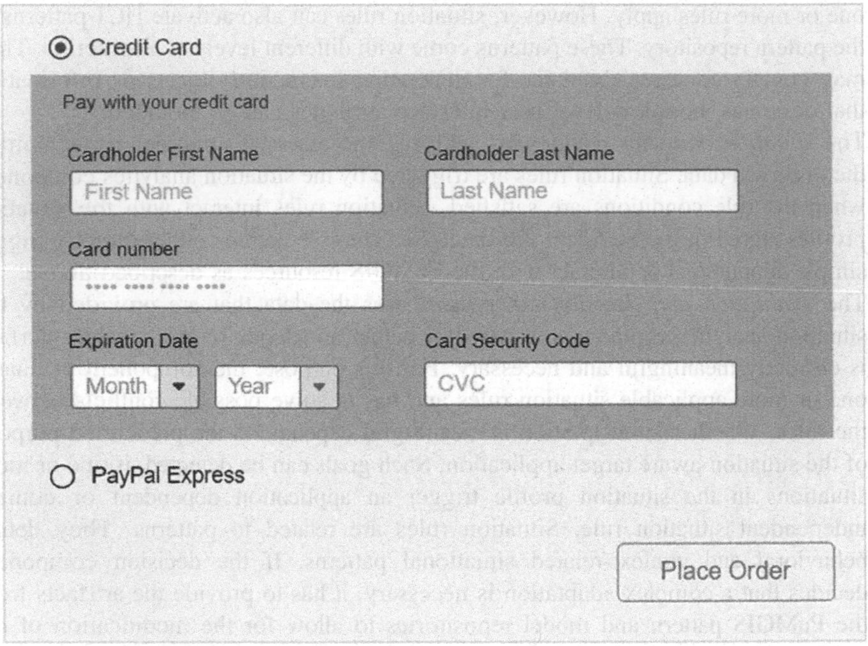

Fig. 3. Regular user interface without adaptation

In our example (Fig. 3), the system, by exploiting the collected eyetracking data, can recognize, whether the user has a problem with a form field. With the help of the API of the eye tracking system SitAdapt 2.0 receives the data about the X and Y coordinates (Table 1) of the user's eyes. The recording component synchronizes these data with other data, for example facial expression recognition data and adds a timestamp to these data. In our example, the eye tracking data are temporal data. The data base writer stores this information from the recording component in the *Rethink* database. In the rule editor, the application developer can create a rule (Fig. 4) for displaying a help text for a form field (e.g., *card security code*). A new rule is created in the rule editor by specifying a range for the X and Y coordinates. If the coordinates move within this area within 5 s (around a certain form field), a certain action should be triggered. In this example, the display of a help text (Fig. 5).

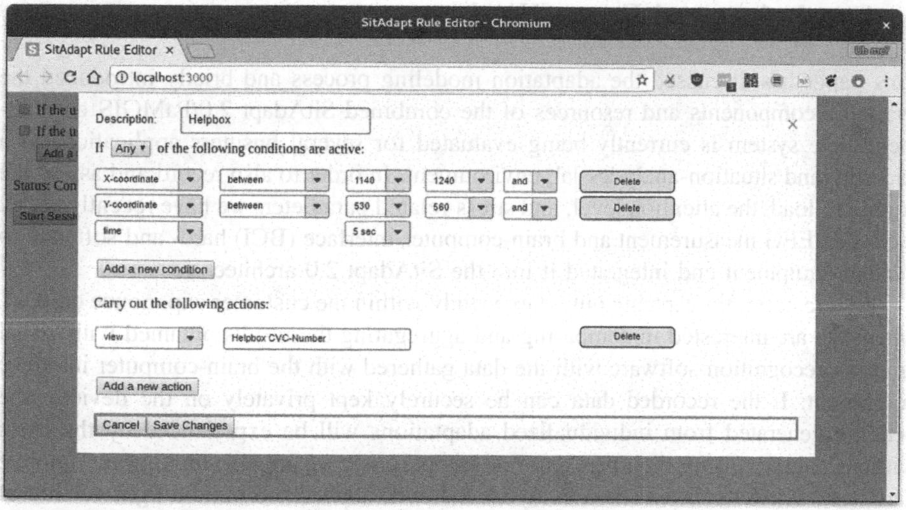

Fig. 4. SitAdapt 2.0 Rule editor

The situation analytics component analyzes and assesses the situation by exploiting the observed data. The rule *(helptext CVC)* is triggered by the situation analytics component. The evaluation and decision component is exploiting the collected data and checking possible conflicts, if more than one rule is triggered at the same time. The adaptation component finally generates the necessary modifications of the displayed user interface (Fig. 5).

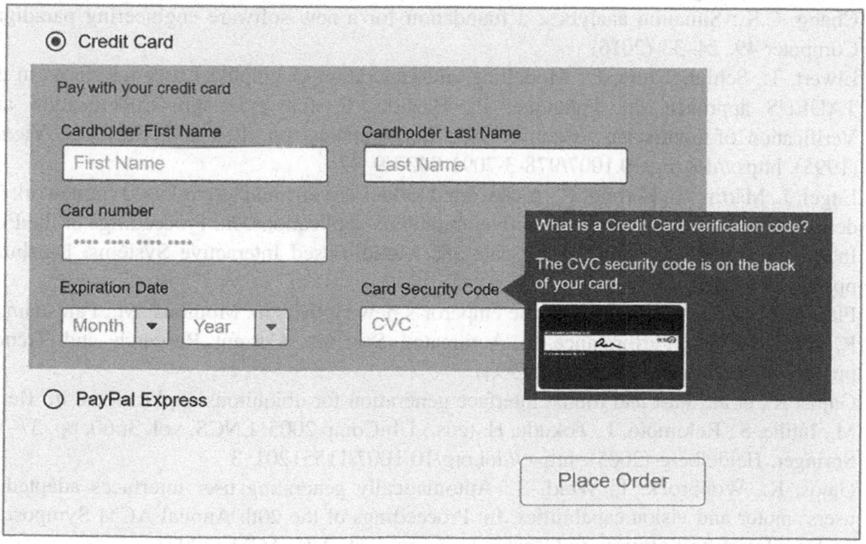

Fig. 5. Adapted user interface

3   Conclusions and Future Work

This paper has discussed the adaptation modeling process and briefly introduced the available components and resources of the combined SitAdapt 2.0/PaMGIS environment. The system is currently being evaluated for several business applications in a usability and situation-analytics-lab environment. In order to also record and assess the cognitive load, the attention level, and stress-related parameters we have recently added the g.Tec EEG measurement and brain-computer interface (BCI) hard- and software to our lab equipment and integrated it into the SitAdapt 2.0 architecture.

We are currently carrying out a large study within the customer experience domain, where we are interested in comparing and aggregating the results obtained with visual emotion recognition software with the data gathered with the brain-computer interface equipment. If the recorded data can be securely kept privately on the devices, the benefits generated from individualized adaptations will be experienced by the users without compromising their privacy. For this purpose, we are also looking into mobile hard- and software for situation analytics that will allow us to build a light version of the SitAdapt 2.0 system. Such a system can be integrated into mobile platforms and bring situation-aware applications to the end user.

References

1. Akiki, P.A., et al.: Integrating adaptive user interface capabilities in enterprise applications. In: Proceedings of the 36th International Conference on Software Engineering (ICSE 2014), pp. 712–723. ACM (2014)
2. Calvary, G., Coutaz, J., Bouillon, L., et al.: The CAMELEON reference framework (2002). http://giove.isti.cnr.it/projects/cameleon/pdf/CAMELEON%20D1.1RefFramework.pdf. Accessed 25 Aug 2016
3. Chang, C.K.: Situation analytics: a foundation for a new software engineering paradigm. Computer **49**, 24–33 (2016)
4. Elwert, T., Schlungbaum, E.: Modelling and generation of graphical user interfaces in the TADEUS approach. In: Palanque, P., Bastide, R. (eds.) Design, Specification and Verification of Interactive Systems 1995. Eurographics, pp. 193–208. Springer, Vienna (1995). https://doi.org/10.1007/978-3-7091-9437-9_12
5. Engel, J., Märtin, C., Forbrig, P.: A concerted model-driven and pattern-based framework for developing user interfaces of interactive ubiquitous applications. In: Proceedings of the First International Workshop on Large-Scale and Model-Based Interactive Systems, Duisburg, pp. 35–41 (2015)
6. Flach, J.M.: Situation awareness: the emperor's new clothes. In: Mouloua, M., Parasuaman, R. (eds.) Human Performance in Automated Systems: Current Research and Trends, pp. 241–248. Erlbaum, Mahwah (1994)
7. Gajos, K., et al.: Fast and robust interface generation for ubiquitous applications. In: Beigl, M., Intille, S., Rekimoto, J., Tokuda, H. (eds.) UbiComp 2005. LNCS, vol. 3660, pp. 37–55. Springer, Heidelberg (2005). https://doi.org/10.1007/11551201_3
8. Gajos, K., Wobbrock, J., Weld, S.: Automatically generating user interfaces adapted to users' motor and vision capabilities. In: Proceedings of the 20th Annual ACM Symposium on User Interface Software and Technology, pp. 231–240. ACM (2007)

9. Gajos, K., Weld, D.: SUPPLE: automatically generating user interfaces. In: Proceedings of the 9th International Conference on Intelligent User Interfaces, pp. 93–100. ACM (2004)

10. Gajos, K., Weld, D., Wobbrock, J.: Automatically generating personalized user interfaces with SUPPLE. Artif. Intell. **174**, 910–950 (2010)

11. Gajos, K., Weld, D.: Preference elicitation for interface optimization. In: UIST 2005: Proceedings of the 18th Annual ACM Symposium on User Interface Software and Technology, New York, USA, pp. 173–182 (2005)

12. Gajos, K., Weld, S., Wobbrock, J.: Decision-theoretic user interface generation. In: Association for the Advancement of Artificial Intelligence (AAAI 2008), pp. 1532–1536. AAAI Press (2008)

13. Märtin, C., et al.: Situation analytics and model-based user interface development: a synergetic approach for building runtime-adaptive business applications. Complex Syst. Inform. Model. Q. CSIMQ **115**(20), 1–19 (2019). https://doi.org/10.7250/csimq.2019-20.01

14. Schilit, B.N., Theimer, M.M.: Disseminating active map information to mobile hosts. IEEE Netw. **8**(5), 22–32 (1994)

15. Yigitbas, E., Sauer, S., Engels, G.: A model-based framework for multi-adaptive migratory user interfaces. In: Kurosu, M. (ed.) HCI 2015, Part II. LNCS, vol. 9170, pp. 563–572. Springer, Cham (2015). https://doi.org/10.1007/978-3-319-20916-6_52

16. Yigitbas, E., Sauer, S., Engels, G.: Adapt-UI: an IDE supporting model-driven development of self-adaptive UIs. In: Proceedings of EICS 2017, 26–29 June 2017, Lisbon, Portugal. ACM (2017)

Ethnographic Practice and the Problem of Context in Interaction Design Education

Michael Lahey[✉]

Kennesaw State University, Marietta, GA 30060, USA
mlahey@kennesaw.edu

Abstract. This paper investigates the concept of context as it relates to inter-action design education. Based on the results of research in which interaction design students suggest that the need to learn business contexts are as important as understanding user contexts, I argue for the application of ethnographic methods to the problem of teaching the contexts of business. This is a novel approach that shifts the historical focus of ethnographic practices in interaction design from analyzing users to analyzing the business field. To do this, I first explain some terms—context, interaction design, and ethnography. Second, I analyze the results of the survey and interview session to get a full sense of the importance of context to interaction design students. Finally, I explain the value of incorporating ethnographic practices.

Keywords: Ethnography · Context · Interaction design education · Method

1 Introduction

Context is a word you hear a lot about if you are interested in interaction design. On *UXPlanet*, Tiffany Eaton suggests that User Experience (UX) design is "rooted in context" [1]. YuTing Chu writes on *Medium* that the "context of use is often neglected or not given the attention it deserves" [2]. Andy Budd, founder of Clearleft, writes that it is important for "UX team[s] to understand and feed into the wider context" [3]. On the *Web Designer Depot*, Kiley Meehan states that, "context is key for effective UX design" [4]. Stephanie Akkaoui Hughes, in a talk at Interaction 14, says, "do not design interactions, design the context for interactions" [5]. While we might quibble with specific points made above about how context is defined in relation to interaction design, context is clearly an important node of discourse that shapes how interaction designers understand their own practices.

This genesis of this paper started with a question: How do you teach context? As a coordinator of an interaction design program, this is a question that has vexed me. How do we get interaction-designers-in-training to understand the importance of context? Furthermore, what contexts do we argue are the most important? To answer this question, I completed a survey of 41 students and a face-to-face interview of 19 students to learn what new, intermediate, and advanced interaction design students understand context to mean. I wanted to understand what contexts they find the most relevant and meaningful to their education. Asking students what context means to them allows me to better understand their views of an admittedly messy word.

© Springer Nature Switzerland AG 2020
M. Kurosu (Ed.): HCII 2020, LNCS 12181, pp. 82–96, 2020.
https://doi.org/10.1007/978-3-030-49059-1_6

Furthermore, their views are valuable to understand how we might translate educational goals regarding context into concepts that they understand and find useful.

The results of this research, which will be discussed in more detail below, are that all students, no matter their point of matriculation in the program, understand the concept of context to be important. A major source of contextual information that they believe they need to know are the contexts (social and context of use) of users. This shouldn't be shocking, as user-centered design is the dominant design paradigm in the United States today.[1] Before students even enroll in an interaction design program, they have often heard the phrase "user experience design," know that it is related to interaction design in some way, and have at least some vague sense that the user is important to these approaches.

However, the more advanced the student, the more likely they are to think that learning business contexts is equally important to understanding user contexts. Put another way, understanding business contexts is as important as championing a user-centered approach itself. For, if an interaction designer cannot argue for the importance of their design philosophy within the many competing interests in a business environment, then how can they create engaging designs?

While interaction design programs position themselves as "user-centered," I am less certain that all interaction design programs have an equally intense focus on how the concept of user-centered design translates into business contexts. Thus, as an interaction design educator, I want to think about what strategies we employ to help students with the problem of navigating business contexts.

Building on student belief that learning to navigate business contexts is as important as learning user-centered design, I argue for a specific way this can be achieved, namely, incorporating ethnographic approaches more fully into interaction design curriculums. Ethnography can broadly be defined as the systematic study of and writing on human cultures. Ethnographic practices have long been incorporated into design through an applied ethnographic approach to various stages of user testing.

What I am suggesting goes beyond this approach. I believe ethnographic approaches to understanding users can be flipped to focus on business contexts. This is because the methods ethnographers learn to understand participants in the research field are equally apt to understanding participants in the field of business. In this way, the interaction designer would turn their office—all the other departments and stakeholders—into another set of users whose goals they must understand. This approach is strategic and acknowledges a focus on users, i.e., user-centered design, is not always the chief determinate of why or what products/services get made. Through learning how to reframe ethnographic methods for the business field, interaction-designer-in-training gain what Lakoff and Johnson call an "equipment for living" [6]—to be better able to understand their position within the field, i.e., their workplace.

To argue for utilizing an ethnographic approach in interaction design education as a tool to translate user-centered design into business contexts, I first explain some terms—context, interaction design, and ethnography. Second, I analyze the results of the

---

[1] Human-centered design and design thinking grew in fits and starts since the 1960s, from the work of such designers and theorists as Nigel Cross, Don Norman, Victor Papinek, and Horst Rittel.

survey and interview session to get a full sense of the importance of context to interaction design students. Finally, I explain the value of incorporating ethnographic practices.

2 Defining Terms

Before I discuss more fully why ethnographic methods are important for interaction designers-in-training, I want to define some key terms that will be used throughout the paper.

2.1 Context

The word "context" will be used in different ways throughout this paper and each use needs to be explained. The Miriam-Webster dictionary defines context as "the parts of discourse that surround a word or passage and can throw light on its meaning." Secondarily, it is defined as "the interrelated conditions in which something exists or occurs: environment, setting" [7]. In this sense, context is that "stuff" that surrounds a text. A goal of this paper is, in part, to interrogate student understandings of what context means. Their understandings, in large part, discussed in Sect. 3, hew close to the way context is used in popular discourse.

In Sect. 4, I will mention specific implementations of the word context within anthropological traditions. Marilyn Strathern argues that contextualizing knowledge is one of the epistemological foundations of twentieth-century anthropology [8]. While anthropology is often understood to interrogate cultural or social context, the concept of context in anthropology has been used to "denote a bewildering variety of characteristics, domains and environments" [9, p. 26]. While there is no stable way context has been deployed in anthropology, anthropologists have long problematized the concept as it relates to the interpretation of cultures and interrogating the role of the observer in observation [10].[2] I will speak of context as it relates to Clifford Geertz' interpretive cultural anthropology. In this view, cultures are texts that can be read for meaning. Geertz coined the term "thick description," or the belief that the more information you learn about a phenomenon will lead to better interpretations [13]. I reference this view because of its pedagogical value to teach ethnographic practices to designers.

Finally, I will discuss how various disciplines designing human-computer interactions have grappled with the importance of contexts to technological use. Design scholars such as Cennydd Bowles break context down into seven categories: device,

---

[2] This problematization of the concept of context is not limited to anthropology. For instance, Paul Dourish notes the co-constitutive nature of text and context, where context is an emergent feature of the interaction between things. Put another way, the activity makes the context as much as the context makes the activity [11]. This view resonates with cultural studies scholars such as Jennifer Daryl Slack, who suggests that a cultural study of a phenomena maps a context by bringing together —or articulating—various parts [12]. In this way, the context is created in the active connection of parts and is not something that exists outside of those parts.

environmental, time, activity, individual, location, and social [14]. This means that context as a framing device can covers everything from software design decisions related to information architecture [15] to the meanings and practices users bring to technological engagement. In Sects. 3 and 4, when referencing different relationships between context and technological use, I will specifically identify the contextual frame utilized.

2.2 Interaction Design

Interaction design is defined by Alan Cooper, the founder of the Cooper design firm, as the design of "behavior in complex technical systems" [16, p. xxii]. Cooper drew the term "interaction design" from Bill Moggridge, and a similar definition is mirrored on the webpage of Interaction Design Association (IxDA) [17]. Goal-Directed Design, Cooper's preferred method for implementing interaction design, is transdisciplinary, borrowing from anthropology, psychology, traditional graphic design, and engineering disciplines. This approach imagines interaction design as part of what Don Norman refers to as the total experience a user has with a product or service [18].

While there are seemingly infinite approaches on how to do interaction design, with each business using its own design guidelines, when I speak of interaction design in this paper, I am directly referring to the Goal-Directed Design (GDD) model unless otherwise noted. Why? GDD helped set the agenda for what might constitute applied interaction design. For instance, Cooper's firm pioneered the use of personas in interaction design. Additionally, Alan Cooper, was a founding board member of the IxDA, a popular international mouthpiece for organizing interaction design discourse. In other words, by focusing on a variant of interaction design that has influenced so many others, I am covering a wide range of what interaction design might mean.

That said, I would be remiss if I didn't point out the discursive messiness that exists in naming conventions today regarding the intersections between technology and design. In the broad strokes, interaction design feels like a parallel field to human-computer interaction, both of which often draw from common resources and terminology. And both exist somewhere within the larger scope of UX design, a floating signifier that eats everything in its path. A quick Google search shows this discursive messiness in full bloom: "Just How Far Beyond HCI is Interaction Design?" [19], "What is the difference between Interaction Design and UX?" [20], "Human Computer Interaction vs Interaction Design" [21], "What's the difference between UX and HCI?" [22].

In short, depending on your disciplinary home, you might define the terms and processes that encompass interactions between humans and machines differently. Thus, I want to acknowledge that what I say about a specific version of interaction design may not map fully onto all UX or HCI-named programs [23].

2.3 Ethnography

Ethnography can broadly be defined as the systematic study of and writing on human cultures. While it grew out of an anthropological tradition, many disciplines in the social sciences and humanities use ethnography today. As with any research practices, there are debates about approach and implementation. So, for the purposes of this paper, I want to define the components that generically describe what ethnography is, what it hopes to accomplish, and some of its main tools.

Ethnography is a qualitative method built on getting the observer (the researcher) into a field (a space—virtual or otherwise—in which data is observed and collected) [24]. To do so, an ethnographer formulates a research question, however broad, which acts as a hypothesis. While in the field, the ethnographer interviews participants (i.e., people in the field), jots down observations, and ruminates on participant experiences in field notes. In addition to interviews and observation, the ethnographer also collects other sources of data which depend on the specific nature of the field setting—ephemera, magazine articles, government reports, et cetera. Through significant time spent in the field, carrying out participant observation, and conversation, the ethnographer begins to gain a sense of the local, embodied meanings of participants in that field.

The ultimate goal of this practice is to understand participants from their perspective. Thus, ethnography is local, embodied, and contextual. In short, an ethnographer aims to understand the role cultural practices play on shaping and expressing the world views of participants. Put another way: What does the world mean to the participant? In this view, people "create meaning about their own worlds" in everyday activities [25, p. 24].

Ethnographic practices are already deeply interwoven into interaction design. When people talk about ethnography as it relates to design, it is often called applied ethnography. Applied ethnography refers to a range of strategies for bringing ethnographic practices into the private sector [26, 27]. In general, this means a truncation of the time and scope that ethnographers often employ to work within the rigors of a stakeholder-based environment. Alan Cooper argues that while ethnographers "spend years living in the cultures they study and record," applied ethnographers (or, in this case, interaction designers) have a more modest goal of understanding the "behaviors and rituals of people interacting with individual products" [16, pp. 45–46]. One will often see ethnographic practices referred to as Contextual Inquiry [28].

3   Interaction Design Student Perception of Context

What follows is a description of an online survey regarding interaction design student comprehension of the concept of context, a follow-up face-to-face interview with a subset of students, and an analysis of the results of both parts of the study.

3.1   Online Survey Description

During the month of November in 2019, an online survey titled "Understanding Context in Interaction Design Education" was published that targeted interaction design students at Kennesaw State University. Of the 60 students who received an invitation, 41 completed the survey. The goal of the survey was to understand how interaction-designers-in-training understand the concept of context through open-ended questions (See Appendix A). Students were asked to identify the classes they have already completed so that they could be categorized into 3 groups—new, intermediate, and advanced.

18 respondents were coded as new. These students are defined as those having taken less than 4 classes in major, none of which could be the core method class for doing interaction design (Interaction Design I). This class teaches Goal-Directed Design and introduces ethnographic approaches to user testing through Contextual Inquiry. These students were the newest in the program. They all had at least a vague sense of what interaction design meant even if these meanings might diverge wildly. These students could also not have participated in an internship.

9 respondents were coded as intermediate. These students are defined as having taken more 4 classes in major but less than 7, one of which had to be the core methods class. These students have all read Don Norman's *The Design of Everyday Things* by this point as well as have been introduced to Goal-Directed Design. They have a firmer grasp of what interaction design means to them. These students could also not have participated in an internship.

14 students were coded as advanced. These students are defined as having taken more than 7 classes in major, which would include the core interaction design method class and might include the second interaction design method class (Interaction Design II). They might also have taken the ethnographic methods class (Ethnography for Designers). The responses of students who had completed Ethnography for Designers were analyzed within this group but coded as distinct.

How Would You Define the Word "Context"? Students were remarkably consistent across new, intermediate, and advanced groups when defining the concept of context. When asked to relay "just the first thoughts that come to your mind. Please do not look up answers" they all responded with definitions consistent with the dictionary definitions of context. Of the 41 responses, 39 defined context using the synonyms like "situation" (15 respondents), "surround" (9 respondents), "setting" (8 respondents), "circumstance" (5 respondents), and "bigger picture" (2 respondents).

Of these respondents, 9 specifically used the word "meaning" to suggest that it was the "stuff" that surrounds "something" (another favorite word in responses, 17 mentions) that gives that "something" its meaning. This implies that the thing itself (the text) has no meaning without its other "stuff." And this "stuff" was most often referred to as "information" (11 mentions).

What Types of "Context" Do Interaction Designers Need to Know? Responses to this question on the online survey were coded into different categories. The categories are listed in descending order relative to response rate:

User Context—General. This category is for respondents who specify user context as important to interaction designers but provided no specific detail. 26 respondents fall into this category (14 new, 7 intermediate, 5 advanced).

User Context—Social Context. This category is for respondents who specify social context or cultural information as important. 9 respondents fall in this category (6 new, 1 intermediate, 2 advanced).

Business Context—General. This category is for respondents who specify business concerns as important for interaction designers. 9 respondents fall in this category (1 new, 1 intermediate, 7 advanced).

User Context—Location. This category is for respondents who specify location information regarding products/services as important. 8 respondents fall in this category (3 new, 0 intermediate, 5 advanced).

User Context—Usability. This category is for respondents who specify usability-based concerns such as how the product is used. 8 respondents fall in this category (3 new, 2 intermediate, 3 advanced).

Business Context—Competition. This category is for respondents who specify understanding market competition for the product/service as important. 3 respondents fall in this category (1 new, 0 intermediate, 2 advanced).

Current Trends. This category is for respondents who specify knowing current design trends as important. 3 respondents fall in this category (2 new, 1 intermediate, 0 advanced).

User Context—Device. This category is for respondents who specify knowing the device for which you will be designing as important. 3 respondents fall in this category (0 new, 3 intermediate, 0 advanced).

User Context—Problem. This category is for respondents who specify fully understanding the design problem as important. 3 respondents fall in this category (0 new, 1 intermediate, 2 advanced).

General Knowledge. This category is for respondents that specify knowing as much as possible about all contexts is important. 2 respondents fall in this category (0 new, 1 intermediate, 1 advanced).

Historical Trends. This category is for the respondent that specify historical design trends as important. 1 respondent falls in this category (1 new, 0 intermediate, 0 advanced).

3.2   Face-to-Face Group Exercise and Interview

At the end of the online survey all respondents were asked if they would be willing to complete a face-to-face, group interview of no more than 1 h. 19 respondents chosen were chosen (7 new, 6 intermediate, 6 advanced) based on relatively equal representation between respondents coded as new, intermediate, and advanced. This session was run as an exercise and interview, where students were grouped by new, intermediate, and advanced. Each group was given paper, writing utensils, and a prompt that read: "What are the most important contextual things an interaction designer needs to know? Put them in rank order. Write them on the paper provided." Groups were given 20 min to discuss, write down, and order their answers. Each group presented their ranking system and we collectively discussed the implications of the results.

New Student Group. Contextual rankings: (1) demographic information, (2) user interaction, (3) parameters and limitations, (4) research, (5) branding and aesthetics, (6) platforms, (7) delivery and final product, (8) competition.

Intermediate Student Group. Contextual rankings: (1) user/customer goals, (2) client goals, (3) demographics, (4) research, (5) branding, (6) prior knowledge/experience, (7) medium/interface, (8) design expectations.

Advanced Student Group. Their responses were broken up into two categories: business context and user context. Business context: (1) time, (2) money, (3) team dynamics, (4) brand, (5) competition, (6) platform integration. User context: (1) demographics, (2) environment, (3) experience/attitude of user. The lists were then combined into a single ranking: (1) time, (2) money, (3) team dynamics, (4) demographics, (5) environment, (6) experience/attitude of user.

Interview Session. The groups responded to questions meant to understand how they selected these contextual categories and to elaborate on potentially unclear meanings. The results of that discussion are listed in Sect. 3.3.

3.3 Analysis

The analysis of the online survey and face-to-face interview session has been broken down into three specific themes.

The Context of Users is Vital. This should come as no surprise to hear from students trained in a major that teaches some variant of UX design. 38 of the 41 participants had already read Don Norman's *The Design of Everyday Things*. Most—some new students, all intermediate and advanced students—had taken a class devoted to teaching psychological principles of screen design. 23 of the 41 participants had also taken a class teaching specific methods to interaction design including hands-on exercises related to user testing.

We see this focus on the importance of user contexts in Sect. 3.1 in how many respondents listed some type of user context as important in the online survey. We also see the same focus in the results of the face-to-face exercise. For instance, in our discussion of the importance of demographic information, a participant from the intermediate student group said that, while demographic information is important, they ranked user testing as more important because demographics "do not define all that a user is." They went on to elaborate that understanding the user's motivations was the most important thing to know.

The More Advanced the Student, the More They Believe Business Contexts are Important. It was far more intriguing to see the association between the amount of time in the major and the growing concern with business contexts. In the online survey, a significant portion of advance students listed business context as important with 7 advanced students listing it in a general sense and the 2 remaining advanced students listing business competition as important. This concern was mirrored in the face-to-face discussion when a representative from the advanced student group said they would rank business concerns as the top three (time, money, team dynamics) "if we are forced to mix our user and business rankings." Another advanced student said that, "we need to research stakeholder goals as much as user goals." When pressed on this, the student said, "we were thinking realistically that, as much as we want to design for the user, we have to design for what we are allocated and that comes down to time, money, and team." Another advanced student suggested that all design is determined by the maturity of the company and that user goals had to work within whatever the structure of the business would allow.

Concern about learning business contexts was most prevalent in advanced students but not limited to them. During the face-to-face session, new students listed some business contexts such as parameters received from stakeholders and competition on their contextual ranking. An intermediate student, during the face-to-face session, said, "we cannot just focus on users, we must understand what are their [stakeholder] goals for a product." Another intermediate student said that, "the business goals need to go more upfront."

The More Advanced the Student, the More They Believe Any and All Contextual Information is Important. In a survey response, an advanced student said that all knowledge was important: "How people will use the design. Where they will be. More identifying information about the user. I feel like there are a million different things that could help provide context to the design and it's up to the designer to gain as much knowledge as possible to build something that properly fits the user." During the face-to-face session, another advanced student said, "we just need to know the whole environment." When pressed to explain this, the student replied, "we just need to know everything—the product, the goals of the stakeholders, the locations it is used in, who is using it, how they're using it, [user] attitudes, just everything."

4   The Value of Ethnographic Approaches

A clear thread in the research above is that learning business contexts is important to the way students understand successful interaction design practice. While advanced students still see user-centered design at the core of their self-definitions, they are far more likely to see business contexts to be as (or more) important. From this research, it appears that the more classes an interaction designer takes, the more networking events they go to (a requirement for advanced students in the major), and the more internship experiences they have, will lead students to focus more on how to operate within the field of business. In many ways, this makes sense; as students get closer to the job market, they become more interested in how they might fit within the overall framework of business culture.

The results of the online survey and face-to-face interview led me to ask: How are interaction design educators preparing students for a transition to business contexts? Furthermore, how can we ensure that a focus on users that pervades interaction design today can survive in an environment of multiple and often competing interests?

All 5 advanced students who had taken Ethnography for Designers[3] responded that it was an important class to help them learn about context. One student said that it helped them learn not only "the context of the consumer to the product but the context of the product itself and how it relates to other systems."

---

[3] In this class, students take a deep dive into learning ethnography, the differences between ethnography and applied ethnography, and complete an ethnographic field report.

This led me to ask: How can we reposition ethnographic practice as not only useful to understanding users but as a tool to help interaction designers understand business contexts? When methods for understanding users—ethnographically based or not—are taught within interaction design programs, they are often taught specifically to interpret users. As stated above, an ethnographic approach could also be utilized in a strategic way, shifting its focus from user interpretation to interpreting the culture, values, and meanings of business contexts. This would help create interaction designers more attuned to their overall environment and could help them more effectively implement user-centered strategies in the workplace.

4.1 Reframing Ethnographic Practice

In this section, I will highlight what ethnographic practice already do well for teaching the value of user context before explaining how it can be flipped to focus on business contest. This means exchanging one field, that of the users, for another. The interaction designer would turn their office—all the other departments and stakeholders—into another set of users whose goals they must understand.

Ethnographic Practice Focuses on Interpretation. When doing ethnography, a researcher enters a field, or the place in which research takes place. A goal of ethnography is that researcher acknowledges that their relationship to participants is shaped by this condition. In the field, humans are participants and, from the perspective of interpretive cultural anthropology, the interactions of humans between themselves, with the researcher, and the environment around them can be read for meaning. The researcher is to describe and interpret the field around them through the lens of culture—"a system of inherited conceptions expressed in symbolic forms" [13, p. 89] through which humans communicate, perpetuate, and develop their attitudes about life.

To bridge the gap between researcher and participant, ethnographers take an emic view of culture, or an "insider's perspective." Thus, an ethnographer's interpretation of that culture should be rooted in the perspective of the participants. We can see this practice mirrored in interaction design education through the goal of empathizing with users. The key is being able to understand a user's sense of how the world works (as it relates to your product/service). Cooper calls this understand a user's mental model [16, pp. 17–19] whereas Norman refers to this as understanding a user's conceptual model [18, pp. 25–31]. The point is to not suggest that a user's mental model is incorrect but to understand how that informs their strategies for engagement.

In the same way that interaction designers aim to understand the mental models employed by users, interaction designers can shift this perception to their fellow employees and clients. This shift allows the designer to become a researcher in their own workplace. This means taking seriously that each person in a job has a different mental model for how the business works. This very well could be rooted in the goals and agendas of their department. By consciously organizing the workplace around the concept of mental models, the designer can acknowledge that it is no longer a given that each and every person's focus within an organization is the same or is user-centered. And even if they are focused on users, the solutions they offer might diverge radically.

Ethnographic Practice Focuses on Self-reflexivity. A key component of doing ethnography is understanding the assumptions that the researcher brings into the field. Any attempt by an ethnographer to make sense of participants in the field should happen alongside a self-inquisitive approach that interrogates their own assumptions. The acknowledgement that the ethnographer's observation is part of the process of constructing meaning helps the ethnographer to be wary of simplistic notions of interpretation. That is because good ethnographic practice calls attention to its own authority and is sensitive to how this shapes power imbalances [10, p. 9]. The comparison of the ethnographer's own communicative practices with that of the participants helps the ethnographer avoid the fallacy of normalcy.

Ironically, ethnographic self-reflexivity is meant as a way to fight what Cooper calls "self-reflexive design," or the problem of designers designing for their goals and not user goals [16, p. 65]. Many approaches to interaction design have built in modes to address the problem of designer assumptions. Goal-Directed design includes multiple stages where designers interrogate assumptions, from the forming and subsequent testing of a persona hypothesis [16, pp. 46–47] to the process of building design requirements [16, pp. 110–111].

Building off the concept of using mental models to understand fellow workers in the business field, the designer as "workplace ethnographer" must acknowledge their mental models as well. This means that acknowledging that satisfying user goals is something that shapes your practice within the business field. In doing so, the designer can uncover their own assumptions about how businesses—from stakeholders to the members of other departments—should operate. In fact, Lean UX, an approach to interaction design put forth by Jeff Gothelf and Josh Seiden that retrofits interaction design practice for Lean environments and Agile approaches, asks designers to fill out assumption worksheets that not only cover user expectations but business expectations as well [29, pp. 18–19].

Ethnographic Practice Focuses on Imbalances of Power. Ethnographers cannot view the field as a neutral given. Rather, the field is a place that is "multisubjective, power-laden, and incongruent" [10, p. 15]. It is a goal of the ethnographer to acknowledge this, incorporate it into their understanding of local meanings, and, as stated above, understand their own power to shape relationships in the field through their very presence.

A shift toward focusing ethnographic practices into the workplace means that the designer acknowledges that any utterances made in the workplace are not neutral but subtended by sophisticated entanglements of power. The act of watching and interpreting fellow worker practice means understanding how perceptions of power shape these interactions. Thus, interaction designers need to incorporate power dynamics into how they understand others in the workplace.

Ethnographic Practice Focuses on Rigorous Environmental Description. Another goal of the ethnographer is to thickly describe the lives of participants [13]. However, rich data from one source creates pitfalls. The process of collecting data from multiple sources is referred to as triangulation, or the comparing and triangulating of field notes with other sources [30]. This means that data collection should be a rigorous approach sustained by multiple sources: jottings, field notes, interviews, collecting records, describing the structure of the field, etc.

The process of rigorous data collection from multiple sources works as a way to undo any assumptions a research has about participants in their field. This means that interaction designers aiming to understanding their business context should be collecting significant and varied information that does not rely on single sources or single informants.

4.2   Implementing a Business Contextual Ethnographic Approach

A practical implementation of this approach could be as an addendum to an internship. It would mean co-oping the idea of journaling, a common practice used by students to document and reflect on their internship experience, by overlaying ethnographic principles to the structure of the journal.

For instance, in Ethnography for Designers, I have designed an assignment that frames how students should structure field notes that builds off Dell Hymes' SPEAKING model [31]. This model, built specifically for sociolinguistic purposes, breaks down social interactions in categories based off specific categories: S (setting), P (participants), E (ends, or social business), A (acts, or sequence of events), K (key, or tone of interactions), I (instrumentality, or kind of language used), N (norms, or what is "ordinary" behavior in that setting), and G—genre, (or recognized ways of interaction).

This assignment follows a previous assignment in which students are given free rein as to how to analyze some type of social situation. This assignment adds the above categories to give students a sense of what they should be looking for in hopes of a richer interpretation of events. Finally, students were then asked what they want to adapt from this framing exercise for their final project—an ethnographic report of chosen participants which includes a field notes component.

This same type of structure could be used for internship journaling, where students are prompted to analyze scenarios not only from the impact it has on them but from an extra perspective in which they aim to identify what is going on for other participants. This would allow interaction-designers-in-training to refocus approaches they learned for implementing user testing in the design process into the actual situation of being at an internship. This would mean applying all the benefits of an ethnographic approach —interpretation, self-reflexivity, attentiveness to power imbalances, and thick description—to understanding where they stand in the business field. Furthermore, it would allow them to start forming strategies for how they will argue for the importance of user-centered strategies in business contexts in the future.

5   Conclusion

While there is often no substitute to being in the field, the goal of this paper is to think about how we can still begin to prepare students for post-collegiate transitions. To do this, I asked a hypothetical question: What would happen if we took ethnographic methods generally pointed toward uncovering user goals and refocused them on the dynamics of power and relationships in the field of business?

According to student perceptions of what is relevant to their careers as interaction designers, understanding user contexts is critical but understanding how to transition a belief in user-centered design into business contexts rife with competing interests is equally as important.

This paper proposes utilizing ethnographic methods to prepare students for the competing interests of the business field. The beauty of this approach is interaction design programs that are teaching a robust version interaction design (as opposed to programs focusing more specifically on designing screens) are already implementing ethnographic methods in some of their classes.[4] Thus, the operational cost of this approach is minimal. This means I am not proposing a significant outlay of resources for programs that most likely are already heavily burdened.

If, however, you work in a program that could be teaching ethnographic methods more fully, this approach is a great opportunity for interdisciplinary outreach to your local anthropology and sociology department. This would strengthen your department's approach to interaction design by creating multiple perspectives on problem solving.

Appendix A

Online Survey "Understanding Context in Interaction Design Education".

<u>Questions</u>

1. What is your name?
2. Which of the Interactive Design degree classes have you taken (or are currently)?
3. How would you define the word "context"? (Just the first thoughts that come to your mind.)
4. What types of "context" do interaction designs need to know?
5. Which class in Interactive Design taught you the most about context? List the class and explain.
6. Did any classes outside of Interactive Design teach you about the importance of context? Is so, which ones and why?
7. Would you be willing to complete a face-to-face, group interview of no more than 1 h?

References

1. Design is rooted in context (2020). https://uxplanet.org/design-is-rooted-in-context-361aed57d9c6. Accessed 13 Jan 2020
2. How the context of use improves product design and user experience, medium (2020). https://medium.com/nyc-design/how-context-of-use-improves-product-design-and-user-experience-3299d2f0a166. Accessed 13 Jan 2020

---

[4] I do not wish to imply that the very fact of teaching ethnographic approaches means that it is being done well. See Räsänen and Nyce's work on the role of anthropology is HCI research [32].

3. How context is bridging the gap between UX and service design, clearleft (2020). https://clearleft.com/posts/how-context-is-bridging-the-gap-between-ux-and-service-design. Accessed 13 Jan 2020
4. Context is key for effective UX design, web designer depot (2020). https://www.webdesignerdepot.com/2017/02/context-is-key-for-effective-ux-design. Accessed 13 Jan 2020
5. Human interaction: physical and virtual Stephanie Akkaoui Hughes – interaction 14 (2020). https://vimeo.com/87226293. Accessed 13 Jan 2020
6. Lakoff, G., Johnson, M.: Metaphors We Live By. University of Chicago Press, Chicago (2003)
7. Context: Miriam-Webster (2020). https://www.merriam-webster.com/dictionary/context. Accessed 13 Jan 2020
8. Strathern, M.: Foreward. In: Strathern's, M. (ed.) Shifting Contexts: Transformations in Anthropological Knowledge, pp. 1–12. Routledge, London (1995)
9. Dilley, R.: The problem of context. In: Dilley's, R. (ed.) The Problem of Context (Methodology and History in Anthropology), pp. 1–46. Berghahn Books, New York (1999)
10. Clifford, J., Marcus, G.E. (eds.): Writing Culture: The Poetics and Politics of Ethnography. University of California Press, Berkeley (2010)
11. Dourish, P.: What we talk about when we talk about context. Pers. Ubiquit. Comput. **8**(1), 19–30 (2004)
12. Slack, J.D.: The theory and method of articulation in cultural studies. In: Morey, D., Chen's, K.H. (eds.) Critical Dialogues in Cultural Studies, pp. 112–127. Routledge, London (1996)
13. Geertz, C.: The Interpretation of Cultures, 3rd edn. Basic Books, New York (2017)
14. Designing with context (2020). https://www.cennydd.com/blog/designing-with-context. Accessed 13 Jan 2020
15. Hinton, A.: Understanding Context: Environment, Language, and Information Architecture. O'Reilly Media, Sebastopol (2014)
16. Cooper, A., Reimann, R., Cronin, D., Noessel, C.: About Face: The Essentials of Interaction Design, 4th edn. Wiley, Indianapolis (2014)
17. IxDA About & History (2019). https://ixda.org/ixda-global/about-history/. Accessed 02 Dec 2019
18. Norman, D.: The Design of Everyday Things. Revised and Expanded. Basic Books, New York (2013)
19. Just how far beyond HCI is interaction design? Boxes & Arrows (2020). http://boxesandarrows.com/just-how-far-beyond-hci-is-interaction-design/. Accessed 13 Jan 2020
20. What is the difference between Interaction Design and UX Design? Interaction Design Foundation (2020). https://www.interaction-design.org/literature/article/what-is-the-difference-between-interaction-design-and-ux-design. Accessed 13 Jan 2020
21. Human computer interaction vs interaction design, stack overflow (2020). https://stackoverflow.com/questions/18830802/human-computer-interaction-vs-interaction-design. Accessed 13 Jan 2020
22. What's the difference between UX and HCI? Quora (2020). https://www.quora.com/Whats-the-difference-between-UX-and-HCI. Accessed 13 Jan 2020
23. There is No Such Thing as an Interaction Design Degree, Medium (2020). https://medium.com/ixda/there-is-no-such-thing-as-an-interaction-design-degree-5d853cd547d3. Accessed 13 Jan 2020
24. Hoey, B.: A simple introduction to the practice of ethnography and guide to ethnographic fieldnotes. Marshall University Digital Scholar, pp. 1–10 (2014)
25. Ladner, S.: Practical Ethnography: A Guide to Doing Ethnography in the Private Sector. Routledge, New York (2014)

26. Schesul, J.J., LeCompte, M.D.: Essential Ethnographic Methods: A Mixed Methods Approach. AltaMira Press, Lanham (2013)
27. Pelto, P.: Applied Ethnography: Guidelines for Field Research. Left Coast Press, Walnut Creek (2013)
28. Beyer, H., Holtzblatt, K.: Contextual Design. Morgan Kaufmann Publishers, Burlington (1998)
29. Gothelf, J., Seiden, J.: Lean UX: Great Products with Agile Teams, 2nd edn. O'Reilly Media, Sebastopol (2016)
30. Monaghan, L.: Speaking of ethnography. In: Monaghan, L., Goodman, J.E., Robinson's, J. M. (eds.) A Cultural Approach to Interpersonal Communication, 2nd edn, pp. 34–37. Wiley-Blackwell, London (2012)
31. Hymes, D.: The ethnography of speaking. In: Anthropology and Human Behavior, pp. 13–53 (1962)
32. Räsänen, M., Nyce, J.: Rewriting context and analysis: bringing anthropology into HCI research. In: Pinder, S. (ed.) Advances in Human-Computer Interaction, pp. 397–414. InTech Education and Publishing, Vienna (2008)

Design Interface and Modeling Technique

Julia C. Lee and Lawrence J. Henschen[✉]

Northwestern University, Evanston, IL 60208, USA
j-leeh@northwestern.edu,
henschen@eecs.northwestern.edu

Abstract. HCI (human-computer interaction) has contributed greatly to the information industry revolution. When used to display and allow interaction through system models, it helps humans to understand systems and processes whose complexity is well beyond pencil-and-paper exploration. An appropriate model with a well-design human-computer interface helps system designers understand today's complex systems and helps humans (both designers and other stakeholders) understand each other. This understanding facilitates system analysis, verification, refinement, improvement, and debugging. We illustrate the advantages of using a good interface design and a rigorous modeling technique by applying one of the most important modelling techniques – Petri Nets – to the popular smart city application domain. We show how this facilitates understanding and communication between system engineers and other project participants and stakeholders.

Keywords: Interface · Smart city · Modelling · Petri Net

1 Introduction

Smart cities are already becoming a reality and will continue to develop and evolve into more complex and sophisticated systems for the foreseeable future [1–4]. The smart cities of the future will be extremely complex composites of systems that were most likely developed independently, systems such as traffic control and energy management. Moreover, they will have a very dynamic nature – as more kinds of systems relevant to city management and operation are developed they will be integrated into existing smart cities.

Smart city projects also have launched a worldwide campaign of involvement of management and public in modern technology. All the projects in different places of the world are no longer just "pure" technical projects. They are also social/economic projects. They cannot be done just by groups of engineers. They require continuous involvement of all the stockholders [4]. They require management/authority prompt decisions; they require enormous public feedback/requests; they need the technical parties to present their design/implementation ideas in a convincing and intuitive ways. All the parties continuously interact with each other. Interfaces for interaction are important for understanding each other.

The implementation of a smart city is concretized with modern technologies. So the presentation/interface of a technical idea to/with the non-technical parties is one of the

© Springer Nature Switzerland AG 2020
M. Kurosu (Ed.): HCII 2020, LNCS 12181, pp. 97–111, 2020.
https://doi.org/10.1007/978-3-030-49059-1_7

key issues for good decisions and comprehensive requirements/feedback. From another point of view, engineers need to have a more systematic presentation of their technical ideas/designs. If some methods can serve as their design tool as well as their presentation method, that would be an ideal way. When engineers come up with a design idea, they use modeling techniques to present their idea to their technical partners. Models are high level views of the design/system and can be easily detailed into a lower level design. Models provide consistent and rigorous views of the whole system across all the various components of the system, in contrast to verbal descriptions. We argue that certain types of design models can also be good presentations of the design and good interfaces to communicate the design idea with the non-technical stockholders of the system to be designed/implemented.

We note that many modelling techniques would be relevant for high-level modelling of a system – Petri Nets for shared resources [5], control and dataflow models [6], Finite State Machines (FSMs) and statecharts [7, 8] because at any given time the system is in a particular state, etc. The Finite State Machine model is one of the modeling techniques that is used very often in the engineering world. Petri Nets can model Finite State Machine [5]. More precisely, Finite State Machine is a subset of the more general technique – Petri Net. So we focus on Petri Net as our design interface between the technical parties and the non-technical parties in a project like the ones in smart city initiatives.

We begin with explanation about Petri Net modelling. Since we use it as a presentation interface to non-technical partners, we will need to do the introduction in a more intuitive way by using examples. On the other hand, since the model should be a "real Petri Net" model of the system, we cannot compromise the important properties of Petri Net. In Sect. 3 we will give some simpler examples to show how Petri Net can be vividly intuitive as well as formally rigorous. In Sect. 4 we use a street lighting system as an example in a smart city to further discuss our argument. In Sect. 5 we point out some ideas related to "smart city like" socio-economic-technical projects.

2 What is Petri Net?

Petri Net modeling was first introduced by Carl Adam Petri in his PhD dissertation in 1962 [5]. Since then, much research on this modelling technique has been done, and many extensions (e.g., Petri Nets with time or transition priorities) have been proposed. It is used as a modeling tool widely in the engineering world.

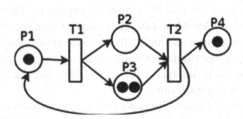

Fig. 1. A simple Petri Net

A Petri Net contains three sets of basic elements: a set of places P; a set of transitions T; and a set of flow relations F. Graphically places are represented by circles, transitions are represented by rectangles, and flows are represented by directed arrows. An important restriction on flow relations is that the flow relation can only be drawn from place to transition or from transition to place, but not from place to place and not from transition to transition. Each place can have one or more markers, or "dots", up to a limit, k, for that place; the limit is determined by the application being modelled. If no limit is specified, it is assumed to be infinite. Each flow has a weight, w; if no weight is indicated in the graph, the weight for that flow is assumed to be 1. Figure 1 shows an example of a basic Petri Net. In this Petri Net, there are 4 places: P1, P2, P3, P4 and 2 transitions: T1 and T2. There are 7 flows: P1 $\rightarrow$ T1, T1 $\rightarrow$P2, T1 $\rightarrow$P3, P2 $\rightarrow$ T2, P3 $\rightarrow$T2, T2 $\rightarrow$ P4, T2 $\rightarrow$ P1. There are no numbers marked on the flows, so by default the weights of all the flows are 1. There is 1 mark in P1, 0 marks in P2, 2 marks in P3, and 1 mark in P4. Since we did not have any notes or definitions about the limitations of number of marks for all the places in the Petri Net in Fig. 1, we assume the limitation is infinite. That is all the places can hold as many marks as they can get.

The above description is about the initial status of a Petri Net. The value of Petri Net is not to describe a static picture/condition of some sort. Its value as a modeling tool is to be used to describe/model a dynamic process. Let us take a look at the dynamics that it can represent. When we talk about the word "transition", it almost naturally means a dynamic. When something happens/changes, we say a transition occurs. For a transition to occur, some condition(s) must be satisfied. When water turns into ice, the temperature must be lower than the frozen point. When stopped traffic starts to move forward in an intersection, the traffic light has to turn to green. When an assembly station can start the next product, the parts for the product must have arrived, etc. For Petri Net to model a class of dynamic processes (not just one or two or some number of processes), we need to define the conditions for the transitions in a Petri Net to occur or to fire. The definition of how transitions can fire endows Petri Net with a very general power to represent/model dynamic systems.

We need to introduce more terms before we can get to the conditions for a transition in a Petri Net to fire. We define the "preset" of a transition as the places that have a flow coming out of them and flowing into the transition. Note that there can be more than one place for a transition with flows flowing to the transition. We define the "postset" of a transition as the places that have a flow coming from the transition to those places. Preset and postset are the places where the conditions for a transition to fire hold. More precisely the conditions are directly related to the marks in those places and capacities to hold marks and the weights on the flows. Let's give some formulas to describe the conditions for a transitions to fire: 1) all the places in the preset of the transition must have enough marks to be consumed during the firing – the number of marks in a place in the preset needs to be no less than the weight of the flow coming out of it and flowing into the transition; 2) all the places in the postset of the transition need to have enough room to accept the additional marks produced from the firing of the transition – the capacity of a place in the postset needs to be no-less than weight of the flow from the transition to it plus the number of marks currently in this place. The firing of the transition will remove from each place in the preset the number of marks equal to the weight of the flow out of that place. It will add to each place in the postset the number of marks equal to the weight on the flow from the transition into that place.

The conditions for a transition to fire in a Petri Net also defines the conditions after the transition fires because we know what are the changes in the number of marks in the places in preset and postset of the transition fired.

Let us observe the behavior of the Petri Net in Fig. 1 based on the transition firing definition above. There is only one place P1 in the preset of Transition T1. P1 has one mark in it, and the flow P1 → T1 has weight 1, so the condition in definition part 1) is satisfied. There are two places in the postset of T1 – P2 and P3. P2 has no marks in it before T1 fires, so it will have 1 mark after T1 fires because the weight T1 → P2 is the default 1. P3 has 2 marks before T1 fires, so it will have 3 marks after T1 fires because the weight of T1 → P3 is also 1 by default. P1 lost 1 mark after T1 fires; it becomes empty after T1 fires. Since there are no specified limits of capacities for all the places, the post condition is also satisfied. T1 will fire. After T1 fires, T2 can then fire because it's pre-conditions and post-conditions are satisfied after T1 fires. After T2 fires, P4 will have one more mark, and P1 will get one mark. It can be seen easily that this Petri Net will continue the firing pattern T1 – T2 – T1 – T2 – ... under the assumption that all the places having unlimited capacity. In practice, unlimited capacity is not a reality. So the designer of the system will set the capacity based on the situation. For a complex system, capacity setting can be determined by running the Petri Net model. For example, in the Petri Net of Fig. 1, capacities of P1 and P2 can be set to 1. The capacity of P3 can be set to 3. The capacity of P4 will be determined by how many times the system will be running. Say, if it should only run 5 times, then the capacity of P4 should be set to 6. After 5 times the system will stop running.

For those readers who prefer a more formal definition we give the following formal definition of the Petri Net in Fig. 1 as an illustration of a formal definition. Since this paper is focused on the representational characteristics of Petri Net in practical applications we will not give formal definitions for the subsequent examples.

$$PT = \{P, T, F, W, K, M_0\} \quad \text{where}$$

$P = \{P1, P2, P3, P4\}$	(Places)
$T = \{T1, T2\}$	(transitions)
$F = \{P1 \to T1, T1 \to P2, T1 \to P3, P2 \to T2, P3 \to T2, T2 \to P4, T2 \to P1\}$	
	(flows)
$W = \{1, 1, 1, 1, 1, 1, 1\}$	(weights of flows)
$K = \{\infty, \infty, \infty, \infty\}$	(if allow continuous firing)
or $\{1, 1, 3, 6\}$	(if allow firing 5 times)
	(capacities of places)
$M_0 = \{1, 0, 2, 1\}$	(Initial marking)

3   Example to Illustrate Petri Net Use

3.1   Modelling a Two-Way Intersection

Figure 2a depicts a two-way-one-lane intersection where vehicle traffic can only go north to south in one direction and west to east in the other direction. Since there is only one lane in each direction, the intersection can only be used by one vehicle at a time.

We will use the simple Petri Net of Fig. 2b to model the dynamics of a two-way-one-lane traffic intersection. Places P1, P2, and P3 represent cars "waiting to cross the intersection", "crossing the intersection", and "out of the intersection" for traffic going in the north/south direction. Places P4, P5, and P6 represent similar situations for traffic going in the west/east direction. P7 represents the intersection itself, with one dot in P7 meaning that the intersection is currently unoccupied or available. One dot in P1 means that a car is waiting on the north side of the intersection and ready to cross the intersection if it is available. Similarly, a dot in P4 means that a car is at the west side of the intersection and ready to cross to the east side if the intersection is available. T1 represents that the north side car gets into the intersection transition. In order for transition T1 to occur there must be one dot in each place P1 and P7, namely the intersection must be empty and a car is waiting in the north side. T2 represents the transition from P2 to P3, namely that the north-coming car has passed through the intersection and the intersection is again empty. Similarly for T3 and T4.

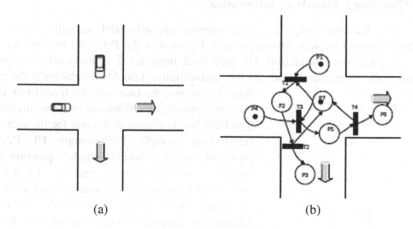

| (a) | (b) |

Fig. 2 (a) 2-way intersection (b) Petri Net model

There can be several situations. First if the north-coming car arrives slightly ahead of the west-coming car, it can pass the intersection immediately because the inter-section is available - a dot is in P7. So transition T1 fires, dots are removed from P1 and P7, and a dot is added to P2, meaning the north-coming car is using the intersection to pass.

If there are cars on both the north side and west side waiting to cross the inter-section, then there will be a contention on who gets the right of way. The basic Petri

Net concept does not have a mechanism to determine which transition gets to fire first when two or more transitions are ready to fire. In other words, there is a nondeterminism implied by the basic definition. If the two streets are heavily travelled, there could be lines of cars waiting in each direction, so that P1 and P4 both have dots. The traffic law can define who gets the right of way, Petri Net can be modified to define a priority for transitions to fire to model this.

Modifications to the Petri Net in Fig. 1 can represent more complex situations. For example, suppose the intersection is inside a city. Any car passing through the intersection will come to another intersection in one city block. That city block can hold a maximum number of cars. We may therefore allow places like P1 and P3 (cars waiting and cars passed through) to hold multiple dots, each dot representing one car in that place. P1 could have from 0 to N1 dots representing the number of cars waiting. P3 could have from 0 to N2 dots representing the number of cars in the next block. Then, the post-condition for T2 that the number of dots in P3 cannot exceed N2 would prevent T2 from firing if the next block was already filled with cars. A north/south car that had moved into the intersection would have to wait. Of course, that car should never have entered the intersection, although in real life drivers do often block intersections. To model this case more accurately, a new Petri Net would likely be drawn. We present this minor modification only to illustrate some of the basic concepts, like capacity and pre- and post-conditions.

3.2   Modelling a Four-Way Intersection

Let us extend the first example to a 4-way intersection and model the traffic pattern with Petri Net. Figure 3 depicts the intersection. Figure 4 is the Petri Net that models the traffic pattern at the intersection. On each road there are 2 lanes to allow opposite direction traffic on the same road. So, the intersection can hold two vehicles at the same time. Of course, the two vehicles have to be traveling in opposite directions not in cross directions. The Petri Net is similar to the one for the two-way intersection example. For example P1, P2, P3 represent the south-bound vehicle's position with respect to the intersection, and T1, T2 are the transitions representing the south-bound vehicle's movement from "before intersection" to "within intersection" and from "within intersection" to "out of the intersection" respectively. Since there are two lanes to allow opposite direction traffic, we added places and transitions: P8, P9, P10, T5, T6 for north-bound vehicles and P11, P12, P13, T7, T8 for west-bound vehicles. Since the intersection can now hold two vehicles at the same time, P7 has two dots in it.

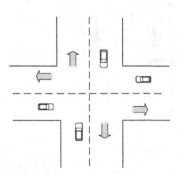

Fig. 3. 4-way intersection

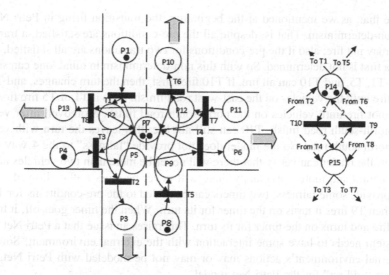

Fig. 4. Petri Net model for 4-way intersection traffic

The 2 dots in P7 can exclude more than two vehicles entering the intersection, but this cannot prevent two cross direction vehicles entering the intersection at the same time which could introduce collision. More mechanism is needed to prevent this situation. In real life, traffic light could be introduced to prevent cross traffic to happen. Petri Net can model a traffic light, but to model a full traffic light will need a more complex Petri Net. We choose to simplify the Petri Net so that the "mutual exclusion" power of Petri Net can be seen by the reader easily.

We introduce more places and transitions to the Petri Net in Fig. 4. We put the added parts to the right side so the picture would not be to "messy" to be understood. However, the connections to the other parts of the graph are clearly marked with labels. Let us explain the meaning of the two new places and two new transitions. P14 represents that the north-south-road has the green light or are allowed to enter the intersection and proceed. P15 represents that the east-west-road has the green light or are allowed to enter the intersection and proceed. Transitions T9 and T10 represent the changes of the turns from east-west to north-south and vice versa. Initially there are two dots in P14 meaning it is the turn for vehicles on the north-south road. For vehicles in the P1 position to enter the intersection T1 needs to fire. Now T1 has three pre-conditions: 1) a vehicle is in P1, 2) the intersection has room, 3) it is the turn for the north-south road. In the current figure all 3 pre-conditions are satisfied. So vehicle in P1 can enter the intersection and proceed. When leaving the intersection T2 puts back one dot in P7 and puts back one in P14. At the same time a vehicle in P8 can also enter the intersection because all the pre-conditions for T5 to fire are satisfied. When both vehicles get out of the intersection, there are still two dots in P7 and two dots in P14. At this time T10 can fire and will put two dots in P15. Now it is the turn for vehicles on the east-west road.

Note that, as we mentioned at the beginning, the transition firing in Petri Net has some non-determinism. That is, despite all the pre-conditions are satisfied, a transition may or may not fire; also if the pre-conditions for two transitions are all satisfied, which one fires first is not determined. So with this non-determinism in mind, one can see that initially T1, T5, and T10 can all fire. If T10 fires first, then the turn changes, and T1, T5 cannot fire until the vehicles on the east-west road finish. Also if T1 or T5 fire first, then T10 cannot fire until vehicles on the north-south road finish. Moreover, after vehicles on the north-south road finish, T10 can still not fire; this leaves the turn with vehicles on the north-south road. So the model does not provide "fairness" to the 4-way traffic. However, the reader can verify that there will never be more than two vehicles allowed in intersection and more importantly there will never be cross traffic allowed.

To provide some fairness, two timers can be added to the pre-conditions for T9 and T10. When T9 fires it turns on the timer for its turn. When the timer goes off, it triggers T10 to fire and turns on the timer for its turn. This raises an issue that a Petri Net model of a system needs to have some interaction with the external environment. Sometime the external environment's actions may or may not be modeled with Petri Net, but it can be an "add-on" for the Petri Net model.

4   Smart City Street Light

In this section we present two examples to illustrate many of the concepts described in Sects. 1 and 2, such as how one can model the ways different parts and subsystems of a smart city interact with each other, how dataflow between different subsystems can be modeled, and why a variety of models is necessary to properly model the smart city. We will emphasize the presentation capacity of Petri Net while sketching the high level design model of the systems in question.

We have purposely kept these examples simple. Their purpose is to illustrate various points, not to model sophisticated real-life systems. Any of these examples fully worked out would take more space to accurately represent and explain than allowed for this entire paper.

4.1   Example 1. Smart Light Pole

Smart cities will be composed of smart components. One important part would be a smart street light system [9]. The smart street light system should serve three major purposes: first, of course, is to illuminate the streets when necessary; second the system should be energy efficient; third the system should be environmentally-friendly; fourth, but not necessarily the last, the street light system should be integrated into the smart city platform. Let's look at a model using Petri Net as its representation interface as well as its high level design.

In this model, we assume that the street lighting system is controlled/changed by three major factors:

- Time of a day – say, schedule the on/off time of the street light by a clock. Turn the light on when evening starts, and turn the light off when dawn comes. Of course, the schedule can be different from season to season.
- Ambient light – this factor takes into account when severe weather is taking place or a solar eclipse is taking place during day time. When the ambient light gets dark, the street light should be turned on even during the day time off schedule.
- Motion of vehicle or human – this factor takes into account when vehicles or human traffic takes place in the evening. In late evening, when the city gets less traffic, the street light can be scheduled to dim in order to save energy. But traffic appearance will resume the light to full luminance.

A smart street light system can be implemented as a set of smart light poles [8]. Smart light poles put the control of the light locally. This implementation not only saves the communication effort that a central controlled system would need, it also makes the control directly react to the nearest environmental change. Therefore, it will act more promptly and appropriately for the local situation. Also this implementation isolates the necessary change into the areas that really need the change. This will increase the efficiency of the entire system. Figure 5 shows a simplified Petri Net model for such a smart light pole.

We first explain the meaning of the Petri Net components – places and transitions. In this Petri Net, there are 12 places and 10 transitions. The meanings of places and transitions are listed below the Petri Net graph. Normally in a Petri Net, the arrangement of the positions of the places and transition is not of importance as long as the number of them and the interconnections of them are the same as the formal definition of the Petri Net. We purposely arrange the positions and transitions in a way so that the presentation characteristic of the Petri Net figure can be easily seen by the readers. In Fig. 5, the top row represents the environmental factors. The middle row represents all the transitions that change the status of the traffic light. The bottom row represents the three states of the traffic light. One thing needs to be pointed out is that in a theoretical model of Petri Net, the environmental changes that impact the Petri Net status are either excluded or are figured into part of the Petri Net. We choose to leave the environmental part open because 1) the environmental factors do impact the Petri Net status; 2) but it is too complex to formally model the environmental change into part of the smart pole Petri Net. We simplify the environmental change by a dot appearing in appropriate places. For example, when ambient light gets dimmed, a dot will appear in P7; when motion is detected in range, a dot will appearing in P9, and so on.

We would like to give more explanations/descriptions so that the graphical display can be easily understood by the readers. We divide the places into 4 groups. The first group in the bottom row of the figure is associated with the light. P1, P2, P3 represent the 3 possible states of the light, namely off, dimmed, and on. The second group in the middle of the top row includes P4, P5 that represent the daily schedule condition based on time. P4 is the time condition for turning off the street light in the morning, and P5 is the time condition for turning on the street light in the evening. The third group on the left side of the top row includes P6, P7, and P8 that represent the ambient light conditions. P6 represents that ambient light is high, e.g. a bright sunny day. P7 represents that ambient light is dimmed, e.g. a dark cloudy condition. P8 represents that ambient light is very low – the same as in the night. This can also be in the case of total solar eclipse. Sometimes the very dark and thick cloud can also create this condition. The fourth group on the right side of the top row includes 4 places: P9, P10, P11, and P12. P9 and P10 represent the traffic condition, e.g. vehicle or pedestrians moving close. P9 represents that motion is within the range of the detection for this light pole. P10 represents motion is not detected within the range of the detection for this light pole. There are two places, P11 and P12 that are used to count how many objects get in and get out of the detection range of the light pole. The meaning of these two places will be further explained in the later paragraphs.

The transitions in the middle row are associated with changing of the street light states. Transitions are "triggered" by the changes in the conditions in each of the groups, but ultimately cause the light change under the different conditions. For example, T1 represents that the light changes from off to dimmed (for energy conservation, the street light in the evening is always in the dimmed state unless motion is detected in range), T2 represents that the light changes from dimmed to on. T3 represents that the light changes from on to off. T6 also represents that the light changes from off to dim but under different conditions. The change represented by T1 is caused by time or normal daily schedule. The change represented by T6 is cause by ambient light changing to dim during daylight because of the weather condition. Since this change happens in daytime schedule, P4 is also a pre-condition of this transition. The light change from dimmed to on can be caused by motion detected in the evening schedule (T2, P5, P9), and this change can also be caused by the change from partial solar eclipse to a total solar eclipse during daytime (T7, P4, P8). All the transitions from T1 to T8 are associated with light changing under different conditions. Based on the list below Fig. 5 and the definitions given in Sect. 2, readers can easily figure out the meaning of each transition. Keep in mind that, after all, a light pole is all about how to control the light. T9 and T10 are transitions associated with communication between this local smart light pole and the control unit in a higher level.

We illustrate the operation by stepping through a sequence of transitions. Suppose the initial state is that the light is dimmed (P2 has a dot); it's time for evening schedule (there is a dot in P5); the ambient light is low (P8 has a dot), and there is no motion detected (P10 has a dot). Suppose now that the sun comes up. The ambient light sensor removes the dot in P8 and places a dot in P6. A short while later the clock icon removes the dot from P5 and places a dot in P4 because it is now time for the light to go off. The three conditions for T4 to fire are now satisfied. T4 fires, removing the dot from P2 and placing a dot in P1; the light goes off. T4 also puts dots back to P4 and P6 respectively to maintain the conditions of "daytime schedule", "ambient light is high", and "no motion detected". Note that when daytime schedule is coming, the light could also be on (not dimmed) due to motion detected. In that case T3 will be activated instead of T4.

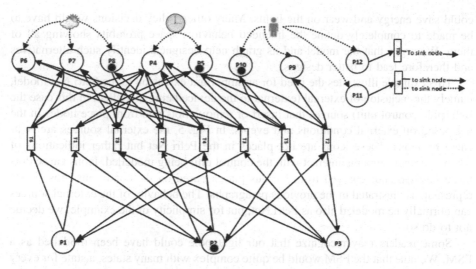

Fig. 5. Petri Net model for a smart light pole

P1: street light is off   P6: ambient light high
P2: street light is dimmed   P7: ambient light dim
P3: street light is on   P8: ambient light low
P4: It is daytime schedule   P9: motion within range
P5: It is evening schedule   P10: motion out of range
P11: count moving object in   P12: count moving object out

T1: off to dim condition 1   T5: on to dim condition 1
T2: dim to on condition 1   T6: off to dim condition 2
T3: on to off   T7: dim to on condition 2
T4: dim to off   T8: on to dim condition 2
T9: send in-count to sink   T10: send out-count to sink

Now suppose sometime during the day a storm occurs. The sunny/cloudy icon will remove the dot from P6 and place a dot in P7. The two conditions for T6 to fire are now satisfied. T6 fires, removing the dot from P1, placing a dot in P2 (light changes to dim), and restoring the dot to P7. Note that P4 also participates in this transition because it is still in daytime schedule. We have purposely kept the model and this sample transition sequence simple for space considerations. For example, in the stepping through in the previous paragraph the sun light may pass through dim for a brief while before reaching high. We could have modelled the movement of dots between P4 and P5 as transitions whose pre-conditions included signals from the clock icon. As we mentioned before, we choose to make environmental changes not part of a more complex Petri Net, by assuming the corresponding icons move the corresponding dots into proper places.

This Petri Net models specific policy decisions made by the city planners. For example, the lights should not turn fully on from the off state but rather go to dim mode first. If conditions warrant, the light will then move from dim to full on. Such policies could save energy and wear on the lights. Many other policy decisions would have to be made to completely define the intended behavior; space prohibits showing all of them. We argue that the model and its graph help designers identify such alternatives and therefore lead to better designs.

This example illustrates the need for an important extension to the Petri Net model, namely the inclusion of external (external to the device being modelled, in this case the light pole control unit) sources that insert or remove dots into/from place nodes in the net based on external conditions and events. In Fig. 5, the external sources are indicated by icons. These icons are not places in the Petri Net but rather indications of where external elements interact with the control unit being modelled. Icons cause dots to be inserted and removed from various places based on the conditions those icons represent, as illustrated in the previous paragraphs. The behavior of the external sources can normally be modeled also as Petri Net, but for simplicity of the example, we decide not to do so.

Some readers may recognize that our light pole could have been modelled as a FSM. We note that the FSM would be quite complex with many states, a state for every combination of current light status, time, motion, and ambient light. More importantly, the natural modularization inherent in the system would be lost. In the Petri Net we have grouped the places concerned with ambient light, for example, so that it is clear from the graph that these belong together and represent one component relevant to the light pole. Similarly for the clock and the motion sensor.

4.2   Example 2. Dataflow and Data Processing

A significant aspect of smart cities, as with most IoT systems, is the transmission of data around the system and the processing of that data in the proper module within the system. Suppose now that each smart light pole transmits information about the motion in its range to a sink node in the smart city system. The function of the sink node is to collect the data from all the smart light poles in the city or on a street or in a district, perform some preliminary computations, possibly send information back to the light poles, and transmit aggregate data to the smart city's central processing system for further and deeper analysis. This requires modelling at a higher level than an individual light pole.

Figure 6 shows the structure of this part of the smart city. The details of individual light poles are not shown except for the places relevant to collecting motion data and transmitting it to the sink. The sink has a modeling component for each light pole, in our case a small Petri Net (although other models could also be used). Each one of these nets has a timer, a place to receive dots representing objects entering the range of the corresponding light pole, a place to receive dots representing that objects have left the range of the light pole, and similar places for transmitting information from the sink to the data center.

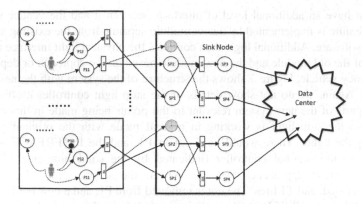

Fig. 6. Motion data collecting and processing

The simplest case for this problem is for the sink to detect when some vehicles may be stuck in the area near the light pole. In this case, when the light pole senses a new vehicle it places a dot in P11, which causes T9 to fire. This sends a message to the sink, placing a dot in SP2. It also causes the sink clock to set a timer for a reasonable amount of time for the vehicle to pass through the area. If the light pole senses a vehicle leaving the area, it places a dot in P12, which causes T10 to fire, placing a dot in SP1. In the sink, if SP1 gets a dot before the corresponding time expires, ST1 will fire; the data center will be notified that another vehicle has passed completely through the area. If when the time expires there are no dots in SP1, i.e., the vehicle did not pass through, ST2 will fire, notifying the data center that there is a possible incident. More sophisticated behavior could be modelled by the addition of information in the messages to the sink and processing capabilities in the sink itself. For example, the light pole could label the vehicles with ids or even take snapshots of the license plates and include that in the message to the sink. The sink, then, could match exiting vehicles with vehicles that had entered the pole's space and identify the vehicle that may have been involved in the incident. A mechanism in each unit might be needed to remove "orphan" dot(s), i.e., dots corresponding to congested vehicles. A timer for each vehicle is needed.

Note that the addition of an SDL and/or dataflow model would be appropriate here to define channels, communication properties, and computation. As with almost any application, a single model is not enough. For example, an SDL model might leave out the internal details of the light pole and sink and simply focus on the channels and communication (channel properties such as type and capacity, number of channels, type of messages on each channel, blocking vs. non-blocking, etc.).

4.3 Exmple 3. Addition of a New System

Our last example illustrates another situation that can occur when integrating a new module into an existing system. Suppose the city engineers want to add a feature to the stop lights that allows an emergency vehicle to force the lights to flash in all four directions. Suppose also that the stop-light control software is proprietary and that the vendor will not allow any modifications. This leads to the conclusion that the physical lights must have an additional level of interface between it and the vendor software. The new feature is implemented by a new module separate from the existing stop-light controller software. Additional logic then connects the physical light interface to one or the other of the old module and the new module based on the approach or departure of an emergency vehicle. Figure 7 shows the structure of the system with the new feature integrated. Again, we do not show details of the stop light controller itself; we only show the parts of the new system relevant to the points being made in this example.

Suppose the stop light is working in normal mode with the original controller controlling the lights. There would be a dot in P1, and the INTERFACE would be connected to the original controller (indicated by the solid blue line). When an emergency vehicle approaches the intersection, the second precondition for T1 becomes satisfied, and T1 fires. The dot is removed from P1, and a new dot is placed in P2. In addition, the INTERFACE is disconnected from the original controller and connected to the emergency controller. When the emergency vehicle leaves the area, T2 preconditions are satisfied, the dot moves back to P1, and the original controller is again connected to the INTERFACE.

This example illustrates how the existence of appropriate models helps designers identify points in an existing system that need to be examined when adding a new feature. In this case, the model of the stop-light controller combined with the restriction that the software cannot be modified leads to the obvious solution shown in Fig. 7. Without such a model, the engineers would have to pour through hundreds or thousands of pages of text. Good modeling software has the ability to zoom in or zoom out. In this case, a user would zoom out to the level indicated in the figure because the internal details of the existing controller are not changeable.

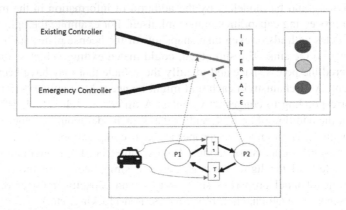

Fig. 7. Stop light system with emergency override added

5 Conclusion

We have presented several examples to show how modelling techniques can help in the design of smart city systems. Such models give manageable overviews of the system that can be understood by both engineers and city management personnel. They can identify points that need careful consideration when the system evolves and help formulate guidelines and requirements for new systems that are to be added. Models show data paths and expose the nature of the data that must pass between subsystems. Modelling systems can zoom in or out to expose or hide details as relevant. Models can concisely represent policy decisions made by city management. Models are generally more precise than word description and, hence, easier to reveal mistakes and inconsistence. We pointed out that a smart city system will need to use several different kinds of modelling techniques. We have also indicated that several extensions to current modelling techniques will be necessary to properly model how external actors interact with the smart city system. We have also illustrated with our examples that the proper presentation of the models in a well—designed human-computer interface facilitates the understanding of the design and, therefore, the analysis and improvement of the systems being designed.

Smart city, and IoT in general, is a worldwide initiative that merges the technical, environmental, and social issues all into one platform. It provides opportunities to peoples from all different areas of the entire world because these are also the stake holders in smart cities and the IoT. We will continue to investigate new techniques capable of adequately modelling these complex systems.

References

1. Airaksinen, M., Kokkala, M.: Smart city - research highlights. VTT Technical Research Centre of Finland Ltd., Espoo (2015). ISBN 978-951-38-8287-7
2. AT&T: Digital Infrastructure (2017). https://www.business.att.com/products/digital-infrastructure.html. Accessed 11 July 2018
3. Juniper Research: Smart cities – what's in it for citizens (2018). www.juniperresearch.com. Accessed 11 Sept 2018
4. Gascó-Hernandez, M.: Building a smart city: lesson from Barcelona. Commun. ACM **61**(4), 50–57 (2018)
5. Murata, T.: Petri Nets: properties, analysis and applications. Proc. IEEE **77**, 541–580 (1989)
6. Khedker, U.P., Sanyal, A., Karkare, B.: Data Flow Analysis: Theory and Practice. CRC Press, New York (2009)
7. Harel, D., Politi, M.: Modeling Reactive Systems with Statecharts: The STATEMATE Approach. McGraw-Hill, Boston (1998)
8. Marwedel, P.: Embedded System Design: Embedded Systems Foundations of Cyber-Physical Systems, 2nd edn edn. Springer, New York (2011). https://doi.org/10.1007/978-94-007-0257-8
9. Moss, R.: Building a smart city? Start with smart street lights (2018). https://www.insight.tech/cities/building-a-smart-city-start-with-smart-streetlights. Accessed 6 Oct 2018

Spreading Awareness About Quality in Interaction and UX to Young Generations

Antonio Opromolla(✉), Valentina Volpi, and Carlo Maria Medaglia

Link Campus University, Via del Casale di San Pio V 44, 00165 Rome, Italy
{a.opromolla,v.volpi,c.medaglia}@unilink.it

Abstract. In a scenario where the whole society is more and more complex, due to the increasing of the interactions and relations created by the technological evolution, it is essential to develop training models that allow to interface with these technological and social ecosystems in a sustainable way, providing specific, transversal and interdisciplinary skills to new professionals. They should be able to identify the needs of people and society and to find new (digital and non-digital) solutions and services based on them. In this context, one of the challenges concerns how to train young generations for the achievement of these objectives, first of all in creating services and products which allow people to have an effective, efficacy and satisfying experience (taking into consideration the Quality in Interaction and User Experience criteria). This contribution discusses some experiences carried out by the authors related to the engagement of high school students in learning processes oriented to how designing solutions and services according to this vision, by also identifying some key points to take into account to spread awareness about these topics to young generations.

Keywords: Training · Young generations · New professions · Quality in Interaction · User Experience

1 Introduction

Nowadays the job placement of young generations is a more and more challenging objective. In fact, in a scenario where the whole society is more and more complex, also the characteristics of the work are changing and the job search and definition become a more and more difficult operation.

The complexity of society has increased with the increasing of the interactions created by the technological evolution, which has been multiplying the connections and relations, not only among people, but also among different environments [1]. Such a complexity, defined by an enormous amount of processes and the inability to regulate cause-effect links within them, has to be managed. For this purpose, it is essential to develop training models that allow to interface with these complex technological and social ecosystems in a sustainable way, providing specific, transversal and interdisciplinary skills. One of the essential elements is the training on openness, collaboration and co-creation, the only prerequisites for obtaining a systemic vision, which gives evidence to the relationships between the phenomena that are part of the same ecosystem [2].

© Springer Nature Switzerland AG 2020
M. Kurosu (Ed.): HCII 2020, LNCS 12181, pp. 112–124, 2020.
https://doi.org/10.1007/978-3-030-49059-1_8

In order to achieve these objectives, it is essential to focus on the training of professionals who are able to encourage the construction of cross-cutting sustainable development processes. In fact, the need is not only of technicians who deal with technological products, but also of professionals able to identify the needs of people and society and to transform them in (at the same time digital and non-digital) solutions and services which people can access.

As a consequence, one of the challenges concerns how to introduce young generations to the need of new professions who address these social and technological issues [3]. Moreover, in an era where digital media are part of daily activities of people it is important to train professionals able to create services and products which allow people to have an effective, efficacy and satisfying experience during the interaction. Indeed, the focus is on QiI - Quality in Interaction, an expression which indicates the quality of solutions and services perceived by people [4] (for example in terms of the organization of the elements in the interface, visual layout, respect of the brand identity elements), and on the UX - User Experience, which indicates how services and solutions match with people expectations in specific social and physical contexts [5]. In particular, the focus of UX is not only on the use of a specific solution, but more on the perception, emotions and reactions that users can have also before and after the use of the solution itself. For this reason, in the UX, the context in which the interaction occurs plays a central role [6].

In this context, it is fundamental to create processes which aim at making young people aware of how the described field can represent the area of their future work. In the Italian context, in the last four years, all the students of the last three years of high schools have been involved in the ASL - Alternanza Scuola-Lavoro (School-Work Alternation) project, an innovative teaching methods which, according to the principle of "open school" helped students to consolidate the knowledge acquired at school and to test their attitudes "in the field" [7]. In fact, the aim of this framework, and of its evolution, the PCTO - Percorsi per le Competenze Trasversali e per l'Orientamento (Paths for Transversal Skills and Orientation) project, is to engage students in practical work experiences in real workplaces to both integrate the knowledge acquired in the classroom and develop interdisciplinary and transversal skills. These types of training frameworks can represent important tools for spreading the skills related to the design of solutions for the complex society to young generations.

This contribution discusses some experiences related to the engagement of high school students in learning processes (under the framework of ASL and PCTO) addressed to how to design interactive solutions in the more and more complex society. The focus has been both on the UX and on the QiI. The contribution is organized as follows. Next paragraph shows some works derived from the academic literature which discussed approaches and experiences of engagement of young generation in the world of digital media professions. The third and fourth paragraphs show the characteristics of the experiences carried out by the authors in this specific field, by discussing the specific purposes of the carried out activities, the organization of these learning processes and the employed tools, and the final outcomes. Then, the conclusions emerged by the carried out activities and some indications to better improve the applied tools and methods.

2 Related Work

As society changes because of techno-socio-economic factors, new skill and competences are required. Indeed, young people are the main subjects interested in receiving a proper education for digital media professions. 21st century skills, which include communicative, social and creative meta-competences in addition to cognitive skills [8], are the direct expressions of this need. The study of Dede [9] makes an overview of the different, but generally consistent, frameworks for 21st century skills. Basically, these skills are characterized by a special attention on learning and thinking capacity to solve complex problems, especially in a collaborative way, as well as on having a proper digital literacy for elaborating information and communicating, and on having more intangible personal and professional qualities for working and living in a complex world.

However new teaching methods are required too in order to satisfy this educational need, especially when the subject is the design and creation of interactive systems (both digital and human). On this point, the study of Saavedra [10] shows that for teaching to students to communicate, collaborate and problem-solve with people worldwide (the key of success in today world), educators require precisely the sorts of skills deemed critical for the next generation. Indeed, Wagner [11] makes evident how these skills are essential not only for careers and college, but for citizenship too.

Focusing on the approaches that support the teaching and learning of these skills, on the one hand, many academic studies concern the use of ICT as learning tools, referring in particular to the e-learning domain and its evolution [12]. In the dynamic context of this approach, the learner-centered framework for e-learning, which values and supports diverse learners and learning contexts where technology is in service to learners (mainly facilitating networking and collaboration) [13], and the blended learning methodology, which combines different learning environments (classroom, online and mobile), offer a suitable framework for the education of digital media professionals. For example, the study of Al-Huneidi [14] proposed a model that applies and combines Constructivism and Conversation theories in Blended Learning environment, in which the student is an active maker of knowledge, so increasing both the level of communication and interaction between students, and, as a result, the learning quality, experience and outcomes.

On the other hand, for issues related to design problems, a project - or problem as well - learning methodology is a very diffuse and effective instrument too, as it has the capacity to create vibrant and active learning environments and to create fundamental skills to address specific problems in complex, real-world settings [15–17]. In the academic literature several studies highlight the need for extending the process of knowledge construction and design that actively involves both learners and teachers typically used in some domains - such as architecture - to disciplines related to ICT design education. For example the study of Pittarello [18] gives some useful advices on how to improve in this sense HCI education experience. In detail, the study presents the development of an educational experience, where both learners and teachers were actively involved in a process of knowledge construction and project design, focused on design thinking (and taking advantage of a platform for remote learning) for increasing the design skills of the students and diminishing the gap between research and industry.

The study of Sheer [8] shows as Design Thinking, that is a team-based learning method, offers teachers support towards interdisciplinary practice-oriented and holistic modes of constructivist learning in projects that helps in dealing with complex phenomena by assuming diverse solution paths based on problem perception. Design Thinking also support in developing individual potentials, giving more confidence towards collaboration, and fostering a positive relationship between teacher and students. Based on the Design Thinking concept, the study of Clemente [19] discusses a learning toolkit to promote higher education students' creative and critical thinking skills demonstrating the importance of carefully designed didactic interventions and instruments to improve such skills.

For younger generations all these principles applies too. For example, the study of Carroll [20] presents a project involving a middle school aiming at making design thinking part of classroom instructional practices as a model of learning to prepare students to 21st Century challenges. The study highlights that design thinking is an approach to learning that succeed in developing children's creative confidence. Another important theme for young generation education is their involvement in learning experience that improve their digital literacy by making them critically understanding digital technologies. In this sense, the study of Hague [21] remarks upon supporting students' digital literacy in the classroom at both primary and secondary level and gives key insights and practical ideas for addressing a range of issues faced by school leaders and teachers in this context. For example, to make students knowing when digital technologies are appropriate and helpful to the task at hand (and when they are not), as well as to make them knowing how culture and society influence digital media understanding. The opportunities to integrate design thinking in digital learning and digital scholarship initiatives are discussed by the study of Burdick [22], where the design thinking results to near-perfect fit with the concerns of new media educators, as they both ask for teaching and learning common skills in line with the needs of our current moment.

As a general observation emerging from the studies presented in this paragraph, both digital tools and creative ones converging in an interdisciplinary learning experience are essential for engage and prepare young generation to the world of digital media professions. Moreover, Constructivism approach is particularly effective in preparing students for problem solving in complex environment. In this regard, Design Thinking itself offers a way for implement constructivist learning, that is fundamental in HCI training education and in the development of 21st century skills.

3 First Experience Aimed at Spreading Awareness in Quality in Interaction and User Experience

In this paragraph, the authors intend to discuss one of the experiences during which high school students have been involved in a learning process addressed to how to design interactive solutions. The focus is on the "Be APPtive!" event, a contest carried out in Link Campus University, which involved about 80 young students from different high schools of Rome.

3.1 Purposes

The purpose of the "Be APPtive!" contest was to encourage the young participants in creating some interactive solutions having as central topic the "wellbeing". They were free to focus on the elements they felt closest to in terms of personal, community or global challenges, specific context of use, employed technologies and platforms, interaction with the whole environment, etc. In particular, as shown in the following paragraph, the participants were asked to reflect both in terms of UX (in particular by investigating the problems to face and the user needs in specific fields) and of QiI (in particular by encouraging them in creating low-fidelity prototypes of the designed solution).

3.2 Organization and Tools

The "Be APPtive!" contest has been organized in the following phases:

1. *Build your team!*: during this phase the work teams have been created. Through some games, the 6 team leaders have been identified and the participants split in the related teams.
2. *This is your challenge!*: during this phase the general topic on which to design the interactive solution has been presented to the participants. In order to stimulate participants on this topic, some inspiring ideas have been presented.
3. *Find the best idea!*: during this phase the participants chose the type of user to design for and the problems to be addressed, decided the concept of the solution and established a pay off that would identify it.
4. *Create the experience!*: during this phase, the participants established the main functions of the interactive solution, created the information architecture and pro-totyped the three main interfaces of the solution.
5. *Pitch!*: during this phase the participants presented their idea to three experts who judged their work and rewarded the three most deserving teams.
6. *Your competences for your future*: the last phase involved experts who told the participants some specific applications of the digital media professions in the complex society.

The organization required one facilitator who led the overall contest, by showing the activities to carry out, and a second facilitator who led the discussion and the activities in the single team. Different tools have been employed during the contest, in order to let easier the activities of the teams:

1. one presentation, which showed the participants the activities;
2. inspiring ideas and personas, with the aim to stimulate the ideas behind the solution to be designed and to fix the characteristics of the user for whom to design. In

particular, participants have been provided both with a mind map representing some fields of application of the chosen topic and with a short description for different kinds of personas (see the Fig. 1);

Fig. 1. Inspiring personas helped the participants to identify the characteristics of the user to design for.

3. operational canvases, with the aim to work more easily on the single activities of the workshop, by fixing the decisions made by the team members from time to time. The provided canvases helped participants at: defining the specific problem to solve, fixing the basic elements of the concept solution, identifying the features of the solution and providing a description for each of them and organizing the defined features. In the Fig. 2 the canvas corresponding to the identification of the features solution.

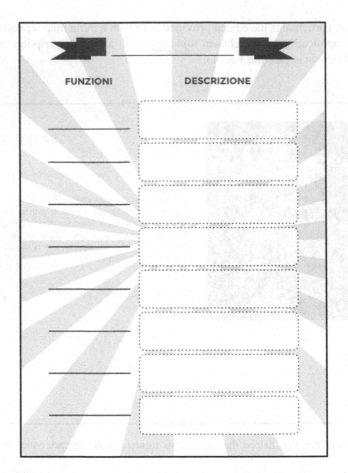

Fig. 2. One of the operative canvases provided to the participants. In this case, it helped the participants to identify the features of the solution.

4. final canvases, with the aim to fix the final version of the solution and to use as presentation tools during the pitch. The provided canvases aimed at showing: the team and the team members, the concept of the solution, the main three interfaces of the designed solution. In the Fig. 3 the canvas presenting the solution.

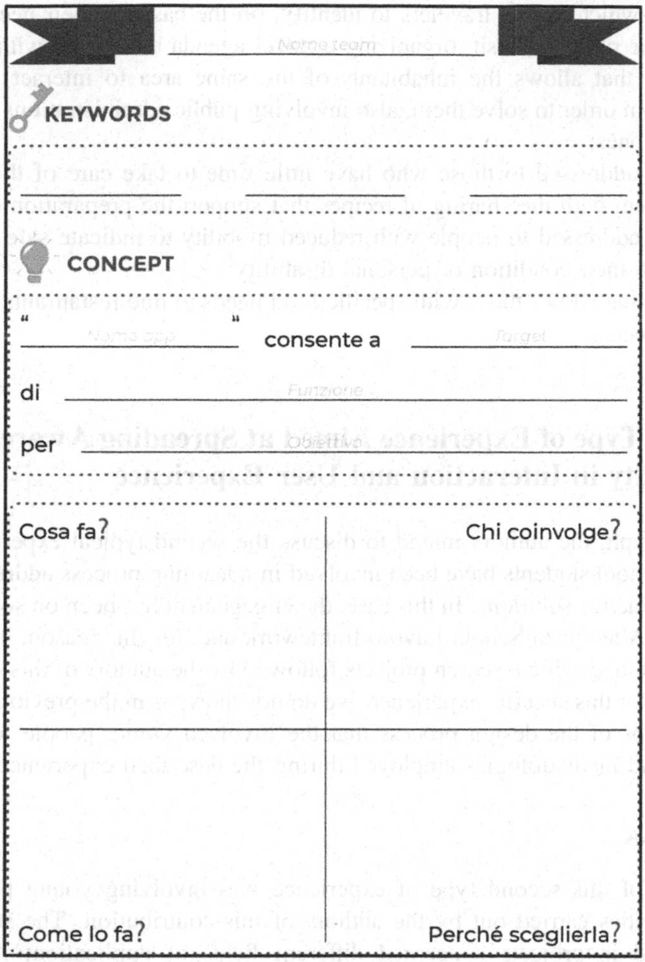

Fig. 3. One of the final canvases provided to the participants. In this case, it helped the participants to show the concept of the designed solution.

3.3 Outcomes

As already mentioned in the previous paragraphs, the central topic of the "Be APP-tive!" contest has been "wellbeing". The participants have been involved in ideating some solutions for this specific field. Following, some of the ideas developed:

- a solution that connects people in order to organize sporting activities within areas of the city that are undervalued;
- a solution which connects young and old people to encourage an exchange of knowledge and skills, in order to enter or re-integrate them into the world of work;
- a solution that puts disabled people in contact with self-sufficient people, in order to establish a relationship of mutual help on various issues;

- a solution which allows travelers to identify, on the basis of their needs and preferences, the places to visit, organizing a travel agenda associated with their route;
- a solution that allows the inhabitants of the same area to interact on common problems, in order to solve them, also involving public administrations for the most important ones;
- a solution addressed to those who have little time to take care of their nutrition, helping them with the sharing of recipes that support the preparation of food;
- a solution addressed to people with reduced mobility to indicate safe and suitable routes with their condition of personal disability;
- a solution that allows those with specific food needs to find restaurants that suitable for their needs.

4 Second Type of Experience Aimed at Spreading Awareness in Quality in Interaction and User Experience

In this paragraph, the authors intend to discuss the second typical experience during which high school students have been involved in a learning process addressed to how to design interactive solutions. In this case, the engagement has been on some activities in the ASL - Alternanza Scuola-Lavoro framework and, for this reason, students have been involved in specific research projects followed by the authors of this contribution. In particular, for this specific experience, we do not show, as in the previous paragraph, the single steps of the design process that the involved young people followed, but some tools and methodologies employed during the described experience.

4.1 Purposes

The purpose of this second type of experience was involving young people in the research activities carried out by the authors of this contribution. The students have been involved in projects concerned different fields of application: mobility and transport sector, sustainability in urban environment, climate change etc. Each project required different activities and, for this reason, different expertise. In this way different kinds of engagement of young people in UX and QiI activities have been tested. This was a central difference with the experience described in the paragraph 3. Indeed, if in that case the focus was on testing their engagement in specific phases for the design of a single solution, in this case the focus was on a more general engagement addressed to varied tasks for different projects. In the next sub-paragraph, the main required tasks are identified.

Also for this type of experience, the presence of a tutor which managed the activities carried out by the young people and give them some initial inputs related to the concepts of UX and QiI was important. Moreover, the use of specific supports (such as canvases to fill) which help the participants to perform the single required tasks was another central element of this type of experience.

4.2 Outcomes

The young participants have been involved in specific laboratories, each of which requiring the participation of almost 15 people and two tutors.

Following, some activities of the laboratories that, on the basis of these experiences, can give the best results in terms of involvement of young people:

1. *Analysis of the user habits and identification of user needs*, in particular in relation to areas of design which affect young people. For this activity the application of qualitative methods (e.g.: focus group, interactive workshops, interviews, etc.) is required to encourage the emergence of data and general considerations.
2. *Identification of best practices*, that they carry out both starting from what they know and from desk researches. For the output of this activity to be comprehensive and focused, a specific canvas which contains for each solution the elements to be investigated should be created.
3. *Production of alternative versions of the concept solution*, by working in small groups. A key point is that offering them the possibility of reflecting on specific steps of the experience that they want users have with the solutions creates more engaging ideas.
4. *Discussion about different ideas and creation of a merged idea.* Starting from more than one concept solution, they have been involved in creating only one, by keeping the strengths of the different versions produced.
5. *Creation of low fidelity prototypes* with essential icons and a basic workflows (that is to say the creation of the essential part of the information architecture of the solution).
6. *Identification of interesting design trends*, that can give the opportunity to innovate specific interactive solutions according to the more recent modes of interaction.
7. *Usability evaluation*, which allows to involve the young people in creating interactive solutions easier to use.

5 Conclusions and Future Work

The paper focuses on how spreading to young generations the activities related to the design of interactive solutions centered on human needs and facing the main social and global challenges. The paper intends to focus on the importance to spread awareness about the topics and activities of UX and QiI (for the realization of new digital and non-digital solutions and services) to young generations not only in an academic context but also during the high school, in order to make them aware of the possible careers in this sector.

In particular, this contribution shows the findings of two kinds of experience, carried out by the authors, by emphasizing not only the specific tasks required to the involved young people, but also the elements on which they can give a valuable contribution.

The paper wants to demonstrate how different formats of engagement of the young people in these topics can be applied. Indeed the paragraphs 3 and 4 show two very different experiences, with different characteristics. On the one side, the contest gives the opportunity of experimenting the creative skills of people, allowing them to find innovative solutions starting from general inputs. On the other side, the engagement on specific research projects allows to create structured activities with specific outcomes to reach.

The central element of the presented experiences does not consist so much in the quality of the produced ideas or contributions, but more than anything else in the stimuli given to the involved participants regarding the topics of QiI and UX. Indeed, these experiences require a further study from their part, in order to better understand if this field can be of interest for their future work. However, beyond that, the participants have had the occasion of understand how technological solutions are not detached from the more general social, environmental and economic system in which they are, but how at the same time they influence and are influenced by the processes underway in society. Using not digital work tools encourages the participants to better reflect on social aspects rather than on technological ones, in order to really solve some real problems and meeting the real people needs.

Moreover, these experiences are positive elements also due to the development and the reinforcement of soft skills for young people, which are necessary in the complex society as described above. These skills concern, for example: working in a team, which allows to interact with people who can have different points of view and opinion; working in an unknown context, which allows to get used to finding solutions in an unpredictable environment; showing and communicating the results of their own work; etc.

However, in order to get young people familiar with these concepts, it is necessary to facilitate some processes. For example, the use of a clear and engaging language is a very important starting point: the use of technical expressions should be avoided and making the words simple with a clear indication of single steps to perform is necessary.

Moreover, the use of game elements which can encourage them to carry out the different activities is considered as a strength. In the first experience presented in this contribution, game dynamics have been applied in order to identify the team leaders, to define the identity of the team and in order to reward the team that worked best. Indeed, these dynamics allow to engage people in a pleasant way, alternating group challenges and collaboration.

Another important element to consider is to create occasions in which the theoretical and practical parts are balanced. Indeed, the more positive experiences are able to give short theoretical contributions, which show the ratio at the basis of the single required activities and the most important best practices, and then a more extended practical exercise, during which the participants are engaged in producing some contributions directly associated with the first part. In this sense, also the presence of a tutor or teacher is on the one side a fundamental element, but on the other side this figure should leave people free to produce and experiment.

In the future, the authors intend to improve the methods and tools shown in this contribution and also finding new possible opportunities to spread awareness about Quality in Interaction and User Experience to young generations. At the same time, the authors will continue to create new occasions (i.e.: laboratories, workshops, contests) in order to reach these objectives.

References

1. Castells, M.: The Theory of the Network Society. MPG Books Ltd., Bodmin (2016)
2. Downes, S.: New models of open and distributed learning. In: Jemni, M., Kinshuk, K.M. (eds.) Open Education: from OERs to MOOCs. Lecture Notes in Educational Technology, pp. 1–22. Springer, Berlin (2017). https://doi.org/10.1007/978-3-662-52925-6_1
3. Perna, M.C.: Motivating young people to pursue the professions of the future (2019). https://www.gettingsmart.com/2019/03/motivating-young-people-to-pursue-the-professions-of-the-future/
4. Rentroia-Bonito, M.A., Jorge, J., Ghaoui, C.: An exploratory analysis of the role of emotions in e-learning. In: Encyclopedia of Networked and Virtual Organizations, pp. 563–571. IGI Global (2008)
5. Kaikkonen, A., Kekäläinen, A., Cankar, M., Kallio, T.: Will laboratory test results be valid in mobile contexts? In: Lumsden, J. (ed.) Handbook of Research on User Interface Design and Evaluation for Mobile Technology, pp. 897–909. IGI Global, Hershey (2008)
6. ISO 9241-210:2019: Ergonomics of human-system interaction—Part 210: Human-centred design for interactive systems
7. Ministero dell'Istruzione, dell'Università e della Ricerca: Alternanza Scuola-Lavoro. http://www.alternanza.miur.gov.it/cos-e-alternanza.html
8. Scheer, A., Noweski, C., Meinel, C.: Transforming constructivist learning into action: design thinking in education. Des. Technol. Educ. Int. J. **17**(3), 8–19 (2012)
9. Dede, C.: Comparing frameworks for 21st century skills. In: Bellanca, J., Brandt, R. (eds.) 21st Century Skills, pp. 51–76. Solution Tree Press, Bloomington (2010)
10. Saavedra, A.R., Opfer, V.D.: Learning 21st-century skills requires 21st-century teaching. Phi Delta Kappan **94**(2), 8–13 (2012)
11. Wagner, T.: The Global Achievement Gap: Why Even Our Best Schools Don't Teach the New Survival Skills Our Children Need–And What We Can Do About It. Basic Books, Hachette (2010)
12. Jochems, W., van Merriënboer, J., Koper, R. (eds.): Integrated e-Learning: Implications for Pedagogy, Technology and Organization. RoutledgeFalmer, London (2004)
13. McCombs, B.L., Vakili, D.: A learner-centered framework for e-learning. Teach. Coll. Rec. **107**(8), 1582–1600 (2005)
14. Al-Huneidi, A., Schreurs, J.: Constructivism based blended learning in higher education. In: Lytras, M.D., Ruan, D., Tennyson, R.D., Ordonez De Pablos, P., García Peñalvo, F.J., Rusu, L. (eds.) WSKS 2011. CCIS, vol. 278, pp. 581–591. Springer, Heidelberg (2013). https://doi.org/10.1007/978-3-642-35879-1_74
15. Savery, R.J.: Overview of problem-based learning: definitions and distinctions. Interdisc. J. Prob. Learn. **1**(1), 9–20 (2006)
16. Barrett, T., Moore, S. (eds.): New Approaches to Problem-Based Learning: Revitalizing Your Practice in Higher Education. Routledge, New York (2011)
17. Dochy, F., Segers, M., Van den Bossche, P., Gijbels, D.: Effects of problem-based learning: a meta-analysis. Learn. Instr. **13**(5), 533–568 (2003)

18. Pittarello, F., Pellegrini, T.: HCI and education: a blended design experience. Multimed. Tools Appl. **76**, 4895–4923 (2017)
19. Clemente, V., Vieira, R., Tschimmel, K.: A learning toolkit to promote creative and critical thinking in product design and development through design thinking, pp. 1–6 (2016)
20. Carroll, M., Goldman, S., Britos, L., Koh, J., Royalty, A., Hornstein, M.: Destination, imagination and the fires within: design thinking in a middle school classroom. Int. J. Art Des. Educ. **29**(1), 37–53 (2010)
21. Hague, C., Payton, S.: Digital Literacy Across the Curriculum. Futurelab, Bristol (2010)
22. Burdick, A., Willis, H.: Digital learning, digital scholarship and design thinking. Des. Stud. **32**(6), 546–556 (2011)

Ask Me No Questions: Increasing Empirical Evidence for a Qualitative Approach to Technology Acceptance

Brian Pickering[1]([✉])[ⓘ], Rachael Bartholomew[2], Mariet Nouri Janian[3], Borja López Moreno[4], and Michael Surridge[1]

[1] Electronics and Computer Science, University of Southampton, Southampton SO16 7NS, UK
{J.B.Pickering,ms8}@soton.ac.uk
[2] Oxford Computer Consultants, Oxford OX1 2EP, UK
Rachael.Bartholomew@oxfordcc.co.uk
[3] Fondazione Centro San Raffaele, Via Lazzaro Spallanzani, 15, 20129 Milan, Italy
nourijanian.mariet@hsr.it
[4] Biocruces Bizkaia Institute, Cruces Plaza, 48903 Barakaldo, Bizkaia, Spain
BORJA.LOPEZMORENO@osakidetza.eus

Abstract. The Technology Acceptance Model and its derivatives position *Perceived Ease of Use*, sometimes mediated by *Perceived Usefulness,* as the primary indicator of an intention to adopt. However, an initial study cast doubt on such a causal relationship: poor ease-of-use scores using a standard instrument did not necessarily correspond to poor usefulness comments from users. We follow up in this paper to explore reproducibility and generalizability. Using secondary review of results from testing and validation activities, we find confirmation that the *post hoc* measurement of *Perceived Ease of Use* is less important to participants than their concern for task-oriented usefulness. An ambivalent relationship obtains, therefore, between quantitative measures of *Perceived Ease of Use* and qualitative review of comments on *Perceived Usefulness* across three sites in Italy, Spain and the UK. Participants seem to prioritize their professional responsibilities and focus on how the technology under test might support them in their role. We therefore offer an explanation based on psychological theories of work and suggest a controlled follow-on study exploring the narrative content of technology acceptance.

Keywords: Technology acceptance · User adoption · Mixed methods · System usability · Technology affordance · Job Characteristics Model · Job demand-control model

1 Introduction

The simplicity and assumed power of the technology acceptance model (TAM) [1, 2] accounts for its continued popularity [3]. In its simplest form, the model claims that *Perceived Ease of Use* (PEOU) predicts a potential user's *Attitude Towards* using,

© Springer Nature Switzerland AG 2020
M. Kurosu (Ed.): HCII 2020, LNCS 12181, pp. 125–136, 2020.
https://doi.org/10.1007/978-3-030-49059-1_9

which in turn leads to the *Behavioral Intention* to adopt the technology. This effect is often mediated by *Perceived Usefulness* (PU). At the same time, there is increasing evidence that the model is not able to deliver against its potential [4, 5]. Later iterations [6, 7] confound its original elegance with contextual factors (job relevance, voluntariness, etc.) and adopter characteristics (gender, self-efficacy, etc.). It is unclear whether such extensions simply make explicit the *external variables* Davis et al. identified [1] or underplay more significant failings [8, 9]. TAM starts to abandon simple measures of PEOU and PU, introducing contextual factors mirrored in its competitor, the Diffusion of Innovation theory (DOI) [3, 10]. It may even undermine significant issues in technology design [11]. Human and social factors need to be given greater prominence [12], especially affect [13]. Indeed, technology is not simply a passive component, but may have an important and equal role in a complex human-machine network [14].

1.1 Investigating Conditions of Technology Acceptance

Although ostensibly easily accessible, PEOU may not be as instrumental in determining technology acceptance and adoption as once thought. We previously reported an exploratory study questioning the dominance of PEOU [15], operationalized via the System Usability Scale (SUS) [16]. Adopting a mixed-methods approach, we identified conflicting results for two cohorts working in healthcare in Italy and in Spain. In both cases, SUS scores were below threshold, suggesting that the technology was not easy to use and therefore in line with TAM predicting that it would not be acceptable. This was the case for a cohort of ICT professionals in Italy. However, a mixed group of ICT users and managers in the Spanish study working collaboratively were more responsive to the technology, developing a task-focused narrative where specific scenarios might enhance and support them in their day-to-day responsibilities. We speculated at the time that the effect may be due to priming (i.e., usability) or the collaborative conditions under which the Spanish trial but not the Italian one was run (engaging with one another to use the technology encouraged a more rounded view of its PU). We need to consider, though, whether different effects between the Italian and Spanish cohorts may be the result of some other artefact. In this paper, therefore, the goal is to validate the *reproducibility* and *generalizability* of our previous findings. That being the case, we also consider how to take this work further.

2   Method

As a baseline technology, we used a security modelling tool which finds risks and offers mitigation strategies in cyber physical systems [17, 18]. The technology was chosen initially since organizations often struggle to identify exposures to risk, as do human agents when faced with complex ICT systems [19]. From the earlier study [15], we predict that PU is not dependent on PEOU, provided that responses are elicited via appropriate methods to allow participants to respond more freely.

2.1 Research Questions

To investigate further the issue of technology acceptance, we focus in this paper on two questions:

RQ1: Do we see the same effects emerge consistently?
RQ2: Do we see similar effects with a different cohort on a related task?

These are intended to address concerns about *reproducibility* (RQ1) and *generalizability* (RQ2).

2.2 Design

There were three studies: one in Italy, one in Spain and one in the UK, each with two iterations making a total of six sub studies[1]. These studies were carried out originally as technology validation trials, with the initial round intended as formative and the second and final round as summative. They had not been specifically designed to explore user acceptance or adoption, and so were not planned or run with the types of controls associated with much empirical work. However, we claim greater ecological validity in that these were effectively field observations. For the Italian and Spanish trials, the technology was used as a standalone, visual design tool intended to promote understanding of cybersecurity within a healthcare environment. In the UK, by contrast, the base technology was integrated into an online social care service.

2.3 Participants

For the first iteration of Italian and Spanish trials, two small cohorts of self-selecting IT professionals were recruited, 5 in Italy and 4 in Spain. All participants had up to 20-years' experience representing different IT disciplines. Five Italian engineers and developers from the hospital's IT department were recruited in the Ospedale San Raffaele (OSR) in Milan, including Application Development & Management; Service Desk; Privacy, Procurement & Control; CRM, Business Intelligence & Process; and Enabling Services & Security. Four self-selecting participants from the Biocruces Bizkaia Health Research Institute in Spain including a Bioinformatics Technician, a Computer Science Engineer, a Software Developer and a Database Manager. In the second round, two participants in each country returned (a software developer and system administrator in Italy; and the Bioinformatics Technician and Database Manager for the first round in Spain). In the UK, 8 participants working for a social care organization took part; roughly half were IT professionals and the others volunteers. In the second, 14 participants split between IT, Charities and management roles took part.

---

[1] The Italian and Spanish studies obtained local ethical approval. For the UK studies, this was approved by the University of Southampton Faculty of Physical Science and Engineering faculty ethics committee, Ref: ERGO/FPSE/31262.

2.4   Data Collection

For the Italian and Spanish trials using the technology as a standalone visual design tool, participants were given a target scenario involving the secure country-to-country transfer of healthcare data. The security of the data is, of course, paramount for both legal [20] and ethical reasons [21]. Using the visual design tool, participants were asked to draw up an appropriate cyber technical system and to comment how realistic the risks and mitigation strategies were that had been automatically generated by the tool. In the first round, Italian participants worked in pairs, whereas the Spanish participants all worked as a group. In the second iteration, the two participants at each site worked together. The two co-authors (MNJ and BLM respectively) supported them and made notes during subsequent discussions when participants were encouraged to "think aloud" about their experience of using the technology.

For the UK trials, the domain was switched to social care. Here, there is still the legislative responsibility to protect personal data. However, the focus now is on effective delivery of social care. The technology was therefore integrated with an existing online social care service to handle privacy and data security. Participants were asked to role-play users as they carried out typical tasks with the service. They were then asked to fill in a privacy and a usability questionnaire. The co-author (RB) facilitated both sessions and provided support if needed. She also conducted semi structured interviews with participants about their response to the service as it handled the tasks they were attempting to complete.

2.5   Data Analysis

We adopted a mixed-methods design to re-analyze the original results which used quantitative instruments and semi-structured interviews. Using both qualitative and quantitative methods has become increasingly common certainly within healthcare [22]. For the first iterations in Italy and Spain, the SUS was used to estimate PEOU [15, 16], providing an overall usability score with scores below 68 regarded as poor. In the UK, by contrast, a locally generated instrument was used based on the company's experience with technology trials and rollout. Scores were reported in relation to the Likert label they most closely approached: for instance, a score of 4 as "Agree", and of 5 as "Strongly Agree".

For the semi-structured interviews, thematic analysis [23] was used across all sites and iterations, focusing on two main themes: PEOU and PU. The notes the researchers took to record what participants said were first analyzed, therefore, to identify the main themes. Subsequently valence (positive *versus* negative) was assigned to each of the utterances associated with the themes.

3   Analysis

As previously reported [15], during the first iteration neither the Italian nor the Spanish participants on average rated PEOU, operationalized via the SUS, above the standard threshold, a score of 68, with some individual scores a lot higher and some lower. Comments from the Italian participants confirmed PU to be poor. By contrast, the

Spanish cohort were more positive and began to describe potential benefits to the organization for identifying risk and introducing consistency. The first question then (RQ1) was to establish whether this trend was repeated for the second iteration.

3.1   Investigating Reproducibility

We validated the reproducibility of the findings with results from a second iteration of testing with the same participants and an updated, improved version of the technology. During this iteration, PEOU was not measured explicitly, focus was placed instead on encouraging participants to describe their response to the technology. Table 1 summarizes comments related to PEOU and PU by valence for both Italian and Spanish participants together. For instance, there were 6 negative comments on PEOU, but 11 positive comments on PU. The Italian participants did criticize some aspects of the user interface (UI) and tool (performance and visual presentation) and felt the technology required prior experience (3 negative comments on PEOU).

Table 1. Summary of *positive, neutral* and *negative* comments from Italian and Spanish participants.

	Positive	Neutral	Negative
PEOU	2	0	6
PU	11	1	2

However, both the Italian and Spanish participants commented on the potential for process improvement: the tool would effectively take an essentially manual ("whiteboard") one currently to a much more efficient semi-automated one (9 positive comments about PU).

Italian User 2:   *Because the same kind of process we are doing but by using whiteboard, in mind or talking with the people. When we have to do a project and we build an infrastructure, usually we are not aware of all the threats and possible solutions that are available. I think this tool can help us a lot in finding threats and solutions.*

What is more, understanding the concept underlying the technology, the other participant starts to think beyond the immediate context of the validation exercise and the *Perceived Usefulness* of the design tool for their own needs:

Italian User 1:   *If my job was this, I think that probably it would help me a lot.*

And then subsequently:

Italian User 1:   *The technology itself is not that difficult to understand but for me it will be difficult to think what structure I have to design just because it is not my job.*

This participant goes on later to criticize specific features of the UI: the search function, the color palate and the lack of a zoom function in the design canvas. Yet, when asked whether the technology would help those whose responsibility is to design, implement and run secure infrastructures, the same user simply observes: "*Yes, I think so*". So, the user is aware of specific shortcomings in the UI, and yet believes overall the technology is easy to use. More importantly, although not applicable to their own job role, they start to make sense of the technology when considering what other colleagues might need and how they might benefit from using it.

The Spanish users also note issues with performance and some difficulty with descriptive labels in the UI (3 negative comments on PEOU). However, they also highlighted the potential usefulness of the technology for a range of colleagues (architects, engineers and implementers) to visualize and understand issues associated with a complex infrastructure (2 positive comments on PU).

Spanish User 2:   *Building a technology infrastructure [with this tool] has recently attained widespread attention in the Engineering of the structure of a system. It helps architects, engineers and constructors to visualize what is to be built in simulated environment and to identify potential threats.*

Both Italian and Spanish participants, therefore, explore the potential usefulness for their respective organizations. Even if they can see no direct benefit to themselves, they are still able to appreciate how the technology might fit for others. Without the priming task of SUS, they seem to downplay PEOU, focusing instead on the umbrella issues of the security of health data and potential utility of the technology. One of the Italian participants even suggests that performance issues would be acceptable given the advantages available.

Italian User 2:   *I think doing this task in real life is so time consuming so the tool is somehow justified to take this much time.*

Accommodating technology shortcomings on account of potential benefit has been attested elsewhere [24, 25]. However, the experience of these limited validation trials suggests that potential adopters are willing to explore potential rather than simply reject on the basis of poor usability.

The earlier results [15] are therefore confirmed in terms of reproducibility. Despite the small number of participants, they were able to identify how the technology might fit within their organization to improve existing processes even if not directly relevant to them. They are still aware, of course, that the technology under test has some way to go to improve usability. However, this has not distracted them from seeing potential. Indeed, they have even been willing to think of ways that technical shortcomings might be tolerated if not completely overlooked.

3.2 Investigating Generalizability

To address questions of generalizability, we revisited the results of a previous validation test, based on the same underlying technology trialed for social care in the UK.

This time, the technology had been embedded within an online social care service. Results were available for two iterations with overlapping, though non-identical participants, 8 in the first round and 14 in the second. Instead of the SUS, participants were asked to rate both their attitude to privacy [26, 27] and technology usability. Participants reported broad agreement on a 5-point Likert scale for both usability and usefulness, and for each iteration, with 1 = Strongly Disagree, and 5 = Strongly Agree. For the first cohort, usability was ranked at 4.33 (median score) and usefulness at 4.00; these correspond to a judgement of "Agree". For the second iteration, the median scores were 3.92 (usability) and 4.00 (usefulness). Wilcoxon signed-rank tests showed that there were no significant differences between usability versus usefulness for either iteration ($Z = -1.378$, $p > 0.05$ for the first, and $Z = -0.120$, $p > 0.05$ for the second). In both cases, therefore, usability and usefulness were rated equally well. If PEOU really is a predictor for intention to adopt, mediated by PU, then we would expect user attitude to be broadly positive when discussing the technology.

Table 2. Summary of *positive, neutral* and *negative* comments from English participants.

Iteration		Positive	Negative
First	PEOU	3	12
	PU	12	4
Second	PEOU	4	48
	PU	8	20

A qualitative analysis of outputs from semi-structured interviews is summarized in Table 2. For each of the two iterations (first and second), the valence of attitudes to PEOU and PU is markedly negative overall. There is a greater willingness in the first iteration of testing to explore usefulness (16 *versus* 15) than in the second (28 *versus* 52). Yet, social care participants do see potential benefits, not least for their own interactions with automated services:

P4 (1st iteration):   *I would consider using this in daily life*

P2 (2nd iteration):   *I trust that it works, its transparent and makes me feel secure*

P10 (2nd iteration):   *The platform is a sensible idea – when is it coming out!*

P11 (2nd iteration):   *Most people don't realise what they have signed up to, and tick a terms box without reading it – this should wake them up to realising the consequences*

These sorts of comment suggest that the technology performs a specific job, namely provide the client (the data subject) with easy-to-use control of their own privacy. It informs the preferences they might want to make without forcing them to run through all the possible consequences: this is the type of empowerment that legislation was intended for and which users (data subjects) may simply be unable to understand and exploit [28].

But on the other, just as the Spanish and Italian participants thought of how the technology might help their colleagues, so the UK social care workers are concerned for their service users – who may be vulnerable or simply not have the experience with technology – and how they would react to such a system elicits a different and more critical response:

P4 (1st iteration):   *if my mum were to use it she would need a walkthrough or a guide. For instance like the [ABC] sign up process is a guided journey, [the service application needs] to be more guided*

P8 (1st iteration):   *I'm not confident that someone less tech-savvy (e.g. an ABC client) would [find it easy to use]*

P6 (2nd iteration):   *"intuitive web-based dashboard" language would be difficult to understand for some people*

This ambivalence in reaction was not reflected, of course, in the quantitative metrics where usability and usefulness were equally and positively rated. It may well be that participants responded to the survey questions from their *own* perspective rather than thinking about their clients. Those metrics would predict a willingness to explore the potential of the technology, which is found in what they say. Yet their comments on usefulness and usability include their clients for the most part. This may reflect the fact that the validation protocol required them to perform a series of typical tasks that the service users (their clients) might encounter. So, as far as usability and usefulness is concerned, they would typically focus only on how it affects the participants in achieving the tasks they'd been set. However, there is an added consideration with usability specifically with the social care services they provide for their clients in the UK: those validating the platform with its enhanced security settings have a responsibility not only to see appropriate controls in place to protect personal and sensitive data, but they also have a responsibility to their clients and how they would get on with the technology.

As far as generalizability is concerned, this second set of results in a different setting (UK social care) suggests that there is indeed no clear-cut relationship between PEOU and PU in terms of adopter intention. Others have also concluded that a direct causal relationship is not as robust as often claimed [29, 30]. But there is evidence too that any such relationship is at best ambiguous in multiple contexts and across different participants. Where those participants are encouraged to explore, their responses to the technology under test and not simply score it via quantitative survey questions focus on making sense of the technology in the contexts they see as relevant.

4 Discussion

A *post hoc* survey designed to capture a user's perceptions of technology usability is problematic for several reasons. The SUS and similar instruments rely on the user's memory of their experience rather than their experience itself. Further, assuming that the user is actually reporting their own experience rather than their expectations of how someone else might view the technology may not be justified. Additionally, of course, if they are experienced users, they may be more critical of less significant features or even biased towards others which they would not implement themselves. The different iterations of the original TAM by Venkatesh and his colleagues [7, 8] start to introduce mediating factors such as experience, willingness and self-efficacy. Even Davis had originally allowed for *external variables* [1] influencing *Perceived Ease-of-Use* and *Perceived Usefulness* but without attempting any systematic investigation. Thatcher and his colleagues are more explicit and position technology adoption within a broader socio-technical context beyond *Perceived Ease-of-Use* and *Perceived Usefulness* [31]. It should be no surprise, therefore, to find ambivalent indications of ease-of-use responses coupled with more comprehensive verbal evaluation of the possibilities afforded by the technology.

The main characteristic that all participants across iterations and sites share is their existing professional association with technology, as users, developers or service providers. Only the (UI) developers are likely to be concerned directly with the look and feel of the technology. The first Italian participant in the second iteration demonstrates this with their very specific comments about the UI, but free form responses identifying potential usefulness of the technology (see above). Instead, the focus for the participants here is on their professional responsibilities. Referring to DOI theory [10] and extrapolating from the documented TAM case for clinicians [29, 32] where organizational context and personal belief systems have an effect, these users are contractually and morally obliged to deliver secure, privacy enhancing services.

Adding to the technology characteristics operationalized initially via PEOU and PU (TAM) and perceived advantage, complexity and ease of integration (DOI), Hackman & Oldham's formulation of the Job Characteristics Model (JCM) [33] and Karasesk's Job Demand Control Model (JDC) [34] provide additional insight in terms of job characteristics and psychological state. In JCM job characteristic *Task significance* is high (i.e., the privacy and security of user data) with punitive fines for data protection breaches [20] and a loss of data subject trust [35]. This leads to *High job strain* (JDC) and therefore increased psychological stress. We believe that there is evidence in our re-analysis of participant responses to the technology under test of a realization of the potential for such technology to handle the *Task significance* amid public concern and regulatory change. In so doing, this reduces the risk of psychological strain. This in turn enhances the *experienced meaningfulness* and *knowledge of results* [33]. According to the original JCM, such outcomes would increase job satisfaction, performance and motivation.

In psychological terms not only does the individuals regain control (JCM) and reduce sources of stress (JDC), but shifts their focus away from the burden of regulatory and operational responsibility towards the driving force for their doing their job. Their motivation has shifted from extrinsic constraints and risk to the intrinsic realization of increased personal autonomy and feelings of competence [36].

5 Limitations and Future Work

Repurposing secondary data by reworking the results from previous studies may be criticized from an empirical methodology perspective. Participants in the original studies had different expectations from the experimental setup, and no appropriate controls to reduce the potential and unwanted influence of confounding factors. It may be argued, for instance, that the participants were sensitive to the demand characteristics of the situation: they are aware that the facilitator represents the technology and so may be more measured in their judgements. Opportunity sampling may conversely have reduced the potential for independent evaluation: these are technology users already and so perhaps compare the technology under test with what they know.

Equally, we would argue that the re-interpretation of the language they use to describe their experience provides a richer perspective on how they view the technology. These informal responses of potential adopters correspond more closely to a DOI approach: we are not simply looking at technology features and how they might influence adoption, but also the ability of potential users to see how the technology fits, and how they communicate their perceptions to others [10]. So, if language is the basis of the social construction of meaning [37] then it affords a more rounded understanding of how technology is likely to fulfill the needs of potential adopters. Exploring how individuals make sense of experience [38], creating a task-oriented progressive narrative which suits their own needs [39], we intend to explore technology acceptance in a follow-on, primary data study eliciting responses to the technology used in the studies reported here as it is seen to fulfil the practical needs of a controlled and cohesive group of potential adopters.

6 Conclusion

The Technology Acceptance Model predicts a strong causal relationship between *Perceived Ease of Use* and *Perceived Usefulness*. The claim is that if users find a technology easy to use then they would see its usability. However, revisiting validation tests across cohorts of IT and social care professionals in health and social care has called into question this assumed causal relationship. Allowing users to engage with a technology in context seems to encourage a more pragmatic perspective. Once potential adopters begin to make sense of the target technology as it addresses their needs, they are willing to accept shortcomings in its implementation. Planned research will in future explore the spontaneous use of narrative as a methodology to identify the intention to adopt.

Acknowledgements. This work was conducting with support of the OPERANDO (EU H2020 research grant No 653704) and of the SHiELD project (EU H2020 research grant No 727301).

References

1. Davis, F.D., Bagozzi, R.P., Warshaw, P.R.: User acceptance of computer technology: a comparison of two theoretical models. Manag. Sci. **35**, 982–1003 (1989). https://doi.org/10.1287/mnsc.35.8.982
2. Davis, F.D.: Perceived usefulness, perceived ease of use, and user acceptance of information technology. MIS Q. **13**, 319–340 (1989)
3. Taherdoost, H.: A review of technology acceptance and adoption models and theories. Procedia Manuf. **22**, 960–967 (2018)

4. Chuttur, M.Y.: Overview of the technology acceptance model: origins, developments and future directions. Sprouts: Working Pap. Inf. Syst. **9**, 1–21 (2009)

5. Bagozzi, R.P.: The legacy of the technology acceptance model and a proposal for a paradigm shift. J. Assoc. Inf. Syst. **8**, 244–254 (2007)

6. Venkatesh, V., Morris, M.G., Davis, G.B., Davis, F.D.: User acceptance of information technology: toward a unified view. MIS Q. **27**, 425–478 (2003)

7. Venkatesh, V., Bala, H.: Technology acceptance model 3 and a research agenda on interventions. Decis. Sci. **39**, 273–315 (2008)

8. King, W.R., He, J.: A meta-analysis of the technology acceptance model. Inf. Manag. **43**, 740–755 (2006)

9. Holden, R.J., Karsh, B.-T.: The technology acceptance model: its past and its future in health care. J. Biomed. Inform. **43**, 159–172 (2010)

10. Rogers, E.: The Diffusion of Innovations. The Free Press, New York (2003)

11. Benbasat, I., Barki, H.: Quo vadis TAM? J. Assoc. Inf. Syst. **8**, 7 (2007)

12. Legris, P., Ingham, J., Collerette, P.: Why do people use information technology? A critical review of the technology acceptance model. Inf. Manag. **40**, 191–204 (2003)

13. Perlusz, S.: Emotions and technology acceptance: development and validation of a technology affect scale. In: 2004 IEEE International Engineering Management Conference (IEEE Cat. No. 04CH37574), pp. 845–847. IEEE (2004)

14. Latour, B.: Reassembling the Social-an Introduction to Actor-Network-Theory. Oxford University Press, Oxford (2005)

15. Pickering, B., Janian, M.N., López Moreno, B., Micheletti, A., Sanno, A., Surridge, M.: Seeing potential is more important than usability: revisiting technology acceptance. In: Marcus, A., Wang, W. (eds.) HCII 2019. LNCS, vol. 11586, pp. 238–249. Springer, Cham (2019). https://doi.org/10.1007/978-3-030-23535-2_18

16. Brooke, J.: SUS-A quick and dirty usability scale. In: Usability Evaluation in Industry, p. 189, 4–7 (1996)

17. Chakravarthy, A., Chen, X., Nasser, B., Surridge, M.: Trustworthy systems design using semantic risk modelling. In: 1st International Conference on Cyber Security for Sustainable Society, United Kingdom (2015)

18. Surridge, M., et al.: Modelling Compliance Threats and Security Analysis of Cross Border Health Data Exchange. In: Attiogbé, C., Ferrarotti, F., Maabout, S. (eds.) MEDI 2019. CCIS, vol. 1085, pp. 180–189. Springer, Cham (2019). https://doi.org/10.1007/978-3-030-32213-7_14

19. Pfleeger, S.L., Caputo, D.D.: Leveraging behavioral science to mitigate cyber security. Comput. Secur. **31**, 597–611 (2012)

20. European Commission: Regulation (EU) 2016/679 of the European Parliament and of the Council of 27 April 2016 (2016)

21. Boyd, K.M.: Medical ethics: principles, persons, and perspectives: from controversy to conversation. J. Med. Ethics **31**, 481–486 (2005)

22. Lilford, R.J., Foster, J., Pringle, M.: Evaluating eHealth: how to make evaluation more methodologically robust. PLoS Med. **6**, e1000186 (2009)

23. Braun, V., Clarke, V.: Using thematic analysis in psychology. Qual. Res. Psychol. **3**, 77–101 (2006)

24. Lee, J.D., See, K.A.: Trust in automation: Designing for appropriate reliance. Hum. Factors: J. Hum. Factors Ergon. Soc. **46**, 50–80 (2004)

25. Turkle, S.: Alone Together: Why We Expect More From Technology and Less From Each Other. Basic Books, New York (2017)

26. Bellman, S., Johnson, E.J., Kobrin, S.J., Lohse, G.L.: International differences in information privacy concerns: a global survey of consumers. Inf. Soc. **20**, 313–324 (2004)

27. Smith, H.J., Milberg, S.J., Burke, S.J.: Information privacy: measuring individuals' concerns about organizational practices. MIS Q. **20**, 167–196 (1996)
28. Acquisti, A., Brandimarte, L., Loewenstein, G.: Privacy and human behavior in the age of information. Science **347**, 509–514 (2015)
29. Yarbrough, A.K., Smith, T.B.: Technology acceptance among physicians: a new take on TAM. Med. Care Res. Rev. **64**, 650–672 (2007)
30. Turner, M., Kitchenham, B., Brereton, P., Charters, S., Budgen, D.: Does the technology acceptance model predict actual use? A systematic literature review. Inf. Softw. Technol. **52**, 463–479 (2010)
31. Thatcher, J.B., McKnight, D.H., Baker, E.W., Arsal, R.E., Roberts, N.H.: the role of trust in postadoption IT exploration: an empirical examination of knowledge management systems. IEEE Trans. Eng. Manag. **58**, 56–70 (2011)
32. Dearing, J.W.: Applying diffusion of innovation theory to intervention development. Res. Soc. Work Pract. **19**, 503–518 (2009)
33. Hackman, J.R., Oldham, G.R.: Motivation through the design of work: test of a theory. Organ. Behav. Hum. Perform. **16**, 250–279 (1976)
34. Van der Doef, M., Maes, S.: The job demand-control (-support) model and psychological well-being: a review of 20 years of empirical research. Work Stress **13**, 87–114 (1999)
35. Lewicki, R.J., Wiethoff, C.: Trust, trust development, and trust repair. In: The Handbook of Conflict Resolution: Theory and Practice, vol. 1, pp. 86–107 (2000)
36. Ryan, R.M., Deci, E.L.: Intrinsic and extrinsic motivations: classic definitions and new directions. Contemp. Educ. Psychol. **25**, 54–67 (2000)
37. Miranda, S.M., Saunders, C.S.: The social construction of meaning: an alternative perspective on information sharing. Inf. Syst. Res. **14**, 87–106 (2003)
38. Murray, M.: Narrative psychology and narrative analysis. In: Camic, P.M., Rhodes, J.E., Yardley, L. (eds.) Qualitative Research in Psychology: Expanding perspectives in methodology and design, pp. 95–112. American Psychological Association, Washington, DC (2003)
39. Gergen, K.J., Gergen, M.M.: Narrative form and the construction of psychological science. In: Sarbin, T. (ed.) Narrative Psychology: The Storied Nature of Human Conduct, pp. 22–44. Praeger, New York (1986)

Anthropomorphic Design for Everyday Objects

Shi Qiu[✉]

Department of Design, Shanghai Jiao Tong University, Shanghai, China
qiushi11@sjtu.edu.cn

Abstract. Eye contact is important during social interactions. It is known as one of the most compelling social signals which can boost people's physiological arousal. However, people tend to feel that they are making eye contacts with other people rather than with objects. In this paper, our research is motivated to explore the possibility of gaze communication between a person and an inanimate object. By anthropomorphizing everyday objects, we try to create social interactions and a sense of emotional bond between people and inanimate objects, inspired by anthropomorphic design. Based on the eye-tracking technology, we implement a coffee machine system with two small responsive displays which called "artificial eyes". In the system, when a person looks at the artificial eyes, they will look back and try to establish the eye contact with that person. When a person stares at the artificial eyes for a while, indicating the needs of using the coffee machine, the artificial eyes will look down and pour the coffee out automatically. Finally, we present the experimental plan to compare the user's perceptions between the interactive-gaze condition and the random-gaze condition of the artificial eyes.

Keywords: Anthropomorphism · Eye tracking · Eye contact · Gaze sensitive object · Social interaction

1 Introduction

Eye contact is important to establish the relationships between people. Since the visual modality is dominant for most people, eye contact is an essential type of the nonverbal communication. Eyes can reflect our interest, honesty, trust and comfort in communication. Establishing good eye contacts during conversation is the key to creating positive connections with other people. When a person initiates interactions with another person, eye contact must come first. However, people tend to feel that they are making eye contacts with other people rather than with the objects. The feeling of being look back when gazing at someone/something should influence our social behavior.

Previous studies in the HCI field related to gaze interaction were mostly confined to the digital or virtual environment, such as to be an input modality to interact with an object while playing video games [20] or to point or select an object during human-computer interaction [13]. In our research, an eye tracker is used to detect the user's gaze and to help the object to understand how it should react based on the gaze data it has retrieved from the eye tracker. Depending on the gaze behavior as the input

© Springer Nature Switzerland AG 2020
M. Kurosu (Ed.): HCII 2020, LNCS 12181, pp. 137–146, 2020.
https://doi.org/10.1007/978-3-030-49059-1_10

modality, we explore to anthropomorphize everyday objects, such as the coffee machine, the cup, the laptop, to create social interactions and a sense of emotional bond between people and these inanimate objects. We develop a coffee machine system with the artificial eyes. When a person looks at the artificial eyes, they will look back and try to establish the "eye contact" with that person. When a person stares at the artificial eyes for a while, indicating the needs of using the coffee machine, the artificial eyes will look down and pour the coffee out automatically. By applying artificial eyes on the coffee machine, we intend to design the object to have its personality traits.

2   Related Work

Webster's New Collegiate Dictionary (1977) defines "anthropomorphism" as the "attribution of human characteristics to nonhuman things or events." This term is originated from the Greek "anthropos" for "human" and "morphe" for "shape" or "form", describing people's tendency to attribute human characteristics to non-lifelike artifacts [8]. Adding familiar humanlike qualities to a less familiar non-humanlike entity can make the entity become more familiar, explainable, or predictable [9].

The phenomenon of anthropomorphism has been intensively studied in social science. In familiarity thesis [10], it states that anthropomorphism allows us to explain things we do not understand based on that we do understand, and what we understand best is ourselves. The familiarity thesis provides a primarily cognitive motivation for anthropomorphism: understanding the world based on a mental model of the world that people are most familiar with. In contrast to the familiarity thesis, the comfort thesis [10] is an emotional motivation for anthropomorphism. According to this thesis, anthropomorphism is "an attempt to feel like we can define and influence the world if it is more like us than not" [10]. People tend to be uncomfortable with things that are not like them and try to make things be like themselves to reduce that discomfort. The psychological discussion of anthropomorphism is not neutral, but is in fact value laden and defines our interaction with the environment [4]. In the social thesis the act of anthropomorphizing reflects values and possesses the potential for social consequence [4]. Phenomenological intersujectivity states that anthropomorphism is a reflection of how we experience the world. It argues that we experience objects that seem to be animated by human consciousness and cause the distinction between self and other to be blurred, and that anthropomorphism is a pragmatic reaction to such objects to make sense of them [12].

Carl DiSalvo et al. [7] explained the anthropomorphic product reflect human-like qualities that include the physical characteristics of shape and size as well as qualities of behavior and interaction. Based on these, we classify the anthropomorphic products into two categories: (1) physical appearance, and (2) behavior and interaction.

2.1   Physical Appearance

Henry the Hoover [21] is a vacuum cleaner which has a big friendly and smiley face. By adding the name and the face to the form of a vacuum cleaner, this product makes itself become a person's friend. Its anthropomorphic form projects human values, aiming at sparking people's social and nurturing instincts, ultimately selling the product [15]. Anthropomorphism also could be on a more abstract level. For example, designers try to endow the products with bodily features such as postures. As shown in Fig. 1, the Dulcinea lamp [19] adopts a retreating posture, the 'back' is turned towards the person, and the position of the 'head' slightly lowered while the 'spine' is erect all the way from bottom to top. This posture is associated with interactions as serene, humble and non-intrusive. Such visual-spatial features may resonate with people, because they are associated with the implicit postures in our daily social interactions [6].

Fig. 1. Dulcinea lamp by Mimmo Paladino [19].

2.2 Behavior and Interaction

In the design of the interactive systems, anthropomorphism also plays an important role and is reflected in not only the appearance, but also behavior and interaction. An interactive cup system [1] was developed to display human-like behaviors based on the eye tracking technology (Fig. 2). In this system, a cup that can move up to indicate "Are you looking at me?" When a person looks at it, it goes back to its initial state. If the user maintains the gaze at the cup after it moves up, it will turn itself around and ensure the handle of the cup to point towards the user and offer "Would you like to have a cup of coffee?" The cup itself can express its shyness when the user staring at it for a longer time. Osawa et al. [16] presented a 'transitional explainer', an agent that instructed people about the features of the multi-function printer (MFP) by mixing real-world and virtual-world representations. In this system, people interacted with the transitional agent to learn how to use the MFP. The agent could hide its real eyes and arms in a virtual-world mode, and extended them in a real-world mode. Afterwards, they evaluated the system and demonstrated that 'transitional explainer' supported users' understanding of how to manipulate the MFP and enhanced users' motivation to use it.

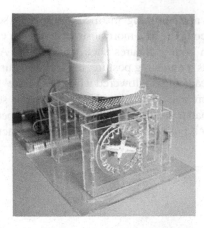

Fig. 2. Working prototype of the interactive cup that reacts to human's eye gaze [1].

3   Design Concept

The relationship between people and objects becomes less engaging as the technology grows. For example: brewing a cup of coffee is more convenient nowadays. We just have to load the coffee capsule into the machine and simply push a button. In our design concept, we aimed at creating a new and interesting interaction between the person and the object by applying the artificial eyes on the coffee machine. We clarified and visualized the concept design by using scenarios, which were developed at the early stages of the concept design. Instead of considering human behavior and experience via the formal analysis and modeling of well-specified tasks, scenario-based design is a relatively lightweight method for envisioning future use possibilities [5].

A coffee machine is the everyday object chosen for this research, because it is a common object that we often use in our daily lives. Since people have been already familiar with the coffee machine, we do not have to introduce the function and how to use it. Every morning, when we arrive at the office, the first thing that we do is to use the coffee machine to pour out a cup of coffee to start the day. We load the coffee capsule into the machine and just push a button. We place a coffee cup to the coffee machine and wait for pouring out the coffee. In this process, it is a one-sided behavior between a person and the object. However, what if we design the coffee machine with the artificial eyes that can show eye gestures to communicate with the person, the experience of using the coffee machine will become quite different and interesting.

The artificial eyes on the coffee machine can blink and try to grab the attention from the person. If the person looks at the artificial eyes, they will look back to establish the "eye contact" (Fig. 3). If the person maintains his/her gaze which demonstrates the intention to use the coffee machine, the artificial eyes will look down and pour out the coffee automatically (Fig. 4).

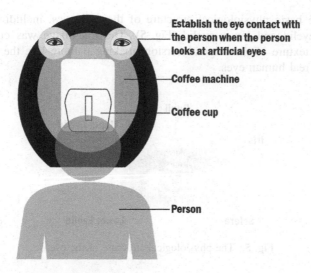

Fig. 3. The artificial eyes establish the eye contact with the person when the person looks at them.

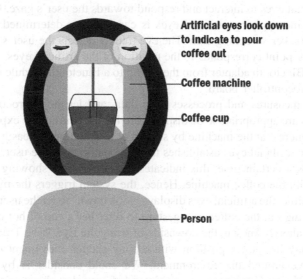

Fig. 4. The artificial eyes look down to indicate pouring the coffee out.

4 Prototype Design

We modified the eye image of the artificial eyes based on the open-source design of the electronic animated eyes [17]. This existed system consists of Teensy 3.2 microcontroller board that can control two eyes, two 1.5" OLED displays to output gaze animations and enclosures produced by 3D printer. The software can handle analog joystick for movement, and buttons for eye blinks or winks. Gaze animations are inspired by the basic physiological structure of the real eyes, including iris, pupil, sclera, upper eyelid and lower eyelid (Fig. 5). The iris image was customized by decreasing the texture of the original version, making it more like the cartoon eyes rather than the real human eyes.

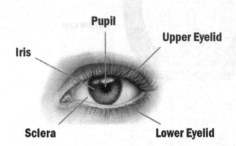

Fig. 5. The physiological structure of the eye.

In the prior work, we used an Eye Tribe Tracker to detect the eye gaze from the user. To create a system that is responsive towards the user's gaze, a Java program has been developed to calculate and reveal the location of the gaze point on the screen. To enable the artificial eyes to interact and respond towards the user's gaze, the position of the coffee machine applying artificial eyes is carefully pre-determined, and must be within the eye tracker's tracking area. The eye tracker detects the user's eye gaze, and if the user's gaze point corresponds to the position of the artificial eyes, a command is sent out via the Bluetooth adapter from the laptop to a Bluetooth module connected to a Teensy 3.2 microcontroller board.

The system measures and processes gaze data, and let the microcontroller know which behaviors are appropriate to be displayed to the user during the experiment. If the user shows an interest at the machine by staring at it, the system measures the fixation duration, and the artificial eyes establishes the eye contact with the user. If the fixation duration exceeds a certain time, this indicates that the user is showing an interest to interact more with the coffee machine. Hence, the system triggers the microcontroller, and at the same time, the artificial eyes displays "look down" to let the user know that the machine is pouring out the coffee as a gesture to offer her a cup of hot coffee.

As we have already known, the downside of using the Eye Tribe Tracker is that the user needs to stay in one fix position without any sudden movement or without the freedom to move around the environment. We could consider is by mounting an Omron Human Vision Components to our intended everyday object and let the device to communicate with our system. This board can perceive people's nonverbal behavior including the user's gaze direction at very high speed and accuracy, and the user is not required to stay in one place for the board to process the environment.

5   Experimental Design

We plan an experiment that uses the artificial eyes system as a test bed to find out how the user will perceive the artificial eyes. We hypothesize that there will be a significant difference of the users' perceptions towards different gaze patterns of the artificial eyes.

A within-subject design will be used in the experiment and it includes one independent variable with three levels (1. coffee machine without eyes, 2. coffee machine with the random-gaze eyes, and 3. coffee machine with the interactive-gaze eyes) and one dependent variable (the users' perceptions towards the artificial eyes). We have described the interactive-gaze condition in Sect. 3 and 4. In the random-gaze condition, the artificial eyes randomly display "look at" and "look away" eye gestures, and each eye gesture on average for a period of 1 s (0–2 s) in any state [3]. We will also test the coffee machine without the artificial eyes, which is considered as a control condition in the experiment.

5.1   Participants and Setup

In the experiment, the participant will sit in front of a round table where towards the coffee machine with the artificial eyes. The placement of the coffee machine will be very crucial and must correspond with the system's targeted area. The position of the participant is also important and must be paralleled to the Eye Tribe Tracker's tracking area. It is necessary to center aligned the tracker and adjusted it towards the participant's face for the maximum trackability. The Eye Tribe Tracker connected to a laptop will be installed 40 to 60 cm away from the participant. When it is calibrated, the eye tracking software calculates the participant's eye gaze coordinates with an average accuracy of around 0.5 to 1° of the visual angle. In order to stabilize and track the accurate gaze, we have to place a pillow on the chair to fix the neck of the participant. The observational camera captures the whole scene. An overview of the experimental setup in the coffee room is shown in Fig. 6.

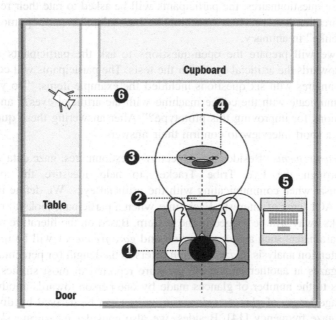

Fig. 6. Overhead view of the experimental setup in the coffee room: (1) the pillow to fix the neck of the participant; (2) the Eye Tribe Tracker; (3) the artificial eyes; (4) the coffee machine; (5) the laptop; (6) the observational camera.

5.2   Measurements

Objective and subjective measures of the artificial eyes will be deployed throughout this experiment.

Subjective Measurements. We will use a subjective questionnaire to measure the users' perceptions towards the coffee machine with artificial eyes, including five subjective measures: social presence, anthropomorphism, animacy, likeability, and perceived intelligence.

Social Presence. Social presence will be measured using Retained Items of the Networked Minds Social Presence Measure (NMSPM) [11] with a seven-point Likert-type scale (from not at all true to very true). The questionnaire consists of six subscales with 36 items. The six subscales are: (1) co-presence, (2) attentional allocation, (3) perceived message understanding, (4) perceived affective understanding, (5) perceived affective interdependence, and (6) perceived behavioral interdependence. Example items in co-presence and attentional allocation are: "(My partner) caught my attention" and "I remained focused on (my partner) throughout our interaction." In the questionnaire, we will modify the wording "my partner" to "the artificial eyes" in all items, which can make the participants easy to understand the recent scenario.

Anthropomorphism, Animacy, Likeability, and Perceived Intelligence. These five dimensions will be measured using the questionnaires of anthropomorphism, animacy, likeability, and perceived intelligence [2]. The questionnaire of anthropomorphism, likeability, and perceived intelligence has 5 items respectively and animacy has 6 items. In these questionnaires, the participants will be asked to rate their responses on the 5-point direction levels such as "machinelike-humanlike" in anthropomorphism and "artificial-lifelike" in animacy.

Besides, we will prepare the open-questions to ask the participants about their perceptions towards the artificial eyes after the tests. The participants will complete the open questionnaires with six questions included the example items: "Do you want to interact/communicate with the coffee machine with the artificial eyes?" and "What is your suggestions for improving this prototype?" After answering these questions, we will conduct a short interview to confirm their answers.

Objective Measurements. Besides the subjective questionnaires, gaze data will be also collected through the Eye Tribe Tracker to help measure the participants' attention/arousal when communicating with the artificial eyes. We define the artificial eyes area as AOI (area of interest). Each time when a participant looks at the artificial eyes and looks away will be logged in the system. Based on the literature review [18], some gaze parameters such as *gaze duration* and *gaze frequency* will be important for the further attention analysis. *Gaze duration* refers to the length (or percentage) of time one person gazes at another and is the measure reported in most studies. *Gaze frequency* refers to the number of glances made by one person towards another. A measure of average length of glances (*glance duration*) can be derived by dividing gaze duration by gaze frequency [14]. Besides, we also consider measuring skin conductivity, heartrate, and heart variance which are three popular measurements to provide a good indication of the user's arousal in real time [2].

6 Conclusion

In this research, we try to explore the possibility of creating gaze communication between a person and an inanimate object. By anthropomorphizing everyday objects, we create social interactions and a sense of emotional bond between people and inanimate objects. We start our preliminary study with the everyday object coffee machine and the artificial eyes. In our future work, we will extend our scenario to the special user group in the natural settings such as the elderly who live in care homes to interact with the artificial eyes. We try to enrich the meaning of the everyday objects: beyond the functionality and become the social companion for the elderly.

Acknowledgements. We thank our colleagues at the Industrial Design Department in Eindhoven University of Technology who offer helpful suggestions and ideas for this pilot study.

References

1. Anas, S.A.B., Qiu, S., Rauterberg, M., Hu, J.: Exploring Gaze in interacting with everyday objects with an interactive cup. In: HAI 2016 - Proceedings of the 4th International Conference on Human Agent Interaction, October 2016, pp. 345–348 (2016)
2. Bartneck, C., Kulić, D., Croft, E., Zoghbi, S.: Measurement instruments for the anthropomorphism, animacy, likeability, perceived intelligence, and perceived safety of robots. Int. J. Soc. Robot. **1**(1), 71–81 (2009)
3. Bee, N., et al.:. Discovering eye gaze behavior during human-agent conversation in an interactive storytelling application. In: International Conference on Multimodal Interfaces and the Workshop on Machine Learning for Multimodal Interaction, ICMI-MLMI 2010, 8 p. (2010). Article 9
4. Caporeal, L.R., Heyes, C.M.: Why anthropomorphize? Folk psychology and other stories. In: Anthropomorphism, Anecdotes, and Animals, pp. 59–73 (1997)
5. Carroll, J.M.: Scenario-based design. In: Handbook of Human-Computer Interaction, 2nd edn., pp. 383–406. Elsevier (1997)
6. Dael, N., Mortillaro, M., Scherer, K.R.: Emotion expression in body action and posture. Emotion **12**(5), 1085–1101 (2012)
7. DiSalvo, C., Gemperle, F.: From seduction to fulfillment: the use of anthropomorphic form in design. In: Proceedings of the International Conference on Designing Pleasurable Products and Interfaces, pp. 67–72 (2003)
8. Duffy, B.R.: Anthropomorphism and the social robot. Robot. Auton. Syst. **42**(3–4), 177–190 (2003)
9. Epley, N., Waytz, A., Cacioppo, J.T.: On seeing human: a three-factor theory of anthropomorphism. Psychol. Rev. **114**(4), 864–886 (2007)
10. Guthrie, S.E.: Anthropomorphism: a definition and a theory. In: Anthropomorphism, Anecdotes, and Animals, pp. 50–58 (1997)
11. Harms, C., Biocca, F.: Internal consistency and reliability of the networked minds measure of social presence. In: 2004 Seventh Annual International Workshop: Presence, pp. 246–251. Universidad Politecnica de Valencia, Valencia (2004)
12. Jackson, M.: Familiar and foreign bodies: a phenomenological exploration of the human-technology interface. J. Roy. Anthropol. Inst. **8**(2), 333–346 (2002)

13. Kangas, J., Špakov, O., Majaranta, P., Rantala, J.: Defining gaze interaction events. In: CHI 2013 Workshop on "Gaze Interaction in the Post-WIMP World, pp. 1–4 (2013)
14. Kleinke, C.L.: Compliance to requests made by gazing and touching experimenters in field settings. J. Exp. Soc. Psychol. **13**(3), 218–223 (1977)
15. Marcus, A.: The cult of cute: the challenge of user experience design. Interactions **9**(6), 31–37 (2015)
16. Osawa, H., Kayano, W., Miura, T., Endo, W.: Transitional explainer: instruct functions in the real world and onscreen in multi-function printer. In: HAI 2015 - Proceedings of the 3rd International Conference on Human-Agent Interaction, pp. 11–18 (2015)
17. Overview—Electronic Animated Eyes for ARM Microcontrollers—Adafruit Learning System: https://learn.adafruit.com/animated-electronic-eyes/overview. Accessed 14 Jan 2020
18. Russo, N.F.: Eye contact, interpersonal distance, and the equilibrium theory. J. Pers. Soc. Psychol. **31**(3), 497–502 (1975)
19. Van Rompay, T., Ludden, G.: Types of embodiment in design: the embodied foundations of meaning and affect in product design. Int. J. Des. **9**(1), 1–11 (2015)
20. Sundstedt, V.: Gazing at games: an introduction to eye tracking control. Synth. Lect. Comput. Graph. Animat. **5**(1), 1–113 (2012)
21. The Henry Hoover Range - What are the Differences in 2020? http://www.thehenryrange.co.uk/the-henry-hoover-range-what-are-the-differences/. Accessed 14 Jan 2020

UX in IxD - User Experience in Interaction Design

Miroslav Sili[1(✉)], Johannes Kropf[1], and Sten Hanke[2]

[1] Center for Health & Bioresources, AIT Austrian Institute of Technology
GmbH, Vienna, Austria
miroslav.sili@ait.ac.at
[2] Institute of eHealth FH Joanneum GmbH, Graz, Austria

Abstract. User experience and the user experience design process are essential
and mandatory factors in product design. Moreover, the field of product design
provides valuable approaches that target the long-standing engagement of the
user and the offered product. This work builds upon this knowledge and
investigates different concepts and methods from the product design field and
their added values for the interaction design of new interactive systems and HCI
artifacts. The work lists and elaborates and investigates five approaches that
serve as a basis for the future extensive research work that targets the development of a dynamic user model used to investigate the impact of different
interaction design styles on the targeting end-user.

Keywords: User experience · UX · User experience design · UxD · Interaction
design · IxD · Quality of experience · HCI

1 Introduction

Situated in the Active and Assisted Living (AAL)-field of practice for more than one
and a half decades, we have been experienced the demand for diversity in building
Information and Communication Technology (ICT)-based solutions. We have been
asked to design and develop various applications, targeting numerous and complex
goals, in different research projects. Guided by concrete user needs and project-specific
parameters, we have been created ICT prototypes ranging from traditional single
device-based applications, over to multi device-based applications, over to adaptive
and personal assistance-based applications to so-called tangible applications. This
variety illustrates that application design nowadays is not necessarily limited to one
design style, e.g., manifested as a classical Graphical User Interface (GUI)-based
application. Application designers can draw on different interaction design styles to
realize the intended interactive system and its HCI artifacts.

This experience formed our curiosity about the question of whether a holistic view
across all different interaction design styles can be useful for the design process of new
interactive systems and their Human-Computer Interaction (HCI) artifacts and consequently useful for the targeting end-user? These considerations formed the basis for an
extensive research work that questions the impact of different interaction design styles

© Springer Nature Switzerland AG 2020
M. Kurosu (Ed.): HCII 2020, LNCS 12181, pp. 147–159, 2020.
https://doi.org/10.1007/978-3-030-49059-1_11

on the targeting end-user supposed to use the intended, to-be designed interactive system.

This work contributes towards the investigation of this research question and represents one fundamental part of the mentioned extensive work. In this paper, we will focus on the literature-based elaboration of concepts and methods that target users' satisfaction in products and HCI artifacts. We investigate the User eXperience (UX) field on a non-functional level with the aim to identify desirable aspects in interactive system design and in human-system interaction. These aspects are considered as key elements towards the long-term user-product engagement. Figure 1 illustrates the work-flow of the overall research. Previously published work is highlighted in blue, this work is highlighted in red, and the future work is highlighted in purple.

Fig. 1. The workflow of the overall research. Previously published work highlighted in blue, the contribution of this work highlighted in red, and the future work highlighted in purple. (Color figure online)

The overall research can be summarized as follow: Prototypes developed in the AAL field of practice serve the starting point for the development of a so-called Interaction Design Research Framework (IxD-FW). Based on these prototypes we have been developed a listing of considerable interaction design styles which we further named Interaction Design Opportunities (IxDOs). Those IxDOs range from classical application-based IxDO, over more advanced adaptive IxDO towards complex so-called companion-based IxDO. The depicted IxDO Research Grid (IxDO-RG) and the cross-cutting issues define the methodological approach for the investigation of IxDOs in terms of characteristics and relationships. This work was published under the title "Interaction Design in the Active and Assistive Living Field of Practice" [16]. The task "IxD and Pleasure", as outlined in Fig. 1, is a successor of the task "cross-cutting issues". Thus, this work contributes towards the identification of these IxD and pleasure-oriented aspects which in turn serve as the basis for the development of the dynamic user model. The user model represents the preliminary result of the IxD-FW and serves as the main toolset for the investigation of the research question and the impact of IxDOs on the targeting user, respectively.

The work is structured as follows: Sect. 2 provides definitions of key terms used in this work and highlights their relationships. Section 3 focusses on the literature-based elaboration of UX concepts and methods that target the mentioned long-term user-product engagement. Section 4 discusses their added values and outlines the mentioned further work which is based on this work.

2 Interaction Design and the Relation to User Experience Design

Before we start to elaborate concepts and methods able to increase users' satisfaction it is necessary to frame the key terms used in this work. The following section defines these key terms, namely Interaction Design (IxD), UX, and User eXperience Design (UxD), and highlights their relationships.

IxD is the basic element and an indispensable condition in the HCI design process. The Interaction Design Association defines IxD as follows: "Interaction Design (IxD) defines the structure and behavior of interactive systems. Interaction Designers strive to create meaningful relationships between people and the products and services that they use, from computers to mobile devices to appliances and beyond" [3]. The second key term, UX is defined as follows: "Person's perceptions and responses resulting from the use and/or anticipated use of a product, system or service" [15].

These definitions highlight the close relation between IxD and UX. Moreover, IxD can be seen as the toolset for UX since UX describes a person's perceptions and responses resulting from the use of the product and IxD is the process that aims to create meaningful relationships between people and products.

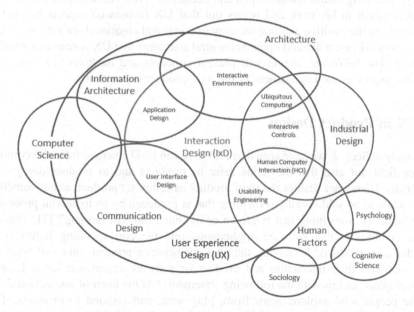

Fig. 2. Disciplines of UX illustrating that IxD (highlighted in green) is conducted of- and influenced by several disciplines. Image adapted from Envis Precisely [8] (Color figure online)

This relationship becomes also very clear by observing the disciplines of UxD as depicted in Fig. 2. The infographic approach visualizes some of the players of this inter-active field and it illustrates that IxD is conducted of- and influenced by several disciplines. Additionally, the visualization illustrates that IxD represents the core component of the UxD. This observation has far-reaching implications. From this broader point of view, it is unambiguous that designers and developers of modern interactive systems are requested to consider and to build upon users' experiences and utilize aspects and methods which can influence and shape future users' experiences. This is collectively what is meant by the UxD process and IxD represents the main toolset for designers and developers in this operational setting.

So far, we have seen that in the field of interactive system design IxD represents the main toolset for UX evocation. Moreover, Fig. 2 highlighted that UxD is a multi-faceted field conducted of several disciplines. However, this work aims the elaboration of concepts and methods which are able to increase users' satisfaction in user-system interaction. Thus, it is necessary to focus on the satisfaction aspect in order to reach this goal.

Here again, UX plays an essential role since the literature defines UX also as something that is associated with positive feelings. Law confirms this view in his work "Understanding, Scoping and Defining User eXperience: A Survey Approach" by the following statement: "UX highlights non-utilitarian aspects of such interactions, shifting the focus to user affect, sensation, and the meaning as well as the value of such interactions in everyday life. Hence, UX is seen as something desirable, though what exactly something means remains open and debatable" [10]. Hassenzahl underlines the desirable aspect in his work and points out that UX focuses on aspects beyond the functional, on the positive and that the experimental and emotional are no coincidence [7]. In this work, we will build upon this central statement that UX is seen as something desirable. The following section will present concepts and methods that utilize this desirable aspect as the key element in the user-product interaction.

3 UX in Product Design

Previously in Sect. 2, we have seen that IxD, UX and UxD emerged from the computer science field but also that the terms refer to products and to product design. The Cambridge Dictionary defines the term product as follows: "product, noun, something that is made to be sold, usually something that is produced by an industrial process or, less commonly, something that is grown or obtained through farming" [1]. This definition emphasizes that software applications and the corresponding hardware are considered as products. Moreover, the analogy between products and soft-ware artifacts continues their interaction and product or software experience level. Lauralee Alben emphasizes this with the following statement: "At the heart of interaction design are the people who explore, learn from, play with, and respond to products. Their experiences, as they use a range of products, from off the shelf software to websites, from electronic games to medical diagnostic equipment, are what effective interaction design is all about" [2]. The analogy was also highlighted in Sect. 2 with the statement "Interaction Design (IxD) defines the structure and behavior of interactive systems. Interaction Designers strive to create meaningful relationships between people and the products and services that they use, from computers to mobile devices to appliances and beyond" [3]. Thus, it is reasonable to build upon this analogy and to start to investigate desirable aspects for software design by observing desirable aspects in product design. The following sections (Sect. 3.1 till Sect. 3.5) presents five approaches that target this desirable aspect in the design and the development of products.

3.1   Quality of Experience

An argumentative and integrative literature review regarding desirable UX aspects leads to the work of Lauralee Alben with the title "Defining the criteria for effective interaction design" [2]. Lauralee lists in her work eight criteria that influence the quality of user experience. In this work, the term "quality" is not used as a measurement instrument but rather as an epitome for successful and satisfying user experience. The key characteristics of the eight criteria can be summarized as follows:

- Understanding of users: This criterion focuses on the understanding of user needs, tasks, and environments of users for whom the product will be designed.
- Learnable & Usable: This criterion addresses usability attributes, but it also focuses on the question if the product communicates a sense of its purpose. The goal is to provide self-evident and self-revealing products that support different ways people will approach and use it.
- Need & Desired: This criterion targets the identification of user needs and user desires. On a broader level, this criterion also questions the valuable contribution of the product for the user with respect to social, economic, and environmental inclusion.
- Effective design process: This criterion focuses on the design process, applied methodology, and user involvement in the design process.
- Mutable: This criterion focuses on the particular needs and preferences of individuals and groups. Moreover, the criterion addresses also the ability of the product to change and to evolve on changing conditions.
- Appropriate: This criterion questions if the product can solve the right problem on the right level. Additionally, the criterion addresses efficiency aspects and the practice of the product.
- Aesthetic experience: This criterion focuses on pleasing aspects such as aesthetic pleasure and sensual satisfaction. This includes also the consistency of spirit and style.
- Manageable: The last criterion addresses the entire context of use and questions if the product can support the user in tasks such as installation, training, maintenance, cost, and supplies. These questions need to be addressed on the individual as well as on the organizational level.

The listing highlighted the characteristics of the eight criteria. It is remarkable that these criteria can be grouped into two clusters. The first cluster targets added values for the end-users. The cluster is conducted of criteria "Learnable & Usable", "Mutable", "Appropriate", and "Aesthetic experience". The second cluster targets the design process and is conducted of the criteria "Understanding of users", "Need & Desired", "Effective design process", and "Manageable". Thus, according to this work, desirable products do not emerge only out of user-centric aspects located in the first cluster, but out of the combination of these user-centric aspects and the appropriate design process which is formed by criteria of the second cluster.

However, the presented work addresses UX on the meta-level. In order to make the desirable aspect in UxD more graspable will focus from now on the mentioned user-centric point of view targeting the added values for the end-users.

3.2   Framework of Product Experience

Here again, an argumentative and integrative literature review on desirable aspects in product design leads to the work of Pieter Desmet and Paul Hekkert with the title "Framework of Product Experience" [5]. In this work, the authors introduce a general framework for product experience that applies to all affective responses that can be experienced in human-product interaction. One of the remarkable parts of the work is the presented concept of "core affect" which is based on Russel's model that describes affective states using two axes [17] as illustrated in Fig. 3. The x-axis represents the valence which ranges from unpleasant on the left to pleasant to the right. The y-axis represents the arousal which ranges from low arousal at the bottom to the high arousal at the top. The product's relevant emotions are arranged in a circular shape at the end of each axis.

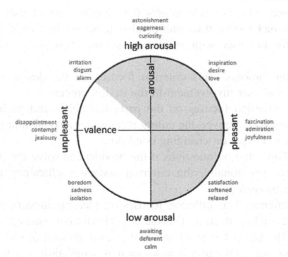

Fig. 3. Illustration of desirable affective responses (highlighted in yellow) that a designer might wish to trigger at the user during the human-product interaction based on the circumplex model of core affects [5, 17] (Color figure online)

Since this model represents product relevant emotions, we can use it to emphasize desirable aspects of human-product interaction, which are mainly from pleasure-providing nature. Figure 3 highlights those aspects by the yellow circle segment which ranges from low arousal attribute on the bottom, over the pleasant attribute to the right, over to high arousal on the top. It is worth to mention that this representation of desirable aspects incorporates even some of the rather unpleasant affective responses such as alarm, disgust, or irritation. One could argue that the design of desired products targets the exclusion of these unpleasant affects, but this is not always the designers' intention. One can think, for instance, of a task where the designers are asked to design an application that aims the evocation of irritation, e.g., for a horror movie game. The desirable affective responses, for this purpose, would be in this unpleasant quadrant.

However, the circumplex model might be able to summarize desirable affective responses in human-product interaction, but it does not describe how these affects could be intentionally evoked. Later, in their work, Desmet and Hekkert present the framework of product experience which is conducted of three distinct components, namely (a) aesthetic pleasure, (b) attribution of meaning, and (c) emotional response. The authors describe that on the aesthetic level we consider a product's capacity to delight one or more of sensory modalities. At the level of meaning, cognition comes into play and lead to cognitive processes, like interpretation, memory retrieval, and associations. Through this process, we are able to assess the personal or symbolic significance of products. The emotional level, we refer to those affective like love and disgust, fear and desire, pride and despair. The remarkable aspect of the framework is that he components build relationships with each other. According to this, aesthetic experience and/or experience of meaning can evoke an emotional experience to the user.

Thus, in a broader manner, aesthetic and meaning experiences can trigger all affective responses that have been presented in the circumplex model of core effects [5]. However, even if the framework seems to be very useful for physical products, it has also some limitations when applying on software artifacts in a general manner. For instance, the social context plays a minor role in the presented framework. This aspect, on another hand, is especially for communication-related software artifacts a subject of matter, although the authors emphasize the importance of the social context as follows: " … In addition, the experience is always influenced by the context (e.g., physical, social, economic) in which the interaction takes place" [5].

3.3 The Psychology of Decision Making in UX

An interesting approach in the field of UX was presented by Joe Leech in his talk "The psychology of decision making in UX" [11]. In his talk, Joe was referring to two ways of thinking, namely "thinking fast" and "thinking slow" and how to design for those two sets of systems. The concept of two ways of thinking comes from the field of psychology and was introduced by Daniel Kahneman in his work "Thinking, Fast and Slow" [9]. Daniel argues that we have two systems in our brain; one that allows us to make decisions quickly, based on emotions and one system that allows us to make decisions slowly, based on previous experience that allows us to predict what is going to happen.

Joe takes up this concept and summarizes the design aspects as the following three-step ruleset:

- Design for the slow: Match the mental model.
- Design for the fast: Evoke the emotion.
- Do first and second.

The rule set highlights that our decision-making process is influenced by our mental model, our emotions, and by the designer which is in need to address both aspects in the same manner in order to provide a positive UX. The matching of the mental model is a multi-level process. On the one hand, it is related to aspects such as usability and accessibility including at least four of five usability attributes (learnability, efficiency, memorability, and error tolerance). On the other hand, it is related to the application fields, the workflows, and the interaction styles that are suited for the targeting user. However, the presented three-step rule set underlines that, next to pragmatic attributes, the emotional experience plays a major role in the acceptability of products. This goes along with the previously presented framework of product experience.

3.4   The Kano Model and Approaches for Delightful UX

A second, inspiring presentation on this field was given by Jared Spool in his talk "Building a Winning UX Strategy Using the Kano model" [14]. Jared utilizes the Kano model, as presented in this work [12], to highlight some useful design aspects but also to highlight some design failures. According to the Kano model, there are three types of product requirements, namely basic needs, performance needs, and delighters that influence customer satisfaction as depicted in Fig. 4. James Moultrie summarizes the three types of product requirements of the Kano model as follows [13]:

- Basic needs: "attributes which must be present in order for the product to be successful".
- Performance needs: " … are directly correlated to customer satisfaction. Increased functionality or quality of execution will result in increased customer satisfaction".
- Delighters: "Customers get great satisfaction from a feature - and are willing to pay a price premium. … these features are often unexpected by customers and they can be difficult to establish as needs up front. … But, it should be remembered that customer expectations change over time, and a cup holder in a car may be today's delighter, but tomorrow it will be expected" [9].

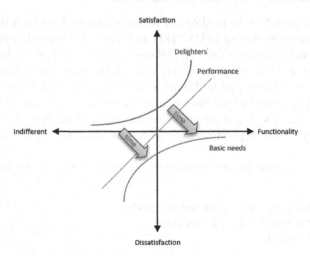

Fig. 4. Description of how attributes' values change over time in the Kano model from delighting towards basic needs [13]

Here again, regarding this work, the interesting product requirements are the delighters. Spool argues further and based on Dana's Chisnell framework [4] that there are three different approaches for making experience delightful, namely: pleasure (in Dana's model referred to as mindfulness), flow, and meaning. Dana describes these approaches as follows:

- "Mindfulness in design is about a pleasing awareness. In relationships, it can mean infatuation. It's knowing that this is good, that this makes me happy. It's satisfying. … As the designer, you demonstrate that you have the user in mind and you understand her goals".
- "Flow describes the state that people enter when they are fully focused … in a task or activity. As the designer, you incorporate psychological cues, language, social cues, and reinforcement to subtly motivate users to keep working or playing longer than they might without those design cues".
- "Meaning comes from a feeling of fellowship, contributing, and making the world a better place. …As a designer, help users know where they fit in and what their effect is by thinking through exactly what you want the emotional and behavioral effects to be of using your design. You demonstrate intention (in the yogic sense) through clarity, simplicity, funneling, modeling outcomes" [4].

If we compare these three aspects with the presented framework of product experience, we can see some parallels. The mindfulness addresses pleasure aspects as the aesthetic experience targets the same goal. The meaning targets in both models the cognitive well-being. And the flow approach in Dana's framework describes in a global manner the positive emotional experience so that users keep using the system for a longer period of time.

3.5 The Pragmatic/Hedonic Model

So far, we have seen that the UxD and especially the design of desirable products is driven by two main characteristics, namely (a) the product needs to fulfill user's practicable needs, e.g., match the mental model, provide usability, satisfy basic needs, and (b) the product needs also to fulfill user's impracticable wishes, e.g., to evoke emotional experiences, to delight the user, and to embrace joy. Marc Hassenzahl addresses this two-folded goal in his work "The hedonic/pragmatic model of user experience" [6].

Hassenzahl argues that the model assumes that people perceive interactive products along two different dimensions, namely (a) the pragmatic dimension that refers to the product's perceived ability to support the achievement of "do-goals", and (b) the hedonic dimension that refers to the product's perceived ability to support the achievement of "be-goals". This correlates with the previously mentioned observation of driving forces in UxD and the design of desirable products. The fulfillment of users' practicable needs represents the pragmatic dimension; the "do-goal" for the product and the consideration of users' impracticable wishes represent the hedonic dimension, the "be-goals" for the product.

Hassenzahl argues further that the model distinguishes three different facets of the hedonic dimension, namely stimulation, identification, and evocation whereas the only one facet of the pragmatic dimension remains the manipulations [6]. However, the remarkable point in Hassenzahls's model is that product characters emerge from the specific combination of pragmatic and hedonic attributes. In his opinion, pragmatic and hedonic attributes are independent of each other and people's perception of pragmatic and hedonic attributes can be either weak or strong. Thus, the hedonic attribute is arranged along the y-axis and the pragmatic attribute is arranged along the x-axis. As argues earlier, both attributes can be perceived as weak or as strong.

Hassenzahl calls a product with strong pragmatic and weak hedonic attributes as an ACT product. As opposite, a product with strong hedonic and weak pragmatic attributes is named as a SELF product. The ACT product is inextricably linked to its users' behavior goal whereas the SELF product is inextricably linked to users' self, e.g., their ideas, memories, and relationships. Furthermore, he calls a product with weak hedonic and weak pragmatic attributes simply unwanted and a product with strong hedonic and strong pragmatic attributes as a product that is perceived as desirable by the user. This is remarkable since this work investigates pleasure-oriented aspects with the aim to establish a long-standing engagement of the user with the offered interactive system. Products that are perceived as desirable contribute definitively to this goal.

In summary, the UX literature research identified an additional dimension towards successful products. The well-known and mandatory dimensions functionality and usability need to be enriched by the dimension desirability in order to provide successful products and thus also successful software artifacts. At this point it needs to be mentioned that usability, considering all five usability aspects, already conducts the "engaging" aspect. However, in this and in the overreaching research work, usability is considered as a basic user need. The perception of desirability, in contrast, goes a step beyond the satisfaction of basic needs. It delights users, it evokes users' emotional experience, and it embraces joy.

4   Summary, Conclusions and Outlook

This work emerged out of the Active and Assisted Living (AAL) context and it represents a contribution towards an extensive research work that questions whether and how far different interaction design styles influence users' system acceptance rate. In order to be able to investigate this research question in a structured manner, it is necessary to divide the research field into manageable units. This work represents one such manageable unit and it focuses on the literature-based elaboration of concepts and methods able to increase users' satisfaction.

In Sect. 2 the focus was on the definition of key terms relevant for this work. Moreover, the section highlighted the relationships between the key terms IxD, UX, and UxD. Section 3 highlighted the analogy between software applications and products. This transition was the basis for the literature-based elaboration of five concepts and methods that target the identification of desirable aspects in product design. Since software applications are considered as products this work assumes that the presented concepts and methods have also added values for the HCI and the design of software artifacts.

Concepts and methods elaborated in this work serve as the foundation for future research and the development of the mentioned user model. Nevertheless, this section will conclude the five elaborated concepts and methods and emphasize the key messages and the added values for the aimed user model.

The first concept, namely the eight criteria that influence the quality of user experience was presented in Sect. 3.1. The concept highlighted that designers are requested to broaden their view in order to design and develop desirable products. It is from uttermost importance to consider the design process in an equal manner as the user-centric aspects which are directly linked to the product such as usability or the aesthetical experience. However, the work presents the eight criteria rather on a meta-level and it is lacking concrete recommendations on how to address these criteria. Nevertheless, the concept can be seen as a starting point for a further state-of-the-art approach investigation with respect to the eight presented criteria.

The framework of product experience was presented in Sect. 3.2. It highlighted that the overall goal of the user-product interaction is the evocation of emotional experience. In other words, products have the ability to delight users if they can provoke users' emotions. The experience of aesthetics and the experience of meaning are the driving forces in this setting. However, even if the provocation of emotional experience seems to be reasonable it needs to be considered that emotional experience is a variable size. It is variable in terms of intensity and duration. Thus, the user-product interaction that is perceived as delightful today might not be delightful any more tomorrow. Nevertheless, the user model will tie on the concept of emotional experience as a key factor to delight the user. Moreover, the aesthetic and the meaning aspects will serve as attributes for the estimation of individual pleasure types within the mentioned user model.

In Sect. 3.3 the focus was on different interaction design techniques that influence users' decision-making process. Here again, the ruleset emphasizes that the mental model and the evocation of emotions play an essential role in the user's decision-making process. This confirms assertions made in the framework of product experience. The mentioned interaction design purposes, namely the design for the slow and the design for the fast will play integral components in the elaboration of the future research task "IxD and Pleasure" as depicted in Fig. 1.

The fourth concept, namely the Kano model was presented in Sect. 3.4. The model underlies the previously presented argument of emotional experience degradation. It argues that delightful innovations become over time basic needs. Thus, designers are requested to consider the value change over time and to address this incessant condition in advance. Next to this aspect, the model focused on three approaches able to make the experience delightful. Here again, we see some parallels to the present framework of product experience and the presented interaction design techniques that influence users' decision-making process. Users' perception of pleasure, cognitive well-being, and the positive emotional experience are named as key factors in this work. These factors will also be used in the mentioned user model.

The last concept, the hedonic/pragmatic model, was presented in Sect. 3.4. The model underlines and frames all mentioned concepts (expect the design process dimension presented in the first concept in Sect. 3.1) in a structured way. All user-centric attributes such as pleasure, emotional experience, aesthetic, and cognitive well-being can be assigned to the "self" and "desired" quadrants. All prevailing attributes such as functionality, usability, and the match of the mental model can be assigned to the "act" and "desired" quadrants. Indeed, this powerful concept will play an essential role in the development of the user model. Moreover, the concept will become the most influential contribution to this goal.

In Summary and as highlighted in Fig. 1, the future work will be on the identification of interaction design types and the elaboration of pleasure types which serve as the basis for the development of the dynamic user model. The user model will be used as the main toolset for the investigation of the overall research question and the impact of IxDOs on the targeting user, respectively. These works and the elaborated results will be published in subsequent research papers.

Acknowledgment. This work summarizes individual aspects of the PhD thesis of Miroslav Sili with the title "UX in the AAL Field of Practice - Interaction Design Framework Targeting Long-Standing User Engagement with Interactive Systems". The aspects have been revised and extended in collaboration with the co-authors in order to form a compact and self-contained representation of the dedicated research task within the overall PhD work.

References

1. PRODCUT   Cambridge   Dictionary.   https://dictionary.cambridge.org/de/worterbuch/englisch/product. Accessed 14 Feb 2020
2. Alben, L.: Defining the criteria for effective interaction design. Interactions **3**, 11–15 (1996)
3. About & History - Interaction Design Association - IxDA. http://ixda.org/ixda-global/about-history. Accessed 14 Feb 2020
4. Chisnell, D.: Beyond frustration: three levels of happy design. UX Mag. (2010). Article no: 536
5. Desmet, P., Hekkert, P.: Framework of product experience. Int. J. Des. **1**, 57–66 (2007)
6. Hassenzahl, M.: The thing and I: understanding the relationship between user and product. In: Blythe, M., Monk, A. (eds.) Funology 2. HIS, pp. 301–313. Springer, Cham (2018). https://doi.org/10.1007/978-3-319-68213-6_19
7. Hassenzahl, M., Tractinsky, N.: User experience - a research agenda. Behav. Inf. Technol. **25**, 91–97 (2006)
8. The Disciplines of User Experience Design by Envis Precisely. https://github.com/envisprecisely/disciplines-of-ux/blob/master/The-Disciplines-of-User-Experience-Design
9. Kahneman, D., Egan, P.: Thinking, Fast and Slow. Farrar, Straus and Giroux, New York (2011)
10. Law, E.L.-C., Roto, V., Hassenzahl, M., Vermeeren, A.P., Kort, J.: Understanding, scoping and defining user experience: a survey approach. In: Proceedings of the SIGCHI Conference on Human Factors in Computing Systems, pp. 719–728 (2009)
11. The psychology of decision making in UX - Video Archive - The Conference by Media Evolution. https://videos.theconference.se/joe-leech-the-psychology-of-decision-making-in. Accessed 14 Feb 2020
12. Matzler, K., Hinterhuber, H.H.: How to make product development projects more successful by integrating Kano's model of customer satisfaction into quality function deployment. Technovation **18**, 25–38 (1998)
13. Kano Model. https://www.ifm.eng.cam.ac.uk/research/dmg/tools-and-techniques/kano-model. Assessed 14 Feb 2020

14. Building A Winning UX Strategy using the Kano Model. https://blog.usievents.com/build ing-a-winning-ux-strategy-using-the-kano-model-ou-comment-aboutir-a-une-experience-util isateur-optimisee-par-jared-spool. Accessed 14 Feb 2020
15. ISO - ISO 9241-210_2010 - Ergonomics of human-system interaction — Part 210_ Human-centred design for interactive systems. https://www.iso.org/standard/52075.html. Accessed 14 Feb 2020
16. Sili, M., Kropf, J., Hanke, S.: Interaction design in the active and assistive living field of practice. In: Zhou, J., Salvendy, G. (eds.) HCII 2019. LNCS, vol. 11593, pp. 480–492. Springer, Cham (2019). https://doi.org/10.1007/978-3-030-22015-0_37
17. Russell, J.A.: A circumplex model of affect. J. Pers. Soc. Psychol. **39**(6), 1161 (1980)

Human Computer Interfaces Reconsidered: A Conceptual Model for Understanding User Interfaces

Susanne Koch Stigberg(✉) 📵

Faculty of Computer Sciences, Østfold University College, Halden, Norway
susanne.k.stigberg@hiof.no

Abstract. The article assesses how human computer interfaces are conceptualized in HCI textbooks and proposes a revised model for understanding user interfaces. In the last decade a variety of novel user interfaces has been introduced. Both new input and output technologies allow users to communicate with digital artifacts in almost limitless ways. However, our understanding of the human computer interface originates from early HCI research, based on the desktop metaphor, including the user, the system, input and output. This article raises the question, how do we conceptualize user interfaces in our own research and for our teaching. The review reveals that there is no consistent understanding of interface concepts in HCI textbooks and that there is a bias towards the desktop metaphor. As a candidate for an updated interface definition, I propose a revised interface model, including 5 concepts: interface paradigm, interaction technique, interaction style, interface platform and interface device. Finally, I report on two examples, how I have used the interface model in the classroom.

Keywords: HCI theory · Interface model · Interface paradigm · Interaction style

1 Introduction

What is a human computer interface? Seemingly, an easy question to answer. Dix et al. [3] describe that both "input and output together form the interface", which "sits between the user and the system". This definition originates from early HCI research based on the desktop computer interface. Nowadays, there are many different types of user interfaces and selecting a suitable input and output for a new digital product can be a challenging exercise. Preece et al. [12] state that "numerous adjectives have been used to describe the different kinds of interfaces that have been developed, including graphical, command, speech, multimodal, invisible, ambient, affective, mobile, intelligent, adaptive, smart, tangible, touchless, and natural. Some of the interface types are primarily concerned with a function (e.g. to be intelligent, to be adaptive, to be ambient, to be smart), while others focus on the interaction style used (e.g. command, graphical, multimedia), the input/output device used (e.g. pen-based, speech-based, gesture-based), or the platform being designed for (e.g. tablet, mobile, PC, wearable)".

© Springer Nature Switzerland AG 2020
M. Kurosu (Ed.): HCII 2020, LNCS 12181, pp. 160–171, 2020.
https://doi.org/10.1007/978-3-030-49059-1_12

To grasp a comprehensive understanding of these diverse user interface concepts can be difficult for students and we, as a research community, should reconsider the interface definition and provide a more nuanced interface model. The goal of this article is to provide an overview of the terminology used in popular HCI textbooks to describe user interfaces and to suggest a revised model that clarifies how these concepts are interrelated. The model can be used in academic for teaching about user interfaces, in practice to provide a framework when designing user interfaces, and as a scaffold inviting the research community to contribute additional content. The second chapter provides a review on how user interfaces are introduced in four different HCI textbooks [3, 5, 12, 13]. In chapter three, I present a revised interface model based on that review. In chapter four, I illustrate how I have used that model in my own teaching, before concluding the article with a discussion in chapter five.

2 Review of Interface Terminology

Abowd and Beale [1] illustrate the human computer interaction in their HCI framework including 4 parts: user, input system, and output (see Fig. 1) based on Norman's action cycle [9], there the input and output define the user interface. Hinckley and Wigdor [5] define that "a user interface is the representation of the system – the summation of all its input devices, conceptual models, and interaction techniques – with which the user interacts", hinting that the term is more complex than input and output. For several years, I have taught basic HCI courses and struggled to find an HCI textbook, that provides a comprehensive model of the user interface, describing the interaction between user and system in more detail, including different aspects of the interface from technology to social context. This led me to review four popular HCI textbooks studying: How are user interfaces conceptualized in HCI textbooks? Table 1 presents an overview of found interface terminology that are described further in this chapter.

Table 1. Found interface terminology in HCI textbooks

	Preece et al. [12]	Shneiderman et al. [13]	Dix et al. [3]	Hinckley and Wigdor [5]
Interaction device	Chapter 7	Chapter 10	Chapter 2	Only input devices
Interaction type	Chapter 3	–	–	–
Interface types	Chapter 7	–	–	–
Interaction style	–	Chapter 7–11	Chapter 3	–
Interaction technique	Chapter 7	–	Chapter 3, 4, 8	Input technologies
Interaction paradigm	Chapter 3	–	Chapter 4	Examples

2.1 Interaction Device

Interaction devices are the physical artifacts used as input and output channel. Shneiderman et al. [13] discuss interaction devices extensively in chapter 10 including different types of keyboards and keypads, pointing devices and displays. Similar, Dix et al. [1] present input and output devices as an essential part of chapter 2: the computer, describing text entry devices, positioning and pointing devices, display devices, devices for virtual reality, and 3D interaction, as well as physical controls, sensors and special devices. In contrast, Preece et al. [12] mention devices marginal as part of interface types in chapter 7. Hinckley and Wigdor [5] focus on input devices such as pointing devices, pen-based, voice, gesture input as well as muscle and background sensing. They take a more technical approach describing such input devices as collections of transducers that sense physical properties of people, places, or things e.g. the mouse including a relative motion sensor, physical buttons, and a wheel for scrolling.

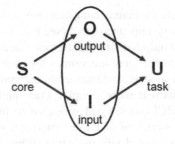

Fig. 1. Interaction framework by Abowd and Beale [1]

2.2 Interaction Type

Preece et al. [12] describe an interaction type as a description of what the user is doing when interacting with a system. They present five interaction types in chapter 3. Instructing comprises issuing commands and selecting options. The conversing type describes interactions with a system as if having a conversation. Both types could be applied to natural and command language interaction style described in 2.4. Manipulating covers interactions with objects in a virtual or physical space by manipulating them, comparable to direct manipulation interaction style presented in 2.4. The exploring type involves moving through virtual or physical environments and a responding interaction occurs when the system initiates the interaction and the user chooses whether to respond. In contrast to the previous four interaction types, which focus on how the user interacts with the system, responding focuses on who initiates the interaction. That means that an interaction could have different types, i.e. responding and conversing, or responding and manipulating.

2.3 Interface Type

In contrast to interaction type, as a way of thinking about how to support users' activities, Preece et al. [12] define interface type as the kind of interface used to support an interaction. In chapter 7 they present an overview of 20 interface types: command, graphical, multimedia, virtual reality, web, mobile, appliance, voice, pen, touch, gesture, haptic, multimodal, shareable, tangible, augmented reality, wearables, robots and drones, brain-computer interaction, and smart. The chapter is a potpourri of different interface devices, techniques, design principles, example interfaces as well as research and design issues.

2.4 Interaction Style

Interaction styles are the "bread and butter" of the interface [13]. They describe conventions, familiar objects and metaphors that help to minimize the learning curve for users and allows them to quickly become productive. Shneiderman et al. [13] describe five interaction styles in part 3 of the book (chapter 7–11). Chapter 7 discusses direct manipulation and how it can be used in an interface. Direct manipulation (DM) was introduced by Xerox PARC and then widely disseminated by Shneiderman [14] and comprises of three principles:

- continuous representation of objects and actions of interest
- physical actions and button pressing instead of complex syntax
- rapid, incremental, reversible actions with immediate feedback on the object of interest.

Shneiderman et al. [13] categorizes user interfaces implementing the DM metaphor by looking at the translational distance between users and the presentation of the metaphor, which will be referred to as strength, from weak DM interfaces such as traditional desktop interfaces or early video game controller to strong DM interfaces such as tangible interfaces or virtual reality applications. Dix et al. [3] discuss DM in chapter 4 as an interaction paradigm. Preece et al. [12] present DM as a framework implementing the manipulating interaction type.

Two other interaction styles, are navigation and menu selection, as well as form fill-in, described in Shneiderman et al. [13] chapter 8. Preece et al. [12] discuss these interaction styles in chapter 7 as part of graphical user interfaces and WIMP. Dix et al. [3] reviews these interaction styles in chapter 3.

Finally, Shneiderman et al. [13] present interaction styles related to natural and command languages ranging from command line interfaces to speech assistants. Similar, Dix et al. [3] include command line and natural language as interaction styles. Preece et al. [12] present command-based and speech interface types fitting instructing and conversing interaction types. Similar, Soegaard [11] defines command language, form fill-in, menu selection and direct manipulation as primary interaction styles originating from the desktop metaphor.

2.5   Interaction Technique

An interaction technique is a way of using a physical input device to perform a generic task in a human-computer dialogue [7]. It is a way to carry out an interactive task, based on using a set of input and output devices or technologies. The term is found in Hinckley and Wigdor [5] chapter 9 "Input technologies and techniques". They describe interaction technique "the fusion of input and output, consisting of all hardware and software elements, that provides a way for the user to accomplish a task, given a particular conceptual model". They provide examples such as the pinch-to-zoom technique for touch-screen services or drag-and-drop as a way to move items in the desktop metaphor. Interaction techniques vary across input devices and interaction paradigms, based on the device's strengths and the user's physical abilities and comfort when using the device.

2.6   Interaction Paradigm

Preece et al. [12], Dix et al. [3] and Hinckley and Wigdor [5] introduce the term interaction paradigm. Preece et al. [12] describe an interaction paradigm as an inspiration for a conceptual model, a general approach adopted by a community for carrying out research with shared assumptions, concepts, values and practices". They list a number of example paradigms without further explanation, e.g. desktop, ubiquitous computing, in the wild, wearable computing, Internet of Things. Dix et al. [3] use the term paradigm in chapter 4 as examples of effective strategies for building interactive systems. Provided examples range from the usability paradigm, the introduction of time-sharing computers, through the WIMP and web, to ubiquitous and context-aware computing. Similar Hinckley and Wigdor [5] use the term paradigm describing the WIMP desktop interface as a paradigm that has been designed for multi-modal control with a keyboard and a mouse using a cursor.

3   User Interfaces Reconsidered

Even though terms and concepts are overlapping in textbooks, there is no coherent understanding of the terminology used to discuss user interfaces. Preece et al. [12] introduce interaction type and interface type, there as other textbooks utilize interaction style instead. Furthermore, concepts such as interaction paradigm are explained differently in all textbooks. Another notable insight from the review is the bias towards the desktop metaphor, which is discussed in great detail in all textbooks. Reasonably, most interface terminology originates from desktop interfaces; however, discussing and conceptualizing a variety of interfaces is necessary for a broader understanding of user interface concept. In the following, I propose a revised interface model (see Fig. 2) aiming for a general interface definition including five key concepts:

- interface paradigm
- interaction technique
- interaction style
- interface platform
- interface devices

I choose to use to differentiate these key concepts using the terms interaction and interface. Interaction focusing on users' activity with the system and the conceptual model of doing so as found in Preece et al. [12] and interface focusing on the technology (software and hardware) that affords these activities. In the model (see Fig. 2), I define an interface paradigm, that encloses a number of interaction techniques. On the right side, the interface paradigm requires an interface platform, a combination of interface devices. On the left side, the interface paradigm implements an interaction style. In the following I will describe the interface model in more detail.

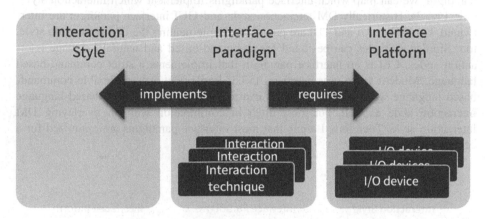

Fig. 2. Proposed interface model relating five key concepts for describing user interfaces

3.1 Interface Paradigm

Preece et al. [12] define paradigm as "a general approach adopted by a community for carrying out research with shared assumptions, concepts, values and practices", whereas Dix et al. [3] use the term paradigm as examples of effective strategies for building interactive systems. Here I propose the concept interface paradigm for describing common user interface types established in both research and practice with accompanying theory, principles and guidelines. The literature presents numerous UIs: command line interfaces (CLI) [10], graphical user interfaces (GUI), natural user interface (NUI) [16] or mobile user interfaces [8], tangible user interfaces (TUI) [6], wearable user interfaces (WUI) [17], or voice user interfaces (VUI) [2]. The list is far from complete but provides an indication to the variety of user interfaces introduced in the HCI community. Most of these interface paradigms consist of a set of associated interaction techniques, a collection of ways to carry out interactive tasks. GUIs built on WIMP and include interaction techniques such as drag-and-drop, click, or double click. Mobile UIs heavily rely on touchscreen and include interaction techniques such as touch gestures (e.g. swipe or pinch-to-zoom). Novel interface paradigms have yet to define a common set of interaction techniques. But grouping similar interfaces into an interface paradigm might help to synthesize shared interaction techniques.

3.2 Interaction Style

The review found two competing concepts focusing on how the user interacts with the machine in a general way. Preece et al. [12] present the concept of interaction type, whereas Shneiderman et al. [13] and Dix et al. [3] introduce the term interaction style. I choose the term interaction style as well, as it seems to be the mutual choice in the community [11]. The reviewed textbooks propose 5 interaction styles: direct manipulation (DM), form fill-in, menu selection, command-based and natural language all originating from the desktop metaphor. If we relate interaction style and interface paradigm, we can map which interface paradigms implement which interaction styles (e.g. Fig. 3). Historically DM interaction style and GUI interface paradigm are intertwined, but Mobile UI and TUI are paradigms implementing the DM interaction style, too. Similar examples can be found for command-based and natural language interaction styles. CLI is an interface paradigm that implements a strict command-based language. Modern voice user interfaces (VUI) implement a more flexible command-based language style. GUI applications can make use of a command-based language interaction style as well, but most often in combination with an overlaying DM interaction style. Therefore, I argue that most interface paradigms are optimized for a certain interaction style.

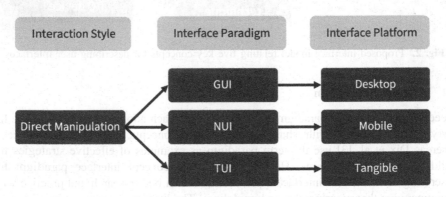

Fig. 3. Interface model sorted by DM interaction style

I support Shneiderman et al. [13] categorization of user interfaces implementing the DM interaction style by looking at the translational distance between users and the presentation of the metaphor, which will be referred to as strength, from weak DM interfaces such as GUI to strong DM interfaces such as TUI or virtual reality applications. I argue for a similar categorization for user interfaces implementing a command-based language interaction style by looking at language flexibility. Traditional command-line interfaces (CLI) request a strict and limited command-based language with little to no flexibility, whereas VUIs such as Siri[1], Google[2] or Alexa[3] are "tolerant for variations, robust, and exhibit slight touches of natural language flexibility" [10].

There might be interface paradigms that implement other interaction styles. Wearable or ambient interfaces rely often on indirect sensing and adapt user's actions and context without conscious human interactions. Preece et al. [12] propose an responding interaction type for these kinds of interfaces. There is no clear match among the enumerated interaction styles. Relating novel interface paradigms and established interaction styles might help to highlight incompatibilities and gaps in the theory and stimulate discussion in the community.

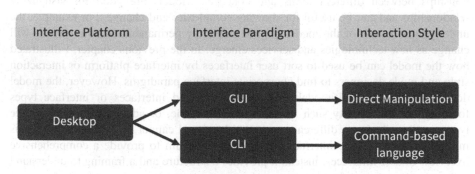

Fig. 4. Interface model sorted by Desktop interface platform

3.3 Interface Platform

The interface platform describes a recognized combination of input and output devices such as desktop, mobile, wearable, tangible, or ambient. It tells us something about the physical objects we interact with. E.g. interfaces for the desktop can assume to have access to a screen as an output device and keyboard and mouse as input devices. Applications for Mobile platform can rely on touchscreen as interface device plus a number of additional sensors such as microphone, GPS, or camera. Other platforms can be defined more loosely, tangible platform usually request physical objects that holds digital information and there their shape and place can be physical manipulated to manage that information (e.g. marble answering machine [18]). The wearable platform indicates that input and output devices are of smaller size so they can be worn. The ambient platform informs that input and output devices are integrated into the user's surrounding. Different interaction paradigms require different platforms. For example, a GUI requires a desktop platform, while Mobile UI is adapted for a mobile platform. Relating interface platform and interface paradigm presents us with an overview of common user interfaces and interaction styles for certain hardware settings

---

[1] https://www.apple.com/siri/.

[2] https://en.wikipedia.org/wiki/Google_Home.

[3] https://en.wikipedia.org/wiki/Amazon_Alexa.

(e.g. Fig. 4). It might guide designers choosing an appropriate interface paradigm for a given platform and preferred interaction style. Furthermore, Hinckley and Wigdor [5] point out that many novel interface platforms rely on elements of a GUI (such as buttons, sliders, checkboxes, and windows), while ignoring that these are optimized for mouse and keyboard which might not be present on their platform. They emphasize that "new modalities require new user interfaces and interaction techniques if one wishes to make the most of their capabilities" [5].

3.4 Interface Model Limitations

Creating an interface model was my approach to structure the field and see the relationships between different terms and concepts. Models are good for visualizing relationships and can be useful for showing complexity and change. For example, the underlying structure of the model may be relatively permanent, but the content will change as new technologies and services emerge. In the previous chapter, I illustrated how the model can be used to sort user interfaces by interface platform or interaction style and guide designers to find appropriate interface paradigms. However, the model does not adjust to multimodal interfaces, specialized interfaces or interface types focusing on functionality such as intelligent, shareable, or adaptive. These interface types are described at a different conceptual level and cannot be explained using this model. Furthermore, the interface model does not claim to provide a comprehensive overview of user interfaces, instead it provides a structure and a framing to understand and compare user interfaces.

4 Experiences from Teaching

In my academic role, the model has been useful for teaching interface terminology and introducing user interfaces beyond the desktop through several ways:

- It offers the students a structure and a lingua franca for describing user interfaces.
- It allows students to explore user interfaces from the three main concepts.
- It enables students to compare user interfaces.
- It illustrates gaps in current research and practice.
- It indicates possible issues when adapting user interfaces across platforms.

In the following, I outline two examples from my own teaching. It is a short experience report, on how I have used the interface model in the classroom. I do not make a claim for its generalizability or effectiveness.

4.1 The Music Player

When teaching user interfaces, I present students with an assignment to design a new music player. Most of the students start right away sketching ideas and wireframes for a mobile music application. When I ask them, why they choose a mobile app, they mention that it is the only thing they know. Next, I ask them to find examples of digital music players and add them to the model. Mostly, they find examples of mobile apps, and desktop media players, but also voice user interfaces for the home media central. Then, I ask the students to insert their examples into the interface model. The right side of the model describing the interface platform and devices, is the easiest part for the students to answer. It is straight forward to list the hardware parts of the examples such as screen, speakers, mouse and keyboard for desktop, touchscreen and speakers for mobile and microphone and speakers for voice user interfaces. Usually we discuss the interaction style next and students express that mobile app and desktop application are more alike, than voice user interfaces. Lastly, I present names for the interface paradigm such as GUI, Mobile UI and VUI and students add interaction techniques they know about. At the end of this exercise, we have an interface model conceptualizing three example user interfaces for a music player on different interface platforms and implementing different interaction styles, something that I struggled with before using the interface model. Additionally, I bring a toniebox[4] to class, a tangible music player for kids, as another example of a music player and the students discuss how the device relates to the previous examples using the interface model.

4.2 Student Projects

Student projects are part of most HCI related bachelor courses we teach, to enable students to explore theory in practice. Students ideate and prototype novel interactive experiences for given platforms and themes. This year students are asked to transform analog content from children books about programming into interactive experiences ranging from digital board games, to interactive wall art or novel audio books to engage children in programming and computational thinking. The interface model can be used in students' design work in two ways: 1) Finding and comparing related work during early research. Students often struggle to find the right keywords during research phase in their project. The interface model supports them to create keywords based on the three different concepts to frame their search. Furthermore, they can compare and select found examples based on these concepts. 2) Communicating their interface ideas to each other, course responsible and examiner. The model provides them with a limited set of concepts, that they can use to describe their user interface and act as a design rationale for their choices.

5 Conclusion

In the last decade numerous novel user interfaces have been introduced that are beyond the desktop [7] or post-WIMP [15]. I found myself struggling to provide students with a comprehensive overview of user interfaces and a set of concepts to describe and compare these interfaces. The contribution of this article is three-fold:1) It provides a review of interface terminology from four popular HCI textbooks. I found a total of 6 concepts related to interfaces: interaction type, interface type, interaction style, interaction device, interaction paradigm, interaction technique. Although these are recurring

---

[4] https://tonies.com.

in several books, there is no consistent understanding of these concepts in the books. Furthermore, I found a bias towards the desktop metaphor, which is discussed in detail in all textbooks. 2) I propose a revised interface model relating 5 key concepts: interface paradigm, interaction technique, interaction style, interface platform and interface device. The model is explained in detail including examples and limitations. 3) Finally, I report on how I have used the interface model in the classroom without making a claim for its generalizability or effectiveness. The examples should be understood as a rationale for the necessity of such an interface model, as well as inspiration for teaching about interfaces. To grasp a comprehensive understanding of all diverse user interface concepts, found in the textbooks, can be difficult for students and we should reconsider the current interface definitions and provide a more nuanced interface model. I challenge the research community to critically assess the proposed interface model as a candidate and invite you to utilize, revise or reject the model.

References

1. Abowd, G.D., Beale, R.: Users, systems and interfaces: a unifying framework for interaction. In: HCI 1991 People and Computers VI, pp. 73–87 (1991)
2. Cohen, M.H., et al.: Voice User Interface Design. Addison-Wesley Professional, Boston (2004)
3. Dix, A., et al.: Human-Computer Interaction. Pearson/Prentice-Hall, Upper Saddle River (2003)
4. Foley, J.D., et al.: Computer Graphics: Principles and Practice. Addison-Wesley Professional, Boston (1996)
5. Hinckley, K., Wigdor, D.: Input technologies and techniques. In: The human-Computer Interaction Handbook: Fundamentals, Evolving Technologies and Emerging Applications, pp. 151–168 (2002)
6. Ishii, H., Ullmer, B.: Tangible bits: towards seamless interfaces between people, bits and atoms. In: Proceedings of the ACM SIGCHI Conference on Human Factors in Computing Systems, pp. 234–241. ACM, New York (1997). https://doi.org/10.1145/258549.258715
7. Kaptelinin, V., Czerwinski, M.: Beyond the desktop metaphor in seven dimensions. In: Beyond the Desktop Metaphor: Designing Integrated Digital Work Environments, pp. 335–354. MITP (2007)
8. Neil, T.: Mobile Design Pattern Gallery: UI Patterns for Smartphone Apps. O'Reilly Media Inc., Newton (2014)
9. Norman, D.: The Design of Everyday Things: Revised and Expanded Edition. Basic Books, New York (2013)
10. Norman, D.: The next UI breakthrough: command lines. Interactions **14**(3), 44–45 (2007)
11. Papantoniou, B., et al.: The glossary of human computer interaction. Online Source Httpswww Interact.-Des. Orgliteraturebook-Gloss.–Humancomputer-Interact, 23 April 2019 (2016)
12. Preece, J., et al.: Interaction Design: Beyond Human-Computer Interaction. Wiley, Hoboken (2019)
13. Shneiderman, B., et al.: Designing the User Interface: Strategies for Effective Human-Computer Interaction. Pearson Education (2016)

14. Shneiderman, B.: Direct manipulation: a step beyond programming languages. In: Proceedings of the Joint Conference on Easier and More Productive Use of Computer Systems (Part-II): Human Interface and the User Interface-Volume 1981, p. 143 (1981)

15. Van Dam, A.: Post-WIMP user interfaces. Commun. ACM **40**(2), 63–67 (1997)

16. Wigdor, D., Wixon, D.: Brave NUI World: Designing Natural User Interfaces for Touch and Gesture. Elsevier, Amsterdam (2011)

17. Witt, H., et al.: The WUI-toolkit: a model-driven UI development framework for wearable user interfaces. In: 27th International Conference on Distributed Computing Systems Workshops (ICDCSW 2007), p. 43 (2007). https://doi.org/10.1109/ICDCSW.2007.80

18. List of Physical Visualizations. http://dataphys.org/list/durrell-bishops-marble-answering-machine/. Accessed 24 Feb 2020

Wizardry in Distributed Participatory Design

From Design to Implementation

Malin Wik$^{(\boxtimes)}$ ⓘ and Akhona Khumalo ⓘ

Karlstad University, Karlstad, Sweden
malin.wik@kau.se

Abstract. Many participatory design methods and techniques assume that the designer and the participant are in the same location. In this study, we explore methods for Distributed Participatory Design. Combining the Wizard-of-Oz technique with oral discussions, in three iterations, we allowed users to actively participate, over distance, in designing a solution for their Events Management and Booking System. A video prototype was captured and used as a specification to communicate the system requirements. System development issues that arose were captured in a log and used to explore the effectiveness of such a specification in the development process. The results show that using wizardry in distributed participatory design is a viable method for allowing active participation and that video prototypes can sufficiently communicate system requirements.

Keywords: Distributed participatory design · Wizard of Oz · Video prototyping · Requirements specification

1 Introduction

Distributed Participatory Design (DPD) offers great opportunities. It reduces the need for travel and can bring design expertise to the participants and bring content and field expertise to the designer. DPD also poses challenges, but these can be overcome with tools that support collaboration in the essential channels of interaction design, namely the user interface.

This paper will discuss a case demonstrating both sides of the coin. The study furthermore explores the advantages and disadvantages of using the outcome of the DPD sessions, namely, an interactive prototype as the requirements specification (or at least to demonstrate the specifications) and the effectiveness of such a specification in the resultant developed solution.

1.1 Background

The original participatory design projects in the 1970s involved the workers of one organization as workplaces went through the process of digitalization [1]. Today, organizations may need information systems and groupware that allow them to interact and cooperate with branches in different geographical locations or even with other organizations.

© Springer Nature Switzerland AG 2020
M. Kurosu (Ed.): HCII 2020, LNCS 12181, pp. 172–186, 2020.
https://doi.org/10.1007/978-3-030-49059-1_13

The field of Computer-Supported Cooperative Work (CSCW) deals with the issues of cooperation over time and space, and the field of Information Systems and Software Engineering deals among other things with the issues of distributed development and outsourcing [2]. But the design of the groupware allowing these collaborations to happen is also a question for the field of Human-Computer Interaction. The participatory design processes of today should allow for active participation of users in different geographical locations and, which might be even more challenging, from different organizations [3]. Many of the methods and techniques applied in participatory design processes, however, assume that the designer and the participant is in the same location.

One key issue of Distributed Participatory Design is thus mitigating the geographical distance, without removing the design process and the participants from the context of use [4]. There have been some advances on the matter, but still the available literature on distributed participatory design (DPD) is limited.

2 Related Work

2.1 Distributed Participatory Design (DPD)

Some studies within Distributed Participatory Design have focused on how to enable participation via distance. [5] for example report on a project in the late '90s where email and web-based prototypes were used to facilitate collaboration between users and developers in a distributed development project of groupware. New designs were communicated using web-based prototypes which the users, after receiving email notification of a new prototype made available, were asked to test. Mailing lists were used for the majority of the communication such as feedback on prototypes, questions from the developers to the users, decision making [5].

In [6] a tool, DisCo, for asynchronous and distributed co-design between children and adults was developed and tested. The participants were asked to design a reading game using the tool. The authors found that the participants demanded more from the tool than participants in analogous co-design sessions had done when it came to sketching their designs. Furthermore, the authors found the co-design sessions needed more facilitation, meaning the participants needed clear instructions of when to do what.

The study reported by [7] explored how to "remotely discuss, develop and test GUI prototypes with users and stakeholders" using a web-based prototyping tool (the technique, GUI-ii, will be introduced in Sect. 2.4).

[8] recently report on a distributed participatory design in a crowdsourced systems development context, but seem to focus on the distribution and participation of the developers rather than the future users.

[4] explored requirements for a web-based groupware rendering distributed participatory design but did not explore techniques for distributed participation in themselves. Another study that is within the DPD field, but do not include methods for distributed participation is reported in [9], in which the authors report on their participatory design methods used in a distributed and inter-contextual setting.

2.2 Requirements Specifications

In 2003 [10] discuss the difficulties of requirements engineering for multimedia systems. While *multimedia system* may sound a bit outdated, multimedia in that work refers generally to the "extrovert parts" of a system and the important role they play – i.e. the interactive graphical user interface (GUI) of a system. The authors argue system requirements should be defined in ways that make them easy to verify and measure, but note that interactive systems contain many properties that are difficult to explicitly express and measure. [10] recommend the multimedia requirements to be visualized rather than written, for example through interactive prototypes.

Capturing System Requirements on Video. [11] suggest that using video representations provide a means to capture and communicate interactive aspects of a system, such as dynamic content and usage scenarios.

[12] ascertain the effectiveness and efficiency of videos in requirements elicitation and validation and find that under time pressure videos clarify requirements better than use cases. They do not explore the use of videos in design and development but propose these processes could benefit from video documentation.

[13] emphasise that the main focus of videos is the design statement, not the quality of the videos. The authors add that the ease of availing videos digitally has made them more attractive for expressing and documenting interaction design ideas.

2.3 Active Participation

Already in 1991, [14] noted the importance of what they label *envisionment*. By this concept, the authors refer to a process that allows the future user to actively use a prototype and influence it. This, in contrast to a user attending a demonstration, reading a system description or reviewing prototypes of different fidelity, let the user experience the system design. The breakdowns can lead to changes in the design and thus in the future system. *Envisionment* is important in revealing issues that would, otherwise, not be revealed until the final system is in place [14].

Envisionment is similar to what [15] term *genuine user participation*. Without genuine user participation, the users are viewed as informants, asked only to share their view of their work in interviews, surveys or perhaps by involving them in final system testing. Instead [15] propose the participation should be a mutual learning process between a user and IT designer, and that the users should have a say in what affects their working conditions. How people participate is just as important as who participate.

In this paper, we refer to *envisionment* and *genuine user participation* as *active participation* for the sake of simplicity. The active participation of future users has in the present study been encouraged by utilizing GUI interaction interviews (GUI-ii), which is a method explained in the following subsection.

2.4 Graphical User Interface Interaction Interviews (GUI-ii)

Graphical User Interface interaction interviews (GUI-ii) is a method which can be used over distance to explore a graphical user interface, often in the form of an explorative and interactive prototype [7].

By using GUI-ii, the fact that the designer is a human can be fully appreciated. The participant and the designer (who could just as well be another participant or a system developer) can interact as in a face-to-face interview or rather a design workshop, but via distance with the interactive graphical user interface between them [7] but also facilitated by voice communication. This way discussions about the design are carried out in direct relation to the interface, where both participant and the designer can see and follow each other's interactions, instead of having to link discussions to external artifacts [5].

2.5   Tools for Distributed Participatory Design

There are numerous prototyping tools at hand for the designer creating prototypes. The problem is, however, that a majority of the tools do not incorporate structures allowing *active participation,* which is vital to the participatory design process. In some tools the designer can decide on the interaction design beforehand by linking elements together, making the prototype appear as functioning. Very few of these tools, however, allow the designer to view the participant's interactions, make swift changes in the interaction or graphical design and let the participant interact with the prototype with inputs beyond clicks. To circumvent these limitations the Wizard-of-Oz tool Ozlab [16], developed at Karlstad University, was used to create the explorative prototypes and conduct the GUI-ii sessions.

Ozlab: Interactive Prototyping and Testing Tool. When using a Wizard-of-Oz setup, the prototype appears functional enough for the participant to perform her tasks and achieving her goals [16, 17]. In reality, all system responses are controlled by the human experimenter, the wizard, who can follow all interactions of the participant and may rapidly modify the interface in the meantime, evaluating changes directly. Allowing for swift changes in interaction design is an advantage of using a human wizard instead of preprogrammed responses in the prototype.

The participants get to see directly how their suggestions would look and feel. [18] argue this direct response give the participants a feeling of control as well as it increases their engagement and motivation to continue participating in the system development process.

3   The Study

In three iterations with five participants in each iteration (n = 3 × 5), GUI-ii was employed in the design of an Events Equipment Booking and Management system. The stakeholders of the system had the opportunity to interact with an Ozlab-based prototype of the system and give oral feedback while doing so. The designer was in Sweden while the participants were in South Africa.

This study is limited to synchronous participation since the method used, i.e. the Wizard-of-Oz technique, is based on the interaction between two humans. Synchronous participation may pose a challenge if the participant and the designer are in varying time zones. However, it worked out well during this study since the time difference between Sweden and South Africa is 0–1 h (depending on Daylight Saving Time).

Participants were emailed a consent form and instructions. Both the consent form and instructions were discussed with the participant, and participants were asked to give consent verbally before a session commenced and then email the signed consent form. One selected company employee was requested to collect the physically signed consent forms and email scanned copies in the first and third iterations. In the second iteration, the participants were asked to email the consent forms themselves. This was because printing facilities were not always readily available at the start of a session.

After the three iterations a video prototype was created. Thereafter the implementation of the system began, using the video prototype as a requirements specification.

The whole process is described in some detail in the following paragraphs.

3.1 Initial Requirements Gathering and Creation of Prototypes

At the beginning of the study, preliminary informal interviews were held with two of the company employees in an open-ended manner to get an introduction to the company's existing work process, its shortfalls and what the desired system should fulfill. The two participants were the warehouse manager and technical manager at the company. These were considered best suited because they are constantly at the center of the process of briefing, requesting and issuing equipment for events. Following the interviews, three 'rough' designs were put together using Ozlab. These were developed keeping in mind the guidelines discussed by [19] for navigating the interface, organizing the display, getting user's attention and facilitating data entry.

3.2 Iteration 1

Five participants were requested to participate in the GUI-ii sessions to further understand what the ideal system should entail. They could share what they thought would and would not work in ensuring great interactivity for them while helping them execute their work tasks in a better way. The system had to present them with a list of events equipment grouped according to sections (departments), displayed on different pages. The participant would select the desired items and capture the quantities required to make a booking. Recommendations would be shown when some equipment is selected. This feature would assist the capturer to remember items that usually work together, that may otherwise be forgotten.

The first iteration of GUI-ii sessions included discussions on which of three types of proposed designs appealed to the stakeholders. Each participant used all three designs, simultaneously discussing by telephone and gesturing by mouse cursor on the computer screen what they would or would not prefer. Participants were called by the designer at the start of the session and, following introduction to the study and gaining consent to proceed, explained the intent and process of the session and what the participant's role was in the design process. Each session was an hour long.

The participants were requested to make a booking by finding and selecting 15 specified items (of which 2 were pop up recommendations based on other selected equipment) from each of the three different designs. Thinking out loud was encouraged. This provided a means to understand what was going on in their minds as they worked through the designs and allowed for comparison of what people said against what they did - how they carried out the tasks and whether they had ease or difficulty finding the required items.

Participants were tasked with finding a list of equipment for a new booking, opening a previous booking to process a return of equipment and discussed further the need for keeping a history log. The order of designs to be tested was given to the participants in varying sequences. Upon completing interacting with each design, the participants answered a questionnaire that helped communicate and give feedback about what they would like altered and added to make the design more suitable. After the three designs had been evaluated, the participant was asked to select their most preferred design. All participants were stakeholders from the company.

The designs were all well received with the preferred system (one that allowed them to select items using checkboxes) leading by 3:2 to another (which allowed them to select by clicking on an image of the relevant item). A third option allowed the participants to make their selection by using a quantity drop-down box next to each equipment item. Suggestions during discussions included rearranging items to improve the layout and ease of finding equipment. Examples were categorizing items, arranging them in alphabetical order, arranging them from left to right rather than from top to bottom and using colors for different categories. Participants tended to rate the first design option high and then sounded a little hesitant about their previous ratings after the subsequent designs had been tried out.

3.3 Iteration 2

The second iteration was preceded by the designer giving feedback on the findings of the previous GUI-ii sessions and presenting the design that will be used going forward. Here we also discussed and weighted other requirements that had surfaced. The design that had been selected as most favorable in iteration one was updated and explored in iteration two. Five participants took part in the GUI-ii sessions of this iteration by following instructions that required them to carry out various given tasks. These included carrying out an event booking, an equipment-hire, an equipment-return and accessing various other system aspects to discuss proposals and expectations of how these would work. Participants were given a call at the beginning of the session and stayed on the call for the duration of the session.

The initial proposals and the changes that had been made were discussed during the session and thinking out loud was encouraged. The wizard responded to certain events as the participants interacted with the prototype and jotted down what was discussed. Due to lack of availability, the participants of the second iteration were not from the company, but the design in this iteration had been introduced to the company participants. Consequentially though, this allowed us to ascertain if the system was usable, easy to learn, follow and understand, appealing, and pleasant to work on even for someone who was not familiar with the company's current practices. The sessions, therefore, focused less on the intricacies of the functionality within proper context and granularity with regards to details than must be availed in the system. Participants included three people who were in the same career field (Sound Engineering/Events Management).

Each participant answered a questionnaire at the end of the 20-minute session. All participants said they had a pleasant experience; the majority found the tasks easy to complete but pointed out that a small amount of training would be ideal, nonetheless. In comments, the system was appreciated for its simplicity and conciseness but in terms of suggestions of what would heighten their experience, they suggested adding aesthetic details for visual appeal. A slightly challenging aspect some participants mentioned was that they did not know what the items were and in which section/category they could be found. This was despite showing in brackets next to the item in the instruction sheet which section they could be found.

3.4   Iteration 3

The third iteration of GUI-ii sessions presented the participants with a more refined version of the design that had been explored in the second iteration. Suggestions that the participants had put forth during iteration one and two had been incorporated in the design. More color, images, and effects to make the design more interesting were added without impacting on the functionality. Five company participants took part in the GUI-ii sessions. The participants were given tasks to complete and yet again encouraged to openly discuss their experiences as they proceeded because they were on call with the designer for the duration of the session. Following clarification received after the sessions in iteration two, the third iteration presented a version of events booking that better resembles the current process flow.

Unlike the previous sessions, where the participant would make an entire booking selecting equipment items from various departments/sections on their own, the third iteration demonstrated how this would be regulated using permissions. This meant a participant would execute only tasks that were relevant to their department and see an event booking process progress as it would normally be carried out with various users giving their input in the same booking by adding their department's requirements for the event booking until it was signed off. This, to a small extent, also gave the participants an audit trail of that booking, making it easier to know who to liaise with, in the case of dependencies, clashes or other changes. A sign off is done once all equipment requests have been received from various departments and the warehouse is ready to release the booked equipment.

All participants were, however, still able to fully process an equipment-hire from start to finish, process a return of equipment and access bookings lists and history screens. At the end of each session, participants answered a questionnaire that was used to establish if we have maintained simplicity and ease-of-use after introducing further changes and whether all expected functionality was present. The participants stated the prototyped system was easy to use. 3/5 mentioned a small amount of training would be recommended. The aesthetics added to the design were effective in making the design more attractive and all participants were satisfied with how well the prototype functionality represented what is required of the system. Keeping a design simple, showing all the relevant information without having to look for it, making it easy to accomplish tasks with a few clicks, allowing the user to see and be able to edit what they have done, and adding a bit of color and images proved to be a pleasing product.

3.5   From Prototype to Requirements Specification

A phased approach was decided upon and the first three design iterations would focus on providing a way to book equipment for events and pure (dry) hire, a way to handle returns of previously booked equipment and a way to manage inventory by keeping information on what the company has in the warehouse, what is booked out, when it is due back, what conditions the equipment is in and whether equipment is available for the next booking. This phase also includes a booking and equipment search functionality. The second phase would focus on the ability to provide a comprehensive history, keep audit logs of user activities and provide performance information such as what equipment is most hired, high demand periods, etc.

Ozlab prototypes are dependent on the human experimenter responding to the participants' input to appear as fully working. This poses a challenge when it comes to the requirement's specification. The final prototype was thus captured in a video to communicate the interaction design to the participants and as a requirement specification for the system to be built. The video prototype was done by using a screen recording tool, Camtasia (as it happened, version 4 was used for the recording and version 8 for editing), to record the Ozlab prototype in a browser. The prototype was recorded from the view of a user, and it appeared functioning since the designer responded to the input of another designer acting as participant. A voice-over explaining the functionalities seen in the video was added. The video prototype was divided into four parts: Event booking (17 min), Equipment hire (6 min), Lists and Returns (5 min) and Inventory Management (3 min).

The video prototype was shared on a link to a cloud storage space (Box) for the company to review. A video conference, via Zoom, was then held to discuss whether the video prototype gave a true picture of how they expected the system to work. The video prototype was accepted, a few additional requirements were highlighted, and a go-ahead given for development to commence.

3.6   From Video Prototype to System

In order to try to capture what, if any, issues arise when using a video prototype as a demonstration of a requirements specification the designer, who also developed the system was asked to keep record of the development process in a log.

The log had five columns: "Development Area and Date", "Describe the problem, questions, issue", "How did you (try to) solve the problem?", "Classify the issue (if possible)" and "Reported by whom? (note others than you)".

A frequent reoccurring contact between the designer and the participants at the company was advised but proved difficult to withhold. Emails tended to get long waiting times before response. The employees are constantly out of office. Communication was both through formal and informal means. i.e. emails and calls and WhatsApp/text messages.

4   Results

The results reported here have been gathered from reports from the video prototyping process, from the log book kept during the development process and from reports from the GUI-ii sessions.

4.1   The Video Prototyping Process

The designer noted five issues regarding the video prototyping. All issues pertained to how to produce the videos in an efficient manner.

During the video prototyping phase, the designer also noticed four things had been overlooked by both the participants and the designer during the GUI-ii sessions: the possibility to enter two different types of information was missing in the prototypes, that a certain information (return date) was not added automatically in the prototype but should be, and that the possibility to enter certain details (flag as unavailable) was not present in the prototypes.

During the video prototype meeting, the participants also pointed out a few more issues that had been overlooked. For example, the designer had used "Equipment hire" to describe the process when a client contacts the company to hire equipment without needing them to handle the setup. The company, however, use "Dry hire" to describe this type of process.

4.2   Records in the Log

In total the developer noted 44 records in the log. The records form a timeline of the development. For analysis, all records were numbered and the developer's own classifications was used to categorize the records. The developer used varying classifications and thus the records was analyzed to recognize if records under different developer classifications were pertained to the same type of issue. The different types of issues are reported below.

Developer Know-How. At least 17 records were logged that were classified as issues related to developer know-how. These records related to issues such as how to programmatically solve a problem, miscalculations resulting in faulty values, web browser compatibility issues, to issues related to moving from local to remote hosting.

The issues raised in these records were general development issues and therefore did not suggest any relation to design, requirements gathering, specification or whether the prototype had any shortfalls.

Uncertainty of Developer as a Result of Given Data. Eight of the records have to do with uncertainties of the developer as a result of the inventory data produced and shared by the company. For example, the supplies were inconsistently named, some was categorized while other lacked categories and inventory was described in terms of "most" instead of actual count.

While the designer included real inventory in the prototypes, it was first when the database was to be created that the ambiguities was introduced. Thus, the ambiguities and what each decision would entail regarding the interaction design was not depicted in the prototypes and evaluated by the participants in GUI-ii sessions. The company was instead asked to provide the developer with the "correct" data, and engage in more talks in order to clarify uncertainties.

Prototype Misrepresentation. One record had to do with misrepresentation of reality in the prototype. Though this did not mean that in reality what the prototype promised could not be done, it highlighted that some things could, in a prototype, appear much simpler than they are to develop in a real system.

Missed Elements and Functions in Prototypes. Five records pertained to uncertainties arising as a result of not having been explored (sufficiently) during the prototyping stage. Prototypes need not represent entire functionality of the product. This means certain elements or functions, despite having been discussed as requirements, were taken for granted that they will be present in the developed system though not explicitly presented in the prototype. In some instances, the functionality is presented in simple terms without intricately going into detail. During development, however, as was in our case, these may present unforeseen complications.

Other Kinds of Records in the Log. The remaining records had various classifications relating to development considerations that would not have been possible to ascertain from the design process and resultant prototype. Some of these were database structure, data security considerations, the use of special characters and delays resulting from unavailability of end-users.

4.3 Other Findings

These findings are experiences extracted from other reports of the GUI-ii sessions conducted in the three iterations.

Wizardry During Interactivity. Using Ozlab in conjunction with calls to the participants allowed us to better understand what the participant wanted without having to spend time coding the desired functionality. Because the designer, acting as a wizard, could see the mouse moves and clicks the participants were making, the participants would use mouse gesture to point out areas of improvement in the design while explaining on the telephone call. Participants were aware of the designer seeing everything they were doing on the computer but not the wizardry that came into play in terms of the responses they would see when they performed specific actions.

Additionally, the wizard could see what actions seemed harder or took longer even when the participant did not verbalize it. We note however, that this could not be measured as several other issues could come into play and these could not be ruled out. In some instances, where these actions are accompanied by verbal utterances that indicate frustration, this can constitute helpful information in assessing usability.

Iterative Prototype Progression. The iterations facilitate the evolution from one point of the design to the next, making befitting alterations informed by the outcomes of the previous sessions. Participants appreciated seeing their suggestions implemented and getting to experience them as part of a working prototype. Because participants participated one on one with the designer, each one's voices were heard. This allowed for most commonly mention considerations to be accommodated and the lesser ones to be explored further by adding those into future discussions with other participants. This was often followed by many realizing things they may otherwise have overlooked. Another reason to keep all suggestions in mind arose from the fact that different users have different needs that may need to be catered for in order to fulfil their individual (or even departmental) task specifications.

Nature of Discussions. The nature of discussions during and immediately post the GUI-ii sessions was relaxed and open-ended. In thinking out loud, which participants were encouraged to do, no structure can be enforced. Using telephone and Ozlab also had the limitation that neither party on either end of the computer had a visual of the other. Often these two parties did not know each other apart from being informed about participating.

Participants often expressed how they felt about their experiences even before they had to respond to a questionnaire.

Requirements Change. Though preliminary discussions and GUI-ii sessions covered several of the system requirements, some requirements were highlighted at a later stage in the design process. These changes were introduced by participants who had participated in all the discussions and sessions and expressed satisfaction.

Examples in our study included that it was only after the second iteration that it was brought to the designer's attention that the system should cater for incremental bookings and only after the third iteration and during the review of the video prototype that it was brought to the designer's attention that an additional group of users should be included that will be responsible for and limited to starting bookings.

Video Prototype as a Requirements Specification. Using a video of the prototype as a requirements specification proved beneficial to the designer, developer and participants. Playback made it easy to review scenarios and what was adopted in the specification. It was also convenient for the developer to refer back to and easily understand what the developed solution must fulfil.

We point out that a developed solution may not be a perfect replica of the video prototype but should provide as closely matched a system if requirements have not changed drastically and the prototype itself had been approved as a signed-off specification.

Commitment of Participating Organization. We fully appreciate that companies have the highest priority in keeping their business running. The techniques used in this study of a participatory nature and the key prerequisite for stakeholders to actively participate. This goes beyond participating in a GUI-ii session, for example, to includes commitment to the project, timely communication response and participant availability. Committing to project and the developed product may be quick and easier. Commitment to the process requires time and availability.

5 Concluding Discussion

Initially, we set out to discuss and demonstrate methods for Distributed Participatory Design (DPD) and the use of interactive prototypes as a requirements specification (or demonstration of such). Before us, [5, 6] used asynchronous methods for participatory design over distance. In our study, we used the synchronous method called GUI-ii, as demonstrated and proposed in [7]. GUI-ii enabled us to ensure the *active participation* of participants as stressed by [14, 15] over distance.

Without moving forward to the development of the system designed in the GUI-ii sessions, it would not be possible to say as much of the efficiency of the sessions. We decided to create a visual representation, a video prototype, to communicate the interaction design and agreed-upon requirements with the participants. The video prototype was furthermore used as a requirements specification during development. This process was captured in a logbook.

Few Prototype Misrepresentations. In this section, we will bring up something that we have not seen discussed as much in the literature. We think, however, that the category "Prototype misrepresentation" is interesting, although probably not specific for digital prototypes as misrepresentations of implementable system/reality could be introduced in a paper prototype as well.

The majority of the records in the development log was development related. This is expected as the focus shift from interaction design to how to implement the system programmatically. What was a bit unexpected, however, was the few instances of "Prototype misrepresentation" noted in the log.

Many prototyping tools allow the designer to suggest all sorts of design and interaction paradigm regardless of how difficult or even impossible the suggestions are to implement. This holds for Ozlab as well. One might expect that transcending from prototype to implemented system would induce many problems related to prototype misrepresentation (of implementable system/reality).

Interestingly enough, only one record in the log was related to prototype misrepresentation. It should be noted, however, that the designer is also a knowledgeable programmer, why some pitfalls could have been avoided. In any way, the few instances of prototype misrepresentation and the double roles of the designer at least suggest that engaging the system developers in the prototyping process could be a good idea as emphasized in [7], at least if the developers do not immediately shy away from unconventional solutions.

Making Requirements Explicit Supported Mutual Learning Between Developer and Participant. Some functions and wording were overlooked by the designer and the participants in the GUI-ii sessions. One example was the designer's use of "Equipment Hire" instead of "Dry Hire". Perhaps this was overlooked by the participants during the first three iterations in an attempt to be polite, and/or the video prototype made it evident that the wrong term was used as the term "Equipment hire" was repeated in the voice over in the video (as well as in the GUI).

By explicitly communicating the systems requirements via interactive prototypes and video prototypes and allowing active participation, the participants could see how the designer had interpreted their expressed needs (as proposed by [10, 11]) and corrected any misinterpretations and mutual learning was supported as emphasized by [15].

The designer also became aware of missed functions and details while reviewing the video prototype. This might be thanks to how focused one must be on the GUI and the interaction design when editing videos and adding voice over explaining everything visible on the screen.

We thus argue video documentation is beneficial for the design and development, as [12] suggested.

Awareness of overlooked functionality and details may mean that additional requirements are added. These requirements may be crucial or require major changes. Indeed, this is welcome as such valuable information may lead to the design most appropriate to the user and since the prototypes were not programmed, the effort to correct mistakes was minimal.

Informal Discussions Helped in Highlighting Work Process Frustrations. Using a relaxed/informal discussion and introducing both the study and the role they are expected to play played a positive role in getting the participants to open up and share their thoughts about what the system should entail to properly address their needs. This often allowed them to open up also about their current work process frustrations which provided information about how the system could be designed to alleviate these. Because questionnaires were given verbally in such an open communication setting, ratings were often given and substantiated which enriched the data collected. Building rapport with participants to encourage them to open up and share information is a well-known success factor in interviewing [20] and seems to hold for GUI interaction interviews as well.

Active Participation in DPD is Difficult Without Internet Connection. Now, the following issue has not been addressed in this study yet but should be noted nonetheless. The methods for the distributed participatory design used in this study, as well as in [5, 6] rely heavily on the participants' access to an internet connection. Sharing video prototypes, even though made easier by digital means [13], is also difficult without an internet connection. Indeed, the oral discussions during the GUI-ii sessions were held over the telephone, but the exchange of views in the graphical user interface and the wizardry behind the non-programmed prototype would not be possible without a web-based tool such as Ozlab [7, 10, 16]. Without it, the participants' interactions with the prototypes would have to be recorded and then shared with the designer in some other way – thus losing the possibility of not only relating the discussion directly to the interface but also the possibility to swiftly respond to the participants' desires.

From our study, we see that it is possible to conduct participatory design over distance, but that it relies on the use of the internet. Therefore, it might be difficult to ensure active participation as stressed by for example [14, 15] over distance in the most secluded and rural parts of the world.

6 Prospects for HCI and Participatory Design

This study does not include the process of introducing the system to the company and its work processes. There is a risk that more overlooked functions and requirements will emerge once the system is in use.

The participants were able to share their views not only in discussions together with their colleagues (after reviewing the video prototype, for example) but also one-on-one during the GUI-ii sessions. By using GUI-ii, the participant was not only allowed to express his opinions regarding the prototype but also to experience design based on his opinions through use. Another way forward that could be interesting to pursue is to explore the possibilities of the participants to be co-designers over distance (as in [7]) and even let them act as wizards.

Although our study includes not only a demonstration of the distributed participatory design process but also the use of video prototypes in development, we have not seen that our account diverges much from the body of literature in the field of participatory design and, the rather limited body of literature in distributed participatory design. To us, this shows that conducting participatory design and development over distance is not something to shy away from. Using a technique such as the Wizard-of-Oz technique in combination with oral discussions contributes to better clarity in understanding what the user requires and geographical distances between participant and designer can be mitigated.

What remains to do is, however, to connect distributed participatory design with the distributed agile development and outsourcing body of literature.

References

1. Bannon, L., Bardzell, J., Bødker, S.: Introduction: reimagining participatory design–emerging voices. ACM Trans. Comput.-Hum. Interact. **25**, 1–8 (2018)
2. Iivari, N.: Coordinating, contributing, contesting, representing: HCI specialists surviving distributed design. In: De Angeli, A., Bannon, L., Marti, P., Bordin, S. (eds.) Design of Cooperative Systems, pp. 207–223. Springer, Heidelberg (2016). https://doi.org/10.1007/978-3-319-33464-6_13
3. Gumm, D.C., Janneck, M., Finck, M.: Distributed participatory design–a case study. In: Proceedings of the DPD Workshop at NordiCHI (2006)
4. Lazarin, C.A.J., Almeida, L.D.A.: Distributed participatory design web-based groupware: gathering requirements through braindraw. In: Proceedings of the 15th Brazilian Symposium on Human Factors in Computing Systems, pp. 1–10. ACM, New York (2016)
5. Farshchian, B.A., Divitini, M.: Using email and WWW in a distributed participatory design project. ACM SIGGROUP Bull. **20**, 10–15 (1999)
6. Walsh, G., et al.: DisCo: a co-design online tool for asynchronous distributed child and adult design partners. In: Proceedings of the 11th International Conference on Interaction Design and Children, pp. 11–19. Association for Computing Machinery, Bremen (2012)
7. Pettersson, J.S., Wik, M., Andersson, H.: GUI interaction interviews in the evolving map of design research. In: Paspallis, N., Raspopoulos, M., Barry, C., Lang, M., Linger, H., Schneider, C. (eds.) Advances in Information Systems Development: Methods, Tools and Management, pp. 149–167. Springer, Heidelberg (2018). https://doi.org/10.1007/978-3-319-74817-7_10

8. Kautz, K., Bjerknes, G., Fisher, J., Jensen, T.: Distributed participatory design in crowdsourced information systems development. In: 29th Australasian Conference on Information Systems, pp. 1–12. Australian Chapter of the AIS (2018)

9. Obendorf, H., Janneck, M., Finck, M.: Inter-contextual distributed participatory design. Scand. J. Inf. Syst. **21**, 2 (2009)

10. Molin, L., Pettersson, J.S.: How should interactive media be discussed for successful requirements engineering? In: Burnett, R., Brunström, A., Nilsson, A. (eds.) Perspectives on Multimedia: Communication, Media and Information Technology, pp. 69–96. Wiley, New York (2003)

11. Karras, O., Unger-Windeler, C., Glauer, L., Schneider, K.: Video as a by-product of digital prototyping: capturing the dynamic aspect of interaction. In: 2017 IEEE 25th International Requirements Engineering Conference Workshops (REW), pp. 118–124. IEEE, Piscataway (2017)

12. Brill, O., Schneider, K., Knauss, E.: Videos vs. use cases: can videos capture more requirements under time pressure? In: Wieringa, R., Persson, A. (eds.) REFSQ 2010. LNCS, vol. 6182, pp. 30–44. Springer, Heidelberg (2010). https://doi.org/10.1007/978-3-642-14192-8_5

13. Bogdan, C., Ertl, D., Falb, J., Green, A., Kaindl, H.: A case study of remote interdisciplinary designing through video prototypes. In: 2012 45th Hawaii International Conference on System Sciences, pp. 504–513. IEEE, Washington (2012)

14. Bødker, S., Grønbæk, K.: Design in action: from prototyping by demonstration to cooperative prototyping. In: Greenbaum, J., Kyng, M. (eds.) Design at Work: Cooperative Design of Computer Systems, pp. 197–218. Lawrence Erlbaum, Hillsdale (1991)

15. Bødker, K., Kensing, F., Simonsen, J.: Participatory IT Design: Designing for Business and Workplace Realities. MIT Press, USA (2004)

16. Pettersson, J.S., Wik, M.: The longevity of general purpose Wizard-of-Oz tools. In: OzCHI 2015: Proceedings of the Annual Meeting of the Australian Special Interest Group for Computer Human Interaction, pp. 422–426. ACM, New York (2015)

17. Kelley, J.F.: An empirical methodology for writing user-friendly natural language computer applications. In: Proceedings of CHI 1983, pp. 193–196. ACM, New York (1983)

18. Larsson, N., Molin, L.: Rapid prototyping of user interfaces in robot surgery—Wizard of Oz in participatory design. In: Nilsson, A.G., Gustas, R., Wojtkowski, W., Wojtkowski, W.G., Wrycza, S., Zupančič, J. (eds.) Advances in Information Systems Development, pp. 361–371. Springer, New York (2005). https://doi.org/10.1007/978-0-387-36402-5_31

19. Shneiderman, B., Plaisant, C.: Designing the User Interface: Strategies For Effective Human-Computer Interaction. Pearson Education, Bengaluru (2010)

20. King, N., Horrocks, C., Brooks, J.: Interviews in Qualitative Research. Sage, New York (2019)

Research on Information Interface Interaction Design Based on Unconscious Cognition

Wenwen Yang[✉]

School of Design Arts and Media, Nanjing University of Science
and Technology, 200, Xiaolingwei Street, Nanjing 210094, Jiangsu, China
1178569502@qq.com

Abstract. Based on the analysis and summary of the theory of unconscious cognition in cognitive psychology, the guiding role and significance of unconscious cognition in the interaction design of information interface are discussed. Use the unconscious theory to guide the interaction design of the information interface, thereby improving the usability and user experience of the information interface. First of all, this article analyzes the visual stimulus factors that influence the information interface design and the design elements of information layout optimization by using literature and survey methods. Then, I summarized the information interface design requirements and methods that meet unconscious cognition. Finally, an unconscious cognitive behavior model was established to guide the interaction design of the information interface and provide a theoretical basis for the interaction design of the information interface. Information interface design based on the user's unconscious cognition is an important method to optimize the user experience and improve the usability and interaction efficiency of the information interface. It provides new ideas and methods for the research of information interface design.

Keywords: Unconscious cognition · Information interface · Interaction efficiency · User experience

1 Introduction

With the emergence of mobile Internet, intelligent mobile terminals are rapidly popularized. Extremely rich information, the era of big data is coming. Information interface interaction is gradually attached importance to. Users interact with products through the information interface to complete the information interaction process. While interaction emphasizes human-centered, information interaction interface design needs to consider user interaction behavior patterns and user cognitive diversity. To meet the needs of different users' cognitive diversity, it is necessary to study user cognitive commonality, which is reflected in unconscious cognition. Therefore, information interface design in the context of unconscious cognition can better meet the different needs and common needs of different users.

At present regarding the information interaction interface design mainly from the perspective of visual perception, including color, shape, etc. But only for visual stimulation and diversity. Adopting information stacking and block-type indoctrination

© Springer Nature Switzerland AG 2020
M. Kurosu (Ed.): HCII 2020, LNCS 12181, pp. 187–198, 2020.
https://doi.org/10.1007/978-3-030-49059-1_14

and other modes can not bring excellent user experience, and there is not much research on information interface design from the perspective of user cognitive psychology. Therefore, it is of great significance to explore users' unconscious cognitive behavior patterns in cognitive psychology to improve the efficiency of information interface interaction. User-centric products need to study user psychology. The theory of unconscious cognition in cognitive psychology provides a basis for the study of information interface usability, so as to meet users' cognitive needs, improve use efficiency and satisfy users' emotional experience.

2 Unconscious Cognitive Mechanism

2.1 Process of Unconscious Cognitive Information Processing

At first, the concept of unconsciousness was put forward hypothetically and speculatively. Unconsciousness belongs to the non-conscious level, also known as the unconscious, and belongs to the instinctive behavior of human beings. With the rise of cognitive psychology, experimental research on unconscious cognition began to emerge. One of the first experiments was on memory by Ebbinghaus, who isolated the concept of "unconscious memory" from the types of memory. Cognitive load theory in cognitive psychology plays a key role in the study of unconscious cognition, which emphasizes the limitation of psychological resources and the reality of cognitive load problem. Among them, information processing is a term in cognitive psychology, which is the output process of receiving, storing, computing and final behavior of information, or the extraction and processing of the memory stored in the human brain, including long-term memory and short-term memory [1].

More and more cognitive psychologists believe that the cognitive system of human brain includes not only the conscious cognitive system but also the unconscious cognitive system. Explicit cognition is a kind of serial controlled information processing system, which requires intentional attention and willpower. Limited psychological resources; Implicit cognition is a parallel, automated information processing system that requires no conscious attention or mental effort. Psychological resources are infinite [2]. The main research contents of implicit cognition are "implicit learning" and "implicit memory". Implicit learning is a kind of unconscious cognitive processing process. It is not aware of the rules or how to master them, but it has learned the rules. The corresponding "explicit learning" is purposeful, conscious learning to master the law. Implicit memory is unconscious memory based on past experiences and habits, while the corresponding "explicit memory" is associative, which is the recollection of previous conscious memory. It can be seen from the essential differences between implicit memory and explicit memory, implicit learning and explicit learning that the information processing process of unconscious cognition is independent and universal [3]. Automatic processing of information by unconscious cognition shows how users perceive, that is, how to help users understand the logic of machine operation. The process is shown in Fig. 1.

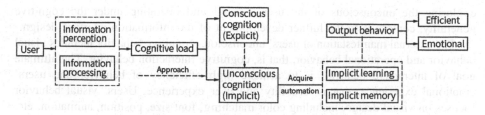

Fig. 1. Process diagram of unconscious cognitive information processing

Unconscious cognitive information processing has its unique advantages.

1. When the information is complex, the unconscious cognition is more efficient in processing the information;
2. Unconscious cognition is not disturbed by the external environment and its own emotions, and plays a stable role and is not susceptible to fluctuations;
3. The process of unconscious cognition is the process of automatic information processing, which is the function of the unconscious mind and has great potential;
4. No need to spend too much mental energy, unlimited psychological resources.

2.2 Research on Unconscious Cognitive Behavior a Subsection Sample

The unconscious cognitive system is a fast, unconscious, completely autonomous system that does not require too much brain power and is subject to emotions and habits rather than conscious control. The unconscious behaviors expressed by the unconscious system of human brain are ubiquitous in People's Daily activities and gradually form users' behavior habits, but are not detected by people. It is an involuntary instinct. A lot of people's behavior is the result of unconscious, but they are not aware of it. Therefore, the interaction between users and products often presents the real needs of users, which are generated unconsciously, but can be expressed by the unconscious behaviors of users. Therefore, this provides a new idea for designers to explore the internal needs of users.

Analyzing users' cognitive behavior characteristics is helpful for designers to make reasonable plans for information layout and presentation form on the information interface. The information in the information interface is not randomly and simply piled up, but has its existence value. It exists to help users obtain or complete an operation task. Moreover, according to different task requirements of users, their cognitive behavior patterns are also different. According to the SPK cognitive model proposed by Rasmussen, human cognitive behavior patterns can be divided into three levels, from low to high, namely skilled cognitive behavior, regular cognitive behavior and knowledge cognitive behavior. The first two are subject to skills and rules, while the knowledge cognitive behavior is not restricted by rules, mainly determined by their own knowledge accumulation and experience. Mainly from the implementation of the knowledge of cognitive behavior on memory access, and cognitive psychology, memory is divided into explicit memory and implicit memory, implicit memory retrieval process that is unconscious cognition process, and its unique advantage that exploring the unconscious of the user's visual and operating under the cognitive generality, contribute to the further development of the information interface design.

The external manifestation of users' unconscious cognitive behavior includes visual behavior and operational behavior, that is, cognitive interaction behavior. The ultimate goal of interactive behavior is to achieve high efficiency of behavior and users' emotional experience, that is, usability and user experience. Users' visual behavior focuses on visual design, including color matching, font size, position, animation, etc. The operation behavior includes click and slide, etc. The evaluation index is the accuracy and efficiency of the operation. The user's visual browsing behavior and operational behavior can be observed, but the motive force of the behavior, namely the user's goal, is uncertain. Different users have different goals, but their behaviors may be the same. The same target may also have the same behaviors. Users' cognitive behaviors are hard to be observed externally.

3 Unconscious Cognitive Behavior and Information Interaction Efficiency

3.1 Extraction of Visual Stimulus Factors in Information Interface

With the rapid expansion of information and crazy into the field of vision, users must be independent access to information resources, excessive information to the user's annoyance. Therefore, information must be selective, orderly and appropriate to convey to the user, which is the responsibility of the information interface. Information user interface is the medium of human-machine and human-information interaction, aiming to help users operate the hardware with the most efficient interactive behavior to achieve their own purposes. The information interface designs information from elements such as color, text, and symbols to achieve the purpose of conveying information and facilitating man-machine communication. As a platform for the communication between people and information, the main task of the information interface is to transform the data-based information into information that conforms to users' cognitive habits and interactive behaviors. The main task here is to start from users' cognitive behavior patterns. 80% of the information resources acquired by people are transmitted by the visual channel, so the visual information interface is the most important one in human-machine interface.

Visual information interface experience is mainly influenced by visual stimuli. In the visual information interface, visual stimuli are received by the user and corresponding behavioral responses are made, including visual behavioral responses and operational behavioral responses. Xie et al. [4] used eye movement tracking technology and unconscious assessment method to design the product interface iteratively, and concluded that the product interface design scheme conforming to unconscious cognitive objectives had better usability and user experience. Therefore, the arrangement and intensity of visual stimuli in the information interface need to be designed reasonably. First of all, in terms of visual behavior, appropriate and appropriate visual stimuli are conducive to ensuring the accuracy of user behavior and improving user experience. Information layout and presentation intensity that do not conform to users' habits and experience often bring unnecessary troubles and confusion to users, and even fail to meet the basic functions of usability, which is fatal to products. Therefore, information interface designers need to understand the cognitive behavior of users under different visual stimuli, so as to design the information layout of the interface reasonably, and find out the maximum visual stimulus factors that affect users' cognitive behavior. Secondly, the operation behavior can be set by the operation task, so that the user can complete the operation process within the specified time, so that the information interface can be evaluated from the user operation accuracy, operation efficiency and other aspects.

Deeply understand users' cognitive behavior, respect users' cognitive behavior law and physiological needs, help designers to understand users' potential cognitive behavior, and assist product design. Figure 2 is the information interface visual stimulus and cognitive behavior model constructed by extracting visual stimulus elements that affect users' cognitive behavior. If the visual stimulation of the information interface conforms to the cognitive model, it will not cause the user's cognitive load; if not, the user's cognitive load will increase, which is reflected in the operation behavior, such as the increase in the number of wrong operations and the increase in the time to complete the operation process. The feedback reflected in the visual and operational behavior will be presented in the form of the user's overall and partial satisfaction evaluation of the interface.

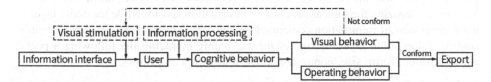

Fig. 2. Visual stimulus and cognitive behavior model of information interface

3.2 Effects of Visual Stimuli on Interaction Efficiency

Interaction includes the interaction within the system, but also includes the interaction between human and machine. Here we mainly talk about human-computer interaction, that is, the interaction between human and system. The process of human-computer interaction is the process in which the information interface acts on the human brain. Information is transmitted to the human brain for processing and processing, and then the human brain responds to achieve human-information interaction. The evaluation criteria of a good information interaction design mainly include usability and user experience. User experience emphasizes user emotion, whether the interaction process is smooth, efficient and comfortable, whether the use process is pleasant. Usability emphasizes whether it meets the needs of users. The purpose of information interface interaction design is to study the interaction efficiency of information interface. Starting from the unconscious cognitive behavior of users, the design methods and principles to improve the interaction efficiency of information interface are studied mainly by information layout.

The information layout that meets the user's interactive behavior habits can greatly improve the quality of information interface, shorten users' cognitive process, reduce cognitive load and improve interaction efficiency. The key points of visual element design to satisfy the user's habit of interaction and improve interaction efficiency include visual element attribute, visual element meaning, visual element grouping and layout. First, the design of visual elements should accord with the characteristics of users' visual search behavior to facilitate users to find information. Second, reduce the cognitive load of visual elements and avoid the visual elements that are difficult to understand and unclear.

The essence of the relationship between visual stimulus, visual behavior and operational behavior is to explore the interactive behavior patterns under different visual stimuli to provide design reference and theoretical basis for information interface designers. To explore whether the visual stimulation interface meets the needs of users, and then to judge the success of the information interface. More importantly, the designer should ensure the unity of the overall visual style while ensuring the consistency between the visual stimulus presentation form and the user's interactive habits (visual search habits and operational habits). Only in the design of information interface, visual stimulation is concise and smooth, and irrelevant operations are reduced, users can improve the accuracy and efficiency of operation, find the target in the least time, and complete the operation task.

The form that causes the size of visual stimuli is information layout, which includes the entity layer and the relational layer. The relational layer is the information architecture, emphasizing the logical structure of information layout, while the entity layer is the presentation of information content. Here, the entity layer of information is mainly studied. Information layout design elements, mainly including the following aspects: color, position, form, size, contrast. Specific analysis is as follows:

1. Use color to capture users' psychology and attract users' attention.
2. The layout of information design elements emphasizes their location and conforms to users' visual search behavior and operational habits.
3. Different presentation forms bring different visual feelings to users.
4. Size includes text size and graph size, highlighting information hierarchy through size comparison.
5. In addition to the selection of color system, more important is the contrast between information components and color matching.

Chang [5] used eye-movement tracking technology to optimize the usability of information interface by optimizing information layout elements to achieve the requirements of unconscious cognition. By controlling the variables, the optimal information interface design is obtained by analyzing the test data of the information layout elements. Therefore, the visual stimulus elements of the information interface can be evaluated by the method of unconscious evaluation.

3.3 Construction of Unconscious Cognitive Behavior Model

Improve interaction efficiency, reduce users' cognitive load and learning cost, obtain unconscious cognitive processing, reduce the cognitive load in human-computer interaction process, and make the whole interaction process tend to unconscious cognitive processing state. Only by reducing the brain cost of users in the operation process can the best user experience be achieved. Therefore, the design should be as close as possible to the user's unconscious cognitive processing [6]. Figure 3 shows the model of unconscious cognitive behavior built based on information interface.

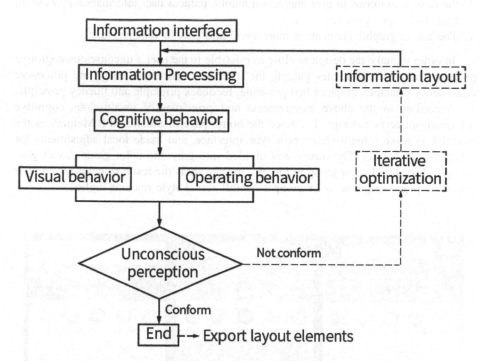

Fig. 3. Model of unconscious cognitive behavior

The evaluation standard of unconscious cognition is the time of visual information search, and the time when the human eye first sees the required information interface elements is taken as the standard to judge whether the unconscious cognition is reached. The unconscious cognition takes 200–250 ms to complete the search [7]. According to the unconscious cognitive behavior model, the information interface layout elements that satisfy the unconscious cognitive process of users can be derived, and the information layout elements can also be optimized. The main points and principles of information layout design are summarized based on the output results and applied to the new information interface design.

The most important factor that attracts attention is the size of visual stimulation. The bigger the visual stimulation is, the more users can pay attention to it. But not bigger the better. Different forms of interaction will also affect users' cognition of interface information. Interaction emphasizes human-centered, so the requirements for information in the whole interaction process are clear, easy to obtain and easy to understand. Requirements for information interface design include:

1. Visual design of the information interface, extracting useful information and available information to facilitate user recognition and understanding.
2. Reasonable information architecture and clear logic.
3. the design conforms to user interaction habits, reduces user information processing time and improves user experience.
4. The use of graphic elements is more vivid and easy to understand.

In order to make the design as close as possible to the user's unconscious cognitive process, four basic principles guiding the interface interaction design are proposed: consistency principle, graphics first principle, feedback principle and fluency principle.

According to the above requirements and principles of unconscious cognitive information interface design, I selected the home page of mobile APP Meituan as the material to make a high-fidelity prototype interface, and made local adjustments for comparative analysis. The survey was divided into gray and color groups, with gray group in Fig. 4 and color group in Fig. 5. Gray group is the result of color group after grayscale processing, and color group's overall visual style remains unified.

Fig. 4. Gray group

Fig. 5. Color group (Color figure online)

The subjective satisfaction of the interface was scored by scale. The scores were given on an isometric 10-point scale, with 1 for worst and 10 for best. After statistical analysis of the data, Table 1 and Table 2 give the average satisfaction scores of the test subjects on three different interfaces, and evaluate them according to good, average and poor grades.

Table 1. Satisfaction score – gray interface

Interface type	Number of people	Average score	Evaluation
Interface 1	24	7.88	Fine
Interface 1	24	7.79	Fine
Interface 1	24	7.88	Fine

Table 2. Satisfaction score – color interface

Interface type	Number of people	Average score	Evaluation
Interface 1	24	6.33	Worse
Interface 1	24	6.17	Worse
Interface 1	24	6.88	Worse

The results showed that the average score of the gray group was 23.54, and that of the color group was 19.38. The score of the gray group was significantly higher than that of the color group. Therefore, the proper use of color in the interface is an important means to design the information interface, but the meaning of the existence of color cannot be denied. The score of interface 2 in the two groups was the lowest, with little difference in the gray group and significant difference in the color group. In the color group, from the icon perspective, interface 2 is more materialized, interface 1 has shadow effect, and interface 3 is flat design. From the perspective of visualization, the contrast between components and background and between components in interface 3 is relatively obvious, which is easy to get users' attention. The same is true from the perspective of color matching. The overall visual effect of the interface 3 visual design is good, the information interface layout is clean and reasonable, easy for users to search visual. Therefore, the principle of information interface interaction design under the unconscious cognition mechanism can optimize the information interface design and make it have better user experience. This survey focuses on visual behavior habits. I conducted another group of surveys on specific operational behaviors and interviewed the results.

According to the user's operation habits, I set the specific operation task as follows: open the APP interface to query the hotel accommodation from January 29 to January 30 in Nanjing, and the operation will be completed when the query is stopped. The specific operation process is to open the hotel accommodation interface – enter the destination – enter the time – query the hotel – end of the task. Figure 6 shows the content of the page for entering the hotel accommodation. This interface is taken as the main part of the study, where the destination and time bar (parameters in the blue box) are independent variables.

Fig. 6. Hotel query interface

I understand the user experience in the process of user operation through interviews. Table 3 shows the statistical results. Besides interview, operation time can also be used as an experimental indicator.

Table 3. User interview record

User	Preference	Reasons
A	Interface 1	Simple
B	Interface 1	Date corresponds to the Sunday
C	Interface 1	Simple
D	Interface 1	Interface 2 "number of each room" information redundancy
E	Interface 1	The arrow icon is indicative
F	Interface 2	"Check-in time" is marked blue, more remarkable
G	Interface 2	"predetermined days" is obvious, easy to get
H	Interface 2	Meet positioning needs

Based on the above analysis and evaluation of the interview records of 7 users, it is concluded that interface 1 and interface 2 have their own advantages and disadvantages. The obvious advantages of interface 1 are simple information layout, reasonable layout rules and indicating that the information conforms to unconscious cognition. But other needs of the user may need to be considered. The prominent advantage of interface 2 is that information highlights important information through color and position, which is convenient for users to operate quickly. The disadvantage is too much information, no reasonable layout. Therefore, through the above assessment of information interface design, it is concluded that information interface design meeting the requirements of unconscious cognition design will have better user experience and use efficiency. The basic requirements of the information interface that conforms to the unconscious cognition are graphic visualization and concise design. Reasonable layout of information, avoid information redundancy, extract useful and available information. To meet the user operation needs, in line with the operation behavior habits and so on.

With the deepening of the research on unconscious cognition in cognitive psychology, the interaction design of information interface guided by the theory of unconscious cognition has become the main research field. By analyzing the unique advantages of the process of unconscious information processing, the unconscious cognitive behavior model is constructed, and the information interaction interface design elements that meet the implicit needs of users are deeply mined. The design elements are used to guide the design of the interaction interface to improve the interaction efficiency and user experience.

4   Interactive Design Method of Unconscious Cognitive Information Interface

The design of unconscious cognitive information interface conforms to the user's behavior habits, which is the application of the behavior habits that the user has but does not know.

In unconscious cognitive theory to guide information interface interaction design, analyze the uniqueness of the unconscious information processing advantages, unconscious cognitive behavioral model was constructed, in unconscious cognitive behavioral model for the extraction of design method in line with the user information layout design elements of the unconscious cognition, excavate deeply the information interaction interface design elements that meet user implicit needs, and in turn use design elements to guide the interactive interface design. And summarized the design method requirements and principles of the unconscious information interface interaction design, so that the unconscious cognitive information interface design has a systematic theoretical system as the support.

5 Conclusion

Information interface interaction design is human-centered, and its ultimate goal is to realize unconscious cognitive interaction design, so as to realize information interaction usability and the best user experience. Unconscious cognitive interaction focuses on the study of users' metaphorical needs.

Through the research and analysis of unconscious cognitive theory and cognitive process, it can help designers to find the neglected users' cognitive behaviors. The unconscious cognitive psychological model satisfies the user's psychological experience and makes the information interaction interface become more friendly information transmission medium. In addition to guiding information interface interaction, the theory of unconscious cognition should also be widely used in the design of other system design products that has close interaction with human, which has more development space.

References

1. Xie, W., Xin, X.: Research on interaction design based on unconscious cognition. Mod. Electron. Technol. **39**(12), 22–25 (2016)
2. Xie, W., Xin, X., Ding, J.: Research on human-machine interface interaction design based on eye movement test. Mech. Design **32**(12), 110–115 (2015)
3. Guo, R.: Implicit cognition-the main cognitive mechanism of immersive language teaching. Lang. Teach. Res. **2016**(12), 22–25 (2016)
4. Chang, F.: Usability evaluation of smartphone APP graphical user interface design based on eye tracker. Packag. Eng. **36**(08), 55–59 (2015)
5. Hu, W.: Evolution and reflection of the unconscious concept: from speculation to demonstration. Guangxi Soc. Sci. **2009**(12), 35–39 (2009)
6. Yang, Z., Zhou, Y., Li, L.: Exploration of unconscious cognition. Psychol. Behav. Res. **2003**(03), 161–165 (2003)
7. Zhang, X.: On implicit cognition. Psychol. Explor. **2000**(02), 40–44 (2000)

Understanding Users

Player Needs First: Understanding Player Needs Before Designing a K-pop Themed Mobile Game

Juan Oreste Braga de Oliveira[✉]
and Antonio Felipe Cumaru Inhamuns[✉]

Black River Studios, Sidia, Manaus, Amazonas, Brazil
{juan.braga, felipe.cumaru}@blackriverstudios.com

Abstract. The aim of this paper is to present how the Game User Survey (GUR) was used to develop a Minimum Viable Product (MVP) for a game, which mixes Idle mechanics with a K-pop thematic. Thus, we discuss about how User experience (UX) research approaches can be used to drive the definitions of the project scope and bring the perspective of the user (in this case, the player) to the development process. We used Design Thinking's Double Diamond as a method. In the end, we present the editions learned and deal with this change in the game research paradigm, where the player is called only to validate the decisions made by the development team.

Keywords: User experience · Games user research · Design thinking · User centered design · Mobile games

1 Introduction: The User Experience in the Games Industry

Digital games are products that create experiences. These experiences are the result of collectively objectified symbolic constructions, are individually subjectified by subjective mechanisms of experience, such as: fun, emotion, entertainment, usability, efficiency and satisfaction [1–3].

Unlike traditional software, which has functional interactions as its main purpose, digital games are created with the objective of providing a positive experience, which can stimulate the cognitive and emotional processing of the player [4, 5]. This recreational nature makes the study of games difficult only by the methods used to analyze the functionality or productivity of the *software* in the field of Human-computer Interaction (HCI). This analysis is necessary, but it is not sufficient to guarantee the product success. In order to explore the subjective aspects of gaming experience, the User experience (UX) methods and techniques were chosen as the main source of this work.

There is no consensus on the definition of the term UX. After a detailed literature review, at least four different understandings about this term could be mentioned: i) for the first group of authors, the focus of the UX definition is on its relationship with the product, being possible to measure the user experience through the observation of objective characteristics such as usability, accessibility, utility, for example [12–15]; ii)

© Springer Nature Switzerland AG 2020
M. Kurosu (Ed.): HCII 2020, LNCS 12181, pp. 201–216, 2020.
https://doi.org/10.1007/978-3-030-49059-1_15

the second group believes that the subjective aspects, which result from the interaction between user and product, are relevant points to be observed. For this, they rely on the theory of emotions, which understands the subjective aspects of the user experience as a product of the emotional field [11, 16]; iii) there are authors who define UX as an approach focused on users, in which it is necessary to understand their needs and motivations first in order to develop a usage experience that meets users expectations [1, 10, 17]; iv) finally, a fourth group of authors defends the commercial aspects, such as the value that the product delivers to the user - as well as the convenience and cost of this experience - as something relevant to be considered by the UX professional [18–20]. There are still studies that see the definition of UX as a combination of all of these aspects [21].

However, other authors point out that this dispersion of concepts and the absence of a clear definition impairs its applicability to digital games, when compared to *Player experience* (PX) [2, 8]. For this work, the notion used comprises primarily what the authors of the third group advocate: an approach centered on the user's needs and motivations.

When talking about the mobile games market, it is clear that the popularization of freemium games has brought a greater focus to the user-centered design approaches. In this sense, finding and removing minor problems in the user experience, particularly if detected in advance by UX techniques, can help to create a game capable of engaging and retaining the player through a good gaming experience [22].

In the games field, any aspect that influences the perception and experience of the player is an issue to be investigated by Game User Research (GUR), an emerging field of study that merges the knowledge coming from HCI, Game Development and Experimental Psychology. The purpose of the GUR is to study the relationship between the user (here called player) and the game, using a set of specific UX techniques and tools that aim to evaluate the experience provided by digital games. In this way, it helps to understand motivations, predict actions, meanwhile looking for new ways to collect users' data and apply it into the game design [23–26]. In essence, a GUR work can impact sales, decrease the incidence of failures and increase the potential for user retention [5].

Given this reality, this article aims to share how took place the efforts of GUR, for the definition of the Minimum Viable Product for a mobile game with a *K-pop* thematic and an idle/incremental mechanics. For this, the Design Thinking method [27] was used, divided into four stages: discovery, definition, development and delivery. The first part describes the development context, which makes room for a brief description of the state of the art of GUR in games. The second part of the article presents the concept of the game and the design methodology used in the development. The third part, contemplates discussions about the results found in the methodological stages, emphasizing the challenges and provocations that were revealed. Finally, the work is concluded presenting the results of the tests performed externally and a brief conclusion based on the findings.

2 Project Context: Concerns and Challenges

In the Games industry, the Game Designer is the professional responsible for "designing" the experience that players will have when playing [28]. For that, this professional applies all his knowledge, and sometimes his repertoire of experience as a player, to combine mechanics and rules and thus achieve his goal.

To assess the gaming experience the Game Designer used to run playtests sessions. In the playtest, a representative group of players is observed while playing the game that the game team intends to evaluate. Throughout the playtest, observers (including the Game Designer) take detailed notes on the players' behavior, both inside and outside the game. These notes are compared with the behavioral responses intended by the game designers to the mechanics they developed [29].

The playtest research approach, despite considering the subjective aspects of the gaming experience (such as fun, for example) differs from the UX approach according to how the user is inserted in the development process. While in the playtest, the user is called only to validate Game Design decisions, in the UX approach the user is invited to participate in research that often precedes the development of a playable prototype, in order to understand what is important and, mainly, what it is not, for a certain group of players.

It is necessary to consider technical issues, but also to explore the perspective of the player and his context of use, in order to capture aspects that reflect his relationship with the game, his satisfaction, motivation and the fulfillment of his expectations. Thus, GUR in this project aimed to help the team of game designers to plan and achieve their design goals. In addition, he helped the production team to prioritize and define the scope of the project.

2.1 The Development Team

The scenario in which this project was developed, had two main challenges: the limited human resources running the research and the low maturity of the team regarding UX processes.

The human resource limitation was due to the fact that there was no UX team dedicated solely to this project. The resources were also allocated to parallel projects. Thus, the role of UX designer was in several hands in the development of the game.

Regarding the team's UX maturity, a diagnosis by observation made by the authors of this article, would place the BRS in stage 3, out of 8 possible according to Nielsen's proposal [30]. In turn, Plewes and Chapman [31] put the maximum level of UX maturity at 6. UX maturity in both studies is directly related to the team's knowledge in user-centered design processes, whose goal is to develop high value products with the best user experience.

For both mentioned authors, stage 5 represents a point at which UX efforts are part of an organization's business and marketing requirements. Above level 5, UX design becomes a strategic part, being applied in the broadest possible perspective to drive a consistent user experience.

Both studies report stage 3 in a similar way. At this stage there is an understanding of the organization in relation to the benefits of a design focused on the user experience, in the case of this work, on the player. However, stage 3 reflects some points diagnosed in the BRS organizational culture: i) The work of UX, Game Design and Art occurring in parallel to the work of Engineering, which hurts the good practices and processes of Software Development [32]; ii) users are consulted regularly on many projects (although perhaps not always in the right way or at the right moment to impact design decisions); iii) there is no specific leadership and team for research demands. It is common that there are demands shared with other areas, in the case of Black River Studios, Art. This reflects the human resource limitations mentioned above.

However, the low maturity of UX is not just a Brazilian reality [33, 34]. In the global gaming industry, UX is still a nascent and little-known area. Participation in lectures at international events such as GDC 2019 and Game UX Summit 2018 served as an empirical experience so that we can see that, except for some big players in the market, most companies still have a low maturity with respect to processes and applications of UX. This inference is an induction based on the experience and observation of the authors of this article, as an assessment of UX maturity was not made as suggested by this methodology.

In view of the barriers presented, the scenario for implementing a user-centered approach was unfavorable. Besides the research itself, there was the challenge of improving the team's maturity regarding UX processes. Thus, the challenges reported here concern not only about carrying-out the research and offering outputs or insight for the game development, but also creating a new culture in the Studio. A culture focused on processes that seek to understand the player first, placing him at the center of discussions about the game MVP.

2.2   About the Game

Pyxis is a mobile game developed by Black River Studios, which is an integral part of Sidia, a R&D subsidiary of Samsung, based in Manaus, Brazil. In this context, the studio develops games that explore new technologies and devices produced by Samsung, the majority customer of the Institute. Seasonally, an internal process of selecting possible game ideas is made. In one of these events, the concept of the Pyxis project was presented, whose essence was to merge the K-pop universe with the idle/incremental mechanics. The idea selection was based on monetization potential, marketing trends and audience reach. Currently, Pyxis is in soft launch with an official launch scheduled for this year.

The objective of the game is to evolve a group of K-pop to the level of stratospheric fame. For this, the player must win the fans through the "points of charm". The sets are a representation of the path of fame, for an anonymous young artist to become an Idol (Korean pop celebrity). To assist you in this journey, the player has upgrades, which can be purchased with the game's currency. These upgrades serve as boosts so that the player gets more fans/money and, thus, can progress in the game.

3   Methodology

This project was developed in four stages, non-linear and iterative, using The Design Thinking Double Diamond method. This method is a synthesis of the common approaches and methods used by designers in product and service projects [27]. Knowing that each project involves a series of variables and particularities, the authors of the method invite those who use it to make adaptations.

At the Black River Studios context, this approach proved to be effective when we considered: i) the type of platform, ii) the short window of time for conducting user surveys, and ii) the development team adopts scrum in their projects [35]. Thus, the project development took place in four distinct phases, which are: a) discover; b) define; c) develop and; d) deliver (see Fig. 1).

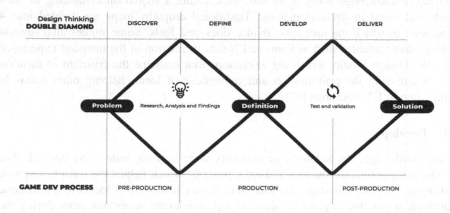

Fig. 1.   Double diamond, adapted to the game development process of Black River Studios.

3.1   Discover

The objective of this stage was to align the team's understanding about the project, develop the first concepts and generate hypotheses to be answered in the next phase. Lasting a week, the team gathered inspirations, insights and research findings. The tools used were: i) CSD Matrix (certainty, assumptions and doubts), tool that organizes what is already known to the team, the hypotheses and assumptions as well as doubts and questions that need immediate response [36], ii) Literature Review, where information on the project's theme was sought from different sources (websites, books, magazines, blogs, papers, etc.). Used to obtain information from other sources - other than users and actors directly involved with the project -, mainly to identify trends in Brazil and abroad, around the theme or similar subjects [37, 38]. Therefore, to improve the structuring of the data, the research was divided into 2 parts: 1) Timeline of events in the K-pop universe; 2) mapping the path for an anonymous young artist to become an Idol.

3.2   Definition

The definition stage aimed to generate opportunities and insights for the project. This stage started with Rapid Ethnography to validate or refute the hypotheses raised in the discovery phase. The divergent results of the initial discoveries were converged on more solid project definitions, to be explored in the next phase. The tools used in this stage were: i) Rapid Ethnography, which are field studies designed to provide a reasonable understanding of users and their activities, due to the limited time in the field of observation [39]. The object of study was the understanding of K-pop by its fans and supporters. The research area was limited to a shopping center in the city of Manaus, which hosted a K-pop event. Organized on the 19th and 20th of January 2019, the K-Weekend [40] had as a draw the solo and group dance competitions, in addition to the booths with merchandising in general; ii) Empathy map, which is a process used to externalize knowledge about users and, thus, create a shared understanding of their needs and assist in decision making. Traditional empathy maps are divided into 4 quadrants, in which the user says, thinks, does and feels. Some studies also suggest adding other variables such as Pains and Needs in relation to the intended experience [41]; iii) Design Studio, which are workshops that combine the criticism of ideation and Design with the prioritization and refinement of ideas, helping other teams to collaborate in UX decisions [42].

3.3   Develop

In the third stage, the solutions or concepts were created, tested and iterated. The development permeated the trial and error process, which helped the team to improve and refine ideas. In this stage, the following were carried out: i) Ideation, a technique that made it possible to generate ideas on top of relevant issues that arose during the previous stages. At this point, it is interesting that several areas are involved, to contribute with different perspectives, which, consequently, makes the final result richer and more assertive [38]. ii) Tests with the user, a qualitative technique that makes use of observations and semi-structured interviews. It was used to collect players' opinions about the art, audio and mechanics of the game. The tests were conducted under the supervision of the UX and Game Design team; iii) Feature sequencer, a technique that assists in the organization and visualization of the functionalities and the incremental delivery sequence of the minimum and viable product, the MVP. In addition to the first MVP, the sequencer assisted in the organization and planning of subsequent deliveries of the game [43].

3.4   Deliver

In this last stage, despite some redefinitions, the game was finalized and delivered for publication in the soft launch model. In this stage, it was carried out: i) Group Interview, a research technique based on collecting qualitative data through the interaction of a group on a theme determined by a researcher/moderator who coordinates and guides the group. The intention of conducting group research is to improve the understanding of how people feel or think about a question, idea, product or service [37].

We emphasize here that the creative process was iterative and incremental. This means that ideas were developed, tested and refined many times, with less consistent ideas being discarded throughout the process. This cycle was essential for the definitions of Game Design, Art and Engineering.

4 Results and Discussions

4.1 Analytical Results of the "Discover" Phase

Starting the work with the CSD Matrix was essential to ensure that the entire development team would be aligned on issues related to the project. This Matrix was built with the certainties, doubts and assumptions of the areas of Art, Engineering, Audio, Q. A., Design and Production, lasting approximately 45 min. Exceptionally, we had the client present at this ceremony. Thus, the assumptions were evaluated and prioritized, with only the most relevant ones being carried out, according to the customer's view. It is worth mentioning that the client's presence speeds up the resolution of the team's doubts and assumptions. At the end of the Matrix, it was found that the team was more confident and aligned about the scope and challenges that the project presented.

We separated the doubts raised in two groups, the first concerning K-pop and the second regarding the consuming public. We started the bibliographic research in an exploratory way, seeking to clarify the doubts related to the thematic axis in question. Therefore, the first findings showed K-pop as a sui generis entertainment product, the result of a series of socio-historical processes in the region of the two Koreas that culminated in the combination of fashion, music and dance with a strong visual and performance appeal [44, 45].

The distinguishing characteristics of K-pop there are: i) the union of elements from hip hop, euro techno, grunge, pop and rap in the songs; ii) the incorporation of contemporary choreographies in the artists' presentations; iii) the creation of song lyrics from the mixture of words in English and Korean; iv) the occasional appearance of Japanese and Chinese onomatopoeia in the songs [46, 47].

K-pop is just one of the elements of Hallyu. Understood by the words "han" for Korea and "ryu" for wave, Hallyu is a term coined to describe the growing global popularity of Korean culture, which includes music, television, films, gastronomy, cosmetics line, etc. [50]. Since modern Korean pop music took shape in the early 1990s, representing the milestone of the 1st generation of this phenomenon, fandoms (fan groups) are now found worldwide, alongside legions of novel aficionados (k-dramas), fashion, movies, food, animations (anime) and Korean games [49, 51].

Naturally, the rules of the game are dictated by the South Korean market. Entertainment agencies understood that the relationship between *Idols* and fans in that country, plays an important role in spreading Korean culture in the rest of the world. In addition, the closeness between fans and *Idols* transcends the physical aspect, creating an emotional bond between them.

Knowing this, the industry works hard on events, promotions, social media, talk shows, variety shows and other public events, in order to explore this connection. In many cases, these fans are treated as assistant producers in strategic decisions. Thus, Idols interact with fans at a level little seen in the Western pop industry, especially the American one. This, of course, creates a much more solid, engaged, profitable and sometimes problematic fan base [46, 47, 58, 59].

Non-Korean fans take on new behaviors as soon as they join K-pop. Initially, their interest in Korean culture comes from the intention to accompany the songs and, soon after, their "bias" (term that refers to the fan's favorite artist). Over time, this ends up influencing the way of acting, thinking, eating and dressing [60, 61]. It is interesting to observe how this group appropriates Korean culture. This behavior is in the context of what scholars call cross-cultural fandoms, characterized by crossing borders between cultures. Thus, the product produced in a cultural context, is reappropriated elsewhere, with another culture [58]. There are studies that contextualize these exchanges as cultural hybridizations. That is, socio-cultural processes in which structures or practices that exist in separate ways, can come together to create new practices, structures and objects [57]. Examples include fanfics, fanzines (magazines), fanfictions (narratives), fanfilms (amateur films or videos), music videos, fanarts (illustrations), spoiling (disclosure of unpublished and/or unofficial information about media content), shipping (cheered by fan favorite couples) and fansubbing (creating subtitles for foreign language content).

Still at this phase, it was run an exploratory interview with a K-pop fan, member of the BTS global fan club. The conversation, which lasted about 1 h, was a key point in the research to understand and clarify the relationship between fans and *K-pop* groups and Idols.

From this interview we started to understand how the relationship of admiration, devotion and love for K-pop, extended to social rituals that went far beyond music. Thus, it was confirmed that to be part of the group of K-pop fans, the individual tends to absorb a certain amount of words, expressions, behaviors, programs and routines. Only by understanding these codes and rituals - or by obtaining that social capital - can the individual be recognized by the group as a kpopper (as K-pop fans are called) [58, 61].

At the end of this first stage of the research, it was realized that the product could not be destined for the South Korean public. Since the specificity of the Asian audience would require a deep immersion from the team, perhaps *in loco,* to understand the nuances of the relationship between South Korean fans and Idols [44, 45]. Of course, travelling to South Korea it was something out of the project scope.

With this understanding, it was possible to assume that the target audience of this project is formed mainly by non-Korean fans. However, it must be considered that different appropriations of *K-pop* emerge according to each country. But at the same time, there are relations of copying attitudes and behaviors with a view to gaining social capital within fandoms.

From all the information and understanding obtained, the following hypotheses were formulated: h1) the main information vehicle is social networks; h2) there is a strong identification with the *Idols;* h3) Kpoppers took notice about K-pop through Japanese culture; h4) K-pop is an element that acts in the construction of the adolescent's identity; h5) consume of products from Japanese culture (*anime*, manga, etc.); h6) consume other products of Korean culture such as *K-dramas*, films, *k-beauty* videos, etc.; h7) Favorite bands are the international top 5 and not the Korean top 5.

4.2   Analytical Results of the Define Phase

The team that went to the field research (see Fig. 2) was composed of three designers and a conceptual artist. It was used a semi-structured questionnaire based on the findings of the previous phase, with closed and open questions. As it was known that K-pop is related to a series of emotional experiences, it was understood that the qualitative approach would offer better results to this project, when compared to a quantitative approach [37]. In addition to testing the hypotheses, the opportunity was taken to present and collect feedback on the concepts of character art developed in parallel with the research.

In the field, it was possible to identify two groups of fans. Group 1, with individuals who experienced the first generation Hallyu, composed of "old fans" (expression mentioned several times during the interviews), aged over 25 years, who essentially consume material from groups of K-pop launched in the period from 2000 to 2012. And Group 2, with individuals who experience the second generation Hallyu, consuming K-pop produced from 2012, represented mainly by teenagers and young adults, aged 13 to 24 years.

Fig. 2. K-Weekend, a 2 day event for K-pop fans in which the field research took in place.

Group 1 has a nostalgic relationship with K-pop, in the sense of remembering experiences from when they were younger. Involvement with the community takes place through organization and participation as jurors in events or just contemplating activities. There is little involvement in online forums, but they still use social networks as the main means of accessing information.

Group 2 has a strong presence on social networks, at events, on online forums etc. A good part of the individuals are part of a dance group, led by a member tasked with learning and transmitting the choreographies to the others. They feel calm when exposing themselves in public, without fear of judgments or prejudices.

Despite the differences, K-pop is a phenomenon that generates a strong bond of friendship and fraternity between supporters, regardless of the generation to which they belong. Fans unite in favor of the popularity of their favorite groups, seeking to increase the fan base. It was also found that there is no space for creations. Covers (imitations of choreographies by large groups) are well valued.

The conceptual arts presented were invalidated by both groups. The characters were associated with the J-pop (Japanese pop music) style, more conceptual and glamorous in relation to K-pop. There was no consensus regarding the definition of the clothing of the K-pop groups, however, the words casual and trend were widely mentioned.

With the understanding acquired so far, it was possible to complete the Definition stage. Three empathy map were created, one based on the first generation of kpoppers and the other two based on the second generation. The empathy map systematically organized the findings of the Discovery and Definition phases of the method, which helped to validate or refute the hypotheses.

The knowledge and insights acquired so far have been converted into opportunities. So, we it was carried out Design Studios workshops, in which a Design team member worked as a facilitator. The Art, Design, Production and Engineering teams participated in this stage. Through co-creation, it was possible to draw features through wireframes, rethink some game design decisions and refine the art of the game.

4.3   Develop Phase Analytical Results

As mentioned earlier, the project's development stage was moving along with the discovery and definition phases. The reason was the urgency to obtain a prototype of medium fidelity of the game, to be presented in the Game Development Conference (GDC), one of the main conferences about electronic games.

Thus, the Art and Engineering teams worked in isolation at various times. The limited scope of this prototype, made most of the opportunities raised so far unfeasible. With that, the application of these would be for another time.

Many feedbacks and insights were obtained during the game's presentation at GDC. In addition, there was a consensus in the team that the prototype was not characterized by the opportunities found and defined in the previous phases. In this sense, several aspects concerning mechanics, art and interactions needed to be refined, reevaluated or removed. What left a stage marked by redefinitions. Not only in the game, but in the team. New members and new understandings made us return to the discovery phase, to review and update the CSD matrix.

Consequently, redefinitions needed to be detailed, measured and prioritized. For this it was used a Feature Sequencer, a technique from method Lean Inception method. Thus, the features were analyzed based on value for the user, development effort and value for the customer. The biggest changes were reflected in the art of the game. Before 2D became 3D, due to the technical feasibility and expertise of the art team that composed the project at that time. In addition, it was designed that the characters should meet archetypes, in order to create connections with the varied profiles of players.

In parallel, a playtest session was organized with K-pop fans and Idle gamers (see Fig. 3). The purpose of the test is was to identify the game's strengths, weaknesses and improvements from the players' perspective. A qualitative approach was used, 12 participants attended to the playtest sessions and the following script was followed: pre-test interview, game session and debriefing.

The playtest main findings were: a) the showtime (rhythm system that offers rewards in game currency the player) was the feature most appreciated by adding an innovative mechanical to an idle/incremental game; b) visuals were well appreciated. It was noticed a homogeneity between UI, VFX, Scenarios and Characters, in the sense that everything seems to be part of the same universe; c) game's songs with second generation references (2NE1, Blackpink, BTS) - mainly influenced by American pop and R&B - offered more insights for the audio to be associated with K-pop; d) K-pop fans and idle/incremental games players have totally different demands. K-pop fans are looking for a fully personalized experience. They would like to customize everything in the game, from the clothes to the songs. Whereas idle games players seek to maximize their winnings.

Fig. 3. Game prototype that was used on playtest sessions.

Despite the differences, it was possible to find similarities between these audiences. There is consensus between the two profiles, about the following: a) skins with boosts and upgrades; b) scenarios where players can see their progress (for example, tours in different countries); c) daily rewards; d) get temporary boosts through video ads; e) seasonal events.

With the findings of this stage and the prioritized redefinitions, the scope of the MVP has been refined. Art, interface and interaction decisions were optimized after new rounds of *Design Studio* workshops with Engineering, Design, Art and Production. The objective here was to build an understanding together, to understand the limits and dependencies of each job, to avoid refractions and to keep the team aligned.

4.4   Analytical Results of the Deliver Phase

At this stage, we return to the discovery stage to revisit some studies. We opted for the Group Interview technique, with two K-pop fans. One of them, a member of the first-generation fan group. And the other, influenced by his younger brother, a member of the new generation of fans. Mediated by two members of the UX team, the objective was to review the hypotheses raised in the definition phase and realign the new members' understanding of the theme. In addition, the ongoing work on the game's conceptual arts and audio has been put under validation. The most relevant findings were: a) regardless of the K-pop generation, the "cute" attribute is present; which validated the concept and proportions of the 3D models of the characters; b) the "box style" concept (which simulates an environment from the perspective of a concert stage), used in the scenarios was strongly validated and associated with VM's (K-pop clips); c) as in the initial interviews, the issue of K-pop clothing is not consensual. However, the use of a unique style of clothing (e.g. high school uniforms) applied under variations according to the archetype of each character proved to be a possibility; d) the songs, created by the audio team, obtained positive feedbacks in general. However, as was found in the playtests, the songs with a sound closer to those of the current generation, with a lot of pop and American R&B influence, were the best evaluated and associated with the K-pop style.

The suggested changes represented a low impact of refraction (compared to the initial phases) and the team embraced and understood the Group Interview as positive. With the data compiled, limits were created in relation to the theme. We used two groups by reference, one more adolescent and the other more adult.

Consequently, game definitions involving the concept of K-pop, need to meet this requirement. In addition, it was defined that the songs should be in accordance with the 2nd generation K-pop, according to the positive data collected both in the playtests and in the group interview. With these findings, it is expected to minimize the uncertainties involved in launching a product for such a specific niche (See Fig. 4).

Fig. 4. The final game interface after receiving all inputs coming from the Research.

5 Conclusion

Creating a game involves complex and intricate decisions. In this context, GUR is a framework that helped us achieve our goals.

Inferring the UX Maturity of Black River Studios development team, even if imprecisely, allowed to design a model with less chance of resistance, according to the reality and profile of the team. As a result, the user-centric approach has shown us that good UX practices go far beyond deliverables of wireframes and comprehensive documentation. The UX approach helped to organize communication between the areas and aligned the understanding of the members. In this way, it was possible to converge knowledge in favor of a more concise MVP that reflects the game's long-term premises. Thus, this research opens room for future projects, both in the sense of evaluating the impacts of the soft launch of this game and in terms of the applicability of GUR in the other projects of BRS to quantify the results of efforts.

However, it was evident that UX is not a role, it is a process under the responsibility of the entire team. Advocating for the best player experience should be a basic premise. In this process, the UX Designer must act as a facilitator. In addition to the organizational sphere, GUR helped bring insights into Game Design, Art and Game Audio, proving to be efficient from the beginning to the current stage of the project.

As for the number of games and products launched daily in the game stores, it can be assumed that considering the user-centered approach is a competitive differential, which may or may not seal the success or failure of a game. This work is expected to encourage provocations and invite enthusiasts and developers to explore new horizons and new approaches in GUR and share them with the community, whether through research or game design. Only then is it possible to build a critical mass and increase the UX maturity of the Brazilian game market as a whole.

References

1. Hassenzahl, M., Tractinsky, N.: User experience - a research agenda. Behav. Inf. Technol. 25(2), 91–97 (2016)
2. Sánchez, J.L.G., Zea, N.P., Gutiérrez, F.L.: Playability: how to identify the player experience in a video game. In: Gross, T., et al. (eds.) INTERACT 2009. LNCS, vol. 5726, pp. 356–359. Springer, Heidelberg (2009). https://doi.org/10.1007/978-3-642-03655-2_39
3. Menezes, F., Silva, I., Frosi, F.: Game user experience (UX): exploring the theory of diegesis. In: 17th SBGAMES Brazilian Symposium on Games and Digital Entertainment on Proceedings, pp 40–48. SBC, Porto Alegre (2017)
4. Pagulayan, R., Keeker, K., Fuller, T., Wixon, D., Romero, R., Gunn, D.: User-centered design in games. In: Jacko, J.A., Sears, A. (eds.) The Human-Computer Interaction Handbook: Fundamentals, Evolving Technologies, and Emerging Applications, pp. 795–822. CRC Press, Boca Raton (2012)
5. Isbister, K., Schaffer, N.: Game Usability: Advancing the Player Experience. CRC Press, New York (2008)

6. Nacke, L.E., Moser, C., Drachen, A., Mirza-Babaei, P., Abney, A., Zhenyu, Z.: Lightweight games user research for indies and non-profit organizations. In: CHI EA 2016 Proceedings of the 2016 CHI Conference Extended Abstracts on Human Factors in Computing Systems, pp 3597–3603. ACM Press, New York (2016)
7. Takatalo, J., Häkkinen, J., Kaistinen, J., Nyman, G.: Presence, involvement, and flow in digital game. In: Bernhaupt, R. (ed.) Evaluating User Experience in Games: Concepts and Methods. Human-Computer Interaction Series, pp. 23–46. Springer, London (2010). https://doi.org/10.1007/978-1-84882-963-3_3
8. Costa, A.F., Nakamura, R.: User experience and player experience: discussion of concepts and their evaluation in the digital games project. In: 15th SBGAMES Brazilian Symposium on Games and Digital Entertainment on Proceedings, pp. 512–517. SBC, Porto Alegre (2015)
9. Law, E.F.C., Roto, V., Hassenzahl, M., Vermeeren, A.P.O.S., Kort, J.: Understanding, scoping and defining user experience: a survey approach. In: CHI 2009 SIGCHI Conference on Human Factors in Computing System on Proceedings, pp 719–728. ACM, New York (2009)
10. Sward, D., Macarthur, G.: Making user experience a business strategy. In: Law, E. (eds.) 21st BCS HCI Group Conference HCI 2007 Towards of a UX Manifesto Workshop, vol. 2, pp. 35–42. BCS, London (2007)
11. Desmet, P.M.A., Hekkert, P.: Framework of product experience. Int. J. Design 1(1), 57–66 (2007)
12. Garret, J.J.: The Elements of User Experience: User Centered Design for the Web. New Riders, Indianapolis (2002)
13. Kuniavsky, M.: Observing the User Experience: A Practitioner's Guide to User Research. Morgan Kaufmann, San Francisco (2003)
14. Morville, P., Rosenfeld, L.: Information for Architecture for the World Wide Web, 3rd edn. O'Reilly Media, Sebastopol (2006)
15. Norman, D., Nielsen, J.: The definition of user experience (UX). https://www.nngroup.com/articles/definition-user-experience/. Accessed 12 June 2019
16. Preece, J., Rogers, Y., Sharp, H.: Interaction Design: Beyond Human-Computer Interaction. Bookman, Porto Alegre (2005)
17. Roto, V.: User experience from product creation perspective. In: Law, E., et al. (eds.) 21st BCS HCI Group Conference HCI 2007 Towards of a UX Manifesto Workshop, vol. 2, pp. 31–34. BCS, London (2007)
18. Cerejo, L.: Creating a hierarchy of user-experience needs. http://www.clickz.com/clickz/column/1696253/creating-hierarchy-user-experienceneeds. Accessed 10 Jan 2019
19. Travis, D.: Why you need a user experience vision (and how to create and publicize it). http://www.userfocus.co.uk/articles/uxvision.html. Accessed 12 June 2019
20. Nyman, N.: The user experience equation. http://www.nnyman.com/personal/2005/11/18/the-user-experience-equation/. Accessed 15 Jan 2019
21. Lopes, E.C.: A (re) vision of the user experience concept: experience as a narrative, monograph of the specialization course in integrated management of digital communication in corporate environments. School of Communications and Arts, University of São Paulo (2012)
22. Tan, M.: Understanding user research: it's not QA or marketing! https://www.gamasutra.com/view/feature/168114/understanding_user_research_its_.php. Accessed 16 Feb 2019
23. El-Nasr, M.S., et al.: Game user research. In: CHI EA 2012 Human Factors in Computing Systems, Extended Abstracts, pp 2679–2682. ACM, New York (2012)
24. Drachen, A., Babaei Pejman, M., Nacke, L.: Games User Research. Oxford University Press, New York (2018)

25. IGDA: SIG spotlight: IGDA games research and user experience SIG. https://www.igda.org/news/news.asp?id=434237&hhSearchTerms=%22User+and+experience%22. Accessed 15 Apr 2019

26. Nayana, C., Ticianne, D., Windson, V.: Analysis of the application of games user research to the evaluation of location-based games. In: 17th IHC Brazilian Symposium on Human Factors in Computer Systems, Extended Proceedings. SBC, Porto Alegre (2018)

27. Design Council: The design process: what is the Double Diamond? http://www.designcouncil.org.uk/newsopinion/design-process-what-double-diamond. Accessed 20 Jan 2019

28. Schell, J.: The Art of Game Design: The Original Book. Elsevier, Rio de Janeiro (2011)

29. GRUX SIG: What is GUR/UX? https://gamesurconf.com/us/what-is-gamesur. Accessed 25 Jan 2019

30. Nielsen, J.: Corporate UX maturity: stages 1–4. http://www.nngroup.com/articles/ux-maturity-stages-1-4. Accessed 18 May 2019

31. Plewes, S., Chapman, L.: A UX maturity model for introducing user experience into the corporate culture. https://www.macadamian.com/learn/introducing-ux-into-corporate-culture/. Accessed 23 Apr 2019

32. Sommerville, I.: Software Engineering, 9th edn. Pearson, São Paulo (2011)

33. Theodoro, G.: The evolution of UX designer in the world of games and the "Designer Unicorn". https://medium.com/@guilhermeteod/. Accessed 06 July 2019

34. Coli: Maturity of the UX market in Brazil in 2017. https://www.infoq.com/br/presentations/matidão-do-mercado-de-ux-no-brasil-em-2017/. Accessed 28 Mar 2019

35. Cumaru, F., Teixeira, N., Braga J.O.: Angest, an absurd game: philosophical reflections on Absurdism inserted in the narrative structure of a game in virtual reality. In: 18th SBGAMES Brazilian Symposium on Games and Digital Entertainment on Proceedings, pp 38–45. SBC, Porto Alegre (2018)

36. Alt, L.: CSD matrix: certainties, assumptions and doubts. http://logobr.org/design-estrategico/matriz-csd/. Accessed 13 June 2019

37. Gil, A.C.: Methods and techniques of social research, 6th edn. Atlas, São Paulo (2018)

38. Silva, M.J.V., Filho, Y.V.S., Adler, I.K., Lucena, B.F., Russo, B.: Design thinking: Business Innovation. MJV Press, Rio de Janeiro (2012)

39. Millen, D.R.: Rapid ethnography. In: Proceedings of 3rd DIS Conference on Designing Interactive Systems Processes, Practices, Methods, and Techniques on Proceedings. ACM, New York (2000)

40. Carvalho, T.H.: Shopping de Manaus receives event for K-Pop fans. https://www.mapinguanerd.com.br/shopping-de-manaus-recebe-evento-para-fas-de-k-pop/. Accessed 18 June 2019

41. Gibbons, S.: The first step in design thinking. https://www.nngroup.com/articles/empathy-mapping/. Accessed 15 June 2019

42. Kaplan: Facilitating an effective design studio workshop. https://www.nngroup.com/articles/facilitating-design-studio-workshop/. Accessed 12 June 2019

43. Carolli, P.: Lean Inception: How to Align People and Build the Right Product. Carolli Editora, São Paulo (2018)

44. Daniel, T.: Korea: The Impossible Country. Tuttle Publishing, North Clarendon (2012)

45. Daniel, T.: A Geek in Korea: Discovering Asia's New Kingdom of Cool. Tuttle Publishing, North Clarendon, VT (2014)

46. Marinescu, V.: The Global Impact of South Korean Popular Culture: Hallyu Unbound. Lexington Books, Lanham (2014)

47. Choi, J.B., Maliangkay, R.: K-pop: The International Rise of the Korean Music Industry. Routledge, Oxon (2014)

48. Todd, D.: History of K-pop. https://www.timetoast.com/timelines/history-of-k-pop. Accessed 15 Jan 2019
49. Mersereau: A brief history of K-pop. https://ontheaside.com/music/a-brief-history-of-k-pop/. Accessed 25 Jan 2019
50. Mente, D.: The Korean Mind: Understanding Contemporary Korean Culture. Tuttle Publishing, North Clarendon (2017)
51. Kwon, E.J., Sintobin, T.M.J.: Korean Wave: discourse analysis on K-pop in US and UK digital newspapers. Master Thesis, Faculteit der Letteren, Specialization in Creative Industries (2017)
52. Benjamin, J.: BTS album earns 2019 Grammy nomination: here's why it's important. https://www.billboard.com/articles/columns/k-town/8489161/bts-2019-grammy-nomination-best-album-packaging. Accessed 15 Jan 2019
53. Souza, R.M.V., Domingos, A.: K-pop: the worldwide spread of South Korean culture. In: Proceedings of 17th INTERCOM Congress of Communication Sciences in the South Region on Proceedings, pp 1–14. Intercom, São Paulo (2016)
54. Koreaboo: 9 Things every trainee MUST Go through before they can debut. https://www.koreaboo.com/lists/9-steps-every-trainee-must-go-prior-debut. Accessed 25 Mar 2019
55. Amaral, A., Tassinari, L.: Cross-cultural fandoms: appropriations in the shipping practices of Brazilian K-POP fans on Facebook. Vozes e Diálogo 1(15) (2016)
56. Bourdieu, P.: The Distinction. Social criticism of the trial. Edusp, São Paulo (2008)
57. Canclini, N.G.: Hybrid Cultures: Strategies for Entering and Exiting Modernity, 2nd edn. Edusp, São Paulo (1998)
58. Chin, B., Morimoto, L.H.: Towards a theory of transcultural fandom. Participat.-J. Audience Recept. Stud. 1(10), 92–108 (2013)
59. Tai, C.: The K-pop superfans who can make, and break, musical careers in South Korea. https://www.scmp.com/culture/music/article/2136573/k-pop-superfans-who-can-make-and-break-musical-careers-south-korea. Accessed 02 Mar 2019
60. Mizumi: Understanding the K-pop idol fan culture. https://medium.com/@isu.mizumi/understanding-the-kpop-idol-fan-culture-b65baea82ec4. Accessed 25 Jan 2019
61. Silva, L.F., Bonfim, M.V.J.: Public Relations and fan culture: study of the behavior of Brazilian K-pop fans on the internet. Leopold.: J. Stud. Commun. Catholic Univ. Santos 123 (44), 49–65 (2018)

Yayy! You Have a New Notification: Co-designing Multi-device Locative Media Experiences with Young People

Dan Fitton[1]([⊠]) [ID], Keith Cheverst[2] [ID], and Janet C. Read[1] [ID]

[1] Child-Computer Interaction Research Group, University of Central Lancashire,
Preston, UK
{DBFitton, JCRead}@UCLan.ac.uk
[2] School of Computing and Communications, InfoLab21, Lancaster University,
Lancaster, UK
kc@comp.lancs.ac.uk

Abstract. This paper explores the involvement of young people in the design of mobile technologies that provide locative media experiences. The specific focus of this work was to understand how multiple devices (phones, tablets and smart watches) could be used within this context. Young people are prolific early adopters and users of mobile technologies. The motivation for involving your people was to gain insights into their ideas and preferences for multi-device usage within the context of locate media experiences. In this work we utilised a design technique specifically developed for use with young people in two design sessions. The designs were analysed in order to gather design insights for mobile technologies providing locative media experiences, and understand the use of multiple devices within the designs created. The key contributions of this work is design insights gathered from young people along with more general findings from running of the design sessions.

Keywords: Children · Child-Computer Interaction · Co-design · Cross-device · Engagement techniques · Locative Media Experiences · Mobile interaction · Teenagers

1 Introduction and Background

The number of available mobile apps continues to grow at an explosive rate: in 2013 the Google Play and the Apple App Store had approximately 750 thousand apps each available for download [1], and by 2015 the number surpassed 1.5 million [43]. Many of these app are location aware [15] and a growing number are aimed at children in both education and entertainment contexts. Apple launched a 'Kids' category in its app store which contains more than 80 thousand apps [47]. Young people are growing up in a digital world awash with new technologies [4, 26, 29] where it is ever more important that we design for them as primary users of technology [20]. The aim of the work presented here was to explore the design of Locative Media technologies with young people, children and teenagers, across a range of different devices (phones, tablets and smart watches). Broadly, the term Locative Media [17, 21] refers to digital media

© Springer Nature Switzerland AG 2020
M. Kurosu (Ed.): HCII 2020, LNCS 12181, pp. 217–233, 2020.
https://doi.org/10.1007/978-3-030-49059-1_16

bound to a specific physical location which is delivered to a mobile device dependent upon the user's location. Previous co-design work relating to Locative Media Experiences (LMEs) has focused primarily on adults e.g. [3, 8]. The design of LME technologies for young people is an underexplored research, especially in the context of different mobile device formats. This paper makes several contributions within this space, firstly the paper presents a set of design insights helpful to other researchers and practitioners designing LME technologies for young people together with the device formats they apply to. Secondly, the paper provides insights into the preferences for different device types within the designs created across two age groups (7–10 and 12–13 years). Finally, the paper highlights the potential usefulness of the specific design technique and following design analysis technique when working with young people. The remainder of this paper discusses related work, the design sessions with two age groups, an analysis of the results and finally a discussion and conclusion.

2   Related Work

2.1   Co-design with Young Children and Teenagers

The last 20 years have seen an explosion in the availability and range of technology for children and as such their adoption of technology has evolved rapidly [28]. There is no doubt that these technologies have changed the landscape of childhood forever [19]. [5] reports that young children are more likely to master technology skills quicker than life skills. Indeed of the 2–5 year olds age group, 70% (in the UK) can play a computer game, while only 43% can ride a bike and 10% can use a smartphone application while only 9% can tie their shoelaces. Further, [5] say that 62% of 10–13 year olds have online presence on social sites such as Facebook and Twitter. More recently [6] reported that 46% of children aged 6–9 play online virtual games, and 16% have a Facebook profile, despite the official age for opening an account being 13. For this reason, it is ever more important that we design for children and teenagers as primary users of technologies, and do this in such a way that is engaging and appropriate for them. Designing for and with children has been a focus of the Interaction Design and Children research community since 2003. Including children as 'design partners' in the design of new and novel technologies is regarded as beneficial for acquiring a better understanding of their use, gathering design ideas and testing out new concepts [9, 37, 42].

As the likes, dislikes, curiosities and requirements differ so greatly between children and teenagers [10, 11, 30], it is often challenging to include them throughout the design process, and special consideration is needed [38]. Further, [32] suggested that children often have difficultly verbalising their thoughts; however over the past decade, there have been huge advances in Child-Computer Interaction and thus, many techniques have been suggested for assisting children and teenagers in design activities where new technologies for them are being developed. Often, such techniques relate to a Participatory Design approach which refers to the involvement of intended users of the technology, as having a critical role as informants in the design of it [18, 39]. The early work by Druin [9] on Cooperative Inquiry brought the idea of engaging children in participatory design to the wider HCI community, methods for engaging children in design are becoming increasingly specialised: for example involving children conversing with aliens [7]. In Fig. 1 [33] present a model for balancing participation amongst experts and intended users.

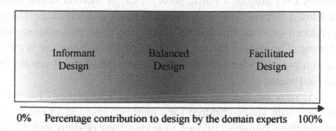

0%   Percentage contribution to design by the domain experts   100%

Fig. 1. IBF model for describing participatory design as a continuum along these modes [33]

One such technique highly relevant to this paper is the Primed Design Activity (PDA) method presented in [14] which discusses the use of scenario sketches and sticky notes for scaffolding design sessions. The technique is particularly relevant to this work as it supports young people in designing mobile apps across multiple different contexts. Adults here are responsible for deciding how to scaffold the design sessions, though they are careful to emphasise that adults are to act as facilitators during the actual session, such as not to impose their ideas on the designs. Achieving this balance between scaffolding sessions and reducing potential bias is highlighted on the IBF Model (see Fig. 1) by [33] which shows the influence of adults in the design process. In more detail, [33] identify three modes of participation in design sessions; informant, balanced and facilitated where i) informant design assumes the design is realised mostly by the design experts, ii) balanced design assumes an equal partnership between the design and domain experts in realising designs, and iii) facilitated design assumes the domain expert (in this case, the school children) takes the lead in designing, with the design expert as a facilitator. They conclude that the IBF model is useful for appropriating participation between design experts (e.g. adults) and domain experts (e.g. children).

The Bluebells [24] design method aims to balance child-centred design with expert design by also using scaffolding techniques for their design sessions. They present three interweaving stages for inclusion and exclusion of children in the design process. These stages are: Before play, During play and After play and are described, respectively, as i) initial fact finding by adults, ii) four design activities with children and iii) adults constructing prototypes. Importantly, the acknowledgement of the constraints of real world product development is reflected strongly in this method. There is an appropriate balance of participation between the design team developing ideas and the end users (in this case children) having timely participation in the design process.

The Warp Speed Design approach to designing tangible games with children aged 9+ is presented in [34]. As a fast-track approach to designing, Warp Speed Design comprises three stages. These are: i) Learning and Idea creation where the researcher acts out a prototype of a game, ii) Children as Interaction Designers where the children plan the activities in the game using pre-prepared worksheets, and iii) Children as Game Designers where even more detail is added, resulting in an almost complete specification for a game. This approach was effective in generating a range of ideas and encouraging team work.

The authors of [31] present a Participatory Design method called Comicboarding which utilises known formats and characters in comics to elicit ideas. The results show that even the children unaccustomed to brainstorming generated as many ideas as those who loved drawing. The authors further suggest that Comicboarding is most useful at a stage in the design process where researchers are confident about certain decisions but want more detailed ideas.

Lastly, in [45] they discuss the use of 'Layered Elaboration' for iteratively generating design ideas with young children for a history game and an energy conservation game. This approach encourages children to revisit their designs and, by using a layer of overhead transparencies, they could add to the ides without destroying earlier design work. They find that the children enjoyed adding to previous designs and presenting their ideas during a group discussion. They conclude that this approach is particularly useful where space and resources are limited. This is due to the portability of the stackable storyboards (which are no bigger than an A4 sheet of paper) and the iterative nature of the technique which allows a number of design partners to provide ideas in a short amount of time.

2.2   Locative Media and Locative Media Experiences

The term Locative Media was coined by Karlis Kalnins in 2003 [17] and denotes the combination of location sensing technologies, such as GPS, with various media [21] that is bound to a specific geographical location. 'Locative' is a grammatical category that conveys location as 'in' or 'next to' [25]. The definition by [2] is pertinent to this paper:

"The locative media that is of most immediate concern is that made by those who create experiences that take into account the geographic locale of interest, typically by elevating that geographic locale beyond its instrumentalized status as a 'latitude longitude coordinated point on earth' to the level of existential, inhabited, experienced and lived place. These locative media experiences may delve "into" the historical surface of a space to reveal past events or stories (whether fictional, confessional or standing on consensus as factual)"

The growing popularity of GPS equipped mobile technologies has allowed for a user's presence in a particular space to be relevant in mobile apps [12]. Such apps have served to increase the opportunity for Locative Media Experiences (LMEs) which track a user's geographic position and return information based on this.

The earliest example of a LME, dating from 2002 (pre-dating the locative media term), is the '34 North 118 West' project (http://34n118w.net/). The project used GPS technology connected to mobile devices to provide users with audio narratives relating to places (and their associated history) as different areas in Los Angeles were encountered.

Further, one of the most widely documented LMEs is the Riot! 1831 experience by [40, 41] which, like the '34 North' project, utilises location-based triggering of content to push audio media to the user as they walk around a public square in the city of Bristol. The study discussed in [41] implies the fact that the riots took place in that actual location contributed significantly to authenticity and the reported user enjoyment of the experience, and further to the sense of immersion experienced by a father and son [40].

Similarly, the authors in [16] describe their study of an LME relating to the historic events in the city of Nottingham. The LME pushes audio narratives to the user, based on their sensed location, as they explore the city. Results show users appreciated listening to spoken narratives and being able to relate them to real locations around the city in order to appreciate historic events.

In [3] the authors describe the development of LMEs using the SHARC framework and, in particular, the development of an LME relating to the cultural heritage for a rural village community.

The aforementioned experiences have been designed by adults, with adults in mind as the primary target users. Further, a great deal of the applications that are intended for children (see for example [44]) are typically designed by adults who often are far from knowing exactly what young users want and need from the technology [28]. In this example, [44] provides a study involving Kurio - a museum guide for families. Although results are positive in engaging children with exhibits (etc.), the actual experiences themselves were designed and created by the researchers based on what they thought the children might want. Contrastingly, the Chawton House project [46] is an example of a project where an experience was designed using a co-design approach with the intended audience of use. In this case, teachers and young children (aged 10–11) were key informants of the design, which resulted in a highly relevant experience for the school children.

3   Method

Two design workshops were carried out in two different schools in the UK, in both cases the MESS Days approach [23] was used where a class circulated between different research studies at intervals. The workshops took place on different days in November and December 2015. The Primed Design Activity (PDA) technique [14] was used for both sessions, whereby the design activities were scaffolded with information sheets, prompting questions and a 'scenario sketch' sheet depicting a usage scenario onto which designs were placed using adhesive notes. In total, 34 children and teenagers (25 Boys and 9 Girls) from the two schools contributed their design ideas.

The aim of each session was to gather ideas from the intended audience of use (in this case, children and teenagers) for an educational and recreational LME for young people. We aimed to generate ideas for a child-friendly LME that increases engagement when visiting, for example, historical sites while on a school trip or family outing.

3.1   Participants

The first school that participated in the study was a primary school. Pupils from the school's computer club were selected by the school to take part and in total 20 children (aged 7–10 years) from four year groups contributed their design ideas. The second school that participated in the study was a High School where 14 pupils, aged 12–13, from one year group contributed their design ideas during their scheduled design and technology class. In both cases the class teacher selected the pupils that took part in the studies and organised the children into groups.

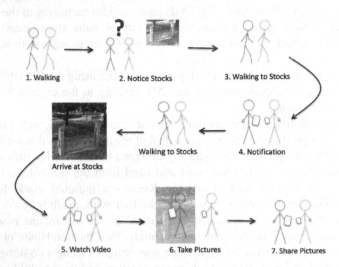

Fig. 2. Scenario Sketch showing a scenario of children noticing the stocks and interacting with technologies to find out more information.

3.2 Apparatus

Each design session was facilitated with a pre-printed A3 scenario sketch depicting a usage scenario (see Fig. 2).

The 'scenario sketch' used in both studies depicted a simplified LME in which two children on a school field trip notice some stocks (historically used as a form of public humiliation punishment) and walk over to them. As they approach the stocks they are notified that there is a video associated with them which they watch on arrival then take pictures of the stocks and share them. Short instructions were provided at each point in the scenario, to assist the children in their understanding of the task. Arrows, text and pictures were used to guide participants through the scenario.

Three different sized Post-it notes were used to represent the three different devices that the children could choose to design for: small, medium and large post-it notes representing a smart-watch, smart-phone and tablet device, respectively. See **Error! Reference source not found.** on the next page as an example utilising a combination of the three sized post-it notes.

The worksheet first required participants to decide at which points in the scenario they would interact with technology, then what technology this would be (phone, tablet or watch), and then design the user interface on an appropriately sized post-it note to be placed on the scenario sketch. The following sub-section provides more detail.

3.3   Procedure

At the start of each design session, the entire group were given an introduction to the work. They were told: i) their designs would be used to assist future research and development of LMEs for young people, ii) that their designs would be considered fairly, but that it was not possible to use all of their ideas, and iii) that they could withhold their designs at the end if they desired (although no pupil did so). All pupils were given an opportunity at this point to ask questions. All assented verbally to taking part and institutional ethical approval was given for carrying out the studies.

The group were asked by one of the researchers to split into pairs, or work individually if desired, and the researchers talked through the worksheet and the types of technology they could design for. The groups were asked about which technologies they were most familiar with - all said they were familiar with a smart-phone (most said they owned one themselves); a majority of the group were familiar with a tablet (either having their own or having played on their parents); very few of the group were familiar with smart-watches (some had seen their parents use one but not actually use it themselves). One of the researchers also asked the group what they use these devices for. Mainly this was for watching videos and playing games. The researchers had a tablet, phone and smart watch to use as props during the introduction and were careful to ensure participants understood the capabilities of a typical smart watch as this was likely to be the most unfamiliar technology.

The pupils were free to choose the technologies used in their designs and researchers were careful not to influence this. Groups had approximately 20 min to work through the scenario, and were told to first read through the scenario and put a star at the points where they envisioned interacting with technology. They were then asked to draw, on the appropriate sizes Post-it note, what they thought the user-interface should look like at each point, and stick them onto the scenario in the place where the interface would be shown. They also annotated their Post-it notes so the researchers could understand them during later analysis.

Researchers were on hand to check the pupils were making progress and to answer any questions. Researchers occasionally probed pupils about their designs to i) help participants expand or better articulate their thoughts or ii) to help interpret what they had drawn, particularly at the primary school where the children found it more difficult to articulate their ideas and annotate their designs.

At the end of the session the groups were asked to talk through their designs then thanked for their time. The researchers noted the age and gender of the groups for later analysis and also made note of any key quotes and comments the participants provided.

3.4   Analysis and Results

Analysis of the designs closely followed the TRAck method discussed in [39] which allows a large sets of designs from young people to be considered by focussing on the key ides conveyed within each design and 'winning' ideas to be democratically chosen. This method was chosen to ensure that all designs were considered equally and from them a set of the most interesting ideas derived in a rigorous way.

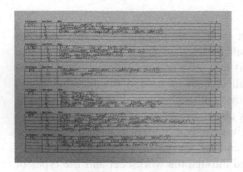

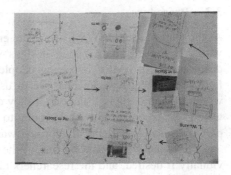

Fig. 3. A completed TRAck Reporting Sheet for designs generated from the PD sessions, the sheet shows the ideas identified within the designs and selections made.

Fig. 4. Completed 'Scenario' worksheet by two high school pupils - showing three different sized post-it notes for the designs for the three technologies and a 'winning' idea of spatial directions to a POI.

Three researchers (two experts in Child-Computer Interaction and one Computer Science PhD Student), all of whom were present during the design sessions, individually examined every design using the TRAck process. A example TRAck recording sheet is shown in Fig. 3.

The TRAck sheet comprised a table with the following headings: i) participant group code (p1–p11 for the primary school group and h1–h7 for the high school group), ii) idea number (a maximum of 5 were allowed per design), and iii) a brief description of the idea found in the design.

In total, 18 designs were generated; however two designs (from the high school group) were incomplete and returned with no interface designs or annotations. Thus, only 16 of the 18 designs were analysed.

Firstly, closely following the TRAck 1:1 process, each design was carefully analysed for a maximum of five candidate ideas to be taken forward to the next stage (recorded on the reporting sheets). From these candidate ideas one is selected from each participant group, in order to be democratic. The evaluators then compared their selected ideas and agree on an overall set of 16 ideas based on popularity.

Next, following TRAck n:n, each evaluator analysed their list of candidate ideas again, but this time selected 16 ideas from any of the designs (not necessarily one from each participant group). Again the evaluators compared their selected ideas and agreed a final set of 16 ideas. It was this final set of ideas that were used to derive the design insights.

Figure 4 shows a completed worksheet with different sized Post-it notes representing the three different technologies. This design also contained a the idea of providing spatial directions to a Point of Interest (POI), such as 'Look left' or 'Walk 10 yards left'.

This 2-stage TRAck process ensured that all (complete) designs were considered during analysis and that if any designs contained more than one valuable idea, these ideas were not lost. This was the case for five designs from which more than one idea was selected for the final list of idea.

Table 1. 16 design insights obtained from analysis of the design ideas, examples of participants ideas drawn in the designs and the device which it was designed for (W: Smart-watch, P: Smart-phone; T: Tablet)

Design Insight	Example from the designs	Device designed for
Spatial directions to a POI	'Stocks Left', 'Walk 10 yards left', 'Stocks nearby!'	W
Perspective Image of POI	Show an image of stocks so I know what to look for	W
Retro notification icons	Big i icon to show I have a notification Camcorder icon to show I have a video to watch	W – P
Photo editing	I can crop it and add filters like Snapchat	P – T
Personalising sound notifications	Choose the tune what I want and change it in the settings	P – W
Option to accept or decline a notification (for information)	Get a message which I can choose to look at or not before it shows on the phone	W
Watch notification prior to showing the information on phone or tablet	Tell me before I get to the stocks then show me the video when I get there	W
Quiz as a fun way of testing how much information you remember	Stocks quiz at the end so I can test what I've learnt	P – T
Multi-media for presenting information	'Watch a video instead of reading lots of text that's boring' Animations and Diagrams as well as the text	T – P
Hints rather than actual directions to get to the next POI	'Look Left'	W
Consistent interface across all 3 devices	'So I can easily switch and watch the video on a bigger screen then go back to the watch to see where to go next'	W - P - T
'More Info' button or link	www link 'to show me more stuff'	P
Game related to POI	Stocks game called 'Super Stock Rescue' where you throw things at people in the stocks Karate chop stocks game	T – P
Summary of POI on Watch	Show me a little bit on the watch then all of it on phone	W
Sharing via social media	Facebook, Twitter, Instagram and Snapchat icons Want to tell my friends 'look at what I'm doing'	P – T
A 'Photo in History'	Add filters to a photo so it looks like I'm in the Stocks	P

4   Results

The 16 final ideas identified from the analysis are presented in Table 1 as design insights. The ideas highlight new ways of displaying information, when compared to how information might be displayed for adults; the children and teenagers here showed enthusiasm for playing games and watching videos to learn information about the stocks - contrasting with text-based information which is likely to be the preferred choice for adults.

Considering Table 1 and Table 2, it is clear to see the interconnections between the different technologies and the participants desire to use a LME across multiple devices at the same time - and further the need to have consistent information displaying on all of the devices being used at that time.

Table 2. Number of designs created by each group for each of the technologies: Smart-watch (W), Smart-phone (P) and Tablet (T) where Pn represents primary school children and Hn represents high school pupils.

		W	P	T	P–T	W–P–T
P1	B8	0	2	0	0	0
P2	G8	2	1	0	0	0
P3	B10 B10	2	0	1	2	0
P4	B9 B9	0	2	2	2	0
P5	B11 B7	1	6	1	0	1
P6	B8 B10	0	4	0	0	0
P7	B10 G8	4	4	3	0	0
P8	B7 G10	1	5	2	0	0
P9	B10 B9	1	2	1	0	0
P10	B10 B10	5	0	0	0	0
P11	B10 G9	0	2	1	0	0
		6	**28**	**11**	**4**	**1**
H1	G12 G13	4	5	4	0	0
H2	G12 G13	1	4	1	0	0
H3	B12 B12	–	–	–	–	–
H4	B13 B11	–	–	–	–	–
H5	B12 B13	3	5	0	0	0
H6	B12 B12	6	3	1	0	0
H7	B12 B13	3	2	1	0	0
		18	**22**	**7**	**0**	**0**

All pupils used multiple post-it notes to convey their ideas and most provided textual descriptions to accompany their designs. Looking at Table 2 it is clear to see that the participants designed across multiple devices, and the spread of designs across the three technologies is interesting; while it was expected that the pupils would primarily design for smart-phones (due to their familiarity with this device), most groups also designed for a smart-watch (12 of 16 groups, with one primary school group designing solely for the smart-watch). Further, the few designs for a tablet device is surprising since this was the next most popular device amongst pupils when questioned at the start of the session. However, one boy aged 9 commented that he 'wouldn't use a tablet - too big to carry around' and similarly a boy aged 13 commented he would prefer to use a smaller device such as the smart-watch to avoid having to keep taking the tablet out of his bag (see Fig. 5). Comments were added to the designs by a researcher at the end of the session.

Reflecting on comments provided by some of the pupils from the high school, the smart-watch likely falls into the 'RICH' category of cool [36] due to its desirability and connotations of 'having a lot of money to spend' if you own this device. Table 2 supports this in that, a higher proportion of high school pupils designed for the smart-watch compared to the primary school children.

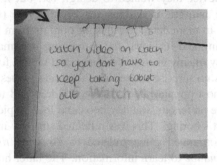

Fig. 5. Comment about the size of the devices, provided by a high school group, and recorded by a researcher at the end of the session. H7 is the classification of the design as group 7 in the high school group.

Table 2 shows the number of post-it notes on each design that relate to the different technologies; in the cases where groups created one post-it design, but associated it with more than one technology, a new column was added to the results table. Further, B & G in column 2 represent the gender of group members, while the numbers represent their ages. We note here that, although most groups annotated their designs with a W, P or T to highlight specifically what technology their design was intended for, several post-it notes did not have labels and thus we categorised them based solely on the size of the post-it note.

5   Discussion

PDA proved a suitable Participatory Design technique to adopt for this work. It was effective in engaging young people in design activities, evidenced through the level of detail in the designs produced by a majority of the primary and high school groups (in total 16/18), and also effective in generating quality designs from which the researchers extracted a number of valuable design ideas. Further, our study showed that the PDA approach is adaptable to different age groups; we used it in two studies involving young people ranging from 7 to 13 years old, and as research shows [13], the motivations, values and understandings even in such a small age gap are significant and each require specific attention. The study also highlighted the flexibility of the PDA approach for effectively capturing a range of ideas across different age groups where their understanding and appropriateness of technologies may differ. We note that the scenarios sketch worksheets highlights a trade-off; the worksheets allowed the participants to understand the scenario quickly and easily, but made the design task relatively prescriptive, relying on the scenario to be representative of a generalised usage scenario for the intended app.

Using post-it notes that ranged in size from small, medium and large to represent the increasing interface sizes of a smart-watch, smart-phone and tablet device (respectively) worked effectively. Indeed, not only were the children and teenagers easily able to choose which device they wanted to design for, but it made it easier for the researchers to tally the number of designs for each device (see Table) during the analysis of the designs. In more detail, the design outputs from the participants of this study provided interesting and fun ideas for conveying information about the stocks. All participants said they mainly use smart-phones and tablets for watching videos and playing games so it was no surprise to see that video and games as ways of conveying information were the most popular amongst the children and teenagers; one primary school child said how he prefers to 'watch videos and look at pictures' rather than read lots of text because 'that's boring'. This was reflected strongly in their designs where a majority of groups incorporated games related to *throwing things at people in the stocks* and videos *on Youtube* to learn information. The latter however may have been influenced by the design of the scenario worksheet and the explicit instruction of 'Watching a Video' after arriving at the stocks. Another interesting idea that had not previously been considered, and which emerged from the designs was the idea of a *Photo in History* where the children can take a photo of themselves in the Stocks using a filter. One comment relating to this from one of the teenage participants was *"Like you can on Snapchat"*.

Fig. 6. Examples of options for sharing pictures to social media platforms.

Moreover, even though no participants said they had used a smart-watch before, and only five in total said they had seen them being used by a family member, the smart-watch was the second most popular device to design for (below smart-phones). We speculate they designed for this device because of the novelty of it and the 'cool' connotations it possesses. One pupil from the High School group expressed how he wanted a smart-watch so that he could *"impress his friends because it would show that [he] is rich"*. While [36] and [22] discuss their studies of 'cool' with respect to teenagers, our study also exposed that the young children here also like the idea of being 'cool' amongst their friends. For example, during the design session, one boy, aged 9, asked if he could *"wear our smart-watch during break-time to show off to his friends"*.

Adding to this notion of 'cool', specifically in the group of teenagers from the High School is the idea of being able to share via social media, which features a lot in their designs - specifically the Facebook, Snapchat and Twitter logo appeared in their designs (See Fig. 6). A comment from one of the teenage participants suggests that it is *"cool to show my friends the photo of me in the stocks like 'look what I'm doing"*.

When considering the technological feasibility of the designs for each of the three devices, it became evident that the participants had little knowledge of the smart-watch. Many of the designs for the watch were ambiguous and not technologically feasible, yet. For example, one pair of primary school children designed entirely for the watch and included ideas such as playing a throw things at me in the stocks game; watching a video on YouTube; viewing a map to see [my] location; and reading text information about the stocks. In addition, one child also commented that "videos should show on my watch to avoid taking out a tablet because it's too big to carry round". This is in comparison with the designs for the smart-phone and tablet devices which were of a much higher quality and more appropriate for the functionalities. This was expected since all participants expressed their familiarity with these technologies at the start of the session.

Furthermore, several groups designed for cross-device interactions. While not all designs here conformed to existing functionalities of the technologies, the ideas behind the designs were of great value and clearly underpin the idea of multi-device applications. One 'winning' idea brought forward from a design shows the desire to have consistent user-interfaces across all three devices to make it easier to work with. Though possibly not feasible yet, this highlights that, where a LME is being consumed across the watch, phone and tablet at the same time, the interface and information should be consistent for clarity and ease of use among children and teenagers.

A key area for future study is reducing the ambiguity inherent in the designs and assisting the later analysis of designs. One possibility would be to have the children to use appropriate wire framing tools such as Balsamiq. However, this would require training the participants to use the software in advance, which was not possible in the case of this study, and may have impacted what was designed.

In terms of limitations of our study, analysis of the designs highlighted a trade-off with using a scenario worksheet to better facilitate the session and generate higher quality design ideas. This could have potentially biased design decisions through the use of specific visual hints, and also simplifying the usage scenario for the intended app. In addition, due to the unfamiliarity of smart-watches and its functionality, the designs for this device are not an accurate representation of a smart-watch and so cannot be fully acknowledged as a cross-device LME. We can improve on this by performing more studies in two or three years time where young people are likely to have a greater familiarity with a smart-watch (or other wearable devices). Further, the design sessions were not recorded and thus no transcripts are available for analysis. This was mainly because: i) it is often difficult to capture transcripts in this type of session (a large group of people in a noisy environment), ii) we did not have sufficient voice recording equipment available at the time to record each individual pairing in the group, iii) the noisy environment would permit good quality sound leading to a time-consuming analysis where researchers try to make sense of the captured data, and iv) ethical issues with capturing data from children. Researchers made comments on the designs once they had been handed in, however some comments and quotes from the children are likely to have been missed. Also, we did ask the participants to present their designs at the end of the session, so in the future we will consider video recording this if possible, to help aid analysis.

6 Conclusion

This paper is the first to explore the design of locative media applications across multiple mobile device formats with young people, furthermore the design technique used allowed participants to show how their designs reacted in different contexts. The outputs from two design sessions with 34 young people, aged 7–14 years, were used to identify 16 design insights for researcher or practitioners wishing to develop technologies that provide LMEs across multiple mobile devices (phones, tablets and smart watches). The PDA technique was used in the design sessions, it helped the participants grasp the unfamiliar concept of a LME, evident through the output of quality design ideas relating to a history-based experience. The scaffolding used in the PDA technique should be considered a trade-off: while it allowed appropriate designs to be created in a short period of time the designs were situated in a closely specified scenario of use. The TRAck approach was used to analyse the designs was helpful in providing a structured and efficient way to consider the ideas evident in all of the 16 designs.

Further analysis of the devices used in each of the designs highlighted a strong preference for phone and smart watch devices and revealed very little evidence for participants considering the use of multiple devices within the same scenario. For many participants the smart-watch was a new and novel device form-factor. It was motivating to observe the enthusiasm of the participants to design for this device; we speculate that this was the case due to the 'cool' traits associated with it. While their designs included some ideas that are not yet feasible in terms of existing functionalities of the smart-watch, they present exciting ways of receiving notifications or viewing information and provide valuable insights into how young people desire to interact with such technologies. We hope that others will find the insights presented here useful in inspiring aspects of their own designs, and also be motivated to consider working with young people through participatory techniques such as PDA.

References

1. App Figures: App Stores Growth Accelerates in 2014 (2015). http://blog.appfigures.com/app-stores-growth-accelerates-in-2014/
2. Bleecker, J., Knowlton, J.: Locative media: a brief bibliography and taxonomy of GPS-enabled locative media. Leonardo Electron. Almanac **14**(3), 24 (2006)
3. Cheverst, K., Turner, H., Do, T., Fitton, D.: Supporting the consumption and co-authoring of locative media experiences for a rural village community: design and field trial evaluation of the SHARC2.0 framework. J. Multimed. Tools Appl. 1–32 (2016)
4. Colwell, J., et al.: Reflective Teaching in Early Education. Bloomsbury Publishing, London (2015)
5. Digital Diaries: A look at how technology affects us from birth onwards (2010). http://www.avg.com/digitaldiaries/2010
6. Digital Diaries: Digital diaries explores how technology is changing childhood and parenting around the world (2014). http://www.avg.com/digitaldiaries/2014
7. Dindler, C., Eriksson, E., Iversen, O.S., Lykke-Olesen, A., Ludvigsen, M.: Mission from Mars: a method for exploring user requirements for children in a narrative space. In: Proceedings of 2005 Conference on Interaction Design and Children, pp. 40–47 (2005)
8. Do, T., Cheverst, K.: The SHARC framework: utilizing personal dropbox accounts to provide a scalable solution to the storage and sharing of community generated locative media. In: EICS 2015, pp. 190–199 (2015)
9. Druin, A., Stewart, J., Proft, D., Bederson, B., Hollan, J.: KidPad: a design collboration between children, technologists, and educators. In: Proceedings of CHI 1997. ACM Press (1997)
10. Druin, A.: The Design of Children's Technology. Morgan Kaufmann, Burlington (1999)
11. Druin, A.: The role of children in the design of new technology. Behav. Inf. Technol. **21**(1), 1–25 (2002)
12. Finan, S.: This must be the place: the importance of place in portable digital media. MSc. University of Dublin (2013)
13. Fitton, D., Read, J., Horton, M., Little, L., Toth, N., Guo, Y.: Constructing the cool wall: a tool to explore teen meanings of cool. PsychNol. J. **10**(2), 141–162 (2012)
14. Fitton, D., Horton, M., Read, J.: Scaffolding design sessions with teenagers: the PDA approach. In: Extended Abstracts CHI 2014, pp. 1183–1188. ACM Press (2014)
15. Frith, J.: Smartphones as Locative Media. Polity Press, Cambridge (2015)
16. FitzGerald, E., Taylor, C., Craven, M.: To the castle! A comparison of two audio guides to enable public discovery of historical events. Pers. Ubiquit. Comput. **17**(4), 749–760 (2013)
17. Galloway A., Ward, M.: Locative media as socialising and spatialising practices: learning from Archaeology. Leonardo Electron. Almanac **14**(3) (2006)
18. Gregory, J.: Scandinavian approaches to participatory design. Int. Journal. Eng. Educ. **19**(1), 62–74 (2003)
19. Healy, J., Anderson, S.: Children and young people's use of technology. Barnardo's NI Policy and Research Unit (2007)
20. Heikkinen, K., et al.: Designing mobile applications for children. User Require. Wirel. **42**, 7 (2015)
21. Hemment, D.: Locative media. Leonardo Electron. Almanac. **14**(3) (2006)
22. Horton, M., Read, J., Fitton, D., Little, L., Toth, N.: Too cool at school - understanding cool teenagers. PsychNol. J. **10**(2), 73–91 (2012)
23. Horton, M., Sim, G., Read, J., Fitton, D., Mazzone, E.: School friendly participatory research activities with children. In: Extended Abstracts CHI 2012, pp. 2099–2104 (2012)

24. Kelly, S.R., Mazzone, E., Horton, M., Read, J.C.: Bluebells: a design method for child-centred product development. In: Proceedings of 4th Nordic conference on Human-computer interaction: changing roles, pp. 361–368, October 2006
25. Lemos, A.: Post-mass media functions, locative media, and informational territories: new ways of thinking about territory, place, and mobility in contemporary society. Space Cult. **13**, 403–420 (2010)
26. Markopoulos, P., Read, J., Hoÿsniemi, J., MacFarlane, S.: Child computer interaction: advances in methodological research. Cognit. Technol. Work **10**(2), 79–81 (2008)
27. Markopoulos, P., Read, J., Hoÿsniemi, J., MacFarlane, S.: Evaluating Children's Interactive Products. Morgan Kaufmann, Burlington (2008)
28. Mazzone, E., Read, J.C., Beale, R.: Design with and for disaffected teenagers. In: Proceedings of 5th Nordic conference on HCI, pp. 290–297 (2008)
29. Marsh, J., Brooks, G., Hughes, J., Ritchie, L., Roberts, S., Wright, K.: Digital beginnings: young children's use of popular culture, media and new technologies. University of Sheffield, Sheffield (2005)
30. McKnight, L., Fitton, D.: Touch-screen technology for children: giving the right instructions and getting the right responses. In: Proceedings of 9th International Conference on Interaction Design and Children, pp. 238–241 (2010)
31. Moraveji, N., Li, J., Ding, J., O'Kelley, P., Woolf, S.: Comicboarding: using comics as proxies for participatory design with children. In: Proceedings of SIGCHI conference on Human factors in computing systems, pp. 1371–1374 (2007)
32. Piaget, J.: To understand is to invent: the future of education. Grossman, New York (1973)
33. Read, J.C., Gregory, P., MacFarlane, S., McManus, B., Gray, P., Patel, R.: An investigation of participatory design with children-informant, balanced and facilitated design. In: Interaction design and Children, pp. 53–64. Shaker, Maastricht (2002)
34. Read, J.: Warp speed design: a rapid design method for use with children. In: Extended. Abstracts CHI 2009, pp. 4681–4686 (2009)
35. Read, J.C., Fitton, D., Mazzone, E.: Using obstructed theatre with child designers to convey requirements. In: Extended Abstracts CHI 2010, pp. 4063–4068 (2010)
36. Read, J., Fitton, D., Cowan, B., Beale, R., Guo, Y., Horton, M.: Understanding and designing cool technologies for teenagers. In: Extended Abstracts CHI 2011, pp. 1567–1572 (2011)
37. Read, J., Gregory, P., Horton, M., Fitton, D., Sim, G., Cassidy, B.: CHECk: a tool to inform and encourage ethical practice in participatory design with children. In: Extended Abstracts CHI 2013, pp. 187–192 (2013)
38. Read, J.C., Fitton, D., Horton, M.: Theatre, PlayDoh and comic strips: designing organic user interfaces with teenage participants. Interact. Comput. **25**(2), 183–198 (2013)
39. Read, J.C., Fitton, D., Horton, M.: Giving ideas an equal chance: inclusion and representation in participatory design with children. In: Proceedings of Interaction Design and Children, pp.105–114 (2014)
40. Reid, J., Geelhoed, E., Hull, R., Cater, K., Clayton, B.: Parallel worlds: immersion in location-based experiences. In: Extended Abstracts CHI 2005, pp. 1733–1736 (2005)
41. Reid, J., Hull, R., Cater, K., Fleuriot, C.: Magic moments in situated mediascapes. In: Proceedings of SIGCHI International Conference on Advances in Computer Entertainment Technology, pp. 290–293 (2005)
42. Scaife, M., Rogers, Y., Aldrich, F., Davies, M.: Designing for or designing with? Informant design for interactive learning environments. In: Proceedings of CHI 1997, pp. 343–350 (1997)
43. The Statistics Portal: Number of apps available in leading app stores as of July 2015 (2015). http://www.statista.com/statistics/276623/number-of-apps-available-in-leading-app-stores/

44. Wakkary, R., et al.: Kurio: a museum guide for families. In: Proceedings of TEI 2009, pp. 215–222 (2009)
45. Walsh, G., et al.: Layered elaboration: a new technique for co-design with children. In: Proceedings of SIGCHI Conference on Human Factors in Computing Systems, pp. 1237–124 (2010)
46. Weal, M.J., et al.: Requirements for in-situ authoring of location based experiences. In: Proceedings of Mobile HCI 2006, pp. 121–128 (2006)
47. Zytnik, M.: School report for apple app store and google play (2014). https://www.adjust.com/company/overview/2014/09/29/kids-apps-report-apple-itunes-google-play/

Observations and Categorisations of Art Practices Associated with AI

Tim Gruchy[✉]

Shanghai Academy of Fine Arts, 99 Shangda Rd, Shanghai 200444, China
timeg@shu.edu.cn

Abstract. In this paper I set out to present a series of categories for artists working with and about Artificial Intelligence [AI]. My approach is more observational than rigidly taxonomic. Having the opportunity to curate a substantial exhibition on this topic, I undertook a year long program of research which encompassed and extended into lengthy conversations with many artists working internationally in the field. This culminated in the exhibition "Future Intelligence" at Tank Museum, Shanghai, 13 December 2019 to 5 January 2020. A number of distinct themes and sub-themes became apparent through this research: Aesthetic and Philosophical, Representation, Identity and Self Awareness, AI and A-life, and Interpretation and Narrative are the major themes. As one would expect, many of the artists and their works explore multiple themes. Additionally, as with all media art practice, artists utilise a large range of diverse approaches to the application of interfaces for audience engagement and interaction, hence I have briefly examined these structurally but not within the thematics. I make specific reference to many, but not all of the artworks that featured in the exhibition as well as a number of other artists and artworks. The paper also presents somewhat of a limited survey of current international practice over the last three years, without attempting to be exhaustive. A more exhaustive list of artists working with AI can be found at AIArtists.org; the global directory of artists working in this field [1].

Keywords: AI art · Artificial intelligence art · Machine learning art · Computational art

1 Aesthetics and Philosophy

Aesthetics and philosophical concerns are both inter-related yet separated at times.

The New Aesthetics - prominent in recent discourse for some time as a mode of thinking about AIs - became popularised under that title as a quasi-movement around artist and theorist James Bridle in 2012. Now no longer considered a current movement, The New Aesthetics is still a highly relevant topic and focus. Some of this pertains to the philosophical implications to do with AIs and aesthetics whilst other artists explore aesthetic relationships and evolution pertaining to the history of human aesthetics and various specific art movements. A number of artists are using various types of machine learning to create works that allude or directly mimic historical styles

© Springer Nature Switzerland AG 2020
M. Kurosu (Ed.): HCII 2020, LNCS 12181, pp. 234–245, 2020.
https://doi.org/10.1007/978-3-030-49059-1_17

or in some cases even specific historical works. For this thematic, AI Aesthetics by Lev Manovich is a key text [2].

1.1

James Bridle [born 1980, lives and works in London] is an important artist, author, thinker and broadcaster whose work across these mediums is focussed acutely on philosophical, aesthetic, political and sociological considerations, concerns and implications of digital technology and AI, in and upon our world today.

In his book New Dark Age: Technology and the End of the Future 2018 [3] he offers a sobering warning about our future. Never has there been more data available to us with which to understand and model the world, but the sheer volume of it seems to be heralding ever increasing in-comprehension rather than the reverse.

New Ways of Seeing 2019 is a four part BBC radio show he wrote and presented. It builds on John Berger's seminal book and BBC series Ways of Seeing 1972 to explore the relationship between how we see the world and how it is made. If we can see it in a different way could it become a better place?

Bridle has produced a plethora of artworks and other projects not all of which utilise AI specifically, but most of which revolve around his primary sets of associative concerns and interests.

1.2

Helena Sarin's work is deeply rooted in aesthetics. Sarin [born, Russia, lives and works in the USA] has an original background in software engineering. She creates suites of two dimensional stills that directly reference different visual languages of historical art. Sarin thus poses questions pertaining to the relations between the possible outcomes of AI induced learning and processing, and historical art movements. She uses exclusively her own analogue drawings and photographs as training data sets for the neural nets, seeking to make work which is aesthetically pleasing with a touch of the enigmatic. Sarin writes about her practice; "reflecting on the characteristics of my analog art - improvised, bold and deeply personal, conveying a sense of fragility, impermanence and imperfect beauty" [4].

1.3

The work and research of Joshua Stanton [born 1981, UK, lives and works in Glasgow] is bound up in his ongoing investigation into the use of AI to push new boundaries for painting with the possibility of creating new emergent aesthetics. He utilises a cyclical feedback process beginning with his own paintings which he inputs into a creative pipeline whereby the AI output feeds back in on itself. Two videos AI Painting 2017 and Generative Style Deep Neural Painting 2017 were included in the exhibition precisely because of their specific aesthetic that, from my perspective, are able to both allude to a history of painting and painterly textures whilst at the same time presenting themselves within an entirely yet somehow unique contemporary moving image medium.

1.4

Tim Gruchy [born 1957, Wales, lives and works in Sydney, Adelaide and Shanghai]

Having been a practising artist all my life and now undertaking the role of curator I thought it was important that I created a new work using AI given the context of the exhibition, to deepen my understanding of the creative terrain. It was particularly the aesthetic and philosophical questions I was drawn to; thus I created Beauty Unbeauty 2019.

Taking the flower as a fundamental human representation of beauty, I began with a data set of flowers drawn from my large personal photo library. I then worked with the Deep Dreaming Generator in what I, like many of the other artists now call a collaboration. Inputing other image data sets I influenced the AI's dreaming in two directions, choosing to call these 'Beauty' and 'Unbeauty' and differentiating outcomes according to my aesthetic judgments both of the influencing data sets and the AI's outcomes. After dreaming my way through literally thousands of images and iterations I then manually built these into very slow, edge of perception slow, animations that appear as time-lapse movies, exhibited in a variant number of spatial and temporal juxtapositions with a little randomness thrown in. In this exhibition I utilised a row of five horizontal flatscreens. It has also been exhibited elsewhere in a three horizontal flatscreen version.

The outcome is a work that has been described as seductive and repulsive in equal parts, a highly accurate descriptor of my undertaking to explore multiple questions concerning beauty, about how human and AI aesthetics are different (if in fact we can say AI's yet possess aesthetic values, I suspect not), and also how artists and AIs can work/collaborate together.

2 Representation

Representation has been fundamental to human artistic expression. AIs represent and reinterpret our visions of self. They also make their own representations of humanity. This occurs in ways we are only just beginning to discern and understand. Interestingly, I am not aware of AIs making images of themselves, and importantly, there is no AI to date that has decided autonomously to make art. Motivationally, art still remains a human endeavour. Many artists are using AIs to evolve and represent a broad morphology of the human form often expressed as an animated morphing, somewhat reminiscent at times of early computer morphing which became available and popularised in the early 1990s. Today, it is the AI automatically determining the form of the change/transition.

2.1

Mario Klingemann [born 1970, Germany, lives and works in Berlin Germany] and Memo Aktens have produced extensive work in this field. Klingemann is regarded as a pioneer in the realm of computer learning, His work in the exhibition also has a specific philosophical context whilst also touching on identity. His work Three Latent Body Problem 2018 is a direct reference to Liu Cixin's acclaimed book series, The Three-Body Problem, itself referring to the classical physics problem. The above work deals with the human body form whilst his other works, Alternative Face 2017, Self Portraits 2018 and Uncanny Mirror 2018 use and manipulate faces in different ways.

Klingemann began learning programming in the 1980s and has worked with AI for over a decade now in a formative practice in the context of art and AI. He works extensively with a type of machine learning program called Generative Adversarial Networks [GANs] which produce a dominant aesthetic of distortion common across his work. He talks of artists searching for the unexpected and mechanisms of external influence, going beyond the conscious mind and GANs being a way of achieving this goal.

2.2

Memo Aktens [born 1975, Istanbul Turkey, lives and works in London] though not represented in the exhibition is a prolific and prodigious artist in the field of AI and beyond.

Akten's Optimising for Beauty 2017 and Dirty Data 2017 are good examples of works dealing with representation. The former uses a dataset of well known celebrity faces fed though a Maximum Likelihood Estimation [MLE] algorithm. The use of MLE algorithms in machine learning is very widespread and they have a propensity for homogenisation and committing towards a dominant truth. This then tends towards the erasure of heterogeneity, something we should all be concerned about in our increasingly divided society.

Social media corporations contribute to the polarising and binary discourse through the use of these types of mechanisms. A similar process has been undertaken in the later work using images of right wing politicians. This time however Aktens has used dirty data. Images that have purposefully not been preened and filtered, cleaned up as it were before being fed to the AI. Thus rather than tending towards a homogenous beauty they move towards the grotesque and distorted, making an entirely different political statement.

Interesting work indeed that touches on many important issues concerning the images we are presented with in the global media and the mechanisms that are now controlling and affecting them.

Aktens' work output is vast and covers many of the themes explored in this paper. It also includes much research and commercial applications.

2.3

Mike Tyka [lives and works in the USA] first studied in the sciences of Biochemistry and Biotech. Around 2015 he began exploring the use of artificial neural networks to artistic ends. In 2017 his Portraits of Imaginary People attracted considerable attention and is an important reference work in relation to the representation issue.

For this work he took literally thousands of pictures of faces from Flickr. These became the source data set for training a GAN. GANs work by utilising two neural networks in adversity. One, the Generator, creates new data with the same statistics as the training set. The other, the Discriminator, tries to distinguish candidates produced by the Generator from the true data set. Initially both perform poorly however as they each learn the output, they become increasingly convincing with the appearance of realism.

The work explores the so-called latent "face space", the underlying multidimensional psychological space of perceived features and properties that specifies how one's perception of which faces are similar to which other faces.

Interestingly, within a year of Tyka's work being produced Nvidia researchers released styleGAN which was then open sourced in early 2019. This provided a ready tool to generate realistic non-original faces, for the fashion and advertising industry. There is also the more sinister potential use of these tools for creating deep fake pictures of video for political or pornographic use.

These explorations cross well over into the Identity category as well as a host of other identity issues. As frequently occurs, artists' explorations of emergent technologies are commercialised and co-opted with great rapidity. These practices also pose a wider issue of long term artistic value.

3   Identity and Self Awareness

Identity and self-awareness are fundamental to the human condition. What does the gradual evolution of another intelligence on Earth do to our sense of identity? How are these two intelligences inter-related? AI generates a breadth of issues relating to self awareness, such as how it can effect and influence human self awareness and notions of the emergence of a sense of self in AIs. Self awareness is a precursor to identity. Identity also has a host of other aspects: gender, race, nationalism to name a few. If AIs are now controlling or at best influencing many of the mechanisms of information exchange and gathering that allow us to understand ourselves and form and inform our sense of identity, then there are some very serious issues at stake.

3.1

Fito Segrera [born 1983, Columbia, lives and works in Czech Republic] began his artistic training in Columbia before moving to New York then Shanghai. His interest and motivation is in attempting to understand the very nature of consciousness in all its forms, particularly human and AI. For Segrera the question "What is it to be?" sits at the core of his practice. Art and programming AIs is just one avenue for his journey of questioning and discovery.

For the exhibition I choose a work Agnosis: The lost memories 2016. If we accept the collective agreement as part of the social contract that gnosis or knowledge is the root of reality and how we experience the world, then our perception of reality is a multi-layered rendering of information over the emptiness of being. Memories are built up as acquired information we are able to retrieve, but much is lost or discarded. The work utilises a system that imposes a technological layer on top of the human perceptual mechanisms, creating an augmented hybrid. The artist went out into the world wearing a head rig that combined a camera with a brain-computer interface [BCI]. The BCI registered moments where his attention dropped, recording brainwaves and the images from these moments. Then using available online services for image recognition and search suggestion, autonomous analyses and interpretations of the 'lost' memories were generated and rendered as abstract virtual 3D sculptures superimposed into the landscape he was traversing at the time.

Simultaneously a log book of autonomously generated machine interpretations or thoughts was produced. Like much of Segrera's work, from highly considered complex intentions and systems comes sets of simple poetic contemplative outcomes. The artist has also undertaken a series of works involving AI and non-anthropomorphic robots.

3.2

Jake Elwes [born 1993, UK, lives and works in London], like many of the artists working in this field, posits his practice as investigations within the recurrent areas of technology, philosophy and ethics. In the exhibition, his work Latent Space 2017 is a propositional question or relationship on the theme of awareness. Using a GAN, one screen generates "at will" a series of humanly recognisable images trained from a database of 14.2 million images, whilst the other screen tries to interpret these as text descriptions.

In GANs the latent space is regarded as having no meaning, but as an observer of this process the audience cannot help but to sense or impose a sense of meaning to the two elements creating a fascinating and compelling engagement.

3.3

Tom White [born 1971, Georgia, lives and works in Wellington, New Zealand] explores AI and machine perception focusing on how machines see the world.

To quote from his website:

"My artwork investigates the Algorithmic Gaze: how machines see, know, and articulate the world. As machine perception becomes more pervasive in our daily lives, the world as seen by computers becomes our dominant reality. Collaborating with AI systems, I create physical abstract prints that are reliably classified by neural networks. It's art by AI, for AI. By giving the algorithms a voice to speak in we are better able to see the world through the eyes of a machine" [5].

The initial process involves both creation and verification by AIs however the final prints are hand printed screen prints and signs. His term for this process is a "perception engine". Though initially recognisable as simplified universally recognisable images, his work – expressed across what seems to be an ever growing series – has much more at play. Primarily his practice is concerned with machine awareness, but by exhibiting images as hand made objects, he engenders other human awareness processes in how the audience perceives then interprets the work.

His practice demonstrates a smart complex set of ideas expressed with consummate simplicity to achieves it's aim of helping one better see a world that is now so thoroughly mediated by machines.

4   AI and A-Life

Regarding Artificial Intelligence and Artificial Life [A-life], it is important to consider pivotal precursors to the explosion of AI in the 2010s and understand it in terms of an evolutionary process. Sentience is only a subset of life or applicable to advanced lifeforms yet they are inextricably inter-related.

A-life has had different meanings over the years, generally it involves computer, robotic and biological simulations of the processes, systems and evolution of natural life. American computer scientist Christopher Langton coined the phrase A-life in the late 1980s. Primarily a scientific pursuit where it has largely been assimilated into other disciplines especially in biological terms, there have been various artistic applications over the past three decades. As a community of thought A-life has been in and out of vogue, however the 'explosion' within AI has brought a renewed interest and vigour.

4.1

In the context of the history of these endeavours, the work of Ernest Edmonds [born 1942, London, lives and works in Sydney and London] is a perfect example. He began painting at an early age, a practice he continued as he undertook formal education in mathematics, philosophy and logic. He began exploring machine learning in the 1960s and how it could be expressed within a formalist artistic context, making artworks that reflected and transmitted light, painting and coding interactive generative works. He has especially explored these digital processes to create systems that enable artworks to manifest a life of their own.

Edmonds has maintained this precise and focused exploration to this day, eschewing populist trends, maintaining his lifelong focus and actually embedding learning over much longer timeframes than are generally popular today to create works that are indicative of the long-view emergence of both the algorithmic evolution and a consistent practice that reflects on this directly.

His recent work Shaping Now 2019 shown in this exhibition is a perfect example. The work presents as a projected screen of colour, time and interaction, and as with much of his work, the imagery references historical connections to the twentieth century Constructivist's structures as well as colour theory deriving from Henri Matisse.

A camera looking at the space in front of the screen monitors the movement of the audience and feeds information to the system that is continuously calculated as activity. This in turn modifies the rule sets to update the colour and form of the display, creating a living abstract image that matures and evolves subject to it's audience over time.

In our age of fast motion and given my own growing predilection for slowness in my own work, I was particularly drawn to the slow paced evolution inbuilt into this work. As I was installing the work and testing it in my studio prior to installation in the exhibition, I at first thought the system was not fully operative and it was only after checking with Edmonds and running it for several days that I began to fully appreciate and understand the true nature and depth of the work.

Over the longer timeframe of the whole exhibition this then extended further. Perhaps single viewing audiences may not understand or appreciate the intentions of the work, but like much conceptual work examination and understanding of the ideas underlying the presented work only enhances the engagement and experience. I enjoyed explaining this to the keen invigilators who were at first mildly disappointed that leaping around energetically in front of the camera did not illicit the usual and anticipated instant gratification. Without exception they all in time appreciated the work in an entirely new way, particularly how it both sat contextually against other works in the exhibition, and against their own expectations. If education and learning are signifiers of sentience then these processes were perfect manifestations contextual to some of the intentions and ideas expressed within the exhibition.

Contributing as an artist, writer and educator in this field over multiple decades, it is easy to understand the importance of Edmonds' enormous contribution to computational art and the art of interaction, and the suitable veneration he has been accorded.

4.2

Jon McCormack [born 1964, Melbourne, Australia, lives and works in Melbourne] is another pioneer albeit from a later generation. He began writing artificial life algorithms in the 1980s which explored what was still a new territory, popularised by artists such as William Latham and others at the time. Just as Latham's works evolved and conceptually pertained to biological evolution, McCormack's work has continued to evolve in context and form, drawing parallels between AI, artificial life and biological behaviour and growth.

For this exhibition he presented a version of The Unknowable 2017, a work originally developed for a massive scale wide aspect wrap around screen in the Wynyard train station in Sydney that was later iterated into a number of other forms. In this instance the 20 min animation was presented as a three screen triptych.

Using his own artificial life algorithms McCormack has created an evolving virtual landscape of flora that evolves through its own sequence of growth, disintegration and fragmentation only to reform anew. The types of flora draw direct reference to plant-life from the Sydney region.

Another of his works Colourfield Lux is a new iteration of Colourfield 2009/2010. Like Edmunds' work Shaping Now, it utilises a screen and camera but in a smaller scale customised design more reminiscent of a domestic mirror. Similarly the camera is being utilised to register light and colour information not figurative imagery. This then feeds a generative ecosystem or artificial life agents in realtime to form symbiotic and stigmergic relationships. Like much of McCormack's work, it possesses underlying environmental concerns originally inspired by James Lovelock's Gaia hypothesis.

To quote the artist from the forthcoming exhibition catalogue: [6]

"In this new iteration – Colourfield Lux – real environmental dependencies are introduced into the virtual simulation. A light and colour sensor receives information about the current dominant colour immediately in front of the work, which feeds back into the virtual ecosystem simulation. This forces the agents to become adaptive to both their simulated and real environments. The evolutionary adaptive nature of the simulation allows the work to display complex dynamics over long time periods, rewarding the viewer over extended engagements. It generates a self-renewing, never ending or repeating sequence through its internal logic that is directed by the environment in which it operates, and so is unique to any particular environment.

The work is realised in a minimal aesthetic style using a circular screen surrounded by a black frame, and is displayed on a wall like a discrete painting. However this painting is always "looking back" at the viewer and responding to them over time. Colourfield Lux forms a mediation on technology, the environment, the self, and the connection between them".

Though these works of McCormack pertain directly to artificial life, other works of his utilise AI more specifically. Drawing Robots 2015/2019 is a swarm of small autonomous AI robots that collaborate to make large scale drawings. AI and robotics are intrinsically related of course but this idea of either individual or swarms of autonomous robots being utilised as drawing machines is an area of practice growing so fast that it is worthy of a paper, if not an entire book on it's own.

In his notes on Drawing Robots, McCormack references two other specific projects as inspiration. The first is Leonel Moura, who for many years has been building autonomous, art-making robots. Moura celebrates the use of autonomous machines to create art-objects "indifferent to concerns about representation, essence or purpose" [7].

Another seminal research project was the Drawbots Project, undertaken by artists, philosophers and scientists at the University of Sussex. He writes: "In 2005 an international, multi-disciplinary, inter-institutional group of researchers began a three-year research project that is attempting to use evolutionary and adaptive systems methodology to make an embodied robot that can exhibit creative behaviour by making marks or drawing" [8].

Across the enormous range of physical design and AI application used by artists, robotic projects and systems exhibit an enormous range of styles, outcomes and register an entire history. An essential reference would be the first compendium of its kind, Robots and Art: Exploring an Unlikely Symbiosis, edited by Damith Herath, Christian Kroos, Stelarc and published by Springer [9].

4.3

A work Metal Life 2016 by Lu Qiuyu [born, lives and works in China] in the exhibition takes a very intriguing, unique and unusual approach to artificial life. Part of an ongoing series, Lu exhibited two pedestals, each of which included an inbuilt bowl containing a portion of liquid metal. On approach and movement from the audience the metal apparently 'comes to life'. In his words:

"What is life? When a drop of liquid metal can hunt for game, digest its prey and move about, can it be said to be alive? Metal Life is a series of interactive installations in which liquid metal "molluscs" are raised. By presenting some interaction paradigms of liquid metal non-rigid interface aesthetically, we are able to make the liquid metal molluscs that inhabit the installation seem to be sentient. When interacting with installation visitors, it exhibits shy, curious, or even slightly insolent behaviour, and prompts its human interlocutor to give some thought to what life actually is".

I found this work to be sublimely intriguing, engaging and seductive in the extreme.

4.4

A number of artists are also looking at the relationship between AI and biological lifeforms and systems. Sofia Crespo [lives and works in Berlin] is a self described Neural artist and her work explores relationships, mechanisms and systems between technology and biology. Biology inspires technology not only in biomemetic ways.

One of her main focuses is the way organic life uses artificial mechanisms to simulate itself and evolve, thus implying the idea that technologies are a biased product of the organic life that created them and not a completely separated object [10].

Six still images from her Neural Zoo 2018 series featured in the exhibition. Exploring the very nature of creativity, she recombines known elements into novel ones to resemble an imagined nature. Our brains immediately recognise, or at least think they recognise, these images, or at least the textures within them. Human perception struggles to make sense of these images within a known reality yet they confound us.

Crespo's video work Panspermia 2019 made in collaboration with Pinar&Viola was also exhibited. It is complied from clips generated entirely with machine learning. Panspermia is the scientific hypothesis that life is distributed throughout the Universe, carried by space dust, meteoroids, asteroids, comets, planetoids, and also possibly by contaminating organisms unintentionally carried on spacecraft. In our present era of AI, space travel and the dystopic threats of the Anthropocene, questions about our origin and the possibilities of taking life off world are pertinent. It also reminded me of Karl Sims Panspermia from 1990 which seems highly relevant and coincidental in the discussion around AI and A-life.

5   Interpretation and Narrative

Using AIs to interpret data is common across most applications and themes. One particular thread of endeavour takes this material and develops it either directly into narratives or as an influencer thereupon narratives. This I find interesting. Using AIs to write stories or screen scripts is an obvious example of this. Sunspring 2016 the short experimental film by director Oscar Sharp and Ross Goodwin, a New York University AI researcher, is an early example. Already there are several websites and other mechanisms that will do this automatically. Although my initial premise for the exhibition did not encompass this type of practice, there were several works that incorporated these concepts in subtler ways.

5.1

British artist and researcher Anna Ridler [born 1985, UK, lives and works in London] uses machine learning to interpret information collections, especially self generated data sets to form new and unusual narratives. These manifest in a range of mediums.

In the exhibition her work Traces of Things 2018 uses material from public and private Maltese pictorial archives to explore the remembering and re-remembering of moments of history. Manifest as stills and video this creates an imagined historical narrative. During the installation period with a mandate from the artists to order a grid of 30 small prints, I found this work unexpectedly profound. The audience is left to interpret their own meaning.

5.2

Posited more as an experiment than an artwork, Bird Songs 2016, by Kyle McDonald [born 1985 USA, lives and works in USA] with Manny Tan and Yotam Mann uses bird sounds from the Macaulay Library's Essential Set for North America. Using a technique called t-SNE [Distributed Stochastic Neighbour Embedding] applied to the sounds only, a mapping that places similar sounds closer together is also applied. This interpretation and organisation is then visually presented with each sound represented by an image from its waveform. Moving a cursor over the map triggers the sound and a popup window with an image and the name of the bird appears. The end result as played by the audience is a highly dynamic interactive composition. Sentence

6   Interfaces

As with all media art practice, artists are using a range of interfaces to determine how audiences engage with their work. Video cameras in two and three dimensions, remain a common unencumbered option. Since Myron Krueger's groundbreaking system work

Videoplace, using 2D cameras in the 1970, through to the explosion of interest that the launch of Kinect in 2010 – the first readily available depth sensing camera and the array of subsequent offerings – cameras both as image generators and multisensors remain one of the fundamental interface options available to artists.

Proximity and motion sensing are used by some artists whilst others rely on the simple mouse or track pad. A few artists are also beginning to work in VR. This extends into Artificial Reality [AR] and Extended Reality [XR]. Creating passive immersive environments is another avenue. Brain Computer Interfaces [BCI] have been around for decades but are rapidly evolving both in terms of systems affordably available to artists and in conceptual approaches. Maurice Benayoun's Valuc of Values 2019/20 [11] is an excellent example of this. With the huge advances being made in the science of this field, it is unquestionably set to become a fascinating area for artists to further explore.

7 Additional Notes

Collaboration is an important dimension. Many of the artists referenced in this paper, myself included, refer to their relationship to the AI component of the work as a collaboration. I believe this is an appropriate descriptor of the process – or at least an aspect of the process – involved when working creatively with AI and thus accurately describes the relationship.

Art was once a purely descriptive and expressive representation of the world guided wholly by the artist's hand, later it became the realm of ideas, sometimes disconnected from the maker's mark. The programmers and engineers of AI software create a mechanism to facilitate a process, however what actually happens within that process is and shall remain beyond our understanding. Thus when artists choose to work with AIs, they may well have a role in establishing the process and data, some even programming the AIs themselves, upon which it feeds, and guide the intentionality of the greater process or idea at work, but importantly, the AI will always bring something of it's own. Thus the true nature and hopefully value of collaboration is embodied in the realm of the practice of artists and AI working together.

Commercial uptake in a changing cultural landscape. The dynamic whereby creative ideas are initiated by artists in the realm of the art world only to be appropriated by the commercial world is well established and acknowledged. This applies to most artistic avenues, however I think it particularly so in the areas of art and technology, AI being no different.

There are other changes at play. New tools, technologies and applications, such as so called smart phones, free up the means of production and provide creative tools and outlets in a manner never dreamed of even a few decades ago. This challenges established thinking and behaviour of what constitutes creative practice, who or what undertakes it, how it is shared as well as complex issues of authorship. The role of the artist, and indeed art, has always changed and evolved and will relentlessly continue to do so.

8 Closing

Artificial Intelligence is unquestionably one of the most important and significant technological shifts pervading the world today. It is compelling and often misunderstood. We consider and imagine a new future transformed by AI, while simultaneously reflecting on the human condition. As we look at AI, it looks back at us, dispassionately consuming vast amounts of input data and processing it in ways we are yet, if ever, to comprehend. The gaze penetrates both directions and offers us cause for reflection.

Artists have always played an important role in helping society understand and assimilate new technologies. The already ubiquitous, all pervasive spread of AIs into a growing number of aspects of our lives has occurred with great rapidity. Their innumerable unknown and often unintended consequences in this mostly commercially driven pursuit, often engendered by the new breed of vast multi-global corporations with huge disparities between their stated aims and reality. Perhaps there has never been a more important time for artists to ask the questions, not all of which are easy or apparent. From this hopefully, humanity can understand our world a little better, imagine it's future and what it is to be intelligent here on Earth and beyond.

References

1. https://aiartists.org/ai-artist-directory. Accessed 30 Jan2020
2. Manovich, L.: AI Aesthetics. Strelka Press, Moscow (2018)
3. Bridle, J.: New Dark Age. Verso, London (2018)
4. Sarin, H.: Future Intelligence Catalogue. SAFA, Shanghai (2020)
5. https://drib.net/about. Accessed 30 Jan 2020
6. McCormack, J.: Future Intelligence Catalogue. SAFA, Shanghai (2020)
7. Moura, L., Pereira, H.G.: Man + Robots | Symbiotic Art. LxXL (2014)
8. For details see the book by Boden, Creativity and Art: Three Roads to Surprise. Oxford University Press (2010)
9. Herath, D., Kroos, C., Stelarc: Robots and Art: Exploring an Unlikely Symbiosis. Springer, Heidelberg (2016). https://doi.org/10.1007/978-981-10-0321-9
10. https://sofiacrespo.com/. Accessed 10 Jan 2020
11. https://www.v-o-v.io/. Accessed 10 Jan 2020

DICT and Seniors: How Can Research Experience Help Us Map Digital Competencies?

Cecília Henriques[1] and Denise Pilar[2(✉)]

[1] Universidade Federal de Santa Catarina, Florianópolis, Brazil
ceciliamhenriques@yahoo.com.br
[2] SAP Labs LATAM, Av. SAP, 188, São Leopoldo, RS, Brazil
denise.pilar@live.com

Abstract. The development of digital competencies is progressive and influenced by use: the more digital resources are used; the more people develop digital competencies. Yet, when considering the elderly public and their specificities, learning to use DICT in Brazil has been driven by short training courses that teach how to use computers and smartphones. For those courses to be more effective and assertive, it is important to map the digital competencies that are already developed by the elderly. Therefore, the question is: how can experience research help in the mapping of digital competencies of elderly users? To answer this question, we carried out an inventory of experience research methods, seeking to identify which among them would be more suitable for mapping digital competencies of the elderly. Next, some data were collected using the identified methods, in order to understand how effective they could be for mapping the digital competencies of this audience. The results show that some methods used in Experience Research are useful for mapping digital competencies and can help researchers and teachers to better direct their research and courses to this specific audience. We expect this proposal to spark and broaden the discussion on the use of DICT by the elderly, user experience, experience research and digital competencies.

Keywords: Digital competencies · Elderly · Experience research

1 Introduction

The increase in life expectancy brings important demands regarding the well-being and inclusion of older people when it comes to ensuring healthy aging and social inclusion of the elderly, especially when considering the elderly as someone who still has much to live, experience, and contribute to their community. In this context, the actions that enable the social inclusion of the elderly are important and, in times of massive use of Digital Information and Communication Technologies (DICT), their digital inclusion, since the technologies have become essential and inevitable, especially when it deals with communication, socialization, education and work.

DICT make older people both delighted and afraid, at the same time: enchanted, particularly by the ease of communication and the ability to access different content and

© Springer Nature Switzerland AG 2020
M. Kurosu (Ed.): HCII 2020, LNCS 12181, pp. 246–256, 2020.
https://doi.org/10.1007/978-3-030-49059-1_18

resources; fearful because, despite favoring family, social, business or financial relationships, for example, they do not always understand how these technologies work, what resources are available, or what are the possibilities for interaction. There is also a concern about safety when using digital devices.

Hence, the need for practices specifically targeted to this age group. In order for DICT to provide a user experience that matches what users want and need, they must meet certain accessibility and usability requirements. However, accessibility and usability alone do not account for the digital inclusion of the elderly, and the development of digital literacy is an important factor to consider. That requires the development of digital competencies, which means that users need to know how to access, analyze, and interpret information that is necessary for learning, for the development of critical thinking and for problem solving. They should also be able to express and disseminate information in a democratic and ethical way, and to retrieve information in a safe and critical manner. Such competencies are considered essential for personal, social, and professional life, especially considering that most of today's daily activities are mediated by digital resources.

The development of digital competencies is progressive and influenced by use: the more digital resources are used, the more people develop digital competencies. Yet, when considering the elderly public and their specificities, learning to use DICT in Brazil has been driven by short training courses that teach how to use computers and smartphones. For those courses to be more effective and assertive, it is important to map the digital competencies that are already developed by the elderly. Therefore, the question is: how can experience research help in the mapping of digital competencies of elderly users? To answer this question, we carried out an inventory of experience research methods, seeking to identify which among them would be more suitable for mapping digital competencies of the elderly. Next, some data were collected using the identified methods, in order to understand how effective they could be for mapping the digital competencies of this audience. Thus, even though the article describes a study for mapping digital competencies, carried out with a group of elderly people, the objective here is to discuss the use of experience research in the mapping of digital competencies of elderly users.

This paper presents an overview of the use of DICT by Brazilian elderly people, in the year of 2019. It also discusses the digital competencies that are considered essential today, as well as the qualitative methods of experience research that can support the mapping of digital competencies of elderly users. Lastly, we present some approaches used to mapping digital competencies with this audience, seeking to be more assertive.

2 Elderly Brazilians

In Brazil, an individual aged 60 or more is considered to be part of the elderly age group. The Elderly Statute, Law n. 10,741, dated October 1, 2003, is the instrument "designed to regulate the rights guaranteed to people aged 60 or over" [1]. Although having begun later than more developed countries, population aging is a process that has been occurring rapidly in Brazil. And it generates changes in the age structure of the population, as there is a decrease in the number of children and young people, and, at the same time, there is an increase in the number of adults and the elderly in the total population. The population aged 60 or over went from 14.2 million in 2000 to 19.6 million in 2010, with a projection of 41.5 million in 2030 and 73.5 million in 2060 [2].

Unlike individual aging, population aging results in social and economic challenges and possibilities that are collective, albeit with direct individual effects, such as the guarantee to social security, health care, social assistance and care, education, work, housing, and, above all, social integration. In addition, the Elderly Statute guarantees to the elderly with absolute priority, "the realization of the right to life, health, food, education, culture, sport, leisure, work, citizenship, freedom, dignity, respect and family, and community coexistence", which explicitly includes the obligation of the family, the community, the society, and the Public Power [1].

Considering, then, that population aging is a reality, in addition to the need for public policies to address the social protection of this public and the guarantee of housing, food, physical health, care and moral health, leisure, work, stability, respect, and non-discrimination, there is still a need to intensify work that protects them from exclusion and social vulnerability, guaranteeing this age group the right to participate in different social spheres, in an inclusive manner, respecting the characteristics specific to their age.

In the meantime, public policies aimed at this age group must consider the specific characteristics of this stage of development, among which stand out: diseases, since over the years, the body is subject to more diseases, especially chronic and associated ones (comorbidities), especially diabetes, hypertension, obesity and hypercholesterolemia [3]; gender differences, since the number of elderly women is greater than that of men[1], "the result of mortality different rates between the sexes, which for the male population are always higher than those observed among women [2].

The increase in life expectancy is also a relevant factor for both men and women, even though women's life expectancy exceeds that of men (which also explains the greater number of women in this age group). Globally, "life expectancy increased from 47 years between 1950–1955, to 65 years between 2000–2005, and is expected to reach 75 years between 2045–2050 [4]. In Brazil, according to data from the 2015 National Household sample survey, the Southeast and South regions recorded the highest percentages of elderly individuals (15.7% and 16.0%, respectively), while the North region (including the Amazon area) recorded the lowest percentages (10, 1%) [5].

In addition, the aging process is slow and gradual, taking different paces, depending on each person, and being influenced, among other factors, by genetics, social, historical, psychological aspects, as well as by diet habits. Although most elderly people have multiple health issues over time, especially chronic, non-communicable diseases, such as diabetes and high blood pressure, the passage of time is not a synonym for dependence [6].

Although most elderly people experience loneliness or social[2] and/or emotional isolation, this is not a natural and permanent state for all of them. Many elderly people

---

[1] The sex ratio for the population over 60 years of age is about 0.8, indicating that there are approximately 80 men for every 100 women [2].

[2] "It implies the scarcity of meaningful and satisfying relationships with regard to the quality of the various types of relationship that a person may have, such as superficial or intimate relationships, relationships with old or recent friends, with co-workers, with neighbors or relatives" [8].

do want to "continue studying and working on something that gives them pleasure. They want to be productive, useful, and active at this life. They don't just want to occupy time, spend time, fill time, waste time. Time, for them, is extremely valuable and cannot be wasted. They don't want to retire from themselves" [7]. They are people who want to work not (only) because of the material need that so much effort demanded from their ancestors, but because they want to find meaning for this moment in life.

In Brazil, many elderly people seek and participate in courses offered mainly by Universities Open to the Third Age (as these stage of life is often referred to as, in Brazil), programs and extension courses offered by Public or Private Universities or specific centers for the elderly, generally maintained by municipal government. These courses are offered, in the majority, in person. The most popular topics include consumer law, basic and daily health care, physiotherapy, nutrition, computer courses, and foreign languages[3]. Such proposals aim at social inclusion, active participation in society, and access to education, either to guarantee the learning that was not possible at a regular age, or for upskilling and personal development.

3   Digital Competencies

In recent years, several terms have been used to describe the skills and competencies of using digital technologies, such as ICT competencies, technology skills, information technology skills, 21st century skills, information literacy, digital literacy and digital competencies. These terms are often also used interchangeably [9]. Digital competency has become an essential concept to describe the knowledge, skills and attitudes that people should have in today's society. It relates to digital literacy and it is one of the eight competencies recognized as essential for lifelong learning by the European Community, and it is also the competency that enables a better insertion in the digital environment, not only through the acquisition of technical competencies, but also through a deeper understanding of the DICT and their interactive and collaborative environments [10].

According to the European Commission, "digital competence involves the safe and critical use of Information Society technologies at work, in free time, and in communication" [10]. It is "underpinned by ICT competencies: the use of computers for obtaining, evaluating, storing, producing, presenting and exchanging information, and to communicate and participate in cooperation networks via Internet" [10]. In addition to this concept, there are those who classify digital competence in dimensions, stating that it can be technical, cognitive, and ethical [11] and that it should enable the person to explore and face new technological situations, in a flexible and critical way,

---

[3] There are many Universities Open to the Elderly in the country, linked to both private and public Universities, which open their doors to the elderly with extension courses on different themes. Examples of these projects, among others: USP60+ (https://prceu.usp.br/usp60/), UATI (https://www3.uepg.br/uati/), UNATI (http://www.unati.uem.br/index.php/), UATI (https://www.pitangui.uepg.br/uati/), UATI (http://www.nuati.uneb.br/saiba%20mais.html), UNATI (http://www.pucrs.br/unati/).

analyzing, selecting and evaluating the data and information. The person should also be able to explore technological possibilities, aiming to solve problems and build shared and collaborative knowledge, while raising awareness of their own responsibilities [11].

Digital competency is also defined in the literature as the competency that allows people to "solve real problems, make decisions, work in collaborative environments, expanding communication spaces in order to participate in formal and informal learning communities, as well as to manage creative and responsible outcomes", since "it consists in having the skills to look for, obtain, process and communicate information, and to transform it into knowledge" [12].

In the specialized literature, it is also defined, among others, as "a set of conditions, resources and available elements applied in a given situation" [13] or as "a set of knowledge, skills and attitudes, strategies and awareness that one needs when using ICTs and digital media to perform tasks, solve problems, communicate, generate information, collaborate, create and share content, build knowledge effectively, efficiently, critically, creatively, autonomously, flexibly, ethically, and reflexively for work, leisure, participation, learning, socialization, consumption, and empowerment" [14].

It is important to mention DigComp, which is the most current document on digital competence and the European frame of reference for the development and understanding of digital competence [15]. Although it is geared towards teachers, it is the material being used as a reference by many professionals. The document presents the areas of digital competence, which can be summarized as follows: a) Information: to be able to identify, locate, retrieve, store, organize, and analyze information, as well as to assess their purpose and importance; b) Communication: to be able to communicate in digital environments, share resources through online tools, connect and collaborate with other people through digital tools, interact and participate in communities and networks; c) Content Creation: Create and edit new content (text, images, videos), integrate and reformulate knowledge and content, create artistic productions, multimedia content and computer programming, knowing how to apply intellectual property rights and licensing; d) Security: personal protection, data protection, digital identity protection, use of security, secure and sustainable use of information; e) Problem solving: identify digital needs and resources. Making decisions when choosing the appropriate digital tool, according to the purpose or need, solving conceptual problems through digital means, solving technical problems, use of technology creatively, updating one's own competence and that of others [15].

Considering specifically elderly Brazilians, five digital competencies were mapped, which are particularly necessary for this audience: Basic internet resources; Web search; Communication by e-mail; Reliable online information; and Virtual Resilience [16]. In addition, the competency of Security and Privacy on the Internet was also mentioned, regarding the use of internet tools to help with preventing theft of personal information [16].

4 Experience Research

Experience research allows to collect data from end users of products and services, to understand the context of use, and to discover these end users' needs. The objective is to obtain a holistic view of the context of use, which allows the researcher to fill in the knowledge gaps that users are not able to communicate directly, as it includes the user's understanding of the tool and how it is used [17, 18]. Therefore, it is a research that focuses on the person and is used, above all, although not only for this purpose, to understand a person's use and experience with digital products. Basically, experience research allows to discover, among other things: what tools people use, why they use them, how these tools are present in users' daily lives, and what advantages and disadvantages the tools have, as well as the user problems the tool solves. As a result of the experience research, it is possible to obtain, among others: 1) The elderly user journey with DICT; 2) Understanding of the context of use of digital tools by the elderly; 3) Personas that represent the elderly subjects of the research.

There are many methods used to collect data in experience research, but, for the purposes of this work, in-depth interviews and observation were selected, as described below, as they allow better understanding of interactions with digital products and offer the opportunity for the research to build rapport with the user, which opens the door to gathering information that would not be disclosed, otherwise.

In-depth individual interviews, which is apparently the most direct way of getting to know a little more about users, as by having time to talk and having a well-structured interview guide, enable the researcher to find out a lot about them and their relationship with digital resources. In addition, the researcher gets the opportunity to investigate the reasons that are behind user actions, and that are key to develop a comprehensive understanding of them. The interview allows to gather information about users, how they use the products and what problems they face, as well as to know their context of use, their vocabulary, social aspects, mental model, etc. [17–19]. Table 1, below, contains the steps for conducting individual in-depth interviews, prepared by Kalbach [17] and Gil [19].

Table 1. Steps for in-depth interviews

Steps	Actions
1	Develop the data collection instrument
2	Define the user profile (or profiles) that will participate in the study
3	Define the number of interviews to be conducted
4	Review and validate the data collection instrument
5	Define the data collection location(s)
6	Develop the informed consent and authorization forms
7	Conduct the interviews
8	Transcribe the data from interviews
9	Analyze the data
10	Write the report

Observation of use is defined as the method in which the researcher meets users, in a conscious and objective way, to capture data and information about who these people are and how they use a particular tool in their daily lives [18]. The main characteristic of observation as a research method is its dependence on a place where it occurs [19]. In the case of experience research, observation is well suited to: 1) discover how people interact with each other or with products or services, making it possible to perceive more clearly how people behave, what they do and how they do something; 2) discover underlying or unconscious thoughts that people have difficulty with or don't know how to express in a formal interview; and 3) overcome assumptions or hypotheses that are not confirmed [18]. Table 2, below, contains the steps for observing the user experience, according to Goodman and Kuniavsky [18] and Gil [19].

Table 2. Steps for observing the user experience.

Steps	Actions
1	Define the scope for the study
2	Define the user profile (or profiles) that will participate in the study
3	Define the observation locations
4	Define times for observation
5	Review study scope
6	Develop the informed consent and authorization forms
7	Conduct observations and record data
8	Systematize the recorded data
9	Analyze the data
10	Write the report

In the following section we describe how the individual in-depth interviews and the user observation were conducted. We also present some of the findings of mapping digital competencies and why the experience research made a difference.

5   Experience Research and the Mapping of Digital Competencies of the Elderly

Considering the proposed objective and the research question we wanted to answer, we chose the methods of individual in-depth interviews and user observation, as previously mentioned. First, we created the data collection instrument, which consisted of open questions about digital competencies, next, we defined participant profile, who should already use mobile tools and social media, such as Facebook or Instagram. Subsequently, we decided to interview six users, from a universe of 55 participants, taking computer classes for the elderly, which were offered by an elderly care center in southern Brazil. All participants had previously participated in a research study to understand the user profile of the elder DICT users.

After reviewing and testing the data collection instrument, we requested authorization from the elderly care center to collect data, and prepared the informed consent and authorization for recording forms, since the interviews would be recorded in audio and/or video. The interviews were conducted along a week, in October 2019. Afterwards, the interviews were transcribed and validated with the participants, before the analysis took place.

The second data collection, user observation, was carried out in the same class, offered by the elderly care center. The level of digital competence and validation of data obtained from individual interviews was defined as the scope of the research. It is important to mention that the scope of the research, the users' profile and the place of observation were defined from the interview data, since these observation sessions were treated as a complementary step in the mapping of digital competencies. The observation period was six hours, divided into six sessions of one hour each. Again, authorization was requested from the elderly care center for data collection and the informed consent and authorization for recording forms were prepared, since the observations would also be recorded on video. Observations were carried out over the last week of October and two weeks in November 2019. The data were systematized and analyzed after each session, followed by a cross analysis at the end of the six sessions.

The analysis of the interviews allowed us to understand that the main activities of the elderly are: accessing social media, chatting with family by voice or video, sending messages or emails, and sharing photos and/or videos. In addition, the use of DICT is influenced, especially by family members, who give smartphones to their elders, as a gift, or request that they get a device in order to facilitate communication, particularly with those who live in distant cities or even neighborhoods. Many elders seem reluctant to purchase the devices, not only because they lack digital competence, but also because the equipment and the internet provider services are expensive.

As for their current digital competencies for using DICT, the elderly state that, at first, it was necessary to attend a training course or to ask for help from family and friends, and after feeling comfortable using their devices, they try to discover new functions and explore the potential of the equipment. However, the main factors that lead them to be less autonomous in this exploration are the fear of damaging the equipment and the uncertainty about where their personal data will end up after being inserted in the device's screen. The main difficulties of use reported by the elderly regard finding information on the devices, accessing software and applications and understanding menus. These difficulties vary depending on their knowledge and experience with computers, due to the following main factors: time of use, and having or not completed a computer or mobile training course. Autonomy for use, on the other hand, was more related to the "level of curiosity" and interest in use.

As for the usage observations, it was possible to notice that many elderly people used devices purchased or donated by their children or grandchildren, which are, generally with little memory and a low capacity processor, not supporting the installation of many applications and crashing frequently. Comments like "my son gave me his old phone" or "my daughter got it for me" are common among them and show that, for many of the participants, the first device comes through the inheritance of a second-hand device from their children or grandchildren, who, in case of trouble using the device, are the first ones the elder seek for help. These assists, however, are punctual and often remove the autonomy of the elderly in executing the action, or learning how to do it, which directly influences the development of digital competencies.

In some sessions, smartphones had to be configured, as most of the elderly were unable to use their own device because some basic settings were inappropriate for them, and they did not know how to change such settings. The biggest complaint of the elderly was about screen time: "my screen turned off" and "why does my screen turn off?" phrases were heard a lot. In the course in which the observations were made, the participants practiced: making voice calls and/or video calls, finding the play store icon on the smartphone, searching for the Facebook and Instagram applications, updating them, uploading images, among other tasks. These challenges demanded that the elderly practiced what they had been learning. As a result, many of the participants began to interact in small groups, when those with a higher level of digital competence would explain to others what they knew about configuration and access to the devices, as well as share their positive and negative user experiences.

Another important finding from the observations was the fact that the elderly use a paper notebook and pen to write down the steps they must take to perform a certain action on the devices. They do this to "help memory," said one participant, as the school does not offer printed teaching material, although many of the students request it, according to the mediator.

But what do individual interviews and user observation have to do with mapping digital competencies? It is common for the mapping of digital competencies to be done through observation and self-assessment questionnaires that use a scale of values (Likert, for example) [16]. However, self-assessment can hinder data collection, since the questions are closed and out of context. Hence, observation, being broader and more comprehensive, plays an important role to help researchers and instructors to map the digital competencies of the elderly.

Considering the research findings and the breadth of data collected, it is safe to say that individual interviews and user observation seem to be more comprehensive to understand the context of use of DICT by the elderly, their needs, problems and benefits that technology brings to their daily lives, as well as to map the digital competencies they already have.

Although this was an initial research, given the characteristics of the elderly public, the individual interviews combined with user observation seemed more pertinent than the questionnaires previously applied, mainly due to the possibility of better understanding the context of using DICT, a weakness of quantitative instruments.

For instructors and instructional designers, for example, what needs to be considered when using individual interviews and user observation for mapping digital competencies is not necessarily what the elderly say they do, but what they mean when they say, for instance, that the reason why they use DICT is because their family insisted, or when they mention they are afraid to use the tools because they do not understand where their data will end up after being entered on the screen. While in a self-assessment questionnaire the answers are already present and all the person has to do is just choose the answer that best matches their personal answer, the interviews allow the elderly to freely share their experience, including feelings and emotions, emphasizing what they consider relevant and, guided by the researcher, reveal data that is essential to understand where they are in terms of digital competence and, with that, guide the creation of future instructional materials and training courses that best address their development needs, since they take into account the existing knowledge.

6 Final Thoughts

Considering that DICT are a given reality and that everyone, regardless of age, is entitled to access and use them, it is necessary to offer the elderly the possibility to learn to use such resources, since new basic competencies are required and necessary for active and effective social participation. On the other hand, digital tools must meet the specific needs of this age group. Furthermore, it is necessary to consider that the new social structure imposed by the digital generates transformations in social practices, now mediated by a great diversity of digital technological platforms. These transformations, although conditioned by digital technologies, depend on human action, which requires the existence of minimal digital competencies to identify, evaluate, and use DICT, as well as to collaborate and participate in the digital world.

The elderly seem to have significant interest in the use of DICT and show a high availability for learning situations. However, the methodologies used in the existing learning options and the materials made available to this group do not seem to address such situations adequately. In addition, the number of courses offered to the elderly has significantly increased, but there are still few proposals that consider their digital competencies in order to develop training courses or learning materials that make use of DICT, or even courses that aim at developing digital competencies.

Studies that contemplate digital competencies for the elderly are important when considering the needs and characteristics of this audience. In the field's literature, especially those articles about courses and learning materials for the elderly, there are few studies that contemplate digital competencies and their mapping, considering age specifics. In addition, the vast majority of works about the elderly, in Brazil, consider the losses that are inherent to human development: cognitive, physical, mental, intellectual, social, or emotional, and are mainly concentrated in the health field, followed by human sciences, multidisciplinary, and social and applied sciences.

In this sense, this work sought not only to report the mapping of digital competencies carried out with a group of elderly people, but also to discuss the use of experience research in the mapping of these competencies with this specific profile. We believe that experience research, especially in-depth individual interviews and user observation are well suited methods, which enable a better understanding of the level of digital competence of the elderly. This is particularly relevant if we consider that the elderly do not always know the terminology used in surveys, which hinders the elaboration of self-assessment questionnaires that can be understood by all elderly users.

Finally, we must emphasize that there are limitations in this work. The main one is the fact that this was a mapping study conducted in one context and cannot be replicated to others, which is typical of qualitative research. Therefore, other studies are necessary to better understand how to map digital competencies using only qualitative methods, and whether these methods can be used with a larger number of elderly users. In the end, the ultimate goal is to learn if that, effectively, would generate value for instructors, instructional designers, researchers and other professionals interested in the topic.

References

1. Lei 10.741, de 01 de outubro de 2003. http://www.planalto.gov.br/ccivil_03/leis/2003/l10.741.htm
2. Ervatti, L.R, Borges, G.M., de Jardim, A.P.: Ministério do Planejamento, Orçamento e Gestão Instituto Brasileiro de Geografia e Estatística. Diretoria de Pesquisas Coordenação de População e Indicadores Sociais Estudos e Análises Informação Demográfica e Socioeconômica, número 3, Mudança Demográfica no Brasil no Início do Século XXI Subsídios para as projeções da população (2015)
3. Envelhecimento e saúde da pessoa idosa, http://bvsms.saude.gov.br/bvs/publicacoes/evelhecimento_saude_pessoa_idosa.pdf
4. World Economic and Social Survey: development in an Ageing World (2007). https://www.un.org/en/development/desa/policy/wess/wess_archive/2007wess.pdf
5. Pesquisa nacional por amostra de domicílios: síntese de indicadores (2015). https://biblioteca.ibge.gov.br/visualizacao/livros/liv98887.pdf
6. Relatório mundial de envelhecimento e saúde (2015). https://sbgg.org.br/wp-content/uploads/2015/10/OMS-ENVELHECIMENTO-2015-port.pdf
7. Goldenberg, M.: A bela velhice. Record, Rio de Janeiro (2013)
8. Neri, A.L., Freire, A.S.: E por falar em boa velhice. Papirus, Campinas (2000)
9. Ilomäki, L., Kantosalo, A., Lakkala, M.: What is digital competence (2010). http://linked-project.wikispaces.com/file/view/Digital_competence_LONG+12.10.2010.docx
10. Recomendação do Parlamento Europeu e do Conselho de 18 de Dezembro de 2006 sobre as competências essenciais para a aprendizagem ao longo da vida (2006). http://eur-lex.europa.eu/LexUriServ/LexUriServ.do?uri=OJ:L:2006:394:0010:0018:PT:PDF
11. Calvani, A., Fini, A., Ranieri, M.: Assessing digital competence in secondary education. issues, models and instruments. In: Leaning, M. (ed.) Issues in information and media literacy: education, practice and pedagogy, 153–172. Informing Science Press, Santa Rosa (2009). https://doi.org/10.17471/2499-4324/299
12. Leiva, J.A.A.: La competencia digital, relación con el resto de competencias básicas. In: Congreso de Inspección de Andalucía: Competencias básicas y modelos de intervención em el aula (2010). http://redes-cealcla.org/inspector/DOCUMENTOS%20Y%20LIBROS/COMPETENCIAS/I%20CONGRESO%20INSPECCION%20ANDALUCIA/downloads/alvarezleiva.pdf
13. Behar, P.A.: Competências em educação à distância. Penso, Porto Alegre (2013)
14. Ferrari, A., Punie, Y., Redecker, C.: Understanding digital competence in the 21st century: an analysis of current frameworks. In: Ravenscroft, A., Lindstaedt, S., Kloos, C.D., Hernández-Leo, D. (eds.) EC-TEL 2012. LNCS, vol. 7563, pp. 79–92. Springer, Heidelberg (2012). https://doi.org/10.1007/978-3-642-33263-0_7
15. DigComp: proposta de um quadro de referência europeu para o desenvolvimento e compreensão da competência digital (2016). http://erte.dge.mec.pt/sites/default/files/Recursos/Estudos/digcomp_proposta_quadro_ref_europeu_compet_digital.pdf
16. Machado, L.R., da Silva Mendes, J.S., Krimberg, L., Silveira, C. Behar, P.A.: Competência digital de idosos: mapeamento e avaliação. In: Educação Temática Digital Campinas, SP, vol. 21 no. 4 pp. 941–959. out./dez (2019) https://doi.org/10.20396/etd.v21i4.8652536
17. Kalbach, J.: Mapeamento de Experiências: um guia para criar valor por meio de jornadas, blueprints e diagramas. Alta Books, Rio de Janeiro (2017)
18. Goodman, E., Kuniavsky, M.: Observing the User Experience, 2nd edn. Elsevier, Miami (2013)
19. Gil, A.C.: Métodos e técnicas de pesquisa social, 6th edn. Atlas, São Paulo (2008)

A Successful Transformation of Work?
An Exploratory Analysis on
Requirements and Evaluation Criteria

Julian Hildebrandt[✉], Johanna Kluge, and Martina Ziefle

Human-Computer Interaction Center (HCIC), Chair of Communication Science,
RWTH Aachen University, Campus-Boulevard, Aachen, Germany
{hildebrandt,kluge,ziefle}@comm.rwth-aachen.de

Abstract. The digital transformation of work is widely discussed by interdisciplinary research, but still, it is not sufficiently explored how different shareholders define a "successful" transformation. Our article aims to close this research gap via a two stepped exploratory approach. As a first step, we derived three dimensions from literature: Requirements, evaluation criteria, and potential conflicts. As a second step, we conducted two focus groups consisting of workers of different job sectors and levels of experience. Thematic qualitative text analysis revealed that successful transformation could be evaluated by an increased outcome quality, decreased working effort, better work life balance and employees' acceptance. It requires suitable competence acquisition programs and a participatory process and should avoid pressure by flexibility, conflicts between worker groups, and conflicts of skill or workforce structure. Results were discussed in order to provide validated instructions on how to supervise and encourage digital transformation, and how to ensure participation of less technology enthusiastic workers.

Keywords: Digital transformation · Future of work · Age · Job crafting · Content analysis

1 Introduction

The digital transformation of work is a manifold and intensively discussed process involving a wide range of technologies, such as information and communication technology (ICT), cloud computing, artificial intelligence, and decision support. Thus, it is addressing several challenges of HCI research, such as adaption and personalization of human needs, human skill support, and demographic change [1]. But still, perspectives on digital transformation benefits are mostly tied to technical and economic evaluation criteria that arise from effectiveness and efficiency.

However, this perspective fails to cover all potentials and risks of digital transformation. The whole working world shifts into a new employer/employee relationship: Instead of job security, employees aim for employability security

© Springer Nature Switzerland AG 2020
M. Kurosu (Ed.): HCII 2020, LNCS 12181, pp. 257–272, 2020.
https://doi.org/10.1007/978-3-030-49059-1_19

and continuous training, while career goals are not achieved by climbing up vertical job ladders but by horizontal changes [2]. Boundaries between work and life disappear [3], and workplaces are more and more disconnected from spatial and temporal constraints [4]. Potential conflicts arise because this transition might impact workers life quality considerably [5], and furthermore precarious jobs of shorter tenures (e.g. *gigwork*) are getting more common. This whole process needs to be actively shaped to provide a participatory changing process and therefor maintain social integrity [6]. Furthermore, potentials like enhanced working motivation, implementation of innovative ideas into workplaces and development of digital skills could only be put into effect by well-researched concepts [7].

Our article contributes to a general concept of employees' participation in digital transformation by identifying an employee-based definition of successful digital transformation, with a side-focus on differences between employer and employee perspectives, as well as requirements for successful transformation and potential conflicts that need to be avoided. The outline of this article is as follows: We provide an overview on digital transformation, as well as possible evaluation criteria in Sect. 2, to transfer those insights into our focus group guideline. Conduction and analysis of these focus group sessions are described in Sect. 3, results of qualitative content analysis are presented in Sect. 4. We discuss these results in order to provide communicative guidelines for an improved digital transformation process in Sect. 5, reflect on limitations in Sect. 6 and summarize our contribution in Sect. 7.

2 Related Work

2.1 Perspectives on Digital Transformation of Work

How is digital transformation different from digitization and digitalization? *Digitization* refers to the process of transferring information from analogue to digital, *digitalization* to the use of digitized information in applications and *digital transformation* to the increasing interconnection of digital applications and data [8]. Even if those terms are built upon each other, there is unfortunately no established term that refers to the process as a whole. Furthermore, practices like telework or other employment or work practices that are enabled by the use of digital technology [9] are arguably not sufficiently covered by the definition, but obviously part of the phenomenon. According to the previous definitions and limitations, we refer to *the Digital Transformation of Work* as the shift from analogue to digital working processes, the introduction of novel digital working processes, the interconnection of applications, as well as the social potentials and practices that are enabled by that. This process is extensive, irreversible, has enormous social implications and is always tied to technology, by the time of this article mostly ICT.

One of the main challenges of the digital transformation of work—beyond interconnecting applications and data—is the overcome of digital divide among workers: Differences in information literacy and digital skills lead to differences in ICT adoption behavior [10] and development of digital skills [11]. Both are by our definition key requirements for digital transformation. Telework (sometimes referred to as *mobile work, remote work* etc.) is one of the first consequences of successful ICT adoption and usage among workers, and defined by performing work outside a firm's premises. It has been shown to have a positive impact on job satisfaction if working processes are well-supported by ICT and the form of spacial flexibility is chosen by the employee, in contrast to the task or the employer [9]. While telework seems as largely beneficial for both employee and employer, it could have been shown to have also a positive impact on organizational commitment and job-related well-being, but also come at the cost of less work intensification and a greater inability to switch-off [12]. However, it is still an growing trend and in the main discussed as beneficial, although the circumstances need to be considered carefully [13].

Another perspective on digital transformation is the participation during the process, which highlights the importance to understand social dynamics as well. *Job-Crafting* is defined as specific form of behaving proactively in changing and reshaping tasks. It has been shown to have a positive impact on individual and team work engagement, creativity and performance, while relying on challenging transformational leaders and being moderated by promotion focus (i.e. aiming for development instead of security needs) as motivation strategy [14]. Communication concepts have to be adapted to different motivational styles to ensure job crafting, which in turn can be directly connected to technology adoption [15]. Furthermore, different worker groups, such as elderly workers require specific training and participation programs to match their needs [16], since such *silver workers* show less motivational aspects, but also less technostress [17]. Employee participation has furthermore been shown to reduce job insecurity [18].

In summary, digital transformation offers huge benefits for workers and companies, but has to fulfil several requirements, such as digital job characteristics and ICT support, as well as job crafting and suitable communication strategies.

2.2 What Defines a Successful Transformation?

Since digital transformation as a global process is still in progress, there is only little known about criteria that define a successful transformation, especially in the context of different stakeholders, e.g. employers and employees.

Employers and companies expect an increase of productivity by the use of digital technology that arises from less working effort or even the replacement of workers. Furthermore they expect increased motivation, an increased ability to participate, and further analysis tools for working time and outcome [19]. On the other hand, there is only little known about what employees expect or want, but they definitely fear reduced job-satisfaction or health that arise from constant availability, as well as the fear of not being able to cope with new technology [20]. Despite specific perspectives, successful transformation could be measured by an increase in life quality, job-satisfaction, efficiency, effectiveness and reduction of insecurity [6], but these rather general criteria are not yet covered by empirical research. How do employees define a successful transformation of work, and what requirements and potential conflict do they identify, specifically in regards to the employer/employee relationship?

3   Methodology

This section describes our focus group design, sample as well as our qualitative analysis procedure.

3.1   Focus Group Design

Both our focus groups were designed semi-structured and guideline based. To keep moderator effects constant, the same moderator was used in both sessions [21], which lasted about 60 min each.

The semi-structured guideline consisted of three sections. As initial step, an explanation video (4:12 min) was shown to the participants to briefly inform about digital transformation. The video covered several aspects, such as raising complexity, the necessity to adapt to digital technology and economic challenges.

The first section of the guideline covered questions regarding the digital status quo of participants workplaces. The second section was about requirements for a successful digital transformation. This section was separated into questions regarding new introduction of digital processes and substitution of analogue processes on the other hand. The following third section covered the main part of the session, addressing evaluation criteria for a successful transformation, at first from the perspective of employees, at second from the perspective of employers. The fourth section addresses potential conflicts during the process of digital transformation.

3.2   Sample Description

Overall, 10 participants (6 female, 4 male), aged from 21 to 56 ($M = 30.2, SD = 9.7$) took part in two separate focus group sessions. Participants were sampled to be employees from distinct industrial sectors and of different ages. All participants volunteered and there was no monetary compensation. All participants agreed to audio recording and were allowed to leave the session at any time.

3.3   Analysis Procedure

As a fist step, both audio recordings were transcribed to text in accordance to the well-established GAT2-Convention [22]. To keep our qualitative analysis inter-subjective and relaible, we used the analysis procedure of thematic content analysis [23], complying with the open coding approach [24] in a consensual variation [25]. We defined both transcriptions as sampling units, the participants contribution to the discussion as recording unit, a single phrase as smallest possible content unit, and a whole coherent statement as context unit.

The initial deductive category system contained *Requirements, Evaluation Criteria* and *Potential Conflicts* as main categories, while Evaluation Criteria is split into *Employees' Perspective* and *Employers' Perspective*. The idea to split Requirements into new introduction of digital processes and substitution of analogue processes was dropped because all coders did not found this difference covered by the actual discussion.

Both transcriptions were analyzed by five professionals independently, by assigning the material inductively and iterative into sub-categories. Those five category systems were combined into the final result among several inter-coder meetings. This final result is unanimous and fully inter-coder reliable.

4   Results

This section presents the results of our qualitative analysis category-wise. We identified 220 content units which we assigned into 45 categories (see Fig. 1). For reasons of legibility, we report employers and employees' perspective on evaluation criteria as separate main categories.

4.1   Main Category 1: Requirements

The first main category addresses conditions and context properties that enable for a successful transformation of work. Results could be inductively assigned into two inductive subcategories: Technology related requirements and process related requirements.

Technology Related. Content units were assigned into this subcategory, if the requirement addressed a specific technology instead of the transformation process itself, i.e. . *The technology should...* vs. *The transformation process should....*

Competence Acquisition

Teaching and Training: Our participants clearly stated that teaching and training about how to use a newly introduced digital technology is necessary to be provided by the company. While the use of digital work technology always seems "super fancy at a first glance, employees obviously need time to get to know a new system". While the question if every technology should come with a training program was quite controversially discussed (i.e. "There was a training program and i was there, but it was so boring i forgot almost everything"), there was broad consensus that employers should not "leave their workers alone" with new technology. Besides training programs, employers should provide multimedia tutorial websites and the possibility of specific support.

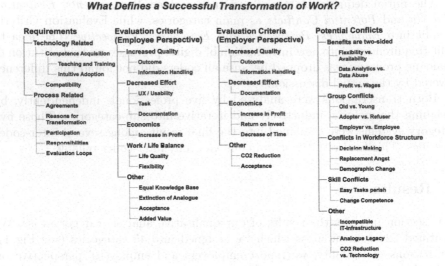

Fig. 1. Final category system as result of thematic content analysis.

Intuitive Adoption: In contrast to the units in the first category, some participants stated that they would clearly disagree on teaching and training, because new software should always be as intuitive as possible. Furthermore, new digital working technology should always provide "learning by doing" and free exploration.

Compatibility. Besides arguments of competence acquisition, subjects also discussed the role of compatibility to existing technology as well as previous knowledge. A successful transformation of work therefor requires an effective use of the fit between the new technology and previously known (e.g. a professional chat applications should not be fundamentally different from a professional workspace application), as well as previous analogue processes (e.g. simply digitize the paper-based process).

Process Related. In contrast to the previous section, units in this subcategory discuss the transformation process independent from specific technology.

Agreements on ICT Usage: All participants agreed that there must be some sort of agreement or communicative etiquette about the use of digital technology, e.g. "no communication after 8PM" or do-not-disturb modi. This discussion is furthermore covered in Sect. 4.4.

Reasons for Transformation: Our subjects discussed the need of reasoning by the employer on why the digital transformation took place: "Employers need to justify why technology was introduced, what benefits do they expect and what the overall strategy is". Other aspects were covered by the point that digital processes were never fully developed when they are introduced. Overall, our participants demanded a transparent process.

Participation: Regarding the participation during the transformation process, our subjects wanted contact points to be clear: "It is very difficult to give feedback. Most employers do not negotiate updates with software companies". Besides this aspect, employees were seen to gladly take on the role of being part in software improvement iterations.

Responsibilities: As further requirements our subjects identified clear responsibilities. Employers are held responsible for collecting evaluation, providing training and teaching, providing documentation about teaching programs. Employers should act as mediators between users and software companies. The current role of employees was rated as "too proactive" in cases of trouble or need for improvement.

Evaluation Loops: In addition to the last aspect, our participants demanded evaluation loops and discussions without fixed expectations on outcome. The transformation process should be independent of current software solutions and should be replaceable by alternatives at any time. Furthermore, this regular evaluation should cover exhaustive aspects, which are reported in the next section.

4.2 Main Category 2a: Evaluation Criteria (Employees' Perspectives)

This first part of the second main category contains units about the employees' perspective on evaluation criteria of a successful digital transformation of work. Participants covered a wide range of arguments here, hence our coders could identify five subcategories: *Increased Quality, Decreased Effort, Economic Aspects, Work/Life Balance,* and *Other Aspects*.

Increased Quality. Content units were assigned into this category, if the participants statement contained some form of quality improvement as measurement for successful transformation. We could derive *Outcome* and *Information Flow*.

Outcome: One of the key aspects of successful transformation was improved output, regardless if this output refers to "better product quality", "more precision" or "better creative output". Some participants furthermore remained abstract and stated that transformation is successful if "the process works better than before".

Information Handling: The second subcategory refers to the information handling that could be improved, mostly by the use of ICT. Digital information handling "ensures" that important information is omniaccessible and validated.

Decreased Effort. *Decreased Effort*, as second subcategory, covers all aspects that highlight less effort for achieving goals. This subcategory could be refined by *UX/Usability*, *Task* and *Documentation*.

UX/Usability: Participants argued that an important evaluation criterion is that the system is "fun to use and frustration-free", which could be subsumed under the label of UX and usability. A successful transformation "reduces effort for the employees" and is worth the changing costs of the introduction. Furthermore our subjects demanded the feeling of being "supported by the system", even if the overall process might take longer.

Task: Another argument cluster refers to task support. An important criterion is that the task needs to be supported in a positive way. Task support needs to be "of more clarity" and the tool has to be at a "high level of specialization". Digital transformation has to make work easier than before.

Documentation: One rather unpopular part of work is documentation. Digital transformation could reduce working effort specifically in this domain, since every action on a digital device could theoretically be "documented and secured accurate to the second".

Work/Life Balance. This subcategory contains all units that refer to a better relation between work and free time. We could identify *Life Quality* and *Flexibility* as inductive sub-subcategories.

Life Quality: Our participants stated that successful digital transformation could be evaluated by nothing less than an improvement on "life quality and general happiness". The benefit from digital transformation could directly contribute to a more family-friendly workplace and more time for friends and hobbies.

Flexibility: Improved flexibility in terms of Independence of working location and time was also considered as a suitable evaluation criteria for digital transformation, even if it was quite controversially discussed as potential conflict (see Sect. 4.4).

Economic Aspects. This subcategory could be more specifically refined in the employers perspective, but even from the workers point of view, an *Increase in Profit* is one of the key evaluation aspects of digital transformation. A company has to achieve some sort of monetary benefit in advance to the transformation.

Other Aspects. We were able to identify four further categories that could not be assign into any of the other categories. Those were *Equal Knowledge Base*, *Exile of Analogue*, *Acceptance* and *Added Value*.

Equal Knowledge Base: Participants argued that an equal knowledge base, on which "everyone has the same information and skills" might be an indicator of successful digital transformation.

Exile of Analogue: Furthermore, our subjects found that digital transformation could be measured by its consequence. A radical approach of this criteria might even lead to "a prohibition of paper".

Acceptance: Another identified factor was *Acceptance*. Employees should accept the technology and should use them frustration-free and deliberately.

Added Value: As last argument of this category, our participants discussed some *added value*, which was defined as fun, a good working climate and happy workers. All units have in common that this value is emotional and directly derived by the technology.

4.3   Main Category 2b: Evaluation Criteria (Employers' Perspectives)

The second part of this main category addresses the employers perspective and is refined by the same subcategories as the previous section except *Work/Life Balance*. We could replicate the categories *Increased Quality*, *Decreased Effort*, *Economic Aspects*, and *Other Aspects*. The category definitions on sub-category level remained the same as in Sect. 4.2.

Increased Quality. As in the previous section, we could derive *Outcome* and *Information Handling* as sub-subcategories.

Outcome: Our participants argued that the best indicator for a successful transformation of work was either the optimization of outcome products in terms of "product quality, an improved creative output or more effective meetings". Digitally transformed processes could therefor lead to outcome improvement in several terms.

Information Handling: Another aspect of increased quality is covered by this second subcategory: Improved information handling, which is defined as a better "filing, validation and access to information", which in turn might lead to faster working in general.

Decreased Effort. In contrast to the previous section, our participants only mentioned a decreased effort in *Documentation* as evaluation criteria for successful transformation in the employees' perspective.

Documentation: In comparison to the previous results, the units in this category highlight the possibility to monitor working-hours and progress. By digital documentation, the employer has less effort to rate "task process and working hours" based on the systems' documentation.

Economic Aspects. As expected, the economic aspects were discussed more in-depth among the employers perspective. In addition to the previously identified *Increase in Profit*, we could further build subcategories of *Return on Invest* and *Decrease of Time*.

Increase in Profit: This argument could be identified as the key evaluation criteria from the employers perspective. Participants stated that "the employers primary goal is always an increase in profit", no matter if this is reached by "producing more products", a "silent replacement of workers" by not re-employing retiring workers, or just a general increase in efficiency.

Return on Invest: In addition to an increase in profit, a *Return on Invest* could also be identified as key metric: The digital transformation needs to recoup the investment on them, i.e. by reducing personnel costs.

Decrease of Time: As last sub-subcategory of economic aspects, our participants discussed a decrease of required time to complete working tasks. A transformation is evaluated as successful if "workers are able to work faster" afterwards.

Other. We could replicate the category of *Acceptance* under the other evaluation aspects, as well as the new criterion of *CO2-Reduction*.

CO2-Reduction: Participants argued that digital transformation could lead to a reduction of CO2-Emissions, i.e. if face-to-face meetings are substituted by video calls.

Acceptance: At last, employers could evaluate a successful digital transformation by its acceptance among workers. Participants argued that digital transformation "needs to be lived and accepted among the whole company". This was set to the conditions of transparency and further analytics, such as the question of e.g. under which circumstances video calls are preferred over face-to-face meetings.

4.4   Main Category 3: Potential Conflicts

This last main category covers potential conflicts that arise from digital transformation. Based on the content units, we identified five sub-categories: *Benefits are Two-Sided*, *Group Conflicts*, *Workforce Structure*, *Skill Conflicts*, and *Other*.

Benefits Are Two-Sided. To be classified as two-sided benefit, content units had to match the criteria to contain a trade-off or a different framing of the same benefit, such as *Flexibility vs. Availability*, *Data Analytics vs. Data Abuse*, and *Profit vs. Wages*.

Flexibility vs. Availability: The ambiguity of flexibility was mentioned as most problematic regarding digital transformation, since being able to work everywhere and at any time was discussed as beneficial and disadvantageous, as this anchor example indicates: "My computer is always within reach and theoretically i am able to work until i fall asleep and this is a curse and a blessing. In addition, i have to be available to my boss all around the clock". On the other hand, flexibility is wanted by both employers and employees, even if the quality of free time might be reduced. Another conflict is shown in the common practice that overtime work is usually not documented when it takes place at home.

Data Analytics vs. Data Abuse: The possibility of current documentation (see Sect. 4.2) keeps the conflict of data abuse. In the worst case, digital transformation could lead to constant and unjustifiable surveillance. Hence, "Data protection in all its facets" needs to be provided, but interests are conflicting.

Profit vs. Wages: Another two-sided benefit addresses the question who profits from the increase in productivity that is made possible by digital transformation. Employees such as employers benefit from an increase in profit, "but on the other hand, the profit usually does not get its way to the employee".

Group Conflicts. Some of the mentioned conflicts are directly addressing conflicts between distinct groups within a company, such as *Old vs. Young, Adopter vs. Refuser* and *Employer vs. Employees.*

Old vs. Young: Participants argued, that specifically older workers that learned analogue processes refuse to adopt to digital technology. In addition, older employees are usually in higher positions than younger employees and hold therefore more decision competence. Furthermore "training programs are neither made nor attractive for workers that are about to be retired".

Adopter vs. Refuser: Besides older vs. younger workers there are two groups that seem similar within the underlying motivation: Technology adopter vs. refuser, since "one kind of worker is able to adopt to new technology, while the other refuses it, maybe even because he might be able to work on a machine, but is not able to learn the underlying concepts of controlling the machine by programming code".

Employer vs. Employees: Employers were seen to "enjoy a more digital lifestyle in their daily life than the ordinary worker, and therefore feels better about digital chance". And on a more general level, the conflict arises from the practice that employers decide about tools and processes that are used by different persons. Thus, if problems arise, the communication from user (i.e. employee) to decider (i.e. employer) must be ensured.

Workforce Structure. This section covers conflicts that arise from differences in the workforce structure, but are not relatable to distinct groups, but rahter processes and practices. Sub-categories are: *Decision Making, Replacement Angst,* and *Demographic Change.*

Decision Making: This conflict is derived from the question of who decides about rules and policies that arise from digital transformation. Policies like "No access to work after 8PM" that contribute to a healthy lifestyle "are not easily implemented by workers because the one who makes the suggestion might seem lazy".

Replacement Angst: Even if our subjects were aware that digitalization in general leads to new types of jobs and not just to a reduction, the fear of being replaced was mentioned as arising conflict.

Demographic Change: In addition to the previous result regarding replacement, another conflict arises from the problem that demographic change leads to less suitable candidates for open job applications.

Skill Conflicts. This section addresses two conflicts that arise from a shifting of required competences: *Easy Tasks Perish* and *Change Competence.*

Easy Tasks Perish: Our participants mentioned that "stupid parts of work persist while the challenging tasks remain". This conflict is two-fold since workers need to be trained to solve more challenging tasks, and their overall job is being reduced to this challenging tasks only.

Change Competence: Furthermore, our participants argued that the acquisition of new competences and the general "adaptation to changes becomes a skill itself".

Other. As in the previous main categories, we were not able to assign every unit into categories of more abstract levels. As other potential conflicts we identified *Incompatible IT-Infrastructure, Analogue Legacy* and *CO2-Reduction vs. Technology.*

Incompatible IT-Infrastructure: Some participants argued that digital technology is "all well and good, but worthless if the conditions are not suitable". According to this, digital technology must be adopted to a bigger context from matching hardware to matching policies.

Analogue Legacy: This refers to processes as well as technologies prior to the transformation. Content units in this category referred to the conflict that arises from insufficient digitalization, i.e. "processes that are to an extent of 70% digital, but also need notes on a sheet of paper".

CO2-Reduction vs. Technology: This aspect was surprisingly controversial discussed. Participants argued that a conflict arises from CO2-Reduction, because higher technological complexity leads to more energy consumption, since "more computing power is needed".

5   Discussion

Our study answers the research question of employees' evaluation criteria for a successful digital transformation of work, as well as requirements and potential conflicts.

Regarding requirements we were able to replicate previous findings regarding competence acquisition, specifically teaching and training [16]. Employees want training programs to be individually tailored for different target groups, specifically addressing different previous knowledge and learning styles. This is furthermore covered by all potential group conflicts we were able to identify. Based on this finding, we highly recommend to rather provide multimedia documentation and interactive tutorials than face-to-face training programs. If training programs are to be provided, they should not be mandatory. Further results regarding requirements show that employers and companies should proactively make their transformation progress transparent, participative and well structured. This requirement complements the previous work by Hetland et al., since even motivated workers expect transformational leaders to behave proactive [14]. Employees want digital transformation to be an iterative and openly discussed process. We recommend to re-evaluate benefits and discuss further developments between workers and management level. Employers are furthermore expected to mediate between workers and software developers.

Addressing the evaluation criteria, we did not find fundamental differences between employees' and employers' perspectives. Both perspectives contain economic benefits, even if these are more specifically mentioned in the employer perspective. Our results contribute therefor to the most obvious criterion found in literature: Digital transformation should lead to an economic benefit, even though it is enabled by more product outcome or less production time. Furthermore, our results show that digital transformation should reduce working effort in regards of task complexity and documentation. Apart from that, novel processes should definitely be user-centered designed, since results furthermore highlight the crucial role of user experience and usability for technology acceptance. A successful digital transformation could be evaluated by economic benefit, increased outcome quality, decreased working effort in regards to task complexity and documentation, as well as technology acceptance, an equal knowledge base among workers, and an increase in work life balance. Apart from that, the resulting process should be totally digital. While some of these criteria are easily to be measured (e.g. profit), others need to be carefully operationalized. These results could contribute to a digital transformation controlling tool for middle management, as well as for education material and training programs. Further research should aim at a quantitative prioritization of these factors, since these are mostly trade-offs. Future research questions should examine how economic benefits are evaluated in comparison to e.g. an equal knowledge base. This is quite important to explore, since employees' interest in company benefits might drop due to shorter tenures and less vertical career possibilities [2].

Conflicts that need to be avoided address two sided benefits, such as the ambiguity of flexibility we found to be quite exhaustively discussed in the literature. Technologies and policies that provide a valid and fair possibility to take remote work into account need to be addressed by future research, i.e. how could after-work hours or small tasks be passed into account to regular working times? This might be a profound but rather complex interdisciplinary challenge for economics, psychology and social science. Unexpectedly, our participants discussed about CO_2 reduction as evaluation criteria as well as potential conflict for digital transformation. This idea of *green IT* was not covered by our literature, since this topic became more and more popular during the year of 2019. Further research should address social, as well as economic potentials of CO_2-reduction as part of an overall modernization strategy for future companies.

6   Limitations

As mentioned in Sect. 3, our sample was of employees only, thus all our employer related results are in fact employees changing their perspective. However, since employers are very hard to recruit for empirical research, we consider this a valid approach as first step into the domain of comparing employer and employee perspectives. Furthermore we found that it was quite hard to make subjects aware of the topic of digital transformation in contrast to digitization and digitalization. This underlines the complexity of the whole process, as well as the interconnectivity between those steps. This is covered by the result that participants often use those terms interchangeably with digital technology or ICT in particular. In summary we think that employees can adapt to their employers perspective on the whole digital process and their economic perspective quite well, but they might not be suitable for samples that aim to address digital transformation (in the notion of Kelly [2]) explicitly. Future research could try to overcome the problem of limited availability of employers by sampling employees with decision making competence, e.g. middle management.

7   Conclusion

To answer the research question of how employees define a successful digital transformation of work, we conducted a thematic content analysis on two focus group sessions. Results cover requirements, specific evaluation criteria, and potential conflicts. A successful transformation requires suitable training programs for different worker profiles, as well as a transparent and participatory dialogue between employees and management level about reasons for digital transformation, responsibility roles and furthermore open and unbiased evaluation loops. Employees define successful transformation by increased outcome quality, decreased working effort, economically beneficial, and flexibility enhancing. Furthermore transformation could be measured by technology acceptance, its consequence (i.e. no analogue remnants), and CO2-Reduction. Potential conflicts arise from ambivalent benefits, such as flexibility or documentation data analysis, as well as group conflicts among workers, or conflicts in the structure of workforce or tasks.

The results highlight the importance of letting employees participate in digital transformation and contribute to a better understanding on requirements and communication strategies. Further studies should examine further relationships by the use of quantitative methods such as conjoint analysis or structural equation modelling to answer the question on how workers could be encouraged to participate in digital transformation. As a parallel step, employers or members of middle management should be interviewed about digital transformation to complement our results.

Acknowledgments. We would like to thank Julianne Monissen, Anna Rohowsky, Lena Lummertzheim and Susanne Gohr for sharing their methodological expertise during our qualitative analysis. Furthermore, we would like to thank all participants of both our focus groups. This research was funded by the Project SiTra 4.0 (German Ministry for research and education, reference no. 02L15A000- 02L15A004).

References

1. Stephanidis, C., et al.: Seven HCI grand challenges. Int. J. Hum.-Comput. Interact. **35**(14), 1229–1269 (2019)
2. Stone, K.V.: From Widgets to Digits: Employment Regulation for the Changing Workplace. Cambridge University Press, Cambridge (2004)
3. Kelliher, C., Richardson, J., Boiarintseva, G.: All of work? All of life? Reconceptualising work-life balance for the 21st century. Hum. Resour. Manage. J. **29**(2), 97–112 (2019)
4. Vilhelmson, B., Thulin, E.: Who and where are the flexible workers? Exploring the current diffusion of telework in Sweden. New Technol. Work Employ. **31**(1), 77–96 (2016)
5. Waller, A.D., Ragsdell, G.: The impact of e-mail on work-life balance. In: Aslib Proceedings. Emerald Group Publishing Limited (2012)
6. Cherry, M.A.: Beyond misclassification: the digital transformation of work. Comp. Lab. L. Pol'y J. **37**, 577 (2015)
7. Oldham, G.R., Da Silva, N.: The impact of digital technology on the generation and implementation of creative ideas in the workplace. Comput. Hum. Behav. **42**, 5–11 (2015)
8. Erfurth, C.: The digital turn: on the quest for holistic approaches. In: Fahrnberger, G., Gopinathan, S., Parida, L. (eds.) ICDCIT 2019. LNCS, vol. 11319, pp. 24–30. Springer, Cham (2019). https://doi.org/10.1007/978-3-030-05366-6_2
9. Neirotti, P., Raguseo, E., Gastaldi, L.: Designing flexible work practices for job satisfaction: the relation between job characteristics and work disaggregation in different types of work arrangements. New Technol. Work Employ. **34**(2), 116–138 (2019)

10. Yu, T.K., Lin, M.L., Liao, Y.K.: Understanding factors influencing information communication technology adoption behavior: the moderators of information literacy and digital skills. Comput. Hum. Behav. **71**, 196–208 (2017)

11. van Laar, E., van Deursen, A.J., van Dijk, J.A., de Haan, J.: Determinants of 21st-century digital skills: a large-scale survey among working professionals. Comput. Hum. Behav. **100**, 93–104 (2019)

12. Felstead, A., Henseke, G.: Assessing the growth of remote working and its consequences for effort, well-being and work-life balance. New Technol. Work Employ. **32**(3), 195–212 (2017)

13. Boell, S.K., Cecez-Kecmanovic, D., Campbell, J.: Telework paradoxes and practices: the importance of the nature of work. New Technol. Work Employ. **31**(2), 114–131 (2016)

14. Hetland, J., Hetland, H., Bakker, A.B., Demerouti, E.: Daily transformational leadership and employee job crafting: the role of promotion focus. Eur. Manag. J. **36**(6), 746–756 (2018)

15. Petrou, P., Demerouti, E., Schaufeli, W.B.: Crafting the change: the role of employee job crafting behaviors for successful organizational change. J. Manag. **44**(5), 1766–1792 (2018)

16. Hildebrandt, J., Kluge, J., Ziefle, M.: Work in progress: barriers and concerns of elderly workers towards the digital transformation of work. In: Zhou, J., Salvendy, G. (eds.) HCII 2019. LNCS, vol. 11592, pp. 158–169. Springer, Cham (2019). https://doi.org/10.1007/978-3-030-22012-9_12

17. Kluge, J., Hildebrandt, J., Ziefle, M.: The golden age of silver workers? In: Zhou, J., Salvendy, G. (eds.) HCII 2019. LNCS, vol. 11593, pp. 520–532. Springer, Cham (2019). https://doi.org/10.1007/978-3-030-22015-0_40

18. Gallie, D., Felstead, A., Green, F., Inanc, H.: The hidden face of job insecurity. Work Employ Soc. **31**(1), 36–53 (2017)

19. Haddud, A., McAllen, D.: Digital workplace management: exploring aspects related to culture, innovation, and leadership. In: 2018 Portland International Conference on Management of Engineering and Technology (PICMET), pp. 1–6. IEEE (2018)

20. Schwarzmüller, T., Brosi, P., Duman, D., Welpe, I.M.: How does the digital transformation affect organizations? Key themes of change in work design and leadership. Mrev Manage. Rev. **29**(2), 114–138 (2018)

21. Hanington, B., Martin, B.: Universal Methods of Design: 100 Ways to Research Complex Problems, Develop Innovative Ideas, and Design Effective Solutions. Rockport Publishers, Beverly (2012)

22. Selting, M., Auer, P., et al.: A system for transcribing talk-in-interaction: GAT 2 translated and adapted for english by elizabeth couper-kuhlen and dagmar barth-weingarten. Gesprächsforschung-Online-Zeitschrift zur verbalen Interaktion **12**, 1–51 (2011)

23. Kuckartz, U.: Qualitative Text Analysis: A Guide to Methods, Practice and Using Software. Sage, London (2014)

24. Elo, S., Kyngäs, H.: The qualitative content analysis process. J. Adv. Nurs. **62**(1), 107–115 (2008)

25. Van den Berg, A., Struwig, M.: Guidelines for researchers using an adapted consensual qualitative research approach in management research. Electron. J. Bus. Res. Methods **15**(2) (2017)

Insights into the Work of Editors of Digital Scholarly Editions for Correspondences

Tobias Holstein[1,2]([✉])[ID] and Uta Störl[2][ID]

[1] Mälardalen University, Västerås, Sweden
research@tobiasholstein.de
[2] Darmstadt University of Applied Sciences, Darmstadt, Germany

Abstract. Digital scholarly editions are one way to preserve the great literary value of correspondences for future generations. They serve as a repository of data, enriched through annotations, textual-comments and contextual information, which is the result of a manifold and extensive groundwork and research effort. The workflow and tasks of editors provide insight into how such editions are created. This is of particular interest because with better tools and environments for creating digital scholarly editions, higher efficiency can be reached.

Thus, in this paper, we provide an insight into work of editors, by analysing their workflow and related tasks, in context of a digital scholarly edition for correspondences project, and point out challenges, limitations and solutions. We confirm that there is a necessity for tools and advanced features for editors by showing examples from editorial work. Furthermore, the design process and its interconnections to software engineering and digital humanities are presented.

Keywords: Digital scholarly edition · Task analysis · Insights · Design process · Interdisciplinary · Digital humanities · Double diamond design process

1 Introduction

Benjamin Franklin Wedekind (1864–1918) was a German playwright, probably best-known for his play Spring Awakening, and book author. During his life, Wedekind maintained a manifold of correspondences via postal mail, i.e. letters and postcards. Wedekind's correspondences are of great literary value and must be preserved for future generations [4]. Currently, there are about 3500 correspondence items that are known and accessible, but further artefacts are regularly discovered during research on known artefacts. Those are to be transcribed, critically annotated, categorised and commented, which is the basis of the digital scholarly edition of Frank Wedekind. In order to further clarify the term digital edition, the categorisation of Franzini et al. [7] is quoted as follows:

© Springer Nature Switzerland AG 2020
M. Kurosu (Ed.): HCII 2020, LNCS 12181, pp. 273–292, 2020.
https://doi.org/10.1007/978-3-030-49059-1_20

S-Scholarly: An edition must be critical, must have critical components. A pure facsimile is not an edition, a digital library is not an edition.
D-Digital: A digital edition cannot be converted to a printed edition without substantial loss of content or functionality. Vice versa: a retro-digitised printed edition is not a scholarly digital edition (but it may evolve into a scholarly digital edition through new content or functionalities).
Edition: An edition must represent its material (usually as transcribed/edited text) – a catalogue, an index, a descriptive database is not an edition

Sahle states that digital scholarly editions "offer the opportunity to overcome the limitations of print technology" [13] and argues that progressing from print to digital editions opened new perspectives regarding accessibility, searchability, usability and computability. Digital and print editions can be differentiated as follows: "digital editions follow a digital paradigm", in comparison to print editions that follow(ed) a paradigm that "was shaped by the technical limitations and cultural practices of typography and book printing" [13].

Digital scholarly editions serve, from a computer science perspective, as a repository for data. This data can be enriched through annotations and comments by editors, which can provide additional information such as interconnections or relations. The data could be used to investigate and analyse relations between correspondences and an author's literary work, to research connections to other authors or to get a better understanding of the society of the past.

There are two roles that we find important to differentiate here: the *author/editor* of digital scholarly editions, and its counterpart the *information seeker*. Both well-known expressions from the information retrieval (IR) domain. The author creates data, that the information seeker is supposed to be able to search in, to browse, etc. If an author creates an incomplete or incorrect annotated text, the information seeker might not be able to find it later on. Authors can also be information seekers, e.g., when existing data is used to support the process of creating/annotating new content.

As an editor one has to conduct a manifold and extensive groundwork, which is necessary to create a digital scholarly edition, that requires expert knowledge, and a vast amount of time and effort. Usually, editors have to cope with a manifold of tools and applications, such as image processing tools (for facsimiles), text annotation/mining and database tools. We have briefly compared tools and applications that were suggested in related work and in online communities (with focus on digital humanities) as well as online courses. However, many tools are either tailored for specific domains/purposes that require a deep technical knowledge, have technical constraints (i.e. require specific platforms), are out-dated or even incompatible with current operating systems, or proprietary software, which naturally comes with various limitations and constraints.

We share the point of view of Sahle, who stated that "a digital edition is more like a workplace or a laboratory" [13], and thus posed the question of how to create a workplace, also referred to as "virtual research environment", that is easy and efficient to use. Franzini et al. [8] created a survey to investigate the expectations and requirements of digital editions and found that "digital editions are imperfect tools unable to meet the expectations of every single user", and suggested to "explore the extent to which creators of digital editions engage with their target users during the preparation and development stages of the project". Therefore, an understanding of how authors create digital scholarly editions, for whom they are created, and what user expectations and requirements for scholarly digital editions are, remains an important research endeavour.

Our contribution is therefore threefold. First, we provide an insight into the work of editors, by analysing their tasks, in the context of a digital scholarly edition for correspondences of Wedekind. We show typical challenges in the process of creating a digital scholarly edition. Second, we show that there is a necessity of providing tools and advanced features for editors of digital scholarly editions for correspondences based on our evaluation and in correlation of related work. Third, we describe our design process and outline the methods that work and did not work, to guide future researchers in the same situation. This includes the challenges of working in an interdisciplinary team of researchers from humanities and computer science, such as terminology, different knowledge of technology and experiences in using software.

2   Related Work

Baillot et al. [1] state that "Scholarly editions are generally conceived by scholars for scholars". They differentiate between "Digital scholarly editions" and "scholarly print editions". According to Baillot et al. digital editions have higher accessibility, provide the potential "to address and actually reach other readers". However, it appears that the developers of this edition are also seen to be the users. Assumptions are made and features implemented, but insights about the actual users are only accessed by evaluating log files later on.

Pohl et al. [12] describe new approaches towards user research and software architecture and depict a differentiation between maintaining software and adding new features at the same time. Issues about outdated or old systems in this domain are reported and challenges outlined.

We found that most publications neglect the important part of how data is actually prepared and efficiently entered into the system and rather focus on how data is presented, shared or used (e.g., [21]). Thus, we also conducted a competitive analysis focused on usability and data input based on the catalogue of digital editions provided by Franzini et al. [8]. The results showed a variety of methods, such as manually editing XML files [6] to comply to the TEI correspDesc XML standard [17] custom plugins for Microsoft Word that transform Word documents into TEI [15] or WYSIWYG editors [14,18].

3   Design and Development Process

In this project, we introduced a user-centred design process based on the double diamond design process [20], which utilises the principle of divergent and convergent thinking and serves as a guideline to find the right problem(s) and the right solution(s) [11]. The overall aim is to improve the computer-aided work [3] of editors of digital scholarly editions. Thus, we utilise our interdisciplinary team of researchers from digital humanities, interaction design and computer science to design, develop and test concepts, prototypes and new releases of the digital scholarly edition.

In parallel, we use a second process, from software engineering (SE), which is the basis for maintaining and incrementally extending/improving the existing software. The SE process handles tasks for the supporting platform (e.g., updates of server operating system, Java EE stack, etc.) and other tasks, such as automated database backups or security (e.g. SSL Certificates, firewall settings, etc.). The software is already used by researchers and is therefor a productive system, which requires frequent maintenance to ensure its availability and stability.

For completion, we also sketch the process used by the researchers in digital humanities. In Fig. 1 we depict the processes as parallel tracks of processes to show the methods and interconnections in one time line. Our process is similar to the Agile UX Approach (e.g. explained by Schwartz [16]), but due to a small team size and variable/temporary team members (e.g., master students writing their thesis), we adapted the process to our needs.

Thus in design phases, before a software release is created, we collect insights by conducting contextual inquiries, interviews and workshops. Low- to high-fidelity prototypes are built and tested with users, and the knowledge and feedback gained are used to implement features for the target stack. We use a separate test environment (same hardware and stack setup as the productive system) for testing new releases before the productive system is updated. After releases are rolled out, they are used by real users, and we gather feedback through contextual inquires, focus groups or usability tests. Users also frequently document and report issues via email, which can be roughly categorised into: software-related bugs (something does not work at all), usability related (something does not work well), and utility-related (we need something to ...). All of those are managed in "GitLab", which serves as a central point for information (e.g., design guidelines, interview data, bug reports, technical documentation, etc.). Thus, the knowledge gained before and after software releases, influences and informs future design decisions in this process.

One benefit of utilising two different processes is supporting different types of work within the project, such as technology-focused research (e.g., database query performance, improving the technology stack, etc.) and design-focused research (e.g., optimising the application's usefulness (utility + usability)). This is also an advantage for side projects, such as a student writing a master thesis. Students have their time frame and schedule and thus produce artefacts and solutions, but also insights into specific problems. Their solutions can (and most often do) solve problems discovered/documented in either of the two high-level processes.

3.1   Design Process

The double diamond design process is split into four phases: *discover*, *decide*, *develop* and *deliver*. The process is iterative but not necessarily sequential, which

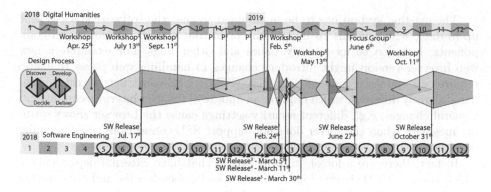

Fig. 1. High level view of the Design Process and its intertwining and interconnections with the processes of the digital humanities research group and the software engineering process

means it is possible to jump between phases, if necessary. The design process in Fig. 1 shows, that certain phases might also overlap, due to parallel work or the fact that in the time frame between two software releases, users will file error and bug reports always for the newest release, and thus their feedback for the last release overlaps with the *develop* phase, where we build prototypes or implement new releases. Frequent feedback, e.g. via email or conversations, is not depicted in the process seen in Fig. 1.

In the design process several methods are used, such as contextual inquires, task analysis, competitive analysis, building low-fidelity prototypes, conducted interviews as well as focus groups, sketching. High-fidelity prototypes can be time-intensive, and it is sometimes faster to directly implement a solution for the actual target platform using the SE process. This takes a considerably high effort, but the chance of failure shrinks, because of previous iterations and user tests in the design process. A result from the software engineering process is usually a new software release, which is then used in the design process to conduct user studies, etc.

The design process is the central part of this project. It is used to build the bridge between two domains, i.e. digital humanities and computer science (technology). From a high-level perspective, the design process allows us to be between human and technology, and thus have to opportunity to observe, document, facilitate communication and to work in and with both sides. This is also an opportunity to encourage interdisciplinary work between domains and to break existing barriers, e.g., by organising workshops with participants from (digital) humanities and computer science (see Workshops in Fig. 1).

3.2   Software Engineering—Maintenance, Utility and Usability

Since maintenance and software architecture is not part of this paper, we will not display the SE process in all details, but rather outline its use from the perspective of the design process as follows.

The existing system has to be maintained so that the software stack is kept up-to-date, which means to update the operating system, platform and components, but also to fix security issues and other bugs. For example, a new web browser version might introduce changes in handling web pages that also requires an update of the software. E.g. HTML/CSS constructs might be rendered slightly different, which requires an update of the user interface component. General changes, e.g., different security settings cause the browser shows warning messages when the server does not support SSL connections, might require updates.

In fact, there are a lot of "moving" parts that have external dependencies, which come with their development cycles and dependencies and thus having a separate SE process to tackle those challenges and limitations proved to be useful.

Implementing new features that involve new frameworks, components, libraries, etc. is another reason to commit to a well-defined SE process. E.g., using continuous integration and deployment to automatise the release of new versions removes a lot of manual workloads. The rising complexity of software, that is increased with every new feature, requires the use of well established SE methods.

Users are usually not interested in how their solution is built, but rather care about whether the system is up and running. However, as soon as problems appear and the software does not run as expected, they cannot work in their established process or have to skip certain parts of it. This is especially critical in the context of a digital scholarly edition, which "as a publication is a process rather than a product. It grows incrementally not only before its final release, but also during its availability to the public" [13]. Thus, breaking the process in any form means not only stopping the incremental growth but also to disrupt its availability. Therefore, it is necessary to facilitate best practices from the well-established software engineering domain, to provide state of the art technology and methods for digital scholarly editions and their underlying platforms.

4 Interviews

To understand the process of creating scholarly digital editions, we conducted a qualitative study based on the method of qualitative, semi-structured interviewing and on-site contextual inquiry [2]. The results are insights into the work of editors, i.e. experts of the field, and their tools.

4.1 Methodology

We interviewed four experts in the domain of humanities (see Table 1), who currently work with digital scholarly editions. Three of those experts (P1, P2, P3) have studied Wedekind and his correspondence, publications and artefacts in depth. One participant (P2) has studied Wedekind for more than 30 years and published multiple print editions. Due to time constraints, we scheduled

Table 1. Details about interview participants.

	Gender	Age	Job description	Role	Wedekind research	Experience
P1	F	30–40	Researcher (M.A.)	Editor	2–5 years	10–20 years
P2	M	70–80	Professor	Editor	30–40 years	40–50 years
P3	M	40–50	Researcher (PhD)	Editor	5–10 years	20–30 years
P4	M	30–40	Researcher (PhD)	Inform. Seeker	–	10–20 years

and conducted all interviews within 3 month from November 2018 to January 2019.

The interviews of P1, P2, and P3 were separated into two parts. The first part was a contextual inquiry with the editors at their workplace. We observed their work with the initial editor system (described in [18,19]), took notes and documented the workflow by taking photos (see Figs. 2, 4, and 3) and videos of the screen. We recorded a total of about 7 h of audio recordings, which we transcribed. The editor system had the same version in all interviews.

The second part of the interview was a semi-structured interview, with questions about digital scholarly editions, the expert's expectations, research purpose and usage. Due to the remote location of the interviews and time constraints, we conducted the contextual inquiry and the interview on the same day, but with a break of about one hour between both.

We also interviewed one expert (P4), who is not directly involved in the Wedekind research but worked with digital editions, and used the same semi-structured interview guideline.

Terms and expressions were translated from German to English, in the form of an analogous translation, in order to present and describe the tasks and workflow in the following sections.

5   Task Analysis and Work Flow

Based on observations during the contextual inquiries, bug reports, email discussions and workshops, we analysed tasks and workflow. Usually, digital scholarly edition "projects start with digital facsimiles and subsequently create transcriptions and edited versions of the text" [13]. However, in this project, we observed a more complex process. E.g., it requires a not to be underestimated preliminary effort to track down and to acquire documents or digital facsimiles (see Sect. 5.2). Analogue documents have to be digitised (see Sect. 5.3) and the vast amount of files have to be managed (see Sect. 5.4). While this sections seems to be ordered in a timely manner, please note that tasks are often done in parallel, not necessarily sequential, and also iterative.

5.1 Correspondence Item

The herein analysed digital scholarly edition contains correspondence items. Those come in many different types of correspondence, such as letters, post-cards, or drafts/notes. These items are either handwritten, typewritten or pre-printed (or a combination of those). An item can be written and/or signed by multiple authors and can contain multiple languages (e.g., quotes from another language such as French). The common script used around 1900 is "Kurrent", but also Latin and the use of typewriters became more common. In summary, correspondence items may contain mixtures of writing styles in Kurrent, Latin, or typewritten text, by one or multiple authors and in one or multiple languages. E.g., a post-card contains pre-printed text (e.g., the description of the picture on the back of a post-card), an addressees address written in Latin, and a German text written in Kurrent quoting french phrases. Also, some authors add draw-ings, sketches or other markings, for example musical notes in Fig. 4c, as shown by P2 during the interview.

5.2 Acquisition

Correspondence items may be available as paper copy of an original (see Fig. 2c), as digital scan, i.e. facsimile (in various file formats, Fig. 4a on the right screen), or as original (see Fig. 2b). The latter involves either a local or remote repository, such as a library, an archive or a private collection, where the correspondence items are stored and organisational effort to find, request and get access to relevant items. Additionally, artefacts and their facsimiles might be subject to copyrights and thus additional legal paperwork in the form of contracts or agree-ments have to be considered and managed by the editors. Certain obligations might affect how facsimiles can be presented online, such as the requirement of showing copyright information below the image, adding additional thank you notes, restricting the size/resolution in case of download options, or restricting the download of the facsimile. Also, copyrights last for a certain period, for exam-ple, dependent on the date of death of the author. Editors have to take this into consideration, and the digital scholarly edition system must comply with laws and regulations, which leads to additional requirements for the implementation.

5.3 Digitisation

After analogue documents have been found, they need to be digitised, i.e. scan-ning/photographing the physical document, which as an artefact is then called "facsimile" Some facilities, such as archives and libraries, offer the service of digitisation for a service fee or provide facsimiles directly. In some circumstances those facilities might lack the resources for digitisation, thus researchers have to travel to the facility (with equipment) and digitise documents themselves (see Fig. 2a). Thus, researchers have to be familiar with digitisation software, the camera equipment and the best practices for digitising documents, such as using a colour reference chart that is required for colour calibration later on (see

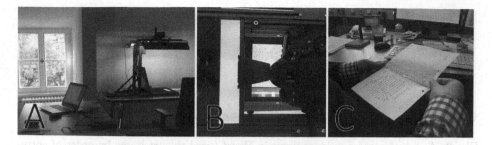

Fig. 2. A: Set-up (camera/laptop) by research team to digitise artefacts; B: Camera Point of View, showing an correspondence item and a colour reference chart; C: Researcher measuring a paper copy of an correspondence item.

Fig. 2b). The reference chart also allows to determining the size of the given object in the photograph, which can be a utility/feature in the digital scholarly edition system.

5.4 Document Management

Handling multiple thousand files like facsimiles/images, contracts, word documents, makes rigorous file management necessary. The research group of P1 and P3 use a shared Group network drive for all project-related files. They defined three main folders: (A) "letter lists", (B) "scans from sites" and (C) "transcriptions", with the following content:

A contains two Excel-Files called "Letters to Wedekind" and "Letters from Wedekind", which contain information about the current state of progress and metadata (e.g., author, date, place of writing, etc.) for each correspondence item.

B contains facsimile files organised in folders named from A to Z with sub-folders in the format "City, Name of Facility", e.g., "Zurich, Central Library".

C contains transcriptions, additional material, such as biographies, and necessary facsimiles, which have been copied from folder B and renamed so that the filename can be used to identify the contained letter or part of a letter. The files are organised in a folder from A to Z with sub-folders for each correspondent in the format "Lastname, Firstname", e.g., "Zweig, Stefan". This means the folder "Zweig, Stefan" contains all material related to the correspondence of "Frank Wedekind" and "Stefan Zweig".

5.5 Meta Data

Before the actual transcription takes place, metadata of the document has to be documented. The editors "set the framework and define the subject" [13] of the digital scholarly edition. Currently, the following metadata and categories are documented (if available): place of writing, date of writing, author, coauthor, addressee, document type (letter, draft, postcard, etc.), materiality, site of

Fig. 3. A: list of correspondence items in Word (used to sort items by order of correspondence); B: Logging the state of the transcription correspondence item in a Word document; C: Excel sheet showing a list of correspondence items with additional information about transcription states and other metadata

recipient, information of publication/print, information of location (where the originals are), copyright information. The materiality of the physical document contains information about fonts, writing style, writing tools (e.g., pencil, pen, ink, etc.), type of paper. Additional notes (free-text fields) can be added, e.g., to describe additional features. Notes are also used to denote how metadata was determined, e.g., if the diary of a person was the source of the information.

Since adding data sets of correspondence partners (person entities) is time extensive, the research team of P1 and P3 decided to create place, city and person entities in the database in advance to speed up the annotation process later on. This is possible through information from the Excel files described in Sect. 5.4. Entities can also contain additional contextual information such as a biography for a person. Creating the person entity is not seen to be a problem since for many things there are already databases with the necessary information available (P3). However, completely unknown persons, that appear in this context for the first time and have never been mentioned anywhere else, might require additional research. Another example is the change of city or street names, places and countries within the last century. Researchers use for example phone books from the time of the correspondence, which are often available from archives/libraries (as can be seen in Fig. 3b), in order to validate street names.

5.6   Transcription

We observed different setups and workflows for transcribing and reviewing correspondence items in the contextual inquiries. P1 and P3 use a Desktop-PC with two screens, one showing the facsimile and another one for the word processing software or web browser (see Fig. 4a). P2 uses a Laptop, thus single screen, but works with copies/printouts of facsimiles (see 4c). P1, P2 and P3 use keyboard and mouse, and P2 did not use the touchpad of the laptop.

The research group of P1 and P3 decided to create a template in the form of a Word file, which is used to collect metadata, transcription and other information of a correspondence item in a single document. The Word file is the work basis for all following steps. P2 and P3 explained that one Word file is used to collect a complete correspondence, but P3 stated also that this depends on the number

Fig. 4. A: Work place set-up with two screens; B: Using an external archive to research street names in phone books; C: Paper copy of a correspondence item showing hand drawn music notes.

of correspondence items and the workflow of the editor. Some editors in the research group use one Word file per correspondence item.

All editors of this digital scholarly edition adapted the workflow of transcribing to a Word file first. Multiple reasons have been identified. System crashes and software errors in early prototypes/releases of the system could have caused, yet unsaved, transcriptions to get lost (P2, P3), thus the Word file also serves as a backup for transcriptions, metadata and other notes. The file can contain a whole correspondence, instead of a single correspondence item (P3). This is important for large correspondences, where often additional notes are taken, which the current system lacks functionality for (P3). It becomes easier to find the order of correspondence and to determine a possible time range for unknown dates of writing of correspondence items when an overview of the whole correspondence is accessible (P3). P3 also stated that the digital scholarly edition system provides "very little methodological control", which can easily lead to mistakes.

An initial transcription is done by one editor and usually reviewed by at least one, most often two or more other editors. A review in this context means, that another editor collates the transcription, metadata, annotations and comments for correctness and completeness. Deciphering handwriting can be difficult because the language and thus expressions might differ from nowadays language. Therefore a discussion about the meaning of certain characters/words might be required before a conclusion can be made. P2 described the review process as letting the reviewer read the text from the original document out loud so that the editor can check/confirm the transcription. P3 explained a similar review process. Thus, at least two people read the same original document, which allows detecting miss-readings, wrong interpretations of handwriting or other errors. P2 also stated that at least two people review the transcription and that this is necessary to ensure the quality of the transcription. P1 and P3 use a Word file with the transcription, metadata and comments for review. The word comment function is used to add comments and mark problematic areas or cases of uncertainty with text markings. Editors can leave notes for the reviewer, to point to a specific already known problem.

5.7 Annotations

Sahle states that textual criticism, comments, annotations and contextual texts "have to substantiate the claim that this is the best possible representation of the editorial subject" [13]. Therefore this digital edition provides a What-You-See-Is-What-You-Get (WYSIWYG) Editor, the key component for annotating, commenting and adding contextual texts to a transcription.

There are different types of annotations available: visual annotations, e.g. font-type, underlining, strike, and bold or italic font; annotation of entities, such as person, city, literary work or events; damages in the material of the original correspondence item, e.g., when parts of the text were unreadable due to water damage.

Editors apply annotations in a different order and in different stages. P2 prepares a Word file with transcriptions and annotations. Custom markings are added in form of sign/letter combinations, for unsupported or digital edition specific annotations. Copy/paste is used to transfer the text to the WYSIWYG Editor, which converts some of the Word formats automatically to corresponding annotations. The rest of the custom markings have to be replaced with annotations from the WYSIWYG Editor, which are internally handled an XML structure.

P3 and P1 use similar custom markings, such as `<lat>jours fixes<lat>`, to mark that this part of the text was written in Latin font, instead of the default font "Kurrent". The `<lat>` custom marking is manually replaced with an annotation in the WYSIWYG Editor later on. P3 describes the first step as "to get the text into the database" and the second step as formal indexing, which means to find and annotate entities in the transcribed text, such as a city, person or place. While P1 adds contextual comments directly after annotating entities, P3 states that this step is done later on.

5.8 Editorial Guidelines

"The most basic exigency in traditional editing – State your rules and follow them! – is as well the central law and starting point of all digital editing" [13]. Due to software updates and increased possibilities, editorial guidelines might be subject to change. This might be caused by an increased functionality of the digital scholarly edition, such as support of further annotations. Editorial guidelines describe how correspondence items are annotated, transcribed and presented, but also provide information about the scholarly edition itself, its purpose and aim.

6 Interdisciplinary Work

Working in an interdisciplinary team has the advantage (and luxury) of discussing and defining common guidelines to optimise working together. In this section, we describe the methods that were most beneficial for this team.

6.1   Workshops

We regularly organise workshops with the researchers of the digital scholarly edition, in which new concepts, ideas, issues and possible solutions are discussed. It is a critical but constructive process, which also supports the knowledge transfer from computer science to digital humanities and vice versa. Discussions include, for example, explaining the limitations, constraints or feasibility of certain ideas in regard of technology, the advantages and disadvantages of certain design decisions (e.g, non-responsive vs responsive design), and to look into bugs/errors that were reported with the team.

E.g., an important improvement for the digital editions' website was the switch to responsive design and accessibility (according to WCAG). Responsive design allows viewing the same content on different devices. The content is adjusted based on the available browser space. This, however, might interfere with the expectation of having content that is always aligned/adjusted in the same way, as it is in a PDF or a printed book. We used a workshop to present test pages that exemplify how responsive design will affect the presentation of the content of the digital scholarly edition. One example is depicted in Fig. 5. Eventually, this led to changes in how content was formatted, i.e. aligned, to avoid issues in the presentation of content for mobile devices.

We recommend interdisciplinary workshops to support the knowledge exchange. It is important that computer scientists understand the requirements of the digital humanities, but it is also important that editors understand the constraints and possibilities of technology.

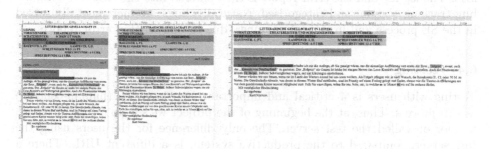

Fig. 5. Mock-up for a Workshop to show how different screen sizes, orientation and resolution affect the layout of an example text

6.2   Focus Groups

Focus groups "involving multiple participants can be useful for understanding a range of perspectives, but execution and analysis can be complicated by the dynamics of individuals working in a group" [9]. We can confirm the positive effect of Focus groups regarding the understanding of a range of different perspectives. Our interdisciplinary team organised a focus group with 7 students as part of a seminar lecture about letter culture around 1900. A homework exercise was given in advance, which included 8–10 tasks about finding certain information on the digital scholarly editions website. This was used as a basis for discussion during the meeting. The students of age from 20 to 25 explained how they used the website, and what solutions they found for the given tasks. They also discovered usability issues, suggested improvements and complained about the choice of colours (among other things).

The most important take away from this focus group was, however, reports about how and when students used the website. One student told that she browsed and read letters published in the digital scholarly edition while taking the bus to the university using her mobile phone. Having had a long discussion about the usefulness of responsive design and other design choices weeks before that, made the team aware of different contexts of use and in consequence the importance of responsive design.

The constructive feedback of this focus group led to further improvements of the digital scholarly editions web site.

6.3   Feedback and Error Reports

We defined a very easy rule about how to handle bug reports in this project. Editors should not waste time in filing bug reports, instead, it should be made as easy and comfortable as possible. Our rule states that all error reports are sent to our mailing list with a short error description, time of the error, a screenshot (if possible) and any other useful information. After receiving an error report, log files are checked for detailed error descriptions, which the system automatically logs. The log file and the error report is then entered into the ticket system, i.e. bug tracking system, and categorised. Naturally, bugs are incrementally solved in the SE process and in a timely manner, due to well-written error reports.

6.4   Testing

Testing with users is a critical and important step in every (human-centred) design process. Thus, at the beginning of the project we set up a second server, further on called the test server. The only difference for the users using the test server, compared to the productive system, is a different URL. There a username/password prompt is shown to protect the test website from being crawled by search engines, which could confuse visitors when they accidentally end up on the test server instead of the productive system.

The test server is used for internal tests, and every pre-release version is tested before it enters the productive system. We have tried remote tests with researchers, but due to the lack of dedicated time for testing, users did not engage with the system as they would with the productive system. This means instead of following the process for entering metadata strictly by the guidelines, users on the test system skipped steps and entered less metadata, annotations and contextual information as usual. Thus, many errors were not found and were later rolled out to the productive system, even though they system was also tested by the software engineers. This shows again that "Designers Are Not Users" [10] and that testing with real users is absolutely inevitable.

In order to cope with this, we blocked some time for testing in workshops and meetings, and used the contextual inquires to gain insight on pre-releases.

6.5 Sketching, Low-Fidelity Prototypes, and Live-Coding

The domain of Digital humanities has a strong focus on text, but it is difficult to convey ideas for interaction styles, page layouts and more via text. Instead, in workshops and meetings, we use sketches, paper prototypes, and sometimes clickable low-fidelity prototypes to show how certain ideas, concepts and thus solutions could be implemented. In workshops, the whiteboard is also often used to discuss identified problems and solutions. Figure 6 shows an example sketch, where the transcription and commenting functions are shown next to a facsimile viewer.

In some workshops, the principles of live-coding were used to test different variants of how content is presented on the digital editions web site. The browser's developer tools were utilised to change style sheets and HTML structures to show and explain features and possibilities. A screenshot from the live coding session is shown in Fig. 7.

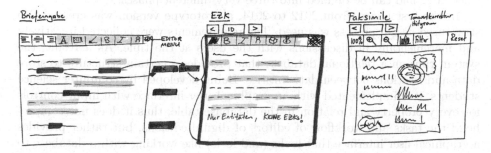

Fig. 6. Sketches of different states of the WYSIWYA Editor (left&middle) and a facsimile viewer (right)

7 Discussion

There are two perspectives that are important to differentiate, but at the same time are intertwined with each other. The first perspective takes the side of the editor, who is entering data into the system. The second perspective is the side of the user (e.g., students, researchers, etc.) that use the data for various purposes, such as literature research.

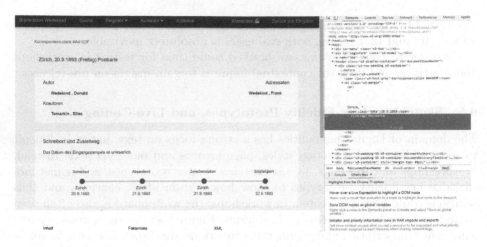

Fig. 7. Live-Coding: changing HTML/CSS of the web site during a workshop presentation using a browser's developer tools.

7.1 Iterative and Incremental Process

Any given system comes with certain constraints. The project has been running since 2012 and can be divided into three very different phases.

In the first phase, from 2012 to 2014, a prototype version was created. No structured design process was used. The requirements were collected iteratively and incrementally in discussions with the users at the time. As a result, the system runs on a relational database that provides a certain structure to store data and relations between data entities. Being developed by computer science students, it is implemented with an graphical user interface with input controls for every property and relation in the database table, thus it does not comprehend the tasks and workflow of editors of digital editions, but rather provides a graphical user interface that looks (and feels) like working with a database to store and archive correspondence items.

This comes with positive, but also negative aspects. Positive is, that there is a relational model of how data is stored and connected, thus it provides a fixed, consistent and clear structure with data fields expecting certain formatted data input. This allows to check the data for consistency using standard queries (e.g., via SQL queries).

However, being confined to the given structure, editors can struggle to enter data that had not been expected, foreseen while the data model was created. This is a natural problem when we consider the tasks and the workflow of editors. We will come back to this point later.

From 2014 to 2018, the system was not further developed in terms of IT, but the editors have already entered a number of documents and other artefacts. This data is now stored in the selected structure in the database.

In the third phase of the project, since 2018, the project has been worked on intensively by a new and larger group of editors and a professional software developer. The new and more users naturally lead to new requirements. Correspondence items are entered incrementally, sometimes as bulk package of multiple correspondence items between two authors. Thus, in the process of entering, annotating and commenting those items, discoveries are being made and those interesting details, patterns, relations, etc. might want to be annotated, commented or stored by editors. This leads to discussions between editors in the research group, of how this information might be entered into the system. We have observed multiple different cases of storing data that circumvents, i.e. exploits, the given data structure.

Therefore, since 2018, we have been further developing the system based on these new requirements and used the double diamond design process as a guideline for design methods. Ideas, needs and wishes are regularly discussed in common interdisciplinary workshops. This allows to conclude that the work process of digital editors is incremental and iterative, and it connects to the software engineering process on multiple occasions.

There are two main types of new requirements: (D) The nature of the data was not correctly recorded; (A) Annotations are missing in order to record the contents of the letter text with editorial accuracy.

As an example of category (D), only persons were originally intended as correspondence partners. During scientific research and the discovery of further correspondence items, it turned out that journals can also be correspondence partners. Of course, journals have completely different characteristics than persons and therefore the data model of the database must be adapted. The adaptation of a relational schema for already existing data is a complex process that has to be carried out very carefully.

Sometimes it also happens that editors enter unexpected data in data fields outside the intended purpose as workaround, might lead to ambiguous data where unambiguous data was expected. This can affect algorithms that create statistics based on this field. Consequently, algorithms must be adapted. Generally speaking, due to the newly introduced complexity in the data fields, new evaluations have to be carried out or the data model has to be changed to take these new requirements into account, which also requires the transformation of existing data.

There are also interesting challenges regarding annotations (A). The number and variants of annotations in the field of edition science are very large and diverse. Here it is important to convey that only true TEI annotations can be evaluated later. Characters that (as in print editions) can be used to mark them up make the search later more difficult or even impossible. Editors use existing annotations, but combine/cascade annotations or define certain characters in combination with an annotation to define a new annotation that the system did not previously provide. E.g. a text annotated as "bold" is used to show printed text (not written by hand or typewriter) on a post card. Another example is the combination of square brackets and text annotated as italic: `<p>[<hi><i>Dank für die</i></hi>] Glückwünsche,</p>`. E.g., those combinations might be expected to be found via search function (perspective of information seekers), because they can be easily mistaken for real annotations in the presentation of the text. Here it is important to establish a process that allows missing annotation types to be added to the WYSIWYG Editor in order to avoid those and other quality problems later on.

7.2   From Print Edition Tool and Mindset Towards Digital Editions

"What You See Is What You Get" (WYSIWYG) is not a fitting expression for the work in digital editions anymore. Digital editions offer much more possibilities, even because they are interactive, interconnected and dynamic. Annotations are one of the reasons, and the more we can use information technology to parse and understand text (either through automated text mining, or manual annotations or contextual comments) the more opportunities we can create. We suggest to call it "What You See Is What You Annotated" (WYSIWYA) instead, showing that we moved away from 'just' visual formatting as it was standard for print editions.

From the perspective of information retrieval, annotations are a way of indexing the content and thus allowing information seekers to find information better and in different ways. Thus, a WYSIWYA Editor that allows to efficiently add annotations, contextual information and comments to transcribed texts, can reduce the time to build a digital scholarly edition. Time saved due to not being required to enter and fill complex XML structures manually, can be used for research or for improving the digital scholarly edition. Once WYSIWYA Editors are configurable to dynamically support new annotations, as needed by the editors, it will allow to add new levels of contextual enrichment to transcribed text. This can then be used to improve the annotation task for new transcriptions, by detecting similar text patterns, or by suggesting entities that have been used in the remainder of a correspondence. Since it is a scholarly edition, the editor must be in control of what is annotated and annotations have to be verified by an editor.

In workshops and discussions many different ideas came up to improve the work of editors of digital scholarly editions. Those ideas reach from visual representation, statistical analysis of correspondence items and automatic validation mechanisms. All of them aim towards a more efficient process of creating a digital scholarly edition. The quest on how to improve the work of digital scholarly edition editors is yet to complete, however, first prototypes look promising.

8   Conclusion

In this paper insights into the work of editors and researchers of an digital scholarly edition were presented, and the design and development processes were described. The identified tasks and workflows showed limitations and typical challenges in creating a digital scholarly edition. We showed that a solution is a interdisciplinary design process that connects the domain of digital humanities and software engineering. Working in an interdisciplinary team in-between two domains, require methods for discussions and knowledge exchange, such as regular and frequent workshops. It is beneficial to dive into the respective other domain, in order to build up domain knowledge and terminology, which in consequence improves the communication between domains.

Methods from the design process should be adapted as necessary. There is a multitude of methods available, which allows to pick the ones that work best in the team, instead of wasting time for methods that are not accepted or just don't work in the particular case. We used an incremental, iterative, not necessarily sequential design process in parallel to an "agile" software engineering process, which allowed to tackle the problems of each domain individually. This creates space for creative exploratory means, but also allows to be exploitative to solve and optimise deeply technical issues. We suggest to make use of both, to explore opportunities and to break out of establishes patterns, but to also investigate and optimise technology. To create the next generation digital scholarly edition, one will need to have both: a well designed, useful and usable interface to help and support the user to achieve its goals, while at the same time providing a platform that is highly functional, stable, maintainable, extendable and adaptable to fulfil the user's needs. Developers and designers shall not forget to answer the question of "who is the user?", "what are the tasks?" and "what does the user need?" (i.e., finding the right problem(s)), before starting to build the right solution(s).

With this paper we have provided specific tasks and shown different workflows of how editors and creators of digital scholarly editions work. Based on the gained insight we are now able to continue to improve the next generation of a platform for digital scholarly editions.

References

1. Baillot, A., Busch, A.: Editing for man and machine. In: Users of Scholarly Editions: Editorial Anticipations of Reading, Studying and Consulting. Variants (Journal of the European Society for Textual Scholarship), Leicester, United Kingdom, vol. 13, November 2015. https://halshs.archives-ouvertes.fr/halshs-01233380, actes à venir dans the Journal of the European Society for Textual Scholarship
2. Beyer, H., Holtzblatt, K.: Contextual Design: Defining Customer-Centered Systems. Morgan Kaufmann Publishers Inc., San Francisco (1997)
3. Bruderer, H.: There are no digital humanities (2018). https://cacm.acm.org/blogs/blog-cacm/232969-there-are-no-digital-humanities/fulltext
4. Deutsche Forschungsgemeinschaft (DFG): Edition der Korrespondenz Frank Wedekinds als Online-Volltextdatenbank (2017). https://gepris.dfg.de/gepris/projekt/389236467?context=projekt&task=showDetail&id=389236467
5. Driscoll, M.J., Pierazzo, E. (eds.): Digital Scholarly Editing: Theories and Practices, vol. 4, 1st edn. Open Book Publishers, Cambridge (2016)
6. Entrup, B., Binder, F., Lobin, H.: Extending the possibilities for collaborative work with TEI/XML through the usage of a wiki system. In: Proceedings of the 1st International Workshop on Collaborative Annotations in Shared Environment: Metadata, Vocabularies and Techniques in the Digital Humanities, DH-CASE 2013, pp. 9:1–9:4. ACM, New York (2013). https://doi.org/10.1145/2517978.2517988. http://doi.acm.org/10.1145/2517978.2517988

7. Franzini, G., Terras, M., Mahony, S.: A Catalogue of Digital Editions. In: Digital Scholarly Editing: Theories and Practices, 1 edn., vol. 4 of [5], pp. 161–182 (2016)
8. Franzini, G., Terras, M., Mahony, S.: Digital editions of text: surveying user requirements in the digital humanities. J. Comput. Cult. Herit. **12**(1), 11–123 (2019). https://doi.org/10.1145/3230671. http://doi.acm.org/10.1145/3230671
9. Lazar, J., Feng, J.H., Hochheiser, H.: Chapter 8 - interviews and focus groups. In: Lazar, J., Feng, J.H., Hochheiser, H. (eds.) Research Methods in Human Computer Interaction (2 edn.), pp. 187–228. Morgan Kaufmann, Boston (2017). https://doi.org/10.1016/B978-0-12-805390-4.00008-X. http://www.sciencedirect.com/science/article/pii/B978012805390400008X
10. Nielsen, J.: Usability Engineering. Morgan Kaufmann Publishers Inc., San Francisco (1993)
11. Norman, D.A.: The Design of Everyday Things, vol. 16 (2013). https://doi.org/10.1002/hfm.20127
12. Pohl, O., Notroff, A.: New approaches towards user research and software architecture in research software engineering: a humanities example. Gesellschaft für Informatik e.V. *GI* (2019). https://doi.org/10.5446/42509. Accessed 25 Jan 2020
13. Sahle, P.: What is a Scholarly Digital Edition?. In: Digital Scholarly Editing: Theories and Practices, 1 edn., vol. 4 of [5], pp. 19–39 (2016)
14. Schmidt, D.: Towards an interoperable digital scholarly edition. J. Text Encoding Initiat. (2014). https://doi.org/10.4000/jtei.979
15. Scholz, G., Zanol, I.: Ernst Tollers Briefe in digitaler Edition. Zeitschrift für digitale Geisteswissenschaften (2018). http://zfdg.de/2018_005
16. Schwartz, L.: Agile-user experience design: an agile and user-centered process? In: ICSEA 2013. pp. 346–351 (2013). https://www.thinkmind.org/index.php?view=article&articleid=icsea_2013_12_20_10176
17. Stadler, P., Illetschko, M., Seifert, S.: Towards a model for encoding correspondence in the TEI: developing and implementing <correspDesc>. J. Text Encoding Initiat. (2016). https://doi.org/10.4000/jtei.1433
18. Steierwald, U., Störl, U., Vinçon, H., Gründling, S.: Die online-edition der Briefe von und an Frank Wedekind. Eine virtuelle Kontextualisierung von Korrespondenzen. In: Medienwandel / Medienwechsel in der Editionswissenschaft, editio / Beihefte, pp. 229–240. De Gruyter, Berlin (2012). https://doi.org/10.1515/9783110300437.229. https://www.degruyter.com/view/books/9783110300437/9783110300437.229/9783110300437.229.xml
19. Störl, U., Martin, A.: Brieftextrevisionen in den digital humanities: die online-Volltextdatenbank für Briefe von und an Frank Wedekind. In: Textrevisionen. Beiträge der Internationalen Fachtagung der Arbeitsgemeinschaft für germanistische Edition, Graz, 17. bis 20. Februar 2016, editio/Beihefte, pp. 199–208. De Gruyter, Berlin (2017). https://doi.org/10.1515/9783110495058
20. The British Design Council: The Design Process: What is the Double Diamond? (2015). https://www.designcouncil.org.uk/news-opinion/design-process-what-double-diamond
21. Thoden, K., Stiller, J., Bulatovic, N., Meiners, H.L., Boukhelifa, N.: User-centered design practices in digital humanities - experiences from DARIAH and CENDARI. ABI Technik **37**, 2–11 (2017). https://doi.org/10.1515/abitech-2017-0002

The Behaviour Observations of Using Rearview Mirror with Distance Indicator

Cheng-Yong Huang[✉]

Department of Arts and Design, National Dong Hwa University,
No. 1, Sec. 2, Da Hsueh Rd. Shoufeng, Hualien 97401, Taiwan R.O.C.
yong@gms.ndhu.edu.tw

Abstract. The mixed modes of transport in Taiwan as well as the placement of parking lots on both sides of the roads have meant that car and scooter accidents are caused by the improper opening of car doors. The cause of a portion of these accidents have been related to the driver wrongly judging the distance of an oncoming vehicle through their rearview mirror. In order to solve this problem, the author has developed a rearview mirror with a distance indicator. Furthermore, he created a behavior observation experiment which compared using a rearview mirror with a distance indicator to using a traditional rearview mirror, as well as turning around and using one's naked eyes, to judge the distance of a traffic cone. The results showed that using a rearview mirror with a distance indicator was not as effective for judging distance as using one's naked eyes, but it was more effective than using a traditional rearview mirror. It is commonly held that men have a better ability to judge the distance of an oncoming vehicle from behind than women do. However, for female drivers, a rearview mirror with a distance indicator was able to improve the accuracy of their estimates of judging the distance of a traffic cone from behind to the level of that of the men. This method was also more effective for them than observing with their naked eyes and using a traditional rearview mirror.

Keywords: Behaviour observation · Rearview mirror with distance indicator · Door crash

1 Introduction

Taiwan is an island that lies in East Asia. On its left coast is the Pacific Ocean and the Taiwan Strait separates Taiwan from the Asian continent. The surface area of Taiwan is around 36,000 square kilometre and in 2019 the population reached approximately 23.6 million people. Taiwan has a very high population density, ranking tenth in the world. However, the population has been distributed unevenly. People are mainly concentrated in cities in the west side of Taiwan. For example, Taipei City's population density has reached 10,000 people per square kilometre; it is extremely crowded and congested. Therefore, traffic is a very major problem in Taiwan. There is a distinct difference when one compares the proportion of cars and scooters in Taiwan to that in areas in Western countries. In Taiwan, the principal mode of transport is the scooter. This is related to Taiwan's narrow land and densely populated terrain, as well as the

© Springer Nature Switzerland AG 2020
M. Kurosu (Ed.): HCII 2020, LNCS 12181, pp. 293–307, 2020.
https://doi.org/10.1007/978-3-030-49059-1_21

availability of mass rapid transport (MRT) systems. Hence the country's inhabitants use scooters as the primary mode of transport, and cars are the secondary mode. As shown in Fig. 1, apart from on expressways, all roads have scooters driving on them.

Fig. 1. Scooters are the primary mode of transportation for Taiwan's inhabitants (image source: Wikipedia-traffic in Taipei).

The number of scooters in Taiwan is the highest of any motorized vehicle in the world [1]. Figures from November 2019 show that the number of scooter licenses obtained from the Motor Vehicles Offices was approximately 13,970,000, the number of car driver licenses obtained was around 8,100,000. The number of scooters are roughly 1.72 times that of the number of cars. Scooters will often drive along the outer side of the road, however, on this outer side of the road, there will often also be car parking lots. Consequently, Taiwan's scooter drivers are often driving alongside car parking lots. Thus oftentimes, drivers of cars parked by the roadside will open their car doors and the scooter rider coming from behind will not have time to dodge the open door and hence, injure themselves. A mode of transport such as the scooter has more difficulty being controlled, no matter if it is braking, suddenly changing direction, or any dodging action. Therefore, on the roads, the scooter is the unlucky vehicle. In addition, during collision, it lacks any protection mechanism for the driver. These factors mean that the areas of the body that are exposed on rider of a scooter become extremely weak [2–4].

If we compare the danger of riding a scooter to that of driving a car, we can see that in the USA, the risk of death when riding a scooter is 37 times that of being a passenger in a car [5]. In Europe, the risk of being injured when riding a scooter is 13 times that of the risk faced as a passenger in a car [6]. Huang observed the actions of car drivers opening their car doors in three car parking locations. There were divided into two-way roads with more cars and scooters, four lane roads with more cars, and two-way roads with fewer cars and scooters. He conducted human factors experiments using Auto-CAD. The results showed that car drivers had four methods for checking to see if there were any oncoming vehicles from behind before opening their car door. The first method was simply opening the door without checking for any oncoming vehicles from behind at all. The second method was to look at the rearview mirror to check for any oncoming vehicles from behind before opening the door. The third method was to turn their body to check their left window for any oncoming vehicles from behind before opening the door. The fourth method was first to open the door a little, then look through the gap in the door to check for any oncoming vehicles from behind before opening the door fully. 43% of people looked at the rearview mirror to check for any oncoming vehicles from behind before opening the door. Therefore, we can see from this that the majority of car drivers used their rearview mirror to check for oncoming vehicles from behind before opening the door. Even though the majority of car drivers do this, so many vehicle accidents are caused by the car door being opened at an unsuitable moment, these accidents are caused by the misjudgment of the distance of an oncoming vehicle when using the rearview mirror [7]. In order to prevent accidents caused this way, the author obtained a patent for a car rearview mirror with a distance indicator in 2015, as shown in Fig. 2. The main goal of this research is to understand the benefits of and difference in using a car rearview mirror with a distance indicator as opposed to a traditional rearview mirror from a human engineering and usability engineering angle.

Fig. 2. Rearview mirror with a distance indicator

2 Literature Review

2.1 Door Crash Accident

Due to the high numbers of vehicles in Taiwan, parking spaces are always placed on the sides of the roads for the temporary parking of cars. However, scooters often travel on the side of the road, and when car drivers temporarily stop by the side of the road and open their car doors, they are encroaching upon the right of way of the scooter drivers. When these car drivers do not notice oncoming vehicles when opening their doors, door crash accidents where the scooter crashes into the car door, can occur. The scooter drivers who fall to the ground as a result of these crashes are also vulnerable to oncoming vehicles from behind crashing into them, causing even more serious casualties. The door crash accidents are as shown in Fig. 3.

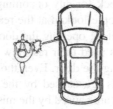

Fig. 3. Diagram of door crash.

With regards to investigative research conducted pertaining to inappropriate opening of car doors, it was found that in other countries, vehicle accidents caused by opening the car door at an inappropriate time were very rare. However, in the advanced Western countries of Europe and the USA, riding bicycles is prevalent. Hence, there is some research that has mentioned accidents related to bicycles being hit by car doors. Here, door crash accidents are talking about bicycles crashing into the car doors of stationary cars. The first thing that happens is the cyclist crashes into the door, and then secondly, is seriously injured as a result of falling to the ground. This is especially true for riders who are not wearing a safety helmet [8]. Although there are articles which have not yet been published which discuss the inappropriateness and the risk of a door crash when bicycle lanes are placed next to parking lots, the majority of traditional bicycle lanes exist in the "door zone" of the opening car doors as car doors are able to extend around 90–105 cm outwards when open. And usually, bicycle lanes are only a little wider than 90–105 cm. This increases the risk of causing a cyclist to crash into a car door, despite bike riders riding in the middle of the bicycle lane. Whether riding in the bicycle lane or not, cyclists are often told to leave the space of a car door between them and roadside vehicles. This increases the field of vision of the drivers who have parked their cars on the roadside as well as the extent to which the cyclists are visible [9].

From police reports on accidents, hospital publications and a video recording of an accident, Johnson et al. analyzed the characteristics and risk factors pertaining to the collision of cyclists with car doors. In Virginia, Australia, the majority of casualties from these types of accidents were males above the age of 18, and the locations of the accidents were all roads with a maximum speed limit of 60 kph [10]. Pei collected material from the UK's traffic accident database and in the area regarding bicycles being hit by car doors, found that it was easy for accidents related to cyclists colliding with doors of parked cars to happen in cycle lanes. Additionally, when taxis stopped to allow passengers to alight, this type of accident also occurred frequently. These types of accidents also happened more commonly on single lane roads, and where it differs from Australia is that a larger proportion of the accidents happened to female cyclists [11].

According to Pai, as mentioned in the article about document investigation into accidents regarding scooter rights on roads, the majority of typically destructive vehicle accidents often happen at crossroads. The path of the car enters the path of the scooter, which infringes upon the road rights of the scooter rider [12]. Accidents of this nature mainly involve the driver not noticing the scooter driving by; this indicates the problem that scooters are not visible enough. Hurt et al. say that another type of car-scooter accident involves the car driver wrongly judging the speed and the distance of the approaching vehicles. The driver relies on his sight to judge the distance and speed at the intersection. However, the scooter lacks the front bonnet which a car has, causing its speed and distance to be measured inaccurately [13].

2.2   Human Factors Automobile Design

Human factors engineering is an important field of study within the realm of engineering technology. It researches the interaction between humans, machines and the environment, and how they are able to integrate with one another. It allows the machines that are designed and environmental systems to suit the characteristics of the human physiology and psychology. It is a field of study that aims to achieve the goals of better efficiency, safety, health and comfort of the manufactured product. The word ergonomics comes from the Greek root word "ergon", its meaning is to work and toil. The meaning of "nomos" is discipline and rules. The two words combined give the meaning of the rule of human work. In our world, there is no unified term for the field of human factors engineering, however there is a small number of nomenclature widely used. Human factors engineering is also widely known as human engineering or ergonomics. They research the interaction between humans, machines and the environment, and how they are able to integrate with each other. They allow the machines that are designed and environmental systems to suit the characteristics of the human physiology and psychology. They are fields of study that aim to achieve the goals of better efficiency, safety, health and comfort of the manufactured product [14].

Human factors engineering projects related to automobiles have included the interaction between cars and their drivers or their passengers, for example, the headrest, safety airbag and secure seat. There are human factors engineering projects related to cars and their outer environment, for example nearby cars, scooters and pedestrians, include reversing sensors, third brake lights and blind spot warning systems. However, there are very few human factors engineering projects related to protecting the people or vehicles outside the car. Now, artificial intelligence (AI) has produced an adaptive cruise control (ACC) system which can automatically detect pedestrians and vehicles within a certain range, automatically braking when it senses something close by. Additionally, students in the design departments of National Taiwan University and I-Shou University have designed a "truck warning system", which uses infrared rays to emit a "warning region" from the inner wheel of large trucks when turning, to remind the masses to stay away. This reduces the chances of accidents happening. However, it is a pity that it has not yet been installed on big trucks. Currently, there are no effective or widely used human factors engineering designs related to the improper opening of car doors. This area needs further research and development. In terms of observations of vehicle related behaviour, Michelle & Steiner used the method of following vehicles to investigate the behaviour of drivers. They used school bus drivers as the target of their investigations. They recorded the drivers' physiology and psychology, and used the means of external provocations to arouse their engagement in aggressive driving behaviour. The experiment required the drivers to fill in questionnaires after the session. It found that 25% of the drivers were not affected by the provocations. The rest of the drivers had a noticeable change in heart rate and blood pressure. All the drivers felt that they would not sound the horn in an aggressive way when encountering the provocation [15].

3 Experiment Design

In order to avoid accidents related to the improper opening of car doors, Huang discovered from his behavioural investigations related to car door opening that car drivers had four methods for opening their car door. The first method was simply opening the door and getting out of the car. The second method was to look at the rearview mirror to check for any oncoming vehicles from behind before opening the door. The third method was first to open the door a little, then look through the gap in the door to check for any oncoming vehicles from behind before opening the door fully. The fourth method was to turn their body to check their left window for any oncoming vehicles from behind before opening the door. Over half of the drivers used a rearview mirror to check for oncoming vehicles [7].

Human factors engineering research is split into descriptive research, experimental research and evaluation research. Descriptive research often focuses on collecting data on the characteristics of the population, for example, surveys into the dimensions of the human body, or the abilities and limits of humans under different conditions. Descriptive research provides the basis of the information needed to make decisions on design. The purpose of experimental research is to determine the impact of some variables towards behaviour. It is often based upon design problems which have arisen during concrete situations, or variables and behaviours predicted in theoretical situations which need to be verified [16]. For example, Garg et al. evaluated the impact safety belts have on the range of arm movement. Evaluation research and experimental research are similar, they differ in that the "some variables" mentioned in evaluation research refers to some systems or products. Evaluation research and descriptive research also have similarities; they attempt to describe the results and the behaviour of humans when using systems or products [17].

Within the realm of human factors engineering, usability engineering and research into behavioral observations, researchers have a choice of two different research settings: field and laboratory. The benefits of field environments lie in the fact that the related variables of the task, the environmental conditions and the special characteristics of the experiment subjects are in line with real-life situations. Therefore, there are more chances for the results obtained to be extended for use in real-life situations [16]. In order to understand the behaviours observed pertaining to using different rearview mirrors to measure the distance of vehicles, if this research is conducted in a laboratory there is no way to understand the split second response of car drivers when opening car doors, thus the choice was made that research conducted in the field environment would be more suitable in this case.

The main purpose of this research is to conduct behaviour observation experiments when using rearview mirrors to observe oncoming vehicles, in order to prevent the improper opening of car doors. The main focus is on the experiment subjects' ability to judge the distance of oncoming vehicles from behind. In order to effectively achieve the aims of the research plan, we must consider the measurements of human factors engineering, the typical operations of usability engineering as well as record behaviour observations, combining the patent of distance indicators on rearview mirrors to conduct behaviour observations of drivers opening car doors. Figure 4 shows the schematic diagram of a rearview mirror with distance indicators of 10 m, 15 m and 30 m.

Fig. 4. Schematic diagram of real experiment setup of rearview mirror with distance indicator.

The experiment subjects sought for this research were people aged 20 and above who hold a car driver's licence. Firstly, we recorded the basic details of each experiment subject relevant to the experiment, including age, driving experience, and whether their primary mode of transport is the car. They were asked to sign a consent form on the ethics of behaviour experiment research. Next, the experiment assistant was asked to simply explain the experiment process, then ask the experiment subjects to sit in the driver's seat of the experiment car. We told them three ways that they could judge the distance behind them. The first way was to judge it using the original rearview mirror. The second way was by using the rearview mirror with a distance indicator. The third way was to open the car door and turn one's head to look behind in order to judge the distance. After this, the experiment assistant picked a distance from 10 m, 15 m and 20 m at random to place a traffic cone at. He then returned to the driver's seat and asked the experiment subject the distance predicted using the three different methods. The person in blue was the assistant, the experiment subject was already in the car. As shown in Fig. 5, the data obtained from the experiment underwent many different types of statistical analysis. When all three distances were tested, we asked the experiment subject to fill in a questionnaire to understand their thoughts on and impressions of using the rearview mirror with a distance indicator and so on. This will be of use as materials to consider in order to improve the design of the rearview mirror with distance indicator later on.

Fig. 5. Photograph of the experiment.

4   Experiment Results

51 experiment subjects in total were found for this experiment, including 24 men and 17 women, aged between 20 and 65. However, the majority of the subjects were young people. The subjects had varied amounts of driving experience, between 1 and 20 years. Their educational levels were mostly concentrated in holding a bachelor's or a master's degree. Since social media was used to seek experiment subjects, therefore students stood in the majority of people found. 31 experiment subjects used the car as their primary mode of transport. Most of the experiment subjects knew about accidents which occurred due to the improper opening of car doors and also knew of the two-step

door opening method. 14 of the experiment subjects had experienced minor accidents related to the improper opening of car doors. The purpose of the behaviour observation experiment was to allow these 51 experiment subjects to judge three different traffic cone distances (10 m, 15 m and 20 m) using three different methods (standard rearview mirror, rearview mirror with distance indicator and turning their body to look behind them). The variables included 1. The traffic cone distance that the experiment subjects reported (unit of measurement: cm) as well as 2. The discrepancy in the absolute values of the distances (the value reported by the experiment subjects minus the distance of the traffic cone, to get the absolute value). The data underwent one-way analysis of variance (ANOVA) and univariate analysis of variance and is described in later chapters.

4.1   Determining the One-Way ANOVA of Different Methods of Judging Different Distances

51 experiment subjects predicted the distance of the traffic cones (split into distances of 10 m, 15 m and 20 m). This data underwent one-way ANOVA; the variables were the judgement of the distance and the discrepancy in absolute values of the distances. The results for the 10 m distance are shown in Table 1. We can see from the results that the shortest mean distance judged was when using the rearview mirror with distance indicator, and the most accurate measurement was when using one's naked eyes to see the object directly. The highest discrepancy seen was when using a standard rearview mirror to judge the distance. Using one-way ANOVA, it was also found that there was a statistically significant difference. Post-hoc tests found that the discrepancy seen when using a standard rearview mirror was bigger than when using a rearview mirror with distance indicator. The discrepancy seen when using one's naked eyes to see the object directly was also bigger than when using the rearview mirror with distance indicator. Both were statistically significant differences. In terms of the discrepancy in absolute values of the distances, the size of the discrepancy was as follows, standard rearview mirror > using one's naked eyes to see the object directly > rearview mirror with distance indicator. However, in the statistics there were no statistically significant discrepancies.

The statistical results for the 15 m distance are shown in Table 2. The results are close to that of the 10 m distance. The size of the measurement of the distance is as follows: using a rearview mirror with distance indicator < using one's naked eyes to see the object directly < using a standard rearview mirror. The shortest mean distance judged was when using the rearview mirror with distance indicator, and the most accurate measurement was when using one's naked eyes to see the object directly. The highest discrepancy seen was when using a standard rearview mirror to judge the distance. The results of the post-hoc tests were the same as that of the 10 m distance; there were statistically significant differences. In terms of the discrepancy in absolute values of the distances, it was the same as that of the 10 m distance, there were no statistically significant discrepancies. It is worth noting that if we compare 15 m to 10 m, the standard deviation in the judgement of distance and the mean of the gap in absolute value has also gotten relatively larger.

The statistical results for the 20 m distance are shown in Table 3. The results are entirely different from that of the 10 m and 15 m distances. The length of the distance measurement is as follows: using a rearview mirror with distance indicator < using one's naked eyes to see the object directly < using a standard rearview mirror. The most accurate measurement was when using the rearview mirror with distance indicator. However, the standard deviation was two times greater than that of the other two methods. This means that at a distance of 20 m, there was a bigger difference in the experiment subjects' measurements using the rearview mirror with distance indicator. In terms of measuring the distance using the three different methods, there was no statistically significant difference. However, after post-hoc test comparisons of the discrepancy in absolute values of the distances we discovered that the mean distance discrepancy of the standard rearview mirrors was smaller than that of the rearview mirror with distance indicator. This was statistically significant.

From the one-way ANOVA of each of the three different distances and three different methods for measurement mentioned above, we discovered that the most accurate way to judge the distance is still by using one's naked eyes to see the object directly. The second most accurate method is to use a rearview mirror with distance indicator. The least accurate way to judge distance was by using a standard rearview mirror. When using a rearview mirror with distance indicator to judge the distance of 10 m and 15 m, the absolute value of the distance discrepancy was the smallest, meaning that the accuracy of using a rearview mirror with distance indicator is high, and the experiment subjects had the smallest margin for error using this method.

Table 1. One-way ANOVA of different methods to measure distance of object at 10 m.

		N	Mean	Std. deviation	F	Sig.	Post Hoc Test
Distance judged	Standard	51	11.2882	3.48498	4.982	.008*	1 > 2*
	Indicator	51	9.2549	3.35764			3 > 2*
	Naked eyes	51	10.4020	2.91551			
	Total	153	10.3150	3.34620			
Discrepancy in absolute values of the distances	Standard	51	2.9275	2.25753	1.535	0.219	
	Indicator	51	2.2353	2.59683			
	Naked eyes	51	2.2647	1.85289			
	Total	153	2.4758	2.26428			

*. The mean different is significant at the 0.05 level.
The traffic cone is 10 m away from the rear of the car.

Table 2. One-way ANOVA of different methods to measure distance of object at 15 m.

		N	Mean	Std. deviation	F	Sig.	Post Hoc Test
Distance judged	Standard	51	16.7941	3.87063	5.122	.007*	1 > 2*
	Indicator	51	14.1667	3.98706			3 > 2*
	Naked eyes	51	15.6569	4.58093			
	Total	153	15.5392	4.26912			
Discrepancy in absolute values of the distances	Standard	51	3.2255	2.76643	0.298	.743	
	Indicator	51	2.8529	2.88148			
	Naked eyes	51	3.2647	3.24862			
	Total	153	3.1144	2.95887			

*. The mean different is significant at the 0.05 level.
The traffic cone is 15 m away from the rear of the car.

Table 3. One-way ANOVA of different methods to measure distance of object at 20 m.

		N	Mean	Std. deviation	F	Sig.	Post Hoc Test
Distance judged	Standard	51	21.4903	3.33090	.764	.467	
	Indicator	51	20.3627	5.93387			
	Naked eyes	51	21.0490	4.27815			
	Total	153	20.9673	4.63350			
Discrepancy in absolute values of the distances	Standard	51	2.2353	2.87464	2.407	.094	2 > 3*
	Indicator	51	3.7941	4.54552			
	Naked eyes	51	2.6765	3.48113			
	Total	153	2.9020	3.73288			

*. The mean different is significant at the 0.05 level.
The traffic cone is 20 m away from the rear of the car.

4.2   Univariate Analysis of Variance with Regards to Gender and Different Methods for Judging Distance

In univariate analysis of variance with regards to gender and different methods for judging distance, the dependent variable is the absolute value of the distance discrepancy. From descriptive statistical analysis (as shown in Table 4), we can see that the mean distance discrepancy of men when using the three different methods for judging distance of the object are as follows: using a standard rearview mirror < using one's naked eyes to see the object directly < using a rearview mirror with distance indicator. Therefore, men had a smaller margin of error when using the standard rearview mirror. The mean distance discrepancy of women when using the three different methods for judging distance of the object are as follows: using a rearview mirror with distance indicator < using one's naked eyes to see the object directly < using a standard rearview mirror. Therefore, women had a smaller margin of error when using the rearview mirror with distance indicator. This kind of result is also shown when the data underwent univariate analysis of variance with regards to gender and different methods for judging distance. There are no statistically significant discrepancies in terms of the different methods for judging distance, but there are statistically significant discrepancies in terms of gender. Genders have mutual influence in terms of methods for judging distance (as shown in Table 5). From Fig. 6, we can also see that women fared the best when using a rearview mirror with distance indicator. The distance discrepancy of the mean absolute value between the genders when using the method of a rearview mirror with distance indicator when compared to the two other methods for judging distance was almost identical. Hence, for women, a rearview mirror with distance indicator was able to increase their accuracy of judging the distance of oncoming vehicles from behind.

Table 4. Descriptive statistical analysis of gender and different methods for judging distance.

Dependent variable: gap absolute value				
Distance judged	Gender	Mean	Std. deviation	N
Standard	Male	2.1304	1.94212	102
	Female	4.1275	3.34790	51
	Total	2.7961	2.66184	153
Indicator	Male	2.9020	3.65806	102
	Female	3.0784	3.14861	51
	Total	2.9608	3.48707	153
Naked eyes	Male	2.4951	3.01276	102
	Female	3.2157	2.81648	51
	Total	2.7353	2.95918	153
Total	Male	2.5092	2.96405	306
	Female	3.4739	3.12660	153
	Total	2.8307	3.04996	459

Table 5. Univariate analysis of variance of gender and different methods for judging distance.

Dependent variable: gap absolute value

Source	Type III sum of squares	df	Mean square	F	Sig.
Corrected model	158.479a	5	31.696	3.500	.004
Intercept	3651.229	1	3651.229	403.224	.000
Distance judged	5.088	2	2.544	.281	.755
Gender	94.927	1	94.927	10.483	.001*
Distance judged*gender	59.386	2	29.693	3.279	.039*
Error	4101.958	453	9.055		
Total	7938.390	459			
Corrected total	4260.437	458			

a. R Squared = .037 (Adjusted R Squared = .027)

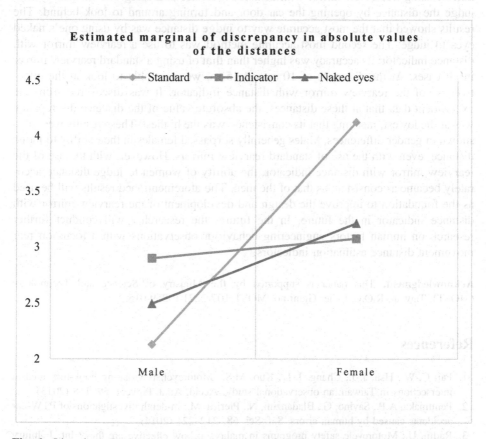

Fig. 6. Line chart of discrepancy in absolute values of the distances between the genders and the three methods of judging distance.

5 Conclusion

Taiwan has a densely populated terrain. In the cities, there are car parking spaces on both sides of the roads. Additionally, when one factors in the mixed transportation modes of cars and scooters in Taiwan, it means that vehicle accidents are easily caused by the improper opening of car doors. In Taiwan, most drivers will use their rearview mirror to look out for oncoming vehicles from behind. There are a portion of accidents caused by the improper opening of car doors due to the misjudgement of the distance of the oncoming vehicle when using a standard rearview mirror. Therefore, the author developed a rearview mirror with a distance indicator in order to solve the problem of judging the distance of oncoming vehicles from behind. For the purpose of this research, a behaviour observation experiment was conducted by putting three distances of traffic cones behind a car and asking the experiment subjects to estimate their distances. The three methods for judging the distances were using a traditional rearview mirror, using a rearview mirror with distance indicator and using one's naked eyes to judge the distance by opening the car door and turning around to look behind. The results showed that the most accurate way to judge distance was by using one's naked eyes to judge. The second most accurate method was to use a rearview mirror with distance indicator; its accuracy was higher than that of using a standard rearview mirror in all cases. At the distances of 10 m and 15 m, we were able to look at the effectiveness of the rearview mirror with distance indicator. It was discovered from the experiment data that at these distances, the absolute value of the distance discrepancy was at the lowest, meaning that its consistency was the highest. These results were also shown in gender differences. Males generally surpassed females in their ability to judge distance, even with the use of standard rearview mirrors. However, with the use of the rearview mirror with distance indicator, the ability of women to judge distance accurately became as consistent as that of the men. The aforementioned results will be used as the foundation to improve the design and development of the rearview mirror with distance indicator in the future. In the future, the researcher will conduct further research on human factors engineering behaviour observations with a focus on rear movement distance estimation indicators.

Acknowledgment. This paper is supported by the Ministry of Science and Technology (MOST), Taiwan, R.O.C. under Grant no. MOST 107-2221-E-259-015.

References

1. Pai, C.-W., Hsu, J.-J., Chang, J.-L., Kuo, M.S.: Motorcyclists violating hook-turn area at intersections in Taiwan: an observational study. Accid. Anal. Prevent. **59**, 1–8 (2013)
2. Penumaka, A.P., Savino, G., Bladanzini, N., Pierini, M.: In-depth investigations of PTW-car accidents caused by human errors. Saf. Sci. **68**, 212–221 (2014)
3. Radin, U.: Motorcycle safety programs in malaysia: how effective are they? Int. J. Injury Control Saf. Promot. **13**(2), 71–79 (2006)
4. Lin, M.R., Kraus, J.F.: A review of risk factors and patterns of motorcycle injuries. Accid. Anal. Prev. **41**(4), 710–722 (2009)

5. Traffic safety facts. http://www-nrd.nhtsa.dot.gov/pubs/811159.pdf. Accessed 16 Jan 2020
6. Motorcycle Road Safety Report 2012-Strategies for Preventing Accidents on the European Roads. https://www.dekra-roadsafety.com/media/dekra-vsr-2012-en.pdf. Accessed 16 Jan 2020
7. Huang, C.-Y.: Observations of drivers' behavior when opening car doors. Proc. Manuf. **3**, 2753–2760 (2015)
8. Dennerlein, J., Meeker, J.: Occupational injuries among boston bicycle messengers. Am. J. Ind. Med. **42**(6), 519–525 (2002)
9. Hunter, W., Stewart, R.: An evaluation of bike lanes adjacent to motor vehicle parking. University of North Carolina Highway Safety Research Center (1999)
10. Johnson, M., Newstead, S., Oxley, J., Judith, C.: Cyclists and open vehicle doors: crash characteristics and risk factors. Saf. Sci. **59**, 135–140 (2013)
11. Pai, C.-W.: Overtaking, rear-end, and door crashes involving bicycles: an empirical investigation. Accid. Anal. Prev. **43**, 1228–1235 (2011)
12. Pai, C.-W.: Motorcyclists right-of-way accidents-a literature review. Accid. Anal. Prev. **43**, 971–982 (2011)
13. Hurt, H., Ouellet, J., Thom, D.: Motorcycle accident cause factors and identification of countermeasures volume 1: technical report (1981)
14. Berkowitz, J.P., Casali, S.P.: Influence of age on the ability to hear telephone ringers of different spectral content. In: Proceedings of the Human Factors Society 34th Annual Meeting, vol. 1, pp. 132–136 (1990)
15. Michelle, A.R., Steiner, M.: Provoked driver aggression and status: a field study. Transp. Res. Part F **3**, 167–179 (2000)
16. Salvendy, G.: Handbook of Human Factors and Ergonomics. Wiley, Hoboken (2005)
17. Garg, A., Bakken, G., Saxena, U.: Effect of seat belts and shoulder harnesses on functional arm reach. Hum. Factors **24**, 367–372 (1982)

Research on Method of Acquiring and Screening of Personalized Functional Requirements of Smart Watches for the Elderly Based on Kano Model

Shengqing Huang, Quan Gu, Jie Zhang[✉], and Chaoxiang Yang

School of Art Design and Media, East China University of Science
and Technology, NO. 130 Meilong Road, Xuhui District,
Shanghai 200237, China
hsq_0702@163.com, 850137117@qq.com

Abstract. To solve the problem that there are many functions of the smartwatch for the elderly, but they do not meet the real needs of users, this paper investigate to use Kano model to obtain the personalized functional requirements of smartwatch for the elderly and the order of the demands importance degrees, in order to provide guidance for the design and development of the smartwatch for the elderly. Uses Kano model combined clustering method to identify and screen the personalized functional requirements of the elderly smartwatch in the current market, in order to determine their attributes of Kano demand and the hierarchical model of the personalized requirements of the elderly smartwatch was constructed. Then it uses entropy method combined with Kano model to calculate the weight of the personalized function requirements items of the bottom of the hierarchy model,analyze the user's personalized function requirements index for the elderly smartwatch, and determines the importance order of the personalized requirements items to guide the design of the elderly smartwatch. Based on the user's personalized functional requirements, the hierarchical model of the elderly smartwatch's individual demands was constructed, which intuitively reflected the importance ranking of the target user's personalized requirements for each function, and provided certain reference for the smartwatch suppliers who are about to engage in mass customization production. Personalized requirements acquisition and screen method research can improve the user satisfaction of the elderly smartwatch, so that the mass customization of the elderly smartwatch manufacturers can reduce costs and improve customer satisfaction.

Keywords: Kano model · Demand hierarchical model · Individual demand · Elderly smartwatch · Mass customization · Demand screening

1 Introduction

As a newly emerged electronic product in recent years, smartwatches have gradually evolved from electronic watches to smart devices that are connected to mobile devices such as mobile phones. They have gradually entered people's normal production and life and provided convenience for people's good lives. The first is to provide people

© Springer Nature Switzerland AG 2020
M. Kurosu (Ed.): HCII 2020, LNCS 12181, pp. 308–323, 2020.
https://doi.org/10.1007/978-3-030-49059-1_22

with auxiliary monitoring in the field of personal sports. Smartwatches are in a blowout situation in the wearable device market. Because of their portability and immediacy. Due to the advent of an aging society, the demand for smart watches for the elderly has gradually grown. Functions such as physical condition monitoring, fall reminders, and emergency contacts can provide greater support for the Senior life, such as monitor their health, and take care of and assist the elderly [1]. With the advent of the intelligent era, elderly wearable devices such as smart watches can greatly enrich the retirement life of the elderly, and also form a bond of communication and connection between the elderly and their caregivers, accurately meeting the individual needs of smart watches for the elderly and caregivers will have broad market prospects. But the current smart watch market is fiercely competitive, with many brands, and consumer groups, especially the elderly, have not yet been widely accepted. The reason is that smart watches have many functions, and the elderly have natural insensitivity to electronic products as they age, and fail to take into account the real personality needs of the elderly in different conditions Inconsistent needs of users and monitors are not well distinguished, resulting in a waste of product functions, poor user experience, difficult operation and other problems [2]. So customize the smart functions of the elderly smart watches to meet the individual needs while reducing the complexity of operation is next research direction of elderly smart watches.

1.1 Kano Theory

The Kano model was formally proposed by Kano and other scholars in 1984. According to the relationship between the product's objective performance and the customer's subjective perception, the Kano model proposed five different dimensions of the quality of different impacts on user satisfaction and dissatisfaction [3], according to the Kano evaluation table, the quality attributes corresponding to the needs of different categories of users can be determined. The current combination of Kano model with different theories and methods is mainly studied in two aspects. First, the application field Tan explored the integration path between House of Product Quality (QFD) and Kano, and proved the feasibility of the method in web design and the creation of attractive products and the promotion of new product development experiments [4, 5], Li Yanlai used the concept of Kano factor to Determining the importance of user needs in the QFD [6]. Secondly, in terms of Kano model application method research, Chen Xiang proposed to use fuzzy clustering method to classify user needs into three types: essential requirements, unitary requirements and charm requirements [7], Berger pointed out that when there are multiple maximum values of the Kano category attribution of a certain quality characteristic or the values are very close, the Kano model will not be able to provide a clear attribution category for him, and he proposes to calculate the "relative customer satisfaction coefficient ratio", to determine the attributes of Kano categories with extremely close attributions [8], Yao Xiang et al. used the Affinity Diagram method combined with the Kano model to perform functional tomography of elderly wearable devices based on user needs [9], Chen Bobo proposed the "maximum lead", improve the determination method of Kano category [10], Nie Daan et al., When studying the relationship between user needs and product quality characteristics, found that there is a fault in mass customization, and proposed multi-classification of user needs based on the Kano model product synchronization design [11].

1.2 Personalized Requirements and Wearable Devices

Personalized requirements are understood from a narrow perspective as customized requirements. Tseng proposed a method of expressing customers' personalized needs through a classification tree and parameter setting, and improved the selection method of a given product [12], Dan Bin studied a mass customization environment, under the customer demand information classification model and its expression method, this method can support customers to describe requirements in a self-service way conveniently via the Internet [13], Tang Zhongjun and others used the Kano model to conduct research on personalized demand acquisition methods, and proposed to use the entropy method combined with the Kano model to calculate the weights of personalized demand items, and empirically verified the effectiveness of the method [14], Hou Zhi et al. Discussed the functional relationship between user satisfaction and product quality, and adjusted the coefficients to determine the importance of different needs [15].

In the field of elderly wearable devices, Hongtu Chen proposed that intelligent wearable devices for elderly people should design human-computer interaction systems that are both patient-centric and monitoring personnel-centric [2], Dou Jinhua and others use emotional computing models to design the development of home intelligent service robots for elderly users. Through computer simulation and 3D simulation, combined with data visualization to construct intelligent product interaction systems with emotional understanding and feedback functions [16], Costas Boletsis and others use smart watches to monitor patients with dementia Physical health status can be provided by providing additional important information to formal caregivers [17].

To sum up, in the field of smart watch equipment, there are still some shortcomings: first, the use of Kano models for customer personalized application research is less, especially for acquisition and demand level aspect analysis; The second is that the relationship between users and monitors in the field of elderly smart watches is relatively complex, the product users are relatively complex, and the research on the weight of complex user needs is slightly inadequate; The third is that research on the acquisition of customized needs focuses on the research on single user acquisition technology and expression has not been studied to screen the complex user customization personalized functional requirements.

2 Methodology

2.1 Framework

This article will propose a personalized functional requirements(PFR) acquisition and screening method based on the Kano model, use the Kano model method to determine the demand category, identify and filter the personalized demand, and analyze its hierarchy, and finally determine the real personalized requirements for the product order of importance weight of PFR (see Fig. 1).

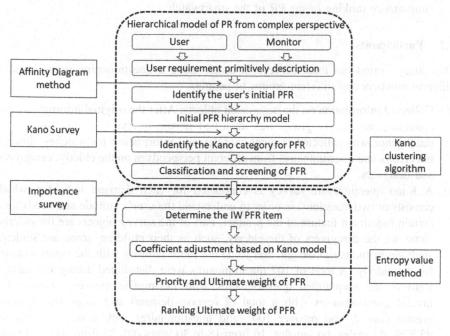

Fig. 1. A conceptual framework that combines Affinity Diagram method, Kano model, and entropy method for personalized demand acquisition and screening.

(1) Observed user originality requirements at smart watches for the elderly on the market. Through observation, interview, questionnaire collect original descriptions of PFR or suggest.

(2) Initial user needs are often repetitive and similar, there are also overlaps or unclear concepts. So this study combines Affinity Diagram method to transform, merge and delete the original information, to identify the user's initial PFR.

(3) Exclude cards with the same or similar content, and categorize them upward to form a demand hierarchy, and create an initial hierarchical model of the personalized requirements.

(4) Carry out a Kano questionnaire survey on users, process the survey data, and determine the Kano attributes of the PFR.

(5) Differentiate different types of customer needs, and filter the user's classification attributes to confirm the true personal attributes of customers.

(6) Investigate the screened personalized needs to design an importance questionnaire and conduct an importance questionnaire in the form of an expert questionnaire. This paper designs a questionnaire based on the 5-level Likert scale for the importance of the user's personalized needs screened above. Sorting the questionnaire data to obtain the initial importance of the user of the elderly smart watch.

(7) Select the corresponding adjustment coefficient according to the Kano category of PFR, and calculate its weight using the entropy method.

(8) According to the final weight value in order from large to small, to get the importance ranking of the PR of the smartwatch.

2.2 Participants

This study carried out three surveys in order, using a questionnaire in the form of different numbers and different groups of people.

a) Collected information on the designated objects. After the original information was collected, the elderly group was identified as the interviewee, and the elderly intelligence was collected original user demand information for watches, through interviews and questionnaires from different perspectives on the elderly, caregivers, and designers.

b) A Kano questionnaire survey is conducted for each demand indicator, which consists of two questions, in order to understand the user's attitude and needs for a certain functional feature of the product. Part of the survey objects are the elderly, some are the caregivers of the elderly, such as their children, some are students studying in industrial design, and some are more familiar with the smart watches for the elderly. A total of 107 questionnaires were distributed during the survey. Remove the unqualified questionnaires with incomplete answers, remove the invalid questionnaires with a total of reverse demand and suspicious demand greater than 2, and recover 104 valid questionnaires with a recovery rate of 95.32%. 44 males, 60 females, 16 from 18 to 30 years old, 25 from 30 to 50 years old, 17 from 50 to 60 years old, 26 from 60 to 70 years old, 11 from 70 to 80 years old, and 9 from 80 years old.

c) The user demand value of elderly smart watches is divided into 5 types, including very important, important, general, unimportant and very unimportant, which correspond to 9, 7, 5, 3, and 1, respectively. The sampling method of this survey is the same as the previous Kano survey. A total of 72 questionnaires were distributed and 62 valid questionnaires were recovered, the effective recovery rate was 86.11%. 26 persons over 60 years old, 36 persons under 60 years old.

2.3 Collection and Classification of Primary User Requirements Information

Identifying the elderly group as the interviewee, the original user needs information of the elderly smart watch was collected through interviews and questionnaires through different perspectives on the elderly, caregivers, and designers, including 10 designs division, 8 elderly users, 10 caregiver users, aged between 22 and 70 years. A total of 42 original user requirements information for elderly smart watches were collected. The process is as follows: 1. Gather information. Write all collected data into cards, and group cards with similar or similar content; 2. Hierarchical classification information. Remove cards with the same or similar content, and categorize them upwards to form a demand level, that is, "level 1, level 2, and level 3 demand" and name it; 3. Organize the cards to create an initial level model of personalized needs for the elderly smart watch among them, there are 8 first-level demand indicators, 17 second-level demand indicators, and 42 third-level demand indicators, as shown in Table 1.

Table 1. Initial hierarchy model of personalized needs for elderly smart watches

Level 1 demand	Level 2 demand	Level 3 demand
Communication social function	Communication social function	Receive message
		Receive mail
		Two-way telephony
		Real-time video
Monitoring and alarm function	Abnormal alarm function	Fall in the alarm
		Abnormal physical indicators alarm
		One key emergency alarm
	Networked communication system	Interworking of community hospitals
	Remote monitoring function	Caregiver information
		Monitor remotely
		Electronic fence
Positioning and navigation function	Route navigation	Navigation
		Map aided
	Real time positioning	Positioning
Monitoring of behavioral signs	Signs to measure	Monitor blood pressure
		Monitoring the heart rate
		Monitor oxygen saturation
		Monitoring sleep quality
	Sport management	Meter step function
		Track of motion
		Motion monitoring timing
		Sports instruction management
Remind function	Fixed action reminder	Drink water to remind
		Take medicine to remind
		Sedentary remind
	Custom reminder	Custom alarm
Voice interaction control function	The voice function	Intelligent voice recognition and input
	Interactive function	Control smart home
		Sleep mode

(*continued*)

Table 1. (*continued*)

Level 1 demand	Level 2 demand	Level 3 demand
Entertainment payment function	Leisure and entertainment	Remote camera
		Play music
		Play video
	Mobile payment	QR code payment
		NFC
Basic performance	Basic information display	Time and date display
		Physical monitoring status display
		Weather forecast
	Stable software features	Rapid response
		Easy to operate
	Stable physical properties	Long standby
		Waterproof
		Anti-impact

2.4 Identify PFR Categories and Evaluate and Screen Based on Kano Model

User demand is an important guide in the product design process. According to the "three-level demand index" in the initial hierarchical model of the functions of the elderly smart watch, a total of 42 items are made. For the personalized demand items at the bottom of the initial model, a detailed Kano survey is made questionnaire, determine the Kano category of the personalized demand item. Each requirement index of the questionnaire consists of two questions, in order to understand the user's attitude and needs for a certain functional feature of the product.

(1) For the personalized demand items at the bottom of the initial model, set forward and reverse questions respectively, and design a Kano questionnaire.

(2) Kano survey conducted. According to the survey results, analyze the corresponding Kano evaluation table to obtain the membership degree of each demand item for each Kano category. In the Kano evaluation table, "M" indicates necessary requirements and "O" indicates expected requirements "A" means charm demand, "I" means no difference demand, "R" means reverse demand, and "Q" means answer to question. The forward problem is to measure the user's attitude when the elderly smart watch has a functional feature, and the reverse problem is to measure the user's attitude when the elderly smart watch does not have a functional feature.

(3) According to the principle of the Kano model, customers will have different satisfaction changes for different types of functions when purchasing products, and will pay different attention to different types of functions when customizing products, whether a certain function is satisfied or not. There will be different changes in satisfaction for different customers, so different types of customer needs must be treated differently, and the list should be filtered according to different

personalized needs to determine the custom attributes of the product. Classify PFR based on data results, and use the Kano evaluation table (Table 2) as the classification principle. The data processing results and analysis are shown in Table 3.

Table 2. Kano's evaluation table

Functional	Dysfunctional				
	Like	Must-be	Neutral	Live-with	Dislike
Like	Q	A	A	A	O
Must-be	R	I	I	I	M
Neutral	R	I	I	I	M
Live-with	R	I	I	I	M
Dislike	R	R	R	R	Q

Source by Matzler and Hinterhuber (1998).

Table 3. Classification list of PFR for elderly smart watches

Primary requirements	User demand classification data statistics					Kano classification	Filter
	M	O	A	I	R		
Receive message	41	30	12	21	0	M(O)	Cull
two-way telephony,	19	45	21	19	0	O	Retention
Real-time video	10	25	30	38	1	I(A)	Special keep
Monitor blood pressure	31	38	18	17	0	O(M)	Retention
......	......	......	......	......	......	......	......
QR code payment	3	9	26	37	29	I(R)	Cull
NFC	2	5	10	36	51	R	Cull
Weather forecast	7	19	36	42	0	I(A)	Special keep
Anti-impact	30	35	18	21	0	O(M)	Retention

(4) The principle of requirements screening is as follows: Type M requirements are those that customers believe products must meet. They should not appear when selecting product customization requirements, but must be basically satisfied in the final physical product. Type O requirements are expectations that customers are very concerned about, requirements should appear prominently during customization to ensure that customers can make a quick choice; Class A requirements are requirements that can surprise customers, the importance of customization is second only to O requirements, customization can be extremely important, greatly improve customer satisfaction; Class I requirements are those that customers do not pay attention to or a small number of customers, which can be eliminated during customization to minimize product maintenance costs without affecting customer

satisfaction, and can also be set in customization options for special needs, they are met under special conditions; R-type requirements are product requirements that customers do not want to appear and must be eliminated when customizing, because its appearance will adversely affect customer satisfaction. The above screening principles can be summarized as shown in Table 4.

Table 4. Kano model-based PFR screening principle

PFR categories	M	O	A	I	R
Filter results	Cull	Reservation	Reservation	Special keep	Cull

2.5 Personalized Functional Requirements Weight Calculation

The determination of the importance of the user's individual needs is mainly to reflect the degree of influence of each requirement on user satisfaction. Through weight calculation, the importance can be divided from several demand indicators, so as to obtain the ranking of the importance among the requirements. This research investigates the screening of personalized needs to design an importance questionnaire and an expert questionnaire, By sorting out the questionnaire data, using SPSS Statistics 26 analysis software to average and standard deviation the various personalized needs data of the elderly smart watches, thereby obtaining the basic importance of the users of the elderly smart watches.

According to the Kano category of the personalized demand item, the respective adjustment coefficient k_j is selected. Then, the initial weight(IW) is adjusted according to k_j to obtain the ultimate weight (UW)of the personalized functional requirements term. The weight adjustment process is shown in Table 5. The Kano model reflects the degree to which the product satisfies the user's satisfaction in meeting the needs of users with different quality attributes. In actual surveys, the necessary requirements are the requirements that customers can easily perceive, the initial weight is generally high, but it is used to improve customer satisfaction, the contribution of degree is small; While the demand for charm is usually an unexpected surprise demand from customers, its initial weight is generally low, but its contribution to improving customer satisfaction is large, when determining the importance of personalized demand items, not only should the customer's importance evaluation information be considered, but also the efficiency of the personalized demand items to improve customer satisfaction should be considered, especially in some of the divergent needs that need to be weighted, make effective adjustments. Therefore, this paper proposes a weight adjustment process based on the Kano model to calculate the final weight of personalized demand terms, as follows:

(1) Select the adjustment coefficient k according to the Kano category of the personalized demand item. In the Kano model, the relationship between customer satisfaction and demand satisfaction can be quantified by a function with parameters, and the relationship can be expressed as:

$$s = p_i k_n$$

Where s is the importance of end-user demand, p_i is the importance of original user demand, $i = 1, 2, 3, \ldots, m$, k_n is the adjustment coefficient for each Kano category, $n = 1, 2, 3, \ldots, n$. Compared with the necessary requirements, the charm requirements can greatly increase user satisfaction. Therefore, for category O requirements, $k = 1$; for category A requirements, $k > 1$; for category I requirements, $k = 0$; for category R Demand, $k < 0$. The value of k is generally determined by the researcher's experience. Referring to previous studies, the adjustment coefficients corresponding to the Kano classification requirements are shown in Table 5.

Table 5. Kano adjustment factor k value

Kano classification	Adjustment coefficient
M	0.5
O	1.0
O(M)	1.25
A	2
I(A)	1.5
I	0.25

(2) Adjust the initial importance according to the value of k to determine the final weight of the personalized demand item. Let the final importance of the personalized functional requirement be w'_i, then:

$$w'_i = \frac{w_i k_i}{\sum_{i=1}^{n} w_i k_i} (i = 1, 2, \ldots, n)$$

Where w_i is the initial weight of the i-th personalized demand, k_i is its corresponding adjustment coefficient, and finally $\sum_{i=1}^{n} w'_i = 1$. Finally determine the ultimate importance weight ranking of PFR.

3 Results

3.1 Personalized Functional Requirements Screening Results

Hierarchical reorganization of the personalized demand items according to the selection principle, and determined that 26 personalized needs were finally obtained. As can be seen from Table 3, the basic needs (M) of the users for the elderly wearable devices are message receiving, fast and stable software and interface display; the expected needs (O) are falls, emergency alarms, remote monitoring, monitoring and partial reminders Functions and stable physical characteristics such as long-lasting power; some requirements such as route navigation, control of smart home functions, community hospital interoperability, real-time video recording, weather display, and drinking water reminder functions have shown a two-way demand among user needs [I(A)], the number of non-differentiated and attractive needs is similar, indicating that their functions are different among users, which is the personalized needs of some users, and is the key observation object of this research; the non-differentiated requirements (I) are for receiving mail, Social entertainment functions such as music playback and time display. According to the screening principle of the Kano evaluation table, 26 items of personalized needs screening results of smart watches for the elderly can be obtained, as shown in Table 6.

Table 6. Screening results of PFR

1. Two-way telephony	7. Real-time video	13. Fall in the alarm	19. Step counting	25. Positioning
2. Caregiver information	8. Long standby	14. navigation	20. Drink water to remind	26. Waterproof
3. Monitoring the heart rate	9. Control smart home	15. Custom alarm	21. Take medicine to remind	
4. Monitor blood pressure	10. Monitor remotely	16. Map assistance	22. One key emergency alarm	
5. Electronic fence	11. Anti-impact	17. Easy to operate	23. Weather forecast	
6. Monitor oxygen saturation	12. Abnormal physical indicators alarm	18. Interworking of community hospitals	24. Exercise guidance function	

3.2 Priority Ranking of Personalized Functional Requirements

By sorting the questionnaire data, using SPSS data statistics and analysis software to average and standard deviation the various personalized needs data of the elderly smart watches, thereby obtaining the basic importance of the users of the elderly smart watches, Confirmed the initial weight of the Personalized functional requirements (IW) (Table 7).

Table 7. Confirmed the initial weight of the PFR

Sort	PFR	IW	Standard deviation
1	One key emergency alarm	8	1.482
2	Easy to operate	7.97	1.482
3	Long standby	7.65	1.839
4	Caregiver information	7.58	1.553
5	Abnormal physical indicators alarm	7.52	1.844
6	Fall in the alarm	7.48	2.252
7	Waterproof	7.45	1.826
8	Anti-impact	7.39	1.653
9	Positioning	7.35	2.001
10	Monitor remotely	7.26	1.828
11	Two-way telephony	7.13	2.108
12	Monitor blood pressure	7.13	1.979
13	Monitoring the heart rate	7.06	2.202
14	Weather forecast	6.52	1.835
15	Navigation	6.35	2.136
16	Interworking of community hospitals	6.29	1.885
17	Electronic fence	6.29	1.987
18	Take medicine to remind	6.23	1.824
19	Monitor oxygen saturation	5.87	2.551
20	Map assistance	5.77	2.243
21	Step counting	5.74	1.924
22	Custom alarm	5.68	2.345
23	Exercise guidance	5.39	1.692
24	Drink water to remind	5.39	1.731
25	Real-time video	5.32	2.267
26	Control smart home	5.03	1.792

Adjust the initial importance according to the corresponding k value of PFR to determine the final weight of the personalized demand item. According to the ultimate weight value (UW), it is sorted from large to small, and the importance ranking of the personalized demand items of the smart watch is obtained (see Table 8).

Table 8. Ultimate weight and ranking of PFR for elderly smartwatches

Sort	PFR	Kano classification	Adjustment coefficient	IW	UW
1	One key emergency alarm	O(M)	1.25	8	0.049407
2	Weather forecast	I(A)	1.5	6.52	0.04832
3	Navigation	I(A)	1.5	6.35	0.04706
4	Interworking of community hospitals	I(A)	1.5	6.29	0.046616
5	Waterproof	O(M)	1.25	7.45	0.04601
6	Anti-impact	O(M)	1.25	7.39	0.04564
7	Positioning	O(M)	1.25	7.35	0.045393
8	Monitor blood pressure	O(M)	1.25	7.13	0.044034
9	Monitoring the heart rate	O(M)	1.25	7.06	0.043602
10	Map assistance	I(A)	1.5	5.77	0.042762
11	Exercise guidance	I(A)	1.5	5.39	0.039946
12	Drink water to remind	I(A)	1.5	5.39	0.039946
13	Real-time video	I(A)	1.5	5.32	0.039427
14	Easy to operate	O	1	7.97	0.039377
15	Long standby	O	1	7.65	0.037796
16	Caregiver information	O	1	7.58	0.037451
17	Control smart home	I(A)	1.5	5.03	0.037278
18	Abnormal physical indicators alarm	O	1	7.52	0.037154
19	Fall in the alarm	O	1	7.48	0.036957
20	Monitor remotely	O	1	7.26	0.03587
21	Two-way telephony	O	1	7.13	0.035227
22	Custom alarm	O(M)	1.25	5.68	0.035079
23	Electronic fence	O	1	6.29	0.031077
24	Monitor oxygen saturation	O	1	5.87	0.029002
25	Take medicine to remind	O(I)	0.5	6.23	0.01539
26	Step counting	O(I)	0.5	5.74	0.01418

4 Discussion

4.1 Kano Attributes of PFR and Personalized Customization Relationship

The UW ranking is integrated into the final personalized demand hierarchy model of the elderly smart watch. We find that the UW of the PFR item can reflect its importance more accurately to a certain extent. Sort the personalized demand items according to the UW, and then you can get the ranking of the PFR. The results show that users have a high degree of importance when they have both the desired attribute (O) and the required attribute (M), such as accident alarm system, monitoring function, positioning function, and stable physical characteristics, which are necessary in the retention function. When the user has dual attributes of charm attributes and non-differentiation attributes [I(A)], we define him as a user with divergent functions, although its main attribute is indiscriminate, many users feel the charm factor, so the functions are often the user's personalized needs, it have high importance in this research, it is also the object of this study. It can be observed that the weather and route navigation functions that are ranked higher are in line with the habits of the elderly. It is a commonly used function in life, so it leads to divergence of needs. Such features can be opened for users to choose during mass customization.

Other works have sorted PFR which have the Kano attributes I(A). According to this sorting, manufacturing companies can identify the key points in product development and mass customization production, and prioritize limited resources to the necessary requirements. PFR can also focus on development, and at the same time grasp the focus when there are needs or design contradictions, in particular, focus on the research of I (A) function requirements, purposefully promote the product to target users, and finally realize the customization of demand items. This can provide a reference for the refinement of product requirements to guide the completion of subsequent product design.

4.2 Role of Mass Customization for Smart Watches for the Elderly

In the actual design project, if the target user is an elderly person aged 60-70 who is in good health or suffers from a chronic disease, this type of elderly person has better self-care ability and has certain social needs, a regular diet and life, and daily travel. The weather and route navigation have certain requirements, but the ability of the physiological body to reduce disease resistance after aging, such as chronic diseases such as coronary heart disease and hypertension, is prone to emergencies. Considering these physiological conditions of the target user, this type of population is targeted Elderly smart watches can purposefully meet user needs, select basic needs O (M)/M functions, such as alarm systems and monitoring systems, stable physical characteristics, and add a small number of expected demand (O) functions with higher demand indicators, the caregiver can receive information and two-way conversation can be satisfied, in order to increase product competitiveness, using the above basic functions as a template to provide target users with personalized demand with no-differentiated demand/ characteristic difference I (A) attributes with high demand indicators, to provide personalized services, such functions can be customized and selected or guided by a combination of functions, such as combining weather forecasting and navigation functions to meet the daily needs of some users, or to meet the needs of community hospitals and real-time video recording, which can screen out the potential needs of users to the greatest extent and meet the minimum cost to get the maximum user satisfaction.

5 Conclusions and Future Works

This paper proposes a method for user's personalized functional requirements acquisition and analysis based on the Kano model. It uses the Affinity Diagram method to sort out product functions, conducts research on personalized functional requirements for elderly smart watches, and applies the principles of the Kano model to existing function classification, followed by screening of personalized functional requirements, researching the importance weight of the screened personalized functional requirements, prioritizing the importance weight of smart watches' PFR, finally determining the product's the customizable attribute items accurately calculate the user's objective requirements for the elderly smart watches and their customization priorities, and provide a scientific basis for the development and design of subsequent products.

This method can provide guidance for manufacturers who organize mass customization production, so that enterprises can not only maintain lower product maintenance costs, but also better meet the individual needs of customers, and increase customer satisfaction under the general situation of mass customization capabilities. It is not only suitable for the function development and design of new products for elderly smart watches, but also for the development and design of new product functions for other elderly wearable products, making the design of elderly products more humane. In addition, this article uses three-level demand indicators for the functional characteristics of elderly wearable devices, to reduce product development time and complexity, use two-level demand indicators for analysis. This research does not translate the research results into actual products for research. In the future, it will expand from single-user requirements research to complexity and multiple user perspectives for personalized demand classification research, and apply user demand analysis to actual projects.

Acknowledgements. The authors thank Li Mengjia from Gannan Normal University, and Li Ming from ECUST, and all the participating users fill out the questionnaire patiently and carefully. The authors would also like to thank all participants and the anonymous reviewers for their extensive feedback to improve the quality of the paper.

References

1. Best, R., Souders, D.J., Charness, N., Mitzner, T.L., Rogers, W.A.: The role of health status in older adults' perceptions of the usefulness of eHealth technology. In: Zhou, J., Salvendy, G. (eds.) ITAP 2015. LNCS, vol. 9194, pp. 3–14. Springer, Cham (2015). https://doi.org/10.1007/978-3-319-20913-5_1
2. Boletsis, C., McCallum, S., Landmark, B.F.: The use of smartwatches for health monitoring in home-based dementia care. In: Zhou, J., Salvendy, G. (eds.) ITAP 2015. LNCS, vol. 9194, pp. 15–26. Springer, Cham (2015). https://doi.org/10.1007/978-3-319-20913-5_2
3. Kano, N., et al: Attractive quality and must-be quality. J. Jpn. Soc. Qual. Control 39–48 (1984)
4. Tan, K.C., Shen, X.X.: Integrating Kano's model in the planning matrix of quality function deployment. Total Qual. Manag. **11**, 1141–1151 (2000)

5. Tan, K.C., Xie, M., Shen, X.X.: Development of innovative products using Kano's model and quality function deployment. Int. J. Innov. Manag. **3**, 271–286 (1999)
6. Li, Y., Tang, J., Yao, J., Xu, J.: Integrated method for determining the final importance of customer demand in the house of quality. Comput. Integr. Manufact. Syst. **14**, 1015–1022 (2008)
7. Chen, X., Qiu, D.: Research on product design based on fuzzy Kano model and TOPSIS method. J. Graph. 316–320 (2019)
8. Berger, C.: Kano's methods for understanding customer-defined quality. Center Qual. Manag. J. 3–36 (1993)
9. Yao, X., Hu, R., Yang, Y., Hu, H.: Research on the functional level of wearable devices for the elderly based on user demand. Packag. Eng. 159–165 (2018)
10. Chen, B., Qi, J., Huang, Y., Shu, H.: Improvement on the judgment method of quality factor evaluation tendency in KANO model. J. Beijing Univ. Posts Telecommun. (Soc. Sci. Edn.) 51–54 (2007)
11. Nie, D., Li, Y., Ma, G., Ma, T.: Synchronous multi-product design method based on user demand classification. Comput. Integr. Manufact. Syst. 1131–1137 (2010)
12. Tseng, M., Radke, A.: Production planning and control for mass customization – a review of enabling technologies. In: Fogliatto, F., da Silveira, G. (eds.) Mass Customization. Springer Series in Advanced Manufacturing, pp. 195–218. Springer, London (2011). https://doi.org/10.1007/978-1-84996-489-0_10
13. Dan, B., Wang, J., Liu, Y.: Research on customer demand information classification model and its expression method in mass customization. Comput. Integr. Manufact. Syst. 1504–1511 (2008)
14. Tang, Z., Long, Y.: Research on personalized demand acquisition method based on KANO model. Soft Sci. 127–131 (2012)
15. Hou, Z., Chen, S.: Research on user demand importance adjustment method based on Kano model. Comput. Integr. Manufact. Syst. 1786–1789 (2005)
16. Chen, H., Levkoff, S.E.: Delivering telemonitoring care to digitally disadvantaged older adults: human-computer interaction (HCI) design recommendations. In: Zhou, J., Salvendy, G. (eds.) ITAP 2015. LNCS, vol. 9194, pp. 50–60. Springer, Cham (2015). https://doi.org/10.1007/978-3-319-20913-5_5
17. Dou, J., Qin, J.: Research on emotional interaction design of vulnerable groups based on emotional computing. Packag. Eng. 7–11 (2017)

Human Factors Engineering Development Process in Civil Aircraft Flight Deck Design and Integration

Fei Li[✉], Xianchao Ma, Yuan Wang, Yao Zhu, Jing Zhang,
and Pu Hong

Shanghai Aircraft Design and Research Institute, No. 5188, Jinke Road, Pudong,
Shanghai 201210, China
lifei@comac.cc

Abstract. The Flight Crew error has been identified as a factor in two-thirds to three-fourths of recent aviation accidents and incidents, including several recent high-profile cases. A practical Human Factors Engineering Process (HFEP) during the whole life cycle of Civil Aircraft Flight Deck was introduced in this paper, which including a number of activities and the relative timing of Human Factors Engineering (HFE) activities with respect to the design phases, as well as the purpose, inputs, core tasks, Outputs and checklist for completion, and recommended practices of each activity of the HFEP.

Keywords: Human Factors Engineering · Development process · Civil flight deck

1 Introduction

All elements of the Flight Deck are influenced by human performance, especially the flight crews. In turn, human performance is influenced by many aspects of Flight Deck design, including the equipment that flight crews interface with, training they receive and procedures they use. These aspects of Flight Deck and system design are addressed by HFE [1].

In the past, human factors engineering analysis has been mostly accomplished on a case-by-case basis, in a somewhat understand manner. This has led to three main problems [2].

- Inconsistencies in the design process itself.
- Untimely application of human engineering principles.
- Lack of systems integration.

A structured HFEP is an approach to solve the above problems. Experience has shown that when HFE activities are performed independently from other engineering activities, their impact and effectiveness is greatly decreased. In fact, addressing the human factors aspects of the Flight Deck is an activity that is best conducted early and continuously throughout the Civil Aircraft engineering design and development life cycle and not something that happens only at the end of a program during the formal

© Springer Nature Switzerland AG 2020
M. Kurosu (Ed.): HCII 2020, LNCS 12181, pp. 324–333, 2020.
https://doi.org/10.1007/978-3-030-49059-1_23

certification test phase. As such, there may be some information generated as part of the engineering design process that could be used for certification as well.

2   Goals and Overviews of the HFEP

The primary goal of the Civil Aircraft Flight Deck HFEP is to provide a systematic method for integrating HFE into Flight Deck analysis, design, evaluation, and implementation to achieve safe, efficient, and reliable operation. Other goals include the following:

- Providing design criteria to guide HFE implementation.
- Integrating an HFEP that can be practically implemented.
- Ensuring flight crews can perform tasks within the established safety, time, and performance criteria with the Human-Machine Interfaces (HMI) provided.
- Providing acceptable workload levels for flight crews.
- Providing a design that helps prevent human error and provides for error prevention, detection, and recovery capability.
- Providing a high-quality interface between flight crews and Flight Deck systems that ensures safe operation, and alerts flight crews on either non-normal or emergency condition.

Figure 1 represents the overview of Civil Aircraft Flight Deck HFEP, which including a number of activities and the relative timing of HFE activities with respect to the design phases.

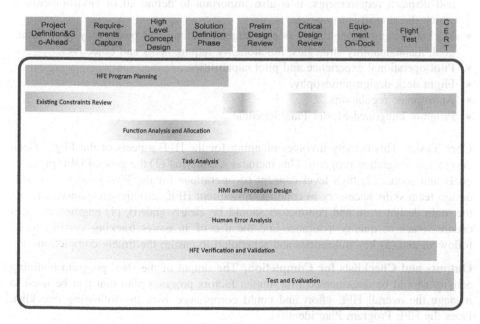

Fig. 1.   An overview of the Civil Aircraft Flight Deck HFEP

However, Flight Deck integration is an iterative process. While the activities are presented below in serial fashion, they will be performed throughout the course of the Aircraft design and development program and will occur in parallel with each other. Thus, for example, there may be a preliminary allocation of function before any analysis work begins, e.g., as part of a preliminary specification of Flight Deck systems. However, the allocation will be analysed further as part of that HFE activity to better specify the basis for allocating functions. The function allocation may be revised across the design process as the design becomes more detailed and evaluations of systems performance are made.

3   Detail Description of the Activities in HFEP

3.1   HFE Program Planning

Purpose and Objectives. The main purpose and objective of HFE program planning is to integrated HFE into the Flight Deck Design and Integration Process. To achieve the key goal and attribute of the HFE Progress identified in Sect. 2, HFE should be fully integrated into the overall Aircraft development and engineering process. This will help ensure timely and complete interaction with other engineering activities.

Inputs. The inputs include but are not limited to:

- Aircraft mission and operational requirements, including mission range and duration, airline company standard operating procedures, as well as landing capability and dispatch requirements. It is also important to define all of environments in which the aircraft is to operate.
- Market strategy drivers, such as cost targets, training and proficiency goal, safety goal, maintainability strategies, functionality requirements and objectives.
- Pilot operational experience and pilot capabilities.
- Flight deck design philosophy.
- Appropriate regulations.
- Program Integrated Master Plan/Schedule.

Core Tasks. This activity involves planning for the HFE aspects of the Flight Deck design and integration program. This includes identifying (1) the general HFE program goals and scope, (2) high-level concept of operations for the Flight Deck, (3) HFE design team skills necessary to conduct subsequent HFE activities (responsibilities of the main design team and contractors should be clearly stated), (4) engineering procedures (such as quality assurance and the use of an issues tracking system) to be followed, and (5) key milestones and scheduled to ensure the timely completion.

Outputs and Checklists for Completion. The output of the HFE program planning activity should be documented in a human factors program plan that can be used to manage the overall HFE effort and could compliance with the following checklist. Does the HFE Program Plan identify:

- general HFE program goals and scope?
- high-level concept of operations for the Flight Deck?
- HFE design team skills necessary to conduct subsequent HFE activities?
- engineering procedures (such as QA and use of an issues tracking system) to be followed?
- key milestones and scheduled to ensure the timely completion?

Are the results of the planning activity documented in a human factors program plan that can be used to manage the overall HFE effort?

Recommended Practices. Engage appropriate multi-disciplinary team. The team should consist of pilots, Flight Deck design and integration, systems engineers, mechanical engineers, Engineering/Program Management specialists, and human factors engineers. An effective skill set includes:

- Flight operations (line pilots are important in uncovering unintended uses of prior designs).
- Human factors.
- Systems engineering.
- Certification.
- Airspace operations, e.g., Air Traffic Management (ATM), Airport and/or Airline Operational Communications (AOC).
- Program Management.

3.2 Existing Constraints Review

Purpose and Objectives. Existing Constraints imposed on the Flight Deck integration mainly include the operational experience and capabilities of the flight crew [3] and the expected operating environment [2] of the Civil Aircraft. Existing Constraints Review (ECR) is used to identify all the potential conflicts and issues between the Flight Deck design proposal and all the constraints mentioned above.

Inputs. The inputs include but are not limited to:

- Flight crew operational experience and capabilities, including general human anthropometry, perceptual and cognitive abilities.
- Human reliability data.
- Expected operation environment. This may include routing (e.g., polar, oceanic, non-ICAO), aircraft limitations (e.g., cruise altitude, range, speed), atmospheric conditions, runway types and conditions, desert and/or arctic operations, and type of maintenance support, etc.

Core Tasks. ECR is performed to understand (1) current or planned work practices so the potential impact of planned changes, such as the introduction of new systems and new responsibilities and tasks or the introduction of new performance schedules, can be assessed, (2) operational problems and issues may be addressed in a new design or modification of an existing design, and (3) relevant domain experience with candidate system technology approaches.

Outputs and Checklists for Completion. The outputs of this activity is an identification of the flight crew capabilities and operating environment in which the aircraft and Flight Deck systems will have to perform and definition of the unique requirements of Flight Deck system which will provide for safe and efficient operation within that environments. And the completion checklist should be:

- Are ECR documents maintained and readily accessible to the design team?
- Do they provide a clear indication of issues identified, the design activities to which they are relevant, and their importance?

Recommended Practices. ECRs should be held periodically during the project/program cycle, as designs change, operations change, or other developments occur. OERs should be implemented as a series, first as a stand-alone, and then subsequent one as an element of the existing design review cycle.

3.3   Function Analysis and Allocation

Purpose and Objectives. The overall purpose of function analysis and allocation is to ensure that functional requirements are sufficiently defined and analyzed so that the allocation of functions to the available resources can take advantage of the strengths of each. In other words, make use of automation and human capabilities in ways that maximize overall function accomplishment.

Inputs. The inputs include but are not limited to:

- A clear definition of the intended function of the Flight Deck/system including how the flight crew will use it.
- Flight Deck philosophy, especially the automation design principles.
- Aircraft operational concept.

Core Tasks. The core tasks may include:

- Conduct Function Analysis and trade-off. Use a "top-down" approach, which starting at the "top" of the hierarchy with the system's high-level mission and goals, to divided the aircraft level functions into the sub-functions until which could be accomplished by a single system or flight crew.
- Define Scenarios for evaluation.
- Conduct Function Allocation Evaluation. This analysis is performed for each scenario. As the whole function analysis and allocation process is iterative, this analysis can begin at the earliest design stages. Allocations can be refined or adjusted as more information about performance is known and evaluations are conducted.
- Evaluate Allocations across Scenarios.
- Evaluate Overall Personnel Role.
- Verify Allocations.

Outputs and Checklists for Completion. The specification of which functions should be carried out by the users and which by the technology. And the completion checklist should be:

- Have the various functions needed to achieve the mission been described?
- Has the allocation of responsibility for conducting functions, or parts of functions, to personnel, to automatic systems, or to some combination of the two been made?
- Is the allocation made on the basis of a function analysis to determine what is required to perform the function?
- Have the roles and responsibilities of personnel and automation in the performance of system functions, including how they may be changed as a result of various types of failure conditions?

Recommended Practices. These design decisions determine the extent to which a given job, task, function or responsibility is to be automated or assigned to human performance. The decisions should be based on many factors, such as relative capabilities and limitations of humans versus technology in terms of reliability, speed, accuracy, strength, flexibility of response, financial cost, the importance of successful or timely accomplishment of tasks and user well-being. They should not simply be based on determining which functions the technology is capable of performing and then simply allocating the remaining functions to users, relying on their flexibility to make the system work. The resulting human functions should form a meaningful set of tasks. Representative users should generally be involved in these decisions. Function allocation analysis is a continuous and ongoing process. While initially qualitative evaluations as discussed here are necessary, allocation acceptability is continuously evaluated as part of later design activities. When mockups, simulators, and other tools become available, function allocations can be evaluated by measuring actual performance.

3.4 Task Analysis

Purpose and Objectives. Each sub-function can be broken down into tasks. The objective of task analysis is to specify the requirements for successful task performance, e.g., what alarms, information, controls, communications, and procedures are needed for flight crew to accomplish their assigned functions.

Inputs. The inputs include but are not limited to:

- Function definition and documented, organized, and consistent set of requirements.
- Baseline flight deck definition and operational procedures.
- Flight deck design philosophy.

Core Tasks. The core tasks may include:

- Identify Tasks need to be analysed. It may not be necessary to perform task analysis on all tasks. For example, if a system function is well known and essentially unchanged from predecessor systems, it may not be necessary to reanalyse it.

- Develop High-Level Task Descriptions. Including purpose, task initiation, pre-conditions, time constraints, task termination and task failure criteria.
- Develop Detailed Task Descriptions. Including low-level description, completeness of the task decomposition, consequence tasks, evaluation results of time-critical tasks, and additional considerations as needed.
- Assign Tasks to Flight Crew. Tasks need to be assigned to individual Flight Crew according to each flight phase.
- Identify Task Requirements. Including information requirements, decision-making requirements, response requirements, communication requirements, workload, task support requirements and workplace factors. These requirements are a major input to HMI and procedure design, as well as training.

Outputs and Checklists for Completion. The outputs of this activity are a set of tasks performance requirements. And the completion checklist should be:

- Do the task analyses specify the requirements for successful task performance, e.g., what alarms, information, controls, communications, and procedures are needed?

Recommended Practices. Two parameters to consider in allocating tasks between crew members and aircraft systems are keeping both the pilot workload and "pilot in the loop" activities at the appropriate level.

3.5 Human Error Analysis

Purpose and Objectives. This activity is performed to evaluate the potential for, and mechanisms of, human error in Flight Crew operations and identify the appropriate methods to decrease the probability or to mitigate the hazard.

Inputs. The inputs include but are not limited to:

- Relevant Operational Experience Reviews.
- Incident and accident databases.
- Flight Crew tasks definition.
- Flight Deck System behaviour.

Core Tasks. The core tasks may include:

- Identify critical Flight Crew tasks to analyse. Especially for the complex and/or novelty systems. As well as conventional systems operations during high workload flight phase.
- Criticality Safety analysis. Analyse the hazards due to the flight crew error to define the associated level of protections.

Outputs and Checklists for Completion. Have significant Flight Crew tasks (i.e., those that impact mission success, the safety of system operations, and where Flight Crew safety is an issue) been identified and analyzed in detail? Have these been evaluated with sufficient detail so that error tolerant design strategies (minimize Flight Crew errors, allow their detection, and provide recovery capability) can be applied to manage them, e.g., through the design of Human-System Interfaces, procedures, training, and automation?

Recommended Practices. Fault Tree Analysis and Human Factors Process Failure Mode and Effects Analysis (HFPFMEA) are the two practical analysis techniques [4].

3.6   Human-Machine Interface and Procedure Design

Purpose and Objectives. This activity is performed to develop the Flight Deck detail HMI proposal and Flight Crew procedure.

Inputs. The inputs include but are not limited to:

- Flight Deck design philosophy.
- Aircraft mission and operational requirements.
- List of HMI issues associated with requirements.
- Technology capabilities.

Core Tasks. The core tasks may include:

- HMI requirements capture. The analyses discussed in previous sections result in requirements for the HMI and procedures.
- Flight crew concept of operation. Alternative operation concept of meeting the requirements should be identified or developed previously and comes down to the final concept via trade-off evaluations, usability evaluations and performance-based tests and evaluations.
- Develop Display Formats and Controls Scheme.
- HMI detail design and implementation.

Outputs and Checklists for Completion. At the end of this step (when it is decided to do formal testing for certification), documents required to be completed may be revised to include the final HMI and procedure design specifications. And the completion checklist should be:

- Does the HMI provide the resources needed by Flight Crew to interact with the systems?
- Do HMIs and procedures that (1) reflect the system's functional and physical design, (2) meet flight crew task requirements, (3) exhibit the general characteristics of well-designed HMI and procedures, and (4) are easy to learn and use?

Recommended Practices

- Engage a multi-disciplinary team for both design and regulatory agency teams.
- Quick iteration of solutions and evaluations.
- Provide the higher-level documents such as the Flight Deck Design Philosophy and Flight Crew Operational Requirements, and rationale/assumption document to all team members.
- Where system is complete enough, involve currently flying line pilots in evaluations.

3.7   HFE Verification and Validation

Purpose and Objectives. The goal of this step is to show compliance to the applicable human factors related regulations and to achieve final certification authority approval of compliance to the human factors related regulations, based on the deliverables presented.

Inputs. The inputs include but are not limited to:

- Certification Plan for human factors compliance.
- Test plan and test procedures including human factors considerations.

Core Tasks. The core tasks may include:

- Formal Testing. Formal testing is done on an article or component that conforms to the proposed type design in form, fit, and function.
- Tasks and activities for the applicant include the submission of all agreed-upon human factors data.
- Tasks and activities for the certification authority include reviewing all human factors data and determining if all human factors related regulations have been complied with.

Outputs and Checklists for Completion. The results of human factors test and analyses will be included in a formal test or compliance report. The certification authority communicates to the applicant the outcomes of the certification authority review: approval or disapproval.

Recommended Practices. Develop a common understanding between the certification authority and the applicant about the relevant human factors aspects and potential issues related to the applicant's product. Establish an ongoing dialog with the certification authority during the design evolution through regularly scheduled familiarization meetings at each stage of development, including early prototype development and evaluation.

3.8   Test and Evaluation

This activity is an integral part of the entire HFEP and spans the full Civil Aircraft Flight Deck design life cycle. Overall objectives are to validate HFE requirements, Various engineering evaluation techniques include:

- Interviews of users.
- Procedure evaluations (e.g., complexity, number of steps).
- Walk-throughs using drawings.
- Reach analysis via computer modelling.
- Time-line analysis for assessing task demands and workload.
- Operational sequence diagrams.
- Usability or heuristic evaluations.
- Walk-throughs using drawings, mock-ups, or prototypes.
- Performance-based tests, such as can be conducted on a full-mission simulator.

4 Summary and Conclusions

The Civil Aircraft Flight Deck system design include controls, displays, crew alerts, checklists, and procedures. HFE issues relate to all aspects of the Flight Crews, across the spectrum of expected operating conditions (nominal, non-normal, and emergency). This paper introduced a HFEP to identify and manage the HFE issue under a structive way, which has been proven to be more practical.

However, this process is not mandatory and users of this information can either utilize the process and or develop another procedure tailored to their particular development and/or environment.

Acknowledgements. The author gratefully acknowledges the helpful reviews by Prof. Xianchao Ma and Ph.D. Dayong Dong and useful discussions with Dr. Wenjun Dong, Ms. Yao Zhu, Mr. Pu Hong, Ms. Jing Zhang and Miss. Yuan Wang.

References

1. Adelstein, B., Hobbs, A.: Design, Development, Testing, and Evaluation: Human Factors Engineering, NASA/TM-2006-214535 (2006)
2. SAE ARP4033: Pilot-System Integration, chapter 6, p. 3
3. SAE ARP5056: Flight Crew Interface Considerations in the Flight Deck Design Process for Part 25 Aircraft, chapter 5, p. 9
4. JSC: Human Reliability Analysis (HRA) Final Report. Volume VII: Human Error Analysis Methodology, JSC report 29867 (2002)

Documentation Tasks with Tablet or Smartphone in the Workplace: A Study with Respect to OSH

Patricia Tegtmeier[✉], Christiane Adomeit, and Sascha Wischniewski

Federal Institute for Occupational Safety and Health (BAuA),
Frierich-Henkel-Weg 1-25, 44149 Dortmund, Germany
tegtmeier.patricia@baua.bund.de

Abstract. Integrating smart mobile devices into the workplace creates new opportunities and challenges for occupational health and safety. This study includes a time series on mental and physical strain during the use of smart mobile devices in order to obtain initial indications regarding a healthy length of use at work.

Sixty-four healthy subjects documented pictures via checklists on either a smartphone or a tablet in two 30-minute trials. Meanwhile participants rated their subjective physical and mental load on an 11-point one-item Likert scale several times. In addition, they estimated musculoskeletal neck discomfort prior to the experiment, and immediately after each of the two trials. Multilevel analysis (MLA) was performed to explore effects of time and the mobile device on the ratings of physical and mental load, as well as the musculoskeletal discomfort.

In the MLA, physical and mental load ratings were positively associated with time and trial. Device was an additional predictor of mental load ratings. Best-fitting model for neck discomfort ratings included time, device, and gender as predictors.

For both mobile devices, the participants physical and mental load increased significantly over time though mean ratings did not reach scores above moderate. No effects of users' age or technophilia were observed. Likewise, musculoskeletal discomfort ratings concerning the neck were significantly higher after the documentation task compared to prior. This research provides only a first insight about possible challenges regarding prolonged use of tablet-pc and smartphones at work. Further research appears worthwhile.

Keywords: Smart devices · Mental load · Physical load · Discomfort

1 Background

Since the 1970s, the paperless future workplace has been predicted, and with the advent of laptops, tablets, smartphones, and other smart mobile devices in addition to, or as replacement for pen and paper, it seems to have finally arrived. As data for Germany by D21 Digital Index [1] demonstrate, job-related and/or private usage of various digital devices developed somewhat differently over the past years. In 2015 smartphone,

© Springer Nature Switzerland AG 2020
M. Kurosu (Ed.): HCII 2020, LNCS 12181, pp. 334–347, 2020.
https://doi.org/10.1007/978-3-030-49059-1_24

laptop, and desktop-pc usage all ranged around 60% and 35% of the respondents used tablet-pcs. Ever since, data indicate a rise of smartphone usage up to 75% in 2018, while laptop- and tablet-pc use remained comparatively stable at 64% and 34%, whereas usage of desktops decreased down to 43% over the same period. Everywhere, mobile devices enable retrieval and documentation of information and knowledge, e.g. electronic care documentation, taking orders in a café, or mobile occupational safety and health risk assessment, without media breaks independent from a specific work-place [2, 3]. They offer the potential to simultaneously improve the workflow and work design. Integrating these smart mobile devices into the workplace creates new opportunities and challenges for occupational health and safety. Unfortunately, already existing recommendations are only partly transferable and there is only a small number of studies specifically addressing smartphone and tablet use in the workplace [4, 5].

However, the extensive research concerning kinematics, and/or muscle activity while using touchscreen devices can give some insight on physical demands placed by touchscreen devices. Operating touchscreen devices requires prolonged visual feedback and thumbs can play a more prominent role, due to texting or operating the device through multi-touch gestures than when using a keyboard. Researchers studying smartphone and tablet use in general, reported highly repetitive hand or arm move-ments and/or prolonged working in unfavorable postures especially of the neck, wrist and thumb [6–11]. Depending on study design, researchers reported downward head tilts of more than 20° some exceeding 40° compared to a neutral upright posture [11–14]. In their study Namwongsa et al. [15] assessed the level of ergonomic risk to smartphone users while texting a short sequence using the Rapid Upper Limb Assessment (RULA [16]) tool. The RULA results found identified the high ergonomics risk of smartphone users. External keyboards could relieve shoulders, wrists and thumbs during long text input. However, this restricts the inherent mobility of the smart devices. Most studies observed periods of smartphone use of less than half an hour. Recently Han et al. [17] researched postural conditions over a period of eight hours in non-controlled environments with and without smartphone use in a group of students. They reported participants to have spent about 20% of their time in postures with a 20–30° head-down tilt, regardless of smartphone use. Nevertheless, they found participants spent longer times in head-down tilt postures of above 30° while using their smart-phone. Some researchers identified the intensity of use as a predictor of pain in the neck, arm or wrist as well as psychological discomfort.

Overall, some suggestions regarding the length of use of smart mobile devices in the workplace would be sensible. However, as intensity of use was determined very differently throughout various studies (retrospective self-information on summative use, quantity or speed of texting, etc.), no reliable values for a safe length of use with regard to physical load could be derived so far. Furthermore, except for usability tests of specific apps, research addressing mental load while using various touchscreen devices at work is even scarcer.

Therefore, the aim of our study was a time-based analysis of mental and physical load during the use of smart mobile devices, in order to provide a first step regarding a healthy length of use in the workplace and defining needs for future research.

2 Methods

2.1 Participants

Sixty-four healthy volunteers, aged 18–65 years, balanced for gender participated in this study. In order to control for possible age effects concerning physical abilities, the sample was stratified in two age groups: aged 19 to 40 years or 41 years and above. All participants had normal or corrected-to-normal vision and were without ongoing musculoskeletal symptoms or surgical interventions in the thumb and upper extremities within the past six months. Participants were recruited from the local community via public notice boards as well as lab internal mailing lists. They received an expense allowance of 10 € per hour.

The number of subjects was initially determined for a repeated measures ANOVA including 8 groups (device (2) × age group (2) × start position (2)) and 30 repeated measures (2 trials with 15 measures) with a 0.5 correlation between them and with an effect size 0.2), confidence level (alpha 5%) and desired power (80%) in G*Power Version 3.1.9.2). Due to technical problems, the experiment was aborted in two cases. The associated data were excluded and two additional participants recruited.

2.2 Task

A typical application of smart mobile devices in the workplace are documenting tasks. Hence, the chosen task involved documenting the contents of various photos via a selective list. Half of the participants performed the task on a smartphone and half of them on a small tablet-pc while holding the device (between-design) in a laboratory setting. The way of holding the device (one- or two-handed) was up to the participants und could be varied freely during the experiment.

Successively, varying pictures were projected onto a wall. Participants used corresponding lists on their particular touchscreen device to document whether certain contents were visible on each photo or not via marking checkboxes by tapping with a finger (thus, resulting in an equal amount of possible taps per photo whether an specific content was visible or not). Photos changed automatically at an interval of 20 s. This interval was derived from a pre-test: Participants should be documenting a photo all the time without idling, and at the same time be able to edit at least two thirds of the respective list. They were informed that it would not be possible to edit a list completely and to change to the next list whenever the picture changed. Participants were free to start with any item on the list while tapping the checkboxes as fast and as accurately as possible.

Following a sequence of six photos, participants saw an 11-point subjective assessment scale. Based on this visual anchor, they verbally assessed their current physical and mental load 1 (not at all) to 11 (very severe) which was noted by the experimenter. Based on internal requirements concerning injury prevention, a subjective physical load exceeding the level 8 was defined as a stop criterion for a trial. Afterwards the next picture sequence started. Each participant executed the task in two 30-min trials once seated/once standing (within-design) with a 10-min break in between.

2.3   Material

Half of the participants used a Galaxy Tab A T280 (7″ display, size $187 \times 109 \times 9$ mm, weight 283 g), the remaining 32 a Samsung Galaxy Note 8 N950F (6,3″ display, size $162.5 \times 74.8 \times 8.6$ mm, weight 195 g). There were 180 pdf files on the devices, each containing a list with 15 items and corresponding editable yes/no checkboxes.

The graphical material included 180 different photographs (all landscape oriented) organized in a PowerPoint presentation. These were projected via beamer onto the wall opposite from the participants (distance 3 m) with a size of approximately 100×150 cm.

2.4   Dependent Variables

Participants rated their subjective physical and mental load on a visual numerical 11-point one-item Likert scale from 1 (not at all) to 11 (very severe), at two-minute intervals during the documenting task.

In addition, they estimated musculoskeletal discomfort prior to the experiment, and immediately after each of the two trials, likewise on 11-point Likert scales. The questionnaire included a body map and highlighted specific musculoskeletal areas (i.e. neck), based on studies by Berolo et al. [18] and Lin et al. [19].

In addition, sociodemographic data (age, gender) and technophilia (questionnaire ATI, 5-point Likert scale) were collected at the beginning of the experiment.

Other variables observed (results not reported in this paper) were posture in respect to RULA as well as performance regarding correct tapped checkboxes, errors, and omissions in the documentation task.

2.5   Procedure

After providing consent to a protocol approved by the ethics board of the Federal Institute for OSH, Germany, participants filled in the questionnaires regarding technophilia as well as the musculoskeletal discomfort prior to the experiment along with the sociodemographic data. Afterwards, they made themselves familiar with the documentation task, the technology, and the 11-point subjective assessment scale used. They documented a six-picture sequence (2 min) to get some experience with the task as well as the items on the list prior to the actual data collection.

Subsequently, the first trial started. The order of the first position adopted (sitting or standing) was randomized so that half of the participants documented standing first. In the seated condition, participants used a general lecture chair without armrests. After 30 min or after reaching the stop criterion described above, the participants filled in the questionnaire about musculoskeletal discomfort a second time. After a 10-min break, the second trial started for each participant in the second position. Finally, each participant completed the musculoskeletal discomfort questionnaire one last time.

2.6 Statistical Analysis

Individuals needed different amounts of time indicating their physical and mental load while documenting, but each trial terminated after 30 min. This resulted in a somewhat unbalanced design with 10 to 14 measurements per participant and trial. No participant completed all of the 15 possible ratings and less than 60% of the participants rated 14 or 13 times. Therefore, only the first 12 ratings of each trial and participant were included in the subsequent analyses. To handle (the still) incomplete data, a multi-level analysis (MLA) was performed using SPSS 25. The explored effects included time and trial (level 1), mobile device, and age group (level 2) on the ratings of physical and mental load, as well as the musculoskeletal discomfort in the neck.

To find the best-fit model, a "bottom-up" modeling strategy was applied using the likelihood ratio test to compare between models (ML estimations). The best-fit model for each dependent variable was recalculated using restricted maximum likelihood estimation (REML) estimations. The measure of the effects was expressed by betas (B) with 95% confidence intervals. Significance was considered at p-value of <.05. The residuals were checked for normality and homoscedasticity based on the best-fit model.

3 Results

Participants included in the current analysis had a mean age of 41 (SD 15.0) and separated for the two age groups 27 (SD 6.1) 54 (SD 7.0) respectively. They had a mean ATI score of 4.1 (SD 1.1) on the 5-point scale. A post hoc one-sample t-test was run to determine whether the recruited group was different from mean, defined as a score of 3.0. ATI score was statistically significantly well above average, $t(63) = 7.739$, $p < .001$, indicating rather high technophilia.

Table 1. Mean values, associated standard deviations (SD) and number of participants [N] physical load ratings separated for trial and device

Tablet												
Trial	1	2	3	4	5	6	7	8	9	10	11	12
1	**1.4**	**1.5**	**1.6**	**1.8**	**2.0**	**2.1**	**2.2**	**2.5**	**2.6**	**2.8**	**3.0**	**3.1**
	(0.7)	(0.7)	(0.8)	(0.9)	(1.0)	(1.1)	(1.1)	(1.2)	(1.3)	(1.3)	(1.4)	(1.4)
	[32]	[32]	[32]	[32]	[32]	[32]	[32]	[32]	[32]	[32]	[31]	[30]
2	**1.7**	**1.9**	**2.2**	**2.3**	**2.5**	**2.7**	**2.7**	**2.9**	**2.9**	**3.1**	**3.1**	**3.4**
	(0.7)	(0.8)	(1.0)	(1.1)	(1.2)	(1.4)	(1.4)	(1.6)	(1.7)	(1.7)	(1.8)	(2.0)
	[32]	[32]	[32]	[32]	[32]	[32]	[32]	[32]	[32]	[32]	[32]	[32]
Smartphone												
1	**1.4**	**1.6**	**1.8**	**2.0**	**2.2**	**2.3**	**2.3**	**2.6**	**2.8**	**3.0**	**3.1**	**3.0**
	(0.9)	(0.9)	(1.0)	(1.2)	(1.2)	(1.2)	(1.3)	(1.5)	(1.3)	(1.4)	(1.5)	(1.3)
	[32]	[32]	[32]	[32]	[32]	[32]	[32]	[32]	[32]	[32]	[31]	[28]
2	**1.8**	**2.1**	**2.4**	**2.6**	**2.8**	**3.0**	**3.2**	**3.4**	**3.5**	**3.6**	**3.8**	**3.7**
	(0.9)	(1.0)	(1.1)	(1.1)	(1.2)	(1.5)	(1.5)	(1.5)	(1.5)	(1.5)	(1.7)	(1.6)
	[32]	[32]	[32]	[32]	[32]	[32]	[32]	[32]	[32]	[32]	[32]	[31]

Neck discomfort, as rated on the 11-point scale, ranged from 1.9 points (SD 1.6) prior to the experiment to 2.7 (SD 2.0) after the first trial and 2.9 (SD 2.3) after the second trial.

Table 1 and 2 display mean values and standard deviations of physical and mental load ratings over time separated for device and trial as well as number of participants giving a rating at that point in time.

Table 2. Mean values, associated standard deviations (SD) and number of participants [N] mental load separated for trial and device

Tablet											
Trial	1	2	3	4	5	6	7	8	9	10	11	12
1	**2.0**	**2.1**	**2.3**	**2.4**	**2.5**	**2.3**	**2.3**	**2.5**	**2.6**	**2.5**	**2.7**	**2.7**
	(1.1)	(1.0)	(1.1)	(1.1)	(1.1)	(1.0)	(1.0)	(1.1)	(1.2)	(1.1)	(1.3)	(1.3)
	[32]	[32]	[32]	[32]	[32]	[32]	[32]	[32]	[32]	[32]	[31]	[30]
2	**1.8**	**2.0**	**2.1**	**2.2**	**2.3**	**2.4**	**2.5**	**2.7**	**2.7**	**2.7**	**2.9**	**3.0**
	(0.7)	(0.9)	(0.9)	(0.9)	(1.0)	(1.0)	(1.1)	(1.3)	(1.3)	(1.3)	(1.3)	(1.4)
	[32]	[32]	[32]	[32]	[32]	[32]	[32]	[32]	[32]	[32]	[32]	[32]
Smartphone											
1	**2.8**	**2.9**	**2.9**	**3.0**	**3.1**	**3.1**	**3.2**	**3.4**	**3.4**	**3.4**	**3.5**	**3.5**
	(1.8)	(1.5)	(1.7)	(1.5)	(1.5)	(1.6)	(1.7)	(1.6)	(1.7)	(1.6)	(1.6)	(1.7)
	[32]	[32]	[32]	[32]	[32]	[32]	[32]	[32]	[32]	[32]	[31]	[28]
2	**2.8**	**3.0**	**3.1**	**3.4**	**3.4**	**3.6**	**3.6**	**3.9**	**3.8**	**3.9**	**4.0**	**4.0**
	(1.2)	(1.4)	(1.4)	(1.6)	(1.5)	(1.5)	(1.6)	(1.6)	(1.6)	(1.6)	(1.7)	(1.6)
	[32]	[32]	[32]	[32]	[32]	[32]	[32]	[32]	[32]	[32]	[32]	[31]

3.1   Model Fit

As a first step in the model building process, we built an empty model (intercept only) for each dependent variable and calculated ICCs based on these empty models. The resulting ICCs ($ICC_{\text{physical load}}$ = .403, $ICC_{\text{mental load}}$ = .699, $ICC_{\text{neck discomfort}}$ = .654) provided evidence for individual variation in the outcome variables with regard to time. Therefore, for all variables reported, multilevel modeling was applied.

Similar modeling approaches for mental and physical load were used. Models of time, trial, touchscreen device, and possible influence of age, technophilia, and gender on mental and physical load ratings at 24 time points were compared.

As can be seen from Table 3, the best-fit model (m7) regarding mental load included time, trial (both random intercept and random slope), a first level interaction between time and trial and a second level effect of device. The best-fit model for physical load ratings (m6) contained time and trial only. Age, technophilia, and gender were no significant predictors of mental or physical load ratings.

Table 3. Bottom-up model comparison (full maximum likelihood estimation) for mental and physical load ratings (12 points in time) based on deviance and number of estimated parameters; each model was contrasted against the previous best one

	Measure	Deviance	P	Difference		
				chi-square	df	p
model 1	mental	3870	3			–
(intercept only)	physical	4798	3			–
model 2	mental	3730	4	140	1	<0.001
(time fixed slope)	physical	4439	4	359	1	<0.001
model 3	mental	3232	6	498	2	<0.001
(time random slope)	physical	3738	6	700	2	<0.001
model 4	mental	3043	7	189	2	<0.001
(m3+trial fixed slope)	physical	3309	7	430	1	<0.001
model 5	mental	3021	8	22	1	<0.001
(m4+time-trial interaction)	physical	3309	8	0	1	0.827
model 6	mental (m5)	2696	11	325	3	<0.001
(trial random slope)	physical (m4)	*2806	10	502	3	<0.001
model 7	mental	*2684	12	12	1	0.001
(m6+device)	physical	2805	11	1	1	0.323
model 8	mental (m7)	2681	14	3	2	0.234
(+cross-level interaction)	physical (-)					
model 9	mental (m7)	2684	13	0	1	0.550
(+age)	physical (m6)	2803	11	3	1	0.074
model 10	mental (m7)	2684	13	0	1	0.741
(+technophilia)	physical (m6)	2803	11	3	1	0.094
model 11	mental (m7)	2684	13	0	1	0.944
(+gender)	physical (m6)	2806	11	0	1	0.655

Note: df = Degrees of Freedom; Deviance = −2 log likelihood; P = number of estimated parameters; p = p value (deviating values with same deviance and parameters are due to display without decimal places); * indicates the best fitting model.

The model strategy on neck discomfort ratings progressively included time (three points in time), touchscreen device, and possible influence of age, technophilia, and gender.

Table 4 summarizes the results of model comparisons using the likelihood ratio test. The best-fit model (m8) incorporated the effect of time of rating (fixed effect as well as random intercept and random slope), device and an effect of gender without any cross-level interactions.

Table 4. Bottom-up model comparison (full maximum likelihood estimation) for neck discomfort ratings (3 points in time) based on deviance and number of estimated parameters; each model was contrasted against the previous best one

	Measure	Deviance	P	Difference		
				chi-square	df	p
model 1 (intercept only)	neck	731	3	–	–	–
model 2 (time fixed slope)	neck	707	4	24	1	<0.001
model 3 (time random slope)	neck	682	6	25	2	<0.001
model 4 (m3+device)	neck	675	7	7	1	0.011
model 5 (m4+cross-level interaction)	neck	675	8	0	1	0.726
model 6 (m4+age)	neck	674	8	1	1	0.432
model 7 (m4+technophilia)	neck	674	8	1	1	0.411
model 8 (m4+gender)	neck	*669	8	6	1	0.012
model 9 (m5+cross-level interaction)	neck	666	10	3	2	0.206

Note: df = Degrees of Freedom; Deviance = −2 log likelihood; P = number of estimated parameters; p = p value (deviating values with same deviance and parameters are due to display without decimal places); * indicates the best fitting model.

3.2 Perceived Physical Load

Based on the best-fit model, predictor estimates were recalculated using REML. The final model revealed a progressive rate of increase for physical load ratings ($\beta = 0.162$, $p < 0.001$). Ratings given in the first trial were lower than in the second ($\beta = -1.430$, $p < 0.001$).

As can be seen in the random effects estimations (Table 5), individual perceived physical load over time had significant variance concerning the intercept ($\beta = 0.835$, $p < 0.001$) and growth rate ($\beta = 0.012$, $p < 0.001$). In addition, participants' ratings differed between trials on initial level ($\beta = -0.600$, $p = 0.002$) and slope ($\beta = 2.082$, $p < 0.001$). In addition, the significant covariance of the random effects for trial with negative sign ($\beta = -0.092$, $p < 0.001$) showed that a lower intercept in the second trial is accompanied with a lower individual increase of physical load over time.

Table 5. Effects final model physical load based on REML

	beta	Std. error	p	Lower 95%	Upper 95%
Fixed effects					
Intercept	1.399	0.117	<0.001	1.165	1.634
Time	0.162	0.014	<0.001	0.133	0.190
Trial	−1.430	0.187	<0.001	−1.805	−1.056
Random					
Residuals	0.141	0.009	<0.001	0.224	0.261
Time intercept	0.835	0.157	<0.001	0.578	1.207
Time slope	0.012	0.002	<0.001	0.008	0.178
Time inter.-slope covariance	−0.019	0.014	0.168	−0.046	0.008
Trial intercept	−0.600	0.191	0.002	−0.974	−0.225
Trial slope	2.082	0.400	<0.001	1.428	3.034
Trial inter.-slope covariance	−0.092	0.025	<0.001	−0.141	−0.043

3.3   Perceived Mental Load

In the recalculated best-fit model (REML) subjective mental load increased statistically significantly as a function of time ($\beta = 0.065$, $p < 0.001$) and from first to second trial ($\beta = -1.270$, $p < 0.001$). Additionally, there was a time-trial interaction ($\beta = 0.040$, $p < 0.001$) indicating a steeper increase of perceived mental load over time in the second trial compared to the first. The device used also had a significant effect on the dependent variable ($\beta = 0.995$, $p < 0.001$): ratings of smartphone users were overall higher (Table 6).

Table 6. Effects final model mental load based on REML

	beta	Std. error	p	Lower 95%	Upper 95%
Fixed effects					
Intercept	1.941	0.215	<0.001	1.513	2.368
Time	0.065	0.013	<0.001	0.039	0.091
Trial	−1.270	0.173	<0.001	−1.612	−0.927
Time x trial	0.040	0.007	<0.001	0.026	0.053
Device	0.995	0.269	<0.001	0.457	1.533
Random					
Residuals	0.221	0.009	<0.001	0.205	0.239
Time intercept	1.723	0.319	<0.001	1.199	2.476
Time slope	0.010	0.002	<0.001	0.007	0.014
Time inter.-slope covariance	−0.036	0.018	0.042	−0.071	−0.001
Trial intercept	−0.210	0.206	0.310	−0.614	0.195
Trial slope	1.347	0.268	<0.001	0.912	1.988
Trial inter.-slope covariance	−0.084	0.020	<0.001	−0.123	−0.046

Equivalent to the physical load, random effects estimations indicate inter-individual differences between participants' ratings over time initial level ($\beta = 1.723$, $p < 0.001$) and slope ($\beta = 0.010$, $p < 0.001$). Covariance of the random effects time ($\beta = -0.036$, $p = 0.042$) reach significance with higher overall intercept going along with a flatter slope over all 24 ratings. For trial, only the random effects for slope varied significantly between first and second trial ($\beta = 1.374$, $p < 0.001$).

3.4 Neck Discomfort

Using REML, the best fitting model (Table 7) produced a general intercept estimate of 1.065 ($p = 0.001$) for neck discomfort ratings on the 11-point scale. Neck discomfort increased over time ($\beta = 0.492$, $p < 0.001$). The effects of device ($\beta = 0.975$, $p = 0.009$) and gender ($\beta = 0.911$, $p = 0.014$) were statistically significant, with higher discomfort ratings given by smartphone users and females.

Table 7. Effects final model neck discomfort based on REML

	beta	Std. error	p	Lower 95%	Upper 95%
Fixed effects					
Intercept	1.065	0.313	0.001	0.438	1.691
Time	0.492	0.112	<0.001	0.268	0.716
Device	0.975	0.361	0.009	0.253	1.698
Gender	0.911	0.361	0.014	0.188	1.633
Random					
Residuals	0.732	0.129	<0.001	0.517	1.035
Time intercept	1.497	0.396	<0.001	0.891	2.516
Time slope	0.440	0.157	0.005	0.218	0.887
Time inter.-slope covariance	0.244	0.178	0.171	−0.105	0.593

Random effects estimations documented individual variance in neck discomfort over the three ratings in time with respect to intercept ($\beta = 1.497$, $p < 0.001$) and slope ($\beta = 0.440$, $p = 0.005$) without statistically significant covariance.

4   Discussion

Since differences in weight and size between the tablet-pc and the smartphone were not particularly large, missing effects of the device used on physical load ratings are not particularly surprising. Figure 1 depicts the participants' ratings of physical load as a function of time documenting on the specific smart device. The plotted ratings for physical load showed a steady increase independent of the device used. However, the absolute magnitude of the increase was small compared to the 11-point scale used for the ratings. Initially starting with a first higher rating, mental load likewise increased between the different time points and the two trials (Fig. 2) albeit with a flatter slope and not using the entire 11-point scale.

As for both mobile devices mean ratings did not reach scores above moderate, there is no reason not to use them as work equipment for documentation tasks similar to the checklist variant used here.

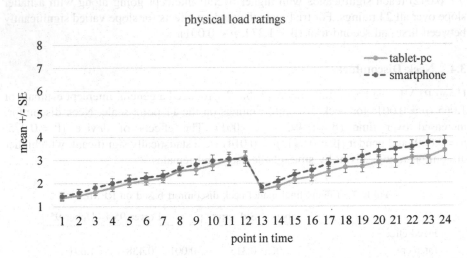

Fig. 1. A comparison of mean physical load ratings over time, and for the first (starting with rating 1) and second trial (starting with rating 13) between smartphone and tablet-pc users

The higher starting point for perceived physical load in the second run (time 1 vs. 13) is an indication that the ten-minute break was not enough for a complete physical recovery. There is no difference in slope between trials. Ratings for physical load furthermore reached no plateau in one of the two half-hour trials. Therefore, even with intermitted breaks, the task might reach higher physical load ratings in the course of a working day.

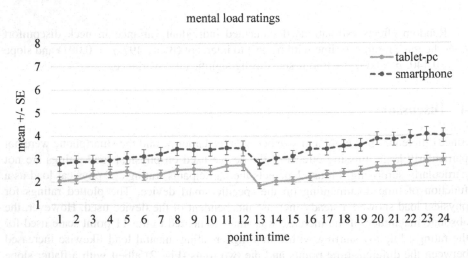

Fig. 2. A comparison of mean mental load ratings over time, and for the first trial (starting with rating 1) and second trial (starting with rating 13) between smartphone and tablet-pc users

In contrast to the physical load ratings, there was no significant difference in the initial rating between first and second trial (Fig. 2). Instead, mental load showed a steeper increase in the second trial. Here, the short break between trials seemed to be subjectively sufficient for recovery. The steeper increase in the second trial indicated a still inadequate regeneration in the longer run (Fig. 3).

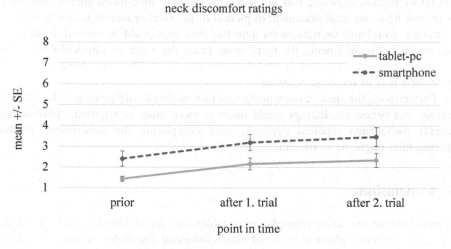

Fig. 3. Ratings of perceived neck discomfort prior to the experiment and after each trial, for both devices (smartphone and tablet-pc)

As with mental and physical load ratings, there was a small but significant increase in neck discomfort over time indicating an effect of device use. Higher ratings for neck discomfort by women as found in the data is not very surprising, as prevalence of neck pain in women is generally more pronounced [20].

In contrast, the differences in the devices in both neck discomfort and mental load ratings appeared somewhat puzzling. Especially since, apart from the higher initial value, there were no further differences in the increase in ratings over time between the two devices. A post hoc comparison of tablet-pc and smartphone group revealed no accidental systematic differences with regard to age or technophilia, which might have influenced the ratings. In addition, no effects of users' age or technophilia were observed for any of the dependent variable.

One explanation might be different expectations with regard to both devices. As mentioned before smartphone use is very common. One can therefore assume that personal experiences with this device might have influenced expectations in the corresponding group. In addition, various media have linked musculoskeletal discomfort in the neck and smartphone use in the past. Participants knew prior to completing the questionnaire regarding musculoskeletal discomfort which device they would use. Thus, expectations might have influenced the perceived neck discomfort in a kind of nocebo-effect or simple have drawn more attention to the neck region. Similarly, own experience in handling a smartphone may have led to increased expectations for effort and thus induced the higher initial value in mental load ratings. On the other hand, variables not recorded here can also be responsible for the differences between devices. A joint examination of mental load ratings and e.g. usability expectations and/or ratings of the specific devices used in subsequent experiments could provide helpful information here.

Findings should be interpreted taking into account the study's limitations. Due to the exploratory nature of the study, as well as concerns for participants' safety and health, we might have chosen trial duration too short. Although longer than in most laboratory studies, exposure was not sufficient to study time-based effects effectively, as in both trials, no local maximum or plateau of physical or mental load was reached. Therefore, no reliable indications for a healthy timespan could be derived. In addition, due to internal requirements, the participants knew the value on physical rating scale that represented the termination criteria (see Sect. 2.2). This may have resulted in systematic bias in response behavior.

Furthermore, the specific documentations task required only tapping a checklist, no texting was necessary. Ratings might differ if more input is required. Additionally, several participants reported eyestrain after completing the experiment. Further investigation might be worthwhile.

5   Conclusions

Results indicate that using smartphones or tablets-pcs for mobile documentation tasks increases subjective physical load and musculoskeletal discomfort steadily over time. However, ratings did not reach scores above average physical or mental load. Therefore, provided the task does not exceed the time span tested, smartphone or tablet use for mobile documentation tasks seems to pose no fundamental risk for employees with respect to OSH. The presented results do not allow an assessment regarding a prolonged use of touchscreen devices over the course of a working week.

This research provides only a first insight about possible work related challenges regarding prolonged use of smart mobile devices with respect to discomfort and strain. Further research integrating different tasks, a longer usage, as well as ratings for eye discomfort appears worthwhile.

Acknowledgments. The study was part of the research and development project "Prevention for safe and healthy working with digital technologies (PräDiTec)" which is funded by the German Federal Ministry of Education and Research (BMBF) within the Program "Innovations for Tomorrow's Production, Services, and Work" (funding number 02L16D034) and managed by the Project Management Agency Karlsruhe (PTKA). The authors are responsible for the contents of this publication.

References

1. Initiative D21: D21-Digital-Indes 2018/2019. Jährliches Lagebild zur Digitalen Gesellschaft. Initiative D21 e.V., Berlin (2019)
2. Eurofound and the International Labour Office: Working anytime, anywhere: The effects on the world of work, Publications Office of the European Union, Luxembourg, and the International Labour Office, Geneva (2017)

3. Messenger, J., Gschwind, L.: Three generations of telework: new ICT and the (r)evolution from home office to virtual office. New Technol. Work Employ. **31**(3), 195–208 (2016)
4. Janneck, M., Jent, S., Weber, P., Nissen, H.: Ergonomics to go: designing the mobile workspace. Int. J. Hum.-Comput. Interact. **34**(11), 1052–1062 (2018)
5. Gross, B., Bretschneider-Hagemes, M., Stefan, A., Rissler, J.: Monitors vs. smart glasses: a study on cognitive workload of digital information systems on Forklift trucks. In: Duffy, V. G. (ed.) Digital Human Modeling: Applications in Health, Safety, Ergonomics, and Risk Management, vol. 10917, pp. 569–578 (2018)
6. Otten, E.W., Karn, K.S., Parsons, K.S.: Defining thumb reach envelopes for handheld devices. Hum. Fact. **55**, 48–60 (2013)
7. Xiong, J., Muraki, S.: An ergonomics study of thumb movements on smartphone touch screen. Ergonomics **57**, 943–955 (2014)
8. Pereira, A., Miller, T., Huang, Y.-M., Odell, D., Rempel, D.: Holding a tablet computer with one hand: effect of tablet design features on biomechanics and subjective usability among users with small hands. Ergonomics **56**(9), 1363–1375 (2013)
9. Gustafsson, E., Coenen, P., Campbell, A., Straker, L.: Texting with touchscreen and keypad phones - a comparison of thumb kinematics, upper limb muscle activity, exertion, discomfort, and performance. Appl. Ergon. **70**, 232–239 (2018)
10. Kietrys, D.M., Gerg, M.J., Dropkin, J., Gold, J.E.: Mobile input device type, texting style and screen size influence upper extremity and trapezius muscle activity, and cervical posture while texting. Appl. Ergon. **50**, 98–104 (2015)
11. Ning, X., Huang, Y., Hu, B., Nimbarte, A.D.: Neck kinematics and muscle activity during mobile device operations. Int. J. Ind. Ergon. **48**, 10–15 (2015)
12. Vasavada, A.N., Nevins, D.D., Monda, S.M., Hughes, E., Lin, D.C.: Gravitational demand on the neck musculature during tablet computer use. Ergonomics **58**(6), 990–1004 (2015)
13. Young, J.G., Trudeau, M.B., Odell, D., Marinelli, K., Dennerlein, J.T.: Touch-screen tablet user configurations and case-supported tilt affect head and neck flexion angles. Work **41**(1), 81–91 (2012)
14. Stawarz, K., Benedyk, R.: Bent necks and twisted wrists: exploring the impact of touch-screen tablets on the posture of office workers. In: Proceedings of the 27th International BCS Human Computer Interaction Conference. British Computer Society, Uxbridge, pp. 41–47 (2013)
15. Namwongsa, S., Puntumetakul, R., Neubert, M.S., Chaiklieng, S., Boucaut, R.: Ergonomic risk assessment of smartphone users using the Rapid Upper Limb Assessment (RULA) tool. PLoS ONE **13**(8), 16 (2018)
16. McAtamney, L., Corlett, E.N.: RULA: a survey method for the investigation of work-related upper limb disorders. Appl. Ergon. **24**(2), 91–99 (1993)
17. Han, H., Lee, S., Shin, G.: Naturalistic data collection of head posture during smartphone use. Ergonomics **62**(3), 444–448 (2019)
18. Berolo, S., Wells, R.P., Amick III, B.C.: Musculoskeletal symptoms among mobile hand-held device users and their relationship to device use: a preliminary study in a Canadian university population. Appl. Ergon. **42**(2), 371–378 (2011)
19. Lin, M.I.B., Hong, R.H., Chang, J.H., Ke, X.M.: Usage position and virtual keyboard design affect upper-body kinematics, discomfort, and usability during prolonged tablet typing. PLoS ONE **10**(12), 21 (2015)
20. Fejer, R., Kyvik, K.O., Hartvigsen, J.: The prevalence of neck pain in the world population: a systematic critical review of the literature. Eur. Spine J. **15**(6), 834–848 (2006)

Research on the Design of Interactive Waiting Interface Based on the Elderly User Experience

Haoyu Xu[✉]

School of Design Art and Media, Nanjing University of Science and Technology,
Nanjing, People's Republic of China
516478512@qq.com

Abstract. Objective: The design of interaction interface for the elderly user experience has been studied at home and abroad, but in the design of interaction waiting interface, there is a lack of research on the vulnerable group of the elderly. The purpose of this paper is to study the relationship between the elderly user experience and the design of interactive waiting interface, and optimize the current elderly user experience in interactive waiting. Methods: to use the method of user experience and user behavior characteristics analysis to make a comprehensive analysis of the elderly's physiology and psychology, and to combine with the design principles of interactive waiting interface. Results: through the experiment, we can get the emotional effect In order to improve the user experience of the elderly users in the process of interactive waiting, it is better to reduce the time perception of the elderly users in the process of interactive waiting.

Keywords: Elderly user experience · Interactive waiting interface design · User behavior analysis · Emotionalization · Time perception

1 Introduction

At the beginning of the twenty-first Century, China has entered the aging society. At present, the aging problem of the age structure of China's social population is becoming more and more serious. According to the statistics released by the National Bureau of statistics in 2019, by 2018, the proportion of the elderly over 60 accounted for 11.9% of the total population, an increase of nearly 5.0% compared with the same period in 2000, which shows that the degree of aging in China is deepening [1]. Some experts predict that by the middle of the 21st century, China's aging population will reach one third of the total population. It can be seen that China's aging population will accelerate its development.

Due to the limitation of hardware technology, page loading, network speed and other reasons, users often have to fall into a waiting state. This kind of state takes a certain time cost for users, and it is easy to generate some negative emotions, and gradually form a bad user experience. This kind of waiting state will make users anxious or even mad because of the length of time [2]. At present, the research on interactive waiting interface is more focused on the ordinary young Internet users, but less on the elderly Internet users over 60 years old. Due to the decline of various

© Springer Nature Switzerland AG 2020
M. Kurosu (Ed.): HCII 2020, LNCS 12181, pp. 348–359, 2020.
https://doi.org/10.1007/978-3-030-49059-1_25

functions of the body and the slow down of the brain reaction speed and learning ability, the design of interactive waiting interface should consider the physiological barriers, specific psychological characteristics and skills barriers. When designing the waiting interface for the elderly, designers should pay attention to the simple and clear information transmission, fault tolerance and empathy, so that the elderly can participate in the design. The design of the interactive waiting interface blames all the negative experience of the elderly waiting on their own reasons. The designers should fully understand and respect it, and design a special interactive waiting interface for the elderly netizens, so that they can overcome the problems caused by the negative emotions caused by the special physical reasons and objective factors.

2 Research on the Basic Theory of User Experience and Interactive Waiting Interface

2.1 Design Principles of User Experience

1. Ensure the security of users and their related network information
   Different from other traditional products such as tools and transportation, the security of network products in interactive design does not mean the physical threat, but the information security and personal privacy of people. Because the user is in the process of interaction and waiting for the specific background operation information is not very clear, and at this time the background often appears the peak of system processing information, the user will doubt the security of the system. And because the users are the old group, they are far less familiar with the operation than the young group, so they will be more insecure.
2. Keep users in a comfortable operating environment
   In the interaction design based on user experience, it is a high-level design to provide users with comfort throughout the whole process principles and objectives. Whether it is the "natural harmony" in human-computer interaction, the "people-oriented" design purpose, or the "user centered" core idea in user experience design [3], its purpose is to enable technology to serve and adapt to people. Users can completely get rid of the shackles brought by traditional product design, and enjoy comfortable and pleasant interaction experience when achieving the purpose of information transmission.
3. The comprehensibility of information and the convenience of system operation
   For the elderly users, the interaction information of the system should be easy for the elderly to understand and learn, it is convenient to use and the design procedure is simplified as much as possible. The simple and convenient interactive waiting interface can effectively alleviate the waiting anxiety of the elderly users, reduce the cognitive load of waiting, and make the elderly users have a better interaction experience. This is similar to the previous David Mamet's "kiss" principle (keep it simple and stupid), i.e. the "lazy person principle" [4].
4. Optimize the efficiency of waiting interface interaction
   Users can interact with information system smoothly according to the above three principles, which cannot be proved the interaction efficiency of the whole

information system is the highest, which only shows that the "user centered" system process design is good. Only when the whole information system is highly coordinated in software, hardware, technology, information architecture and system logic, can the efficiency of the whole interaction experience be optimized.

5. Hierarchy of principles

Safety, comfort and convenience are the premise of the whole human-computer interaction system to achieve the goal of high efficiency, and ensuring safety is the premise of the elements used. On the basis of ensuring the security, the most important thing is that the system can achieve convenience, and the second is to achieve user comfort through the design of user experience (Fig. 1).

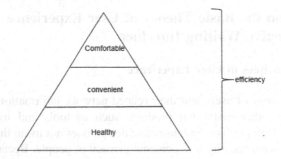

Fig. 1. Principles and relations of user experience of interactive waiting interface

2.2   User Experience at the User Level of the Elderly

The three levels of product design mentioned by Donald Norman in his early emotional design are instinct level, behavior level and reflection level. These three levels are intertwined and have an impact on product design.

Based on Norman's theory, the design of the elderly user interface should mainly include the analysis and research of the elderly user's operation behavior, such as the color of the interface, the layout of the page, etc.; the friendliness of the system interface, such as whether the interaction of the interface can reach the most effective cooperation form of the input and output of the elderly user information; the research and design of the elderly user's emotion Teachers need to stand in the perspective of the elderly users to design and think about whether to meet the needs of the elderly at different levels.

2.3   Concept of Interactive Waiting Interface

In daily life, when people use PC or mobile app, "waiting" is a common interaction state, which often appears in the process of using. Generally, the reason for the interaction waiting may be caused by hardware, or the system needs to deal with a large amount of information in a short time, resulting in a short-term stagnation state; another is that the design of the interaction interface has certain defects, resulting in the user's waiting state.

In general, the user enters interactive instructions on the interface, which are sent to the server after receiving the instructions in the front section, and the server returns to the interface after receiving the instructions to pass the information to the user [5]. However, the user can not perceive the whole background interaction process, and the waiting time is different in different network environment. This unknown waiting will greatly affect the user's use experience.

2.4 Characteristics and Classification of Interactive Waiting Interface

In the design of loading interface, we should consider the different user environment, input task, system operation function and logical architecture comprehensively, and choose the best loading interface category to provide good user experience for different users. Different waiting interface design types will also bring different user experience (Fig. 2).

1. Full screen interactive waiting interface
   This loading interface is to occupy all the user's operation interfaces during the waiting period. This often occurs in the initial stage of system loading, the replacement of a large amount of information, and the replacement of representative scenarios. The advantage of this type of interface design is that it can give users a clear prompt of loading waiting, so that users can know in time that they are in the state of interaction waiting. Usually, in the full screen loading interface, the user can't perform other operations except to choose to cancel loading. Classic cases include the loading of wechat initial interface, the search waiting status of idle fish, etc.

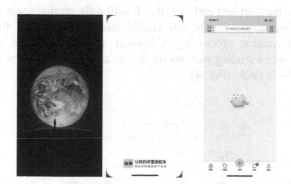

Fig. 2. Wechat and free fish loading interface

2. Occupation loading interface
   This loading interface usually takes up most of the system's resources in the process of user interaction and waiting, so that the system can only process the current data and cannot perform other operations. This kind of waiting interface design is suitable for the installation of large-scale software and programs, the update of application programs, etc. Such as the scenario when the IOS system of apple is updated (Fig. 3).

Fig. 3. IOS system update

3. Background waiting loading interface

This form of waiting interface generally hides the data information processed in the background, which means that the system loading process will not be used to the user's screen and system for a long time. Because the user is waiting for the load while taking the form of operating in the background of the system, so the user will not have long-term waiting problems and can get a smooth interactive operation process. This multi task loading mode will not cause trouble to users in the process of waiting for the start and end of tasks. It will only remind users after the system finishes loading tasks, which will enable users to focus on the operation of important information processing. Common software includes the background display status when sending pictures on Weibo and the scene when sending pictures in wechat friends circle (Fig. 4).

Fig. 4. Background loading mode when uploading pictures on Weibo

4. Modeless loading interface

In the traditional mode loading, the information content of the whole interface is presented to the user after the image and text are all loaded in the process of loading the interface. This loading mode is slow in efficiency, requires high hardware configuration and network speed, and is not friendly to the elderly users. The non modal loading form is to load the text and picture information of the loading interface separately. It will first present the main picture and text content to the user, so that the loading process can be ended without interfering with the user's operation. The advantage of this loading form is to quickly improve the reading and operation efficiency of users and understand the information content of the page. However, there is a risk that users will lose the key information of the page, which leads to the failure of users to completely establish the closed-loop role of information acquisition. This kind of application software is generally suitable for content reading. In the design of the activity page, attention should be paid not to put important information on the pictures, because it is easy for users to ignore the information and may not be able to load the pictures so that users miss important information. The design cases of non modal interactive waiting interface include the loading interface of qunar app and the loading of Taobao webpage (Fig. 5).

Fig. 5. Where to load web pages in non modal mode

3   Study on the Influencing Factors of the Design of User Interaction Waiting Interface for the Elderly

3.1   Influencing Factors of Elderly Users

In the design of interactive waiting interface, for the elderly, the elderly factor is one of the most important links in the whole design process. In the process of in-depth research of the elderly users, it is conducive to improve the understanding of the real interaction needs of the elderly, so as to ensure that the whole interaction waiting interface is designed to meet the interaction principle of the elderly user experience.

The old age is the end of a person's life. With the increase of people's age, all functions of human body begin to enter into the degradation stage, such as the decline of body function, the decline of immunity, the decline of organ function and so on. However, this process must be experienced by everyone in his life. For the special physical and psychological conditions of the elderly, designers should fully understand and respect them. In the process, from the perspective of the elderly group, they should solve the problems and deficiencies in the interactive waiting interface design. In the process of interaction between the elderly and the interface, physiological factors play a significant role. To explore the physiological factors of the elderly group is one of the preconditions for the design of user experience waiting interface for the elderly.

(1) Sensory elements

People's senses are mainly divided into vision, hearing, smell, touch and taste, usually called "five senses". 80% of people's perception of external things is obtained through vision, which is an important sense channel for the connection between the outside world and people [6]. Visual perception is the most used way to interact with users in the interface, and it is also the same in the interaction waiting interface design. Due to the increase of age, the visual ability of the elderly users will gradually decline, and the contrast perception ability of the interface will decline. In order to enable them to identify the target timely and accurately, create tasks, and wait for the design of the interface, they need to achieve a stronger picture face ratio than the young people. The elderly will also suffer from "presbyopia" which will lead to a decrease in their ability to adjust the close visual focus [7]. At the same time, the old people's ability to adjust the light generated by the environment will also be reduced, which will directly lead to their ability to recognize color far less than the young people.

In the process of loading the interface, the elderly users can also be fed back through sound effects. Although the use of auditory system is not as frequent as visual perception, it is also a key interaction mode in the design of interactive waiting interface. Especially when the elderly are in some special environment, such as strong sunlight, the vision of the elderly will be disturbed by strong light, and only through the auditory transmission to know the information. In the design of auditory feedback, we should consider that some old people have hearing impairment, generally they are not particularly sensitive to the high frequency band. Hearing impairment of the elderly will not only interfere with their access to interface information, but also affect their language and understanding, further affect their social interaction, which will lead to a strong sense of loneliness and inferiority.

With the development of science and technology, the sense of touch on the interface has gradually changed from unfamiliar to familiar. This is mainly reflected in the application platform of smart phones, and the common way is to use the screen vibration to let users sense the feedback of the interface. Tactile approach will let users get a better user experience, which will let their attention fully into the interaction. Compared with the young people, the old people's central nervous system response ability is also more sluggish, which will make their requirements for interface tactile perception more obvious. In the sense of smell, interface interaction is seldom used at present.

(2) Analysis of psychological characteristics

After retirement, most of the elderly often have a series of psychological problems because they often live alone or with their partners and lack of social contact. The first is the social and family roles suddenly change and bring about the unaccustomed. In the past, they used to be the useful labor force in the unit and the pillar in the family. With the growth of age, their self-worth is increasingly not reflected, which will cause a psychological gap for the elderly. Especially for the empty nest old people who live alone and their children are not around, their psychological problems are especially serious. Many old people will have depression and loneliness. Their spiritual world is not fully released. These special psychological characteristics will also be reflected in the special needs of the elderly in the use of electronic products. Designers should also consider the special psychological needs of the elderly when studying the elderly user experience, so as to give them a better interactive experience.

3.2   Influence of Behavior Factors

The physical flexibility of the elderly will be inversely proportional to their age, and many elderly people will reflect that their physical flexibility is far less than that of their youth. Mainly reflected in their muscles began to relax, the control of the body decreased, the movement became clumsy and so on. These are caused by the atrophy of tissue cells and cerebellum, which will directly lead to the decline of the old people's ability to respond to operation and the decline of movement coordination.

In the design of some important waiting interface information, we should take into account some misoperations that may occur in the elderly due to the aging of hand joints and the decline of response ability, and try to avoid the consequences of these misoperations.

3.3   Influence of Scene Factors

Scene factors include the external environment when the elderly interact with the interface, such as lighting environment, communication environment and other relevant environment. These changes in the environment will affect the interaction experience of the elderly. Compared with the rabbit, it will move from the indoor with relatively weak light to the outdoor. The stimulation of strong light will make the vision of the elderly inadaptable. The designer should consider the interference brought by this change to the elderly, and use appropriate design to improve this inadaptability and improve the user experience.

For the elderly as a special group, the change of scene is a challenge to them. The cognitive ability of the elderly is closely related to the environment. When the scene used by the elderly changes, they will be unable to adapt in a short time. Therefore, we should be flexible in the design of the interactive waiting interface for the elderly, close to the familiar way of operation, and reduce the cognitive burden of the elderly as much as possible.

4 Design Strategy of Interactive Waiting Interface Based on Elderly User Experience

4.1 Transfer of Interface Information

Through the basic text information and picture information to the elderly users to transmit the current system loading situation, which will help the elderly know the specific time they need to wait in advance, reduce the anxiety caused by the unknown. Generally, it can be solved from the text, color and layout of the waiting interface.

(1) Interface text

In terms of font design, the recognition of the old people for the song and Kai typefaces is lower than that for the fine and bold typefaces. Under the same stroke, the recognition degree of Ming style is greater than that of Kai style and bold style [8]. The more strokes the characters have, the greater the probability of recognition errors the elderly will have, and the hollow font and round font are not suitable for the elderly. The font size is best controlled between 14pt and 16pt, and the light has a great impact on the recognition ability of the elderly. The more light is, the higher the recognition ability of the elderly [9].

(2) Color of interface

Compared with the young people, the old people's color perception is much weaker and their discrimination ability is also poor. Some experiments have found that the color matching with the highest visual recognition of the elderly is yellow blue, followed by blue purple and purple red. In addition, in terms of text readability, the best one is white characters on blue background. In the interface color matching, the old people are different from the young people. The young people pursue the simple and clean interface, prefer the color with low color saturation, and the interface design with weak contrast is more thin and popular with the young people. The elderly prefer the color matching with high brightness and purity, and the interface effect with strong contrast.

(3) Layout of interface

Some studies have found that in terms of text, text with wireframe will attract more attention of the elderly and improve their visual search efficiency. In terms of pictures, the old people like static pictures or dynamic design with slow switching [10], which is also different from the young people. The young people prefer the effect with rich dynamic effects and cool pictures, because it will attract their attention. When waiting for the interface design, avoid the strong flashing picture effect. In typesetting, horizontal arrangement is more convenient to read than vertical arrangement. The layout adopts the network format, with concise and clear information transmission as the design criteria.

4.2 Emotional Design

The loading of the page should be designed in an emotional way so that the elderly will not have negative emotions in the process of waiting. We can adopt vivid and interesting loading elements to attract the attention of elderly users, so as to improve the elderly user experience. In emotional design, we should also fully combine the special psychological characteristics of the elderly, their sense of belonging to the society and family, and the design of the interface should embody humanistic care everywhere. In the process of interface loading, the elderly should not have the psychology of giving up the follow-up operation. On the basis of understanding, respecting and caring for the elderly, the waiting interface is designed.

4.3   Hide Loading Process

The elderly users' judgment on the waiting time of mobile product interaction is from the beginning of waiting interface to the end of content loading. Enhance the way of switching between each interface to weaken or hide the loading time of the interface, and let the elderly users feel the whole interaction process is smooth and smooth through the loading process of the hidden interface. This can optimize the user experience of the elderly in the waiting state of the interface loading.

However, it should be noted that the elderly users are different from the young users. The animation effect of jump should not be too intense. The whole process should be relaxed to meet the physiological characteristics of the elderly and the expectations of the elderly in the interactive waiting.

4.4   Multi Channel Feedback Form

According to the special physiological characteristics of elderly users, multi-channel interaction should be considered when waiting for the interface design. It is convenient to transfer the information of the system by using multiple ways of interactive and cooperative operation. This way is conducive to help the elderly users of different groups of obstacles to get a good interactive experience. And the multi-channel interaction will also increase the pleasure of the elderly and enhance the user experience. For example, when the microblog client pulls down and refreshes, in addition to the reminder of loading icon, it will be accompanied by rhythmic sound effect to show the loading status of the current user. These methods can deliver clear loading information to the elderly users through a variety of different information channels. Multi channel feedback can effectively optimize the interaction experience of the elderly.

5   Experimental Design of the Effect of Interactive Waiting Interface Loading Mode on the Waiting Experience of Elderly Users

5.1   Experiment Purpose and Process

At present, the research on the design of mobile interactive waiting interface for the elderly user experience is in a blank state, and there is no actual experimental conclusion and in-depth research. This experiment mainly uses the knowledge of cognitive psychology of the elderly to study the elderly's perception of waiting time for mobile applications and the changes of their psychological state. The experimental procedure consists of four parts: the selection of experimental samples, the determination of experimental personnel, the task of experiment and the statistical analysis of experimental results.

5.2   Selection of Experimental Samples

The experimental equipment will choose the same mobile phone as the brand hardware and software configuration, which is to ensure the accuracy of the experimental results. The test samples all use the method of color removal to avoid unnecessary interference of the interface color to the participants. Also, the time status bar should be hidden to avoid the interference of time information to participants. Set the actual waiting time of the samples set in the experiment to 5.0 s, which is based on the report on user behavior of mobile application published by Baidu in 2018. When the waiting time of mobile interface interaction exceeds 5.0 s, 70% of users choose to exit the interface. In this experiment, Taobao, an e-commerce product frequently used by the elderly, will be used as the experimental sample. Sample 1 is a blank loading page, sample 2 is a conceptual interface loading model, and the rotating icon is selected as the loading prompt element. Sample 3 is an emotional loading mode, and the loaded prompt element is a family portrait that can make the elderly have emotional resonance. Sample 5 is a dynamic element that is used to constantly switch.

5.3   Determination of Laboratory Personnel

According to the data of China Internet Statistics Center, the sex ratio of domestic Internet users is 55.6:44.4, and the number between 50 and 70 years old accounts for 11.7% of the total number of Chinese Internet users. In this experiment, 30 elderly volunteers will be recruited in the form of social recruitment, 16 males and 14 females. Participants were controlled between 50 and 70 years old. The professional background of the participants covers many industries, and they have some experience in online e-commerce platform shopping.

5.4   Experiment Task and Process Design

Task 1: let the subjects click the logo of Taobao Search page, and when the interface is loaded to the next level, they can carry out the next operation. When the participants completed the test of samples 2–4, they were graded according to their time perception during the waiting process. 5.0 points were given to the samples with the shortest self perception time, and 1.0 points (one decimal place) to the samples with the longest self perception time.

Before the beginning of the experiment, the experimenter will take the rating scale to inform the subjects of the scoring principle and the purpose of the experiment. Before the experiment, all subjects will be familiar with the process of sample 1 and carefully feel the waiting time of interaction. During the experiment, all the experimental samples will be randomly provided to the subjects for experiment, which is to avoid the influence of the test sequence of the samples on the subjects.

Task 2: according to the results of task 1, two experimental samples with the shortest perceptual time of elderly users were counted and tested by the same group of testers. At the end of the two samples, the subjects were asked to score and record the scores. Similarly, in order to avoid the interference of sample sequence factors, two samples were randomly provided to the subjects.

6 Summary

With the rapid development of the Internet industry and the gradual popularization of 5g technology, more and more elderly people begin to enter the network use army, and the elderly pay more and more attention to user experience and demand satisfaction. The common interface design for the elderly user experience has been designed at home and abroad, but the interaction waiting interface design is lack of attention to vulnerable groups. Therefore, it is urgent to pay attention to the design of the interactive waiting interface for the elderly. The design of the loading interface for the elderly user experience proposed in this paper is based on the special psychological and physiological characteristics of the elderly. By using the methods of user research and behavior analysis, it is verified that the behavior characteristics and psychological characteristics of the elderly will affect their users' Internet access For. And design experiments, using four different forms of page loading on the elderly users' time perception.

References

1. Stable growth of population, significant improvement of population quality [EB/OL]. Http://www.gov.cn/xinwen/2019-08/22/content_.htm. Accessed 22 Sept 2019
2. Hu, M.: User Experience Research and Design Strategy of Human-Computer Interaction Waiting State – Research on Interactive Waiting Design based on Cognitive Psychology. School of Design and Art, Beijing University of Technology, Beijing (2015)
3. Meng, X., Li, X.: Human Computer Interaction Technology – Principle and Application. Tsinghua University Press, Beijing (2004)
4. Baidu Encyclopedia. Lazy principle entry. Https://baike.baidu.com/item/lazyprinciple
5. Fu, Y.: Research on Interactive Waiting Experience Design of Mobile Products Based on Time Perception. School of Design and Art, Hunan University, Changsha (2017)
6. Peng, J.: Research on the Interaction Design of the App Interface of the Elderly Smart Phone Based on User Experience. School of Art Design and Media, East China University of Science and Technology, Shanghai (2013)
7. Wang, A., Guo, J., Zhang, Q.: Research on the packaging design of intelligent pharmaceutical products for the visual characteristics of the elderly. Packag. Eng. 39(2), 55–59 (2018)
8. Chen, M.: The Effect of LCD Text and Background Color Combination on Visual Recognition of the Elderly. Institute of Industrial Design, Yunlin University of Science and Technology, Taiwan (2002)
9. Cai, B.: Visual Search Performance of the Elderly in Direct Layout Design. Master of Design Institute, University of Science and Technology, Taiwan (2002)

Usability, User Experience and Quality

Evaluating the Usability and the Accessibility of Saudi E-Government Websites

Nourah Aloboud[1](✉), Raghad Alotaibi[2], and Amani Alqahtani[1]

[1] King Abdulaziz City for Science and Technology, Riyadh, Saudi Arabia
{naloboud, asjalqahtani}@kacst.edu.sa
[2] College of Computer and Information Sciences,
King Saud University, Riyadh, Saudi Arabia
436201236@student.ksu.edu.sa

Abstract. E-government services provide citizens with an efficient way to manage their information. Achieving usability and accessibility within e-government websites is vital due to its role in facilitating online transactions for citizens. This paper provides an empirical study to investigate the usability and the accessibility of a representative Saudi e-government website. The usability of each of the tested Saudi e-government websites was evaluated based on Nilsson's 10 heuristics. The accessibility was examined based on Web Content Accessibility Guidelines (WCAG 2.0) principles and used two automated tools. The results of the usability test shows few usability issues. However, our study shows that the minimum level of WCAG 2.0 accessibility conformance level was not met by the tested Saudi e-government sites. Finally, a list of some practical recommendations regarding accessibility and usability evaluations that could be generalized to other e-governments websites is provided.

Keywords: Web accessibility · WCAG 2.0 · Accessibility · Usability · E-government · Saudi Arabia

1 Introduction

Offering government services via the World Wide Web has grown due to its role in reducing costs and facilitating the delivery of services to the public sector. The services provided by e-government can be categorized into three types [1]: government-to-citizens (G2C), government-to-business (G2B), and government-to-government (G2G). G2C is an example of communication between a government (the service provider) and its citizens. Examples of e-government services include submitting job applications or renewing citizen's identification cards, driver's licenses, or passports. The Saudi Arabian government has recognized the importance of e-government. Thus, the Ministry of Communication and Information Technology in Saudi Arabia established a program known as "YESSER" that aims to specify the standards and regulations of e-government services [2]. The YESSER program has succeeded in making significant steps to improve e-government, such as creating standards and documents that assist in supporting it. At present, Saudi Arabia provides a number of e-

© Springer Nature Switzerland AG 2020
M. Kurosu (Ed.): HCII 2020, LNCS 12181, pp. 363–372, 2020.
https://doi.org/10.1007/978-3-030-49059-1_26

government websites, such as Abshir, and some have achieved a Digital Excellence Award (DEA) for their design [3].

E-government is used by a wide range of users with different backgrounds, including people with disabilities, the elderly, educated, uneducated, and foreigner users. These users might confront several obstacles when using these services. Thus, ensuring the usability (ease of use) and the accessibility (access to all) of services is crucial to facilitate online transactions for citizens. The objective of this study is to provide a useful evaluation for future development by assessing the usability and the accessibility of a representative number of Saudi e-government websites. These improvements could help citizens complete their tasks and effectively use e-government services. Five e-government sub-websites offered by the Ministry of Labor and Social Development where evaluated. The ministry has a Saudi e-government website that aims to provide support to the community by working with citizens and authorities to empower the general public. The evaluated sites are Musaned, Taqat, Labor Education, Citizen Account, and Your Voice Heard. These sites provide business-to-consumer services. The usability evaluations were assessed in both versions, Arabic and English, except for the Citizen Account website, which does not provide an English version. The accessibility evaluation was conducted on only the Arabic version.

The two assessments conducted were the accessibility and usability evaluations. First, for the accessibility evaluation, we used a combination of automated and manual methods. In the manual evaluation, three evaluators examined the selected services based on the principles of the Web Content Accessibility Guidelines (WCAG 2.0) [4]. The objective was to determine the compliance of the tested subjects with WCAG 2.0 principles and conformance levels (level A, AA, and AAA). Two automated tools were selected, the AChecker tool and the Total Validator. Both tools are publicly available and have the capability to assess WCAG 2.0 conformance levels. Second, for the usability evaluation, three expert reviewers evaluated the services based on Nilsson's 10 heuristics [5].

This study aims to provide two main contributions. First, an empirical study was conducted to test the usability of e-government websites in Saudi Arabia. Second, an empirical study was undertaken to measure the accessibility of e-government websites in Saudi Arabia. The intention is to provide some recommendations for future developments. In Sect. 2, we begin by discussing some of the studies that have been conducted on e-government services. Section 3 includes a description of our methodology, and the selected test subjects are introduced. In Sect. 4, we present the study results and discussion by answering two questions on (RQ1) the usability of the e-services and (RQ2) the accessibility of the e-services. Section 5 includes a list of some recommendations regarding accessibility and usability evaluations that could be generalized to other e-governments websites and discusses the limitations of our study. Finally, we provide conclusions and suggestions for future works in Sect. 6.

2   Literature Review

A number of empirical studies have been conducted to measure the usability and the accessibility of e-government services. This is to help governments improve the efficiency of their services and to encourage their citizens to use online government services.

Khan and Buragga [7] evaluated the usability and accessibility of two e-government websites in Saudi Arabia, Saudi Railways and Saudi Post. The usability test was evaluated using a heuristic evaluation. In regard to the accessibility evaluation, the websites were first evaluated using W3C WCAGs and then their results were compared utilizing web accessibility tools. The study shows that the examined websites were not compatible with code standards. Moreover, recommendations were proposed to enhance the examined websites. Eidaroos, Probets, and Dearnley [3] examined two Saudi e-government websites by using customized heuristic principles. The usability checklist involved nine principles: consistency, links and navigation tools, help for users, features and functions, data entry forms, visual design, accessibility to visually impaired users, security and privacy, and the precision of information. The results identified several usability issues in the examined e-government websites.

Al-Faries et al. [1] conducted an empirical study to evaluate the accessibility and the usability of a sample of Saudi e-government services. The usability evaluation was accomplished using an expert review, while the WCAG 2.0 guidelines were used to evaluate the accessibility of the websites. The usability outcomes show that the websites under test were well designed except that some of the violations of the guidelines made the websites less user friendly. However, none of the evaluated services completely fulfilled the WCAG 2.0 accessibility guidelines. The most discovered accessibility issues included using text alternatives for non-text elements (level A), accessibility of the keyboard (level A), and compatibility (level AAA). Al-Khalifa [8] used a heuristic evaluation to evaluate the usability of the homepage of 14 Saudi government websites. The heuristic checklist is based on the ISO 9241-151 and the Travis checklist. They also considered the general design heuristics provided by Yesser. The evaluation results identified many usability problems and highlighted areas for improvements.

Al-Khalifa [9] evaluated the accessibility of 36 Saudi government homepage Arabic version websites. The accessibility test was evaluated using WCAG 2.0, which was provided by the W3C. WCAG 2.0 consists of four general principles: perceivable, operable, understandable, and robust. The study shows that the examined websites did not pass the minimum WCAG 2.0 accessibility guidelines. Al-Khalifa et al. [6] re-evaluated the same websites that had been visited previously in a study carried out in 2010 that showed a serious problem in that the sites had not reached the minimum requirement of WCAG 2.0 guidelines, implying a lack of equality between disabled and nondisabled people in benefiting from online governmental services. The authors sought to track how Saudi e-government accessibility had evolved after a lapse of 5 years. The results showed an improvement in the accessibility of Saudi government websites since 2010, yet future recommendations were highlighted to further improve their accessibility.

However, some of the above studies only tested the main page, which is not representative of an entire web page. Some studies have focused on testing the services in terms of only the usability, while some others have focused on finding only the accessibility issues in these web pages. Our aim is to test both the usability and accessibility of the entire website of the Ministry of Labor and Social Development of Saudi Arabia.

3   Methodology

The objective of this study is to provide a useful evaluation for future development by assessing the usability and the accessibility of top Saudi e-government websites. These improvements could help citizens in completing their goals while effectively and efficiently using e-government services in a satisfying way.

3.1   The Subject Under Test

Five e-government sub-websites offered from the Ministry of Labor and Social Development were evaluated. The ministry is a Saudi e-government website that aims to provide support to the community by working with citizens and authorities to empower the general public. The following sub-websites were evaluated between June 15, 2019, and July 29, 2019: Musaned, Taqat, Labor Education, Citizen Account, and Your Voice Heard. The sites provide business-to-consumer services. The usability was evaluated in both versions: Arabic and English, with the exception of the Citizen Account website, which does not provide an English version. The accessibility evaluation was conducted on the Arabic version.

3.2   Evaluation Process

Two assessments were conducted: one on accessibility and the other on usability. First, for the accessibility examination, we used a combination of automated and manual methods. For the automated evaluation, three evaluators examined the selected services based on WCAG 2.0 principles [4]. The objective was to determine the compliance of the tested subjects with WCAG 2.0 level A, AA, and AAA principles. For the automated assessment, two tools were selected, the AChecker tool and the Total Validator. They were chosen because they are publically available. Moreover, they are capability of assessing WCAG 2.0 (A, AA, and AAA) conformance levels.

Second, in terms of the usability evaluation, three expert reviewers evaluated the services. The usability was evaluated using Nilsson's 10 heuristics [5]. The expert reviewer went through the e-government services several times, examining the page dialogs and elements by cross referencing them with the usability heuristics [5]. Finally, any heuristic violations, including their severity, were recorded.

4 Results and Discussions

4.1 Accessibility Evaluation

The result of the accessibility evaluation revealed that the examined Saudi government websites had a total of 441 violations. Moreover, the outcome of the evaluations showed that none of the examined websites met the lowest accessibility conformance level. According to the conformance levels, level A had the highest number of violations at 68% (see Fig. 1). The results of the assessment point to an unsatisfactory level of accessibility for the evaluated e-government websites. The following subsections present descriptions of the average violation outcomes per criteria for each principle.

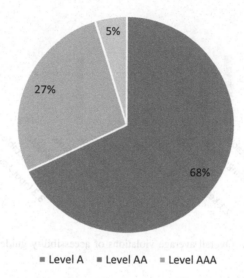

Fig. 1. Percentage distribution according to conformance level

Principle 1: Perceivable. The most commonly violated criterion for the perceivable principle was guideline 1.4, which reached 84 violations (see Fig. 1). This guideline emphasizes making it easier for users with visual and hearing disabilities to separate the foreground information from the background. The most commonly violated success criterion (SC) in this guideline was criterion 1.4.4 at level AA, which supports individual with low vision by making them able to control the content text size. This violation results in a medium impact on the design.

Moreover, guideline 1.3 had the second highest number of violated guidelines (80). The basis for this guideline was to encourage the creation of adaptable site content that can be browsed in several ways by all users without affecting the structure or the information. The only failed SC in this guideline was 1.3.1 (info and relationships) on level A. The last most frequently failed guideline was guideline 1.1, which had approximately 47 violations. The intent of the guideline was to promote text alternatives for any non-text content.

Principle 2: Operable. The purpose of the operable accessibility principle was to ensure the operability of the components and the navigation of user interfaces (see Fig. 2). In this study, guideline 2.4, which concerns the ability of a user to easily navigate the websites, had the highest number of failures SC (77). The most violated SC in this guideline was 2.4.4 (link purpose) on level A and 2.4.6 (headings and labels) on level AA.

Finally, all the tested websites violated guideline 2.1 (keyboard accessible). This is because the websites' functions could not be fully accessible from the keyboard.

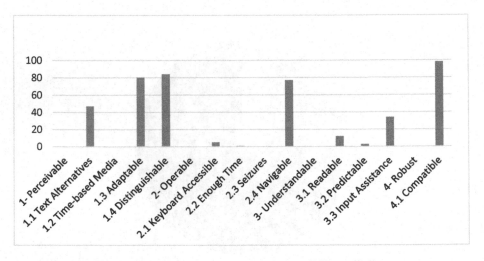

Fig. 2. Overall average violations of accessibility guidelines

Principle 3: Understandable. The understandable principle aimed to ensure that the users are able to understand the information and the operations in the user interface (see Fig. 2). Guideline 3.3 is the most common violated guideline in this principle, with approximately 34 violations. This guideline intended to help users evade and modify mistakes. The failed SC in this guideline was 3.3.2 (labels or instructions), which belongs to the lowest conformance, level A.

Guideline 3.1 is about making text content readable and understandable. Evaluating the tested websites for this guideline showed the fulfillment of several SCs, for example, unusual words (SC 3.1.3), pronunciation (SC 3.1.6), and reading level (SC 3.1.5). The only failed SC in this guideline was 3.1.1 (language of page) on level (A), which had approximately 12 violations.

Finally, the last violated guideline was guideline 3.2, which had approximately three violations. Guideline 3.2 is about ensuring the web pages' work in a predictable way. Two SCs failed in this guideline, which were 3.2.3 (consistent navigation) and 3.2.4 (consistent identification) both identified to be on level AA compliance.

Principle 4: Robust. The robust accessibility principle states that content should be accessible to all users via different types of technologies that meet the users' accessibility needs (see Fig. 2). The robust principle consists of the compatibility guideline (4.1), which works toward the support of compatibility with present and upcoming user agents. The websites that were examined contained a total of 98 compatibility guideline violations, which was the highest number of violations across all the websites. The two failed SCs in this guideline were 4.1.1 parsing (level A) and 4.1.2 name, role, value (level A). For example, in regards to parsing SC, start and end tags were not applied as specified in the specifications. In terms of name, role, value SC, several elements in the evaluated web pages did not have a "name," "value," or "role" allocated to them, which disabled the compatibility with assistive technology.

4.2   Usability Evaluation

This section provides the results of the usability evaluation based on Nilsson's 10 heuristics, and the overall findings are illustrated in Table 1 for the Arabic version and Table 2 for the English version. The outcomes show an excellent effort on these websites. This was the case for the "match between system and the real world" heuristic, for example, as the use of familiar icons, the logistic order of the menu choices, and avoidance of computer jargon words were appropriate. Moreover, one of the strengths was the effective design of the help system on the websites in that the user could easily access the help system and return to work. Other common strengths were the use of a consistent and simple color throughout the system and the use of brief and clear error messages.

Table 1. Number of violations and their types for each website: Arabic version

Name	Number of guideline violations
Musaned	Consistency and standards (3), error prevention (1), and visibility of system status (2)
Labor education	Visibility of system status (2), error prevention (1), and aesthetic and minimalist design (1)
Taqat	Consistency and standards (3), error prevention (1), visibility of system status (2), user control and freedom (1), and aesthetic and minimalist design (1)
Your voice heard	Error prevention (1)
Citizen account	Consistency and standards (2), help users recognize, diagnose and recover from errors (1), aesthetic and minimalist design (4), and error prevention (1)

The most major and repetitive usability issues were found to lie within the borders of consistency and standards, visibility of system status, and help users recognize, diagnose, and recover from errors for both the Arabic and English versions. For instance, in terms of consistency and standards, the navigation bar was inconsistent across all pages of the website. Inconsistencies were also noted in the menu design of the system. For the visibility of system status, the system did not highlight the current selected option. Moreover, no visual feedback was provided about the currently selected choices on the menu. In regards to error prevention, one of the repetitive violations across all the websites was that the data entry screens did not indicate the number of character spaces available in a field. Moreover, one major weakness was found in the Tagat website in that the user was unable to cancel an in-progress operation. Although a small number of usability issues were observed, they could hinder the users from utilizing these websites.

Table 2. Number of violations and their types for each website: English version

Name	Number of guideline violations
Musaned	Consistency and standards (3), visibility of system status (1), and Error prevention (1)
Labor education	Visibility of system status (2), error prevention (1), and aesthetic and minimalist design (1)
Taqat	Visibility of system status (2), user control and freedom (1), consistency and standards (3), error prevention (1), and aesthetic and minimalist design (2)
Your voice heard	Error prevention (1)

5 Practical Recommendations and Limitations

5.1 Practical Recommendations

Based on our study outcomes, the Saudi e-government should apply the following recommendations to address the accessibility and usability issues:

- The Saudi e-government should determine the best design for accessibility and usability standards that conform to international guidelines.
- The e-government should make it mandatory for web developers and administrators to apply these guidelines and standards.
- The Saudi e-government should provide web developers and administrators the needed training in regard to the accessibility and usability standards, which includes training on the tools, resources, and methods.
- The e-government should conduct continuous evaluations of their portals to discern any limitations.
- Awareness about the importance of applying accessibility and usability should be raised among developers and the administration.

5.2 Practical Limitations

This study has some limitations. First, manually evaluating the usability and accessibility of e-government websites is prone to errors. In addition to the manual accessibility evaluation, we evaluated the sites using automated tools. However, not all the accessibility barriers could be automatically detected. It is recommended that further evaluations be undertaken with end users to help show any difficulties faced by real users. Another limitation is the restriction of our accessibility evaluation on one of the Arabic versions of the tested websites that does not have an English version.

6 Conclusion

The accessibility and the usability of five Saudi E-governments websites were examined in this study. First, the accessibility study was accomplished by a combination of manual and automated methods. In the manual evaluation, three evaluators examined the selected services based on the WCAG 2.0 principles. In regard to the automated evaluation, the websites were evaluated using two tools, the AChecker tool and the Total Validator. Second, the usability evaluation was conducted using Nilsson's 10 heuristics.

The results of the usability evaluation show few usability issues. Thus, minor efforts are recommended to improve the usability of the tested websites. However, the outcomes of the accessibility evaluation point to an unsatisfactory level of accessibility for the evaluated e-government websites. By examining the WCAG 2.0 general principles (perceivable, operable, understandable, and robust), we found that none of these principles were attained in level A. The main violations were compatibility (level A), distinguishability (level AA, AAA), adaptability (level A), and navigability (level AA, AA, AAA). Finally, the study provides some recommendations for enhancing e-government websites in general to be more useful for all citizens and residents.

References

1. Al-Faries, A., Al-Khalifa, H.S., Al-Razgan, M.S., Al-Duwais, M.: Evaluating the accessibility and usability of top Saudi e-government services. In: Janowski, T., Holm, J., Estevez, E. (eds.) Proceedings of the 7th International Conference on Theory and Practice of Electronic Governance (ICEGOV 2013), pp. 60–63. ACM, New York (2013)
2. Yesser: Guidelines for government websites. http://www.yesser.gov.sa/english/documents/Guidelines_for_Government_Websites_en.pdf. Accessed 12 July 2019
3. Eidaroos, A., Probets, S., Dearnley, J.: Heuristic evaluation for e-government websites in Saudi Arabia. In: Proceedings of the Third Saudi International Conference, 5–6 June, pp. 5–6 (2009)
4. W3.org Homepage. Understanding WCAG20. http://www.w3.org/TR/UNDERSTANDING WCAG20/conformance.html. Accessed 12 July 2019
5. Nielsen, J.: Heuristic evaluation. In: Nielsen, J., Mack, R.L. (eds.) Usability Inspection Methods, pp. 25–62. Wiley, New York (1994)
6. Al-Khalifa, H.S., Baazeem, I., Alamer, R.: Revisiting the accessibility of Saudi Arabia government websites. Univ. Access Inf. Soc. 16, 1027–1039 (2017). https://doi.org/10.1007/s10209-016-0495-7
7. Khan, M.A., Buragga, K.A.: Effectiveness of accessibility and usability of government websites in Saudi Arabia. Can. J. Pure Appl. Sci. 4(2), 1227–1231 (2010)

8. Al-Khalifa, H.S.: Heuristic evaluation of the usability of e-government websites: a case from Saudi Arabia. In: Proceedings of the 4th International Conference on Theory and Practice of Electronic Governance, pp. 238–242. ACM, Beijing (2010)
9. Al-Khalifa, H.S.: Exploring the accessibility of Saudi Arabia e-government websites: preliminary results. In: ICEGOV, Proceedings of the 4th International Conference on Theory and Practice of Electronic Governance, Beijing, China, pp. 274–278 (2010)

Research on Evaluation Index System of Artificial Intelligence Design Based on User Experience

Qianwen Chen(✉) and Haowei Wang

School of Design Art and Media, Nanjing University of Science and Technology, Nanjing, Jiangsu, People's Republic of China
1501796143@qq.com

Abstract. In order to provide evaluation methods for the interface by AI design at the user experience side. First, this paper analyzes the human-computer interaction model, the display characteristics of the interface, and summarizes the influence factors of the interface on the user experience. Then studied the existing methods of building evaluation system. After that, using rough set theory and fuzzy analytic hierarchy process, the evaluation index system of user experience based interface design is established. According to the evaluation system, we can provide a meaningful optimization strategy for improving the user experience of the interface, in order to provide a better experience for the user in the process of using the AI design interface.

Keywords: Artificial intelligence design · User experience · Evaluation system

1 Introduction

In the 21st century, a new generation of information technology represented by artificial intelligence is booming all over the world. Artificial intelligence has injected new power into social development [1]. At the same time, it has profoundly changed people's production and life style. AI technology has penetrated into all aspects of life: personalized recommendation on mobile phones and voice navigation are inseparable from it.

In the current social background, it is undeniable that designers are also involved in the wave of artificial intelligence. In the field of design, artificial intelligence also has a very good performance. Adobe's Sensei can assist with drawing revision and video processing [2]; Prism can move the style of one image to another [3]. Take Alibaba smart "Luban" for example, 8000 designs can be made per second. Artificial intelligence can not only help designers to make posters, videos, but also assist in web interface design. Wix, the service provider of the station, has launched the artificial intelligence system ADI [4]. Even if users do not have graphic design foundation and computer knowledge, they can easily design an interface and create a website. In the future, there are bound to be more interfaces designed by artificial intelligence.

So what can AI provide for web page interface design? How does this affect the user experience of the interface? Under the guidance of artificial intelligence, what is

© Springer Nature Switzerland AG 2020
M. Kurosu (Ed.): HCII 2020, LNCS 12181, pp. 373–386, 2020.
https://doi.org/10.1007/978-3-030-49059-1_27

the difference of user experience of the interface? In order to make AI assist human designers in better design activities, human designers need to fully understand the advantages and disadvantages of AI designers in the design of web interface. Using statistical method to establish an evaluation index system to evaluate the user experience of interface design. It can help human designers to separate the excellent work of artificial intelligence design, reduce the burden of human designers, and optimize the user experience of web pages. Provide more theoretical support for designers. So that designers can better cooperate with AI design for design activities.

1.1 Background

On January 2, 2020, China Internet Network Information Center released the 44th statistical report on the development of China's Internet [5]. By June 2019, the number of Chinese Internet users had reached 854 million, with a penetration rate of 61.2%. We have entered the era of mobile devices and information technology. In an information system, the interface is the most direct contact between the system and the user, and it is the medium of information exchange between the user and the system. Good interface interaction design can not only meet the basic needs of users to find information, but also enable users to complete tasks effectively and satisfactorily, bringing users a pleasant experience [6].

The popularity of artificial intelligence has stimulated the upsurge of using artificial intelligence in mainstream services and technologies for the public. The emergence of artificial intelligence is also likely to change the way designers work in the near future. At present, artificial intelligence station building is a very big innovation in the field of design. For example, Weebly, Squarespace and QIFEIYE. The result of intelligent platform building algorithm is that the computer can help users design a website. When users design web pages through the platform, they are first required to input the user's nature of the website, and then input different properties and parameters of the interface according to the prompts. At the same time, users can also improve the design according to the template provided on the platform. Then the platform will retrieve from its own database and finally generate a website. With this tool, even if there is no graphic design basis and related computer knowledge users can easily and quickly design a website.

"User experience" has become a hot word in the Internet industry in recent years. Some large Internet companies have set up a separate department, user experience department, to study and improve the user experience of their products. In order to provide a good user experience, we must first identify the needs of users. Artificial intelligence + big data can provide accurate information and grasp the real needs of users. For example: when the user is older, the text and controls in the interface can be appropriately enlarged; according to the user's usage habits, the columns with different browsing rates can be rearranged to improve the user's usage rate and loyalty. Although AI can achieve accurate data collection and delivery, design is a perceptual creation process, which is one of the insufficiencies of computers. On the basis of fully understanding AI, designers should complement its advantages and optimize the user experience of web interface.

1.2   Research Status

In 2019, Microsoft Research Institute collected more than 150 design suggestions, refined and verified them, and finally integrated them into an artificial intelligence interaction guide, which divides the interaction process into four stages by time [7]. Some scholars, such as Tullis. T.S [8], have extracted four indexes of interface information density, object clustering degree, layout complexity and information extraction time for static digital interface evaluation, and then determined the model to predict the number of user searches and interface satisfaction. Streveler and Wasserman [9] put forward a quantitative research method to evaluate the layout system of the interface, to determine the indicators and algorithm accuracy of the expert user evaluation screen layout. The existing evaluation system research has interface oriented, artificial intelligence interactive design oriented, but there is no specific evaluation index system for AI generated interface.

The second section of this paper analyzes the factors that affect the user experience, the third section combs the methods and principles of the establishment of the evaluation index system, and the fourth section establishes the evaluation index system based on the results of the above two sections.

2   Influencing Factors of User Experience

In order to build a user experience based evaluation system, designers need to systematically analyze and summarize each node in the interaction. It can help designers to find design points by exploring the mechanism of communication and information transfer between the interface and users when they contact and use the web interface. After that, the factors that affect user experience are analyzed.

From the traditional human-computer interaction model, it can be concluded that human in the process of interaction involves three aspects: human, machine and environment. Users tend to see the machine as a tool for accomplishing tasks. With the development of artificial intelligence technology, the interactive object gradually changes from "machine" to "robot", which has the properties of "machine" and "human". In the process of changing from "machine" to "human", users have the expectation of communication for operation, but also more desire for natural interaction. Therefore, designers should not only summarize the existing theories, but also analyze the experience of human interaction.

In interface design, user experience is related to user's personal factors, environmental factors and information factors. Personal factors refer to the influence of user differences on user experience. Environmental factors refer to the environment in which users are in when receiving information. Information is all information presented to users through the interface.

2.1   Personal Factors

User Differentiation. The impact of personal factors on user experience involves the differences of each user. Because the evaluation of user experience is relatively subjective, the evaluation of an interface involves individual differences. Individual difference mainly refers to the psychological and physiological differences based on the culture, life experience, and cognitive experience that users receive in the process of receiving information. These differences make the user experience affected to some extent, and have different feelings for the interface. Nowadays, artificial intelligence technology can depict the user's portrait through data collection, and understand the user's preferences. In the design of interface, if the interface is facing all user groups, the general design principle is adopted. For special users, special design principles must be adopted.

Perceptual Analysis. Users can feel external things and products through vision, hearing, touch, smell and taste. With the support of artificial intelligence technology, the machine adds cameras, microphones, loudspeakers, etc., and has the ability of language understanding, image recognition, gesture recognition and voice communication. With the development of technology, the interaction channels between human and machine are more and more diverse, and the user experience brought by it is more natural. Therefore, in the interface evaluation system, the perception factors of the interface can be evaluated from the perspective of multi-channel.

Emotional Composition. Emotion is the attitude experience of human subject consciousness to objective things. Users' emotion evaluation standards have obvious task differences and individual differences. After analysis, several factors of emotional evaluation are summarized: first, when users contact the interface, they have the expectation of interface evaluation and communication in mind. At the end of interaction, users will compare the differences between pre use and post use emotions. If the user obtains more emotion after completing the task than the initial emotion, the interface will have a positive emotion for the user. The second is the realization of users' individual expression and values. When users choose products, they tend to choose products or interfaces that match their personality and values. It also confirms that users pay more and more attention to individual expression in Marlowe's demand.

Cognitive Load. Sweller [10] believes that the user's cognitive resources need to be consumed in the interface operation. When the cognitive resources needed by all operations exceed all cognitive resources owned by users, it will lead to insufficient resource allocation and excessive cognitive load. From the previous research results, we can see that cognitive load is the proportion of cognitive resources allocated to a task among all cognitive resources. Cognitive load plays an important role in interface design rating.

PAAS and Van merrinboer proposed that there are three factors that affect cognitive load: task environment characteristics, learner subject characteristics and the interaction between learners and task environment [11]. The task environment characteristics has a great relationship with the information content and presentation mode in the interface. If there are too many useless or less useful information and low frequency information in an interface, it will bring high cognitive load to the user, which will cause some interference when the user identifies the interface, easy to forget and misread, and waste the user's cognitive resources. If users need more cognitive resources to learn how to use the interface, it will also bring some obstacles to users' perception and understanding. So in the interface design, the more information the interface presents, the better, but at the same time, the cognitive load of users should be considered. Therefore, when evaluating the interface, we should pay attention to the balance between information and cognition.

2.2 Environmental Factor

Environmental factors in the application of products mainly refer to the impact of the user's environment on decision-making, including temperature, humidity, lighting environment, sound, etc. [12]. For the user to contact or use the interface, the environmental factors are not as complex as the user to use the product, but also less important than the human factors and machine factors. A good light environment can make the information presented in the interface clear and complete to the user. The acoustic environment can ensure the concentration of the operator's attention and the smoothness of the auditory channel. The gas environment and thermal environment can ensure the psychological and emotional stability of the operator. The environmental factors can meet the specified requirements by improving the internal and external conditions of the control room [13].

2.3 Information Factor

Information factor is the most important factor that affects user experience. All information of the interface includes the content, presentation and interaction of information.

Contents of the Interface. The information content of the interface mainly refers to the visual elements such as icon, navigation, color, text, picture, tab, etc. When arranging the contents in the interface, the levels should be clear to ensure the priority of important tasks. At the same time, the interface logic should be clear, so that users know where they are. Appropriate control design makes the interface look more beautiful and has a certain role in prompting. The framework and hierarchical structure of a website have been set up. The content updated regularly will make the whole website fuller and improve the user experience.

Information Presentation of the Interface. The interface is usually composed of some small information modules, which are represented as different controls in the interface. Each control is presented in different ways in the interface, and the structure of the interface is formed by various combinations of controls. The diversity of interface presentation is reflected in the diversity of each control and combination form. It is the combination of layout, navigation and menu of the interface. For example, the combination of the same control and different colors can represent different states of the control. Also like the different layout of the same number of controls.

Interface Interaction. The development of artificial intelligence drives the development and change of human-computer interaction technology. The anthropomorphic interaction can bring better user experience to users. When people first interact with machines, they tend to regard machines as a tool, and people adapt to the behavior of machines. The anthropomorphic design requires that the machine can communicate with the user like a human, and can make personalized adjustment according to the user's needs and operation. So the designer should study what kind of response the user expects the interface to make and what kind of feedback it will have after the operation. When the user has enough knowledge of an interface, he can be in an active position and gain psychological security. The user's understanding of the interface includes the operation aspect and the understanding of their own state. During interaction, the user is clear about what the system can do, how to interact, and how to correct errors in operation. Clear hierarchical relationship and natural operation interface can let users know their own state. In order to continuously adapt the interface to the user, after the operation, the interface can collect feedback from the user after use, and carefully update and adjust the interface after understanding the user behavior.

3 Principles and Methods of Establishing Evaluation Index System

3.1 Principles of Establishing Evaluation Index System

The evaluation index system refers to a number of indexes that represent the characteristics of evaluation objects and their interrelations. When constructing the index system, we should follow several principles. From the overall point of view, when evaluating and listing, we should select indicators with high importance, great influence, comprehensive reflection of all aspects of the system characteristics, and exclude unnecessary or less important indicators. And the meaning of the selected indicators should be simple, clear, clear and easy to understand. There should be clear boundaries between the indicators, and the contents should not be repeated or overlapped with each other, too much and too detailed, so that the indicators are too cumbersome and overlapped with each other, and the indicators should not be too few and too simple, so as to avoid the omission of indicator information and the occurrence of errors and untruths.

From the perspective of each indicator, the selected indicators should have corresponding evaluation criteria. It is better to choose quantifiable indicators. Some indexes that are difficult to be quantified or scored can be described, calculated and analyzed by the way of reflecting the level from the side, such as test, weight and other methods. The evaluation result is easy to quantify, the data collection is simple, and the calculation method is clear.

3.2 The Method of Establishing Evaluation Index System

There are many methods to establish the evaluation index system. There are subjective evaluation methods, such as expert opinion evaluation method and Richter scale method. Mathematical evaluation methods, such as TOPSIS evaluation method, grey correlation degree method, etc. At the same time, with the development of measurement technology, eye tracking technology and EEG technology are more and more widely used.

Rough set theory can deal with uncertain and incomplete information. On the one hand, its mathematical foundation is mature and does not need prior knowledge; on the other hand, it is easy to use. Because the purpose and starting point of the research of rough set theory is to analyze and reason the data directly, find the hidden knowledge and reveal the potential laws, it is a natural data mining or knowledge discovery method [14]. It has a strong complementarity with the theory of dealing with other uncertainty problems, especially the fuzzy theory [15]. Fuzzy set theory has the characteristics of qualitative and quantitative combination, which is widely used in the comprehensive evaluation of various fields. On the basis of fuzzy analytic hierarchy process, rough set theory is used to describe and deal with uncertainty relatively objectively, which can analyze imprecise, inconsistent and incomplete information and complement each other.

According to the primary evaluation index system of interface design, combined with rough set theory and AHP, a specific evaluation model is constructed (Fig. 1).

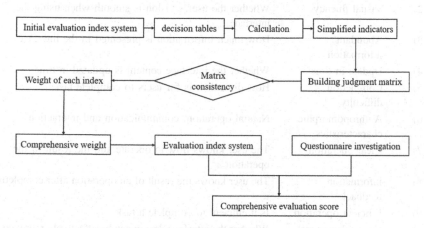

Fig. 1. Interface evaluation system model

4   Establishment of Evaluation Index System

According to the analysis of user, interface information and environment in the third section, several evaluation factors affecting the user experience of interface are listed, and 17 influencing factors and the characteristics of each influencing factor are listed in the table.

Table 1. Influencing factors of user experience

Number	Influence factor	Characterization
(C2)	Multichannel	There are stimulation modes other than visual channels, such as sound, vibration, etc.
(C2)	User expectation	Comparison between the feeling after use and the expectation before use
(C3)	Affection need	Expression of user's personality and emotion
(C4)	Learning cost	The cost of learning how to use the interface
(C5)	Memory cost	Can users remember how to use the system after learning to use it
(C6)	Environmental factor	Light, sound, gas, heat and other factors around the interface
(C7)	Control design	Whether the design style of the control is consistent, and whether it is the user's favorite style
(C8)	Control semantics	Whether the semantics of the control is clear
(C9)	Control properties	Can controls (icons, navigation) help users understand information
(C10)	Interface style	Interface style, such as color, etc.
(C11)	Visual balance	Is the layout of the interface visually balanced
(C12)	Visual fluency	Whether the user's vision is smooth when using the interface
(C13)	Abundant information	How much information is presented in the interface
(C14)	Update in time	Whether the interface content is updated in time
(C15)	Completion difficulty	How difficult it is for users to complete tasks
(C16)	Anthropomorphic characteristics	Natural operation, communication and interaction
(C17)	Clear operation	The user knows how to operate and the result of the operation
(C18)	information feedback	The user knows the result of an operation after completing it
(C19)	Efficient operation	Is it efficient to complete a task
(C20)	Error-tolerant rate	Whether the interface design can be effectively removed or corrected in case of error
(C21)	Distinct levels	Do users clearly know that they are at the level of the system
(C22)	Information structure	Whether the interface level is clear and the user knows his current position
(C23)	Feedback collection	Interface to collect user experience comments and suggestions
(C24)	Update informed	Every time the interface is updated, the user will be informed of the updated contents and functions

The influencing factors of user experience are selected and integrated according to the principle of evaluation index establishment, and 19 influencing factors are reserved. The preliminary evaluation index system is constructed by using the analytic hierarchy process (AHP) method, which is divided into three levels: target level, criterion level and index level. Taking the target oriented evaluation target as the target level index, the basic requirements of the interface constitute the first level index of the evaluation object, and the evaluation factors determined in the first step constitute the third level index system.

Table 2. Preliminary evaluation index system

Target layer	Criterion level		Index level	
User experience based interface design	User factors	(A1)	Multichannel	(B1)
			User expectation	(B2)
			Individual needs	(B3)
			Cognitive load	(B4)
			Control properties	(B5)
			Interface style	(B6)
			Reasonable layout	(B7)
			Visual fluency	(B8)
			Abundant information	(B9)
			Distinct levels	(B10)
	Task interaction	(A3)	Update in time	(B11)
			Completion difficulty	(B12)
			Anthropomorphic characteristics	(B13)
			Clear operation	(B14)
			Information feedback	(B15)
			Efficient operation	(B16)
			Fault tolerance rate	(B17)
			Dynamic iteration	(B18)
	Environmental factor	(A4)	Environmental factor	(B19)

4.1 Evaluation System After Attribute Simplification

Seven interfaces were selected as experimental objects,
i.e.

$$U = \{u_1, u_2, \ldots\ldots, u_7\},$$

The importance of the evaluation results to each secondary index is measured by the five level scale, which is represented by values 1–5 respectively. Establish decision table of primary evaluation index system. The simplified index system is obtained by calculating the distinct function of information system.

Table 3. Simplified evaluation index model

Target layer	Criterion level		Index level	
User experience based interface design	User factors	(A1)	Multichannel	(B1)
			Individual needs	(B2)
			Cognitive load	(B3)
	Information content	(A2)	Control properties	(B4)
			Reasonable layout	(B5)
			Distinct levels	(B6)
			Update in time	(B7)
	Task interaction	(A3)	Anthropomorphic characteristics	(B8)
			Clear operation	(B9)
			Information feedback	(B10)
			Operational fault tolerance	(B11)
			Dynamic iteration	(B12)

4.2 Weight Calculation and Consistency Test

According to the evaluation index model, the judgment matrix of the criterion layer to the target layer and the indicator layer to the criterion layer is constructed, and the corresponding weight value is calculated. According to the scoring method in Table 4 and 5, experts are invited to score the importance of the first level indicators in Table 3, 4 and 5: user factors, information content, task interaction) to find the weight of the first level indicators; then, they score the importance of the second level indicators in Table 1, 2, 3, 4 and 5 to find the weight of each evaluation factor.

Table 4. Scoring of importance of evaluation factors

Importance of factors	Score
Unimportance	1
Less important	2
Commonly	3
More important	4
Very important	5

Through the weight ratio calculated by each criterion layer, the combined weight and vector of the whole system are calculated synthetically, and the final combined weight order of the system is obtained. The specific methods are as follows:

The judgment matrix of the indicator layer to the criterion layer is constructed. Taking the user factor as an example, the judgment matrix of the three factors of multi-channel, individual demand and cognitive load is constructed.

$$P = (P_{A1})_{3*3} = \begin{Bmatrix} 1 & 2.031 & 1.204 \\ 0.492 & 1 & 0.593 \\ 0.831 & 1.688 & 1 \end{Bmatrix}$$

Table 5. AHP analysis results

Term	Feature vector	Weight value	Maximum eigenvalue	CI value
Multichannel	1.291	43.046%	3	0
Individual needs	0.636	21.192%		
Cognitive load	1.073	35.762%		

The eigenvectors are:

$$W_{A1} = (0.375, 0.7500, 1.875)$$

Table 6. Summary of conformance test results

Maximum characteristic root	CI value	RI value	CR value	Consistency test results
3.000	0.000	0.520	0.000	Adopt

Repeat the above calculation process to determine the weight of criterion layer to target layer and indicator layer to corresponding criterion layer as shown in the table. At the same time, the consistency of all judgment matrices is obtained, which meets the ICR < 0.1. It shows that the evaluation system has the reliability required by AHP.

Table 7. Weight of criteria layer to target layer

Criterion level	W_{Ai}
A1	0.26842
A2	0.36052
A3	0.37105

Table 8. Weight of index layer to criterion layer

Index level	W_{Bi}
B1	0.10638
B2	0.05237
B3	0.08838
B4	0.09002
B5	0.10966
B6	0.06874
B7	0.06874
B8	0.09493
B9	0.0982
B10	0.07692
B11	0.07529
B12	0.07038

4.3   Object Evaluation

See Table 5, 6, 7, 8 and 9 for the construction of user preference evaluation criteria; obtain the score of each evaluation index by questionnaire. From the weight value obtained in the previous step, the evaluation value of each AI interface is calculated.

Table 9. User preference scoring

Grade	Importance of factors	Score
1	Excellent	5
2	Good	4
3	Commonly	3
4	Poor	2
5	Very poor	1

5   Conclusion

According to the research on the evaluation system of web page interface based on artificial intelligence, the results of calculation and verification can be concluded as follows:

- From the user's point of view, the multi-channel perception and cognitive load account for a large proportion. Users pay more attention to the multi-channel input of information perception and the cognitive load of the interface. Therefore, in the interface generated by artificial intelligence, in addition to the stimulation of the visual channel, the stimulation of other channels should also be appropriately increased to make the interaction more full. In terms of cognitive load, we should pay attention to the comprehensibility and complexity of interface information to reduce the cost of learning and memory;

- In terms of information content, interface layout has the greatest impact on user experience. Reasonable interface layout and smooth vision bring better experience to users;
- At the task interaction level, explicit operation and anthropomorphic characteristics have the greatest impact on users. In the interaction process, it is the most important for the user to know how to operate the interface, followed by the anthropomorphic and natural interaction to provide a better experience for the user.

In the early stage of this paper, the factors that affect the user experience of AI design interface are selected from three levels of personal, information and environment by consulting the literature. Through simplifying the influencing factors and establishing the corresponding evaluation model in different levels, this paper explores the degree of the influence of the factors on the user experience of AI design interface in the three criteria levels, and measures the influence process with a systematic evaluation system In order to provide a meaningful optimization strategy for improving the user experience of the interface, in order to provide a better interaction experience for the user in the process of using the AI design interface. The lack of this paper is that the interface of research is less, the number of questionnaire survey is less, and leading to the weight of the evaluation index is not persuasive, which needs further improvement and optimization.

References

1. Vocke, C., Constantinescu, C., Popescu, D.: Application potentials of artificial intelligence for the design of innovation processes. Procedia CIRP **84**, 810–813 (2019)
2. Adobe Sensei Homepage. Https://www.adobe.com/cn/sensei.html. Accessed 02 Jan 2020
3. PRISMA Homepage. Http://www.prisma-statement.org/. Accessed 02 Jan 2020
4. Wix Homepage. https://www.wix.com/release/notes/wix-adi. Accessed 02 Jan 2020
5. China Internet Network Information Center Homepage. Http://www.cac.gov.cn/2019-08/30/c_.htm. Accessed 02 Jan 2020
6. Yu, N., Kong, J.: User experience with web browsing on small screens: experimental investigations of mobile-page interface design and homepage design for news websites. Inf. Sci. **330**(10), 427–443 (2016)
7. Amershi, S.: Guidelines for human-AI interaction. In: 2019 CHI Conference on Human Factors in Computing Systems, vol. 5, no. 2 (2019)
8. Thacker, P., Tullis, T.S., Babu, A.J.G.: Application of Tullis visual search model to highlighted and non-highlighted tabular displays. In: Human Factors Perspectives on Human-Computer Interaction: Selections from Proceedings of Human Factors and Ergonomics Society Annual Meetings, Santa Monica, CA, pp. 115–119 (1995)
9. Streveler, D.J., Wasserman, A.I.: Quantitative measures of the spatial properties of screen designs. In: INTERACT Conference Proceedings, North Holland, Amsterdam (1984)
10. Sweller, J.: Cognitive load during problem solving: effects on learning. Cognit. Sci. **12**(2), 257–285 (1988)

11. Van Gerven, P.W.M., Paas, F.G.W.C., Van Merriënboer, J.J.G., Schmidt, H.G.: Cognitive load theory and aging: effects of worked examples on training efficiency. Learn. Instr. **12**(1), 87–105 (2002)
12. Chen, Z., et al.: Assessing affective experience of in-situ environmental walk via wearable biosensors for evidence-based design. Cognit. Syst. Res. **52**, 970–977 (2018)
13. Bonnes, M., Carrus, G.: Environmental Psychology, Overview. Reference Module in Neuroscience and Bio Behavioral Psychology (2017)
14. Zhang, Q., Xie, Q., Wang, G.: A survey on rough set theory and its applications. CAAI Trans. Intell. Technol. **1**(4), 323–333 (2016)
15. Diker, M.: Textures and fuzzy unit operations in rough set theory: an approach to fuzzy rough set models. Fuzzy Sets Syst. **336**(1), 27–53 (2018)

Ecological Momentary Assessment Tools: Lessons Learned from an HCI Perspective

Pietro Crovari(✉) ⑩, Fabio Catania(✉) ⑩, Micol Spitale(✉) ⑩,
and Franca Garzotto(✉) ⑩

Department of Electronics, Information, and Bioengineering (DEIB),
Politecnico di Milano, Milan, Italy
{pietro.crovari,fabio.catania,micol.spitale,franca.garzotto}@polimi.it

Abstract. Ecological Momentary Assessment (EMA) is a popular family of tools in behavioural research that is known for its ability to capture in detail fluctuating phenomena while minimizing bias. They consist of short questions to be answered many times per day. Still, participants often perceive EMA-based studies as burdening, resulting in a low compliance rate. A good design of the EMA study - in terms of what to measure, how to put questions to the users, and when - is fundamental to minimize the above drawback and improve participants' compliance. Our research focuses on the "how" dimension of EMA design, looking at it through the lens of HCI. We performed an empirical study devoted to explore this specific design aspect, exposing 20 users to different formulations of EMA questions in the same domain for 2 weeks. From the study results, we distilled some lessons learned related to the design of the EMA User Experience, which can benefit future designers of this assessment tool.

Keywords: Ecological Momentary Assessment (EMA) · Experience sampling methods (ESM) · Questionnaires design

1 Introduction

Ecological Momentary Assessment (EMA) is a family of techniques widely used in behavioural psychology [30]. EMAs consist of short questions to be answered many times per day. Doing so, the researcher can precisely reconstruct the observed phenomenon along with time [9]. These questionnaires can vary a lot in form, measured variables, and frequency the respondent is asked to answer, but they share some common features [32]:

- *Shortness*: usually, they are made by one or a few questions, such that the time required to answer is minimum [13];
- *Frequency*: a EMA-based research is typically composed of 7 to 15 question per day, depending on the phenomenon observed [48].

© Springer Nature Switzerland AG 2020
M. Kurosu (Ed.): HCII 2020, LNCS 12181, pp. 387–403, 2020.
https://doi.org/10.1007/978-3-030-49059-1_28

- *Medium*: The instrument used to deliver questions changed over time [8]. In the beginning, pen and paper was the most adopted technique, but now EMA is usually prompted on people's smartphone, using one of the many existing mobile application to prompt the questions in the right moment [38].

EMAs are effective to track the fluctuation of behaviours and mental status such as depression [5,28], stress [26], smoke, alcohol, or drug addiction [31,44,45], and mood [10]. For example, recent studies have successfully adopted EMAs to investigate food temptations [25], emotional awareness [41], daily social interactions [49], and suicidal ideation [17]. Mattingly et al. exploited these tools to investigate work conditions [21]. Many factors contributed to the success of EMAs [36]. From the psychological perspective, they are capable of acquiring data in the respondent's natural context, and the possibility of making multiple questions per day allow researchers to monitor the precise fluctuation of the phenomenon observed [9]. From the technological point of view, the success of ubiquitous technologies [43], such as smartphone and wearable devices, gives the possibility of exploiting those technologies to deliver the questions without the necessity for the respondent of carrying extra devices or pen-and-paper based questionnaires [13].

EMAs disrupt "traditional" research protocol of behavioural psychology. In fact, instead of having few, consistent sessions of information collection, such as interviews and long questionnaires, EMA-based studies exploit numerous short questions to be answered frequently. On top of that, they are ecological, meaning that the collection of the information is done in the respondents' environment, minimizing the bias introduced by the location, such as a psychologist's studio, a researcher's laboratory, or a hospital, often perceived as intimidating [35]. These characteristics also contribute to minimize the recall bias, the errors introduced during the recall process [6].

Given their flexibility, EMAs can be applied in many studies, that investigate very different domains [15]. As a consequence, the design choices that lead to the realization of the study are strictly dependent on the study itself. When to prompt an EMA? How many questions per day? Which questions to chose? How to design the questions? Multiple answers or Likert scales [2]? How to aggregate and analyze data? The researcher must choose all these aspects carefully. All the factors can determine the success or the failure of a study. If a question is not prompted in a good moment, or it is formulated badly, the user is not willing to cooperate, giving low-quality answers, or not answering at all. As a consequence, researchers should pay extreme attention in the design of the EMAs, to maximize the amount of data collected and, possibly, the quality. EMAs are still used widely, and many research works focus on how to improve their efficacy. In particular, many studies investigate *when* is the best moment to prompt an EMA, focusing both on defined protocols that specify the right moments and on dynamics algorithms that tailor those moments to the specific user. To the best of our knowledge, though, the literature lacks on analyzing *how* to design EMA-studies, providing a set of lessons learned the research can follow to avoid common pitfalls, in particular under the lens of Human-Computer

Interaction. Adams et al. started an investigation in this direction but proposed a new EMA optimal only in the assessment of physical pain [1].

In this context, this research was born. We want to collect and share a set of insights that can be useful in the design phase of an EMA-based study. We want to elaborate some lessons learned that can be applied to most studies to improve their efficacy. In particular, we focus on a Human-Computer Interaction (HCI) perspective, understanding how the User Experience can be leveraged to improve the outcomes of a study.

In order to develop EMA design lessons learned, we run a study with 20 participant with different age, sex, and background, and we asked them to answer 4 types of EMAs that investigate their mental health status. The EMAs were designed to be very different in the form, length, and effort required to answer. At the end of the collection phase, we interviewed the participants to understand their opinion about the EMAs, how the questions were perceived, to have their insights in the study, and to ask for suggestions for improving the acceptance of the EMAs.

This work brings two major contributions. First, we propose a study on a largely unexplored design dimension of EMA-based study, the HCI perspective. Then, we share the insights collected and we translate this valuable information into design principles that can be applied to most EMA-based studies.

The paper is structured as follow. After an accurate State-of-Art analysis, the study will be described, with particular attention to the final interview process. Then, the paper will explain in detail all the insights we got and how they can influence the design of an EMA questionnaire. The paper will conclude with the elicited design principles and some general considerations that can be effectively adopted in most EMA-based studies.

2   State of Art

Since EMAs evolved from questionnaires to be answered with pen and paper to questions on electronic devices (first palmtop computers, then smartphones), HCI started to investigate the importance of the user interaction in the data collection process.

Researchers tried to improve EMAs to minimize the burden perceived by respondents while answering, and/or trying to maximize their compliance, that is the percentage of answered EMAs among all the prompted ones. The first investigated direction to minimize the perceived burden was the design of questions that minimized user effort. For example, Zhang et al. tried to exploit the action of unlocking the smartphone to collect data from the user [48]. In fact, they designed a set of EMAs that substituted the smartphone unlock screen. The user could answer the question through the same gesture used to unlock the screen normally. Answering the EMA, the users could access the device as if they had regularly unlocked their screen. An experimental study showed that even if these EMAs were perceived as more intrusive with respect to notification-based ones, the compliance was much higher. Intille et al., instead, designed μEMA, a single-question EMA to be prompted on a smartwatch, and showed that its completion rate was higher than the one obtained with a traditional EMA prompted on a smartphone (81.21% vs. 64.54%) [16]. Finally, Yue et al. investigated how pictures could be a new kind of EMA question [47].

Another investigated path is the exploitation of Machine Learning techniques to find the best moments to interrupt the respondents, and prompt EMAs consequently [39]. This problem is also known as Interruptibility problem [46]. Fogarty et al. discovered that sensors on a smartphone are enough to estimate a person's interruptibility [12]. Obuchi et al. [22] used Activity Recognition API to deliver EMAs at Activity Breakpoints, the time instants in which the device revealed a change in the activity detected from the smartphone (e.g., from walking to standing, from sitting to walking, etc.). The improvement in the user compliance was tangible, up to a 70% factor. Okoshi's research group, instead, monitored events internal to the device to estimate users' interruptibility [23].

Finally, many studies tried to exploit user engagement to increase EMA compliance. An economic reward is a widely adopted technique to keep the user motivated. Usually, the reward is proportional to the percentage of EMA fulfilled. This approach is easy to adopt and works effectively but presents two main drawbacks [7]. First, the research is not easily scalable since it requires economic funding to reward each participant [30]. Second, the economic reward increases compliance, but it does not ensure the quality of the data collected. In fact, the reward mechanism does not depend on how the respondents fulfill the EMA, but only on if they do that.

For these reasons, researchers tried to find alternative ways to engage users, to guarantee data quality along time with a good compliance rate. Christensen et al. suggest as a good practice to sensitize the respondents about the importance of the study and make them feel responsible for having good results in the research [7]. To increase the feeling of involvement, Hsieh et al. implemented an online platform that let users have feedback from the answered EMAs. Interestingly, they discovered that the compliance rate increased significantly when the users had the possibility to look at data visualization on the EMAs they had responded to [14]. Finally, Van Berkel et al. demonstrated that with a gamified version of the EMA they designed data quality improved, seeing gamified-EMA users submitting text answers that were 174% longer the ones offered through not gamified EMAs [40].

Even if the literature presents many successful examples of techniques to improve the outcomes of an EMA-based study, either increasing the compliance or improving the quality of the answers, to the best of our knowledge there are no studies that focus on the design of the study, especially from an HCI-perspective.

3   Methodology

In order to maximize the efficacy of our study, we started analyzing a range set of studies based on EMA prompted on smartphones trying to infer the lessons learned from the researchers during their studies. We exploited this knowledge as the starting point for the design of the study procedure, to understand which were the most critical points to be investigated.

The study aimed at collecting information about how people interact with Ecological Momentary Assessment, how different EMAs impacts on the results of a study, and which benefits researchers can obtain by leveraging on the User Experience.

3.1 Setting

We chose to run our data collection study in daycare and therapeutic centers, known to be a very stressful work environment, that usually leads to psychological burnout [4,18,33]. For this reason, such a population could benefit from continuous monitoring through EMAs.

3.2 Population

We recruited 20 people working in 2 therapeutic facilities on a volunteer base. To participate in the study, people were required to have an Android smartphone, at least with OS version 4.1 installed. Most of the enrolled volunteers were women (4 M, 16 F). Participants varied a lot in age, from 23 to 64 ($M = 35, SD = 10.9$), in their educational background, from secondary school diploma to master's degree, and in the role they covered in the centers. The study had been enrolled by psychologists, educators, coordinators, managers, sociomedical operators, and support teachers. The expertise level with the smartphone was not a criterion during the selection process. To each participant, a unique code was assigned to guarantee the respect of their sensible data (P1-P20).

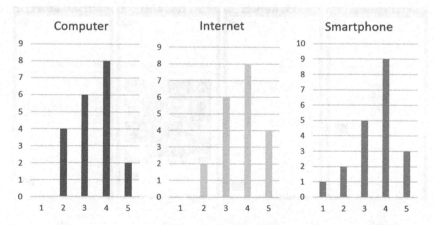

Fig. 1. The graphs summarize the response to the questions asked during the initial interview, as described in Sect. 3.3. The questions were: how much do you feel confident *(left)* with computers? *(center)* with internet? *(right)* with smartphones? Study participants had to answer with a score in [1;5], where 1 meant no confidence, and 5 totally confident.

3.3 Procedure

The study lasted 4 weeks and was divided into three main phases: an *Initial Interview* to collect some demographic information and set up the study, a *EMAs Collection* period, to let the users interact with the various questionnaires, and a *Final Interview*, in which users where interviewed to gather insights on the experience.

Initial Interview. At the beginning of the study, participants were met individually for an initial interview. First, all the participants signed a consent form. After we explained them the study procedure in detail, a mobile application was installed on the volunteers' devices. This application consisted of a customized version of AWARE, an open-source framework born to prompt EMA on mobile devices [11]. Then, volunteers were asked to answer a quick questionnaire investigating the demographic information of the volunteers and their relationship with technology. We asked each participant to express a grade from 0 to 5 according to how confident they felt with Computers, Internet, and Smartphones, where 1 meant no confidence with the technology, and 5 totally confident. These questions aimed to have a better understanding of the population we dealt with. As Fig. 1 shows, most the study participants felt confident with the use of technology, and therefore for the vast majority of the users, the interaction with the smartphone had not to be considered as a major issue for our study. The interview ended with a short training session to teach participants to use the application.

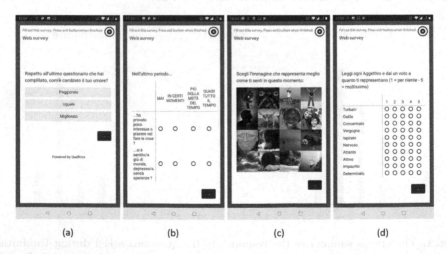

(a)   (b)   (c)   (d)

Fig. 2. The four EMAs prompted during the study. In particular, (a) Three-answers question, (b) PHQ-2, (c) PAM, (d) PANAS. Each time, the application randomly selected one and prompted it

EMAs Collection. For 4 weeks, participants run the AWARE application on their smartphones. During the day, the application prompted an EMA every hour, from 9 AM to 10 PM, for a total of 14 EMAs per day. Every time, an EMA was selected randomly among the four shown in Fig. 2. The questions were designed to be very different in the formulation and in the interaction required to answer. Most of the questions were inspired by widely adopted questionnaires:

1. *Three-Answers*: The user had to say if his/her mood had improved, worsened, or did not change from the last question answered (Fig. 2.a);
2. *PHQ-2*: The short version of PHQ questionnaire [34] consisted on two statements investigating depression to answer with a value from 1 to 4 [19]: *Little interest or pleasure in doing things – Feeling down, depressed or hopeless* (Fig. 2.b);
3. *PAM*: The Photographic Affect Meter (PAM) [24], required the users to select the image that they felt the most represented by (Fig. 2.c);
4. *PANAS*: The short version of Positive Affect and Negative Affect questionnaire [42], asked the users to give a score from 1 to 5 to 10 different adjectives [37]: *determined, upset, attentive, alert, inspired, active, afraid, nervous, upset, ashamed, hostile* (Fig. 2.d).

Users knew about a new EMA to be answered through a notification on their device. In fact, once AWARE created the question, a notification was prompted on the participant's device. When the user clicked on it, the question appeared full-screen. Participants could dismiss the questions clicking on the cross on the top-right corner of the EMA. If the participant did not click on the notification, before generating a new EMA the application destroyed the previous notification, marking the question as not answered.

Final Interview. At the end of the EMAs collection period, participants were met individually for a final interview, to understand how they perceived the EMAs they received and having their insights on the study. The interview followed a semi-structured approach. The questions aimed at exploring the experience with the EMAs and collecting and how the design of the questions influenced the experience. We used the following questions as a starting point:

1. How was your experience with the EMAs?
2. What did you think every time you received a notification? How did you feel?
3. *[Showing a picture of every EMA used during the study]* Please, for every kind of EMA, tell me what you thought when you saw it appear. Then, rank them from the one you liked the most to the one you disliked the most.
4. Which are the main elements that made you decide whether to answer a question or not?
5. Do you think the kind of EMA influenced your decision of responding it?
6. In a work environment such as yours, which are the aspects you would investigate through EMAs?
7. Do you have any other question and or feedback?
8. How do you think we could exploit those data?

4 Results

In this section, the answers to each interview question will be presented, organizing the answers by recurrent topics. Not all the participants were able to end the collection phase successfully, in fact, 7 of them uninstalled the application before the end of the study because their smartphones were not powerful enough to correctly run the application. Anyway, we decided to listen to their insights too, since they provided a valuable contribution to the analysis, keeping in consideration the reasons that led them to abandon the experimentation.

User Experience. Most of the participants [13/20] were comfortable with the experience. P13 and P18 found questions *"quite repetitive"*, while P2 turned the notifications off because he was annoyed by the continuous prompting of notifications. P4, P5, P7, and P20 had issues with the compatibility of the application and their smartphones: even if the Operative System of their device was compliant with the AWARE's requirements, the hardware was not powerful enough to run smoothly such an application.

Intrusiveness. 11 participants told that at the beginning the application was not intrusive, but 5 of them admitted that in the final days of the study they started to feel annoyed by the continuous notifications. P18, instead, became upset in a few days, saying that he *"hated when the notification was prompted while [he] was hanging out with friends"*. P2 said that he had turned off after few days, and since that moment he answered much less EMAs because he did not see them arriving. P1 told that continuous notifications, along with the little variety of the questions, made the experience upsetting. P11 that it was an intrusive and useless experience, because in his opinion, with the questions proposed a person would always have chosen a mild/positive answer unless he/she was severely depressed. Reactions about the questions were quite different, most of the respondents [13/20] did not have a clear opinion about them, but some of the participants [3/20] found the EMAs *"a perfect moment to think about themselves in the everyday routine"* [P14]. P17, instead, said that he felt like judged by the continuous questions and that this fact impacted a lot on the answers given.

EMAs. During the interview, the participants had the possibility of expressing their opinion on the various EMAs used in the study (Fig. 2). For the majority of the participants [14/20], PAM was the preferred question. In fact, according to them, answering by *"choosing an image was much more intuitive and faster than reading a textual EMA"* [P6]. PAM was generally perceived as *"funny and engaging"* [P12]. On the other hand, some participants [P1, P3, P9, and P18] had some reserves on PAM EMA, since they felt constrained by the set of pictures, often perceived as *"too limited"* [P3], or they were *"difficult to interpret"* [P18]. Three Answers question was widely appreciated too. In fact, 11 participants pointed it as the second most preferred EMA, mainly for its shortness [P14, P15, P20] and immediateness [P2, P8, P9]. Even if P5 enjoyed Three Answer EMA, during the interview he expressed some doubts about what a behavioural study can collect from such a short question. Most of the participants did not like PHQ-2, for two main reasons. First, 8 participants found the questions too wordy and admitted that sometimes they did not thoroughly read the question before answering, but they based on their memory. 5 participants, instead, argued the PHQ-2 questionnaire because, in their opinion, questions were too direct and they *"felt obliged to answer in a certain way"* [P7]. Finally, PANAS was the least appreciated question as 13 users pointed out during the interview. 7 of the participants justified this choice with the long-time required to answer to that EMA. On top of that, 6 participants complained about the adjectives on the EMA, saying that giving a score to some of those was not easy. P16 was particularly disappointed by PANAS because he *"always gave a very similar score to all the adjectives"* making him *"feel like a warm person, a person with that as not strong emotion at all"*. Interestingly, in some cases the appreciation of the various EMAs was complementary. In particular, 2 participants, namely P11 and P19, preferred PANAS to all the others EMAs, and found Three Answer the most annoying EMA. These participants justified their choices saying that PANAS was the only question that allowed them to express properly how they felt because the others were too *"short"* [P19] or *"constraining"* [P11]. Both the participants admitted the time necessary to answer an EMA does not influence its likeability, since they considered that time as a time to reflect about themselves, whereas they found much more annoying answering to short questions that they believed to be *"pointless"* [P11].

Influencing Factors. 18 participants affirmed that the location and the activity performed were the main factors to decide whether to respond or not. However, the same group of participants had a very different idea on which are the conditions in which they answered and the ones in which they skipped the questions. More precisely, 9 of the participants said that working hours where a good moment to answer quick questions, whereas the other 9 affirmed that at work they did not want (or have time) to answer EMAs. Similarly, 10 of the participants enjoyed responding EMAs during their spare time, such as at night at home, whereas some of them [P3, P6, and P15] refused to answer EMAs in free time, considering them as "work issues" [P7]. Most of the participants [15/20] agreed that when they were on public transportation they were willing to respond. Some participants elicited concrete contexts in which they were not willing to receive any EMA. For example, when he was using a maps application to get oriented he found that having EMA that opened above the maps to be upsetting. In the same way, P8 participated in a 48-h competition (a hackathon) and, during that time, he deliberately ignored all the EMAs because he did not want to lose the focus on the challenge. Finally, 2 participants said that other variables influenced the most of their decision. P10 noted that when he was in a bad mood, he used to skip more questions, especially the longer ones, such as PANAS. P2, instead, answered EMAs only if he was already using the smartphone when the notification prompted.

Also, the type of EMA prompted played a role in the decision to answer. 7 participants said that the type of questions did not affect the decision to answer because they wanted to be *"collaborative with the study"* [P1]. 8 participants said that the question type influenced the decision only when they had little time to answer, and therefore they skipped long questions such as PANAS, whereas they always responded to faster Questions such as PAM and Three Answers. The remaining 5 participants, instead, *"let [their] personal taste influence the decision, skipping the questions [they] thought to be more tedious"* [P10].

Research Variables. Most of the participants believed that questions like PHQ-2, investigating the depression, were not useful in an environment such as social work, whereas other aspects, like stress, anger, tiredness level, job satisfaction, and emotion regulation, would have provided a much more accurate overview of the employees. P14 suggested to investigate more work-related variables, such as the workload, or the relationship between colleagues, or between colleagues and the families of the assisted. P16, instead, preferred questions to focus on personal introspection and that could lead to moments of personal reflection.

Data Exploitation. Many participants suggested that the collected data, if adequately aggregated, could also have a key role in the strategic decisions within the daycare center. For example, workload information could be used to create a better schedule for the operators [P16], whereas the data about relationships with colleagues could help to do targeted interventions to improve employees' work conditions, and eventually create a more enjoyable environment [P14]. P3 proposed to use EMAs results as KPIs in the quarterly evaluation of the Daycare Center.

5   Lessons Learned

In this section, we describe a set of lessons learned on the design of an EMA-based study that we were able to elicit starting from the literature, the study, and the interviews. These can be considered as a starting point in the design phase of a study.

1 – Keep in Consideration the Participants' Smartphones – EMA applications usually have high requirements in terms of computation and storage capabilities for a smartphone, especially in studies where other sensors data are collected through the smartphone. As a consequence, the researcher should maximize the effort to reduce these requirements as much as possible; otherwise many compatibility problems will arise and, consequently, the results of the study will be compromised. Further precautions can be taken to mitigate this factor; for example, if the EMA application reveals to be battery-draining, participants can be provided with an external battery for their devices.

2 – Find a Good Balance Between the Information Desired and the Effort Required to Answer EMAs – During the process of designing EMAs, the researcher must keep in consideration the effort needed to the respondent to answer the question(s). As a consequence, the choice of the complexity of the question and the interaction pattern of the EMAs should be the one that optimizes the trade-off between the effort required to answer and the information obtained.

3 − Avoid Direct Questions as Much as Possible − In general, the interviews highlighted that direct questions, such as PHQ-2, were perceived worse by study participants. Participants tend to feel judged while answering these kinds of questions and making them less natural in the responses. Additionally, in direct questions respondents have to explicitly admit if something is wrong, inducing the respondents to give false answers.

4 − Prefer Picture-Based EMAs over Textual Ones − Picture-based EMAs are more appreciated for several reasons. First, coherently with Guideline 3, these kinds of EMA are perceived better from the participants since they do not investigate the phenomenon directly. On top of that, users perceive image-based EMAs as more immediate to answer, and therefore less burdening. Finally, as users reported, PAM EMAs are an engaging activity and that can be considered as fun. For this reason, visual contents are an excellent instrument to increase users' appreciation and, consequently, decrease the feeling of burden created by an EMA-based study.

5 − Researcher Through EMAs Is Creating a Moment of Introspection for the Respondents − When people answer to an EMA, they are having a moment of introspection, in which they have the chance of thinking about themselves. The periodical nature of EMA studies can provide to respondents a reminder to think about themselves during the urge of everyday routine. This fact can have immediate benefits in participants' well-being. Additionally, it is an added value to the study that, if adequately underlined during the set-up interview of the studies, can motivate participants to be compliant with the experimentation.

6 − When Data Are Analyzed, Missing Questions Have a Meaning − As interviews highlighted, often the lack of answer has a reason that led the respondent not to answer the EMA. The problem can have very different in nature, depending on the respondent and the moment in which the EMA is prompted. As a consequence, these missing values should not be considered as Missing At Random (MAR) data [29].

7 − Participants Want to Be Involved − The interviews supported Van Berkel's thesis about the importance of users' involvement in the study [40]. In fact, our participants during the interviews argued that having feedback on their answers could have been fun and engaging. The researcher can leverage on the involvement to increase the engagement with the study and, consequently, to obtain better results. There are many ways to increase the participants' involvement, their efficacy depends on the population and the observed phenomena, but making the user feel involved and protagonist of the research is generally a good practice (Table 1).

Table 1. Lessons learned for designing EMA-based studies at a glance

EMA-based studies Lessons Learned
Keep in consideration the participants' smartphones
Find a good balance between the information desired and the effort required to answer EMAs
Avoid direct questions as much as possible
Prefer picture-based EMAs over textual ones
Researcher through EMAs is creating a moment of introspection for the respondents
When data are analyzed, missing questions have a meaning
Participants want to be involved

6 Discussion

In this section, we will discuss some considerations that are worth to be considered from the study and the evicted lessons learned.

Smartphones are a Good Medium for Most People – The study highlighted how smartphones are a good medium for prompting EMAs. The reason is mainly in their pervasiveness [20]. In fact, exploiting smartphones we can have access to a computational device that users have, without the necessity of providing additional hardware, that is expensive for the study designer and burdening for the participant. Additionally, smartphones sensors can be exploited to acquire additional data, that provide further data to the study. On the other hand, as our study highlighted, EMA application can be battery and computationally draining. As a consequence, it is extremely important to optimize the application adopted to avoid this issue. However, there are some cases in which the smartphone is not a good choice. For example, with an aged population accessibility problems may arise [3].

Know Your Population – The interviews showed the importance of the knowing the target population. During the meetings, participants gave insights that could have enhanced the data collection. Knowing users' habits, preferences, and problems can help the design of a better study. Questions can be refined and protocols adjusted to fit participants' needs. If possible, mechanisms of customization, such as adaptive algorithms that exploit Artificial Intelligence and Machine Learning techniques to dynamically adapts the EMAs to the user, should be implemented to tailor the protocol to the single participant as much as possible [27].

Choose the Right Question – The choice of the EMA(s) is the most crucial aspect of any study. The choice of the EMAs can determine the success of the failure of the study. For this reason, researchers should pay extreme attention to their design. There are many variables to be considered, some directly related to the research questions, and others related to the target population. The interviews highlighted that the way a question is formulated has a strong impact on how it is perceived and, consequently, in the answers. In fact, study participants said that they felt judged by direct questions like PHQ-2, and because of that they did not want to answer those questions. On the contrary, they were willing to answer questions they liked, even if they were busy with something else.

Timing – Choosing the right time for prompting the questions is fundamental. EMAs should be prompted often enough to minimize recall bias, but no too often, to minimize the sense of intrusiveness [30]. The time at which questions are prompted strongly influence the compliance. Our interviews showed that there not a *"universally good"* and a *"universally bad"* time, but good and bad moments strictly depends on the single user. Some participants preferred to receive questions in their spare time, others answered only in working ones. Our work highlighted the importance of having a system able to prompt EMAs adapting to the participants' habits. Most of the participants described the time spend to go from home to work, and vice-versa, as a good moment to answer questions.

Engagement of Users – Involving users into the research process can create engagement and, consequently, ensure good compliance to the study. Additionally, answers to the EMA will have a higher quality than the ones obtained with not engaging mechanisms such as remuneration [35]. Other mechanisms, such as gamification, can be exploited to create engagement. Involvement, though, can bring an added value to the research, since there is the possibility of obtaining useful insights from the study participants. During our interviews we had the chance of understanding the participants' point of view, that allowed us to understand the collected data more in detail.

6.1 Limitations and Future Works

Even if the outcomes are interesting, the study presents some limitations. In fact, we run the experimentation with a limited set of participants, 20, and in a very specific scenario, the daycare facilities. Though, the lessons learned we evicted are not scenario-dependent. The research team wants to continue this research on different dimensions. First, we want to conduct a bigger study to refine the lessons learned and collect new interesting insights. Then, the content of the EMAs will be analyzed considering different perspectives, as suggested by the participant of this study, to understand which figures can benefit from the collected data. Finally, another study in a different context will help to understand which other aspects emerge in other contexts.

7   Conclusion

We wanted to collect information about how people interact with Ecological Momentary Assessment, how different EMAs impacts on the results of a study, and which benefits the design of the EMAs can bring to a study. To achieve this result, we ran on-the-field experimentation for 4 weeks with 20 people, who received 15 EMAs per day chosen randomly among 4 possible EMAs. Then, we met singularly the participants in a semi-structured interview. Collected answer revealed many interesting aspects of the study. From those, we were able to elicit a set of lessons learned, useful to the design of most EMA-based studies.

On top of that, we obtained two additional insights. First, we saw that EMA data have a value, not only for behavioral analysis. In fact, Collected data during EMA-based studies are exploitable on different levels beyond research analysis. Many workers in the day centers highlighted how they could benefit from those data. For example, Management could create new KPIs based on the EMAs to measure and evaluate the quality of work in the structures. Human Resources could understand the well being of the employees, and make interventions to improve employees stress level. Finally, dynamics inside the centers could be better studied, finding the problems and understanding which interventions can solve the issues.

Second, we had the possibility to see how Co-design activities are effective to increase participants' engagement. Participants, after the co-design session, were enthusiastic about taking part in such a study, and many of them asked what could they do to help in it. Yet, we do not have quantitative evidence of this aspect, since it was an unexpected outcome of the interview process. Further studies will explore this intuition, see if the improvement is measurable.

Even with the described limitation, the paper explores a set of lessons learned evicted in a real-world scenario that the researcher of an EMA-based study should keep into consideration during the design of the experimentation. Additionally, the insights we gathered allow to understand the participant's perspective in such a study better.

References

1. Adams, P., Murnane, E.L., Elfenbein, M., Wethington, E., Gay, G.: Supporting the self-management of chronic pain conditions with tailored momentary self-assessments. In: Proceedings of the 2017 CHI Conference on Human Factors in Computing Systems, CHI 2017, pp. 1065–1077. ACM, New York (2017). https://doi.org/10.1145/3025453.3025832, http://doi.acm.org/10.1145/3025453.3025832
2. Allen, I.E., Seaman, C.A.: Likert scales and data analyses. Qual. Prog. **40**(7), 64–65 (2007)
3. Arab, F., Malik, Y., Abdulrazak, B.: Evaluation of PhonAge: an adapted smartphone interface for elderly people. In: Kotzé, P., Marsden, G., Lindgaard, G., Wesson, J., Winckler, M. (eds.) INTERACT 2013. LNCS, vol. 8120, pp. 547–554. Springer, Heidelberg (2013). https://doi.org/10.1007/978-3-642-40498-6_44
4. Arches, J.: Social structure, burnout, and job satisfaction. Soc. Work **36**(3), 202–206 (1991)

5. Armey, M.F., Schatten, H.T., Haradhvala, N., Miller, I.W.: Ecological momentary assessment (EMA) of depression-related phenomena. Curr. Opin. Psychol. **4**, 21–25 (2015)
6. Chouinard, E., Walter, S.: Recall bias in case-control studies: an empirical analysis and theoretical framework. J. Clin. Epidemiol. **48**(2), 245–254 (1995)
7. Christensen, T.C., Barrett, L.F., Bliss-Moreau, E., Lebo, K., Kaschub, C.: A practical guide to experience-sampling procedures. J. Happiness Stud. **4**(1), 53–78 (2003)
8. Conner, T.S., Tennen, H., Fleeson, W., Barrett, L.F.: Experience sampling methods: a modern idiographic approach to personality research. Soc. Pers. Psychol. Compass **3**(3), 292–313 (2009)
9. Csikszentmihalyi, M., Larson, R.: Validity and reliability of the experience-sampling method. Flow and the Foundations of Positive Psychology, pp. 35–54. Springer, Dordrecht (2014). https://doi.org/10.1007/978-94-017-9088-8_3
10. Ebner-Priemer, U.W., Trull, T.J.: Ecological momentary assessment of mood disorders and mood dysregulation. Psychol. Assess. **21**(4), 463 (2009)
11. Ferreira, D., Kostakos, V., Dey, A.K.: Aware: mobile context instrumentation framework. Front. ICT **2**, 6 (2015)
12. Fogarty, J., et al.: Predicting human interruptibility with sensors. ACM Trans. Comput.-Hum. Interact. (TOCHI) **12**(1), 119–146 (2005)
13. Hektner, J.M., Schmidt, J.A., Csikszentmihalyi, M.: Experience Sampling Method: Measuring the Quality of Everyday Life. Sage (2007)
14. Hsieh, G., Li, I., Dey, A., Forlizzi, J., Hudson, S.E.: Using visualizations to increase compliance in experience sampling. In: Proceedings of the 10th International Conference on Ubiquitous Computing, pp. 164–167. ACM (2008)
15. Hufford, M.R., Shiffman, S., Paty, J., Stone, A.A.: Ecological momentary assessment: real-world, real-time measurement of patient experience (2001)
16. Intille, S., Haynes, C., Maniar, D., Ponnada, A., Manjourides, J.: μema: microinteraction-based ecological momentary assessment (EMA) using a smartwatch. In: Proceedings of the 2016 ACM International Joint Conference on Pervasive and Ubiquitous Computing, pp. 1124–1128. ACM (2016)
17. Littlewood, D.L., Kyle, S.D., Carter, L.A., Peters, S., Pratt, D., Gooding, P.: Short sleep duration and poor sleep quality predict next-day suicidal ideation: an ecological momentary assessment study. Psychol. Med. **49**(3), 403–411 (2019)
18. Lloyd, C., King, R., Chenoweth, L.: Social work, stress and burnout: a review. J. Ment. Health **11**(3), 255–265 (2002)
19. Löwe, B., Kroenke, K., Gräfe, K.: Detecting and monitoring depression with a two-item questionnaire (PHQ-2). J. Psychosom. Res. **58**(2), 163–171 (2005)
20. Lurie, N.H., et al.: Everywhere and at all times: mobility, consumer decision-making, and choice. Custom. Needs Solut. **5**(1–2), 15–27 (2018)
21. Mattingly, S.M., et al.: The tesserae project: large-scale, longitudinal, in situ, multimodal sensing of information workers. In: Extended Abstracts of the 2019 CHI Conference on Human Factors in Computing Systems, CHI EA 2019, pp. CS11:1–CS11:8. ACM, New York (2019). https://doi.org/10.1145/3290607.3299041, http://doi.acm.org/10.1145/3290607.3299041
22. Obuchi, M., Sasaki, W., Okoshi, T., Nakazawa, J., Tokuda, H.: Investigating interruptibility at activity breakpoints using smartphone activity recognition API. In: Proceedings of the 2016 ACM International Joint Conference on Pervasive and Ubiquitous Computing: Adjunct, pp. 1602–1607. ACM (2016)
23. Okoshi, T., Nozaki, H., Nakazawa, J., Tokuda, H., Ramos, J., Dey, A.K.: Towards attention-aware adaptive notification on smart phones. Pervasive Mob. Comput. **26**, 17–34 (2016)

24. Pollak, J.P., Adams, P., Gay, G.: PAM: a photographic affect meter for frequent, in situ measurement of affect. In: Proceedings of the SIGCHI Conference on Human Factors in Computing Systems, pp. 725–734. ACM (2011)
25. Prinsen, S., Evers, C., Wijngaards, L., van Vliet, R., de Ridder, D.: Does self-licensing benefit self-regulation over time? An ecological momentary assessment study of food temptations. Pers. Soc. Psychol. Bull. (2018)
26. Reichenberger, J., et al.: No haste, more taste: an EMA study of the effects of stress, negative and positive emotions on eating behavior. Biol. Psychol. 131, 54–62 (2018)
27. Riley, W.T., Serrano, K.J., Nilsen, W., Atienza, A.A.: Mobile and wireless technologies in health behavior and the potential for intensively adaptive interventions. Curr. Opin. Psychol. 5, 67–71 (2015)
28. Rooksby, J., Morrison, A., Murray-Rust, D.: Student perspectives on digital phenotyping: the acceptability of using smartphone data to assess mental health. In: Proceedings of the 2019 CHI Conference on Human Factors in Computing Systems, CHI 2019, pp. 425:1–425:14. ACM, New York (2019). https://doi.org/10.1145/3290605.3300655, http://doi.acm.org/10.1145/3290605.3300655
29. Rubin, D.B.: Inference and missing data. Biometrika 63(3), 581–592 (1976)
30. Scollon, C.N., Prieto, C.K., Diener, E.: Experience sampling: promises and pitfalls, strength and weaknesses. In: Diener, E. (ed.) Assessing Well-Being. Social Indicators Research Series, vol. 39, pp. 157–180. Springer, Dordrecht (2009). https://doi.org/10.1007/978-90-481-2354-4_8
31. Shiffman, S.: How many cigarettes did you smoke? Assessing cigarette consumption by global report, time-line follow-back, and ecological momentary assessment. Health Psychol. 28(5), 519 (2009)
32. Shiffman, S., Stone, A.A., Hufford, M.R.: Ecological momentary assessment. Annu. Rev. Clin. Psychol. 4, 1–32 (2008)
33. Söderfeldt, M., Söderfeldt, B., Warg, L.E.: Burnout in social work. Soc. Work 40(5), 638–646 (1995)
34. Spitzer, R.L., Kroenke, K., Williams, J.B., Patient Health Questionnaire Primary Care Study Group, et al.: Validation and utility of a self-report version of PRIME-MD: the PHQ primary care study. Jama 282(18), 1737–1744 (1999)
35. Stone, A.A.: Ecological momentary assessment in survey research. In: Vannette, D.L., Krosnick, J.A. (eds.) The Palgrave Handbook of Survey Research, pp. 221–226. Springer, Cham (2018). https://doi.org/10.1007/978-3-319-54395-6_28
36. Stone, A.A., Shiffman, S.: Ecological momentary assessment (EMA) in behavorial medicine. Ann. Behav. Med. (1994)
37. Thompson, E.R.: Development and validation of an internationally reliable short-form of the positive and negative affect schedule (PANAS). J. Cross Cult. Psychol. 38(2), 227–242 (2007)
38. Trull, T.J., Ebner-Priemer, U.W.: Using experience sampling methods/ecological momentary assessment (ESM/EMA) in clinical assessment and clinical research: introduction to the special section (2009)
39. Turner, L.D., Allen, S.M., Whitaker, R.M.: Interruptibility prediction for ubiquitous systems: conventions and new directions from a growing field. In: Proceedings of the 2015 ACM International Joint Conference on Pervasive and Ubiquitous Computing, pp. 801–812. ACM (2015)
40. Van Berkel, N., Goncalves, J., Hosio, S., Kostakos, V.: Gamification of mobile experience sampling improves data quality and quantity. Proc. ACM Interact. Mob. Wearable Ubiquit. Technol. 1(3), 107 (2017)

41. Versluis, A., Verkuil, B., Lane, R.D., Hagemann, D., Thayer, J.F., Brosschot, J.F.: Ecological momentary assessment of emotional awareness: preliminary evaluation of psychometric properties. Curr. Psychol. 1–9 (2018). https://doi.org/10.1007/s12144-018-0074-6
42. Watson, D., Clark, L.A.: The PANAS-X: manual for the positive and negative affect schedule-expanded form (1999)
43. Weiser, M.: Ubiquitous computing. Computer 10, 71–72 (1993)
44. Witkiewitz, K., Marlatt, G.A.: Relapse prevention for alcohol and drug problems: that was Zen, this is Tao. Am. Psychol. 59(4), 224 (2004)
45. You, C.W., et al.: Soberdiary: a phone-based support system for assisting recovery from alcohol dependence. In: Proceedings of the 33rd Annual ACM Conference on Human Factors in Computing Systems, CHI 2015, pp. 3839–3848. ACM, New York (2015). https://doi.org/10.1145/2702123.2702289, http://doi.acm.org/10.1145/2702123.2702289
46. Yuan, F., Gao, X., Lindqvist, J.: How busy are you?: Predicting the interruptibility intensity of mobile users. In: Proceedings of the 2017 CHI Conference on Human Factors in Computing Systems, CHI 2017, pp. 5346–5360. ACM, New York (2017). https://doi.org/10.1145/3025453.3025946, http://doi.acm.org/10.1145/3025453.3025946
47. Yue, Z., et al.: Photographing information needs: the role of photos in experience sampling method-style research. In: Proceedings of the SIGCHI Conference on Human Factors in Computing Systems, CHI 2014, pp. 1545–1554. ACM, New York (2014). https://doi.org/10.1145/2556288.2557192, http://doi.acm.org/10.1145/2556288.2557192
48. Zhang, X., Pina, L.R., Fogarty, J.: Examining unlock journaling with diaries and reminders for in situ self-report in health and wellness. In: Proceedings of the 2016 CHI Conference on Human Factors in Computing Systems, pp. 5658–5664. ACM (2016)
49. Zhaoyang, R., Sliwinski, M.J., Martire, L.M., Smyth, J.M.: Age differences in adults' daily social interactions: an ecological momentary assessment study. Psychol. Aging 33(4), 607 (2018)

Research on Interactive Usability Evaluation of Mobile Map Navigation Based on User Behavior Pattern

Licheng Deng$^{(\boxtimes)}$ and Zhicheng Ren$^{(\boxtimes)}$

Nanjing University of Science and Technology School of Design Art and Media,
Nanjing 210000, China
532958737@qq.com, 956821843@qq.com

Abstract. According to AHP method and fuzzy comprehensive evaluation method, this paper weighted and verified the interactive usability of mobile terminal map navigation, in order to obtain a reliable interactive usability evaluation system of mobile terminal map navigation. Via questionnaire and statistics analysis, this paper had the results that learnability and fault tolerance had the highest weight value in the first level indexes; and feedback timeliness, comfort in use, information comprehensibility and task completion steps had higher weight value and final scores respectively. The conclusion is that on the subjective emotional level, the first level evaluation index has the greatest influence on learnability; on the information cognitive level, the consistency and memorability of the first level evaluation index have a greater influence; on the objective operational level, the Effectiveness and fault tolerance of the first level evaluation index have a greater influence on the interactive availability of map navigation on the mobile terminal.

Keywords: User behavior mode · Map navigation on mobile terminal · Interactive availability · Evaluation indicator

1 Introduction

With the development of mobile information, map navigation interaction in dynamic environment becomes more and more complex. Facing constantly changing technologies and interactive systems, the user's maladjustment in the interaction process is becoming more and more obvious [1]. Due to the current interaction mode of multi-sensory channel fusion and the application of artificial intelligence technology, the interaction mode, operation process, interface layout and information level of map navigation have been changed, resulting in the user's unclear information, unclear positioning and frequent errors in the use process [1]. Facing the current situation, scholars at home and abroad have proposed many solutions such as deconstruction of human-computer interface, reconstruction of information system, and establishment of evaluation system. However, the current interaction design field has not yet established standard for the application of artificial intelligence technology in map navigation. Therefore, in the field of map navigation interaction at mobile terminal, the influencing

© Springer Nature Switzerland AG 2020
M. Kurosu (Ed.): HCII 2020, LNCS 12181, pp. 404–419, 2020.
https://doi.org/10.1007/978-3-030-49059-1_29

factors of user behavior change and interaction availability. Therefore, the establishment of a systematic and scientific evaluation system is still a matter of concern.

At present, scholars at home and abroad have summed up different evaluation systems according to different specific evaluation objects. Pucillo [2] combines the theory of user experience and interactive availability, and puts forward the model of user experience availability. This is of great help to the research on the evaluation system of map navigation interactive usability in the paper.

Through literature review and questionnaire survey, this paper selected the factors that affect the interactive usability on the subjective emotion, information cognition and objective operation level, established the corresponding evaluation model, explored the influence degree of the factors on the interactive usability of mobile map navigation, and measured the influence degree with a systematic evaluation system, so as to improve the users' experience and interaction quality.

In the first section, this paper summarizes the social status of mobile terminal navigation and the problems of existing solutions. In the second section, based on the efforts made by domestic and foreign scholars in this field, we get the user's behavior mode in the map navigation context and the interactive usability impact level of the corresponding behavior stage. In the third section, we select the evaluation indexes that have a great impact on the interactive usability, and in the fourth section, we evaluate the index weight by experiment and questionnaire scoring, in the fifth section, we calculate the evaluation index score by fuzzy comprehensive evaluation, and in the sixth section, we get the final conclusion.

2   Related Work

2.1   User Behavior Model in the Context of Map Navigation

The user behavior is easily affected by the thinking pattern, which is based on the past experience or rules to quickly evaluate the existing situation. Therefore, in order to eliminate the influence of emotional factors and establish an objective user behavior model, Card et al. [3] proposes a GOMS model, namely goals, operations, methods and selection rules. Based on the four stages of an action in motivational psychology, Norman [4] establishes a user behavior model of human-computer dialogue, which divided human behavior into three parts: goal, execution and evaluation.

In the context of map navigation, the user perceives the environmental information with the navigation system, defines the behavior sequence, executes the action, and completes the action and evaluation finally [5]. At present, researchers have studied user behavior models from various perspectives. From the perspective of user experience, Yang [6] summarizes the logical characteristics of user behavior and the corresponding interface design. Based on the logic of user behavior, Zheng [7] summarizes four design principles of user behavior: consistent behavior, related behavior, similar behavior and behavior contrary. Richard and Jan [8] emphasize the attention to behavior itself in the interaction process, and propose a complete user behavior research process. Wang et al. [9] propose that when users want to complete a certain task, first they need to determine the behavior motivation and have behavior trigger, then they can change the behavior according to the change of using scenes.

To sum up, based on the previous research on user behavior, this paper divided the user behavior into four stages: goal, method, operation and evaluation, which are responding to determination of task, determination of method, sequential execution of action and evaluation of operation effect. The above four stages response to the user determination of destination, selection of navigation mode, entry of navigation mode and the consistency of navigation mode and results (Fig. 1).

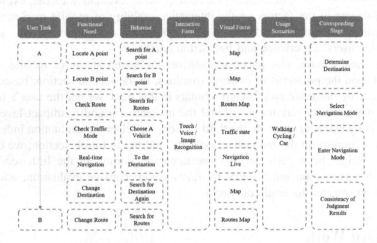

Fig. 1. The user behavior map of navigation

2.2 The Interactive Availability of Map Navigation

At present, the international organization for Standardization (ISO) describes usability as the effectiveness, efficiency and subjective satisfaction of a specific user when using a specific product to complete a specific task in a specific use environment [10]. Nielsen, founder of usability engineering, believes that usability includes learnability, memorability, efficiency, error rate and satisfaction. Nielsen and his colleagues put forward 10 main usability principles: visibility of system state, system should be consistent with the real world, the control and autonomy of users, system consistency and standardization, help users diagnose and repair errors, prevent errors, rely on identification rather than memory, flexibility of operation and minimize design [11] (Fig. 2).

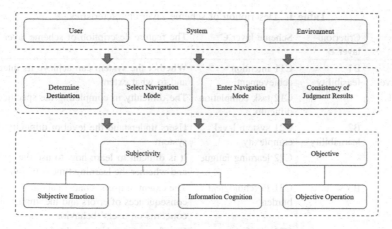

Fig. 2. Ideas of the paper

In a word, this paper combined the four stages of the user in the navigation process to divide the usability target into the subjective emotional level, the information cognitive level and the objective operation level from the subjective and objective interaction usability perspectives.

3 The Formulation of Map Navigation Interactive Availability Evaluation Index

In this paper, when selecting the evaluation indexes of mobile terminal map navigation, we follow the principles of hierarchy, integrity and feasibility.

Based on the above user behavior model, usability goal and usability design principle in the context of mobile terminal map navigation, this paper evaluated the usability of mobile terminal map navigation from the emotional level, cognitive level and objective level. This paper determined the first level evaluation index of navigation interactive usability as feasibility, learnability, security, visibility, memorability and consistency, effectiveness and fault tolerance. There are secondary evaluation indexes under each evaluation objective in the first level. The paper defined the first level as criterion layer, and determined the second level as scheme layer (Table 1).

Table 1. Description of scheme layer characteristics

Target layer A	Criterion layer B	Scheme layer C	The feature description of scheme layer
A1 subjective emotion	B1 feasibility	C11 intention achievement	Whether the system can achieve its intention and to what extent
		C12 task completion difficulty	The difficulty in completing the specified task
	B2 learnability	C21 system level complexity	Users understand the level of difficulty at the system
		C22 learning fatigue	It is difficult to learn how to use the system, and whether the learning time is within 10 min
	B3 security	C31 Psychological burden	The extent of users' concern about the possible consequences of errors and the impact of such concerns on users' behavior
		C32 comfort in use extent	Comfort extent during using process
		C33 help function availability	The usefulness of the help function provided by the system in the event of an unpleasant situation
A2 information cognition	B4 visibility	C41 feedback timeliness	The degree to which the user can timely notice whether the system responds to the current operation
		C42 understanding of system status	The convenience of the current state of the system that users can know in time
	B5 memorability	C51 information density suitability	The reasonable degree of information density that users are exposed to in the process of using
		C52 information quantity suitability	The reasonable degree of the amount of information that users are exposed to in the process of using
	B6 consistency	C61 information comprehensibility	Whether the user can quickly understand the information in the process of using
		C62 Operation Understandability	In the using process, users can quickly understand the operation required to achieve the use purpose
A3 objective operation	B7 effectiveness	C71 task completion steps	The total number of steps after the user completes the specified task
		C72 task completion time	The length of time the user has completed the specified task
	B8 fault tolerance	C81 number of errors	The total number of errors the user has made to complete the specified task
		C82 error correction time	The time from the operation mistakes during the completion of the specified task to the recovery of the correct operation
		C83 error correction method	The way in which the user can recover the correct operation after an error occurs during the completion of the specified task

4 Evaluation Index Weight

4.1 Experiment

Experimental Purpose
The subjects were asked to score the evaluation index according to the specific feelings.

Experimental Equipment
Mobile Baidu map navigation app 10.22.0.960 version.

Participants
Ten participants were invited to participate in the experiment. The age range was from 20 to 30 years old, and the sex ratio was 4:1. The use process was observed in the same use scenario. All subjects had normal hearing, vision and good rest. And a single test lasted about 30 min. In order to avoid the influence of learning effect on the experimental results, the participants were fully familiar with the navigation operation of mobile phones before the experiment. Each subject was not allowed to discuss the problems related to the experiment.

Experimental Process
Set the same navigation destination on Baidu map navigation app, and arrange the participants to complete the same navigation task in the same use scenario. After completing the assigned task, the participants will score the elements according to the relative importance scale of AHP factors. Before the formal experiment, the subjects had 10 min to be familiar with the equipment and scoring rules. During the experiment, the assistant is not allowed to prompt the participants unless they ask for help.

Experimental Result After the subjects completed the assigned navigation task, they were asked to evaluate the first level and second level rating indicators in the approach of AHP. According to the relative importance of the evaluation indicators and the corresponding scale, a judgment matrix was constructed. Finally, the average value was obtained, which is based on the scores of invited people, and a judgment matrix of the average value was constructed (See Table 2). Due to space limitation, only the judgment matrix of the average value of the first level evaluation index is shown here. In this paper, after comprehensive processing, the weight value and other data will be calculated according to the judgment matrix.

410   L. Deng and Z. Ren

Table 2. Judgment matrix of first level evaluation index

	B1	B2	B3	B4	B5	B6	B7	B8
B1	1	1/8	1/4	1/5	½	1/3	1/6	1/6
B2	8	1	5	4	7	6	2	3
B3	4	1/5	1	1/2	3	2	1/3	1/3
B4	5	1/4	2	1	4	3	1/2	1/2
B5	2	1/7	1/3	1/4	1	1/2	1/5	1/5
B6	3	1/6	1/2	1/3	2	1	1/4	1/4
B7	6	1/2	3	2	5	4	1	2
B8	6	1/3	3	2	5	4	1/2	1

4.2 Data Analysis

Calculating Eigenvector and Index Weight of Judgment Matrix
Sum the indexes of each column of judgment matrix A.

$$A_j = \sum_{i=1}^{n_2} a_{ij} \quad i = 1, 2, \ldots, n_1; \ j = 1, 2, \ldots, n_2 \tag{1}$$

In the formulation: n_1 is the number of square matrix rows; n_2 is the number of square matrix arrays.

The new matrix B is obtained by normalizing each index of judgment matrix A.

$$B = \frac{a_{ij}}{A_j} \quad i = 1, 2, \ldots n_1 \ j = 1, 2, \ldots n_2 \tag{2}$$

Sum the indexes of each row of matrix B, and get the eigenvector T_i as follows:

$$T_i = \sum_{j=1}^{n_2} b_{ij} \quad i = 1, 2, \ldots n_1 \ j = 1, 2, \ldots n_2 \tag{3}$$

After the eigenvector T_i is normalized, the index weight W_i is obtained as follows:

$$W_i = |T_i| / \sum |T_i| \quad i = 1, 2, \ldots n_1 \tag{4}$$

After the above steps, the following levels of interactive usability evaluation index weight values are obtained (Table 3).

Table 3. Weight value and ranking of primary evaluation indexes

Evaluating indicator	Weight value
B2 learnability	0.333
B7 effectiveness	0.199
B8 fault tolerance	0.162
B4 visibility	0.115
B3 security	0.077
B6 consistency	0.052
B5 memorability	0.035
B1 feasibility	0.025

Weight analysis of each evaluation index: B2 learnability, B7 effectiveness and B8 fault tolerance are the most important indexes that affect the interactive availability of map navigation on the mobile. B4 visibility and B3 security also have a great impact on the interactive availability of map navigation on the mobile terminal. Among the first level evaluation indexes, the weight value of learnability is the highest, which reflects the users subjective demand for learnability of the interactive system; the second is effectiveness and the third is fault tolerance, which reflect the objective data of the user when using the product objectively; the weight difference among the visibility, security indexes and the top three indexes is small, which indicates that good visibility and security can also greatly improve the interactive usability; B6 consistency, B5 memorability and B1 feasibility account for a relatively small proportion, which have little influence on the interactive usability of map navigation on the mobile, but they are also indispensable factors (Table 4).

Table 4. Weight and ranking of secondary evaluation indexes of interactive availability

Evaluating indicator	Weight value
C41 feedback timeliness	0.875
C71 task completion steps	0.857
C61 information comprehensibility	0.833
C51 information density suitability	0.8
C22 learning fatigue	0.748
C11 intention achievement	0.667
C81 number of errors	0.634
C32 comfort in use	0.584
C31 psychological burden	0.35
C12 task completion difficulty	0.333
C82 error correction time	0.261
C21 system level complexity	0.25
C52 information quantity Suitability	0.2
C62 operation understandability	0.167
c72 task completion time	0.143
c42 understanding of system status	0.125
C83 error correction method	0.106
C33 help function availability	0.061

Numerical analysis of the weight of each evaluation index: C41 feedback timeliness, C71 task completion steps and C61 information comprehensibility are the most important indexes that affect the interactive availability of map navigation on the mobile terminal. C51 information density suitability and C22 learning fatigue also have an important influence on the interactive availability of mobile map navigation. Among the first level evaluation indexes, the weight value of feedback timeliness is the highest, which reflects that users want to get system feedback in time when they are cognizing system information; the second is the operation steps of task completion, which reflects the objective data of users when they are operating products objectively; the weight value of information density suitability and learning fatigue index is not much smaller than the top three indexes' weight value, which indicates that information density suitability and learning fatigue also plays an important role in improving the interactive usability of map navigation on the mobile; the weight values of Comfort in Use and psychological burden are moderate, reflecting the users subjective emotional demands in the interaction process; the relatively small ones are C72 task completion time, C42 system state understanding process, C83 error correction method and C33 help function, which are useful for map guidance on the mobile. The impact of mobile map navigation interactive availability is small, but it should not be ignored when designers want to improve the interactive usability.

Consistency Test of Judgment Matrix
Calculate λ_{max} of Judgment Matrix A.

$$\lambda_{max} = \frac{1}{n_3} \sum (A \cdot W)_i / W_j \quad n_3 \in Z^+ \tag{5}$$

In the formulation: n_3 is the order; Z^+ is the positive integer set; $A \cdot W$ is the multiplication of judgment matrix A and weight set W, $W = (W_1, W_2, W_{n1})$, the result is a column vector.

Calculate the Consistency Index CI of Judgment Matrix A.
The consistency index is calculated by CI. The smaller the CI is, the greater the consistency is. The degree of inconsistency of A is measured by the value of λ - n. The consistency indicators are defined as:

$$CI = \frac{\lambda - n}{n - 1} \tag{6}$$

When CI is close to 0, there is satisfactory consistency; when CI is larger, there is more inconsistency; when CI = 0, there is complete consistency.

In order to measure the size of CI, the random consistency index RI is introduced.

$$RI = \frac{CI_1 + CI_2 + \cdots + CI_n}{n} \tag{7}$$

Considering that the deviation of consistency may be caused by random reasons, when checking whether the judgment matrix has satisfactory consistency, it is necessary to compare CI with random consistency index RI to obtain the test coefficient CR, which is as follows:

$$CR = \frac{CI}{RI} \tag{8}$$

Generally, if CR is in line with CR < 0.1, the judgment matrix is considered to pass the consistency test, otherwise, it will not have satisfactory consistency.

According to the above consistency test steps, we can get (Tables 5 and 6):

Table 5. Consistency test of primary evaluation indexes

Term	Feature vector	Maximum eigenvalue	CI value	RI value	CR value	Consistency test results
B1 feasibility	0.201	8.277	0.04	1.41	0.028	Good
B2 learnability	2.666					
B3 security	0.62					
B4 visibility	0.922					
B5 memorability	0.284					
B6 consistency	0.417					
B7 effectiveness	1.593					
B8 fault tolerance	1.297					

Table 6. Consistency test of secondary evaluation indexes

	Feature vector	Maximum eigenvalue	CI value	RI value	CR value	Consistency test results
C11 intention achievement	1.333	2	0	0	Null	Adopt
C12 task completion difficulty	0.667					
C21 system level complexity	0.5	2	0	0	Null	Adopt
C22 learning fatigue	1.5					
C31 psychological burden	1.063	3.035	0.018	0.52	0.034	Adopt
C32 comfort in use extent	1.752					
C33 help function availability	0.185					
C41 feedback timeliness	1.75	2	0	0	Null	Adopt
C42 understanding of system status	0.25					
C51 information density suitability	1.6	2	0	0	Null	Adopt
C52 information quantity suitability	0.4					
C61 information comprehensibility	1.667	2	0	0	Null	Adopt
C62 operation understandability	0.333					
C71 task completion steps	1.714	2	0	0	Null	Adopt
C72 task completion time	0.286					
C81 number of errors	1.9	3.039	0.019	0.52	0.037	Adopt
C82 error correction time	0.781					
C83 error correction method	0.318					

According to the above data, the weights of the evaluation indexes calculated by AHP in this paper have passed the consistency test. The CI value of the first level evaluation indexes approaches to 0, which has satisfactory consistency and meets the requirements of $CR < 0.1$. The CI value of the second level evaluation indexes of the third group and the eighth group is close to 0, with satisfactory consistency. The CI value of the rest second level evaluation indexes is 0, with consistency. What's more, the CR value meets the requirements of $CR < 0.1$, passing the consistency test.

5   Fuzzy Evaluation Method to Verify Evaluation Indexes

Establish the evaluation object factor domain $U = \{U_1, U_2, U_{n5}\}$, n5 are the number of factors. Create comment set $V = \{V_1, V_2, V_X\}$, X is the number of comments.

In this paper, we set the comment set $V = \{V_1, V_2, V_3, V_4, V_5\}$ and use the 5-point Likert scale to assign 1–5 points to it. 5 points correspond to excellent, 4 points correspond to good, 3 points correspond to medium, 2 points correspond to general, and 1 point corresponds to poorness. V value results are shown in the Table 7:

Table 7. Fuzzy comprehensive evaluation and assignment

Score	Significance
5	Excellent
4	Good
3	Medium
2	General
1	Poor

The fuzzy relation matrix R between the factor index U_i and the evaluation index V_j is established as follows:

$$R = \begin{bmatrix} r_{11} & r_{12} & \cdots & r_{1j} \\ r_{21} & r_{22} & \cdots & r_{2j} \\ \vdots & \vdots & \ddots & \vdots \\ r_{i1} & r_{i2} & \cdots & r_{ij} \end{bmatrix} \tag{9}$$

In the above matrix R: r_{ij} is the membership degree of the i factor index to the j comment, $j = 1, 2... X$.

The fuzzy matrix of matrix R is calculated, and the membership matrix D of standard level to comment set is obtained as follows:

$$D = W. R \tag{10}$$

The fuzzy and comprehensive score E [12] are:

$$E = D. N \qquad (11)$$

In the above formula, N is the set of expert scores.

In this paper, 10 experts are invited to carry out fuzzy evaluation on the evaluation indexes of map navigation interactive usability of mobile terminal. After the fuzzy evaluation matrix is obtained, the comprehensive score is calculated according to the formula of E [12] = D · N, and the full score is 50 points.

It can be seen from the above that the weight value set of the first level evaluation index of the criterion layer is as follows:

$$W_b = \begin{pmatrix} 0.025, 0.333, 0.077, 0.115, 0.035, \\ 0.052, 0.199, 0.162 \end{pmatrix}$$

The second level evaluation index weight sets of scheme level are as follows:

$$W_1 = (0.667, 0.333)$$

$$W_2 = (0.250, 0.748)$$

$$W_3 = (0.350, 0.584, 0.061)$$

$$W_4 = (0.875, 0.125)$$

$$W_5 = (0.800, 0.200)$$

$$W_6 = (0.833, 0.167)$$

$$W_7 = (0.857, 0.143)$$

$$W_8 = (0.634, 0.261, 0.106)$$

According to the above calculation steps, we can get the following formula. The comprehensive evaluation matrix of the first level evaluation index is:

$$R = \begin{bmatrix} D_1 \\ D_2 \\ D_3 \\ D_4 \\ D_5 \\ D_6 \\ D_7 \\ D_8 \end{bmatrix} = \begin{bmatrix} 0.500 & 0.233 & 0.100 & 0.133 & 0.034 \\ 0.375 & 0.275 & 0.226 & 0.099 & 0.025 \\ 0.526 & 0.164 & 0.129 & 0.161 & 0.020 \\ 0.713 & 0.188 & 0.025 & 0.038 & 0.036 \\ 0.520 & 0.340 & 0.040 & 0.060 & 0.040 \\ 0.533 & 0.283 & 0.118 & 0.033 & 0.033 \\ 0.629 & 0.200 & 0.086 & 0.029 & 0.056 \\ 0.485 & 0.116 & 0.121 & 0.174 & 0.104 \end{bmatrix}$$

The final result:

$$D = W_b * R$$

$$= \begin{pmatrix} 0.025 & 0.333 & 0.077 & 0.115 \\ 0.035 & 0.052 & 0.199 & 0.162 \end{pmatrix} \begin{bmatrix} 0.500 & 0.233 & 0.100 & 0.133 & 0.034 \\ 0.375 & 0.275 & 0.226 & 0.099 & 0.025 \\ 0.526 & 0.164 & 0.129 & 0.161 & 0.020 \\ 0.713 & 0.188 & 0.025 & 0.038 & 0.036 \\ 0.520 & 0.340 & 0.040 & 0.060 & 0.040 \\ 0.533 & 0.283 & 0.118 & 0.033 & 0.033 \\ 0.629 & 0.200 & 0.086 & 0.029 & 0.056 \\ 0.485 & 0.116 & 0.121 & 0.174 & 0.104 \end{bmatrix}$$

$$= (0.510 \quad 0.217 \quad 0.135 \quad 0.091 \quad 0.046)$$

The final score is:

$$E_f = D \cdot N = (0.510 \quad 0.217 \quad 0.135 \quad 0.091 \quad 0.046) \begin{bmatrix} 50 \\ 0 \\ 0 \\ 0 \\ 0 \end{bmatrix} = 25.5$$

Similarly, the final score of each evaluation index can be obtained:

According to the above data results, we can conclude that the final evaluation result is excellent. According to the principle of maximum membership, the quality of the interactive usability evaluation system of mobile terminal map navigation established in this paper is excellent (Table 8).

According to the above calculation of membership degree of evaluation indicators at all levels, the following results can be obtained:

- According to the principle of maximum membership, the quality of the first level evaluation index is evaluated as excellent. The weight value of learnability ranks first, which shows that learnability takes a critical position on the interactive availability of mobile map navigation. According to the final calculation score of the secondary index, it can be seen that learning fatigue and system level complexity are essential evaluation factors in the interactive usability evaluation system.
- The maximum membership of the first level evaluation index effectiveness is 0.629, and the ranking of weight value is the second, which proves that this index has an important influence on the interactive availability of map navigation on the objective operation level. According to the final calculation score of the secondary index, it can be seen that task completion steps have a significant influence on interactive usability.
- The maximum membership of the first level evaluation indexes fault tolerance and visibility are 0.485 and 0.713 respectively. The judgment results are excellent and the weight value ranks high, which shows that fault tolerance and visibility also

Table 8. Final scores of primary and secondary evaluation indexes

First level evaluation index	Composite score	Secondary evaluation index	Final score
B1 feasibility	4.032	C11 intention achievement	15.941
		C12 task completion difficulty	14.433
B2 learnability	3.875	C21 system level complexity	10.829
		C22 learning fatigue	13.796
B3 security	4.021	C31 psychological burden	16.164
		C32 comfort in use	16.937
		C33 help function availability	1.412
B4 visibility	4.503	C41 feedback timeliness	22.136
		C42 understanding of system status	4.912
B5 memorability	4.240	C51 information density suitability	18.772
		C52 information quantity suitability	7.416
B6 consistency	4.247	C61 information comprehensibility	18.309
		C62 operation understandability	8.102
B7 effectiveness	4.318	C71 task completion steps	19.991
		C72 task completion time	7.202
B8 fault tolerance	3.696	C81 number of errors	16.755
		C82 error correction time	12.615
		C83 error correction method	1.809

have an important impact on the interactive availability of map navigation. Combined with the final score of secondary indicators, it can be seen that the scores of error number, error correction time and feedback timeliness are high, which are important factors that cannot be ignored.

- The first level evaluation index security has a maximum membership of 0.526, a moderate ranking of weight value. Besides, psychological burden and comfort in use indexes both have a high final score. This situation proves that security index still plays a key role in the interactive usability of map navigation. Interaction designers should consider the subjective feelings of users and pay attention to them in the interaction design.
- The maximum membership degrees of consistency, memorability and feasibility are 0.533, 0.520 and 0.500 respectively. The weight values of these three evaluation indexes rank lower, and their scores are similar. Combined with the final scores of the secondary evaluation indexes, it can be seen that due to different factors such as users' personal experience and status, the users' intention achievement degree and task completion difficulty and information availability are different. In the process of interactive design, interactive designers should pay attention to these factors.

6 Conclusion

According to the calculation and verification results in this paper, the following conclusions can be drawn:

- On the subjective emotional level, learnability and security have the greatest influence on the usability of interaction. Interaction designers should focus on reducing the users' learning fatigue and psychological burden, and improving the users comfort;
- At the level of information cognition, consistency and memorability have a great influence on the usability of interaction. Interaction designers should pay attention to the timeliness of system feedback, the comprehensibility of information and the suitability of information density;
- In the objective operation level, the effectiveness and fault tolerance play a critical role on the interactive usability of map navigation on the mobile terminal. In the interactive design process, the interaction designer should focus on the task completion steps and the number of errors of the system, so as to provide a better interactive experience of map navigation for users.

Through the above literature review and questionnaire survey, this paper analyzed the interactive usability goal of mobile map navigation from the subjective and objective perspective, selected the factors that affect the interactive usability on the subjective emotion, information cognition and objective operation level, established the corresponding evaluation model, and explored the influence of the factors on the interactive usability of mobile map navigation on the three perspectives. The systematic evaluation system is used to measure the impact, so as to provide a meaningful optimization strategy for improving the interactive quality of user map navigation and provide better interactive experience for users in the navigation process of applying artificial intelligence technology. However, due to the small number of people in the questionnaire, the final evaluation system is not comprehensive enough, which needs further improvement and optimization.

Acknowledgement. This work was supported by the help of Bin Jiang and Zhicheng Ren. I would like to extend my sincere gratitude to all those who helped me during the writing of this thesis.

References

1. Jiang, L.J., Li, J.Y., Li, Z.L., Wu, Z.H., Zhang, Y.: Experience measurement of three navigation interfaces in virtual riding. J. Graph. **39**(03), 515–521 (2018)
2. Pucillo, F., Cascini, G.: A framework for user experience, needs and affordances. Des. Stud. **35**(2), 160–179 (2014)
3. Card, S.K., Moran, T.P., Newell, A.: The Psychology of Human-Computer Interaction. L. Erlbaum Associates Inc. (1986)
4. Norman, D.: The Design of Everyday Things. Basic Books inc., New York (2002)

5. Ma, X.C., Zhang, L.: Navigation map information design in the digital age. Packag. Eng. **39**(22), 241–245 (2019)
6. Yang, J.: The behavior logical thinking of smartphone APP user interface design. Packag. Eng. **39**(22), 241–245 (2018)
7. Zheng, L.X.: Product design rules based on the user behaviors. Packag. Eng. **37**(14), 73–76 (2016)
8. Jan, C., Richard, B.: Hidden in Plain Sight. Harper Collins, New York (2013)
9. Wang, W.W., Liu, Y.Z., Yang, X.Y., Liao, K.: Research on cultural and creative product design guided by user behavior and context. Packag. Eng. **40**(24), 27–32 (2019)
10. Cao, Y., He, R.K.: Usability evaluation based on the interaction mode of washing machine control area. Packag. Eng. **40**(20), 81–87 (2019)
11. Nielsen, J.: Usability Engineering. Academic Press, Boston (1993)
12. Zeng, D., Li, K.G, Cheng, H.F, Zhou, Z., Qiu, S.P.: Evaluation method and application of vehicle driving experience based on FCE-AHP. Mod. Manuf. Eng. (11), 67–73 + 106 (2019)

The Problems with Usability Testing

Peter Gregory Dunn[✉] and Alice Hayes

NatWest Group, London, UK
peter.gregory.dunn@gmail.com

Abstract. Most books discussing User Experience (UX) or usability often dedicate sections or entire chapters to an introduction to usability testing as a valid and reliable method to identify issues that occur within a given interface or system [e.g., 1, 3, 6, 10]. Indeed, there is an entire book written about specific methods and application of usability testing [e.g., 6]. Despite the plethora of books discussing usability testing, Rolf Molich and his colleagues have found variance in the usability issues found even amongst agency experts [e.g., 12, 13, 14]. These variances suggest that usability testing might often be inconsistently applied across the UX field. From our experience in industry, we put forth in this paper commonly problems with usability testing, which can result in the inconsistencies applied across the UX field. These problems are contrasted against suggested protocol found in literature, which provides a basis to support discussion of solutions and provide recommendations to new researchers.

Keywords: Usability testing · Evaluation · Research methods

1 The Problem with Usability Testing

Usability testing is the most commonly used method applied by User Experience (UX) professionals to evaluate the usability and the overall experience of a given interactive system [7]. Indeed, textbooks designed for introductory courses in UX, Human-Computer Interaction (HCI), Human-Centred Design (HCD), or similar almost certainly have a section or an entire chapter devoted to usability testing [e.g., 1, 3, 10, 17]. Despite such a focus on usability testing amongst and from UX professionals, several authors have noted variances amongst UX professionals concerning the outcomes of tests run on the same interface [e.g., 11, 12, 13, 14]. Lindgaard and Chattratichart [11] had found that the number of tasks provided in testing was positively correlated to the percentage of problems found and of new problems. So, these findings suggest that some of the variances in UX professionals' usability test results can be explained by how many tasks they cover in their testing. Nonetheless, there is one undeniable truth that can be stated given the results from the CUE studies made by Molich and colleagues [e.g., 12, 13, 14]; As Molich et al. stated [14] the, "simple assumption that we are all doing the same and getting the same results in a usability test is plain wrong." In the present paper, we present a thesis to explain alternative or additional reasons that may explain the variances found amongst UX professionals' usability testing results.

© Springer Nature Switzerland AG 2020
M. Kurosu (Ed.): HCII 2020, LNCS 12181, pp. 420–430, 2020.
https://doi.org/10.1007/978-3-030-49059-1_30

Addressing the variance of usability testing results amongst UX professionals is important because arguably it impacts the perception of those who use UX professional services. Simply put, if stakeholders cannot receive reliable services and findings, how are they to know what is a serious issue from a spurious result? Molich et al.'s CUE showing this variance of usability testing results have also gained substantial attention from the UX field as well, as evidenced by the over 500 citations gained for these papers [i.e., 12, 13, 14]. To address the issue of usability testing variance, we have introduced five potential problems with usability testing, which are supported by both academic evidence as well as some of our own experiences in industry. Recommendations are offered to address each problem. Nonetheless, each problem is introduced in hopes that future researchers will pick up the baton and further investigate the legitimacy and potential impact of each problem.

To provide some additional context, a brief history of usability testing will be reviewed prior to proceeding to identified problems. Finally, in terms of scope, focus is restricted to lab usability testing, and not remote variations of usability testing. This focus is in line with Molich et al.'s papers [e.g., 12, 13, 14], which has served as the impetus for the present paper.

1.1   A Brief History of Usability Testing

It is interesting to note that there are limited academic books and papers written on the history of Human-Computer Interaction (HCI), let alone the history of usability testing specifically [e.g., 15, 17, 19]. Most accounts of HCI in the academic literature generally attribute the origins of the field starting with Xerox PARC back in the late 1970s and early '80s [e.g., 15, 17]. Still, some online sources indicate the beginnings of HCI began in World War I and World War II [e.g., 19, 20]. Whitby [20] specifically discusses the role of evaluation in cockpit design in World War II, as human factors and psychology make their first attempts at scientifically evaluating and improving human performance and the interaction design for a given system (i.e., the cockpit). It is therefore argued that the beginnings of usability testing began during WWII during the 1940's. If one is interested in a more complete historical review of HCI, then Norman [17] is recommended for in an in-depth history.

Early usability testing as described by Norman [17] and Whitby [20] suggests most testing from WWII and during the PARC era was validation testing in nature. Validation testing describes a specific type of usability testing where a given system or interface is tested with specific tasks, which are measured against predetermined usability standards or benchmarks [18]. Since those times, however, Rubin and Chisnell [18] have suggested that the most common type of usability testing among the four they have identified, is assessment testing. Assessment testing is described as a cross between more exploratory research, and a more objective and measured test similar to validation testing. Participants will perform tasks, as with validation testing, but performance is not assessed against predetermined benchmarks. Rubin and Chisnell suggest that quantitative measures are taken, but there is dialogue between participant and facilitator to explore any issues encountered by the participant. In sum, assessment testing lies somewhere along a continuum that describes how to carry out usability testing. It lies between validation testing at one extreme, and exploratory testing at the other, where no tasks are defined, and participants are asked to evaluate the design concept in an exploratory manner. Of note, the fourth and final type of usability testing Rubin and Chisnell identify is comparative usability testing, where researchers compare two systems or interfaces against each other [18]. Furthermore, comparative usability testing is carried out as part of any of the other three usability test types already mentioned above.

Rubin and Chisnell provide a good overview of the different usability testing methods [18, See Figure 1]. The popular assessment testing is problematic, however, because of how it lies on a continuum between two defined extreme forms of testing. Most UX professionals are familiar with usability testing as a method of research via introductory texts [e.g., 1, 3, 18]. The problem as evidenced by Molich's research, however, is in the application of usability testing [e.g., 12, 13, 14]. It is argued that relatively few UX professionals practicing usability testing have been formally trained or familiarized themselves with the few texts that deal specifically with *when* to conduct a usability test, and *how* to facilitate it [e.g., 6, 18]. Therefore, the identified problems are issues that arguably occur as a result of a popular research method applied in UX, by professionals who may have a limited understanding of when and how to apply it (Fig. 1).

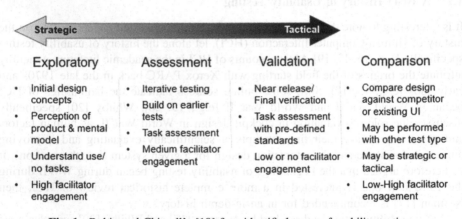

Fig. 1. Rubin and Chisnell's [18] four identified types of usability testing.

2   Identified Problems

2.1   Usability Testing as the Wrong Method

Usability testing is recognized as a keystone and one of the principal methods to evaluate the design and usability of a system during development, before release [e.g., 1, 7, 18]. Arguably, it is used so predominantly and broadly that it is used in various situations or contexts where a different approach is more appropriate. In other words, this *go-to* method for UX professionals is applied too often and in the wrong situations. Too many UX professionals simply use this method as a matter of course, without thinking about: 1) where they are in the design process, 2) the design problem that is being addressed, 3) what information the team requires to move the project forward, 4) the research challenge they are trying to solve.

As early as 2008, Saul Greenberg and Bill Buxton also questioned the broad application of usability testing in their article titled, *Usability Evaluation Considered Harmful (Some of the Time)* [7]. In their influential paper, Greenberg and Buxton argue that while usability testing may be valuable in many contexts, it's heavy push as a central method to use for evaluation in all situations limits our ability to pursue more explorative techniques that enrich our understanding of the problems we are trying to solve. Thereby enabling more creative solutions to these problems. Fundamentally, they argue that it is the responsibility of the researcher to thoughtfully consider the research questions and situation they are trying to address, and from that come up with appropriate method(s) that will effectively address these questions and situation. While CHI has embraced usability evaluation because of its utility in most research contexts, it is not *always* the right approach.

Eight years later, and Hertzum [9] further questioned how usability testing is applied during development and testing of a product or service. While Hertzum does not question the application of the methodology itself, he does question when and how it is best applied during the development process.

These few articles that appear to directly question the broad use of usability testing as a method are testament to the industry's blind faith in its use. Whilst certainly there are many occasions where usability testing is effectively used, these articles indicate there are too many instances when usability testing is incorrectly applied. Figure 2 presents a double diamond approach as described by Austin [2]. Given the double diamond framework, it is argued that usability testing is most effectively used as an assessment research approach as defined by Rubin and Chisnell [18]. Thus, usability testing is limited in providing effective and insightful results in most instances where design is at a more exploratory phase according to the double-diamond process.

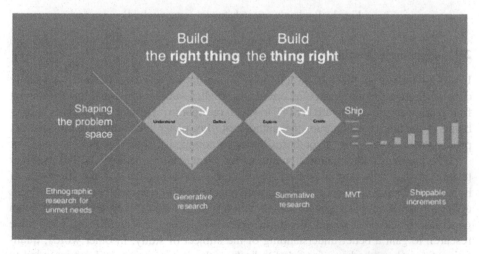

Fig. 2. Double diamond framework as presented by Jane Austin [2].

Recommendation: Choosing the Right Method. One way to support UX professionals choose a more appropriate method of research would be to supply them with a framework, which supports decision of research method given the stage of the project. One such framework that has come from industry, which integrates well with the double-diamond design process, is Emma Boulton's *Research Funnel* [4]. Boulton's Research Funnel separates research into four distinct phases directly linked with the stage of the design project (see Fig. 3). Further fleshing this model out to more strictly define when to conduct usability testing and disseminating that information may prove helpful to the UX industry.

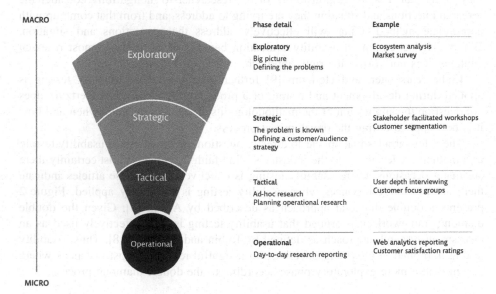

	Phase detail	Example
MACRO		
Exploratory	**Exploratory** Big picture Defining the problems	Ecosystem analysis Market survey
Strategic	**Strategic** The problem is known Defining a customer/audience strategy	Stakeholder facilitated workshops Customer segmentation
Tactical	**Tactical** Ad-hoc research Planning operational research	User depth interviewing Customer focus groups
Operational	**Operational** Day-to-day research reporting	Web analytics reporting Customer satisfaction ratings
MICRO		

Fig. 3. Boulton's research funnel framework [4].

2.2   Hypothesis Testing Versus Objectives Setting

Usability testing in the lab is definitely a qualitative research method, especially considering the literature often recommends smaller sample sizes ranging from about four participants tested iteratively [4], to seven or eight [5]. Despite lab usability testing being a qualitative technique, the authors of this paper have often witnessed UX professionals developing "hypotheses" prior to conducting their research.

The problem with creating hypotheses for a qualitative method like lab usability testing is that it is simply wrong. Hypotheses are generated for the purposes of hypotheses testing is inherently a quantitative technique to statistically make inferences about a population, based on the sample that has been tested [7]. Hypotheses are often generated based on a sound literature review, or indeed, by conducting qualitative research to gain a better understanding of the subject of study. In other words, qualitative research methods are intended to be hypothesis-generating, and not intended to deduce the validity of a given hypothesis.

So why would UX professionals feel they need to create hypotheses for conducting usability testing? Perhaps one reason why the practice is done is to give their stakeholders the appearance that usability testing research is an objective and robust research. Arguably, the authors' experience suggests that UX researchers are often stating *objectives* for the usability testing, but labelling these as *hypotheses* and, sometimes, using wording to mirror what would often be considered an alternative hypothesis. For example, when testing navigation of a shopping journey a hypothesis might say, *most users are unable to complete a shopping journey without assistance*. Such a statement is problematic because it has the potential to bias the UX professional one way or another before any research has taken place. Another example when testing the proposition of a new product might be, *Users will like the proposition because of its properties X, Y, and Z*. Hypotheses like the latter are even more dangerous because, not only do these hypotheses have potential to bias the research, but they also present a danger of the UX professional making baseless claims about the potential success of a product.

Recommendation: Setting Objectives. As Rubin and Chisnell [18] suggest, it is perfectly reasonable to acquire quantitative measures in usability testing. Often these quantitative measures take the form of time to complete task, number of errors, number of prompts, or from survey ratings taken from participants reflecting their attitudes or opinions about the system they just tested. UX practitioners must be careful when collecting these quantitative measures when conducting typical usability tests consisting of approximately five participants. Five participants are nowhere near the required amount to make generalizations about the results of these measures applied to entire population of users. Instead, it must be made clear that, in most cases, UX professionals need to decide on predetermined criteria that these measures must meet to satisfy a defined usability standard. Any other use of quantitative measurement with such small sample sizes is arguably pointless.

2.3   Construction of Protocol

As stated in the introduction, texts intended to provide budding UX professionals with an introduction to this field will often include a section or chapter for usability testing [e.g., 1, 3, 10, 17]. Unfortunately, these texts only provide an overview of the logistics for setting up this kind of research (e.g., participant recruitment, equipment and set up, defining objectives, setting tasks). None of these texts go into sufficient detail concerning how to construct tasks and questions for these sessions, and none provided any reference to books like Rubin and Chisnell [18], or Dumas and Loring [6], which cover this issue with sufficient detail. Rubin and Chisnell have provided a good overview and classification of the types of usability tests, and adequate detail on how one might go about preparing the protocol. Dumas and Loring, however, go into detail on how to prepare, as well as the setting up of tasks and questions.

When comparing the referenced texts meant to train UX professionals on research methods to market research texts meant to train market researchers on proper protocol [e.g., 5, 8], the UX texts are severely lacking in the detail required to properly train professionals on UX research protocol. Indeed, only Dumas and Loring [6] adequately addresses issues for avoiding leading questions, but does not address double-barreled or hypothetical questions, which are addressed in market research texts [e.g., 5, 8]. The lack of providing proper protocol information in texts dealing with usability testing means that there are a lot of UX professionals who simply are ignorant of these issues in questionnaire or interview protocol construction, or it is left to chance that they are properly trained by a UX professional who knows proper interview protocol construction. In our combined 25 years' experience, we have often encountered scripts from UX professionals that contain questions that are leading, double-barreled, or hypothetical questions. All of these types of questions are known to undermine the integrity of the research, and there would almost certainly be variance in results found between professionals were ignorant about avoiding these types of questions, versus professionals who understood how to avoid these questions and construct robust research protocol.

Recommendation: Awareness is Key. Fault for this ignorance amongst some UX professionals for effective and robust protocol construction lies with the UX professional bodies. When compared against market research, the market research texts and, presumably courses, do a better job of educating market researchers in detail on how to carry out various market research methods [e.g., 5, 8]. Ideally, the UX profession has to do a better job in their texts, and arguably coursework in at least some cases, to provide detailed instruction concerning how to construct good research protocol and what types of questions to avoid.

2.4   Facilitation of Usability Testing

Facilitation of usability testing often suffers similar problems to those identified in the previous section concerning the construction of testing protocol. In fact, in our experience, if the test script contains problems with the way questions are constructed, often there are issues with facilitation as well. Also like the previous section, only one book in the UX literature properly covers how to facilitate a usability testing session, and what issues to avoid [i.e., 6]. In their book, Dumas and Loring [6], tackle subjects nearly always overlooked in other books on UX. These subjects include giving participants enough time to speak and sufficiently answer questions, when to interrupt, how and when to prompt during tasks, and how to handle delicate situations that inevitably occur in some sessions. Finally, Dumas and Loring state that there is no perfect usability test, but it is important that facilitators can reflect on their last session and understand what went well and what could be improved.

The results of any given round of usability testing is influenced most by how the testing is facilitated by a UX professional. In our experience, strong facilitators will enable participants to tell a story that expresses where the issues are in the system or interface that is being tested, and most importantly, *why* these issues are important to rectify for the participant. It is the stories, and the reasons why that support these stories that provides powerful results in qualitative research. Strong facilitators grasp the importance of storytelling and understanding the underlying reasons why participants say or do things during testing. They pull this information out of participants, seemingly effortlessly at times. Weaker facilitators who have not been properly trained tend to stay at a surface level, meaning that they do not probe to understand why participants behaved a certain way or provided a given response. These facilitators are prone to identifying an issue without fully gathering an understanding of why the issue is problematic for the user. Furthermore, weaker facilitators are more prone to glaze over issues and miss identifying them. Ultimately, it is argued that results from weaker facilitators, which lack that deeper understanding of issues, makes it more difficult for design teams to effectively address a given issue. Thus, it is argued that this usability testing problem may explain some of the variation found in Molich et al.'s CUE papers [e.g., 12, 13, 14]. It is important that discrepancies between the quality of facilitators is minimized so that more consistent results from usability testing can be obtained regardless of who is the facilitator.

Recommendation: Proper Facilitation Mentoring. Effective facilitation of usability testing can be tougher than it looks (see Fig. 4). Similar to the previous usability testing problem, it is the responsibility of experienced UX professionals and their professional associations to set up mentoring programs. A certification for experienced UX professionals that may mirror that of the Market Research Society (MRS). It would mean proper training regarding facilitation of usability testing among other UX research methods, and novice UX professionals can see what "good" looks like by observing experienced and certified professionals. Experienced UX professionals would then mentor novice UX professionals until a level of competency is achieved in facilitation skills.

Fig. 4. Facilitation in lab usability testing can be tougher than it looks.

2.5 Reporting

Several UX texts do address reporting the results of a usability test [e.g., 1, 10, 18]. Nonetheless, reporting is the culmination of everything the facilitator had done prior to this point. Therefore, if there were problems with the usability testing prior to reporting, then reporting would be influenced accordingly. For instance, we have experienced several instances where UX professionals report on the likelihood that a concept might be a success, based on the responses these professionals gathered during testing. This can be problematic because, as stated earlier, it is statistically not possible to suggest that a concept may or may not be a success based on the opinion of five or six participants in a round of usability testing. While that example might seem blatantly obvious to point out here, there are other more common ways that UX professionals use, which subtly communicate to stakeholders that an inferential statistic is being made from a sample size of about five participants, to their population of users. These ways include using percentages to express success/failure or some other type of behavior (e.g., where participants clicked) during testing; or using the numbers of participants who was successful or unsuccessful in a task out of the total number of participants (e.g., 2 out of 5 failed) when no predetermined standards were agreed on prior to testing. The latter may seem particularly contentious, but we would argue if no predetermined standards were set, then the test is more exploratory in nature and, therefore, *why* these participants failed should take precedence over how many.

How reports are written and delivered can be especially problematic. If reporting as described above does explain some of the variance witnessed in Molich et al.'s research [e.g., 12, 13, 14], then it presents a fundamental issue for the UX profession. Specifically, poor reporting can set improper expectations from naïve stakeholders concerning what can, and what cannot be determined from a usability test. For example, imagine a senior executive stakeholder of a large corporation has invested in usability testing of a new concept the corporation will launch in the coming months. The usability testing report indicates that if certain changes are made, then the concept should be a success. An experienced UX professional would know that such a statement is patently wrong: usability testing can de-risk a new concept, but it cannot determine outright whether or not a concept will be a success. Still, if this is the senior executive's first experience with usability testing, then s/he knows no better, and in its simplest form, one of two things are likely to happen: 1) The concept fails and the senior executive distrusts the practice of usability testing as a whole, of 2) The concept is a success and the senior executive has an expectation set that usability testing can effectively predict the success of a concept. Either way, the experience sets a bad precedent and one that an experience UX professional must unnecessarily overcome to promote the value of UX research.

Recommendation: Texts and Templates. It may be helpful for new UX professionals to read in texts what is and what is not acceptable to report in usability testing reports, and why these rules are in place (e.g., setting expectations as described above). Templates may be used in texts and by experience UX professionals disseminating these templates to less experienced professionals for them to understand what a "good" report looks like.

3 Conclusion

There may exist more problems with usability testing that have not been identified in this paper. Nonetheless, given the literature and through our professional experience, we feel that these five problems identified are the most notable. Therefore, it is argued that the five problems identified in this paper contribute to the variation in perceived quality of UX research in the industry, and must be addressed to help stop inaccurate stakeholder expectations and negative perceptions of UX from other disciplines.

This is not a full treatise about usability testing and its problems. Nonetheless, each problem is introduced in hopes that future researchers will pick up the baton and further investigate the legitimacy and potential impact of each problem. Therefore, we encourage others to test the validity assumptions and arguments made in this paper. As with any researcher, we would be very interested to better understand what drives variation in usability test findings. With that better understanding, it is hoped that the UX community could work toward solutions that would improve the consistency, validity, and efficacy of UX research as a whole.

References

1. Allen, J., Chudley, J.: Smashing UX Design: Foundations for Designing Online User Experiences. Wiley, London (2012)
2. Austin, J.: All the things you need when you want great design. Presented at Turing Fest (2017). https://www.turingfest.com/2017/product/jane-austin. Accessed 24 Feb 2020
3. Benyon, D.: Designing User Experience: A Guide to HCI, UX and Interaction Design, 4th edn. Pearson, Harlow (2019)
4. Boulton, E.: The research funnel. https://medium.com/@emmaboulton/the-reseach-funnel-617b8333ad7f. Accessed 24 Feb 2020
5. Brace, I.: Questionnaire Design: How to Plan, Structure and Write Survey Material for Effective Market Research. Kogan Page, London (2018)
6. Dumas, J.S., Loring, B.A.: Moderating Usability Tests: Principles and Practices for Interacting. Morgan Kaufmann, Burlington (2008)
7. Greenberg, S., Buxton, B.: Usability evaluation considered harmful (some of the time). In: CHI 2008: Conference on Human Factors in Computing Systems 2008, pp. 111–120. ACM, Florence (2008)
8. Hague, P., Cupman, J., Harrison, M., Truman, O.: Market Research in Practice: An Introduction to Gaining Greater Market Insight. 3rd edn. London (2016)
9. Hertzum, M.: Usability testing: too early? Too much talking? Too many problems? J. Usability Stud. 11(3), 83–88 (2016)
10. Krug, S.: Don't Make Me Think: A Common Sense Approach to Web Usability, 2nd edn. New Riders, Berkeley (2006)
11. Lindgaard, G., Chattratichart, J.: Usability testing: what have we overlooked? In: CHI 2007: Proceedings of the SIGCHI Conference on Human Factors in Computing Systems 2007, pp. 1415–1424. ACM, San Jose (2007)
12. Molich, R., et al.: Comparative evaluation of usability tests. In: UPA 1998: Proceedings of the Usability Professionals Association 1998. UPA, Washington, DC (1998). http://www.dialogdesign.dk/tekster/cue1/cue1paper.pdf. Accessed 24 Feb 2020

13. Molich, R., Dumas, J.S.: Comparative usability evaluation (CUE-4). Behav. Inf. Technol. **27** (3), 1–22 (2008)
14. Molich, R., Ede, M.R., Kaasgaard, K., Karyukin, B.: Comparative usability evaluation. Behav. Inf. Technol. **23**(1), 65–74 (2004)
15. Myers, B.A.: A brief history of human computer interaction technology. ACM Interact. **5**(2), 44–54 (1996)
16. Nielsen, J.: How many test users in a usability study. https://www.nngroup.com/articles/how-many-test-users/. Accessed 24 Feb 2020
17. Norman, K.L.: Cyberpsychology: An Introduction to Human-Computer Interaction, 2nd edn. Cambridge University, Cambridge (2017)
18. Rubin, J., Chisnell, D.: Handbook of Usability Testing: How to Plan, Design, and Conduct Effective Tests, 2nd edn. Wiley, Indianapolis (2008)
19. Soegaard, M.: The history of usability: From simplicity to complexity. https://www.smashingmagazine.com/2012/05/the-history-of-usability-from-simplicity-to-complexity/. Accessed 24 Feb 2020
20. Whitby, B.: Flying lessons: what aviation investigations tell other disciplines about user interfaces. https://uxbri.org/2013/#blay-whitby-profile. Accessed 24 Feb 2020

Proposal of Quality in Use in Software Quality

Shin'ichi Fukuzumi[1]([⊠]), Nowky Hirasawa[2], Noriko Wada[3],
Toshihiro Komiyama[4], and Motoei Azuma[5]

[1] RIKEN, Center for AIP, Tokyo, Japan
Shin-ichi.fukuzumi@riken.jp
[2] Otaru University of Commerce, Otaru, Japan
[3] Meditrina, Tokyo, Japan
[4] NEC Corporation, Tokyo, Japan
[5] Waseda University, Tokyo, Japan

Abstract. Both product quality and quality in use which are positioned in software quality model deal with "usability" for users. The former, usability is positioned as one of product quality. The latter, usability is dealt with outcome of use by using product, system and service as quality. Especially, it is necessary for quality in use to consider influence on not only users when interact directly but also wider stakeholders. For this, it is important to prepare a model to realize making a product which usable for users and which effective for almost stakeholders by using the product. In this paper, we cluster four target user groups, they are, "operator of system and/or software", "organization which has responsibility for system and/or software management", "customer using system and/or software" and "Society which exists system and/or software". According to these clustering, we propose four models about quality in use correspond to target users.

Keywords: Software · Quality · Usability · Public · Environment

1 Introduction

From the end of the last century, importance of usability has been considered in not only ergonomics area but also software engineering area. Quality model in SQuaRE (System and software Quality Requirement and Evaluation) series which are dealt with in ISO/IEC JTC1SC7 defined effectiveness, efficiency, satisfaction freedom from risk and context coverage as elements of "Quality in Use" [25010]. Figure 1 shows the Quality in Use model defined in ISO/IEC 25010.

In this figure, three quality characteristics (effectiveness, efficiency, satisfaction) are same as usability elements defined in ergonomics standard ISO 9241-11: 2018 [2]. About freedom from risk and context coverage, though influence on economy and health is described in the definition, there is no concrete contents. Context of use is mainly focused on interaction directly.

© Springer Nature Switzerland AG 2020
M. Kurosu (Ed.): HCII 2020, LNCS 12181, pp. 431–438, 2020.
https://doi.org/10.1007/978-3-030-49059-1_31

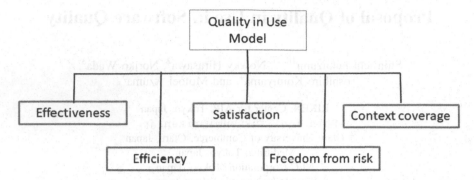

Fig. 1. Quality in Use model defined in ISO/IEC 25010 [1]

However, object of quality in use shall be not only simple direct interaction but also many stakeholders and society which are influence on indirectly by someone use the product, system and service.

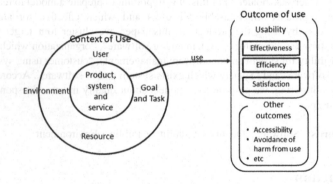

Fig. 2. Usability concept (ISO9241-11, modified) [2]

For example, interaction operator (direct user) with a control panel in electric power supply company, organization (indirect user) who manages and distributes by using the results, residents, government and/or public (stakeholders except direct user/indirect user) who are affected (e.g. black out) by the results used in the organization. In case of self-driving car, direct user is a driver, indirect users are persons' who sits a passenger's seat or customer in commercial car, stakeholders except direct user/indirect user are other cars exist on road or pedestrian or government/local government managed road and traffic networks. It is necessary to expand models after having made use of a conventional quality characteristic as influence on them cannot be represent only by quality characteristics shown in Fig. 1.

As trend of standardization in ergonomics area, ISO 9241-11:2018 (Usability: concept and definition) shows clearly that usability is outcome of "use" in identified context of use. Figure 2 shows the usability concept. Moreover, "accessibility" and "avoidance of harm from use" are positioned as other outcome of use. From these, effective, efficiency and satisfaction are dealt as outcome of use directly.

2 Purpose of Quality in Use

As system and software products are widely used in our life, use of them is influence on not only their direct uses but also organizations and society.

It is responsibility for society of the manufacturer to be controllable these influence as much as possible.

From this, quality is regarded influence on stakeholders by using. The purpose of quality in use is that manufacturers and managers are able to enforce to "use" for improvement of quality by measuring and evaluating [3].

The objectives which are influenced by use of system and software in not only their direct users but also included various kinds of stakeholders. Contents of influence (quality characteristics) are different by the difference of objects. From this, the paper classifies these objects into four groups shown below and quality in use model for each group is defined.

- Operator of system and/or software
- Organization which has responsibility for system and/or software management
- Customer using system and/or software
- Society which exists system and/or software

When "quality in Use" is considered, it is necessary to clarify which group is focused. Because quality models for use of system and product are different by the difference of objects described above influence is different by different of target when considering quality of same product or system by use.

In this paper, terms are defined as follows:

- Definition of "Quality in Use"
  Quality in Use is influence on users and/or public by using product, system or service
  Influence is represented as quality
- Definition of "User"
  Individual or group that interacts with a system or benefits from a system during its utilization (ISO/IEC/IEEE 12207:2017), (ISO/IEC/IEEE 15939:2017) [4, 5].

3 Quality in Use Models

According to the previous section, objects of quality in use are considered to be divided into four groups. Figure 3 show the quality in use models for four groups.

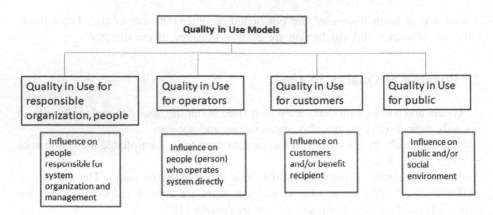

Fig. 3. Quality in use models for four target groups

In this figure, each box about quality in use, that is, "quality in use for responsible organization, people", "quality in use for operators", "quality in use for customers" and "quality in use for public" is object group of quality in use, respectively. Below four boxes describes influence by use.

In this, "quality in use for operators" is correspond to the original quality in use model. As this model mainly focuses on direct user, we consider that elements of usability defined in ISO9241-11:2018 should be adopted as quality characteristics in this model. Quality characteristics for the other three objects shall be defined by terms which represented each influence suitably.

3.1 Quality in Use for Responsible Organization, People

Figure 4 shows a proposal of quality in use model for responsible organization, people.

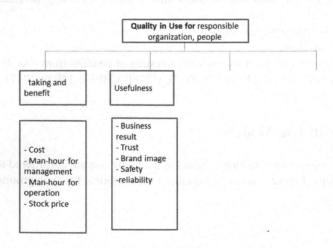

Fig. 4. Quality in use model for responsible organization, people (tentative)

In this figure, there are two quality characteristics. However, there may be any other quality characteristics. It is necessary to discuss them future.

3.2   Quality in Use for Operators

Figure 5 shows the quality in use model for operators.

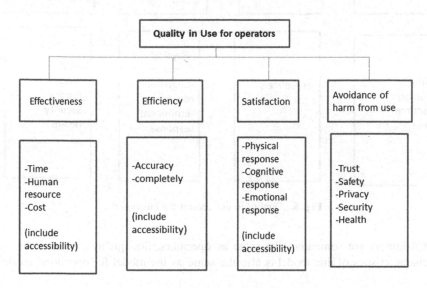

Fig. 5. Quality in use model for operators

This figure is similar to the original quality in use model defined in ISO/IEC25010 and these quality characteristics are similar to "outcome of use" in Fig. 2. From these, this model mainly focus to "direct user". In this figure, "effectiveness", "efficiency" and "satisfaction" are used. About these words, ISO/IEC25062 [6] (parts of SQuaRE series) and ISO9241-11:2018, effectiveness, efficiency and satisfaction are defined as elements of usability. So, quality characteristics of quality in use model for operators are able to consider "outcome of use", they are "usability" and "other outcome of use".

3.3   Quality in Use for Customers

Figure 6 shows the quality in use model for customers.

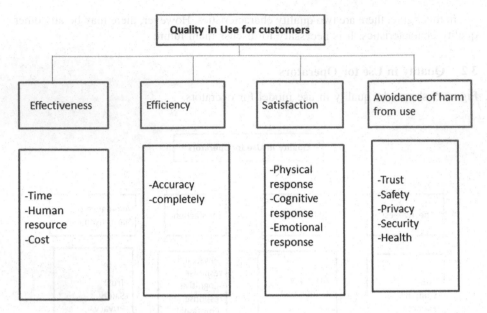

Fig. 6. Quality in use model for customers

Customers are sometimes the same as operators. So, quality characteristics and subcharacteristics of this model is also the same as the model for operators' model.

3.4 Quality in Use for Public

Figure 7 shows the quality in use model for publics.

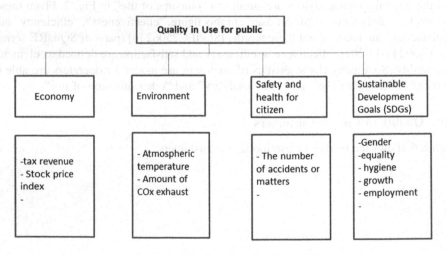

Fig. 7. Quality in use model for public

Subcharacteristics of each quality characteristics in this model may be not only these. And quality (influence) for public shall be considered in not only short term but also long term. About this model, it is necessary to discuss continuously.

3.5 Example

- Electric power supply company
  - Objectives: supply electric power stably
  - "use": operation by operator (in the central control room)
    - Influence on operator: usability
    - Influence on user (organization): interrupted the supply of electricity due to operation error
    - Influence on customer: they cannot use any electric appliances due to interruption of supply of electricity
    - Influence on public: Due to traffic jam caused by stop of signal, increase exhaust gas
  - To reduce these negative influence,
    - Education and training for operators
    - Prompt announcement to customer and/or local government.

4 Discussion

Usability

Usability definition used in SQuaRE series is similar to ISO9241-11:2018. This is along usability concept shown in Fig. 2, that is, "outcome of use". On the other hand, usability sometimes means "efficiency during task (easy to input characters)", "hard to mistakes" and feeling (usable/unusable) during task. As shown in ISO/IEC25062 [6] in SQuaRE series, the former represents "summative" includes during the work, the latter represents "formative". As International Standard, the former is treated as usability. It seems valid that the latter is included in product quality because Nielsen et al. express usability with efficient operation, hard to error, easy to learn, easy to memory [7].

Accessibility

Current accessibility definition is common to both ergonomics and information processing domain, defined as "extent to which products, systems, services, environments and facilities can be used by people from a population with the widest range of needs, characteristics and capabilities to achieve identified goals in identified contexts of use". From this sentence, accessibility can be judged as subcharacteristics of product quality. However, as a note, a sentence "Accessibility for people with disabilities can be specified or measured either as the extent to which a product or system can be used by users with specified disabilities to achieve specified goals with effectiveness, efficiency, freedom from risk and satisfaction in a specified context of use, or by the presence of product properties that support accessibility" is described. As this representation is similar to the definition of usability, accessibility shall be included in quality in use if using this sentence. From this, though accessibility shall be included both product quality and quality in use, it is necessary to pay attention to the use of term "accessibility" because the term is used as different meaning.

5 Conclusion

In this research, we classified objects of quality in use into four groups. Each group has quality model and there are different quality characteristics and subcharacteristics in each quality model. As future work, we will make detail quality model for each object.

References

1. Kosinski, M., Wang, Y.: Deep neural networks are more accurate than humans at detecting sexual orientation from facial images. J. Pers. Soc. Psychol. **114**(2), 246–257 (2010). ISO9241-210: Human-centred design for interactive systems
2. https://www.theguardian.com/technology/2016/mar/24/tay-microsofts-ai-chatbot-gets-a-crash-course-in-racism-from-twitter. 27 Feb 2019
3. https://www.nytimes.com/2018/03/19/technology/uber-driverless-fatality.html. 27 Feb 2019
4. Roto, V., Law, E., Vermeeren, A., Hoonhout, J. (eds.): Use Experience White Paper - Bringing Clarity to the Concept of User Experience, Result from Dagstuhl Seminar on Demarcating User Experience, 15–18 September 2010, pp. 1–12 (2010)
5. IEEE: Global initiative for Ethical Considerations in Artificial Intelligence and Autonomous Systems (2018)
6. Ministry of internal affairs and communications in Japan: AI development guideline (2018). (in Japanese)
7. ISO: fDIS9241-210: Ergonomics of human–system interaction—Part 210: Human-centred design for interactive systems (2019)
8. ISO: PDTR9241-810: Ergonomics—Ergonomics of human-system interaction—Part 810: Human-system issues of robotic, intelligent and autonomous systems (2019)
9. Fukuzumi, S. et al.: Extraction of new guideline items from the view point of ELSI (Ethics, Legal, Social Issues) for service utilized AI. In: Focus on Healthcare Area, 32nd Domestic Conference on Japanese Society for Artificial Intelligence (2018). 3H1-OS-25a-04 (in Japanese)

Accuracy Assessment of ARKit 2 Based Gaze Estimation

Robert Greinacher[1](✉) and Jan-Niklas Voigt-Antons[1,2]

[1] Quality and Usability Lab, Technische Universität Berlin, Berlin, Germany
{greinacher,jan-niklas.voigt-antons}@tu-berlin.de
[2] German Research Center for Artificial Intelligence (DFKI), Berlin, Germany

Abstract. With the growing amount of mobile application usage, assuring a high quality of experience became more and more important. Besides traditional subjective methods to test and prototype new developments, eye tracking is a prominent tool to assess quality and UX of a software product. Although portable eye trackers exist, the technology is still mostly associated with expensive laboratory equipment. To change that and to run quick and cheap eye-tracking studies in the field, attempts have been made to turn everyday hardware like smartphone cameras and webcams into eye trackers. This study explores the possibility of using a standard library of iOS to tackle the vast technical complexity usually coming with such approaches. The accuracy of an eye-tracking system purely based on the ARKit APIs of iOS is evaluated in two user studies (N = 9 & N = 8). The results indicate that an ARKit based gaze tracker provides comparable performance in terms of accuracy (3.18°, or 1.44 cm on screen), while at the same time, it uses far fewer hardware resources and provides a higher sample-rate than any other smartphone eye tracker. Especially the easy to use API is the main advantage over the technical complex systems which rely on their own image analysis for gaze estimation. Privacy implications are discussed.

Keywords: Mobile eye tracking · Accuracy · ARKit

1 Introduction

With over two million apps in each of the two major app stores, user experience (UX) became a crucial aspect of the success of an app [14]. The same goes for the web: since global website accesses using mobile devices outnumbered accesses using desktop computers in 2016 [24], the industry is shifting its efforts to focus on the development of mobile software. Measuring and improving the perceived experience and quality of an application as early as possible in the developmental process is key.

Besides traditional subjective methods, eye tracking is a prominent tool to assess quality and UX of a software product, but as well for market analyses, research, and emerging fields like adaptive software or advanced user interaction concepts. Psychological, physiological, perceptual, and cognitive functions are

© Springer Nature Switzerland AG 2020
M. Kurosu (Ed.): HCII 2020, LNCS 12181, pp. 439–449, 2020.
https://doi.org/10.1007/978-3-030-49059-1_32

Fig. 1. The history of eye-tracking hardware: traditional systems used to be large, heavy, and generally immovable. While the industry started to develop mobile, glasses-like systems, the future of mobile eye-tracking might be as non-intrusive as an ordinary smartphone. Images © 2019 by Tobii AB and Rahul Chakraborty

frequently studied using eye tracker—as one famous quote goes *"Eyes are the window to the soul"*, which dates back to 58 to 68 A.D. For instance, Hoppe and colleagues were able to derive four of the Big Five personality traits (neuroticism, extraversion, agreeableness, conscientiousness) by analyzing eye movement characteristics [13]. Makowski, Landwehr, and colleagues were able to distinguish text readers from each other observing them while reading only a few lines [19,20].

Eye-tracking supports developers, researchers, and creators with fascinating, compelling, and as these examples demonstrate, often important information. Hence, the shrinking cost and size of the corresponding hardware is a well-desired objective. For the general public, there is even greater motivation in learning about this technology: privacy implications that come with less intrusive methods of gaze estimation. We will further elaborate on this aspect during the discussion of this work after we established an understanding of what's possible with current mobile eye-tracking solutions.

Traditionally, expensive and labor-intense lab studies were conducted to make use of the bulky eye-tracking equipment. More modern approaches are wearable systems that are still expensive (see Fig. 1, for example). Using reliable and integrated mobile eye trackers provides plenty of exciting applications. For example, the research community benefits from reduced equipment costs and options to increase the ecological validity of user studies. Also, crowd testing can benefit from eye tracking insights for the first time—if the accuracy of such systems proves to be suitable for the research question at hand.

Because an operation system (OS) usually does not provide direct access to the underlying hardware, but through hardware abstraction layers, we assume to gain more performance from OS provided application programming interfaces (APIs) than by creating own models and analyzing substantial data streams like the live stream of a smartphone camera. This, of course, only works if such interfaces exist with more or less precisely the desired functionality. Building a gaze estimation system in iOS is such an edge case: the Apple's ARKit 2 library [2] offers access to a degree-value of the user's current line of ganze, relative to their face direction. These can then be mapped to screen coordinates.

Every iOS device with version $\geq$11 equipped with Apple's *"TrueDepth"*, can record eye movements in real-time. This translates to a sample rate of 60 Hz, equal to the screen refresh frequency. This is four to six times more data than previous approaches yielded [17]. The main advantages of using the ARKit API compared to extracting eye movements from analyzing the front-facing camera stream are CPU load and thus power efficiency, portability (within the iOS realm), and convenience. Only a few lines of code are necessary to obtain eye movement data while preserving enough CPU headroom for other tasks. For example, reading the eye movements, putting this data through a mapper model in order to obtain screen coordinates (we'll discuss this in more detail) and subsequently updating the position of an user interface (UI) element to indicate the obtained gaze position left on average about one-third of the CPU load of an iPhone XR for other tasks. This is enough to alter content based on gaze position information (real-time adaptive applications), games, gaze controlled interfaces like eye-typing apps (e.g., [11]) or to run crowdsourced usability tests (e.g., [12]).

Since the first products using this technology are already commercially available (see [12]), we conducted two studies to evaluate the accuracy of using the iOS provided interfaces for creating an eye tracker/gaze estimation system. To our knowledge, this is the first study aiming to do so. We first investigated the general accuracy of an ARKit based gaze estimator. Because first impressions of this prototype showed diminishing results over time, we hypothesized a drift of accuracy the longer the calibration lies back in time. Thus, we created a second study to investigate this drift.

1.1 Related Work

In 2018, Khamis and colleagues published a review of mobile device base gaze estimation systems [16]. Amongst others, they pointed out that further research should focus on ecological validity since lab studies often do not reflect real-world challenges and accuracy measurements.

TurkerGaze from 2015 is a model for post hoc webcam gaze estimation, trained with images from hundreds of crowdsourcing workers, offering a reasonably accurate gaze position estimation with a median error of only 1.06° [25]. One year later, WebGazer [22] and its derivative SearchGazer [21] offered live gaze position estimation and analysis and is implemented purely in JavaScript, which makes it feasible to be used for websites on desktop and mobile devices. Both systems achieve an average accuracy of 4.17°. Krafka and colleagues developed a sophisticated system based on a convolutional neural network and trained it with 2.5 M images from 1.5 k people using crowdsourcing [17]. Although the reported accuracy of only 1.8 cm sounds promising, they did not report angles of error but only a euclidean distance in centimeters. Hence, evaluating the quality of their gaze tracking system depends on the distance between the eye and screen. The so far most advanced online eye-tracking system for smartphones using a standard smartphone camera is ScreenGlint with an average accuracy of 2.44° in a fixed head setting [15].

A recent publication by Brousseau et al. from 2020 presented an infrared camera-based 3D model for eye tracking on a smartphone [4]. Gaze positions are estimated using convolutional neural networks on device. The system achieves a gaze bias of 0.72°, with the device free to move in the user's hands at about 30 frames per second. To our knowledge, this is the so far most advanced accuracy of a smartphone gaze-tracker. The group used an industry prototype with direct access to an infrared camera. To this date, these are either rare, or the access is restricted by the OS. For example, the iPhone's *TrueDepth* camera features an infrared camera as well, but developers cannot access its data directly but only through APIs like ARKit. Hence, the approach built by Brousseau et al. could, at the time of this writing, not be transferred to an unmodified iPhone.

Cicek and colleagues demonstrated a similar approach in 2018 [6]. Using ARKit as the technical foundation, they created a head-pointing software for hands-free interaction with the smartphone. They favored head-based pointing over gaze estimation because (amongst others) it requires a more fine-grain calibration and constant ambient lighting. Indeed, when comparing gaze estimation against head-based pointing, previous research concluded head-based pointing is generally more voluntary and stable and thus provides greater accuracy compared to gaze-tracking [3,18].

An interesting work by Abbaszadegan and colleagues from 2018 using an ARKit-based eye and head tracker is TrackMaze [1]. In their game, users maneuvers a virtual ball through a static maze using tilting, eye-tracking, and head-tracking. Apart from game-performance (completion time, wall hits), the authors evaluated ease of use, enjoyment, fatigue. Consistently, the eye-tracking interaction performed worst and provided the least joy, ease of use, and cause the most fatigue.

2   Methods

To test the accuracy of an ARKit based eye-tracker/gaze estimator, we conducted two user studies. First, we investigated the overall accuracy of the eye tracker. In a second study, we repeated the experiment three times to test for a potential drift of accuracy over time. Both tests used a smooth pursuit task to gather samples, as described in the following section.

2.1   Operationalization

In a smooth pursuit task, participants follow a moving dot on the screen with their eyes [8]. While doing so, the eye tracker records and estimates gaze positions. Because we know the exact coordinates of the moving dot, we have a ground truth of the estimated gaze positions. For the analysis, we compare these estimated positions with their corresponding stimulus positions by computing the euclidean distance per sample (see Eq. 1).

$$d(stim, est) = \sqrt{(stim_x - est_x)^2 + (stim_y - est_y)^2} \tag{1}$$

Using the distance between eyes and screen, this can then be translated back to an absolute distance on screen or to the gaze bias angle. Regarding human participants, the literature provides evidence for a response latency of somewhat more than 100 ms [5,23]. Therefore, we disregard the first second of the collected samples per trial. Also, we matched stimulus to gaze positions with an offset of six samples. This way, we account for a delayed response of the eyes relative to the rushing ahead, actual stimulus position. Figure 3 provides a visualization of the matching between stimulus movement and corresponding, estimated gaze position.

2.2   Apparatus and Test Setup

An iOS 12/Swift 4 app was written to make use of ARKit to obtain eye tracking position information. The data were then mapped to screen coordinates. This was done on-device and in real-time using two linear regressors, one for each axis, X and Y, employing the AIToolbox [7]. The mapping model was trained with data from a quick calibration phase before the data collection started.

The device used for the test was an iPhone XR (326 ppi). The raw eye movement data obtained from the ARKit API is relative to the face and does not correct for body or device movement. Hence, any movement adds further variance to the gaze estimation. This proof of concept evaluates the general feasibility of such a system, and its results should justify further elaboration on it, including the development of a device and body movement correction. In order to minimize the impact without such correction mechanics, we chose a controlled lab setting for the user studies. In this setting, we reduced additional movement to a minimum by mounting the smartphone to the desk in front of the participants and using a chin rest for the participants likewise. The distance between participants' eyes and the screen was 26 cm.

2.3   Procedure

After the phone and chin rest were adjusted to fit the participants, we calibrated the mapper model. In the first study, we employed a quick, smooth pursuit task in order to gather samples from many different screen positions to sufficiently map the API outcome values to screen positions. The second study only used a five-point calibration [9]. In the latter case, a stimulus dot was displayed in the center and each corner of the screen for two seconds each. Subsequently, the main data acquisition started. The first experiment consisted of a 28 s long-lasting smooth pursuit task. In the second study, we used three consecutive 34 s long-lasting smooth pursuit tasks with a short break of about 15 s in between.

2.4   Participants

The first study included nine participants, four of whom are female. The average age is 28.3 years ranging from 21 to 39 years of age. None of the participants wear glasses. One of them had contact lenses, which corrected the vision to normal. Three of the eight participants have had previous eye tracking experience. The second study was conducted on a group of eight test participants, four of whom are female. The average recorded age was 27.0, with a range between 20 and 30 years of age. Two of the eight participants have previous eye-tracking experience, none of them wear glasses or contact lenses. Both studies were done in accordance with ethical principles for medical research involving human subjects proposed by the World Medical Association (WMA) Declaration of Helsinki.

3   Results

The first user study revealed a median gaze estimation accuracy of $3.18°$, see Table 1. The correlation between the actual stimulus position and the estimation per axis was statistically significant [10].

Table 1. Results of both user studies combined (dataset 1 and 2), the second study is divided by the three trials. Distances are the euclidean distance between the estimated gaze position and the actual stimulus (see Sect. 2.1), averaged throughout the trial. Pearson correlations between the stimulus and the prediction axis are given in the *cor.* labeled columns. All of which show a statistically significant correlation ($\alpha = .05$). The data of the second study is averaged per participant and then averaged per trial, the standard errors of the mean per trial are 23.52 px, 44.7 px, and 32.03 px respectively.

Dataset	Distance in px	Distance in cm	Distance in $°$	cor. X	cor. Y
1	187 px	1.44 cm	3.18°	.89	.91
2, trial 1	239 px	1.85 cm	4.08°	.88	.85
2, trial 2	329 px	2.54 cm	5.60°	.85	.74
2, trial 3	300 px	2.32 cm	5.11°	.83	.70

The second study was conducted in order to test for a potential drift of accuracy over time. A one way repeated measures ANOVA of the median distance between predicted gaze and stimulus position per trial and participant was employed. Given the eight participants and three trials, this results in 24 observations. A significant effect of the trial was observed ($F = 8.155, p = .004$). Hence, the time since calibration has a significant influence on the accuracy of the gaze estimation. This finding supports our hypothesis of drift over time.

Mauchly's test for sphericity did not provide evidence to conclude that the variances of differences are significantly different ($p > .4$). Jarque Bera test did likewise not show evidence to suggest that the normality of the dependent variable is statistically significantly violated. Therefore, the statistical assumptions of the ANOVA are met.

A Bonferroni corrected posthoc comparison of the trials revealed statistically significant differences between the first and the second trial ($t = -3.343$, $df = 7$, $p = .012$) as well as between the first and the third trial ($t = -3.691$, $df = 7$, $p = .008$). The difference between the second and the third trials did not show significant differences ($t = 1.23$, $df = 7$, $p = .259$) (see Fig. 2).

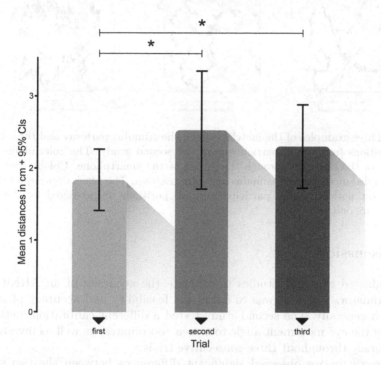

Fig. 2. Comparison of the gaze position estimation accuracy in the three trials of the second experiment. The bars depict the absolute on-screen distance in cm between the estimated gaze and the smooth pursuit stimulus. Approx. 5919 samples were recorded per trial and participant. These were averaged per participant and subsequently summarised in this plot. The standard error of the mean was 0.18 cm in the first trial, 0.35 cm in the second, and 0.25 cm in the third. Whiskers depict 95% confidence intervals. Stars indicate a statistically significant difference ($\alpha = .05$) between groups.

Performance-wise ARKit was accounting for about two-thirds of the CPU load of the entire smartphone system while running the three trials of the test app.

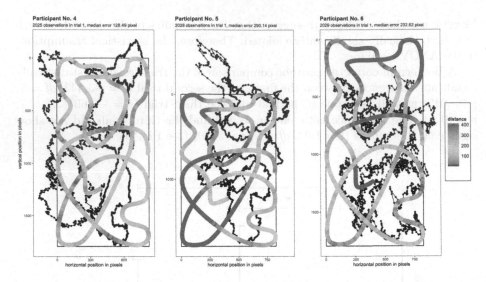

Fig. 3. Three examples of the match between the stimulus pathway and the estimated gaze positions from three participants of the second study. The colorful line is the pathway of the stimulus through the screen of the smartphone. Colour encodes the euclidean distance between stimulus and gaze position. The black dots depict the consecutive estimations of the participants' gaze positions as predicted by the model. (Color figure online)

4   Discussion

We conducted two user studies to evaluate the accuracy of an ARKit based gaze estimator. The first was to assess the feasibility and accuracy of such an approach generally. The second study tested a different calibration method for mapping the eye movement angle to screen coordinates, as well as investigating the accuracy throughout three consecutive trials.

Interestingly, we observed significant differences between the two studies. Setting the two additionals trials of the second study aside, we expected the accuracy of the first trial in both studies to be similar. The two things changed were the calibration and the participants. Regarding the calibration, the more accurate results were obtained in the study with a more sophisticated calibration for the coordinate mapper. This might point towards a potential issue with this component. If this induces additional variance, we could have minimized its impact by mapping the screen positions offline during the analysis phase. This would have allowed us to test different algorithms and training methods. However, in order to test a minimal and, at the same time, fully functional prototype, we decided to do the mapping in real-time and on device. The second difference between the studies was the sample of participants, which boils down to the relatively small sample size. This is a limitation of the presented work. Nevertheless, the results are good enough to motivate further efforts to improve the prototype. Here, head and device movement should be addressed to make the gaze estimation robust for real-world applications outside a controlled lab setting.

We found significant accuracy variations between trials. Eye blinks likely triggered this. We exclude fatigue as a possible error source since the whole experiment lasted only a couple of minutes. Presumably, this is also not caused due to head movements since the experiment was conducted using a chin rests and a desk-mounted smartphone to reduce involuntary movements to a minimum. However, micro-movements could accumulate over time and add to the drift. To avoid drift and to maintain a good gaze position accuracy, even without accounting for head and device movements, multiple calibration steps should be used.

The obtained accuracy of $3.18°$ is comparable to previous approaches [15, 17, 22] using ordinary camera data and machine learning. The accuracy of the presented approach is about one degree better compared to WebGazer and SearchGazer and about $.75°$ worse than what ScreenGlint could measure. Compared to the novel approach by Brousseau et al., the here presented ARKit based gaze estimator performs about 4.4 times worse [4]. Nevertheless, it is essential to point out that this state of the art result comes with significant technical complexity and depends on a particular smartphone hardware configuration. Also, the sample rate of previous systems has been only around 30 Hz compared to the 60 Hz gained with ARKit [4,15] or even only 15–20 Hz [17].

A crucial aspect of this work is an implication to the users' privacy. ARKit offers a straight forward interface to gaze estimation at a quality level sufficient even for some commercial use cases. Also, it is a matter of hours for software manufacturers to integrate eye-tracking functionality into their products. However, while this is very convenient, currently, app developers do not need to ask users for permission to use these powerful tools. Instead, only camera access is requested. However, this is not informative about what can be done after this access is granted. No informed decision of the users is required to implement eye-tracking once the camera access is permitted. For instance, while an online shop app asking for camera accesses might be found suspicious by privacy-sensitive users, social networks often have unrestricted camera access to be able to take a photo and share it. The fact that users cannot know if such a social network provider is scanning their faces to analyze their personality profiles [13] or identify them [20] is a problem that needs to be addressed by Apple as the creator of the iOS platform and the ARKit APIs.

4.1 Conclusion

We assessed a straight forward implementation of a mobile eye tracker system built purely around ARKit 2 [2]. Two user studies were conducted with nine and eight participants, respectively. On the one hand, the obtained gaze estimation accuracy ($3.18°$, or 1.44 cm on screen) is comparable to previous approaches built around ordinary front-facing cameras of smartphones. On the other, this solution outperforms other systems in code complexity, CPU load, sample-rate, and ultimately in developer convenience. Nevertheless, similar to previous smartphone eye trackers, our results consistently show an accuracy which is in the order of magnitude less precise than traditional desktop hardware eye tracker systems. This work is a teaser into what is possible with on-board tools of modern smartphones. Privacy implications are discussed.

Acknowledgment. We appreciate the help of our great team: Danish Ali, Martin Burghart, Tanja Kojic, Luis Meier, Lan Thao Nguyen, Kerstin Pieper, Andres Pinilla, and Sonia Sobol.

References

1. Abbaszadegan, M., Yaghoubi, S., MacKenzie, I.S.: TrackMaze: a comparison of head-tracking, eye-tracking, and tilt as input methods for mobile games. In: Kurosu, M. (ed.) HCI 2018. LNCS, vol. 10903, pp. 393–405. Springer, Cham (2018). https://doi.org/10.1007/978-3-319-91250-9_31
2. Apple: Arkit 2 arfaceanchor - information about the pose, topology, and expression of a face detected in a face-tracking AR session (2018). https://developer.apple.com/documentation/arkit/arfaceanchor
3. Bates, R., Istance, H.O.: Why are eye mice unpopular? a detailed comparison of head and eye controlled assistive technology pointing devices. Univers. Inf. Soc. **2**(3), 280–290 (2003)
4. Brousseau, B., Rose, J., Eizenman, M.: Hybrid eye-tracking on a smartphone with cnn feature extraction and an infrared 3D model. Sensors **20**(2), 543 (2020)
5. Carl, J., Gellman, R.: Human smooth pursuit: stimulus-dependent responses. J. Neurophysiol. **57**(5), 1446–1463 (1987)
6. Cicek, M., Xie, J., Wang, Q., Piramuthu, R.: Mobile head tracking for ecommerce and beyond. arXiv preprint arXiv:1812.07143 (2018)
7. Coble, K.: Aitoolbox. a toolbox of AI modules written in swift: Graphs/trees, support vector machines, neural networks, PCA, k-means, genetic algorithms (2017). https://github.com/KevinCoble/AIToolbox
8. Dodge, R.: Five types of eye movement in the horizontal meridian plane of the field of regard. Am. J. Physiol. Legacy Content **8**(4), 307–329 (1903)
9. Duchowski, A.T.: Eye Tracking Methodology. Theory and Practice. Springer, Cham (2017). https://doi.org/10.1007/978-3-319-57883-5
10. Harrell Jr., F.E., Dupont, C., et al.: HMISC: Harrell miscellaneous. R package version 4.0-3. Online publication (2017)
11. Hawkeye Labs, Inc.: Hawkeye access - browse any website, hands-free, all through eye movements(2018). https://apps.apple.com/de/app/hawkeye-access/id1439231627
12. Hawkeye Labs, I.: Hawkeye - user testing. eye tracking tests on an iphone or ipad, no extra hardware required (2019). https://www.usehawkeye.com/
13. Hoppe, S., Loetscher, T., Morey, S.A., Bulling, A.: Eye movements during everyday behavior predict personality traits. Front. Hum. Neurosci. **12**, 105 (2018)
14. Hsu, C.L., Chen, Y.C., Yang, T.N., Lin, W.K.: Do website features matter in an online gamification context? focusing on the mediating roles of user experience and attitude. Telematics Inform. **34**(4), 196–205 (2017)
15. Huang, M.X., Li, J., Ngai, G., Leong, H.V.: Screenglint: practical, in-situ gaze estimation on smartphones. In: Proceedings of the 2017 CHI Conference on Human Factors in Computing Systems, pp. 2546–2557. ACM (2017)

16. Khamis, M., Alt, F., Bulling, A.: The past, present, and future of gaze-enabled handheld mobile devices: survey and lessons learned. In: Proceedings of the 20th International Conference on Human-Computer Interaction with Mobile Devices and Services, pp. 1–17 (2018)
17. Krafka, K., et al.: Eye tracking for everyone. In: Proceedings of the IEEE Conference on Computer Vision and Pattern Recognition, pp. 2176–2184 (2016)
18. Kytö, M., Ens, B., Piumsomboon, T., Lee, G.A., Billinghurst, M.: Pinpointing: precise head-and eye-based target selection for augmented reality. In: Proceedings of the 2018 CHI Conference on Human Factors in Computing Systems, pp. 1–14 (2018)
19. Landwehr, N., Arzt, S., Scheffer, T., Kliegl, R.: A model of individual differences in gaze control during reading. In: Proceedings of the 2014 Conference on Empirical Methods in Natural Language Processing (EMNLP), pp. 1810–1815 (2014)
20. Makowski, S., Jäger, L.A., Abdelwahab, A., Landwehr, N., Scheffer, T.: A discriminative model for identifying readers and assessing text comprehension from eye movements. In: Berlingerio, M., Bonchi, F., Gärtner, T., Hurley, N., Ifrim, G. (eds.) ECML PKDD 2018. LNCS (LNAI), vol. 11051, pp. 209–225. Springer, Cham (2019). https://doi.org/10.1007/978-3-030-10925-7_13
21. Papoutsaki, A., Laskey, J., Huang, J.: Searchgazer: webcam eye tracking for remote studies of web search. In: Proceedings of the 2017 Conference on Conference Human Information Interaction and Retrieval, pp. 17–26. ACM (2017)
22. Papoutsaki, A., Sangkloy, P., Laskey, J., Daskalova, N., Huang, J., Hays, J.: Webgazer: scalable webcam eye tracking using user interactions. In: Proceedings of the Twenty-Fifth International Joint Conference on Artificial Intelligence-IJCAI 2016 (2016)
23. Robinson, D.A.: The mechanics of human smooth pursuit eye movement. J. Physiol. **180**(3), 569–591 (1965)
24. StatCounter: Mobile and tablet internet usage exceeds desktop for first time worldwide. (2016). http://gs.statcounter.com/press/mobile-and-tablet-internet-usage-exceeds-desktop-for-first-time-worldwide
25. Xu, P., Ehinger, K.A., Zhang, Y., Finkelstein, A., Kulkarni, S.R., Xiao, J.: Turkergaze: Crowdsourcing saliency with webcam based eye tracking. arXiv preprint arXiv:1504.06755 (2015)

Usability of Software–Intensive Systems from Developers' Point of View

Current Status and Future Perspectives of International Standardization of Usability Evaluation

Toshihiro Komiyama[1]([✉]), Shin'ichi Fukuzumi[2], Motoei Azuma[3], Hironori Washizaki[3], and Naohiko Tsuda[3]

[1] NEC Corporation, Tokyo, Japan
t-komiyama@nec.com
[2] RIKEN Center for Advanced Intelligence Project, Tokyo, Japan
shin-ichi.fukuzumi@riken.jp
[3] Waseda University, Tokyo, Japan
{azumam, washizaki}@waseda.jp, 821821@toki.waseda.jp

Abstract. Even though the type of software-intensive systems has transitioned from the mainframe to the client-server and from the client-server to the cloud, usability is one of the significant quality characteristics throughout the transitions. To achieve and improve usability, it is important to ensure a common understanding of usability concepts and to utilize proven usability evaluation technologies. Quality characteristics and subcharacteristics of software-intensive systems, including usability related ones, are defined in the quality models, i.e. product quality model and quality in use model, of ISO/IEC 25010:2011 in ISO/IEC 250nn SQuaRE (Systems and Software Quality Requirements and Evaluation) series. The SQuaRE series also defines quality measures for quality characteristics and subcharacteristics to be used for quality evaluation. The quality models of software-intensive systems are now under revision considering evolved systems and software technologies and influence on various stakeholders, including "Public".

This paper describes the international standardization of usability definition and evaluation from the developers' point of view. First, the overview of the SQuaRE is introduced. Second, concepts and technologies related to usability in the SQuaRE are explained. Third, the study results of the application of the SQuaRE to actual projects are introduced, focusing on usability. Finally, future perspectives of international standardization of usability of software-intensive systems are described.

Keywords: Usability · International standardization · ISO/IEC 250nn SQuaRE series · Quality evaluation · Quality model · Quality measure

© Springer Nature Switzerland AG 2020
M. Kurosu (Ed.): HCII 2020, LNCS 12181, pp. 450–463, 2020.
https://doi.org/10.1007/978-3-030-49059-1_33

1   Introduction

Progress of the information technologies has been expanding the opportunities to use ICT products explicitly or implicitly, and a huge amount of software is being developed and used. Following this trend, the effects of software defects on the lives of individuals, society, and the environment have also increased, leading to a rise in interest in the quality of software. Besides, as it has widely recognized that software is the most significant component to generate the values of information systems, concern to software quality has also increased to ensure and enhance the product values.

The improvement of software quality has been one of the major topics of discussion since the first Software Engineering Conference was held under the sponsorship of NATO (North Atlantic Treaty Organization) in 1968. The engineering approach to quality improvement includes the implementation and enhancement of quality based on the utilization of techniques and tools for design, verification, and validation. Additionally, from the management point of view, an explicit definition of quality goals and technologies for measuring, evaluating and controlling the achievement of the goals are also important.

The quality of the software is not enough in itself if it is simply capable of providing the required functions (functionality) or it is free of defect or failure (reliability). To enhance user satisfaction and provide superiority in market competition with high quality, it is required to consider quality from multilateral viewpoints. These will include ease of use for the user (usability) and the speed between making a processing request and receiving the result (efficiency). Technologies to specify, implement, measure and evaluate significant characteristics to be considered are also necessary.

When an acquirer and a supplier agree on software quality requirements or an acquirer compare and select candidate software products, it would be confused if ways of specifying and evaluating quality differed. From the awareness of such kind of problems, ISO/IEC JTC 1 SC 7/WG 6 (Software Product and System Quality) has proceeded international standardization of the management, modeling, quantification, specification, and evaluation of systems and software product quality.

One of the authors, Mr. Komiyama, described usability evaluation based on ISO/IEC 9126 and 14598 series in 2008 [1]. Currently, those have already replaced with the ISO/IEC 250nn SQuaRE series. This paper is described based on the valid International Standards at this moment.

In the following sections, first, we introduce an overview of the ISO/IEC standards related to systems and software quality requirements and evaluation. Second, we explain the concepts and technologies related to usability from the developers' point of view in the standards. Third, we explain the study results of software quality evaluation using the International Standards. Finally, we discuss future perspectives on the enhancement of usability aspects of the standards.

2   International Standards for Systems and Software Quality Evaluation

2.1   History of Standardization

Based on the basic recognition that software quality should not be evaluated only concerning the number of defects and that arbitrarily selected measures should not be used for software quality evaluation, a proposal for standardization of software quality evaluation was made and the work for international standardization was started at ISO/TC 97/SC 7 in 1985. Since then, the projects for standardization of software quality evaluation were taken over by the joint technical committee of ISO and IEC, ISO/IEC JTC 1, that was organized in 1987 and then assigned to WG 6 in 1992, which was established in ISO/IEC JTC 1 SC 7 (Software engineering). After that, the scope of SC 7 has expanded to systems and software, and WG 6 to systems and software, data and IT services.

Since the start of ISO/TC 97/SC 7 and also ISO/IEC JTC 1 SC 7/WG 6, Prof. Azuma, Waseda University, was assigned to the Convener. Since the start of ISO/IEC JTC 1 SC 7/WG 6, Mr. Komiyama, NEC Corporation, was assigned to the Secretary. In 2015, Mr. Komiyama took over the convenorship and Mr. Sakamoto, NTT Data Corporation was assigned to the Secretary.

In Japan, the Information Technology Research and Standardization Center of the Japanese Standards Association (JSA/INSTAC) established the Technical Committee on Software Quality Evaluation in 1987 and the Information Technology Standards Commission of Japan of the Information Processing Society of Japan (IPSJ/ITSCJ) established the mirror committee of ISO/IEC JTC 1 SC 7/WG 6 in 1992. Technical contributions, such as proposals of work items, submission of working drafts, and submission of comments on proposed draft standards, has done based on the domestic committees' activities. Through these administrative and technical contributions, Japan has been leading the international standardization of software quality evaluation.

As to usability, ISO/TC 159 (Ergonomics)/SC 4 (Ergonomics of human-system interaction) has proceeded international standardization focusing on the usability of interactive systems. Harmonization of usability concepts between JTC 1/SC 7 and TC 159/SC 4 has been done since the establishment of SC 7/WG 6. Dr. Bevan and Dr. Fukuzumi have contributed to this harmonization as liaisons of those SCs.

2.2   Organization of International Standards

"ISO/IEC 9126: Information technology - Software product evaluation - Quality characteristics and guidelines for their use" was issued in 1991 as the first International Standard for software quality evaluation. This standard defines six quality characteristics as viewpoints of software quality evaluation together with the basic evaluation processes.

Later on, the two series of International Standards, i.e., ISO/IEC 9126: Product quality and ISO/IEC 14598: Product evaluation, and two supplementary standards were developed to promote the application of standards in actual businesses and to improve the convenience of audiences.

Those were reorganized from 1999 and currently combined and enhanced as ISO/IEC 250nn SQuaRE (Systems and software Quality Requirements and Evaluation) series. Figure 1 shows the architecture of the SQuaRE series. As shown in Fig. 1, SQuaRE is composed of the following six divisions:

SQuaRE is composed of the following divisions:

- ISO/IEC 2500n - Quality Management Division. The International Standards that form this division define all common models, terms, and definitions referred to by all other standards from the SQuaRE series.
- ISO/IEC 2501n - Quality Model Division. The International Standards that form this division present detailed quality models for systems and software products, quality in use and data. Practical guidance on the use of the quality model is also provided.
- ISO/IEC 2502n - Quality Measurement Division. The International Standards that form this division include a system and software product quality measurement reference model, mathematical definitions of quality measures, and practical guidance for their application.
- ISO/IEC 2503n - Quality Requirements Division. The International Standard that forms this division helps to specify quality requirements.
- ISO/IEC 2504n - Quality Evaluation Division. The International Standards that form this division provide requirements, recommendations, and guidelines for product evaluation, whether performed by independent evaluators, acquirers or developers. The support for documenting a measure as an Evaluation Module is also presented.
- ISO/IEC 25050 25099-Extension Division. The SQuaRE extension (ISO/IEC 25050 to ISO/IEC 25099) is designated to contain system or software product quality International Standards and/or Technical Reports that address specific application domains or that can be used to complement one or more SQuaRE International Standards.

All the International Standards and Technical Specifications are located in one of the divisions. It could be aware of the document number. Table 1 shows the title and outline of International Standards and Technical Specifications in the series.

Currently, further enhancement of the SQuaRE series is underway. Enhancement points are the following:

- Application of SQuaRE to specific fields, such as cloud computing and AI
- Quality engineering
- More practical guidelines for quality evaluation.

As to usability, it was defined as one of the quality characteristics to be considered and implemented through the development of software products in JTC 1/SC 7. On the other hand, usability was defined as influences to operators of interactive systems in their context of use, i.e., effectiveness, efficiency, and satisfaction, in TC 159/SC 4. As a result of continuous discussions on this issue, currently, usability is located as a characteristic of product quality model, and influences to users, such as effectiveness, efficiency, and satisfaction, are dealt with as characteristics of quality in use model. The actual treatment of these characteristics in the models is explained in Sect. 3.

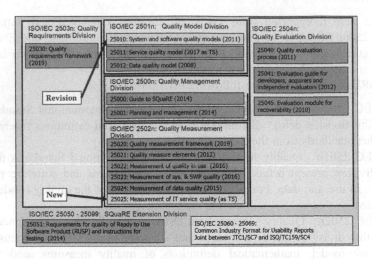

Fig. 1. The architecture of the SQuaRE series

Table 1. List of International Standards and Technical Specifications in the SQuaRE Series

IS/TS No.: Year	Title (Edition)	Outline
ISO/IEC 25000:2014	Systems and software Engineering – Systems and software Quality Requirements and Evaluation (SQuaRE) – Guide to SQuaRE (2nd edition)	Definition of common terms, explanation of basic concepts and guidance of SQuaRE series
ISO/IEC 25001:2014	Systems and software engineering – Systems and software Quality Requirements and Evaluation (SQuaRE) – Planning and management (2nd edition)	Guidance of organizational promotion and support of quantitative quality management
ISO/IEC 25010:2011 (under revision)	Systems and software engineering – Systems and software Quality Requirements and Evaluation (SQuaRE) – System and software quality models	Structured models of product quality and quality in use, and definition of quality (sub) chracteristics of them
ISO/IEC TS 25011:2017	Information technology – Systems and software Quality Requirements and Evaluation (SQuaRE) – Service quality model	Structured model of IT service quality and definition of quality (sub) chracteristics of it
ISO/IEC 25012:2008	Software engineering – Software product Quality Requirements and Evaluation (SQuaRE) – Data quality model	Structured model of data quality and definition of quality (sub) chracteristics of it
ISO/IEC 25020:2019	Systems and software engineering – Systems and software Quality Requirements and Evaluation (SQuaRE) – Quality measurement framework (2nd edition)	Basic concepts of quality measurement
ISO/IEC 25021:2012	Systems and software engineering – Systems and software Quality Requirements and Evaluation (SQuaRE) – Quality measure elements	Definition of quality measure elements composing quality measures
ISO/IEC 25022:2016	Systems and software engineering – Systems and software Quality Requirements and Evaluation (SQuaRE) – Measurement of quality in use	Definition of quality in use measures

(continued)

Table 1. (*continued*)

IS/TS No.: Year	Title (Edition)	Outline
ISO/IEC 25023:2016	Systems and software engineering – Systems and software Quality Requirements and Evaluation (SQuaRE) – Measurement of system and software product quality	Definition of product quality measures
ISO/IEC 25024:2015	Systems and software engineering – Systems and software Quality Requirements and Evaluation (SQuaRE) – Measurement of data quality	Definition of data quality measures
ISO/IEC TS 25025 (under development)	Information technology – Systems and software Quality Requirements and Evaluation (SQuaRE) – Measurement of IT service quality	Definition of IT service quality measures
ISO/IEC 25030:2019	Software engineering – Software product Quality Requirements and Evaluation (SQuaRE) – Quality requirements framework (2nd edition)	Basic concepts of quality requirements
ISO/IEC 25040:2011	Systems and software engineering – Systems and software Quality Requirements and Evaluation (SQuaRE) – Evaluation process	Basic concepts of quality evaluation
ISO/IEC 25041:2012	Systems and software engineering – Systems and software Quality Requirements and Evaluation (SQuaRE) – Evaluation guide for developers, acquirers and independent evaluators	Guidance of quality evaluation for developers, acquires and independent evaluators
ISO/IEC 25051:2014	Software engineering – Systems and software product Quality Requirements and Evaluation (SQuaRE) – Requirements for quality of Ready to Use Software Product (RUSP) and instructions for testing (2nd edition)	Guidance of quality requirements specification and testing for RUSP

3   Usability Within SQuaRE

3.1   Quality Models and Measures of Software-Intensive Systems

ISO/IEC 25010: System and software quality models [2] provides the structured models of system and software quality from the developers' and the users' points of view. We call the former product quality model and the latter quality in use model. Both product quality and quality in use are decomposed into characteristics and then subcharacteristics in these models. Figure 2 shows the product quality model and Fig. 3 shows the quality in use model. As mentioned in Sect. 2 usability is involved in the product quality model and effectiveness, efficiency and satisfaction are involved in the quality in use model.

Systems and software quality evaluation could be classified into three phases, i.e., design to coding, testing and operating, according to the differences of evaluation viewpoints and applicable measures and measurement methods.

The evaluation viewpoints are given by the quality models. The product quality model defines system and software quality from developers' viewpoints and is suitable for design to coding and testing phases. The quality in use model defines it from users' point of view and is suitable for the operating phase.

The quality measures and measurement methods of characteristics and subcharacteristics of product quality model are defined in ISO/IEC 25023 [3], and those of quality in use in ISO/IEC 25022 [4]. ISO/IEC 25023 provides quality measures and measurement methods on internal properties and external properties. The former is suitable for the design and coding phase since it could be calculated using results of static verification and validation of non-operable work products such as review and inspection. The latter is suitable for the testing phase since it could be calculated using the results of behavioral verification and validation of operable products with testing. ISO/IEC 25022 provides quality in use measures and measurement methods, which are suitable for the operating phase. They could be calculated based on the impacts of products to direct and indirect users, which are measured typically using user survey, user performance measurement and user behavior measurement. Table 2 shows examples of two types of product quality measures and quality in use measure.

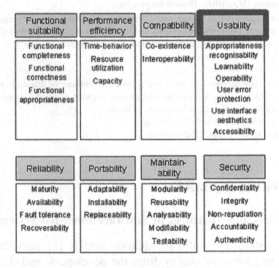

Functional suitability	Performance efficiency	Compatibility	Usability
Functional completeness Functional correctness Functional appropriateness	Time-behavior Resource utilization Capacity	Co-existence Interoperability	Appropriateness recognisability Learnability Operability User error protection Use interface aesthetics Accessibility

Reliability	Portability	Maintainability	Security
Maturity Availability Fault tolerance Recoverability	Adaptability Installability Replaceability	Modularity Reusability Analysability Modifiability Testability	Confidentiality Integrity Non-repudiation Accountability Authenticity

Fig. 2. Product quality model of ISO/IEC 25010

Effectiveness	Efficiency	Satisfaction	Freedom from risk	Context coverage
Effectiveness	Efficiency	Usefulness Trust Pleasure Comfort	Economic risk mitigation Health and safety risk mitigation Environmental risk mitigation	Context completeness Flexibility

Fig. 3. Quality in use model of ISO/IEC 25010

Table 2. Examples of product quality measures of ISO/IEC 25023 and quality in use measures of ISO/IEC 25022

Quality model	Quality characteristics	Quality subcharacteristics	Phase	Name	Measurement Function
Product quality model	Maintainability	Modularity	Design	Cyclomatic complexity adequacy	X = 1 − A/B A = Number of software modules which have a cyclomatic complexity score that exceeds the specified threshold B = Number of software modules implemented
	Reliability	Maturity	Testing	Failure rate	X = A/B A = Number of failures detected during observation time B = Duration of observation
Quality in use model	Effectiveness	Effectiveness	Operation	Tasks completed	X = A/B A = Number of unique tasks completed B = Total number of unique tasks attempted

3.2 Quality Subcharacteristics and Measures of Usability

As shown in Fig. 2, ISO/IEC 25010 positions usability as one of the quality characteristics of the product quality model. It means that usability should be considered in the development phase. Usability is decomposed into six subcharacteristics. Table 3 shows the definitions of usability and its subcharacteristics. The points to evaluate these usability subcharacteristics are as the following:

- Appropriateness Recognizability: To check if the users can understand easily whether the product is suitable for their needs or not.
- Learnability: To check if the users can learn and acquire skills to utilize the product without too much effort.
- Operability: To check if the users can use the product without excessive stress.
- User Error Protection: To check if the product can guard the users not to make errors and if the users can recover easily when they mistake.
- User Interface Aesthetics: To check if the product can appeal to the senses of users.
- Accessibility: To check if the wide range of users having different characteristics and abilities can use the product.

The products which are designed and implemented considering usability and its subcharacteristics are expected to improve some of the quality in use characteristics and subcharacteristics, such as effectiveness, efficiency, and satisfaction, in the operation phase.

For the usability subcharacteristics, ISO/IEC 25023 provides measures for their objective and quantitative evaluation. Table 4 shows some examples of the usability measures to be used in the development phases.

Table 3. Definitions of usability and its subcharacteristics of ISO/IEC 25010

Usability		degree to which a product or system can be used by specified users to achieve specified goals with effectiveness, efficiency and satisfaction in a specified context of use
	Appropriateness	degree to which users can recognize whether a product or system is appropriate for their needs
	Learnablity	degree to which a product or system can be used by specified users to achieve specified goals of learning to use the product or system with effectiveness, efficiency, freedom from risk and satisfaction in a specified context of use
	Operability	degree to which a product or system has attributes that make it easy to operate and control
	User error Protection	degree to which a system protects users against making errors
	User interface aesthetics	degree to which a user interface enables pleasing and satisfying interaction for the user
	Accessibility	degree to which a product or system can be used by people with the widest range of characteristics and capabilities to achieve a specified goal in a specified context of use

Table 4. Examples of usability measures of ISO/IEC 25023

Usability subcharacteristics	Phase	Name	Measurement function
Appropriateness	Design and Testing	Description completeness	X = A/B A = Number of usage scenarios described in the product description or user documents B = Number of usage scenarios of the product
Learnablity	Design and Testing	Error messages understandability	X = A/B A = Number of error messages which state the reason of occurrence and suggest the ways of resolution where this is possible B = Number of error messages implemented
Operability	Design and Testing	Undo capability	X = A/B A = Number of tasks that provide undo capability or prompt for re- confirmation B = Number of tasks for which users could benefit from having re- confirmation or undo capability
User error protection	Design and Testing	Avoidance of user operation error	X = A/B A = Number of user actions and inputs that are protected from causing any system malfunction B = Number of user actions and inputs that could be protected from causing any system malfunction
User interface aesthetics	Design and Testing	Appearance aesthetics of user interfaces	X = A/B A = Number of display interfaces aesthetically pleasing to the users in appearance B = Number of display interfaces
Accessibility	Design and Testing	Accessibility for Users with disabilities	X = A/B A = Number of functions successfully usable by the users with a specific disability B = Number of functions implemented

4   Usability Evaluation Based on SQuaRE

4.1   Overview of Waseda Software Quality Framework: WSQF

The ISO/IEC 250nn SQuaRE series is a useful framework to specify, measure and evaluate quality objectively and multi-directionally. SQuaRE is independent of the domain and type of products. It provides quality models, quality measures and guidelines for quality management, quality requirement specification, and quality measurement and quality evaluation. However, the descriptions of them in SQuaRE are rather general and abstract since it is developed and published as International Standards. It's necessary to concretize them for practical use. It's also expected to clarify the relationships among characteristics and subcharacteristics of product quality model and quality in use model.

Responding to these issues, a project, Establishment of Framework for Software Product Quality Quantification and Total Quality Evaluation through Measurement, Evaluation, and Analysis was established in 2015 and performed until 2017 by Waseda University, funded by the Research Initiative on Advanced Software Engineering (RISE) of the Information-technology Promotion Agency (IPA). The authors, Prof. Azuma and Mr. Komiyama joined and contributed to this project as experts of SQuaRE.

As a result of this study, a comprehensive quality evaluation framework, Waseda Software Quality Framework (WSQF) [5], was created targeting software products developed by third-party such as packaged software or cloud-based applications. The quality measures and measurement methods in the WSQF are based on those in SQuaRE. The WSQF enhanced measures and measurement methods in SQuaRE so that they can be applied to the target software. Furthermore, the WSQF summarizes the obtained measurement results as a comprehensive quality evaluation grouped by multilateral quality characteristics and subcharacteristics.

The WSQF was applied to twenty-one actual software products. As the results, the trends by quality characteristics, relationships among quality characteristics, relationships between quality-in-use and product quality, and relationships between quality characteristics and product context. All the assets and data created and obtained through this study are disclosed as WSQB17: Waseda Software Quality Benchmark [6].

4.2   Practical Measures for Usability

The WSQF defined sixty-six quality measures for product quality and seventeen for quality in use, covering all the quality subcharacteristics of those models. The Goal-Question-Metric (GQM) method [7] is applied to select measures from SQuaRE and define them for not losing the purpose of the measurement. The templates, surveillance sheets or tools are developed and prepared and utilized to obtain measurement data on them. Figure 4 shows examples of usability measures and its template.

Usability Subcharacteristics	SQuaRE ID	WSQF ID	Name	Measurement Function
Operability	UOp-6	UOp.6.1	Rate of Undo support	X = A/B A = Number of functionalities that can be reverted B = Number of functionalities requiring Undo support
Accessibility	UAc-3	UAc.3.1	Rate of functionality accessibility for hearing and visual impairment	X = A/B A=Number of functionalities accessible for hearing and visual impairment B=Number of functionalities

			UOp.6.1			UAc.3.1		
Function ID	Function	Necessity of Undo (NA: if not applicable)	\<Undo type 1\> Possible to go back to previous screen and redo (YES: if possible)	\<Undo type 2\> possible to go back to status before completion and redo (YES: if possible)	\<Undo type 3\> possible to undo and redo (YES: if possible)	Consideration of universal design (YES or NO)	Character size (YES: if possible)	Audio guide (YES: if possible)
MF001	Open document	NA				YES		YES
MF002	Save document	NA				YES		YES
MF003	Delete document			YES		YES		YES
MF004	Edit document				YES	YES	YES	YES
MF005	Search document		YES			YES	YES	YES
...								

Fig. 4. Examples of WSQF usability measures and templates

4.3 Analysis of Relationships Between Usability and Quality in Use

The WSQF measures were applied to twenty-one software products. More than one data could be obtained for fifty-seven out of sixty-six measures on product quality and all seventeen on quality in use. Obtained data are summarized as quality scores of sub-characteristics and then those of characteristics. Correlation analysis of them is performed. Figure 5 shows the correlation coefficient of the quality scores of quality characteristics. As to usability, it was found the following statistically significant results:

- a higher functional-suitability score tends to indicate a lower usability score and,
- a higher portability score tends to indicate higher usability scores.

Statistically significant correlations between usability and effectiveness, efficiency and satisfaction were not observed with the analysis. We expect a further collection of data and analysis to clarify them.

	Perf.	Com.	Usab..	Rel..	Sec..	Mai..	Port.	Effec.	Effic.
Functional-suitability	0.27	0.19	-0.73**	0.35	-0.05	0.47	0.25	-0.23	0.49
Performance-efficiency		0.44	0.24	0.36	-0.17	0.36	0.33	0.32	-0.10
Compatibility			0.04	0.15	-0.06	0.36	-0.07	-0.14	0.05
Usability				0.16	-0.25	0.11	0.47*	-0.13	-0.13
Reliability					0.30	0.38	0.42	-0.08	0.11
Security						-0.06	0.20	0.64	-0.34
Maintainability							0.25	-0.29	0.01
Portability								-0.17	0.63
Effectiveness									0.03
Efficiency									

Fig. 5. Correlation coefficient of quality score by quality characteristics

5 Future Perspectives of International Standardization of Usability Evaluation

The current ISO/IEC 25010 was published in 2011. Revision of ISO/IEC 25010 has initiated in 2019 to catch up on new technology trends of systems and software engineering and also to harmonize with the other SQuaRE documents and with the related International Standards developed within SC7 and by the other SCs. Application results of the SQuaRE, such as the WSQB, will also be considered to make it more practical.

5.1 Reorganization of Document Structure

The current version of ISO/IEC 25010 includes the following three topics:

- Basic concepts of quality model,
- Product quality model,
- Quality in use model.

The first topic is described focusing on quality models for system and software. However, now SQuaRE has ISO/IEC 25012: Data quality model [8] and ISO/IEC TS 25011: Service quality models [9]. The basic concepts should be able to apply not only to system and software but also data and IT services. Also, Quality in use characteristics and subcharacteristics are common between ISO/IEC 25010 and ISO/IEC 25012. They should be structured and defined independently to target entities.

Considering these matters, it was proposed and accepted to sprit the current ISO/IEC 25010 to the following three parts:

- Part 1: Overview and usage

To describe fundamental concepts of quality models commonly applicable to quality in use, system and software products, data and IT services.

- Part 2: Product quality model

To restructure the model considering harmonization with concepts and definitions of Security, Safety, Usability, Scalability, Maturity and so on described in the related International Standards.

- Part 3: Quality in use model

To restructure the model considering types of users and stakeholders affected with system and software products, data and IT services.

Now, these revisions are underway.

5.2 Harmonization with Usability Standards

The definitions of usability, effectiveness, efficiency, and satisfaction in ISO/IEC 25010 are identical with those of ISO 9241-11: Usability: Definitions and concepts [10] prepared by ISO/TC 159 (Ergonomics)/SC 4 (Ergonomics of human-system interaction). Currently SQuaRE deals usability as a characteristic of product quality model and the other three as characteristics of quality in use model. On the other hand, ISO 9241-11 deals usability as an outcome of use and considers it to be composed of effectiveness, efficiency, and satisfaction.

So, we are now considering to move usability from part 2 to part 3 of the new ISO/IEC 25010 change the name and definition of usability in product quality model, such as interaction capability.

The definition of accessibility is not also identical. The necessity of identification shall be decided. Also, accessibility is dealt with as a subcharacteristic of usability in the product quality model of ISO/IEC 25010. On the other hand ISO 9241-11 deals accessibility as one of outcome other than usability. If we move accessibility to quality in use model as an outcome of the product, then a new name and definition will be necessary, such as access capability.

5.3 Enhancement Based on Results of Actual Uses

After the revision of ISO/IEC 25010, quality measures of ISO/IEC 25023 will be revised based on the new product quality model defined in ISO/IEC 25010-2. We expect quality measurement methods of the WSQB are more widely used and improved as a result of actual use. That knowledge will be incorporated into ISO/IEC 25023 revision to make measures for usability and the other quality characteristics and subcharacteristics more practical.

The other expectation to WSQB is further clarification of relationships among characteristics and subcharacteristics of product quality model and quality in use model. If we could obtain more data, correlation analysis based on sufficient sample data may clarify furthermore significant correlations and no significant correlations among them. That may lead to reconsiderations of quality model structure, and quality measures for each characteristic and subcharacteristic. Significant positive and negative correlations within a model and across models will make it possible to evaluate the quality of software-intensive systems more systematically, user-oriented and goal-driven, by considering tradeoff and cause-effect.

6 Conclusion

In this paper, we introduced an overview of the ISO/IEC 250nn SQuaRE series and its viewpoints and measures of usability and explained about the WSQF study results concerning the application of the SQuaRE to actual projects. Based on them, we discussed revision points related to usability evaluation. As future work, we will proceed to collect and analyze quality data using the WSQF and gain and implement useful insights into the SQuaRE to make it more practical and useful.

References

1. Komiyama, T.: Usability evaluation based on international standards for software quality evaluation. NEC Tech. J. 3(2), 27–32 (2008)
2. ISO/IEC 25010: Systems and software engineering—Systems and software Quality Requirements and Evaluation (SQuaRE)—System and software quality models (2011)
3. ISO/IEC 25023: Systems and software engineering—Systems and software Quality Requirements and Evaluation (SQuaRE)—Measurement of system and software product quality (2016)
4. ISO/IEC 25022: Systems and software engineering—Systems and software Quality Requirements and Evaluation (SQuaRE)—Measurement of quality in use (2016)
5. Tsuda, N., et al: WSQF: comprehensive software quality evaluation framework and benchmark based on SQuaRE. In: Proceedings of the 41st International Conference on Software Engineering, pp. 312–321 (2019)
6. WSQB17: Waseda Software Quality Benchmark. http://www.washi.cs.waseda.ac.jp/wsqb/
7. Basili, V.R., et al.: Goal, Question, Metric Paradigm. Wiley, Hoboken (1994). Encyclopedia of Software Engineering
8. ISO/IEC 25012: Software engineering—Software product Quality Requirements and Evaluation (SQuaRE)—Data quality model (2008)
9. ISO/IEC TS 25011: Information technology—Systems and software Quality Requirements and Evaluation (SQuaRE)—Service quality models (20117)
10. ISO 9241-11: Ergonomics of human-system interaction—Part 11: Usability: Definitions and concepts (2018)

An Experimental Study of Typography Using EEG Signal Parameters

Ana Rita Teixeira[1,2(✉)] and Anabela Gomes[3,4]

[1] Coimbra Polytechnic - ESEC, Coimbra, Portugal
ateixeira@ua.pt
[2] IEETA, Aveiro University, Aveiro, Portugal
[3] Coimbra Polytechnic - ISEC, Coimbra, Portugal
[4] Centre for Informatics and Systems,
University of Coimbra, Coimbra, Portugal

Abstract. Brain-Computer Interaction (BCI) technology can be used in several areas having recently gained increased interest with diverse applications in the area of Human Computer Interaction (HCI). In this area one of the central aspects relates to the ease of perceiving information. Typography is one of the central elements that, when properly used, can provide better readability and understanding of the information to be communicated. In this sense, this multidisciplinary work (typography and cognitive neuroscience) examines how the brain processes typographic information using EEG technology. In this context, the main goal of this work is to obtain information about the users when reading several words written in different typefaces and deduce theirs mental states (fatigue, stress, immersion) through user's electroencephalogram signals (EEG). Additionally, several EEG features were extracted, namely the energy of Theta, Alpha and Beta waves, as well as, the variability of these bands' energy. It is considered that this is a preliminary study in this area and may be extended to another type of design features.

Keywords: EEG · Mindwave · Fatigue · Immersion · Stress

1 Introduction

The construct of mental workload can be understood as the level of cognitive engagement which has a direct impact on the effectiveness and quality of a learning process. Mental states can be detected through several noninvasive sensing and imaging technologies, such as, fMRI and EEG [10]. However, not all of these available interfaces are suitable for mental state detection in real life situations. Of the several associated problems, the portability and difficulty of acquisition stand out. In recent years, vast researches have concentrated towards the development of EEG based human computer interface in arrangement to enhancing the quality of life for medical as well as non-medical applications [8]. It can be used in smart city applications such as brain-computer interface in industrial

© Springer Nature Switzerland AG 2020
M. Kurosu (Ed.): HCII 2020, LNCS 12181, pp. 464–473, 2020.
https://doi.org/10.1007/978-3-030-49059-1_34

applications or intelligent wireless wearable EEG solutions for daily life applications [1], [7]. Industry and community of research has been attracted by wireless EEG devices and they are easily available in the market. Such technology can be incorporated to psychology, medical applications, and real-time monitoring of patients. Neurosky Mindwave headset [11] is a portable device and is generally used to detect and measure electrical activity of the user's forehead and transmit the collected data wirelessly, to a computer for further processing [9], [13]. After processing the data base, the signals are categorized into various frequency bands for feature extraction, namely attention, concentration and blinking. In the literature some works describe a variety of EEG features extracted by various algorithms to detect of mental states, such as adaptive auto-regressive parameters, time frequency features and inverse model-based features. Comparing the time frequency features, some works suggested frontal midline theta as a better candidate than frontal alpha activity for use in a BCI-based paradigm designed to detect and modulate emotional reactions. Frontal midline theta was considered to be associated with positive emotional experience and with the relaxation state from anxiety [14]. Theta band waves exist during tasks that require the correlation of increased mental effort and sustained concentration [12]. In the other hand, alpha band waves exist when a person is in relaxation mode, and they may reflect the progress of perceptual processing, memory tasks, and the processing of emotions. Other time frequency features, such as, attention, fatigue, immersion and stress based on power energy of theta, alpha and beta band can be useful to detect mental stage in routine activities. Attention levels can be indicated by several physiological markers, namely eye tracking; eye pupil dilation, which is proportional to attention; the blinking rate, which decreases as attention level increases and the modulation of the EEG activity [15]. Fatigue is a complex state manifested by a lack of alertness, weakness, dizziness, or queasiness, which leads to inefficiency and performance reduction [4]. Immersion is another parameter used. In [6] immersion and concentration are compared and it was found that concentration and immersion states increased alpha waves and theta waves decreased during concentration or increased during immersion. In [2] the immersion is discussed and can be detected in different situations providing the state of immersion as one of the game parameters or to generate a control signal that may be used to provide a warning message or abort the game when the situation of the excessive indulgence in the game reaches. The stress parameter is widely discussed in numerous works with different focuses [3], [5]. The purpose of this study was to analyze mental workload while comparing three types of letters and also their influence in seven words related to emotions. This study aimed to assess mental fatigue, stress and immersion by using electroencephalographic measures during visual screen words. This paper is divided into four sections. Section 2 describes the material and methods followed in experimentation: the participants, the experimental design, the data acquisition and the data processing and analysis. In Sect. 3 the results and how they were used to characterize the stress, fatigue and immersion parameters are also described, and, finally, Sect. 4 contains the conclusions and finally some topics for further work.

2   Materials and Methods

In this section the participants characterization, experimental design as well as the data acquisition and data analysis are described.

2.1   Participants

Thirty participants (9 males and 21 females), aged 18–21 years (mean: 19 ± 0.8 years), were recruited to perform a monotonous reading task. All participants provided informed consent prior to participating in the study. At the beginning of the experiment, a questionnaire was made to each participant in order to obtain a more detailed characterization of the population in question: age, sex, level of education and the existence of visual problems.

2.2   Experimental Design

The experiment was undertaken in a usability laboratory. The experiment was considered correct if there were no interruptions. It consisted of a sequential visualization of seven white "emotional words" (Joy (J), Sadness (S), Love (L), Hate (H), Sympathy (Sy), Unrest (U) and Calmness (C)) written in a black screen, considering three typography fonts and each typefaces respectively:

- Sans Serif – Open Sans;
- Serif – Old London;
- Handwriting – Dancing Script;

Figure 1 presents a sequential example with three screens. The words occurred on the screen in a sequence of 21 possible combinations, Table 1. During this task, each word was presented for 3 s at the center of the screen, followed by a pause with a white screen for 1 s totalizing 83 s, as shown in Fig. 2. Participants only have to see the word and read the word presented in the screen. In total, each participant will be exposed for 83 s to 21 frames with words written in white on

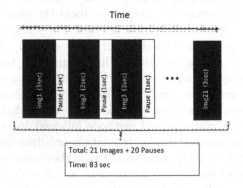

Fig. 1. The timing diagram of the experiment.

Table 1. Coding combinations of typefaces with the selected emotional words.

	Open Sans	Old London	Dancing Script
Joy	J_{OS}	J_{OL}	J_{DS}
Sadness	S_{OS}	S_{OL}	S_{DS}
Love	L_{OS}	L_{OL}	L_{DS}
Hate	H_{OS}	H_{OL}	H_{DS}
Sympathy	Sy_{OS}	Sy_{OL}	Sy_{DS}
Unrest	U_{OS}	U_{OL}	U_{DS}
Calmness	C_{OS}	C_{OL}	C_{DS}

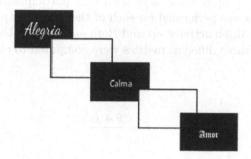

Fig. 2. Experimental time sequence (an example)

a black screen and 20 transition frames in a white screen. It should be noted that the location on the screen, as well as, the size of the words did not change. The participants were also asked not to blink and not to move their eyes and body during the visualization of the screens. The purpose of this procedure is to eliminate ocular and muscular artifacts, thus avoiding signal loss. At the end of the experiment, users were asked to choose on paper which typographic font they preferred and which they found more frequently.

2.3   Data Acquisition

Neurosky's Mindwave is a device that measures brain activity using a sensor on the forehead $(Fp1)$ and a clip located on the left ear that acts as a ground and reference. It can provide a raw signal at a sampling rate of 512 Hz and 12 bits of resolution as well as processed information like power bands. However, bands and indicators are sent at a rate of 1 Hz. The software checks the POORSIG-NAL indicator sent by Neurosky's Mindwave every second. A value of 0 in this indicator guarantees good contact between electrodes and the skin and, therefore, a good quality signal. In the case of poor signal quality, the attention value is rejected and not recorded by the software. The main frequency range of the EEG signal is [0.5–30] Hz, which contains information about mental states and can be divided into 5 main bands, delta waves [0.5–4] Hz, theta waves [4–8] Hz, alpha waves [8–13] Hz, beta waves [13–30] Hz and gamma waves [30–40] Hz. For different brain activities, the power changes of the three bands (theta, alpha and beta) comply with different patterns, which implies that the power of the 3 bands are key indicators of mental states, such as, stress, immersion and fatigue indicators.

2.4   Data Processing Ad Analysis

The EEG signal as well as the signal associated to the power bands, for each participant, were divided into 21 segments of 3 s related to each task (visualization and reading each screen). The average of the segments by group of words and by group of typography was analyzed for each participant and for all participants. This analysis was performed for each of the frequency parameters namely Theta activity - θ, Alpha activity - α and Beta activity - β. Using the frequency information bands three different metrics were computed to characterize mental states, such as :

1. Fatigue (F)

$$F = \frac{\theta + \alpha}{\beta} \tag{1}$$

2. Immersion (I)

$$I = \frac{\theta}{\alpha} \tag{2}$$

3. Stress (S)

$$S = \frac{\beta}{\alpha} \tag{3}$$

The results are reported considering the minimum, maximum, average $\pm$ and standard deviation σ values. Significant level is reported at $p < 0.05$. The average of the parameters values were computed and compared. The three types of letters as well as the relation with the emotions words are analyzed.

3   Results and Discussion

Our study intended to address the following questions:

- Q_1 - Different words written in the same typeface present different energy levels? In what waves?
- Q_2 - The same words written in different typefaces present different energy levels? In what waves?
- Q_3 - Different words written in the same typeface present different levels of fatigue, immersion and stress? In what typefaces (OS, OL and DS)?
- Q_4 - The same words written in different typefaces present different levels of fatigue, immersion and stress? In what typefaces (OS, OL and DS)?

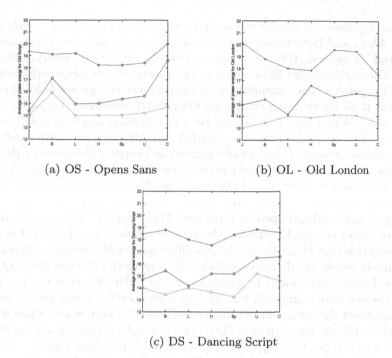

(a) OS - Opens Sans   (b) OL - Old London

(c) DS - Dancing Script

Fig. 3. Variability of the power energy of all participants considering three typefaces: OS - Opens Sans (a); OL - Old London (b) and DS - Dancing Script (c) for each emotional word (Joy (J), Sadness (S), Love (L), Hate (H), Sympathy (Sy), Unrest (U) and Calmness (C))

To answer the first question (Q_1) the levels of energy were compared, in the bands θ, α and β, between words of same typeface, as shown in Fig. 3. A confidence level of 95% was used, where some results stand out. Theta band power levels haven't got a significant statistical difference between all words when written in typeface DS. However, there were differences between H_{OS}-C_{OS} ($p = 0.036$), Sy_{OS}-C_{OS} ($p = 0.013$), J_{OL}-L_{OL} ($p = 0.028$), J_{OL}-H_{OL} ($p = 0.0229$), J_{OL}-C_{OL} ($p = 0.041$), Sy_{OL}-U_{OL} ($p = 0.0154$) and Sy_{OL}-C_{OL} ($p = 0.0154$) in typeface OL. Beta band energy levels show no statistically significant differences between words when written in OS and OL typefaces, but only one difference S_{DS}-U_{DS} ($p = 0.039$). Alpha band energy levels are those where there are most statistically significant differences between different words: J_{OS}-S_{OS} ($p = 0.083$), J_{OS}-C_{OS} ($p = 0.000121$), S_{OS}-L_{OS} ($p = 0.0215$), S_{OS}-H_{OS} ($p = 0.0212$), L_{OS}-C_{OS} ($p = 0.000015$), H_{OS}-C_{OS} ($p = 0.00041$), Sy_{OS}-C_{OS} ($p = 0.00091$) and U_{OS}-C_{OS} ($p = 0.000042$) when written in OS typeface, J_{OL}-H_{OL} ($p = 0.033$), L_{OL}-H_{OL} ($p = 0.0111$) and L_{OL}-U_{OL} ($p = 0.0313$) when written in OL typeface and J_{DS}-C_{DS} ($p = 0.0417$), L_{DS}-U_{DS} ($p = 0.019$) and L_{DS}-C_{DS} ($p = 0.0284$) when written in DS typeface. The word Calmness is the one with the most statistically significant energy differences over a large set of words written in the same typeface. To answer the second question (Q_2) the energy levels in the Theta, Alpha and Beta bands for each word written in different typefaces were compared. In general, there were no statistically significant energy differences in the Theta, Alpha and Beta bands in the various words when written in the different typefaces. The exceptions were the different energy levels for the word Calmness in all bands when comparing OS and OL typefaces (C_{OS}-C_{OL} Theta ($p = 0.0073$), Alpha ($p = 0.0045$) and Beta ($p = 0.025$)) and also in OS and DS typefaces (C_{OS}-C_{DS}) in Theta ($p = 0.016$) and Alpha ($p = 0.084$) bands. The word Sadness presented statistically significant energy differences in the Beta band when we compare this word written in the OS and OL typefaces (S_{OS}-S_{OL} ($p = 0.048$)) and in the OS and DS typefaces (S_{OS}-S_{DS} ($p = 0.014$)). Table 2 presents a descriptive statistical analysis of the values for each of the bands considering all the words grouped by typefaces. Theta band is the one with average values of higher energy. Comparing the various values of the Table 2 it is possible to conclude that there are no obvious differences, with however differences in the different words (as discussed earlier). To answer the $3rd$ question (Q_3) the levels of Fatigue, Stress and Immersion between different words written in the same typeface were compared, highlighting a few points. There are no statistically significant differences in the Immersion levels between words when written in typeface DS. In this typeface (DS), there is only a statistically significant difference in Fatigue L_{DS}-Sy_{DS} ($p = 0.0472$) and Stress S_{DS}-L_{DS} ($p = 0.0189$) levels. There are some statistically significant differences in Fatigue, Stress and Immersion levels in the various typefaces when comparing different words: in Fatigue levels, the pair of words S_{OS}-C_{OS} ($p = 0.0108$), L_{OS}-C_{OS} ($p = 0.0481$), H_{OS}-C_{OS} ($p = 0.0335$) and J_{OL}-L_{OL} ($p = 0.02$) and in Stress levels, the pair of words J_{OS}-C_{OS} ($p = 0.066$), S_{OS}-C_{OS} ($p = 0.0205$), H_{OS}-C_{OS} ($p = 0.033$), U_{OS}-C_{OS} ($p = 0.0464$), S_{OL}-L_{OL} ($p = 0.0189$), L_{OL}-H_{OL} ($p = 0.0034$) and L_{OL}-C_{OL} ($p = 0.0176$). As highlighted in previous analysis, the word Calmness was the one that presented the most statistically significant energy differences in relation to a large set of words, in the analysis of these 3 parameters, when written in the same typeface. According to Table 2, the Fatigue levels show higher mean values in typeface OL, the levels of Immersion and stress present mean values almost equal in all typefaces. Finally, and answering to Q_4, levels of fatigue Eq. 1, immersion Eq. 2 and stress Eq. 3 were compared to each word written in different typefaces. No statistically significant differences in levels immersion for the various words when written in the different typefaces was found. In general, the levels of fatigue and Stress for the various words when written in the different typefaces also did not present significant statistical differences, but only the following: Fatigue levels showed significant statistical differences for C_{OS}-C_{OL} ($p = 0.0363$), C_{DS}-C_{OS} ($p = 0.0051$), J_{DS}-J_{OL} ($p = 0.0325$). Stress levels showed significant statistical differences only for C_{OS}-C_{OL} ($p = 0.00029$).

Table 2. Minimum, maximum, average and standard deviation considering the frequency bands (θ, α and β) and each typeface (OS, OL and DS) respectively

		Min	Max	μ	σ
θ band	OS	12.00	23.82	18,93	3,41
	OL	12,14	23,91	18,70	3,69
	DS	11,45	23,45	18,51	3,59
α band	OS	10,90	23,60	15,88	3,58
	OL	10,39	23,93	15,42	3,53
	DS	10,16	23,88	15,50	3,52
β band	OS	10,22	23,94	14,42	2,71
	OL	9,84	23,73	13,69	1,86
	DS	10,37	23,94	14,06	2,30

Considering all the words grouped by typefaces, a variability analysis of the average values for fatigue, stress and immersion parameters are showed in Fig. 4. We can conclude that, globally, there are no significant differences in terms

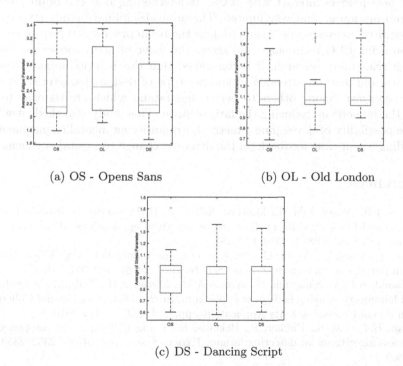

(a) OS - Opens Sans   (b) OL - Old London

(c) DS - Dancing Script

Fig. 4. Variability of the average values: Fatigue values, (F), Immersion values, (I) and Stress values, (S) of all participants considering three types of letter: OS - Opens Sans (a); OL - Old London (b) and DS - Dancing Script (c)

of wave energy and the parameters analyzed. However, by performing a word analysis and considering the different typefaces, significant statistical differences are found, which leads to the conclusion that the analysis methodology as well as the signal acquisition equipment are very promising for the development of a BCI.

4   Conclusions and Further Work

Typography plays a key role in any graphic design, and readability is one of the main aspects to consider. There are several factors that influence the readability of a typeface, such as spacing, contrast, size, shapes, character color, background color, among others. Additionally, typography is a very dynamic communication tool, appealing to the imagination and communicating ideas without ever losing the purpose of what one wants to communicate. For communication to occur without interference it is important to choose the right typeface. This allows a reading to be very or little readable and a person to be quite attentive or not. Consequently, it is a fundamental component of any project. However, typographic fonts are more easily perceived and lead to higher levels of understanding, attention, immersion, stress or fatigue than others. Despite growing knowledge about how readers interact with texts, understanding how the brain processes this information is relatively limited. This multidisciplinary study (typography and cognitive neuroscience) examines how the brain processes typographic information using EEG technology and shows the value of neuroscience methodologies for readability research. It is considered that this is a preliminary study in this area and may be extended to another type of design characteristics: color, shape, contrast among others to better understand which are the way to promote the immersion, reducing the fatigue state. This study also sheds new light on the possibility of developing a metric for quantifying mental engagement and providing a real-time feedback on the dynamic change of mental engagement.

References

1. Aris, I.B., Yusof, S.M.M., Mousavi, S.N., Ali, H.H., Sahbudin, R.K.Z.: Low cost wireless EEG system for medical and non-medical applications. IEEJ Trans. Electron. Inf. Syst. **138**(2), 90–93 (2018)
2. Ga, Y., Choi, T., Yoon, G.: Analysis of game immersion using EEG signal for computer smart interface. J. Sens. Sci. Technol. **24**(6), 392–397 (2015)
3. Hamid, N.H.A., Sulaiman, N., Aris, S.A.M., Murat, Z.H., Taib, M.N.: Evaluation of human stress using EEG power spectrum. In: 2010 6th International Colloquium on Signal Processing & its Applications, pp. 1–4. IEEE, May 2010
4. Jap, B.T., Lal, S., Fischer, P., Bekiaris, E.: Using EEG spectral components to assess algorithms for detecting fatigue. Expert Syst. Appl. **36**(2), 2352–2359, Mar 2009
5. Katahira, K., Yamazaki, Y., Yamaoka, C., Ozaki, H., Nakagawa, S., Nagata, N.: EEG correlates of the flow state: a combination of increased frontal theta and moderate frontocentral alpha rhythm in the mental arithmetic task. Front. Psychol. **9**, 300 (2018)

6. Lim, S., Yeo, M., Yoon, G., Lim, S., Yeo, M., Yoon, G.: Comparison between concentration and immersion based on EEG analysis. Sensors **19**(7), 1669 (2019)
7. Mihajlovic, V., Grundlehner, B., Vullers, R., Penders, J.: Wearable, wireless EEG solutions in daily life applications: what are we missing? IEEE J. Biomed. Health Inform. **19**(1), 6–21 (2015)
8. Minguillon, J., Lopez-Gordo, M.A., Pelayo, F.: Trends in EEG-BCI for daily-life: requirements for artifact removal. Biomed. Signal Process. Control **31**, 407–418 (2017)
9. Molina-Cantero, A.J., Guerrero-Cubero, J., Gómez-González, I.M., Merino-Monge, M., Silva-Silva, J.I.: Characterizing computer access using a one-channel EEG wireless sensor. Sensor **17**, 1525 (2017)
10. Morita, T., Asada, M., Naito, E.: Contribution of neuroimaging studies to understanding development of human cognitive brain functions. Front. Hum. Neurosci. **10**, 464 (2016)
11. Neurosky Mindwave User Guide (2018)
12. Sammler, D., Grigutsch, M., Fritz, T., Koelsch, S.: Music and emotion: electrophysiological correlates of the processing of pleasant and unpleasant music. Psychophysiology **44**(2), 293–304 (2007)
13. Sezer, A., İnel, Y., Seçkin, A.Ç., Uluçınar, U.: The relationship between attention levels and class participation of first-year students in classroom teaching departments. Int. J. Instr. **10**(2), 55 (2017)
14. Suetsugi, M., et al.: Appearance of frontal midline theta activity in patients with generalized anxiety disorder. Neuropsychobiology **41**(2), 108–112 (2000)
15. Vinod, A.P., Guan, C.: Design of an online EEG based neurofeedback game for enhancing attention and memory. In: IEEE Engineering in Medicine and Biology Society (2013)

Research on Evaluation of Perceptual Experience Quality of Web-Based Panoramic Navigation System Based on Cognitive Mechanism

Haowei Wang[✉], Bin Jiang, and Qianwen Chen

School of Design Art & Media, Nanjing University of Science and Technology,
Nanjing, Jiangsu, People's Republic of China
2680383509@qq.com, jb508@163.com

Abstract. In order to improve the application status of panoramic navigation and optimize the user's web browsing experience, an evaluation system is proposed to evaluate the quality of user perceived experience of panoramic navigation. Based on the theory of user perception, cognitive mechanism and the induction of users and perception elements, this paper studies the influencing factors of users' perception experience of Web panoramic navigation system, constructs an evaluation index system and quantifies the weight of each index. Finally, the validity and feasibility of the evaluation system are verified by selecting a representative panoramic navigation system. The evaluation system constructed in this paper provides evaluation system and design reference standard for panoramic navigation design of web pages.

Keywords: Panoramic navigation · Cognitive mechanism · Perceived experience quality · Evaluation system

1 Introduction

In recent years, the application field of virtual reality technology on the Internet platform is more and more extensive, and the application forms are gradually rich. However, due to the neglect of the important role of user experience and cognitive psychology in the field of virtual reality, the panoramic interactive experience of such websites is poor. Panoramic virtual reality is a kind of easy to realize and practical virtual reality technology, which is widely used in various interactive carriers with a broad perspective and strong visual impact. Nowadays, panorama display is not a simple tool for visual scene display. People realize its economic benefits and cultural communication by increasing interaction and information transmission. Among them, web-based panoramic virtual presentation is one of the most practical and economic benefits. It is mainly used in campus, scenic spots, exhibition halls and other environments, so that users can get a very immersive viewing experience through a new form of vision and interaction.

Panorama technology is a kind of virtual reality technology [1]. Compared with the virtual reality technology which needs the investment of 3D scene modeling and

© Springer Nature Switzerland AG 2020
M. Kurosu (Ed.): HCII 2020, LNCS 12181, pp. 474–486, 2020.
https://doi.org/10.1007/978-3-030-49059-1_35

simulation technology, panorama technology has its unique technical and interactive advantages, and has some unique characteristics [2]: 1) panorama technology does not need a lot of data support, and data acquisition and processing are not complex. Only through the real composite image shooting to image splicing, and then to image optimization three steps can be achieved; 2) panoramic technology records the real scene, which is intuitive and real, and the browsing process is fast to obtain visual information, reducing the burden of user operation; 3) the presentation of panorama on the web page does not need too much hardware support, and it can run in real time on the PC. At the same time, the requirements for loading devices are also low, and users are easy to interact in the browsing of virtual scenes on the web; 4) panorama technology presents high quality images, which are not affected by external objective factors.

Based on the above advantages, panorama technology is widely used in multiple scenes to help people realize more intuitive and immersive virtual scene perception and interaction.

2 Related Works

2.1 Current Situation Analysis

As the name implies, panoramic navigation function is added to panorama. Compared with other web pages, panoramic navigation design is a more complex module design process, which involves the dynamic interactive control of panoramic window itself. Panoramic navigation system includes the interactive control of panoramic browsing window and map navigation window, panoramic switching and background data switching, as well as the information perception and transmission in panoramic interactive process Pass [3]. Therefore, in addition to the basic visual perception information available to users, the common web-based panoramic virtual reproduction system interface should also have a map interaction window and a navigation module throughout the whole system. Through investigation, it is found that many panoramic technology applications at this stage stay at the panoramic demonstration level of the scene, while ignoring the navigation function and interaction function module of the system.

The functions of panoramic navigation system mainly include the following three aspects: first, the switch between panoramic view visual mobile browsing and panoramic view; second, Panoramic Map overview and interactive control, real-time feedback of view point dynamics; third, the information content and information transmission methods presented in panoramic navigation, in which information includes text, voice or picture and other information categories acquired by multi-sensory channel.

2.2 Application Characteristics of Panoramic Navigation

Panoramic virtual presentation builds a visual interaction window between the real world, virtual world and users. The interface carries a lot of information such as text, pictures, voice, images, etc., forming a real-time feedback information loop, enhancing the authenticity of user experience, and bringing a strong visual sense. Different web panoramic virtual presentation mode and user's basic attribute requirements determine that panoramic navigation system is different from other web page information interfaces. Panoramic navigation has the following characteristics [4]:

1. Multi perception: in addition to the common visual perception of web browsing, web panoramic virtual navigation may also involve a variety of perception systems such as hearing, but compared with VR and AR users with higher technology, the perceptual channel is slightly thinner.
2. Real time interaction and feedback: panoramic virtual reality technology can output information by means of media and computer. The information transmission and interactive control in Web panoramic navigation system are real-time, intuitive guidance and real-time feedback of user's operation.
3. Autonomy: when browsing the panorama of the web page, the user has strong autonomy, which is mainly manifested in that the user can drag freely in the panorama, and there is no limit to the direction and angle of dragging, and the panorama can also be switched freely according to the requirements of the user, without the distinction of front and back order.
4. Immersion: panoramic virtual technology is applied in web pages to create the junction of virtual and reality in the physical space, especially the panorama is constructed from the real scene images collected from the real scene to create a virtual immersion experience on the physical space for users.

3   Perceptual Experience in Web Panoramic Navigation

3.1   User Perception Theory

User perception theory refers to the process that users perceive human-computer interaction or interaction between users and objects or service providers through senses, thoughts, etc. [5]. Through a lot of literature surveys, the quantitative research on perceived quality is mostly focused on service quality or information quality. Perceived experience quality assessment includes service or interactive experience assessment and information quality assessment.

Cognitive process is the advanced process of human brain to input, transform, store and improve the perceived information, including perception and attention stage, memory stage, thinking and decision-making stage [6]. Perception is the direct reflection of objective things in human brain through multi-channel senses, including sensation and perception; attention is the direction and concentration of psychological activities on certain objects, including selective attention, focused attention, segmented attention and sustained attention; memory is the reflection of human brain on past experience, including the stages of recollection, retention, reproduction and recollection. The information is temporarily stored in the multisensory channel system, then enters the short-term memory and long-term memory through the brain control system, and finally realizes the current task or optimal design through the problem decision-making process.

According to the formation process of cognitive activities in design psychology, the information transfer process of the navigation system is that users receive information and start processing when opening the web page, which has the following four steps [7]:

1. Receiving information: the navigation system interface presents the initialization status of panorama and navigation map, a brief introduction of knowledge background and interactive operation icons, etc., so that users can have a preliminary understanding of the whole system, in order to have a preliminary prediction and a deeper understanding of the subsequent information.

2. Situational experience: in the process of browsing, users can analyze each physical object and place through real scene display, image, animation, voice and other display methods, so as to promote users to form in-depth understanding. In this process, a more immersive interaction mode can also be created to increase the user's participation and interest.

3. Form heuristic cognition: when the user completes the demand, the user obtains the promotion of knowledge or the pleasure of task completion. The cognition obtained from panorama is more profound than that obtained from conventional web browsing.

3.2 Quality Evaluation of Perceptual Experience

Perceptual experience is the user's experience and psychological feeling in the process of information acquisition. It comes from the comparison between the actual situation of user's information perception and the user's expectation. It also determines the user's attitude towards the system and service, the user's evaluation of information quality and the user's satisfaction. Therefore, the quality of user perceived experience is related to the quality of system information and affects each other [8].

The introduction of perceptual experience quality into the theory of cognitive mechanism refers to the evaluation of information quality and information quantity conveyed to users through different presentation methods. From the perspective of perceived quality experience, user perceived experience quality is related to user perceived preference, perceived information and perceived experience [9]. As shown in Fig. 1, the user's perception preference includes the preference of interaction mode and information content itself, which is related to the user's own behavior habits; the perception information quality refers to the system interface information itself, and the evaluation indicators of information quality are complexity, content, applicability, etc.; the perception experience of the user browsing the panoramic navigation system depends on the viewing mode, task triggering, scenario reproduction, etc. and so on.

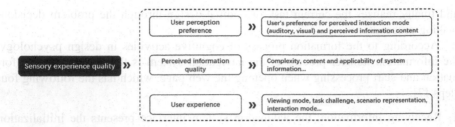

Fig. 1. Influencing factors of perceived experience quality

4   User Perception Elements in Web Panoramic Navigation

4.1   Interface Element

The interface element of Web panoramic navigation system is the visual element perceived by the user's vision, which roughly includes: 1) Panoramic image. Panoramic image is an important part of panoramic navigation system, which requires high definition and smooth image mosaic. 2) Text message. Information can be divided into two types, one is content information, which can deepen users' cognition through information transmission. The other is function information, which is convenient for users to understand the system operation and has guidance. 3) Image. In order to better transmit information, images will be added to the navigation system to deepen users' understanding of information. 4) Icon. There are two kinds of icons, one is system icon. The other is navigation icon, which plays a role of navigation in panoramic navigation of web pages, helping users understand and complete learning tasks. 5) Map. Map elements will be added to the panoramic navigation system. When users browse panorama, they have a certain understanding of the overall situation and their location. 6) Interface layout. Refers to the regional scope and location of each element information presentation.

4.2   Interactive Mode

The user requirements of the navigation system determine the interaction mode. Interaction mode is also a part of user perception. Different interaction modes have different cognitive processes, and the quality of user perception experience will change accordingly. The ways of interaction are as follows: 1) Information presentation. The interaction mode of system information plays a decisive role in the user experience. The information in the web panoramic navigation system is mainly represented by text, pattern, audio commentary and video. 2) Task triggered. A task, challenge, or content triggered by a user in an interaction. 3) Scene reproduction. In order to increase the user's immersion, the system provides a variety of interactive ways of scenario reproduction. 4) Environmental atmosphere. Panoramic navigation sometimes creates an atmosphere, which will increase the interaction of music and dynamic effects.

5 Construction of Evaluation System

According to the above analysis of perception experience quality and perception elements in panoramic navigation system, the following will build evaluation indicators from the perspective of user's cognitive mechanism, focusing on the quantitative indicators of information acquisition quality in user's perception experience quality.

In order to construct the evaluation system of Web panoramic navigation, it is necessary to establish scientific and objective evaluation indexes of user experience quality, in order to better guide decision-making and optimize design. The selection of indicators should follow the principles of consistency, comprehensiveness, effectiveness, independence, hierarchy and measurability with the user's needs, among which the internal relationship between the perceptual elements and perception information quality in Web panoramic navigation system should be constructed according to the principle of hierarchy, which can effectively improve the accuracy, scientificity and operability of the evaluation model.

5.1 Preliminary Determination of Evaluation Index

Based on the research of the above user perception process, cognitive theory and the influencing factors of user perception experience, this paper evaluates the quality of user perception experience when users browse the panoramic navigation system of web pages, and finally constructs the evaluation system, as shown in Table 1.

Table 1 shows that the quality evaluation index of user experience covers the quality evaluation standard of perception elements from the perspective of information quantity and quality, the quality evaluation standard of perception experience from the perspective of interaction process mode and level, and the impact evaluation index of user perception preference from the perspective of user characteristics in all aspects. Three levels of 23 phase indicators transform the factors affecting users' cognitive level in Web panoramic navigation into more specific, intuitive, operable and quantifiable indicators.

Table 1. Hypothesis model of user perceived experience quality evaluation index

Total target layer A	Perceived experience quality evaluation		
Sub target layer Ai	Perceptual element evaluation A1	Perceptual experience evaluation A2	User characteristic evaluation A3
Criterion layer B	Comprehensibility B1	Navigational B5	User preferences B9
Scheme layer C	Difficulty in obtaining content information C11	Intuitive navigation function C51	Preferences for ways to access information C91
	Navigation information understanding C12	Rationality of navigation planning C52	Operating environment preference C92
Criterion layer B	Value B2	Immersion B6	User emotion B10

(continued)

Table 1. (*continued*)

Total target layer A	Perceived experience quality evaluation		
Scheme layer C	Perceived information professionalism C21	Reality of scenario reproduction C61	User experience pleasure C101
	Perceived information objectivity C22	Task challenge difficulty C62	User expectation matching degree C102
Criterion layer B	Diversity B3	Interactive quality B7	Cognitive matching B11
Scheme layer C	Diversity of information content C31	Diversity of interaction modes C71	User cognitive matching C111
	Diversity of information presentation C32	Interesting interactive form C72	User habit matching C112
Criterion layer B	Conciseness B4	Fluency B8	
Scheme layer C	Simplicity of interface layout C41	Panorama browsing fluency C81	
	Clarity of content and information C42	Panorama switching reaction speed C82	
		Feedback real time C83	

5.2 Determine the Weight of Each Index

According to the evaluation index model of user perceived experience quality of panoramic navigation of the above web page, the final evaluation index is formed, and then the weight of each index is determined by AHP [10].

The analytic hierarchy process (AHP) is a simple, flexible and practical multi criteria decision-making method for quantitative analysis of qualitative problems [11]. Its basic principle is to take the complex multi-objective decision-making problem as a system and decompose it into objective layer, criterion layer and scheme layer. On this basis, qualitative and quantitative analysis is carried out to assist decision-making to make optimal design Scheme.

1. Expert rating. First, three experts from design industry are invited to evaluate the importance of the three-level index structure of the evaluation index model. The score is 1–5, and 1–5 respectively corresponds to the importance of "small", "small", "medium", "large" and "large". See Table 2 for scoring data.

Table 2. Scoring data of experts

Criterion layer	Scheme layer	Expert 1	Expert 2	Expert 3
B1	C11	5	5	5
	C12	5	4	5
B2	C21	4	3	3
	C22	4	3	2
B3	C31	4	4	2
	C32	4	4	3
B4	C41	4	4	4
	C42	5	4	3
B5	C51	5	5	3
	C52	5	5	4
B6	C61	4	4	5
	C62	3	2	4
B7	C71	3	4	4
	C72	3	4	5
B8	C81	4	4	4
	C82	4	3	2
	C83	3	5	4
B9	C91	3	3	4
	C92	3	1	2
B10	C101	4	4	5
	C102	5	3	2
B11	C111	4	3	2
	C112	5	2	3

According to the above scoring data, calculate the score of level II criterion level B. For example, for the first expert, $B1 = (score\ C11 + C12)/n1$, $B2 = (score\ C21 + C22)/n2$, ... $B11 = (Score\ C111 + C112)/n11$. In the same way, the scores of the other two experts' secondary indicators are calculated. Finally, the secondary index scores are calculated as shown in Table 3.

Table 3. Criteria layer (secondary index) score

Dimension	Criteria layer	Expert 1	Expert 2	Expert 3
Perceptual element evaluation A1	Comprehensibility B1	5	4.5	5
	Value B2	4	3	2.5
	Diversity B3	4	4	2.5
	Conciseness B4	4.5	4	3.5
Perceptual experience evaluation A2	Navigational B5	5	5	3.5
	Immersion B6	3.5	3	4.5
	Interactive quality B7	3	4	4.5
	Fluency B8	3.667	4	3.333
User characteristic evaluation A3	User preferences B9	3	2	3
	User emotion B10	4.5	3.5	3.5
	Cognitive matching B11	4.5	2.5	2.5

2. Construct judgment matrix. According to the analysis of expert scoring data, establish the judgment matrix of the second level (i.e. B1, B2 ... B11), and the judgment matrix is $\mathbf{P} = (m_{ij})_{a \times b}$

$$P1 = (m_{ij})_{a \times b} = \begin{bmatrix} m_{11} & m_{12} & \cdots & m_{1b} \\ m_{21} & m_{22} & \cdots & m_{2b} \\ \vdots & \vdots & \ddots & \vdots \\ m_{a1} & m_{a2} & \cdots & m_{ab} \end{bmatrix} \tag{1}$$

Among

$$P_{ij} = \frac{Score(B_i)}{Score(B_j)}, \tag{2}$$

m_{ij} refers to the number of J for the ith evaluation index.

In the case of Expert 1, $P_{12} = \frac{Score(B_1)}{Score(B_2)} = \frac{5}{4}$, The final judgment matrix is shown in Fig. 2.

11阶判断矩阵											
评估	B1	B2	B3	B4	B5	B6	B7	B8	B9	B10	B11
B1	1.0000	1.2500	1.2500	1.1111	1.0000	1.4286	1.6667	1.3635	1.6667	1.1111	1.1111
B2	0.8000	1.0000	1.0000	0.8889	0.8000	1.1429	1.3333	1.0908	1.3333	0.8889	0.8889
B3	0.8000	1.0000	1.0000	0.8889	0.8000	1.1429	1.3333	1.0908	1.3333	0.8889	0.8889
B4	0.9000	1.1250	1.1250	1.0000	0.9000	1.2857	1.5000	1.2271	1.5000	1.0000	1.0000
B5	1.0000	1.2500	1.2500	1.1111	1.0000	1.4286	1.6667	1.3635	1.6667	1.1111	1.1111
B6	0.7000	0.8750	0.8750	0.7778	0.7000	1.0000	1.1667	0.9545	1.1667	0.7778	0.7778
B7	0.6000	0.7500	0.7500	0.6667	0.6000	0.8571	1.0000	0.8181	1.0000	0.6667	0.6667
B8	0.7334	0.9168	0.9168	0.8149	0.7334	1.0477	1.2223	1.0000	1.2223	0.8149	0.8149
B9	0.6000	0.7500	0.7500	0.6667	0.6000	0.8571	1.0000	0.8181	1.0000	0.6667	0.6667
B10	0.9000	1.1250	1.1250	1.0000	0.9000	1.2857	1.5000	1.2272	1.5000	1.0000	1.0000
B11	0.9000	1.1250	1.1250	1.0000	0.9000	1.2857	1.5000	1.2272	1.5000	1.0000	1.0000

Fig. 2. Judgment matrix

Calculation:

$$P_1 = (m_{ij})_{a \times b} = \begin{bmatrix} 1 & 1.25 & \cdots & 1.111 \\ 0.8 & 1 & \cdots & 0.889 \\ \vdots & \vdots & \ddots & \vdots \\ 0.9 & 1.125 & \cdots & 1 \end{bmatrix} \tag{3}$$

3. Calculate importance ranking. According to the judgment matrix P_1, the maximum eigenvalue λ_{max} and the corresponding eigenvector are obtained. Among them,

$$P \cdot W = \lambda_{max} W \tag{4}$$

$$\lambda_{max} = \frac{1}{n} \sum_{i=1}^{n} \frac{(P \cdot W)_i}{W_i} \tag{5}$$

After importing the data in the judgment matrix into the excel worksheet, calculate the weight according to the above formula, as shown in Fig. 3.

评估	B1	B2	B3	B4	B5	B6	B7	B8	B9	B10	B11	行内乘积Mi	行内乘积n次方根	权重
B1	1.0000	1.2500	1.2500	1.1111	1.0000	1.4286	1.6667	1.3635	1.6667	1.1111	1.1111	11.5974	1.2496	0.1119
B2	0.8000	1.0000	1.0000	0.8889	0.8000	1.1429	1.3333	1.0908	1.3333	0.8889	0.8889	0.9962	0.9997	0.0896
B3	0.8000	1.0000	1.0000	0.8889	0.8000	1.1429	1.3333	1.0908	1.3333	0.8889	0.8889	0.9962	0.9997	0.0896
B4	0.9000	1.1250	1.1250	1.0000	0.9000	1.2857	1.5000	1.2271	1.5000	1.0000	1.0000	3.6391	1.1246	0.1007
B5	1.0000	1.2500	1.2500	1.1111	1.0000	1.4286	1.6667	1.3635	1.6667	1.1111	1.1111	11.5974	1.2496	0.1119
B6	0.7000	0.8750	0.8750	0.7778	0.7000	1.0000	1.1667	0.9545	1.1667	0.7778	0.7778	0.2294	0.8747	0.0784
B7	0.6000	0.7500	0.7500	0.6667	0.6000	0.8571	1.0000	0.8181	1.0000	0.6667	0.6667	0.0421	0.7497	0.0672
B8	0.7334	0.9168	0.9168	0.8149	0.7334	1.0477	1.2223	1.0000	1.2223	0.8149	0.8149	0.3829	0.9164	0.0821
B9	0.6000	0.7500	0.7500	0.6667	0.6000	0.8571	1.0000	0.8181	1.0000	0.6667	0.6667	0.0421	0.7497	0.0672
B10	0.9000	1.1250	1.1250	1.0000	0.9000	1.2857	1.5000	1.2272	1.5000	1.0000	1.0000	3.6394	1.1246	0.1007
B11	0.9000	1.1250	1.1250	1.0000	0.9000	1.2857	1.5000	1.2272	1.5000	1.0000	1.0000	3.6394	1.1246	0.1007
											乘积总和		11.1629	

The table header spans: 11阶判断矩阵 | 生成权重

Fig. 3. Data analysis of index weight

According to the excel table, after calculation, $\lambda_{max} = 11$, the feature vector W is normalized, that is, the weight distribution of each factor, as shown in Fig. 4, it can be seen that for Expert 1, the weight of each index is: B1 = 0.1119, B2 = 0.0896, B3 = 0.0896, B4 = 0.1007, B5 = 0.1119, B6 = 0.0784, B7 = 0.0672, B8 = 0.0821, B9 = 0.0672, B10 = 0.1007, B11 = 0.1007.

4. Consistency check. When the order of judgment matrix is more than 2, it is often difficult to construct a good consistency judgment matrix, so it is necessary to conduct consistency test to determine whether the weight calculated by the judgment matrix is reasonable. The test formula is:

$$\mathrm{CI} = (\lambda_{max} - n)/(n - 1) \tag{6}$$

RI is the average random consistency index of the judgment matrix, and the reference table of RI value of the judgment matrix of order 1–12 is shown in Table 4:

Table 4. RI reference value of multi order judgment matrix

Degree	1	2	3	4	5	6	7	8	9	10	11	12	13
RI	0	0	0.58	0.90	1.12	1.24	1.32	1.41	1.45	1.49	1.52	1.54	1.56

After calculation, $\lambda_{max} = 11$, CI = 0, CR = 0, so P has satisfactory consistency. The calculation results are shown in Fig. 4.

	PW		λmax	CI	RI	CR
			一致性检验			
B1	1.2313	1.0000	11.0000	0.0000	1.5200	0.0000
B2	0.9851	1.0000				
B3	0.9851	1.0000				
B4	1.1082	1.0000				
B5	1.2313	1.0000				
B6	0.8619	1.0000				
B7	0.7388	1.0000				
B8	0.9031	1.0000				
B9	0.7388	1.0000				
B10	1.1082	1.0000				
B11	1.1082	1.0000				

Fig. 4. Consistency test results

In the same way, each index weight of expert 2 and expert 3 is calculated respectively, and the final weight value of each factor is finally determined.

For expert 2, the weight of each index is: B1 = 0.1130, B2 = 0.0770, B3 = 0.1017, B4 = 0.1017, B5 = 0.1273, B6 = 0.0763, B7 = 0.1017, B8 = 0.1017, B9 = 0.0.0587, B10 = 0.0758, B11 = 0.0651.

For expert 3, the weight of each index is: B1 = 0.1299, B2 = 0.0649, B3 = 0.0669, B4 = 0.0910, B5 = 0.0931, B6 = 0.1168, B7 = 0.1168, B8 = 0.0865, B9 = 0.0780, B10 = 0.0911, B11 = 0.0649.

See Table 5 for the final weight value of each index.

Table 5. Final weight values of criteria level indicators

Second-class index	Final calculated weight
B1	0.1183
B2	0.0772
B3	0.0861
B4	0.0978
B5	0.1108
B6	0.0905
B7	0.0952
B8	0.0901
B9	0.0680
B10	0.0892
B11	0.0769

In the same way, the above calculation method is used to calculate the third level index weight, and finally determine the influence weight of each scheme index layer. See Table 6 for the weight of level III indicators.

Table 6. Final weight of scheme level indicators

Third-class index	Expert 1	Expert 2	Expert 3	Final calculated weight
C11	0.0592	0.0657	0.0592	0.0614
C12	0.0592	0.0526	0.0592	0.0570
C21	0.0386	0.0386	0.0463	0.0412
C22	0.0386	0.0386	0.0309	0.0360
C31	0.0431	0.0431	0.0344	0.0402
C32	0.0431	0.0431	0.0517	0.0460
C41	0.0435	0.0489	0.0559	0.0494
C42	0.0543	0.0489	0.0419	0.0484
C51	0.0554	0.0554	0.0475	0.0528
C52	0.0554	0.0554	0.0633	0.0580
C61	0.0517	0.0603	0.0503	0.0541
C62	0.0388	0.0302	0.0402	0.0364
C71	0.0476	0.0476	0.0423	0.0458
C72	0.0476	0.0476	0.0529	0.0494
C81	0.0328	0.0300	0.0360	0.0329
C82	0.0328	0.0225	0.0180	0.0244
C83	0.0246	0.0375	0.0360	0.0327
C91	0.0340	0.0510	0.0453	0.0434
C92	0.0340	0.0170	0.0227	0.0246
C101	0.0396	0.0510	0.0637	0.0514
C102	0.0496	0.0382	0.0255	0.0378
C111	0.0342	0.0461	0.0308	0.0370
C112	0.0427	0.0308	0.0461	0.0399

6 Conclusion

Based on the research status of Web panoramic navigation system and the analysis of users' pain points based on users' cognition, this paper introduces the theory of users' perception experience, summarizes the users' perception elements in panoramic navigation, determines the influencing factors of users' perception experience quality in Web panoramic navigation, and constructs the index model; according to the analytic hierarchy process, obtains the right of rating index model Finally, we select the "panoramic Forbidden City" system, which is very representative and has a large number of views, to evaluate its improved navigation information and interactive experience, and put forward optimization suggestions.

References

1. Xuejin, H.: Research on the construction and key technology of panoramic map guide system of tourist attractions. J. Hubei Second Normal Univ. **29**(S1), 148–150 (2012)
2. Xuejin, H.: The current situation of panorama technology application and some technical problems. Mod. Sci. **24**, 283 (2009)
3. Guo, C., Cao, F.: The application of 3D panoramic technology in the introduction of tourist attractions. Geospatial Inf. **7**(1), 46–48 (2009)
4. Zhang, X., Lizhang: Research on the application of museum navigation system based on hybrid reality technology. Popular Lit. Art **22**, 122–123 (2019)
5. Tan, Z.: Research on Product Conceptual Design Technology for User Perceived Information. Zhejiang University (2007)
6. Tian, S., Wen, Y.: Research on the design of information system interface navigation based on cognitive psychology. Sci. Technol. Innov. Appl. **32**, 28–29 (2015)
7. Guo, T., Guo, X.: Research on the sensory quality and behavior model of AR museum visitors from the perspective of cognitive load. Decorate **10**, 94–97 (2018)
8. Lu, S.: Empirical Research on the Construction of Information Quality Evaluation System Based on User Experience and Perception. Tianjin Normal University (2012)
9. Liu, B., Lu, S.: Research on the comprehensive evaluation system of information quality based on user experience. Libr. Inf. Work **55**, 56–59 (2011)
10. Xinzhao, Y., Hou, W., Chen, X.: Research on the usability index system of complex information system interface. J. Books **39**(04), 716–722 (2018)
11. Xiangxue, Zhao, Y.: Research on user experience evaluation of mobile music APP based on the theory framework of perceptual expressiveness. Libr. Inf. Knowl. 1–14 (2020)

User Loyalty Analysis of Knowledge Payment Platform

Xin Wang[✉] and Bin Jiang

Nanjing University of Science and Technology, Nanjing 210094, China
1762397996@qq.com, jb508@163.com

Abstract. On the one hand, the rapid development of mobile Internet makes a large amount of free information available, on the other hand, it reduces the efficiency of people to obtain effective information. With the development of economy and the improvement of people's consumption level, knowledge payment products have become an efficient way for more and more learners to obtain knowledge and consultation. Knowledge payment platform users show different in the process of learning needs and expectations, based on the research of the user needs to understand the user's habits, accurate positioning the user's learning and paying willingness, to provide users with higher quality, better experience knowledge paid products and promote the use of user satisfaction and loyalty. This paper takes the user viscosity of the knowledge payment platform as the research object, and obtains the influencing factors of user viscosity through qualitative and quantitative research based on the user experience. On the basis of theoretical research, this paper summarizes the influencing factors of user viscosity of knowledge payment platform, and further studies the influencing factors of user viscosity by questionnaire survey. Finally, the relevant research bias graph affecting the user viscosity of knowledge payment platform is obtained, and corresponding design optimization Suggestions are given based on the survey results. Through the research of this paper, it is helpful for knowledge payment platform to optimize resource allocation and improve user experience and user viscosity. Increase users' willingness to pay and promote the sustainable development of enterprises.

Keywords: Knowledge payment platform · User loyalty · User experience

1 Research Background

Knowledge payment is to turn knowledge into products or services to realize its commercial value. By paying for knowledge, people save the time cost of filtering effective information, thus improving learning efficiency. While paying, users further promote the development of the knowledge payment industry and provide more efficient services, forming a virtuous circle. In recent years, the phenomenon of knowledge payment has become more and more common. According to the research report of research on China's online knowledge payment market in 2018, the scale of China's knowledge payment industry was about 4.9 billion yuan in 2017, and the scale is expected to reach 23.5 billion yuan in 2020 under the combined effect of various factors.

© Springer Nature Switzerland AG 2020
M. Kurosu (Ed.): HCII 2020, LNCS 12181, pp. 487–497, 2020.
https://doi.org/10.1007/978-3-030-49059-1_36

The user viscosity of the knowledge payment platform is the main factor that determines the sustainable development of the platform. In addition to the influence of product quality, the user's continuous payment behavior on the platform also depends on the user's experience in the process from choosing to buy the product to learning the knowledge.At present, various knowledge payment platforms in China are developing vigorously. How to improve user experience in the fierce competition, identify and solve the problems existing in users' use process, explore the potential functions of products and improve users' repurchase rate has become an important factor for the sustainable development of knowledge payment platforms. The research on the influencing factors of user viscosity and satisfaction degree is conducive to understanding the payment behavior of users and providing the correct development direction for the knowledge payment platform. However, as a rapidly developing APP in the application market, the knowledge payment platform is not well studied. This paper hopes to provide theoretical reference for the user experience design of the knowledge payment platform through the systematic study on the factors influencing the user viscosity of the knowledge payment platform.

2   Research Status of Knowledge Payment Platform

2.1   Literature Research Status

CNKI search keywords "knowledge payment", nearly 10 years of relevant literature search results for quantitative visual analysis, get Fig. 1, it can be seen from the figure from 2016 to 2018, the number of relevant literature increased linearly; From 2018 to 2019, relevant researches were in a stable period of development in the industry, and from 2019 to 2020, relevant literatures again showed a continuous upward trend. Through the trend chart of related literature search results in the past 10 years, it can be understood that the knowledge payment platform is still in the state of sustainable development, and the research on the influencing factors of user viscosity is of great significance to its sustainable development.

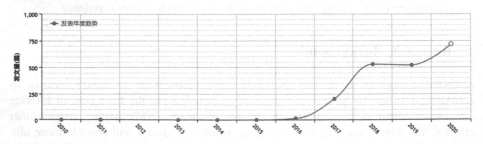

Fig. 1. Relevant literature search results in recent 10 years

2.2 Classification of Knowledge Payment Platforms

According to the mode of knowledge realization, knowledge payment platforms are divided into the following three types: the first type is paid subscription type, such as get, knowledge Live, himalaya and so on. This type appeared relatively early, in the form of audio on-demand, offering premium courses on top of free on-demand courses. At present, the development of this type of knowledge payment platform is more mature and plays a leading role in the knowledge payment platform. The second type is a single paid q&a type, and the answer and value are representative applications of this type. This type of platform takes the platform as the medium. Questioners pay to ask questions through the platform, and respondents get paid for answering questions. Other users can also pay to read the answers. The third type is the paid community type. This type of platform allows users to join a target group through payment. In the community, there will be a community initiator or other users to share experience or news, so that other users in the community can get more effective information. 4G and the upcoming 5G technology to further promote the development of the knowledge payment platform, network platform to provide users with the service implementation of differentiation and the distance, in order to meet the needs of different consumers, knowledge payment platform should according to the trend of the development of the society to provide users with accurate service, meet the demand of users niche, community.

3 Functions and Features of Knowledge Payment Platform

2016 is the first year of the development of the knowledge payment platform. After continuous exploration of various platforms in recent years, the knowledge payment platform has made great progress. During this period, it has experienced the following development stages: exploration period (2012–2014), market launch period (2014–2016), high-speed development period (2016–2018), application mature period (2018–present).

3.1 A Subsection Sample

From the perspective of knowledge payment platform, its function is to turn knowledge into products or services to realize commercial value. From the perspective of consumers, its function is to obtain useful information efficiently. On the surface, the knowledge payment platform builds a bridge between consumers and knowledge, so that the acquisition of knowledge information is not limited by time and space, and users can choose high-quality courses and teachers on their own. If payment platform for knowledge on deep analysis, we can find knowledge payment platform through the network environment will be more with the same learning knowledge demand of users and providers, the platform to realize a large number of producers together with knowledge or services, learners can communicate through the comments section study, this clustering phenomenon to form a new network learning environment and create a good learning atmosphere. These online groups based on the same field of interest have a great possibility to develop from online communication to offline discussion, forming a perfect closed loop of online learning and offline cooperation.

3.2 Knowledge Payment Platform Features

The following characteristics of the knowledge payment platform are summarized through literature reading and the author's use of the knowledge payment APP:

(1) Liberalization of learning: On the one hand, the application of knowledge payment breaks the limitation of the traditional learning environment of fixed place and fixed time to learn knowledge, and enables users to learn online through mobile devices. Learners can replay learning videos according to their learning conditions, making up for the shortage of offline one-time learning. What needs to be paid attention to is that while knowledge payment application brings convenience to users, it is difficult to form a systematic knowledge system and has certain selectivity for the suitable learning field.

(2) Accuracy of content: The user needs of the knowledge payment platform are becoming more and more sophisticated, and the knowledge content at this stage is becoming more and more vertical. Through the platform, users can precisely locate learning products according to their needs and conduct paid learning. Generally, paid courses have trial courses. Users confirm that the learning content meets their needs before purchasing the complete courses.

4 Research on Extraction of Influencing Factors of User Loyalty in Knowledge Payment Platform

4.1 Qualitative Analysis of Factors Affecting User Loyalty

User Feature Extraction

User feature extraction mainly uses the personage method in service design to summarize and classify the basic user's basic characteristics, physiological characteristics and behavior characteristics. The users of the knowledge payment platform are mainly divided into two categories: students with the need to learn new skills, and office workers with the need to improve their ability (Table 1).

Table 1. Student biography model (established by the author)

		Student model1	Student model2	Student model3
Basic Information	Name	Li Yi	Wang Xiao	Zhang Jun
	Gender	Female	Female	Male
	Age	21	24	26
	Job	Bachelor	Master's degree	Dctor
Psychological information	Hobby	Illustration, Make up	Economics, Movie	Fitness
	Lifestyle	Go to class + Rest + Learning illustration	Go to class + Laboratory + Rest + Library	Laboratory + Gym + Rest
	Character	Optimistic and positive	Quiet	Strong self-control
	Payment factor	Paid courses are more systematic	Inspire yourself to learn on time by paying	Higher paid product quality
Behavioral Information	User attitudes towards knowledge payment platforms	Pay to study illustrations, you can have more communication with the teacher, and hope to strengthen the interactivity of the students	I hope to enjoy a perfect learning supervision mechanism after successful payment	At present, the quality of paid products varies, and I hope to strengthen the admission management of lecturers

According to the above student personality model analysis, it can be concluded from the basic information that undergraduate to doctoral students are young and energetic. From psychological information, it can be concluded that their lives are mainly based on learning activities. I can improve myself in the spare time through the knowledge payment platform. From the behavioral habits information, we can understand the attitudes and needs of student users on the knowledge payment platform (Table 2).

Table 2. Worker biography model (established by the author)

		Worker model1	Worker model2	Worker model3
Basic Information	Name	Li Jing	Liu Heng	Niu Wen
	Gender	Female	Male	Male
	Age	24	40	32
	Job	Taobao shop owner	Secondary School Teachers	Designer
Psychological information	Hobby	Photography	Literature	Travel
	Lifestyle	Customer service + delivery + learning photography	Class + Rest + Reading	Go to work + rest(play games) + travel
	Character	Hard work, innovation	Serious	Pursuit of personality
	Payment factor	Great value for money, you can continuously improve your ability	Knowledge payment platform can understand the different opinions of different scholars on ancient thoughts	Constantly update your internal knowledge structure in your spare time
Behavioral Information	User attitudes towards knowledge payment platforms	Intelligently recommend courses based on areas of user interest	It is best to record the learning time while learning; content update reminder	Simplified learning platform interface design

Based on the analysis of the above-mentioned office worker ethnographic model, it can be understood from the basic information that users of the office worker knowledge payment platform have a large age span and are more dispersed than the student group user age. From the psychological information, we can understand that different occupations and different ages of office workers have different hobbies, indicating that the knowledge payment platform should provide knowledge services in more fields to meet the needs of different groups. From behavioral habit information, users expect the platform to make intelligent recommendations, record learning time, and simplify the design of learning interfaces based on the areas of interest to users.

Extraction loyalty of user factors

The author uses literature review to extract user viscosity related research on knowledge payment platform to extract user viscosity influencing factors. Peng Xinyu, Wang Ningning and others in "Analysis of Influencing Factors and Development Strategies of Online Knowledge Payment Behavior" proposed the factors that affect knowledge payment behavior are the content of knowledge products, the popularity of knowledge consumption platforms, the evaluation of other users, the price of knowledge content, creator Visibility, consumer experience. Liu Shuangshuang uses Maslow's Hierarchy of Needs theory to divide user needs into quality of content, perfect after-sales service, social needs, and privilege mechanisms to meet users' respectful needs and self-realization needs, and then proposes a knowledge payment platform design based on user needs in principle.In the "Research on User Experience Design of Knowledge Paid APPs from the Perspective of Micro-learning", Tang Yan proposed "matching user context", "efficiently reaching learning content", "promoting multi-dimensional group co-creation", "leading the establishment of learning habits" and "Five Design Principles to Improve Perceived Fragmentation Achievements. Ma Jingru, Liu Lin and others analyzed the positive factors of satisfaction of users' online knowledge payment behaviors in demand motivation, platform trust, knowledge quality, consumption cost, consumption experience, and marginal knowledge value Measure role. The author summarizes the existing research results and summarizes the following factors affecting the user viscosity of the knowledge payment platform: high-quality learning content, a certain degree of visibility of the lecturer, and reasonable prices; complete after-sales service in terms of functions, meeting user social needs, Guide learning habits, efficient time management design, perfect learning encouragement mechanism, interaction function with lecturer, learning punch design, audio progress bar content positioning function, that is, users can accurately and timely locate learning content and learning mode switching at their own pace Design means that the user can switch the learning mode of graphics, audio, video and so on.

4.2   Quantitative Analysis

The previous article summarizes the user viscosity influencing factors through a persona model and literature review. The above factors are used to conduct a quantitative study on the satisfaction factors of various user viscosity influencing factors through questionnaire surveys and demand level analysis.

Survey questionnaire design

The content of the survey questionnaire is a priority survey of the factors affecting the user viscosity of the knowledge payment platform. Each question of the questionnaire has 6 levels to choose from, level 1 represents the weakest demand, level 6 represents the strongest demand, and so on. The survey participants choose the level of demand that meets their expectations based on their actual situation.

(1) Research purpose: Based on the previous personality model and literature survey of user viscosity influencing factors, design a questionnaire for the questionnaire, and obtain a certain number of user groups for each influencing factor level through the questionnaire survey. In the scientific satisfaction study of the factors affecting user viscosity.

(2) Survey population: The survey population is divided into two parts: college students and office workers.

(3) Questionnaire design content: It is divided into five parts. The first part is the basic information of the interviewee. Through these questions, you can understand the basic situation of the interviewee. The second part is the investigation and analysis of the demand for payment models of knowledge payment platforms, that is, to clarify the degree of user demand for different types of knowledge payment platforms. The third part is the user satisfaction level survey of the knowledge payment platform. The survey questionnaire is formulated based on the influencing factors of user viscosity of the knowledge payment platform summarized above. Through this part, different users' attitudes to the influence factors of user viscosity are obtained. The fourth part is the subjective problem, that is, users can put forward what aspects of the knowledge payment platform still need, as a supplementary factor affecting user viscosity, so as to comprehensively analyze the knowledge payment platform user viscosity.

(4) Survey method: Create a questionnaire through a survey website questionnaire star, and forward the completed questionnaire to generate a QR code and fill it out via WeChat group.

Demand level analysis

A total of 132 questionnaires were successfully collected in this questionnaire survey, and the questionnaire was further collated. For example, some questionnaire answers chose the highest level 6 or the lowest level 1. Such questionnaires do not make the survey data authentic and reliable, so The questionnaire was defined as an invalid questionnaire. After the selection was completed, 124 valid questionnaires were obtained.

Among the valid questionnaires, 49.19% were obtained from basic information, 50.81% were female, and 50% were students and office workers. 92.32% of the respondents had paid knowledge learning experience online. Among those without knowledge paid experience, 50% said that the main reason for no paid purchase was that there was no interested learning direction in paid content. Only 1% of the respondents indicated that they did not trust the knowledge providers of the knowledge payment platform, indicating that consumers have a high degree of trust in the knowledge payment platform. Full use only accounts for 6.25%. Most users cannot learn all the purchased knowledge, to a certain extent, indicating that the user experience design of the platform is not perfect. Most users choose knowledge payment platforms for three main reasons: improving their social competitiveness, enriching themselves to relieve anxiety, and making friends to build social circles.

Through the analysis of the survey results of the demand for the payment model of the knowledge payment platform in the second part of the questionnaire, the average value is calculated for each problem demand level (Fig. 2 and Table 3).

Table 3. Demand level average score (established by the author)

System model of knowledge payment platform	Demand level average score
Paid subscription type	4.233
Single pay question and answer type	3.926
Paid community type	3.584

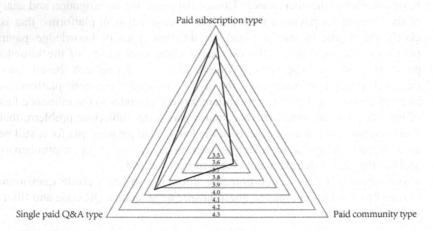

Fig. 2. System model of knowledge payment platform bias graph

A Subsection SampleFrom the above statistics of average demand scores and bias charts, it can be clearly seen that the paid subscription type in this survey object has a higher demand than the single paid Q & A type and paid community type.

According to the user satisfaction level survey of the knowledge payment platform in the third part of the questionnaire, the average value of each question satisfaction level is calculated, and the results are as follows (Table 4):

Table 4. Satisfaction level average score (established by the author)

Knowledge payment platform	User satisfaction level
Paid product quality	4.03
Paid product price	3.96
After sales service	3.92
Interface design	3.85

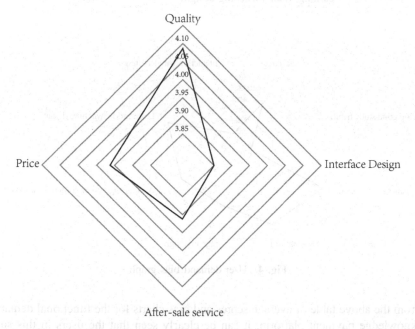

Fig. 3. User satisfaction bias graph

It can be clearly seen from the above satisfaction average statistics table and bias graph that users in this survey have higher satisfaction with the quality of paid content, relatively lower satisfaction with the interface design of the knowledge payment platform, Subsequent development should increase the focus on interface design (Fig. 3).

Through the user demand level investigation of the knowledge payment platform function in Part IV of the questionnaire, the average value of each question demand level is calculated, and the results are as follows (Table 5):

Table 5. Demand level average score (established by the author)

Social circle	3.89
Interact with lecturer	3.75
Develop good study habits	3.70
Time management function	4.04
Learning encouragement	3.98
Sign in design	3.89
Audio progress bar content positioning function	3.94
Learning mode switching design	4.00

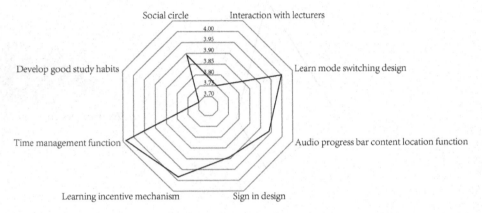

Fig. 4. User demand bias graph

From the above table of average scores and bias charts for the functional demand of the knowledge payment platform, it can be clearly seen that the users in this survey have relatively high demand for time management functions and learning mode switching design. The need to interact with lecturers is relatively low (Fig. 4).

5 Conclusion

With the maturity of the 5G network and the rapid development of the economy, the knowledge payment platform will more and more penetrate into people's daily learning life. Will be an urgent problem for knowledge payment platforms. Through qualitative analysis and quantitative analysis, this paper obtains the current users' satisfaction with the knowledge payment platform and the demand for its various functions, and hopes to provide some directions for the future improvement of the knowledge payment platform.

References

1. Zhao, Z.C., Liu, C.Y.: Investigation and analysis of the use of knowledge research products by college students. Libr. Res. Work **11**, 29–33 (2019)
2. Wu, D.: Research on "Usage and Satisfaction" of Knowledge Paying APP Users. Liao Ning University (2018)
3. Tang, S.: Research on User Experience Design of Knowledge Payment App from the Perspective of Micro-learning. Jiang Nan University (2019)
4. Fang, L.H., X, B.F.: Research on payment models and willingness to pay for knowledge payment platforms. Bus. News (23), 3–4 (2019)
5. Zhang, X.: Paying for knowledge: a new paradigm for knowledge dissemination. Audiovisual (01), 144–145 (2019)
6. Wang, N., Li, Y.J.: Research on the construction of knowledge paying app service system oriented to user needs. Mod. Intell. **39**(10), 66–77 (2019)

A Quantitative Method to Measure Noticeability of Animations in Mobile Interfaces

Qianyao Xu, Yiding Liu, and Yingqing Xu[✉]

Tsinghua University, Beijing 100084, China
xuqy17@mails.tsinghua.edu.cn, yqxu@mail.tsinghua.edu.cn

Abstract. Animations are widely used in mobile user interface design nowadays. By exploiting the noticeability of Motion Garaphics, interface designers can rapidly draw a user's attention to salient objects. Such effects can be achieved by a variety of different visual stimuli including color, shape, size, motion, luminance, and flashing. However, it needs to be better understood and precisely assessed how the different animations affect user attention. In this paper, we analyzed and compared the noticeability of ten different animations. We investigated the extent to which they attract users' attention and generate quantitative indications accordingly. We propose a quantitative method to measure the noticeability of animations in mobile interfaces and point out possible directions for future studies.

Keywords: UI animation · Noticeability · Measurement method · Mobile interfaces

1 Introduction

Animation is a widely adopted design element in mobile user interface (UI). Defined as a visual change that is intentionally constructed within a UI, animations often represent animated UI items, such as a bouncing icon implying users to click. It plays a significant role in the interaction of visual interfaces [1]. By exploiting such visual stimuli, interface designers can rapidly draw a user's attention to salient objects in a mobile interface. A variety of different visual stimuli can be used to achieve prompting effects, including color, shape, size, motion, luminance, and flashing [5]. However, there is a lack of an accurate understanding of how these animations support the prompting effects. It is also unclear how such understanding can facilitate the design practice related to UI animations. We therefore conducted a study to accurately assess the prompting effect of different animations. We explored the noticeability of ten animations via the proposed method. In addition, the eye track record supports the measurements. Results show that different UI animation has different intensity of visual stimuli. The findings can be relevant to a wide variety of applications, especially the mobile UI animations. Designers can use the proposed method to measure

© Springer Nature Switzerland AG 2020
M. Kurosu (Ed.): HCII 2020, LNCS 12181, pp. 498–509, 2020.
https://doi.org/10.1007/978-3-030-49059-1_37

the noticeability of any animation design and apply the appropriate options to their designs. UI animation as a typical form of motion graphics, is not strictly character driven or story based, it plays a significant role in the interaction of visual interfaces. For example, the blinking text cursor in Microsoft MS-DOS system informs the user of where to input and whether the system is ready to read a command. The blink is not a dominant animation but critical in the interaction between the system and the user. Designers often use UI animations to keep users in context, to assist teaching, to enhance the user experience, and to aid data encoding and support the visual discourse [2]. With limited space for information display and user interaction, mobile apps often use animations to enhance their usability and efficiency. However, over-designed animations may be overwhelming, distractive or convoluted for the user to apprehend [2]. Although different design guidelines have emerged, such as the Material Design by Google, none of them provide an accurate indication on the noticeability of different animations. Designers have no clue of how intense the animations are, and which of them is appropriate to apply. Studies on visual perception have examined the noticeability of motion and looming [3]. Apart from these two, there are many other animations to be studied, such as color changing. Inspired by a previous experimental design of visual stimuli test [3], we propose a quantitative framework for measuring the noticeability of mobile UI animations. The framework is based on the involvement of participants with a mobile app that we developed. The app allows participants to complete simple search tasks by gesture interaction: from a grid of different figures with similar identical visual feature. We conducted a study on 18 participants to explore the noticeability of 10 UI animations. In each task, participants are required to search for one specific target among the figures. The result shows that participants spend shorter time when the target figure happens to be animated, compared to when the nontarget figures are animated. We utilize the variance of the search time to indicate the noticeability of an animation. In addition, the eye track record supports the results of the measurement. We believe that this method of measuring noticeability can be extended to other animations to support a wider range of scenarios in UI animation design.

2 Related Work

2.1 UI Animation

Animations have become a prevalent element in mobile UI design [10]. Yet the definition of animation has been ambiguous in different contexts [10]. Some studies include any qualitative changes of an interface into the term "animation" [7]. Other studies mentioned "animation" only to describe the spatial movement of visual components [12]. Liddle defined animation as a intentionally constructed visual change, excluding visual changes resulting from errors or lack of design [10]. It also excludes the predefined animated contents such as videos because they are not part of the interface [10]. Such a definition includes both large-scale visual changes(the transition among UI pages) and small visual changes(a bouncing icon). In our study, we use the term animation to particularly describe the latter While Liddle collapsed the two items to study on guidelines for UI animation.

2.2 Animation and Noticecability

Animations can effectively explain the visual changes to the UI and therefore guide the user's attention [7]. As stated by previous researchers, interactive animations can shift the user's cognitive load to the human perceptual system and therefore reduce the load [8]. It smooths the transition between visual states to assist users in tracking elements and understanding visual changes on the screen [8]. However, an inappropriate use of animations can be distracting and therefore draw the user's attention away from his task at hand [13]. Hence, while there are benefits to integrating animations in user interfaces, they must be used appropriately to create positive effects. User noticeability is defined as the level of a user's cognitive, affective, and behavioral investment while interacting with a digital system [11,12].

2.3 Assessment of Noticeability

There have been diverse works assessing the noticeability of mobile UI animations. Leung has identified three main paradigms for empirically measuring the noticeability and/or distraction effects of highlighting techniques, including measurement by "Dual Task", "Path Deviations", and "Short Exposure Present/Absent" [9]. In the "Dual Task", participants perform two tasks, a primary task such as a game or a "work-like" activity, and a secondary task to detect and respond to the highlighted item. It measures noticeability by the noticing time, the response effectiveness and the detection accuracy. In the "Path Deviations Paradigm", researchers ask participants to point to a target from a grid of items and analyze their pointing trajectories [4,12]. In the "Short Exposure Present/Absent Paradigm", researchers briefly show the participants a series of stimuli and ask them whether they saw the highlighted item or not [5]. Although given the significant role of noticeability and the diverse measurement paradigms, it remains under-explored that a quantitative and objective measurement method on the very domain of mobile UI animations, which involves a particular screen size and unique interaction habits.

3 Method

3.1 The Single Search Task

The feature of the single search task is that only one of the search targets has different characteristics from the others. The search target can be quickly found, such as a red target in a pile of gray objects. The critical attribute of the measurement is the time spent on the search task, and dynamic effects are added to assist or interfere with the search, and the measurement results are compared and analyzed under different parameters.

In this paper, we use letters as the target objects for measurement. In each task, the participant is required to find one target from the provided items. Only one random item of them has a change of state. In a general single search task, participants may ignore the outstanding items because the search target can be roughly predicted. In our task, the change of visual state happens to both the target item and the nontarget items, in which case participants will not fix their visual attention to make any subjective prediction.

The search priority of the participants is mainly reflected by the slope (k) of response time (RT) changing with the number of candidate items. We use the term "hit" and "miss" to represent situations where the animation happens to the target item or a nontarget item. By comparing and analyzing the k value of "hit" and "miss" situations, it is possible to assess how the animation effect affects the search behavior, which we indicate with a calculated score. This score mainly synthesizes two aspects of the animation: the visual attraction of the animation, and how the animated effect affects the noticeability of the target item. In general, when the number of items increases, the RT will also increase accordingly. but after the animation is applied, the reaction process of the participants will be affected.

4   Study

4.1   Set up

The entire task last about 20 min for each participant to complete. The experimental device had a 5.1-in. screen size, a resolution of 1920*1080, a processor of Hisilicon Kirin 960, a running memory of 4 GB, and an operating system of Android 7.0 version. During the experiment, the distance between the glasses and the screen averaged 32.2 cm (ranging from 19 cm to 60 cm). We also used the eye tracker to record the changes of visual focus of participants. The eye tracker was an SMI glass ETG 2w, with a sampling rate of 120 Hz. For the acquisition and processing of eye tracking data, we used BeGaze, version 3.6.52. An eye glasses type of instruments were used for participants with myopic lens, to reduce the experimental offset. An experimental app was developed using the Property Animation module of Android SDK.

A total of 18 enrolled students of Tsinghua University were selected in the experiment. They aged between 20 and 30 years old, with a healthy visual acuity by birth or through correction. Each participant could receive a subsidy of 50 RMB by completing the experiment.

4.2   Task and Stimulus

We develop a mobile app using the Property Animation Module of Android SDK to conduct the single search task test with participants. Within each task,

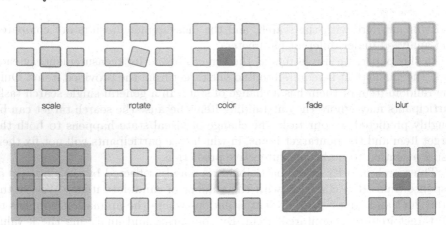

Fig. 1. This diagram demonstrates the ten most common types of highlighting animations. It conceptually represents the items by squares. In our study, the items appear to be letters in the QuartzEF font. (Color figure online)

there are two attributes to be adjusted, the type and the amount of animations. As shown in Fig. 1, we include ten common types of highlighting animations: scaling, rotating, color changing, fading, burring, darkening, flipping, glowing, depth changing and graying out. In the setting page of Fig. 3, we click the "PRE" and "NEXT" to switch the animation type. There are three modes showing different amount of animations. The "MODE 3V", "MODE 6v", and "MODE 8v" set the amount of animation to be three, six and eight. In addition, we use the term "hit" and "miss" to describe whether the animation highlights the target letter or not. The app records the experiment data from the backstage and generates statistic graphics in the "Test Results" of Fig. 3. To counteract the affection of familiarity, we require each participant to complete tasks in two reversed sets of animation sequence as shown in Fig. 2.

No.	Animation Type	Duration(ms)		No.	Animation Type	Duration(ms)
1	scale	1000		1	gray out	2100
2	rotate	1000		2	depth change	2100
3	color	2100		3	glow	2100
4	fade	2100		4	flip	2100
5	blue	2100		5	darken	2100
6	darken	2100		6	blue	2100
7	flip	2100		7	fade	2100
8	glow	2100		8	color	2100
9	depth change	2100		9	rotate	1000
10	gray out	2100		10	scale	1000

Sequence A   Sequence B

Fig. 2. Each participant is required to complete half of their tasks in Sequence A and the other halfs in Sequence B to counteract the error caused by a fixed task sequence.

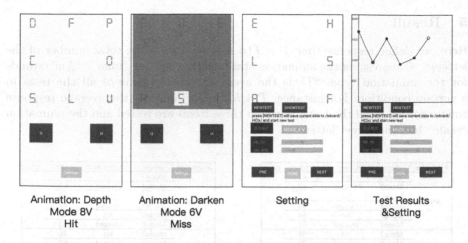

Animation: Depth   Animation: Darken   Setting   Test Results
Mode 8V   Mode 6V   &Setting
Hit   Miss

Fig. 3. The main task interface of the experimental software.

As shown in Fig. 3, within a single search task, the participants face letters arranged in a three by three grid. The letters consist of one target letter and several nontarget items, the amount of which depends on the experiment mode. The target letter is randomly selected to be either the letter "U" or "H" by an equal possibility. The nontarget items are also randomly selected by an equal possibility from the letter "A", "C", "E", "F", "O", "P", "S" ,"L". Each letter randomly locates in the grid by an equal chance. We adopt the QuartzEF font so that all the letters share the same basic elements of the figure. They can be covered by the placeholder figure "8" before appearing in difference. When the letters appear, the participants are required to click on the target letter, either "U" or "H".

4.3 Procedure

We adjust the attributes before each single search task. The chance is 40% that the target letter is highlighted by the animation. In the experiment, the participant starts the task by clicking the "start" button. After 1300 ms, the placeholders turn to different letters, one of which is highlighted by an animation. Then the participant is required to find the target letter, either "U" or "H", and click on the relevant button below. The app simultaneously records the response time (RT), the accuracy of selection, and whether the animation highlights the target letter. We also utilize eye tracking techniques to record the trajectory of their focus point for detailed analysis on their behaviors. The blinking frequency and diameter of pupils are also recorded to identify the intensity of their focus attention.

5   Result

Here, we define response time $T = T(n, s, Ani)$. "n" is the total number of the letters. "s" represents the animation state, either "hit" or "miss". "Ani" stands for the animation type. "T" is the average response time of all the tests in a certain condition. For instance, $T(3, hit, scale)$ denotes the average response time recorded in all the tests, in which three items are tested and the animation "scale" hits the target letter.

animation	mode	hit/missed	amount	total
scale	Mode3	hit	47	
	Mode3	missed	63	
	Mode6	hit	47	348
	Mode6	missed	59	
	Mode8	hit	64	
	Mode8	missed	68	
rotate	Mode3	hit	38	
	Mode3	missed	72	
	Mode6	hit	45	324
	Mode6	missed	56	
	Mode8	hit	59	
	Mode8	missed	54	
color	Mode3	hit	58	
	Mode3	missed	65	
	Mode6	hit	53	341
	Mode6	missed	47	
	Mode8	hit	55	
	Mode8	missed	63	
fade	Mode3	hit	43	
	Mode3	missed	67	
	Mode6	hit	43	303
	Mode6	missed	48	
	Mode8	hit	44	
	Mode8	missed	58	
blur	Mode3	hit	57	
	Mode3	missed	66	
	Mode6	hit	36	317
	Mode6	missed	52	
	Mode8	hit	58	
	Mode8	missed	48	

animation	mode	hit/missed	amount	total
darken	Mode3	hit	54	
	Mode3	missed	67	
	Mode6	hit	40	313
	Mode6	missed	52	
	Mode8	hit	47	
	Mode8	missed	53	
flip	Mode3	hit	45	
	Mode3	missed	68	
	Mode6	hit	43	305
	Mode6	missed	46	
	Mode8	hit	50	
	Mode8	missed	53	
glow	Mode3	hit	54	
	Mode3	missed	64	
	Mode6	hit	42	292
	Mode6	missed	42	
	Mode8	hit	39	
	Mode8	missed	51	
depth	Mode3	hit	40	
	Mode3	missed	77	
	Mode6	hit	35	287
	Mode6	missed	40	
	Mode8	hit	46	
	Mode8	missed	49	
grayout	Mode3	hit	62	
	Mode3	missed	70	
	Mode6	hit	37	309
	Mode6	missed	41	
	Mode8	hit	47	
	Mode8	missed	52	

Fig. 4. The amount of tests for each animation in different conditions were counted.

The noticeability of the animation is mainly reflected by the change of the response time as the letters increase in the search task. Therefore, we also define that the k value,

$$k(n_1, n_2, s, Ani) = \frac{T(n_2, s, Ani) - T(n_1, s, Ani)}{n_2 - n_1}$$

When the number of letters increases, the response time increases accordingly. In a "miss" situation, the response time appears to be longer as the letters increase. In a "hit" situation, the response time gets less longer or even shorter than usual. Our explanation is that such a phenomenon reflects how animation affects the response time. We suppose that,

$$Noticeability = k(n_1, n_2, miss, Ani) - k(n_1, n_2, hit, Ani)$$

Since the response time is an average value, we take the p value of ANOVA as the weight of the k values when calculating the "noticeability". The ANOVA here is not used for the comparison of the average numbers. It is applied as a correction of the "noticeability" value. Specifically, the p(n1, n2) denotes the significance of the average response time difference between two conditions: n1 letters and n2 letters in the search task.

$$\begin{aligned} Noticeability(Ani) \ = \ & (k(3,6,miss,Ani) - k(3,6,hit,Ani)) * (1 - p(3,6)) \\ & + (k(6,8,miss,Ani) - k(6,8,hit,Ani)) * (1 - p(6,8)) \\ & + (k(3,8,miss,Ani) - k(3,8,hit,Ani)) * (1 - p(3,8)) \end{aligned}$$

We use the Microsoft.Office.Interop.Excel in C#.NET library for data analysis. 18 participants are recruited for 3222 search tasks in total. The distribution of different task conditions is listed in Fig. 4. 82 task records are excluded due to the participants' misoperation or overtime response longer than 3000 ms. Based on the ANOVA test for the k value, we found significant differences between "hit" and "miss" in condition (fade, k68), (fade, k38), (flip, k36), (flip, k38), and (color k38).

Among the tested animations, "fade" is the most noticeable one with a noticeability value of 525.83. The noticeability of "fade", "darken", "rotate", "blur" and "glow" are measured as positive, while the rest are measured as negative. The results indicates that 'grayout", "scale", "flip", "color" and "depth" have distracted the participants from target letter searching.

6 Discussion

The method of our study can be potentially utilized in various scenarios of UI design and research. It allows researchers to accurately measure the noticeability of mobile UI animations and establish a comprehensive dataset for future design facilitation. Such outcomes can assist designers to make more effective selections on mobile UI animations in their practice

Through our study, we provide designers with an assessment tool to measure the noticeability of various mobile UI animations. Designers can adopt such a method to conduct studies on their original animation designs. The noticeability of the ten animations, which has been measured and calculated, can serve as a scale for future measurement to be more precisely perceived.

Moreover, we see the development of our tool as a step towards a more systematic framework for the evaluation of mobile UI animations. Such a framework will facilitate mobile UI design by allowing designers to quickly select animations according their noticeability. Given studies on more diverse animations and larger amount of participants, future researchers can collect the noticeability value of more animations with higher reliability. Therefore, a comprehensive framework can be constructed to indicate the noticeability of each animation (Figs. 5 and 6).

Animation	target	response time (avg)			k value			Noticeability
		MODE3	MODE6	MODE8	k36	k68	k38	
fade	Hit	1017	1412	1125	395	-287	108	
	Missing	1132	1142	1419	10	277	287	
	p				0.565	*0.077	**0.035	525.83
darken	Hit	1030	1264	1175	234	-89	145	
	Missing	1228	1412	1539	184	127	311	
	p				0.804	0.633	0.5	152.47
rotate	Hit	963	1177	1055	214	-122	92	
	Missing	1164	1275	1448	111	173	284	
	p				0.204	0.715	0.242	147.62
blur	Hit	1126	1154	1319	28	165	193	
	Missing	1224	1349	1467	125	118	243	
	p				0.504	0.643	0.228	69.93
glow	Hit	1024	1360	1184	336	-176	160	
	Missing	1268	1241	1387	-27	146	119	
	p				0.583	0.503	0.978	7.76
grayout	Hit	1099	1280	1335	181	55	236	
	Missing	1280	1171	1335	-109	164	55	
	p				0.87	0.519	0.623	-53.51
scale	Hit	1198	1154	1177	-44	23	-21	
	Missing	1469	1415	1404	-54	-11	-65	
	p(k)				0.113	0.389	0.32	-59.56
flip	Hit	1111	1220	1187	109	-33	76	
	Missing	1299	1407	1299	108	-108	0	
	p(k)				**0.015	0.639	**0.027	-102.01
color	Hit	998	1136	1334	138	198	336	
	Missing	1367	1385	1615	18	230	248	
	p(k)				0.204	0.926	*0.09	-173.23
depth	Hit	1026	1489	1375	463	-114	349	
	Missing	1176	1133	1409	-43	276	233	
	p(k)				0.11	0.187	0.633	-175.84

Fig. 5. The average response time, the k value, the p value and the Noticeability.

Furthermore, this study provides an effective method for usability tests on mobile UI animations. Once UI designers have created one or more animations. They can conduct usability tests on them with the approach proposed in our study. While conventional usability tests rely on interviews, observation or survey, all of which involves more or less subjective feedback from the participants, this approach measures the noticeability, which reflects the consumed time and operation accuracy. Such a method adds an objective, quantitative dimension to the users' feedback on UI animations, which enhances the understanding of the animations' noticeability.

Besides mobile UI animations, the focus of this study, there exists other forms of animations in diverse user interfaces and devices, such as web applications and VR devices. We expect our approach to enhance future research or usability tests on these animations and eventually facilitate relevant UI design. Moreover, the mobile UI animations and the relevant measurement experiments in our study are all from android operation system. In the future, we can potentially generalize this approach to other platforms such as IOS.

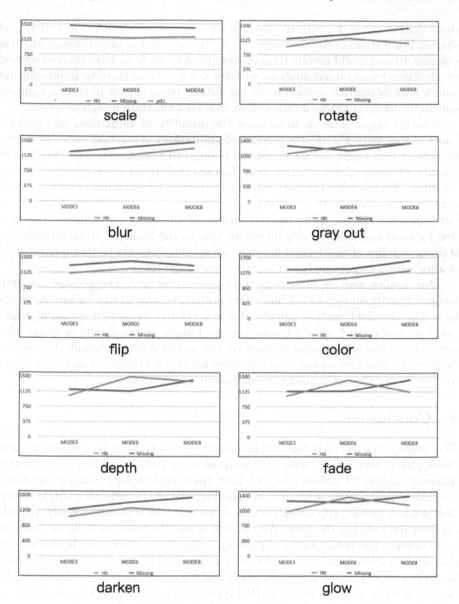

Fig. 6. In each sub-figure, the y axis presents the average response time and the x axis presets the number of the letters in the search task.

7 Limitations and Future Work

Our study has several limitations to address in the future. This work has generated a set of empirical characterizations of different noticeability of different mobile UI animations. However, there are abundant opportunities to extend these findings and to validate them with different intensities, quantity and shapes. For instance, only the letter "U" or "I" are used as target items, which is different to real-world mobile UI components. Although we have derived several implications based on our analysis, we have not validated them by implementing animations in realistic scenarios. In the future research, we intend to validate our implication on the facilitation of mobile UI animation design practices.

Another opportunity is to increase the quantity of animations and participants in the study. Firstly, the amount of animations in one task varies from two to eight, which might not be significant enough to examine the affection by the amount of items. Secondly, this work focuses mainly on a quantitative understanding of measuring the noticeability of mobile UI animations with insights derived from a relatively small sample size of participants. The participants in our study are chosen to be representatives of the users on campus. The limited location and identity may introduce bias to the findings. To investigate the statistic validity of the derived findings, we need to conduct further quantitative studies with a larger number of participants in the future.

Our results may be limited in their generalizability. The present research focused heavily on measuring how users notice the animations on mobile interface. The obtained "noticeability" value is a relative value without an absolute value as a standard scale for comparison. Future works should leverage this method to establish a larger dataset on the noticeability of mobile UI animations, which provides a more comprehensive context for designers and researchers to understand the noticeability of one specific animation.

8 Conclusion

The widespread use of animation in mobile user interfaces is a relatively new development over recent years. Our work aims to understand how user's notice different mobile UI animations and how their noticeability can be measured through a quantitative approach. We conduct the study through a single search task with a mobile app developed on Android, which simultaneously records relevant data during the task. We propose a specific value to indicate, analyze and compare the noticeability of different animations. Given the limitations of this study, we hope that this exploratory research encourages future researchers to study a wider range and a larger amount of UI animations so as to facilitate the design ideation, usability tests and HCI research related to mobile UI animations.

References

1. Baumann, K.: User Interface Design of Electronic Appliances. CRC Press, Boca Raton (2001)
2. Chevalier, F., Riche, N.H., Plaisant, C., et al.: Animations 25 years later: new roles and opportunities. In: Proceedings of the International Working Conference on Advanced Visual Interfaces, pp. 280–287 (2016)
3. Franconeri, S.L., Simons, D.J.: Moving and looming stimuli capture attention. Percept. Psychophys. 65(7), 999–1010 (2003)

4. Gallivan, J.P., Chapman, C.S.: Three-dimensional reach trajectories as a probe of real-time decision-making between multiple competing targets. Front. Neurosci. **8**, 215 (2014)
5. Gutwin, C., Cockburn, A., Coveney, A.: Peripheral popout: the influence of visual angle and stimulus intensity on popout effects. In: Proceedings of the. CHI Conference on Human Factors in Computing Systems, pp. 208–219 (2017)
6. Heer, J., Robertson, G.: Animated transitions in statistical data graphics. IEEE Trans. Visual. Comput. Graph. **13**(6), 1240–1247 (2007)
7. Hudson, S.E., Stasko, J.T.: Animation support in a user interface toolkit: flexible, robust, and reusable abstractions. In: Proceedings of the 6th annual ACM symposium on User interface software and technology, pp. 57–67 (1993)
8. Laurel, B., Mountford, S.J.: The Art of Human-Computer Interface Design. Addison-Wesley Longman Publishing Co., Inc., Boston (1990)
9. Leung, J.: Understanding the noticeability and distraction of interactive highlighting techniques (2017)
10. Liddle, D.: Emerging guidelines for communicating with animation in mobile user interfaces. In: Proceedings of the 34th ACM International Conference on the Design of Communication, pp. 1–9 (2016)
11. Moher, J., Anderson, B.A., Song, J.H.: Dissociable effects of salience on attention and goal-directed action. Curr. Biol. **25**(15), 2040–2046 (2015)
12. Oh, J., Sundar, S.S.: User engagement with interactive media: a communication perspective. In: O'Brien, H., Cairns, P. (eds.) Why Engagement Matters, pp. 177–198. Springer, Cham (2016). https://doi.org/10.1007/978-3-319-27446-1_8
13. Schlienger, C., Conversy, S., Chatty, S., Anquetil, M., Mertz, C.: Improving users' comprehension of changes with animation and sound: an empirical assessment. In: Baranauskas, C., Palanque, P., Abascal, J., Barbosa, S.D.J. (eds.) INTERACT 2007. LNCS, vol. 4662, pp. 207–220. Springer, Heidelberg (2007). https://doi.org/10.1007/978-3-540-74796-3_20
14. Thomas, B.H., Calder, P.: Applying cartoon animation techniques to graphical user interfaces. ACM Trans. Comput.-Hum. Interact. (TOCHI) **8**(3), 198–222 (2001)

Using Reinforcement Learning Agents
to Analyze Player Experience

Tian Zhu[✉], Powen Yao, and Michael Zyda

GamePipe Laboratory, University of Southern California, Los Angeles, CA, USA
{tianzhu,powenyao,zyda}@usc.edu

Abstract. Analyzing player experience often requires collecting lots of gameplay data from human players, which is labor-intensive. In this paper, we present an approach to classify player experience using AI agents. A deep Reinforcement AI agent is deployed to learn abstract representation of game states. Then, machine learning models are trained with the abstract representation to evaluate the player experience. It shows that the abstract representation learned by AI agents can provide important information about how game levels are perceived by players. And the abstract representation can help machine learning models to classify whether player experience is enjoyable.

Keywords: Player experience · Reinforcement learning · Machine learning

1 Introduction

Evaluating player experience is an important task, because it can shed light on how games could be further improved. Since more and more games are coming out each year, it is very useful to have machine learning models that can evaluate player experience. Letting a human player analyze an enormous amount of video game levels is very labor-intensive, as it requires the human player to play all those levels manually. However, machine learning models can be trained with existing data to evaluate game levels automatically.

Different games provide different information to players. In order to build machine learning models for them, different game information must be collected. For example, in a platformer game the model needs the information about where all the platforms are, while in a shooter game the model cares about where the enemies are and what weapons they have. Although games have different mechanics, they can all provide enjoyment to the same player [12], which implies a shared abstract representation should exist across different games [16]. A reinforcement AI agent can be trained to play different games. While the agent learns to play the game, it will evaluate how beneficial each action is under certain game states. Such evaluations from AI agents are universal for different games, thus can be viewed as the abstract representation across different games.

© Springer Nature Switzerland AG 2020
M. Kurosu (Ed.): HCII 2020, LNCS 12181, pp. 510–519, 2020.
https://doi.org/10.1007/978-3-030-49059-1_38

In this paper, we present a general approach to evaluate player experience using a reinforcement AI agent. The AI agent is trained to learn the abstract representation of game states. Machine learning models are built on top of this representation to classify whether game levels are enjoyable or not. Although we apply our approach on one testbed game in this paper, this general approach can be applied to other games as well.

2   Related Work

In [1], game quality metrics are calculated from AI self-play simulations. Those game quality metrics are then used in evolutionary algorithms to produce combinatorial games with better designs. In our paper, gameplay data from AI self-play simulations are also used. Instead of using them to generate better game designs, we use those simulations to help us evaluate real human player experience.

Another work related to ours is [14]. In [14], the relationship between game states and game actions are approximated using adaptive AI. It is similar to using reinforcement learning agents to develop abstract representation of game states in our paper. The relationship between game states and game actions is called relevant entropy, which is used to identify common game design flaws in [14]. Game level events and player behavior are analyzed to help improve the quality of automatically generated game contents in [14], whereas in our paper, game states and AI behavior are analyzed to better predict player experience.

Machine learning techniques have been widely used to evaluate player experience. In [6], Convolutional Neural Networks (CNN) are used to extract game events from gameplay videos, which then can be used to evaluate player experience. In [7], neural networks built on physiological signals are used to predict player experience. However, physiological signal recording devices are not widely available. So, in our paper, we focus on data that can be collected from AI simulations. Long Short-Term Memory Recurrent Neural Networks (LSTM) are neural networks for classifying sequential data. In [15], LSTM is trained on gameplay videos to generate player tailored game content. In our approach, LSTM is trained on the abstract game representation to classify player experience.

Since Deep Q-learning by Google DeepMind [8] has been proved to be successful on Atari games, we deploy the same framework in our paper to train a deep reinforcement agent to collect game state information from a testbed game. The objective of our AI agent is to develop an abstract representation of game states instead of achieving the highest scores for a group of games as in [8]. One advantage of Deep Q-learning is that it can be applied to different games, thus making our approach applicable across different games.

3   Abstract Representation of Game States

When a player plays a video game, the game presents information about the current game state to the player, and the player processes this information to develop an understanding of the game states. Then, the player takes actions accordingly to progress in the game. To analyze player experience, it is important to know what information is presented to the player and how the player perceives that information. In this paper, we use reinforcement learning agents to approximate the player perceptions.

3.1 Deep Q-Learning

Reinforcement learning [8,9] is an area of Machine Learning in which AI agents are trained to take appropriate actions under certain circumstances. During the exploration of the environment, AI agents gradually learn what actions should be performed under different conditions as to maximum cumulative reward. In the context of video games, AI agents are trained to achieve highest possible scores, or to progress as far as possible in a level.

Q-learning is a classic reinforcement learning algorithm. In Q-learning, the agent learns a function that maps environment states and actions to future rewards. This function tells us which actions should be taken to maximize the cumulative rewards under the current game state. In Deep Q-learning [8,9], the function is a deep neural network with environment states as the input and Q-values for each possible actions the agents can perform as the output. Actions with higher Q-values are more likely to lead the agents to higher cumulative reward. Compared to traditional Q-learning, the deep neural network in Deep Q-learning enables it to handle more complicated environment states, like in video games where game states are typically represented as pixel arrays whose dimensions can be enormous.

Consider the actions and its Q-values an agent can take at a certain state. If all actions have similar Q-values, this implies that no matter which actions the agent is going to take, the cumulative reward will not change much. But if one particular action has much higher Q-values, the cumulative reward will be greatly reduced once the less optimal action is taken. In the context of video games, actions with similar Q-values means that a player is less likely to make a wrong decision which can prevent him/her from finishing a level or achieving a high score, whereas a particular action with much higher Q-values implies that the player is currently in an intense game situation in which the player must make a smart choice in order to move forward in the game or get a higher score. In this sense, Q-values approximate the current game states presented to the player.

As described in [2], flow is a mental state in which a person is fully immersed when the person is participating in an activity. One important aspect of achieving flow is the balance between challenges and participant's skill level. In the context of games that provide challenges to the player, the enjoyment comes from conquering challenges of proper difficulty level. We argue that Q-values learnt by AI agents abstract what challenges are presented to the player and how those challenges will change over time when the player proceeds in the game, thus affecting player experience [11].

3.2   Normalized Q-Value Difference

In the simplest form of video games, there is only one control button, like Flappy Bird. In Flappy Bird, a player can push the only button to make a bird jump over pipe obstacles. At any moment, there are two possible actions for the player, jump or not jump. As mentioned above, if those two actions have similar Q-values, then the player is allowed to play freely without making a mistake; otherwise, the player must plan his/her move wisely. Here, we want to know exactly how freely the player can act. Assume that at any game state, two actions (jump or not jump in the game of Flappy Bird) can be taken by the player, and q_1 is the Q-value for the first action and q_2 is the Q-value for the second action. Thus, we define Normalized Q-Value Difference (NQD) as

$$NQD(q_1, q_2) = \frac{|q_1 - q_2|}{max\{q_1, q_2\}} \tag{1}$$

Here $NQD(q_1, q_2)$ calculates the normalized difference between the Q-values of two actions. If $NQD(q_1, q_2)$ is close to 0, it implies that two actions have similar Q-values, then which action to take does not matter too much. If $NQD(q_1, q_2)$ is close to 1, then one action has much higher Q-value, therefore which action to take will have a great impact on game reward. In the case where one Q-value is negative and another one is positive, we set $NQD(q_1, q_2)$ to 1 to make sure $NQD(q_1, q_2)$ is always within the range from 0 to 1.

In some game states, both actions can have very high Q-values, while in some other game states, both actions can have relatively low Q-values. To make those game states comparable, the difference is normalized. Based on the definition of Normalized Q-value Difference, some features are defined for game levels.

Average Q-Value Difference. Average Q-value difference (avg_{QD}) is the average $NQD(q_1, q_2)$ across all game states experienced by a trained AI agent through a game level. Low avg_{QD} value indicates that a player can make decisions more freely in a game level. For example, in some easy game levels, a player can take either action without being punished, thus having low avg_{QD} values.

Standard Deviation Q-Value Difference. Similar to avg_{QD}, Standard deviation Q-value difference (sd_{QD}) is the standard deviation of $NQD(q_1, q_2)$ across all game states experienced by a trained AI through a game level.

Maximum Q-Value Difference. Maximum Q-value difference (max_{QD}) is the maximum $NQD(q_1, q_2)$ across all game states experienced by a trained AI agent through a game level. This value indicates the intensity of the most intense moment in a game level.

Percentage of Intense States. The percentage of intense states ($\%_{QD}$) is the fraction of game states with $NQD(q_1, q_2)$ larger than a certain threshold.

$\%_{QD}$ calculates how often a player will encounter intense moments in a game level. If $\%_{QD}$ is too low, it is possible that the game level is trivial and boring; otherwise, if $\%_{QD}$ is too large, the game level can be too difficult, which is also an unenjoyable experience.

3.3 Level Comparisons

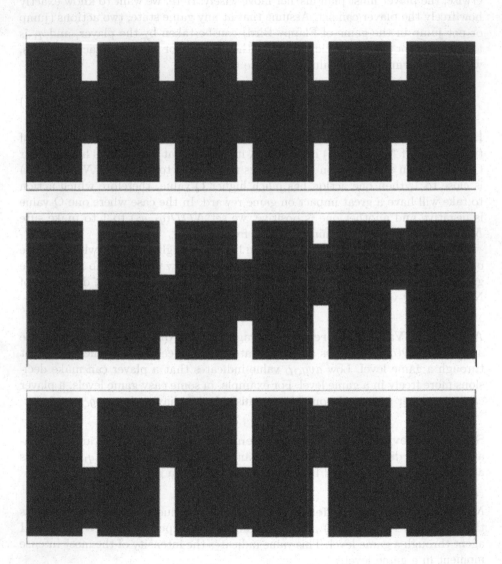

Fig. 1. Three example levels in Flappy game (Level 1 to Level 3, top to bottom)

Table 1. $NQD(q_1, q_2)$ based features for Level 1 to Level 3

Levels	avg_{QD}	sd_{QD}	max_{QD}	$\%_{QD}$
Level 1	0.075	0.104	0.756	0.405
Level 2	0.083	0.140	0.890	0.445
Level 3	0.222	0.253	1.000	0.667

In Table 1, four $NQD(q_1, q_2)$-based features are calculated. Level 1 (top in Fig. 1) is a relatively easy level, in which all fives pipe obstacles remain in the same vertical position. If a player can successfully pass through the first pipe, it will not be too difficult to conquer the remaining pipes. So, this level has the smallest feature values. Level 2 (middle in Fig. 1) is slightly more difficult. In Level 2, a player needs to carefully control the bird to higher and higher positions without colliding with any obstacles. Level 3 (bottom in Fig. 1) is a rather difficult level. There is a big height difference between any two consecutive pipe obstacles. It requires the player to perform jump action at perfect timings so that the player can proceed to the end of this level. Thus, Level 3 has the highest avg_{QD}, sd_{QD}, max_{QD} and the largest amount of intense moments ($\%_{QD}$).

Table 2. $NQD(q_1, q_2)$ based features for easy and hard levels

Levels	avg_{QD}	sd_{QD}	max_{QD}	$\%_{QD}$
Easy	**0.091**	**0.143**	0.888	**0.434**
Hard	**0.114**	**0.162**	0.864	**0.445**

In Table 2, we calculate $NQD(q_1, q_2)$-based features averaged over 100 easy levels and 100 hard levels. All levels are randomly generated. The difficulty is manipulated by limiting the positions of all pipes. In easy levels, all pipes are closer to the center area of the level. In hard levels, the possible height for each pipe is from the floor of the level to the ceiling of the level. Therefore, the height difference between two consecutive pipes could be large. All features, except max_{QD}, are statistically significant (in bold, $p < 0.005$). Again, it shows that the information collected from AI agents can help us distinguish levels with different difficulties.

Table 1 and Table 2 shows that four $NQD(q_1, q_2)$-based features can help us differentiate levels with different properties, because those four features reflect how AI agents interact with a game level. After reinforcement learning, the AI agent is trained to always perform the most optimal action, thus the AI agent can be viewed as an optimal version of a human player. Even though a real human player may never achieve the same level of optimality as an AI agent, we argue that those four $NQD(q_1, q_2)$-based features calculated from the experience of an AI agent is related to the experience of the human player. In the next section, we will show how those features can be used to classify player experience.

4   Player Experience Classification

4.1   Flappy

A game called Flappy is created in Unity3D for this experiment. Flappy has the same game logic as Flappy Bird in which a player can order a controlled bird to jump over pipe obstacles. In Flappy, there are five pipe obstacles that the player needs to pass through in each level. The horizontal distance between consecutive pipe obstacles is fixed throughout the experiment.

In this experiment, we use the same Deep Q-learning structure as in [9] to train our reinforcement AI agent. In the training phase of Deep Q-learning (training time steps is 2e6), random generate levels with five pipe obstacles are presented to the AI agent. In each random level, the height of each pipe obstacle is sampled from a uniform distribution between the level's upper-bound vertical position and lower-bound vertical position. The training is accomplished within the framework of Unity ML [5] and OpenAI Baselines [3].

Also, a human player (Male, 32 years old) is asked to play randomly generated levels. We use only one human participant because we find in our experiment that different players tend to have very different preferences of what constitute as enjoyable levels. After the human player finishes a level, he is asked to label the level as either enjoyable or not enjoyable. After the AI agent is trained, all labelled levels are played again by the AI agent. When the AI agent plays the labelled levels, we record Q-values for each action at each game state. Four features, avg_{QD}, sd_{QD}, max_{QD} and $\%_{QD}$, are calculated for each labeled game level. In total, we collect features for 221 game levels (55% are labeled as enjoyable levels). Two thirds of those game levels are used for training and the remaining one third levels are used for testing.

4.2   Decision Tree

We notice that in the collected data, the four $NQD(q_1, q_2)$-based features are not linearly correlated with the enjoyment of game levels. For example, if $\%_{QD}$ is too high, intense moments in the game occur too often, thus making the game level over-challenging and less enjoyable. On the other hand, if $\%_{QD}$ is too low, almost every moment in the game is trivial, making the game level boring. So, we decided to use Decision Tree which can handle non-linearly separable data [13].

For this experiment, three types of input features are used for classification: game level layout features, $NQD(q_1, q_2)$-based features, and mixed features (game level layout + $NQD(q_1, q_2)$-based features). The game level layout features are the vertical positions of pipe obstacles in each game level. The output of each classifier is a binary label, 1 - the input game level enjoyable, or 0 - the input game level is not enjoyable.

4.3 Long Short-Term Memory

LSTM (Long Short-Term Memory) [4] is a recurrent neural network that can be used to classify sequential data. One advantage of LSTM is its capability to remember information from previous game states. It is a good fit for classifying player experience, because the overall player experience is not determined by a single frame in game but by a sequence of game states presented to the player.

In this paper, we apply LSTM directly on the Normalized Q-value sequences to classify player enjoyment. One issue with LSTM is that the length of Q-value sequence for each level is different. To solve this problem, shorter sequences are pre-padded with 0 to make sure all Q-value sequences have the same length.

4.4 Results

During initial feature analysis, max_{QD} turns out to be close to 1 regardless of whether a game level is enjoyable or not. Therefore, this feature is excluded from classifiers. Including sd_{QD} in the classifiers greatly downgrade the classification performance, so sd_{QD} is also excluded from the classification. In the post-experiment interview with the human player, he reported that he enjoyed different types of levels, ranging from levels of great difficulty to levels of moderate difficulty, even to some tricky easy levels. It implies that the distribution of intense moments across enjoyable levels is not consistent. This can explain why sd_{QD} does not help improve the performance of the classifiers.

The performance metrics of classifiers (Decision Trees with Gini Impurity and max depth 7, LSTM with 16 hidden units) are reported in Table 3.

Table 3. Classifier performance

Features	Accuracy	Recall	Precision	F1
layout	0.60	0.59	0.73	0.65
avg_{QD}	0.52	0.52	0.76	0.62
$\%_{QD}$	0.53	0.54	0.59	0.56
$avg_{QD} + \%_{QD}$	0.48	0.49	0.57	0.53
layout $+ avg_{QD}$	0.58	0.57	0.70	0.63
layout $+ \%_{QD}$	0.77	0.76	0.78	0.77
layout $+ avg_{QD} + \%_{QD}$	0.74	0.72	0.78	0.75
LSTM	0.74	0.68	0.92	0.75

In Table 3, Accuracy is the fraction of correctly predicted levels (including enjoyable and not enjoyable levels). Precision is the fraction of recognized enjoyable levels by our classifiers that are truly enjoyable. Recall is the fraction of enjoyable levels that are successfully identified by our classifiers. F1 is the metric of classification performance considering both precision and recall.

The performance metrics of avg_{QD} classifier and $\%_{QD}$ classifier is better than a random binary classifier (baseline, 50% accuracy), but only to a limited extent. It implies that avg_{QD} and $\%_{QD}$ are related to player experience, but do not encode enough information to serve as a standalone input feature. Without sufficient information from other features, those two features may conflict with each other, and this may cause the classifier with input $avg_{QD} + \%_{QD}$ to be the worst classifier in Table 3.

When incorporating level layout information with avg_{QD} and $\%_{QD}$, the performance of classifiers is improved, which supports our argument that the experience of an AI agent is related to the experience of the human player, and can help improve the performance of player enjoyment classifiers. The Decision Tree classifier with the best overall performance is the one using level layout information and $\%_{QD}$. This classifier outperforms layout+avg_{QD} classifier and layout+$avg_{QD} + \%_{QD}$ classifier. It shows that $\%_{QD}$ is more relevant to player enjoyment, implying that it is important to have the right amount of intense moments in an enjoyable level.

Due to its capability to remember previous game states, the LSTM model also has good performance. And it is the one with the highest Precision and F1 score. Since LSTM model does not use any knowledge of the level layout, it shows that the abstract representation alone learnt by AI agents can provide sufficient information about how the player perceives a game level. Also, this implies that Deep Q-Learning and LSTM can be applied to other games, because they are game-independent.

The results of our experiments support our argument that the AI agent can learn abstract represention of game levels, which can help machine learning models with player experience classification.

5   Conclusion and Future Work

In this paper, a Deep Q-learning agent is trained to play a testbed game. We argue that the abstract representation of game states developed by the AI agent is relevant to the player experience. It is shown by our experiments that machine learning models (Decision Tree and LSTM) trained with the abstract representation can classify player experience with good results, thus making it possible to analyze game levels automatically.

One advantage of learning abstract representation of game states is that the abstract represenation is universal across different games regardless of their game mechanics. Therefore, machine learning models built upon the abstract representation can be adapted to different games. Since Deep Q-learning is also a general framework that can be applied to different games [10], it is possible to transfer knowledge learned from one game to another game. Ideally, we can evaluate player experience for a new game without collecting human player gameplay data from that new game. This will be our topic for future research.

In the future, we can also develop more features based on the abstract representation (Q-values) to further improve the performance of player experience classifiers, especially for games that have more than two actions. Procedural Content Generation is another direction where we can apply our approach. First, the universal abstract represention of enjoyable game levels can be explored. Then, this abstract representation can be transformed into game levels of different geners regardless of their game mechanics.

References

1. Browne, C., Maire, F.: Evolutionary game design. IEEE Trans. Comput. Intell. AI Games **2**(1), 1–16 (2010)
2. Csikszentmihalyi, M.: Beyond Boredom and Anxiety. Jossey-Bass, San Francisco (2000)
3. Dhariwal, P., et al.: Openai baselines (2017). https://github.com/openai/baselines
4. Gers, F.A., Schmidhuber, J., Cummins, F.: Learning to forget: continual prediction with LSTM. In: 9th International Conference on Artificial Neural Networks (ICANN 1999), pp. 850–855 (1999)
5. Juliani, A., et al.: Unity: A general platform for intelligent agents. arXiv preprint arXiv:1809.02627 (2018)
6. Luo, Z., Guzdial, M., Liao, N., Riedl, M.: Player experience extraction from gameplay video. In: Fourteenth Artificial Intelligence and Interactive Digital Entertainment Conference (2018)
7. Martínez, H.P., Garbarino, M., Yannakakis, G.N.: Generic physiological features as predictors of player experience. In: D'Mello, S., Graesser, A., Schuller, B., Martin, J.-C. (eds.) ACII 2011. LNCS, vol. 6974, pp. 267–276. Springer, Heidelberg (2011). https://doi.org/10.1007/978-3-642-24600-5_30
8. Mnih, V., et al.: Playing atari with deep reinforcement learning. arXiv preprint arXiv:1312.5602 (2013)
9. Mnih, V., et al.: Human-level control through deep reinforcement learning. Nature **518**(7540), 529 (2015)
10. Perez-Liebana, D., Liu, J., Khalifa, A., Gaina, R.D., Togelius, J., Lucas, S.M.: General video game ai: a multi-track framework for evaluating agents, games and content generation algorithms. arXiv preprint arXiv:1802.10363 (2018)
11. Rollings, A., Morris, D.: Game Architecture and Design Scottsdale. Coriolis, Los Angeles (2000)
12. Ryan, R.M., Rigby, C.S., Przybylski, A.: The motivational pull of video games: a self-determination theory approach. Motiva. Emot. **30**(4), 344–360 (2006). https://doi.org/10.1007/s11031-006-9051-8
13. Safavian, S.R., Landgrebe, D.: A survey of decision tree classifier methodology. IEEE Trans. Syst. Man Cybern. **21**(3), 660–674 (1991)
14. Salge, C., Mahlmann, T.: Relevant information as a formalised approach to evaluate game mechanics. In: Proceedings of the 2010 IEEE Conference on Computational Intelligence and Games, pp. 281–288. IEEE (2010)
15. Summerville, A., Guzdial, M., Mateas, M., Riedl, M.O.: Learning player tailored content from observation: platformer level generation from video traces using LSTMs. In: Twelfth Artificial Intelligence and Interactive Digital Entertainment Conference (2016)
16. Zhu, T., Wang, B., Zyda, M.: Exploring the similarity between game events for game level analysis and generation. In: Proceedings of the 13th International Conference on the Foundations of Digital Games, p. 8. ACM (2018)

Images, Visualization and Aesthetics in HCI

Generating Graphic Representations of Spoken Interactions Revisited: The Tension Factor and Information Not Uttered in Journalistic Data

Christina Alexandris[1,2], Dimitrios Mourouzidis[1,2(✉)], and Vasilios Floros[1,2]

[1] National and Kapodistrian University of Athens, Athens, Greece
calexandris@gs.uoa.gr, mourouzidisd@gmail.com,
florosbas2002@yahoo.gr
[2] European Communication Institute (ECI), Danube University Krems
and National Technical University of Athens, Athens, Greece

Abstract. The proposed interactive and semi-automatic processing in distinctive modules facilitates the correct perception and evaluation of pragmatic features and paralinguistic features in spoken interaction, especially in discussions and interactions beyond a defined agenda and specified protocol, such as interviews and live conversations in Skype or in the Media. We propose a processing and evaluation framework including a generation of graphical representations and tags corresponding to values and benchmarks depicting the degree of information not uttered and non-neutral elements - including tension - in Speaker behavior in spoken text segments.

Keywords: Spoken journalistic texts · Spoken interaction · Tension · Paralinguistic features · Graphic representations · Cognitive Bias

1 Processing Information Not Uttered in Spoken Journalistic Texts

Pragmatic features in spoken interaction and information conveyed but not uttered by Speakers can pose challenges to applications processing spoken texts that are not domain-specific. The proposed interactive and semi-automatic processing in distinctive modules facilitates the correct perception and evaluation of pragmatic features and paralinguistic features in spoken interaction, especially in discussions and interactions beyond a defined agenda and specified protocol, such as interviews and live conversations in Skype or in the Media.

We propose a processing and evaluation framework including a generation of graphical representations and tags corresponding to values and benchmarks depicting the degree of information not uttered and non-neutral elements in Speaker behavior in spoken text segments. Special focus is placed on the element of tension. The generated tags and values can be used for text classification for the development and collection of empirical data for HCI and HRI applications and for applications such as Sentiment Analysis and Opinion Mining.

© Springer Nature Switzerland AG 2020
M. Kurosu (Ed.): HCII 2020, LNCS 12181, pp. 523–537, 2020.
https://doi.org/10.1007/978-3-030-49059-1_39

Spoken political and journalistic texts may be considered to be a remarkable source of empirical data both for human behaviour and for linguistic phenomena, especially for spoken language. However, with some exceptions, spoken political and journalistic texts are usually underrepresented both in linguistic data for translational and analysis purposes and in Natural Language Processing (NLP) applications. These text types pose challenges for their evaluation, processing and translation since they are usually rich in socio-linguistic and socio-cultural elements, include discussions and interactions beyond a defined agenda and are often not domain-specific. Furthermore, with spoken political and journalistic texts there is always the possibility of different types of targeted audiences - including non-native speakers and the international community. In these cases, essential information, presented either in a subtle form or in an indirect way, is often undetected, especially by the international public.

As the variety and complexity of spoken Human Computer Interaction (HCI) (and Human Robot Interaction - HRI) applications increases, the correct perception and evaluation of information not uttered is an essential requirement in systems with emotion recognition, virtual negotiation, psychological support or decision-making.

Furthermore, Information that is not uttered is problematic in Data Mining and Opinion Mining applications, since they mostly rely on word groups, word sequences and/or sentiment lexica [18], including recent approaches with the use of neural networks [6, 15, 29]. In recent research for Sentiment Analysis from videos (text, audio and video) with the use of a hierarchical architecture for extracting context dependent multimodal utterance features [26], it was observed that, in some cases, the gesture, facial expression or movement may either complement or contradict the semantic content of a spoken utterance, even in domain-specific applications.

The graphic patterns and visual representations are based on the output of an interactive annotation tool for spoken journalistic texts presented in previous research [4]. Specifically, in the interactive annotation tool [4], incoming texts to be processed constitute transcribed data from journalistic texts. The annotation tool was designed to operate with most commercial transcription tools, some of which are available online. The development of the tool is based on data and observations provided by professional journalists (European Communication Institute, Program M.A in Quality Journalism and Digital Technologies, Danube University at Krems, Athena- Research and Innovation Center in Information, Communication and Knowledge Technologies, Athens - Institution of Promotion of Journalism Ath.Vas. Botsi, Athens and the National and Technical University of Athens, Greece). Since processing speed and the option of reusability in multiple languages of the written and spoken political and journalistic texts constitutes a basic target of the proposed approach, strategies typically employed in the construction of Spoken Dialog Systems, such as keyword processing in the form of topic detection, were adapted in the developed annotation tool. The functions of the designed and constructed interactive annotation tool [4] include providing the User-Journalist with (a) the tracked indications of the topics handled in the interview or discussion and (b) the graphic pattern of the discourse structure of the interview or discusion. Furthermore, these functions facilitate the comparison between discourse structures of conversations and interviews with similar topics or the same participants/participant.

2   Generated Graphical Representations and Tags: The "Relevance" Module and Previous Research

Generated graphical representations and annotation options are proposed for identifying the complex types of information presented, in combination to the respective activated modules within a singular annotation and processing framework. All strategies and respective modules presented are based on the Gricean Cooperative Principle [12, 13] in the Speech Acts involved.

Pragmatic features, in particular, indicators of a Speaker's attitude-behavior and intentions, including tension, can be visualized in distinctive generated graphic representations and related annotations. The generated distinct types of graphic patterns presented here contribute to a user-independent evaluation of spoken Human-Human conversation and interaction [3, 21].

In small speech segments with constant and quick change of speaker turns and with discourse structure compatible to models where each participant selects self [27, 34], topic tracking (and topic change) allows the evaluation of speaker behavior and enables the identification of Speaker's intentions and Illocutionary Speech Acts performed [7, 28]. Topic tracking can be applied especially in short speech segments with two or multiple Speakers-Participants [3]. The content of relatively short utterances can be summarized with the use of keywords chosen from each utterance by the user-evaluator [3], with the assistance of the Stanford POS Tagger for the automatic signalization of nouns in each turn taken by the Speakers in the respective segment in the dialog structure. The registered and tracked keywords, treated as local variables, signalize each topic and the relations between topics, since automatic Rhetorical Structure Theory (RST) analysis procedures [30, 36] usually involves larger (written) texts and may not produce the required results.

The implemented "RELEVANCE" Module [21] generates a visual representation from the user's interaction, tracking the corresponding selected topic-keywords in the dialog flow, as well as the chosen types of relations between them. The interactive generation of registered paths is similar to the paths with generated sequences of recognized keywords in spoken dialog systems, in the domains of consumer complaints and mobile phone services call centers [11, 23]. This function is similar to user-independent evaluations of spoken dialog systems [33] for by-passing User bias [9, 22]. Keywords (topics) may be repeated or related to a more general concept (or global variable) [17] or related to keywords (topics) concerning similar functions (corresponding to the Repetition, Generalization and Association relations respectively and the visual representations of Distances 1 (value "1"), 2 (value "2") and 3 (value "3") respectively) [3]. A keyword involving a new command or function is registered as a new topic (New Topic, visual representation of Distance 4, corresponding to value: "0"). The sequence of topics chosen by the user and the perceived relations between them generates a "path" of interaction, forming distinctive visual representations stored in a database currently under development: Topics and words generating diverse reactions and choices from users result to the generation of different forms of generated visual representations for the same conversation and interaction [3, 21].

The generated visual representations depict topics avoided, introduced or repeatedly referred to by each Speaker-Participant, and in specific types of cases may indicate the existence of additional, "hidden" Illocutionary Acts other than "Obtaining Information Asked" or "Providing Information Asked" in a discussion or interview. Thus, the evaluation of Speaker-Participant behavior targets to by-pass Cognitive Bias, specifically, Confidence Bias [16] of the user-evaluator, especially if multiple users-evaluators may produce different forms of generated visual representations for the same conversation and interaction and compared to each other in the database. In this case, chosen relations between topics may describe Lexical Bias [31] and may differ according to political, socio-cultural and linguistic characteristics of the user-evaluator, especially if international users are concerned [5, 19, 25, 35] due to lack of world knowledge of the language community involved [14, 24, 32]. The envisioned further development of generated visual representations is their modeling in a form of graphs, similar to discourse trees [8, 20].

The types of relations-distances between word-topics chosen by the user-evaluator are registered and counted. If the number of (a) the "Repetitions" or (b) the number of the "Generalizations" or (c) the number of the "Topic Switches" exceeds well over 50% of the registered relations-distances between word-topics, the interaction is signalized for further evaluation, containing Illocutionary Acts not restricted to "Obtaining Information Asked" or "Providing Information Asked". The following benchmarks indicate interactions with Illocutionary Acts beyond the predefined framework of the dialog for multiple Speaker discussions and/or short speech segments, where Ds = Number of Distances and Sp = Number of Speaker turns [1]:

- X = Ds $\leq$ Sp (calculating over 50% of "Repetitions" (Distance = 1, value "1")) or "Topic Switches" (Distance = 4, value "0").
- X = Ds > Sp $\times$ Gen (Gen = Sp $\times$ 3 $\div$ 2) (calculating over 50% of "Generalizations" (Distance = 3, value "3").

These benchmarks for dialogs with short speech segments can be referred to as "(Topic) Relevance" benchmarks with a value of "X" or "Relevance (X)" [1].

The above-described values, benchmarks [1] and graphic representations also allow the identification and detection of additional, "hidden" Illocutionary Acts not restricted to "Obtaining Information Asked" or "Providing Information Asked", as defined by the framework of the interview or discussion [21]. Three frequently detected categories of pointers to "hidden" Speech Acts are: "Presence" (reluctance to answer questions, avoidance of topics, polite or symbolic presence in the discussion or interview but not an active participation), "Express Policy" (direct or even blatant expression of opinion or policy- persistence on discussing the same topic of interest or attempts to direct the discussion in the topic(s) or interest) and "Make Impression" (behavior similar to the previous categories - with characteristic prosodic and paralinguistic features). These Speech Act pointers may be connected to each other and may even occur at the same time. The "Make Impression" Speech Act pointer is distinguished from the other two Speech Act pointer since it is identifiable on the Paralinguistic Level [21].

The "[IMPL]" tag is generated after the activation of the above-described "RELEVANCE" Module signalizing the presence of additional, "hidden" Illocutionary Acts performed by the Speakers-Participants. The "[IMPL]" tag may be accompanied by an indication of the "Presence", "Express Policy" or "Make Impression" Speech Act pointer, if applicable. Figure 1 and 2 depict graphical representations of the "RELE-VANCE" Module Output: Generated graphical representation with multiple "Topic Switch" relations [21] and generated graphical representation with multiple "Gener-alization" relations [21], both resulting to the generation of the "[IMPL]" tag.

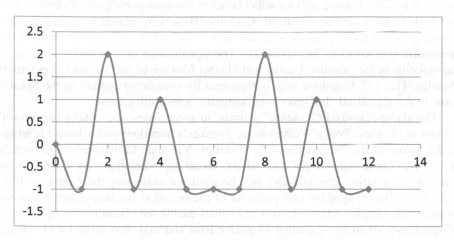

Fig. 1. Generated graphical representation with multiple "Topic Switch" relations (Mourouzidis et al., 2019) producing the [IMPL] tag as output.

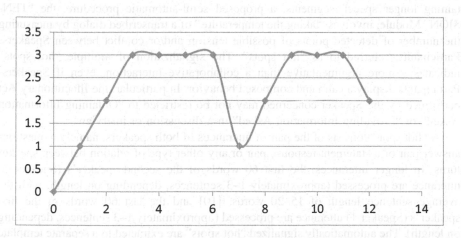

Fig. 2. Generated graphical representation with multiple "Generalization" relations (Mourou-zidis et al., 2019) producing the [IMPL] tag as output.

3 Generating Graphical Representations Revisited: The Tension Factor

The further development of the database containing registered spoken interaction for determining and evaluating Cognitive Bias in spoken journalistic texts [3, 21] involves the processing of discussions and interviews containing larger speech segments. In the case of discussions and interviews containing larger speech segments, the identification of speaker's intentions and "hidden" Illocutionary Act detection follows a process locating points of possible tension and/or conflict between speakers-participants. In points of possible tension and/or conflict between speakers-participants, Cognitive Bias can both be by-passed or registered. Cognitive Bias is by-passed by signalizing and counting the points of possible tension and/or conflict between speakers-participants henceforth referred to as "hot spots" [1]. The signalization of "hot spots" is based on the violation of the Quantity, Quality and Manner Maxims of the Gricean Cooperativity Principle [12, 13]. Cognitive Bias is registered by comparing content of the Speaker turns in the signalized "hot spots" and assigning a respective value.

The above-described "Presence" Pointer, in some cases, the "Make Impression" Pointer or "Express Policy" Pointer to the Speaker's intentions and behavior is related to the values of the "Relevance (X)", "Tension (Y)" and "Collaboration (Z)" benchmarks [1]. These benchmarks and related visual representations are based on the Gricean Cooperative Principle and may be used for evaluating the Cognitive Bias-Confidence Bias [16] of the user-evaluator of the recorded and transcribed discussion or interview. Graphic representations and values enable the evaluation of the behavior of speakers-participants, depicting Cognitive Bias and may also serve for by-passing Confidence Bias of the user-evaluator of the recorded and transcribed discussion or interview.

Targeting to by-pass Cognitive Bias in two-party discussions and interviews containing longer speech segments, a proposed semi-automatic procedure, the "TENSION" Module, involves "taking the temperature" of a transcribed dialog by measuring the number of detected points of possible tension and/or conflict between Speakers-Participants, referred to as "hot spots". The signalization of multiple "hot spots" indicates a more argumentative than a collaborative interaction, even if Speakers-Participants display a calm and composed behavior. In particular, the Illocutionary Act performed by the Speaker concerned may not be restricted to "Obtaining Information Asked" or "Providing Information Asked" in a discussion or interview.

A "hot spot" consists of the pair of utterances of both speakers, namely a question-answer pair or a statement-response pair or any other type of relation between speaker turns. In longer utterances, the first 60 words of the second speaker's (Speaker 2) utterance are processed (approximately 1–3 sentences, depending on length, with the average sentence length of 15–20 words, [10] and the last 60 words of the first speaker's (Speaker 1) utterance are processed (approximately 1–3 sentences, depending on length). The automatically signalized "hot spots" are extracted to a separate template for further processing. The extraction contains not only the detected segments but also the complete utterances consisting of both speaker turns of Speaker 1 and Speaker 2. For a segment of speaker turns to be automatically identified as a "hot spot", at least two of the following three conditions (1), (2) and (3) must apply [1] to one or to both of the speaker's utterances, of which conditions (1), (2) are directly or indirectly related to flouting of Maxims of the Gricean Cooperative Principle [12, 13]. These conditions are the following, with features detectable with a POS Tagger (for example, the Stanford POS Tagger, http://nlp.stanford.edu/software/tagger.shtml) or they may constitute a small set of entries in a specially created lexicon or may be retrieved from existing databases or WordNets:

- (1) Additional, modifying features. In one or in both speakers' utterances in the segment of speaker turns there is at least one phrase containing a sequence of two adjectives (ADJ ADJ) (a) or an adverb and an adjective (or more adjectives) (b) (ADV ADJ) or two adverbs (ADV ADV) (c) (Violation of the Gricean Cooperative Principle in respect to the Maxim of Quantity -"Do not make your contribution more informative than is required") [1].
- (2) Reference to the interaction itself and to its participants with negation. For example, "I" or "you" ((I/You) "don't", "do not","cannot") (a) and in the verb phrase (VP) there is at least one speech-related or behavior verb-stem referring to the dialog itself (b) (for example, "speak", "listen", "guess", "understand") (including to parts of speech other than verbs (i.e. "guessing", "listener"), as well as to words constituting parts of expressions related to speech or behavior ("conclusions", "words", "mouth", "polite", "nonsense", "manners"), (violation of the Gricean Cooperative Principle in respect to the Maxim of Quality -"1- Do not say what you believe to be false", "2 - Do not say that for which you lack adequate evidence") [12, 13] and/or in respect to the Maxim of Manner -Submaxim 2 "Avoid ambiguity") [12, 13] in the utterance of the previous Speaker: considered unacceptable, ambiguous, false or controversial) [1].
- (3) Prosodic emphasis and/or Exclamations. (a) Exclamations include expressions such as "Look", "Wait" and "Stop". (b) Prosodic emphasis, detected in the speech processing module, may occur in one or more of the above-described words of categories (1a, 1b, 1c, 2a and 2b) or in the noun or verb following (modified by) 1a, 1b and 1c [1].

The benchmark for evaluating a remarkable degree of tension in a discussion is signalized by multiple "hot spots" detected and not sporadic occurrences of "hot spots". Thus, the number of 1–2 "hot spot" occurrences in longer speech segments in question (30–45 min) signalizes a low degree of tension. A remarkable degree of tension in a 30–45 min discussion or interview is related to a number of at least 4 detected "hot spots" (where the number of 3 hot spots constitutes a marginal value). Detected points of possible tension and/or conflict are indicated by the following benchmark (where Y = wav file length in minutes divided by ($\div$) the number of "hot spot" signalized speech segments): $Y < 10$. (Example: File length = 35 min, SPEECH SEGMENT-count: 5, Evaluation: 7). These benchmarks for dialogs with long speech segments can be referred to as "Tension" benchmarks with a value of "Y" or "Tension (Y)" [1].

Additionally, each "hot spot" is marked with a (1,1) if both speakers' utterances are considered equally non-collaborative (1, 0) for Speaker 1 (in this case, the journalist-reporter), (0, 1), if the interviewee's (Speaker 2) reaction is not justified in respect to the style and content of the utterance of Speaker 1 and (0, 0), if a "hot spot" speech segment is evaluated by the user not as a point of possible tension and/or conflict between speakers-participants (false "hot spot"- [1]).

Both Speakers may have an equal number of a grading of "1" in all extracted "hot spots" detected or one of the Speakers may have a slightly higher/lower or a considerably higher/lower grading of "1". A grading of "1" in 50% or more of the "hot spots" signalizes that the Illocutionary Act performed by the Speaker concerned is not restricted to "Obtaining Information Asked" or "Providing Information Asked". Speaker behavior indicating that Illocutionary Acts performed are not restricted to the predefined interaction framework is evaluated by the following benchmarks (where Z = the number of "hot spot" signalized speech segments divided by ($\div$): 2 (50%): Sum of Speaker grades $\geq Z$. (Example: SPEAKER1 (1, 1, 1, 0, 1), SPEAKER2 (0, 0, 1, 1, 0), SPEECH-SEGMENT-count "hot spots": 5, sum of grades = 6, 6 $\geq Z$ where $Z = 2.5$). These benchmarks for dialogs with long speech segments can be referred to as "Collaboration" benchmarks with a value of "Z" or "Collaboration (Z)".

In the proposed annotation options, the [IMPL] tag for text segments at sentence, passage or text level signalizes the presence of "hot spot" as a feature related to complex information content, including implied information, intentions, attitude and behavior.

The "[IMPL]" tag is generated after the activation of the above-described "TEN-SION" Module (Fig. 3) signalizing a remarkable degree of tension and uncollaborative behavior between the Speakers-Participants and the presence of additional, "hidden" Illocutionary Acts performed (Figs. 4 and 5).

Spoken text (wav. file length = 35 mins): Sp1 /Sp2 = Speaker1 / Speaker 2

Sp1 / Sp2 -- **Sp1 / Sp2** -Sp1 / Sp2 - **Sp1 / Sp 2** -**Sp1 / Sp 2** -- Spr1 / Sp 2 - **Sp1 / Sp 2**-
----------------[hot-spot-1]-------------[hot-spot-2]--[hot-spot-3]------------[hot-spot-4]-

Y (Tension) < 10 => Generation of "[IMPL]" tag

Fig. 3. "TENSION" Module Output: Signalization of multiple "hot spots" in a spoken text segment for the generation of the "[IMPL]" tag.

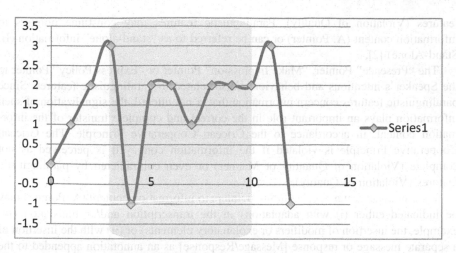

Fig. 4. "Hot spots" -Tension (shaded area between topics) in generated graphical representation producing the [IMPL] tag as output.

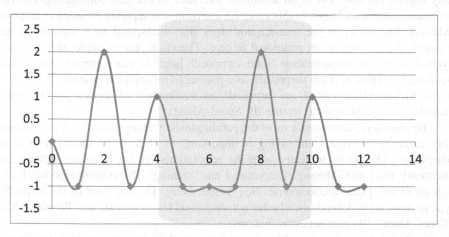

Fig. 5. "Hot spots" -Tension (shaded area between topics) in generated graphical representation with multiple "Topic Switch" relations, producing the [IMPL] tag as output.

4 Generating and Annotating Information Not Uttered in Paralinguistic Features

The generated graphic patterns allow the additional indication of any paralinguistic features influencing the content of the spoken utterances. Since paralinguistic features concern information that is not uttered, the signalization and visualization of such information plays an important role in the correct and complete transfer of the information content, in accordance to the Gricean Cooperative Principle. The Gricean Cooperative Principle is violated if the information conveyed is perceived as not complete (Violation of Quantity or Manner) or even contradicted by paralinguistic features (Violation of Quality). Paralinguistic features may constitute pointers to information content (A. Pointer) or can be referred to as "stand-alone" information (B. Stand-Alone) [2].

The "Presence" Pointer, "Make Impression" Pointer or "Express Policy" Pointer to the Speaker's intentions and behavior is also related to paralinguistic features. Since paralinguistic features concern information that is not uttered, the signalization of such information plays an important role in the correct and complete transfer of the information content, in accordance to the Gricean Cooperative Principle. The Gricean Cooperative Principle is violated if the information conveyed is perceived as not complete (Violation of Quantity or Manner) or even contradicted by paralinguistic features (Violation of Quality).

Paralinguistic features constituting pointers to information content (A. Pointer) may be indicated either (i) with adaptations in the transcription and/or translation (for example, the insertion of modifiers or explanatory elements) or (ii) with the insertion of a separate message or response [Message/Response] as an annotation appended to the transcription of the spoken utterance.

Paralinguistic features referred to as "stand-alone" information (B. Stand-Alone) may require the insertion of an additional utterance in the text constituting the transcription and/or translation. In this case, the insertion of a separate message or response [Message/Response] to the transcription does not correspond to a transcribed text segment but inserted as an additional feature. Therefore, for example, the raising of eyebrows with the interpretation "I am surprised" [and/but this surprises me] [2] may be indicated either as [I am surprised], as a pointer to information content (A. Pointer), or as [Message/Response: I am surprised], as a substitute of spoken information, a "stand-alone" paralinguistic feature (B. Stand-Alone).

The alternative interpretations of the paralinguistic feature (namely, "I am listening very carefully", "What I am saying is important" or "I have no intention of doing otherwise") [2] can be indicated with the annotations "[I am listening], [Please pay attention], [No] and [Message/Response: I am listening], [Message/Response: Please pay attention], [Message/Response: No]" respectively. The insertion of the respective type of annotation depends on whether paralinguistic feature constitute "Pointer" (A) or "Stand-Alone" (B) paralinguistic features.

Similarly, the slight raise of hand outward with the interpretation "Wait a second" [and/but wait] [2] may be either be indicated as [Stop. Wait], as a pointer to information content (A. Pointer), or as [Message/Response: Stop. Wait.], as a substitute of spoken information, a "stand-alone" paralinguistic feature (B. "Stand-Alone"). The alternative interpretations of the paralinguistic feature (namely, "Let me speak", "I disagree with this" or "Stop what you are doing") [2] can be indicated with the annotations "[Let me speak], [No], [Stop] and [Message/Response: Let me speak], [Message/Response: No], [Message/Response: Stop]" respectively. The insertion of the respective type of annotation depends on whether paralinguistic feature constitute "Pointer" (A) or "Stand-Alone" (B) paralinguistic features.

In the proposed framework, the interactive annotation of the previously described prosodic features is combined with the option of indicating the respective paralinguistic features ([facial-expr: type], [gesture: type]), if applicable, and the insertion of the chosen annotations, for example "[facial-expr: eyebrow-raise]" and "[gesture: low-hand-raise]". The insertion of the respective annotation allows the insertion/generation of the appropriate messages, according to the parameters of the language(s) and the speaker(s) concerned.

Paralinguistic features are annotated interactively with the corresponding tags and/or the chosen respective messages. In this case, the generation of the [IMPL] tag for an entire speech segment depends on the user's evaluation of the paralinguistic features concerned. One of the intended functions of the proposed annotation is its use as an additional annotation option to existing transcription tools and speech processing applications. The annotations concern text output generated by Speech Recognition (ASR) module for pre-processing/post-processing, providing options for evaluation, (machine) translation or other processes, including Data Mining applications. The annotation can be run as an additional process or with a possible integration (as upgrade) in existing tools and systems.

In case of the interactive annotation of the paralinguistic features the [IMPL] tag is not automatically generated. This difference is related to the particularities of the information content of paralinguistic features perceived by the user (Figs. 6, 7 and 8).

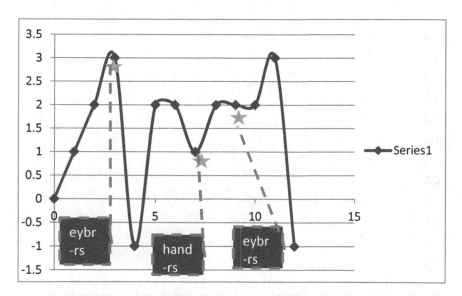

Fig. 6. Paralinguistic information (annotations) in generated graphical representation. The "[facial-expr: eyebrow-raise]" and "[gesture: low-hand-raise]" annotations depicted as "[eybr-rs]" and "[hand-rs]" respectively. The [IMPL] tag is a result of the user's choice and evaluation.

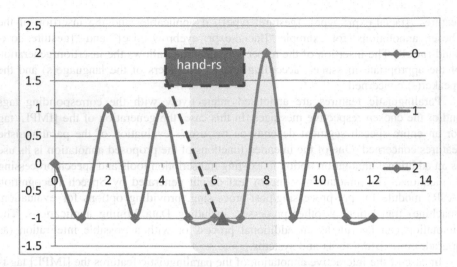

Fig. 7. "Hot spots" -Tension (shaded area between topics) and paralinguistic information (annotations) in generated graphical representation with multiple "Topic Switch" relations, producing the [IMPL] tag as output.

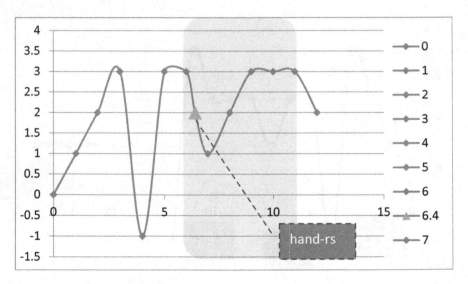

Fig. 8. "Hot spots" -Tension (shaded area between topics) and paralinguistic information (annotation) in generated graphical representation with multiple "Generalization" relations, producing the [IMPL] tag as output.

5 Conclusions and Further Research: Interface Upgrade and Empirical Data for Applications

The present application targets to assist the evaluation and decision-making process in respect to discussions and interviews in the Media (or Skype), providing a graphic representation of the discourse structure and aiming to by-pass Cognitive Bias of the user-evaluator (and/or User-Journalist). The predominate types of relations in the discourse and dialog structure, if applicable, are easily identified by the y level value around which the graphic representation is developed.

The time-frame generation of the linear structure allows the graphic representation to be presented in conjunction with the parallel depiction of speech signals and transcribed texts, a typical feature of most transcription tools. In other words, the alignment of the generated graphic representation with the respective segments of the spoken text enables a possible integration of the present application in existing transcription tools.

Furthermore, the above-described graphic representations and values enable the evaluation of the behavior of speakers-participants, allowing the identification and detection of additional, "hidden" Illocutionary Acts not restricted to "Obtaining Information Asked" or "Providing Information Asked" framework defined by the interview or discussion.

A further development and upgrading of the current interface is necessary for increasing speed and ameliorating user-friendliness. The envisioned upgrade includes the simplification of the existing menu and overall improvement of the graphical user interface (GUI).

In the present application, special focus is placed on tension in spoken political and journalistic texts as a source of empirical data both for human behaviour and for linguistic phenomena, especially when an international public is concerned and where a variety of linguistic and socio-cultural factors is included. With the visibility of all information content, including information not uttered, the proposed processing and annotation approaches may also be used for compiling empirical data for research and/or for the development of HCI- HRI Sentiment Analysis and Opinion Mining applications, as (initial) training and test sets or for Speaker (User) behavior and expectations.

References

1. Alexandris, C.: Evaluating cognitive bias in two-party and multi-party spoken interactions. In: Proceedings from the AAAI Spring Symposium, Stanford University (2019)
2. Alexandris, C.: Visualizing pragmatic features in spoken interaction: intentions, behavior and evaluation. In: Proceedings of the 1st International Conference on Linguistics Research on the Era of Artificial Intelligence – LREAI, Dalian, 25–27 October 2019. Dalian Maritime University (2010)
3. Alexandris, C.: Measuring cognitive bias in spoken interaction and conversation: generating visual representations. In: Beyond Machine Intelligence: Understanding Cognitive Bias and Humanity for Well-Being AI Papers from the AAAI Spring Symposium, Stanford University, Technical Report SS-18-03, pp. 204–206. AAAI Press, Palo Alto (2018)

4. Alexandris, C., Nottas, M., Cambourakis, G.: Interactive evaluation of pragmatic features in spoken journalistic texts. In: Kurosu, M. (ed.) HCI 2015. LNCS, vol. 9171, pp. 259–268. Springer, Cham (2015). https://doi.org/10.1007/978-3-319-21006-3_26
5. Alexandris, C.: English, German and the international "semi-professional" translator: a morphological approach to implied connotative features. J. Lang. Translation. **11**(2), 7–46 (2010)
6. Arockiaraj, C.M.: Applications of neural networks in data mining. Int. J. Eng. Sci. **3**(1), 8–11 (2013)
7. Austin J.L.: How to do things with words. In: Urmson, J.O., Sbisà, M. (eds.), 2nd edn. University Press, Oxford Paperbacks, Oxford (1962)
8. Carlson, L., Marcu, D., Okurowski, M.E.: Building a discourse-tagged corpus in the framework of rhetorical structure theory. In: Kuppevelt, J., Smith, R.W. (eds.) Current and New Directions in Discourse and Dialogue. TLTB, vol. 22, pp. 85–112. Springer, Dordrecht (2003). https://doi.org/10.1007/978-94-010-0019-2_5
9. Cohen, P., et al.: Quickset: multimodal interaction for distributed applications. In: Proceedings of the 5th ACM International Multimedia Conference, Seattle, Washington, pp. 31–40. Association for Computing Machinery (ACM) (1997)
10. Cutts, M.: Oxford Guide to Plain English, 4th edn. Oxford University Press, Oxford (2013)
11. Floros, V., Mourouzidis, D.: Multiple Task Management in a Dialog System for Call Centers. Master's Thesis, Department of Informatics and Telecommunications, National University of Athens, Greece (2016)
12. Grice, H.P.: Studies in the Way of Words. Harvard University Press, Cambridge (1989)
13. Grice, H.P.: Logic and conversation. In: Cole, P., Morgan, J. (eds.) Syntax and Semantics, vol. 3. Academic Press, New York (1975)
14. Hatim, B.: Communication Across Cultures: Translation Theory and Contrastive Text Linguistics. University of Exeter Press, Exeter (1997)
15. Hedderich, M.A., Klakow, D.: Training a neural network in a low-resource setting on automatically annotated noisy data. In: Proceedings of the Workshop on Deep Learning Approaches for Low-Resource NLP, Melbourne, Australia, pp. 12–18. Association for Computational Linguistics-ACL (2018)
16. Hilbert, M.: Toward a synthesis of cognitive biases: how noisy information processing can bias human decision making. Psychol. Bull. **138**(2), 211–237 (2012)
17. Lewis, J.R.: Introduction to Practical Speech User Interface Design for Interactive Voice Response Applications. IBM Software Group, San Diego (2009). USA, Tutorial T09 presented at HCI 2009
18. Liu, B.: Sentiment Analysis and Opinion Mining. Morgan & Claypool, San Rafael (2012)
19. Ma, J.: A comparative analysis of the ambiguity resolution of two English-Chinese MT approaches: RBMT and SMT. Dalian Univ. Technol. J. **31**(3), 114–119 (2010)
20. Marcu, D.: Discourse trees are good indicators of importance in text. In: Mani, I., Maybury, M. (eds.) Advances in Automatic Text Summarization, pp. 123–136. The MIT Press, Cambridge (1999)
21. Mourouzidis, D., Floros, V., Alexandris, C.: Generating graphic representations of spoken interactions from journalistic data. In: Kurosu, M. (ed.) HCII 2019. LNCS, vol. 11566, pp. 559–570. Springer, Cham (2019). https://doi.org/10.1007/978-3-030-22646-6_42
22. Nass, C., Brave, S.: Wired for Speech: How Voice Activates and Advances the Human-Computer Relationship. The MIT Press, Cambridge (2005)
23. Nottas, M., Alexandris, C., Tsopanoglou, A., Bakamidis, S.: A hybrid approach to dialog input in the citzenshield dialog system for consumer complaints. In: Proceedings of HCI 2007, Beijing, People's Republic of China (2007)
24. Paltridge, B.: Discourse Analysis: An Introduction. Bloomsbury Publishing, London (2012)

25. Pan, Y.: Politeness in Chinese face-to-face interaction. In: Advances in Discourse Processes Series, vol. 67. Ablex Publishing Corporation, Stamford (2000)
26. Poria, S., Cambria, E., Hazarika, D., Mazumder, N., Zadeh, A., Morency, L.-P.: Context-dependent sentiment analysis in user-generated videos. In: Proceedings of the 55th Annual Meeting of the Association for Computational Linguistics, Vancouver, Canada, 30 July–4 August 2017, pp. 873–883. Association for Computational Linguistics – ACL (2017). https://doi.org/10.18653/v1/P17-1081
27. Sacks, H., Schegloff, E.A., Jefferson, G.: A simplest systematics for the organization of turn-taking for conversation. Language 50, 696–735 (1974)
28. Searle, J.R.: Speech Acts: An Essay in the Philosophy of Language. Cambridge University Press, Cambridge (1969)
29. Shah, K., Kopru, S., Ruvini, J-D.: Neural network based extreme classification and similarity models for product matching. In: Proceedings of NAACL-HLT 2018, New Orleans, Louisiana, 1–6 June 2018, pp. 8–15. Association for Computational Linguistics-ACL (2018)
30. Stede, M., Taboada, M., Das, D.: Annotation Guidelines for Rhetorical Structure. Manuscript. University of Potsdam and Simon Fraser University, March 2017
31. Trofimova, I.: Observer bias: an interaction of temperament traits with biases in the semantic perception of lexical material. PloSone 9(1), e85677 (2014)
32. Wardhaugh, R.: An Introduction to Sociolinguistics, 2nd edn. Blackwell, Oxford, UK (1992)
33. Williams, J.D., Asadi, K., Zweig, G.: Hybrid Code Networks: practical and efficient end-to-end dialog control with supervised and reinforcement learning. In: Proceedings of the 55th Annual Meeting of the Association for Computational Linguistics, Vancouver, Canada, 30 July–4 August 2017, pp. 665–677. Association for Computational Linguistics (ACL) (2017)
34. Wilson, M., Wilson, T.P.: An oscillator model of the timing of turn taking. Psychon. Bull. Rev. 12(6), 957–968 (2005). https://doi.org/10.3758/BF03206432
35. Yu, Z., Yu, Z., Aoyama, H., Ozeki, M., Nakamura, Y.: Capture, Recognition, and Visualization of Human Semantic Interactions in Meetings. In: Proceedings of PerCom, Mannheim, Germany (2010)
36. Zeldes, A.: rstWeb - a browser-based annotation interface for rhetorical structure theory and discourse relations. In: Proceedings of NAACL-HLT 2016 System Demonstrations. San Diego, CA, pp. 1–5 (2016). http://aclweb.org/anthology/N/N16/N16-3001.pdf

Reflections on Data Visualization Design by Professionals in the Tourism Field

Caroline M. Barroso[1]([⊠]), Caroline Q. Santos[1]([⊠]), Luciana S. Espindola[2]([⊠]),
and Milene S. Silveira[2]([⊠])

[1] UFVJM, Diamantina, Brazil
carol.tijucal@gmail.com, caroline.queiroz@ufvjm.edu.br
[2] PUCRS, Porto Alegre, Brazil
luciana.espindola@acad.pucrs.br, milene.silveira@pucrs.br

Abstract. To extract information and knowledge of the large amounts of data generated nowadays is a need that has been challenging researchers from several fields such as computing, communication, health and applied social sciences. In the context of tourism data in Brazil, from a specific scenario, we noticed that the field's professionals don't use techniques and tools for processing and presenting data collected by them, which may be compromising the extraction of relevant information and knowledge of these data. In order to support these professionals in the reflection on the data and in planning the best way to present them to their target audience, a study was carried out with turismologists, using a customizable visualization model, intended for the planning of interactive narrative views of data. The template allowed these professionals a new way of planning the presentation of their data, as well as knowledge of computer terms and techniques that may be appropriated by them in their data analysis context.

Keywords: Data visualization · HDI · Design · Tourism data

1 Introduction

Optimal use and interaction with large volumes of data demand the development of computational solutions to process it into information and knowledge, supporting decision-makers on their actions. To this extent, computer science researchers have engaged in interdisciplinary efforts to create such solutions to meet the needs of users interested in analyzing data. However, it is known that the available solutions favor users with computational skills over other profiles [30]. This reinforces the need to offer lay professionals computing tools and technologies to facilitate and enable knowledge discovery in their databases. Not long ago, Human-Data Interaction (HDI) [2,12,15] emerged as a new area, focused on supporting human manipulation, analysis, and sense-making of data. HDI is an interdisciplinary area that involves computer science, statistics, sociology, social communication, and psychology, seeking to "deliver personalized,

© Springer Nature Switzerland AG 2020
M. Kurosu (Ed.): HCII 2020, LNCS 12181, pp. 538–554, 2020.
https://doi.org/10.1007/978-3-030-49059-1_40

context-aware, and understandable data from big datasets". Besides that, HDI seeks to bring people closer to data access, enabling a broader understanding of data at hand [3], as well as fostering people's minds with new insights.

Turning the attention specifically to tourism, we focused our studies on data collected between 2009–2014, during an academic research on the tourism demand of Diamantina and region, a small city in the country side of Minas Gerais, Brazil [13,25,26]. A great deal of data was gathered about the tourist profiles, motivations to visit the region, expectations and impressions after consuming local products and services, as well as the degree of satisfaction after knowing the destination. These results are kept in a tourism demand database, which was made available to municipal managers so they could use it for improving infrastructure and local tourism actions. However, despite the availability, decision makers almost did not use this database as it was meant [13]. We believe the reason for it lies in a lack of knowledge about the usage of computational tools to assist on treatment, analysis and data presentation. If so, the gap between data collection and data analysis, involving digital literacy and HDI, could interfere with the extraction of relevant information and knowledge to decision making.

In this scenario, we identified the opportunity to help decision makers, some of them lay in computer skills, by focusing on the process of reflection during visualization design as a strategy to support the data analysis, presentation, and decision making. As such, we used tourism data from Diamantina and region [13,25,26] as an example, and applied the CIViS design model [21] to foster reflection during data visualization design. We conducted individual sessions with professionals working in the tourism sector. According to the participants' respective roles within the sector, we observed that their visualization modeling reflected their goals. In tune with their background and responsibilities, participants expressed concerns in modeling data to support strategic, tacit and operational decision-making.

The remainder of this paper is organized as follows. Background concepts and research base works are presented in Sect. 2. Sections 3 and 4 describe the used methodology and the obtained results, respectively. Section 5 contains a discussion about this research findings. Last, we present our final considerations and goals for future studies in Sect. 6.

2   Background

Data visualization is a field in computer science that aims to help the process of understanding data [8] by those who explore and analyze them, independent of their working area [7]. It is much more than a visual representation of data, because it is, rather, the process of dissecting raw data, which in themselves have little meaning, and presenting the results of their analysis [4], impacting positively both on the decision-making process and on data communication [31,32]. As for their nature, visualizations can be static, like a graph without interaction resources, or dynamic, enabling the interaction with data and the deepening of their exploration [31].

With the field progression, more and more visualization tools have enabled data analysts and researchers to more easily explore large data sets, and to obtain insights, understand the data and generate new knowledge [1]. Some of these visualization tools are: Gephi[1], Tableau[2], Google Sheets [3], and others. Besides that, the JavaScript library called D3.js[4] is widely used for creating interactive visualizations, however, it requires minimal programming knowledge. The big question behind this tool offering is: can lay users easily use or learn to use them? Many of these tools, such as Gephi and Tableau, were considered difficult to learn by data analysts lay in computing [22,23]. It is clear, then, the need to promote digital literacy in computational data analysis tools, training users in the acquisition of data perception and awareness skills, how to interact with them and how to manipulate them.

Hence, it is necessary that data are organized and manipulated according to the user's needs, allowing them to be visualized and analyzed. Only in this way, knowledge and insights can be generated. Even so, data visualization, depending on the way it was designed, may not be able to present the details existing in a database. With that, some researchers in the area proposed the association of visualization with storytelling, adding a narrative dimension to the visualization, so that it tells a story [4–6,9,11,24]. Segel and Heer [24] coined the expression Narrative Visualization, which seeks to improve interpretation and data analysis, such that end users can choose between making synthetic readings (in a linear sequence) or more in-depth ones (in a interactive way) [5,9,24].

Narrative visualization has been a common practice in the field of journalism, and media such as *The Guardian*[5] already incorporate narrative visualizations in their news. Although it has a strong use in journalism, narrative visualization has been introduced in other areas such as the analysis of data from social media [21], being here proposed to be used in tourism. Seeking to support researchers, Lee et al. [11] presented the Visual Data Storytelling Process (VDSP) model, emphasizing that this process requires context definition, information selection as well as the selection of visualization techniques, and the choice of an order for data presentation in the narrative (Fig. 1). This process model can contain several iterations of each component in any order (exploring data, creating a story and telling a story), so the progression does not have to be linear. The model used in this study was inspired by this process, such that the data analyst may occupy any of the remaining roles in this model (scripter, editor, presenter).

2.1   Data in the Tourism Context

Data and information generated in the tourism sector have a great diversity of meanings, with peculiar characteristics of the sector. According to its

---

[1] http://gephi.org/.
[2] http://www.tableausoftware.com/.
[3] http://www.google.com/intl/nl/sheets/about/.
[4] http://d3js.org/.
[5] http://www.theguardian.com/international.

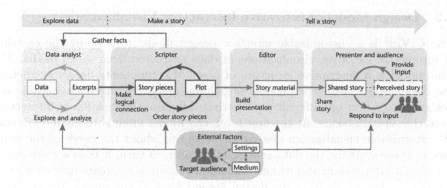

Fig. 1. Visual Data Storytelling Process [11]

characteristics, information can be differentiated for *i)* business management, *ii)* promotion of tourism or *iii)* tourist information. So, it is necessary to understand two expressions that, although seemingly similar, have different meanings: tourism data is related to management, with decision making in the sector, while tourist data is addressing information to the tourist [16]. Each kind of data can generate several types of information to be used in different contexts.

The information generated in the tourism sector can be used by governments, associations, consultants, researchers and analysts, suppliers and intermediaries, and also by tourists. The tourism raw material is information about tourism products and services, that is, information is a key element for the various players in this sector. In this sense, managers who use computational tools to help on data analysis of tourism activity get competitive advantages. In relation to data analysis, the visualization of tourism data uses techniques such as graphs, diagrams, and tables, containing specific information and statistics on the analyzed content [17]. However, much of this analysis is limited to simple statistical techniques, without presenting correlations or integrating data according to some theoretical knowledge [17].

According to Smith [28], tourism is particularly interested on behavioral models explaining causes and consequences of human actions as a source of inspiration in the area. In this sense, tourism managers use fragments from the past, such as monuments, arts, buildings, narratives, songs, among others, to tell stories about tourism in a given location [14]. Despite the challenges of such process in the sector, initiatives were already presented. Sabou et al. [20] developed a prototype system to assist the tourism decision-making process by using linked data technologies, tripling the content of TourMIS[6], a sourof European tourism statistical data used in the study. A researchers' group created a project called Our World in Data whose goal is "to make the knowledge on the big problems accessible and understandable." They created interactive data visualizations with tourism data [19], which can be explored via https://ourworldindata.org/tourism.

---

[6] http://www.tourmis.info/.

2.2   Design Model of Narrative Interactive Visualizations

The CIViS[7] is a customizable interface design model to support the creation of interactive narrative visualizations of data extracted from social media [21]. The model is a descriptive structure of a set of components used to structure the design space, with the purpose of helping designers and data analysts co-designers to reflect on different aspects that influence the creation of interactive narrative visualizations. At the first level, the model intends to guide designers of customizable visualization systems on reflecting about the needs of the main user of these systems, the data analyst. This user, in turn, acts as a co-designer when using the system and its customization resources to create narrative visualizations, thus configuring the design second level of the model. By inserting the data analyst as co-designer through customization, it becomes explicit that the analyst acts as a designer [21].

To support the designer's decisions, CIViS brings components that allow the designer to present the narrative visualization possibilities to the co-designer (data analyst) so that they understand the aspects within the data and decide which to use in their customization. Figure 2a illustrates the CIViS prototype, with sheets representing the scenes, and cards, post-its, and pencils representing the other components. Each component is represented by a card (Fig. 2b) with the front containing the name and icon of the component and the back with an explanation about it, as part of the help system.

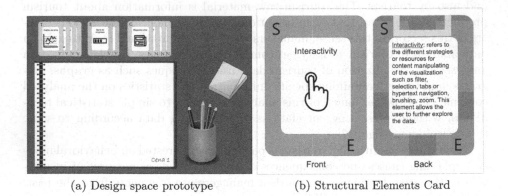

(a) Design space prototype   (b) Structural Elements Card

Fig. 2. CIViS components [21].

The **scene** is the basic structure for the narrative visualization customization, consisting of a space over which the interface elements will be organized. A narrative visualization can have one or more scenes, according to the decisions of the data analyst co-designer. The **narrative visualization models** are based on those proposed by Segel and Heer [24]: Martini Glass Structure,

---

[7] Customizable Interface model to support building narrative Visualizations of data extracted from Social media.

Interactive Slideshow, and Drill-Down Story. These are hybrid models that offer alternatives for balancing the narrative guided by the author (little interactivity) and the freedom of story discovery by the reader (more interactivity). Any chosen model, the co-designer must choose between **genres**: magazine style, annotated chart, partitioned poster, flow chart, comic strip, slide show, and film/video/animation [24]. The choice of genre concerns to how the elements of narrative visualization will be arranged on the interface and how the end user will be able to interact with them, from little (or none) to much interactivity.

Other components on CIViS are: **narrative elements**, which emerge from data (event, actors, location, time); **visualization techniques**, consisting of any technique already consolidated and suitable for the data type (bar graph, line graph, table, heat map, graph, etc.); **visual elements**, to help on the narrative visualization (visual structures, choice of transitions between techniques or scenes, among others); **structural elements**, which assist and facilitate the use of narrative in visualizations (via ordering, interactivity and message mechanisms); and **help system**, based on the Semiotic Engineering [29] method for building help systems [27], which supports designers in decisions on how to speak directly to users and how to make better use of the application.

Through cards, CIViS supports users in the reflection and decision-making process, favoring the understanding about the database, context, and possible solutions. After a study with potential users of the model, it was verified its potential to express decisions regarding the customization of narrative visualizations at the design level [21]. Additionally, the study suggested the model might be suitable to other contexts, being not restricted to social media. This is a reason for choosing it to be a applied in this research on the tourism domain.

2.3 Real Touristic Demand Survey

Considering the challenges of qualified use of information in tourism, Medaglia [13] used as a case study a Survey of Real Touristic Demand in Diamantina (MG) and Region (PDTD[8]) [26], carried out between 2009 and 2014, to explore the fundamentals of organizing tourism information. The PDTD sought to support local tourism development by promoting the use of data by tourism professionals and had as positive points: its simple existence, easy access to information that is difficult to produce, the wealth of information, the good approach to the report contents, the guidance and the existence of motivating information for tourists and help tool for local administration (managers).

Medaglia [13] sought to verify the motivations of tourists visiting Diamantina, discover their interests in visiting other cities in the Diamonds' Circuit[9] and compare their expectations with the degree of satisfaction after experiencing

---

[8] PDTD stands for "Pesquisa de Demanda Turística de Diamantina e Região", in Portuguese.
[9] The Brazilian State of Minas Gerais has 46 tourist circuits involving approximately 600 municipalities. Diamantina is one of the 15 municipalities participating in the Diamonds' Circuit.

the destination. The results pointed out the need to consider accurate tourist information (website, maps, brochures, tourist and traffic signs); provision of good quality services; diversification strategies of products, market and access, in order to increase the staying at the destination for longer periods and decrease its concentration on weekends. For the author, these points are fundamental in the search for local tourism development.

Studying touristic demand is very important for the success of tourist destinations, being among the first steps to achieving the balance between supply and demand through the destination strategic planning. The PDTD made it possible to characterize the (potential) users of this information, resulting in the identification of 17 areas represented by different entities in the Municipal Tourism Council (COMTur)[10], with 8 public, 5 private and 4 representatives of civil society. After defining the user profile, the challenge was to understand the reason why these entities, actors of the local tourism, do not use information generated by the PDTD. Through interviews, despite the positive points, it was identified that the survey has little distribution of printed copies, it is extensive and poorly accessed, it lacks information about the natural surroundings (like waterfalls), as well as other local contexts, such as Carnival and religious events.

From this perspective, the PDTD [26] did not produce the expected effect, highlighting the need to seek for "strategies and products that mix graphs, tables and different text formats, i.e., different organizational formats for the information contained in the PDTD" [13]. By recognizing the data and information organization as a set of procedures to enable people to interact with them, the author pointed to the importance of the mediation in the process of understanding information retrieved from the PDTD. This allowed us to identify in this niche the opportunity for using narrative visualization methods on tourism data, giving rise to the present work.

3   Method

While carrying out this research, we made decisions involving planning, procedures and adjustments, which resulted in the adopted methodology. Initially, we performed a literature review (Sect. 2), containing related researches and also intended to retrieve information collected by the PDTD [26], mainly results from the questionnaires applied to tourists. During the literature review, we got acquainted with the design modeling tool we chose, CIViS [21], originally created for the modeling of interactive narrative visualizations of data from social media. In this sense, we had particular interest on verifying whether CIViS could be suitable to other contexts, namely, tourism data visualization design.

Our proposal to apply the CIViS in this context used as source the results from the PDTD [26], containing data and reports about the specific reality of tourism in Diamantina and region [13]. The work was planned to be conducted in individual sessions with professionals working in the tourism sector, each

---

[10] It is formed by the local government, companies and civil society, to guide the municipal policies of tourism and manage the Municipal Tourism Fund [13].

session consisting of three stages: questionnaire, use of the model to create the visualization design and semi-structured interview with the participants.

In order to ensure the feasibility of the research, we conducted a pilot study containing all the steps of the dynamics: the questionnaire, the use of the model prototype (context, cards and task) and the semi-structured interview. This pilot was meant to help us understand how the dynamics would be, the approximate duration and better ways to explain the model, its components and its use. As a result, we observed the need to facilitate the understanding of the model's step flow by relating its steps with the corresponding cards, creating a short step-by-step to be consulted by the participant during the task. The three stages and corresponding steps of this research can be seen in Fig. 3.

After the pilot study, we proceeded to the proper study in individual sessions. The participant answered the questionnaire, and then, we presented the model and all the materials for carrying out the study: CIViS tutorial, final report from PDTD (with a summary of the research content), the context of the data for using the model, the description of the task to be performed, the table for recording decisions, the CIViS step flow, and the cards, all organized according to the structure of the model prototype. Afterwards, the participant started the task following the step flow and getting to know each card's function. According to what they wanted to narrate, they chose or discarded the cards, being aware that they could go back on this decision at any time, excluding or adding any card. At the end of the three states of this study (questionnaire, modeling and interview), we analyzed the collected data according to qualitative methods [18] allied to the content analysis technique [10].

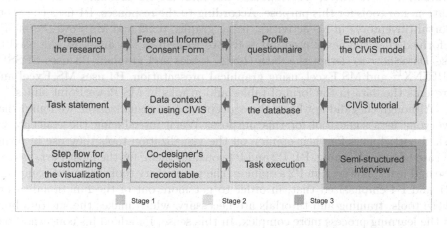

Fig. 3. Research stages and corresponding steps in detail.

4   Results

The dynamics of using CIViS in the context of tourism was carried out between November and December of 2018, with the participation of all the 4 professionals composing a council of advisors for tourism public affairs in Diamantina.

Individual sessions lasted an average of 50 to 60 min. In this section, we present the profile of the participants and the results obtained with the modeling of the narrative visualization.

4.1 Participants' Profiles

The study counted with participants active in different areas of the tourism sector, according to the profiles shown in Table 1. Each participant signed the Free and Informed Consent Form, agreeing to participate in this study, which was divided into three stages: questionnaire, use of the CIViS model to create data visualization, and semi-structured interview.

Table 1. Participants' profile.

ID	Age	Gender	Education	Action on field
P1	30	M	Turismologist	Decision maker
P2	33	F	Turismologist	Decision maker
P3	41	F	Turismologist	Data modeler
P4	37	F	Economist	Data modeler

From the questionnaire we identified that the participants regularly analyze tourism data. However, they reported not knowing the meaning of data visualization, nor tools for this purpose. According to the responses, P1 uses the State Portal (inventory) in his activities, using graphs, texts and MS PowerPoint. P2 informed that she never used any software to help in the analysis, she used to use DataShow to design the data (texts, tables and graphs). P3 uses SPSS[11], SPHINX[12] and MS Excel, using graphical presentation. P4 uses MS Excel and presents the data in the form of tables and graphs in MS PowerPoint slides.

Although they did not know the concept of data visualization, we found that everyone uses some tool for this purpose. When introducing the concept, we asked participants for their opinion on the visualization tools they use in terms of ease of use or learning. P1, P2 and P4 consider them, for the most part, easy to use and learn, however, in P2's opinion, the proprietary tools are more complete. P1 and P4 emphasized that, in order to get more out of the functionalities of these tools, training and tutorials are necessary, which makes the surroundings of the learning process more complex. In this sense, P4 added his concern about the time required to learn these tools, due to the extra training courses. Directing the focus of the discussion to another aspect, P3 understands that the ease of use of the tool *"depends on the data to be worked on and on the audience for whom it is intended, as customizing takes a long time."*

---

[11] http://www.ibm.com/analytics/spss-statistics-software.
[12] http://www.sphinxbrasil.com/.

4.2   Result Analysis per Participant

Each participant gave a different focus on modeling their narrative visualization, exploring different aspects of the data and information contained in the PDTD. P1 planned his visualization seeking to increase the stay in hotels and inns by analysing reports of positive experience. To this end, he highlighted information contained in the 122 questionnaires applied and maintained by PDTD, identifying that 66 tourists considered the accommodation good, 31 excellent, 11 regular, 5 poor and 7 could not say. Of these, 60% chose to stay in hotels and inns, and 61% intended to visit the surroundings (increasing their stay). When creating his model of narrative visualization, P1 sought to highlight: the occupancy rate and guest experience in hotels and inns; information from surrounding cities; average calculation to increase permanence, relating to the means of transport; and, option for guest experience reports. The results of P1's reflections are seen in the Fig. 4a.

As reported in a later interview, P2 created her model of narrative visualization prioritizing simplicity in the organization of the scene, as seen in the Fig. 4b. In her modeling, P2 investigated tourists' motivation to visit Diamantina by analyzing the relationship between PDTD graphs containing information about this motivation. Participant P3 also used graphs available in the PDTD report to investigate the relationship between tourists' origins and the characteristics of their trips to Diamantina. For this, P3 selected 10 graphs of interest, relating them in a narrative visualization model that, according to her expectations, would give rise to 10 different scenes. Due to the restricted time, P3 was able to elaborate only the first scene of her modeling, which, however, was sufficient to record her reflections and intentions, as we see in the Fig. 4c.

Finally, P4 used the PDTD data to model a narrative visualization about the socioeconomic profile of Diamantina tourists in 2014. Initially, the participant chose an image of the city and searched for data about gender, age, income and education. After reflections and analysis, P4 concluded that tourists were equally distributed between genders; they were mostly between 18 and 51 years old (64%); income between R\$ 1,501.00 and R\$ 5,100.00 (56%) or above (35%); and incomplete higher education or above (74%). According to P4, this type of analysis is suitable for identifying the socioeconomic profile of tourists. The result of her narrative visualization model can be seen in the Fig. 4d.

4.3   General Analysis of the Results

From the narrative visualization modeling by each participant, we observed they chose a different set of cards, according to their own goal. During the interview, they reported difficulties with CIViS in respect to the clarity of its cards and also about the terminologies they were presented with. P4 told of a general feeling of what interactivity means, but could not express exactly its meaning in the context of the tool and its components and cards. After the dynamics, P4 came to a curious conclusion that the interactivity in CIViS is about the modeling activity itself, instead of the product of this activity: an interactive

(a) Modeling of P1

(b) Modeling of P2

(c) Modeling of P3

(d) Modeling of P4

Fig. 4. Result of the modeling activity of each participant.

narrative visualization. Even though, after recurring consultations to the tutorial and cards, the model and its usage became overall clear, according to P4.

From another perspective, P1 told about the difficulties of abandoning graphs while analysing data. In his reasoning, the model was meant to foster a storytelling, thus he sought for better ways of doing it by studying the model's cards. P1 accounted he *"thought of creating a story that escaped of the graphs usage a bit, [...] but I was not able with the kind of data I wanted to use."* Additionally, P1 told about the perceived artificiality of using, for instance, a card for zooming in a point of the model, while on the computer the concept is more straightforward. This added another level of difficulty, which he felt was more of the matter of getting used to the modeling tool. In P3's view, the model and its cards are self-explanatory, but only after a guided overview with a savvy modeler, who knows about CIViS and manages to clarify its key points. She explained that if she *"was alone doing the reading, it would be more difficult."*

The participants considered that the sequence of steps for creating the visualization followed an adequate flow for this purpose. In the understanding of P2, this flow helps to direct the modeling, mainly regarding ideas about what is wanted and how to organize it better. P1 initially reported that *"the biggest difficulty was understanding the tools [the components, especially the charts]."* He stressed that prior knowledge of terminologies could facilitate modeling. After the practice, P1 considered that the ideas became clearer, but that he would need more data and more time to organize a richer visualization.

The model itself was considered useful for reflecting about data and its context. For P1, the model presented another way for visualizing data. P2 added by saying that this way of thinking about visualization allowed her to make quick changes and it is accessible. According to her, who declared herself a layperson, it was possible to see the dispositions of the components, understand what could be changed in the modeling, and analyze the whole, because everything is in front of her. Interestingly, P4 believed she was working the a software prototype instead of a design model, but this didn't prevent her from considering the overall approach an easy way for presenting data, offering many possibilities of analysis. All participants told that using CIViS elicited reflections on interactive narrative visualization aspects that they never had thought of before. P1 had an initial expectation that he would not use graphs in the narrative visualization and, during his modeling, he realized that, in order to present the data, it was necessary to use graphs incorporated into the story. P2 gave and interesting account about the reflections lead by the model. She said:

> In fact, it helped me to reflect on what would be more important or not. What would bother me about a page like that. What is really interesting or not, what would make me lose the desire to continue reading, then, it helped me in that sense. [...] Concern and reflection. I never thought so. There are things that bother me and there are things that don't bother me. [...] [For example,] I don't really like [page] models that are too long and flat, that I have to keep scrolling [...] [P2]

When asked if the use of CIViS was able to foster new reflections, P3 gave a rich report based on her prior experience. She told she's been working with the same data (the PDTD) for over a decade, and her vision was already biased. By using the model, she was able to change the perspective from individual questions answered by the PDTD to the relations between these very questions. The possibility of making these relations was exciting for her, she said.

Participant P4 reflected about her prior impression concerning the use of software tools without knowing all the possibilities they offer, and also without seeking to understand the existing resources. As a user, most of time she didn't think about all the possibilities she's been offered, only about what she missed. We note here that the co-designer perceives, then, the designer's intention. This reflection lead to a new one, not as user of a product, but as designer of a visualization. This dynamic made her think about "the information we share." In her words:

> I wonder, are they as clear as possible? Does someone on the other side understand it? This is so important that, what's good all this science for, to discover a bunch of things, and not knowing how to transmit them, specially to those who are not in the same knowledge level. So, this is something to think about [P4].

Aligned with this view, P3 also observed the importance of making oneself understood. By using CIViS, she said she managed to think about data in a structured way, as information, and to put herself in other's shoes: *"as you have to choose the elements, you think and put yourself in the place of who will be accessing the data."* According to her, this was an interesting aspect of the dynamic.

Finally, P3 praised the use of CIViS in the tourism sector. According to her, tourism is a socioeconomic phenomenon, depending of very specific social characteristics, but the sector is more focused on dealing with information coming from economy, treating tourism as a commodity. In her view, the model presents a way to bring closer data coming from tourism and those coming from economy, thus providing a more complete description of tourism.

5   Discussion

We observed that the participants in this research, despite being savvy professionals in the tourism sector, seem not to have digital literacy, being not acquainted to visualization tool specifically designed for the area. They also lacked the perception on how the process of collecting, processing and analyzing data is related to the modeling for a better presentation. This means they were suitable to our research, since they are seniors in tourism area but lay on modeling tools.

Despite one of the goals of Human-Computer Interaction is to facilitate the learning and use of software, this simplification is not always possible. In situations like these, it is necessary to create tools to support use, such as Help, and learning, such as epistemic tools[13]. In this study, we used the CIViS model, which is an epistemic tool dedicated to assist designers and co-designers on the creation of solutions for interactive narrative visualizations in design time. This specific study used the model in the context of data analysts acting as co-designers.

We noticed the models of narrative visualization created by each participant reflected their goals within their work roles. P1, for example, planned his visualization with a focus on increasing the stay of tourists in hotels or inns. For this, he carried out a descriptive analysis of the reports of positive experience available in the PDTD. On the other hand, P2 made a qualitative analysis based on the relationship between PDTD graphs, seeking to investigate the tourist's motivation to visit the destination. Both P1 and P2 are decision makers and, despite using different analytical approaches, we perceive a clear focus on the search for solutions to straightforward problems, respectively: maximizing the stay in hotels, and meeting the expectations of tourists by understanding their motivations to visit the destiny.

In the perspective of data modeling, P3 sought to relate the tourist's place of origin to their destination, in an attempt to highlight the characteristics of the trip. She did this through qualitative analysis of PDTD graphs. In turn, P4 was interested in drawing the socioeconomic profile of the tourist from the

---

[13] Epistemic tool is one that seeks to increase the understanding of a problem and the implications it brings, instead of pointing directly to its solution. [29, p. 56].

data maintained by the PDTD, using a descriptive analysis of these data. Note that both models are dedicated to a description of aspects that can influence decision making, whatever they may be, because the focus of their modeling was on the characterization of the tourist profile, without having a specific question or problem to solve.

Although the four participants are involved in the tourism context, we could see that P1, P2 and P3, as tourism specialists, were concerned with typical issues in the area, such as accommodation, satisfaction and experience, while P4, an economist active in the tourism sector, expressed special interest in socioeconomic aspects, favoring a descriptive analysis of the data. In line with their backgrounds and responsibilities, the participants expressed concern with modeling data to support decision making at a strategic, tacit and operational level, ranging from the possible improvement of the infrastructure at the destination to the satisfaction of the tourist throughout their overall experience (from the origin to the destination).

Regardless of the participants' profile, the use of the model caused reflections on aspects of data analysis that they had not previously thought about. It could be seen that the model, in addition to supporting the design of narrative data visualization, provided analysts with greater insight into what they really wanted to convey and contributed to the organization and structuring of their ideas by relating the data and information they wanted to present.

The model introduced these professionals to a new way of planning and presenting their data, as well as helped them to build knowledge about computing jargon and techniques which they may appropriate and employ in a data analysis context. With this, we consider that the model allowed the tourism professionals, lay people in visualization, to reflect about their data and to plan the data presentation to obtain new insights from it. This comes to meet the goals of HDI, which seeks to bring people closer to the now usual big volumes of data, enabling understanding, awareness and better means to foster decision making.

The results pointed out that the design model helped the professionals to organize ideas, guiding them from a larger down to a narrower scope of decisions about the planning of interactive narrative visualizations. These decisions happened after reflection not only about correlation between data and its presentation, but also about the way the very consumer of a visualization might prefer this data to be presented, which required the analysts to put themselves in the consumer's shoes. The design model also favored the perception of how to bring social and economic aspects closer, enabling a more complete description of the touristic reality on this region, from the perspective of tourism managers.

6   Final Considerations and Future Works

Tourism information (and the way it is presented and analyzed) is very important for the perception and clarity concerning the tourist activity and the development of strategies to foster the growth in this sector. In this sense, Computer Science can support tourism professionals in their relationship with data, from collection and treatment to analysis and reflection on how to best present them to a target audience, which is done through the understanding of this process and by appropriation of the available technologies [2,12,15,30]. In fact, this is one of the goals of the Human-Data Interaction field (HDI).

Considering the high demand for information in the tourism sector, we observed that the approach used for presenting data withing the PDTD did not meet the needs of its users. We believe these professionals need training on the available technologies, prioritizing those which are more intuitive, easy to use, and that allow the manipulation and creation of visualizations, therefore, giving their target audience freedom to explore the data and obtain knowledge.

A contribution of this work is the use of the CIViS model in a different context from the one for which it was conceived (social media data analysis). In the original context, participants were familiar with the concepts and tools, while in this new context of tourism, data analysts considered themselves lay in these aspects. In spite of this difference regarding participants' acquaintance level with such technologies, concepts and tools, professionals from both contexts reported that CIViS fostered reflection on different and better ways to model and present data and information to the target audience. This highlights the importance of investigating how clear and well presented the data needs to be in order to be able to prospect information and knowledge from them. This reinforces the need of evolving this research to create a prototype of a tool to instantiate the CIViS model, which could help us to identify technological aspects to be improved, such as field formats, data manipulation, presentation ways, etc., leading to better ways to allow a rich experience in data exploration.

As future work, we plan to improve the model's tutorial, step flow and some of the cards according to participants' suggestions, as a way to promote greater clarity. We also plan to translate this model from Portuguese to English, in order to promote its usage in other contexts. Another important future work is related to the development of a CIViS workshop. According to participants, they stressed the importance of receiving support from the researcher in loco, by means of a presentation of the model and typical dynamics. Last but not least, we plan to verify the model by first designing visualizations by using CIViS and then asking to end users, consumers of these visualizations, to use them as they wish. This dynamics is meant to be recorded for future analysis and results triangulation, highlighting the strong and weak points of creating visualizations with the support of our model.

References

1. Brooks, M.: Human Centered Tools for Analyzing Online Social Data. Ph.D. thesis. University of Washington, Seattle, WA (2015)
2. Cafaro, F.: Using embodied allegories to design gesture suites for human-data interaction. In: Proceedings of the 2012 ACM Conference on Ubiquitous Computing (UbiComp 2012), p. 560–563. Association for Computing Machinery, New York, NY, USA (2012). https://doi.org/10.1145/2370216.2370309

3. Crabtree, A., Mortier, R.: Human data interaction: historical lessons from social studies and CSCW. In: Boulus-Rødje, N., Ellingsen, G., Bratteteig, T., Aanestad, M., Bjørn, P. (eds.) ECSCW 2015: Proceedings of the 14th European Conference on Computer Supported Cooperative Work, 19–23 September 2015, Oslo, Norway, pp. 3–21. Springer, Cham (2015). https://doi.org/10.1007/978-3-319-20499-4_1
4. Figueiras, A.: How to tell stories using visualization. In: 2014 18th International Conference on Information Visualisation, pp. 18–26. IEEE (2014)
5. Figueiras, A.: Narrative visualization: a case study of how to incorporate narrative elements in existing visualizations. In: Proceedings of the International Conference on Information Visualisation (IV), pp. 46–52 (2014)
6. Gershon, N., Page, W.: What storytelling can do for information visualization. Commun. ACM 44(8), 31–37 (2001)
7. Heer, J., Bostock, M., Ogievetsky, V.: A tour through the visualization zoo. Queue 8(5), 0:20–20:30 (2010)
8. Heer, J., Viégas, F.B., Wattenberg, M.: Voyagers and voyeurs: supporting asynchronous collaborative information visualization. In: Proceedings of the SIGCHI Conference on Human Factors in Computing Systems (CHI), pp. 1029–1038 (2007)
9. Kosara, R., Mackinlay, J.: Storytelling: the next step for visualization. Computer 46(5), 44–50 (2013)
10. Lazar, J., Feng, J.H., Hochheiser, H.: Research Methods in Human-Computer Interaction. Wiley, Hoboken (2010)
11. Lee, B., Riche, N., Isenberg, P., Carpendale, S.: More than telling a story: transforming data into visually shared stories. Comput. Graph. Appl. 35(5), 84–90 (2015)
12. McAuley, D., Mortier, R., Goulding, J.: The dataware manifesto. In: 2011 Third International Conference on Communication Systems and Networks (COMSNETS 2011), pp. 1–6, January 2011. https://doi.org/10.1109/COMSNETS.2011.5716491
13. Medaglia-Silveira, J.: Os desafios do uso qualificado da informação em turismo: o caso da pesquisa de demanda turística real de Diamantina/MG. Tese de doutorado, UFMG, Belo Horizonte, Brasil (2017)
14. Meneses, J.N.C.: História & turismo cultural. Autêntica (2013)
15. Mortier, R., Haddadi, H., Henderson, T., McAuley, D., Crowcroft, J.: Human-datainteraction: the human face of the data-driven society. SSRN2508051 (2014)
16. Nascimento, M.J., Silva, P.S.: Informação: insumo básico para o desenvolvimento do setor de turismo em Santa Catarina. Perspectivas em ciência da informação (Impresso) 9(1), 48–69 (2004)
17. Rabahy, W.A.: Turismo e desenvolvimento: estudos econômicos e estatísticos no planejamento. Editora Manole Ltda (2003)
18. Raupp, F.M., Beuren, I.M.: Metodologia da pesquisa aplicável às ciências. Como elaborar trabalhos monográficos em contabilidade: teoria e prática. São Paulo: Atlas, 76–97 (2006)
19. Roser, M.: Tourism. Our World in Data (2020). https://ourworldindata.org/tourism
20. Sabou, M., Braşoveanu, A.M.P., Arsal, I.: Supporting tourism decision making with linked data. In: Proceedings of the 8th International Conference on Semantic Systems (I-SEMANTICS 2012), pp. 201–204. ACM, New York (2012). https://doi.org/10.1145/2362499.2362533
21. Santos, C.Q.: CIViS: Modelo de design de interface customizável para apoiar a construção de visualizações narrativas interativas de dados extraídos de mídias sociais. Tese de doutorado, Escola Politécnica. PUCRS, Porto Alegre (2018)

22. Santos, C.Q., Silveira, M.S.: What do social media data analysts want? An analysis from the perspective of data visualization. In: Proceedings of the 17th Brazilian Symposium on Human Factors in Computing Systems (IHC 2018), pp. 54:1–54:4. ACM, New York (2018). https://doi.org/10.1145/3274192.3274246. http://doi.acm.org/10.1145/3274192.3274246

23. Santos, C.Q., Silveira, M.S., Manssour, I.H.: Visualization and social media data analysis: preliminary studies about data analysts' perception. In: Proceedings of the Brazilian Symposium on Human Factors in Computer Systems (IHC), pp. 35:1–35:4 (2016)

24. Segel, E., Heer, J.: Narrative visualization: telling stories with data. IEEE Trans. Vis. Comput. Graph. 16(6), 1139–1148 (2010)

25. Silveira, C.E., Medaglia, J.: Desenvolvimento turístico em cidades históricas: estudos de caso de diamantina/MG. (2014)

26. Silveira, C.E., Medaglia, J.: Perfil da demanda turística real de diamantina e região (2014). Accessed 12 Aug 2018

27. Silveira, M.S., Barbosa, S.D., de Souza, C.S.: Model-based design of online help systems. In: Jacob, R.J., Limbourg, Q., Vanderdonckt, J. (eds.) Computer-Aided Design of User Interfaces IV, pp. 29–42. Springer, Dordrecht (2005). https://doi.org/10.1007/1-4020-3304-4_3

28. Smith, S.L.: Tourism Analysis: A Handbook. Routledge, Abingdon (2014)

29. de Souza, C.S.: The Semiotic Engineering of Human-Computer Interaction. MIT press, Cambridge (2005)

30. Strey, M.R., Pereira, R., de Castro Salgado, L.C.: Human data-interaction: a systematic mapping. In: Proceedings of the 17th Brazilian Symposium on Human Factors in Computing Systems (IHC 2018), pp. 27:1–27:12. ACM, New York (2018). https://doi.org/10.1145/3274192.3274219. http://doi.acm.org/10.1145/3274192.3274219

31. Ward, M.O., Grinstein, G., Keim, D.: Interactive Data Visualization: Foundations, Techniques, and Applications. CRC Press, Boca Raton (2015)

32. Ware, C.: Information Visualization: Perception for Design. Elsevier, Amsterdam (2012)

The Image of Presence and the Presence of the Image

Kenneth Feinstein(✉) ®

Sunway University, No. 5, Jalan Universiti, 47500 Bandar Sunway,
Selangor Darul Ehsan, Malaysia
kenf@sunway.edu.my

Abstract. This article traces the development of art from the Renaissance to contemporary media practice. It looks at how images are made in relation to the main theoretical paradigm of the age. Moving from the window metaphor/ Cartesian thought to media art/Ontology it focuses on how presence has been central to how we view and understand images and how they place us in the world. This paper develops the theoretical relationship of art practice based on presence as being central to how our identity is linked to our relationship to otherness through technology.

Keywords: Cultural interface · Information visualization · Technology: interaction design · Multimedia design · New technology and its usefulness · Media art · Experiential art · Expanded cinema · Otherness · Ontology · Window metaphor · Projection

1 Introduction

If we look at all art as being about presence, then what we need to question is the nature of that presence. We all have to be in proximity to a work to see or hear it, but proximity as presence can just mean being at a place at a given time. It does not question the nature of the relationship created in that moment in time and space. In the Western tradition we have had competing approaches to presence which either puts us away from the world or having us search for our place in the world.

Starting with Plato's Cave we have had a tradition of a metaphysics where meaning is hidden from us by the physical world, nature is a screen hiding reality from us. This was picked up by the early Christian Gnostics and has continued on through Descartes and Heidegger's idea of authentic existence.

In contrast the Pythagorean tradition is one where we find meaning in the objects of the world if we are aware of them. This is where the celestial harmonies come into play. The idea is that the metaphysical laws that govern nature are mathematical essence and further they can be made understandable to us through sound as the embodiment of the mathematics. So that harmonies are understood as ratio that relate to ratios found in nature. This is a more phenomenological approach than the Aristotelian model.

The Cave metaphor places us in a condition where our ignorance is not because caused by the act of seeing or hearing, but rather that what we see and hear is designed to obscure the truth. A truth hidden from us. It is only by breaking the confines of life

© Springer Nature Switzerland AG 2020
M. Kurosu (Ed.): HCII 2020, LNCS 12181, pp. 555–568, 2020.
https://doi.org/10.1007/978-3-030-49059-1_41

that we can be in a condition to experience reality. It defines what we see and hear as inherently false. Our relationship to images and sounds is one where they are intended alienate us from the world not put us in relationship to it. Presence becomes one of separation. We are present only in as much as we are conscious of our being other from what we are seeing. Presence is measured by distance away from what we are seeing.

The Pythagorean model is one where nature reveals itself to us. It becomes our responsibility to discover the laws of nature, but they are present before us to be discovered. It is for us to use our senses and logic to be able to makes sense of what we experience in order to have the forces of nature revealed to us. The Pythagorean tuning is one where ratios are used tonal harmonies, where what we experience as harmonious is a physical embodiment of a mathematical proportion. What we understand is an experience which leads us to knowledge.

With both ways of gaining knowledge technology has had an important place. Either as a thing that helps keep the truth away from us or as essential to our ability to live in and make sense of the world. We tend to divide technology into the useful and the meaningful. So that as we understand how we relate to technology the tendency is to look at technology as either inventions or as the embodiment of ideas. Buildings are inventions that help us survive, cathedrals are the embodiment of ideas. It is hammers versus epistemology. It is how we interpret our relationship to technology that also defines what we belief is our place in the world. Does it keep us from the real, being an object of separation or does it enable us to create a relationship with the world? These questions are played out in how we have interpreted our place in time and space through our theory and how we visualize the world.

Dating back to Hesiod's *Works and Days* we can see the idea of a Golden Age in which humanity lived more in tune with nature and thus with no need for technology. Epimetheus' error leads to Prometheus giving fire and the arts to man and the removal of humanity from Arcadia. The arts, *techne*, is the manipulate materials into objects of meaning, *poiesis*. We could see a similar relationship in the Christian idea of the Fall. The casting out of humanity from a natural ideal into a harsh world where tools become necessary because we are no long in a natural order. They exist to help us survive, keeping us in a bare life, but not fundamental to allowing us to access truth.

Or following Bernard Stiegler we can look towards the stories of Epimetheus and Prometheus as a founding myth of a view of humanity in which we are defined by our relationship to technology. [1] where it is the development of technology that enables us to become human. In his interpretation technology is not symbolic of a Fall from Grace, but it through technology that humanity comes to be. Stiegler points out that the Fall myth assumes humanity before technology as an ideal natural state and that it assumes a relationship to technics based on a lack. While it may seem a nice metaphor from evolutionary archeology, we know that it is just a myth. Stiegler reminds us instead of seeing technology as a way of extending ourselves into the world. That the separation of humans as subject and technology as objects is a false construct [1]. We are a technical being not a being who uses tools. Our relationship with technology is how we understand time and our relationship to it. Places us in temporal experiences that can be historical, personal or cultural memory. This sense of time including our understanding of our heritage as well as our knowledge of death places us in the world as temporal beings. This distinction is fundamentally different to the main tradition of

Western philosophy. The movement away from this tradition and how it is embodied through media art practice is the subtext of this work. We will see how philosophical concepts and artistic practice have woven themselves together to great a new world view.

Our relationship to technology is centered on how we navigate our way through the world, how we interact with it and derive meaning in it. How we understand this relationship is central to how we live in the world. And images are a technology that allows us to present ourselves to the world and the world back to us. Through images we can act on a world that is distant and detached from us or it can be a way of enabling a relationship to others and Otherness. As we explore the development of images and their technical aspects, we will be looking at the changes in how we see the relationship of self to others, nature and society.

We will first see this relationship of the theoretical to the metaphorical (visual) in the relationship of the window metaphor to the Cartesian formulation of the *Cogito*. How they both play out a singular understanding of a metaphysics that valorizes presence as a method of separating us from the physical. Making presence also an absence.

2 Separation of Mind and Body

2.1 The Window Metaphor

"One can look at seeing but one can't hear hearing" –Duchamp [2].

With the Renaissance both classical (horizon line) perspective and framed painting were developed. Their development was tied to each other. Even though they are two very different inventions. Perspective allowed of us to see an image of the world as occupying space. While the framed painting placed that space within a context [3].

If we look at painting before and into the Renaissance we find most painting is not only located in churches or palaces, but it is centered more on frescos, alters and stained glass. The relationship between the viewer and the image was different with each form. Where stained glass presented an illuminated image, this would be one that was from an angle higher and at a distance from the viewer. It looked down on you as such as you looked up at it. The stories of Jesus or the saints was speaking down to you. Alters were elevated from the public and at the front of the church. Services were conducted behind it and depending on the time of year a new image was opened up as a form of theatre. The viewer again was assumed to look up at the image and feel that they were gazing upon something distant from them. The engagement with the image was one of separation from it. These images were highly prescribed in content and intended to have an appeal to masses of people in a single viewing.

Lastly, we had frescos. Frescos were large paintings created directly on the wall of a building. Typically, a cathedral, palace or some other grand building where a public gathered. The scale of frescos tended toward having the image appear to be life sized in relation to the viewer. In most cases the image was of a scale so that the entire width would be too large for a viewer to take in. While this allowed for a more proximate relationship with spatialization of the objects in the image was not based on a relationship to a particular viewer. These were views for publics not for individuals. With frescos the scale was one where there was not a distinction of between the image and the world. It would seem as if it was an extension of the world outside. It was as if the wall was not there.

With the development of the framed image the idea that what we see in a painting is analogous the view we have out a window takes shape. The frame around the painting defines the image. It delineates what exists and what doesn't exist within the image's world. Its reality lives only with in its frame. This leads to the image defining itself as separate from the world of the room it is hung in. In the Western tradition windows are used to look out onto another view. As Hans Beltings says, "Real or painted windows symbolize the location of the observing subject, who is looking out the window at the world" [3]. The significance of the window metaphor in painting is that it turns the viewer into the observing subject. As a viewer we are separated from what we see by the frame. It places us in a position of judgement on the view. "In the Renaissance the gaze goes out into the world, so to speak, since it feels itself as the master of what it perceives" [3]. Where stained glass or the alter placed the viewer as one who looked up on to the divine for knowledge and salvation, when at the window the viewer's relationship is reversed. The viewer transforms from being the object of the work speaking down to them into the observing subject determining the meaning of the work. The viewer's gaze is detached from what is viewed, she is on one side looking on to a world distant from her "over there". The frame locates the viewer and at the same time disembodies them from what is being seen. The frame keeps what is seen encased and distant from the viewer. This valorizes the view over presence. The gaze becomes a view of contemplation. This view of contemplation disembodies thought from the physical world, making viewing a metaphysical act. The thought enacted by the view becomes more important than seeing itself. The viewer as the observing subject takes the metaphysical position of pure thought. They only encounter the image through a disengaged view where they stance is now of divine thought. The world is one that exists for contemplation alone, the physical world is a veil hiding reality from us. The act of seeing has become disconnected from what is seen. We look upon a scene that we have no presence within.

2.2   The Cogito

This view of the world is reiterated and codified in René Descartes' *Cogito*. In his critic of Descartes, Gilles Deleuze's analysis of the Cogito is made up of a subject of the statement and the enunciation of that subject [4]. The enunciation become paramount over the subject of the statement. "In other words, the subject cannot produce a statement without being thereby split (scindé) by the statement into a subject of enunciation and a subject of the statement" [4]. This splitting means that the subject of the statement is always a subset of the enunciation. This because the truth if the statement is secondary to the truth of the enunciation itself. The veracity of what I say I see or do is not as important as that I am cognizant of the act of thinking. The thinking comes first and is the primary truth, it becomes the proof of metaphysics as real. While what I say claim to see or experience is only a reflection of thought. The subject of the statement will relate to the world, be it "I am walking", "see a new car" or "I want a new phone". In all cases I am subject and the object of the same statement placing us within and without at the same time. All that I am left with the ability to create statements. Our presence is one that has been split into being in a physical world and removed from it in the same act. While thought establishes identity it also removes that identity from the physical world. This is why the only truth inherent in the Cartesian formula is the enunciation itself. This leaves no room for a reality beyond the act of thinking or as we see with the window metaphor the act of seeing. Only allowing relationships extending beyond the self to being reflective back on to the self. It assumes an independent being that doesn't need presence, because presence only exists by being in relationship to something else. Presence demands that we are present with another. It is the relatedness that defines it. "I am present here with you", or "I am here before this sculpture". To place thought above and before presence it to have being as self, paramount to nature in general. We see nature as alienated from us, therefore other to us in a way which does not allow us to overcome this alienation. The thinking subject, like the observing subject is one that exists through its separation from the world. Its presence takes the form of an absence. The act of thinking or seeing becomes self-referential, only reinforcing my own existence. Leading to a withdrawal from the world while still allowing me to pass judgment upon the world. So that the meaning of the world becomes as a way of allowing me to gain enlightenment. This enlightenment is generally transmitted through a narrative. Talking about a how narrative is transmitted in art, Roland Barthes refers to Diderot's idea of the tableaux vivant. This is an idea where a significant moment is presented to the viewer which is the summation of the narrative presented. This assumes not just a knowledge of the story told, an understanding of a metaphorical vocabulary, but most importantly a viewer who acts as an observing subject [5]. The work is addressed to the viewer. But no matter the scale, and in the case of painters like Jacques Louis David the scale was immense, the viewer presented with an image which meant to have meaning through an alienating distance. David's *Death of Socrates* is an example of the tableaux vivant. The work is immense (129.5 cm × 196.2 cm) creating an experience of gazing upon an image on the scale of a proscenium theatre. The people in the image appear life sized, yet we do not feel that we can enter the image. The space of the image is created to be presentational to the viewer not just because it is encased within a large gold frame, but because the characters are presented as a continual pose parallel to the viewer. The only character looking at us is small and encased in the arch and stairwell. He brings our eye to other figures leaving the scene. While he is looking at us, his situation (we assume he is one of the Athenian authorities who sentences Socrates to death) and scale make him reflexive back on to the main action. His view reflects back on to us as viewers. He mimics us in a way that doesn't bring us into the image, but rather his powerlessness in the scene reminds us of our position as detached viewers. This distancing reinforces a Cartesian view of our relation to the world. What we see may be informative yet it is also not actionable. What we perceive as the world in the image is distinctly not our world. It merely a device for contemplation. This idea of thinking of metaphysical reality as actual and the physical world as only mechanical reduces the animate to the animal and the mind to the human. It assumes that knowledge is found through contemplation and not through the experience. This way of defining the world defines the development of politics, technology and science.

3 Alchemy, Science and Media of Presence

3.1 Experimental Experience

While this world view was the dominant understanding of the world and our place within it from the Renaissance to Heidegger and art reinforced it, other forms of knowledge developed in parallel. Because the Cartesian formula assumed a metaphysical reality that was beyond the physical world it demanded a world view where all experience could become calculation. If the physical world was only the support for the metaphysical then as support it only needs to be mechanical reusable and replaceable. Contrary to this was a history of experimental knowledge which would become science. This path to knowledge assumes that the physical world is real and the path to discovering the metaphysical laws that define it. This tradition of experimental knowledge was the basis of first alchemy and later science. It tried to discover the inner workings of nature through its manifestations. In China alchemy concentrated on extending life and became the basis of Traditional Chinese Medicine (TCM). As a practice it is based on understanding how to balance the forces of nature to an equilibrium that we call health. By contrast Islamic and later Western alchemy looked to the physical laws of nature to find the meaning lying behind it. This led to the birth of chemistry, the development of optics, horizon line perspective, and eventually the division of science from mysticism (the Hermetic arts). In the alchemical tradition knowledge was gained through experimentation. These investigations tend towards the transdisciplinary, as the alchemist was trying to find how differing ways of discovering laws of nature through the act of transmutation. Through transmutation is was assumed that the underlying principles that connected the world would be revealed. This meant that the alchemist was first interested in understanding the metaphysical principles that governed life, but as opposed to the epistemological view as expressed by Thomas Aquinas and Descartes. What made Western alchemy distinct from the Islamic version and from the scientific method was that it tended to use obscure hermetic language to hide the knowledge found. What was discovered by the alchemist was developed through the use of devices, but was not developed so that others would be able to recreate the experience. As such the methodology was highly experiential, but hermetic at the same time. In the early Renaissance the scientific method was developed. Central tenets to it were reproducibility and the presentation of information to a public. The earliest forms of media practice date from this time and are based on these two principles. Looking at the Museo Kircherianum (Kircher Museum), Siegfried Zielinski tells us that, "[t]he museum was also full of marvelous optical and acoustic devices. The concept of technology that Kircher elaborated and presented here was, on a complex level, entirely characteristic of natural magic. Technology stood for the spectrum of artificial constructions where 'the operative force or agent was not obvious to the eye" [6]. It presented the metaphorical ways of seeing and understanding the teachings of the Catholic Church, Athanasius Kircher was a senior Jesuit priest based in the College Rome. He creates audio and visual devices that appear to be magical to the viewer. Because the viewer has no way of knowing how the device operates he is "introducing magic into a technical device, Kircher expands its possibilities and defines it philosophically and aesthetically by treating it within the category of experiments with metamophoses" [6]. This means that the viewer experiences an uncanny moment meant to illuminate them.

Remembered today for *Ars magna sciendi sive combinatoria* (The Great Art of Knowledge or Combinatories) and *Ars magna lucis et umbrae* (The Great Art of Light and Shadow) in which he lays out the devices he utilized and the ideas they represent. His works in the museum were not only the first public museum with media art as we know it today, but it was one of the most popular attractions in its time. Devices recounted as being in the museum include sculptures of heads that speak to the viewer as one passes by, a room where the viewer's head is replaced with various images of a variety of metaphorical animals (referred to as the Metaphor Machine), elaborate sound devices to place disembodies sound in to spaces and a room utilizing magic lanterns to projects image on the wall. These works were designed to appear magical, the viewer was not to be aware of how the effects were created. The transmitted message was of primary importance.

Today we would refer to these works as installations. These pieces presented some of the foundational elements of media art. The viewer was places at the center of the work. Where a framed painting assumed a detached gaze on to the image and a fresco assume a gaze of awe looking to the divine, here the viewer first recognizes themselves in relation to the work. With the hall of speaking heads, the audience experience is individual, the heads only speak while the viewer is in proximity to it. The understanding of proximity to this type of work is not one of being close enough to see it, but rather one where proximity itself is fundamental to the work. The piece reacts to the presence of the viewer meaning that the viewer has to be-with the object to complete the action and have the work actualize itself. It is only through a relationship to the other (the viewer) that the work completes itself as a device and action.

While the Metaphor Machine only makes sense if the viewer recognizes their own body. Presence and recognition of the self in relation to the work is the unique change that happens when we move from traditional image to what Vilém Flusser called the technical image [7]. The Metaphor Machine begins a relationship of placing ourselves into works as a way of finding identity outside of ourselves. Where in the window metaphor I may understand that what I see is addressed to me, there is no need for me to identify with what I see. While with the metaphor Machine self-identity is the operational core of the work.

Simply the major points found in these works are 1) the viewer as the center of the work, 2) the relationship of the work as being-with to the viewer and 3) the ability for the viewer to identify with the work, to incorporate the work into their being. These are the basic principles found in the works that existed in the Kircher Museum. This becomes the beginning of what will become media art practice. These basic elements will be found in later works from the 19th to the 21st centuries. As technology develops and we start to invent apparatuses that create technical images our relationship to images transforms into one centered on our relationship with the other and Otherness. With the invention of the camera and the computer the apparatuses that we use to create images and sounds incorporate interaction into their functionality. As devices they function through feedback, action and reaction, they operate in time and through the feedback loop they make the presence of others necessary for their operation. These devices help us create a sense of identity the is linked to our relationship to the Other.

3.2   The Relationship of Otherness

Central to this article is the argument that the great transition in how we see the world is a movement away from the Cartesian and Heideggerian models of the primacy of the individual into an understanding of our relatedness and responsibility to Otherness. This change which became stronger after the Second World War, has been reflected by and partially driven by the developments of media art and the technical image. This idea is reflected in Deleuze's two volumes on cinema [9, 10] as well as the works of Flusser, most specifically *Into the Universe of Technical Images*.

Since the development of photography, the nature of how images are created changed from the interpretation of an artist to the direct encoding of a moment from reality. Photographs and later moving images, are denotational and temporal in nature. Such images are created because the operator of the apparatus and the subject in the image are in proximity to each other. They share the same time and place. There is a relationship created between the camera operator, the camera and the subject of the image. In the act of photography, in that moment of interplay a relationship between all three is created. Without all parties being present the image cannot exist. The image comes into being through a relationship of being-with. To look at this from the Emmanuel Lévinas' ontology we see that the self, the photographer, can only complete herself as an I through the relationship created with the subject photographed and the interplay with the apparatus. In the act of photographing the subject the photographer is a) creating a relationship with the subject with which the image cannot exist and b) presenting the subject as other that cannot be thematized [11]. Where Heidegger sees Dasein, as being, as authentic only though its self-actualization, Lévinas is telling us that our authenticity can only be through our related ness to others. It though how we interact and how we take on our responsibility to others that we become a self.

We see the face of the other in all that it is. It is that *face* and no other. It is not an interpretation or a metaphor of what that face should mean. Roland Barthes opens *Camera Lucida* with this statement, "I happened on a photograph of Napoleon's youngest brother, Jerome, taken in 1852. And I realized then, with an amazement I have not been able to lessen since: 'I am looking at eyes that looked at the Emperor'" [12]. Here he is emphasizing the how the technological image, in this case the photograph, brings the face of the other in its reality to us. We encounter the presence of that face in its actuality and its temporality. With the photograph there is an excess, things beyond the control of the photographer. We see this in the blurred object, something half in and out of the frame and in a face in the picture. This excess happens because we are encountering an unthematizable other in the act of creating the image. This is the encountering of the Other, which places us in a state of being-with-the-other and of being-in-the-world. By encountering the other in the act of photography or filming we are placing both of us into a moment that is dependent of both of us and acknowledging the authenticity of our existence. With the photograph there is an excess, things beyond the control of the photographer. We see this in the blurred object, something half in and out of the frame and in a face in the picture. This excess happens because we are encountering an unthematizable Other in the act of creating the image.

This moment is created by how we interact with each other and the camera. As a photographer or subject, we also have the same relationship with the camera, the creating apparatus. As we develop new forms of technical images, this inter-relationship, the action and reaction has become a defining part of the systems. Our relationship to the apparatus making the technical image is also one of being-with in time. Flusser defines an apparatus as a device that is operated by a program. Programs are based on our interact with it. We use a program, then see the results and from there decide what needs to be done next. He defines the nature of how we utilize an apparatus as play [7]. We interact with the apparatus as another. What we do is play like and conversational in nature. Our relationship with the apparatus becomes one where being-with-in-the-world moves beyond just the human. It helps establish our responsibility to the Other that goes beyond just people, making us responsible for existence itself. This brings us back to Stiegler's assertion about our relationship to the technical. In an ontological sense it actualizes our being-in-the-world.

As we create technical images these images present us the world and place us as active within it. We it becomes less about reading images as experiencing them, being-with them. Our relationship with technical images becomes one of experiencing as being and presence first and a metaphorical meaning can be found later. Where the tradition of painterly images and theatre was one of distancing the viewer to establish a distance for meaning, as we moved from photography to film, radio and television our relationship to the images became one of identification with characters presented. We started to place ourselves into the stories told. The classic Hollywood film seemed to combine elements of the classic disembodied viewer and the engaged identification of the technical image and this worked well for the first half of the first half of the 20th century, but after the experiences of the Second World War a crisis of how we could come to terms with genocide on an industrial scale came about [8]. Our distance from the story negated through the change of the narrative structure from strong moralizing stories to the opened narratives we find in Neo-realism, New Wave films from around the world [9]. The theoretical movement away from the individual as sole agent of their lives and the ontological understanding of being as part of a greater web was becoming an accepted view. The long-established Cartesian has not disappeared and we can see it in technological and political struggles across the 20th and 21st centuries, but this understanding of an ontological interrelatedness has taken hold in many parts of our cultures. Significantly for us this has been evident in the creation of movements like Fluxus, Lettreism, Situationism and expanded cinema. These movements started to question the relationship of the work to the audience and assumed a more engaged audience for their performances or films [13]. Coming out of this we get the essay film, a form of direct address by the film maker to an audience, Happenings and perfor-mance, media objects, such as Anthony McCall's projection sculptures and environmental/site specific art. All of these works have the same basic tenets we traced Kircher, they are viewer centric and the viewer is expected to identify themselves in relation to the work. What has changed is that as we understand the world differently we approach the work in a different way. The Metaphor Machine was designed to so that the viewers presence still contained elements of a distancing and dislocation, what I see is me and not me. In media art practice we understand the work to create interactions that are more conversational in nature. A work such as Peter Campus' *Anamnesis* places a reflection and a 3 s delayed projection onto the same piece of glass. Both the reflection and the projection are life sized and on a glass in the room acts more like a screen than a window. Here we are experiencing ourselves in relation to time and space. The reflected image reverences our view of ourselves, left is right and vice versa, but the projection corrections that reversal meaning in the screen a viewer can face themselves.

The post-war development of experimental cinematic practice was interested in how to bring moving images out of the back box and into the world [13]. From these tendencies' artists went either in the direction of questioning the structures of cinema or into bringing images into the world. The first tendency is exemplified by Warhol's early films *Sleep* or *Empire* where the use of extended duration questioned the relationship of audience to the image and to the movie theatre experience. In the same direction we can look to Stan VanDerBeek's Movie Drome as trying to create a whole new way of artist and audience to experience the image. VanDerBeek created a space where he would use film and animation as tools of improvisation so that the performance was determined by his relationship to the audience. This being similar to what is found in Javanese, Balinese and Malay wayang kulit (shadow puppetry) where the dalang (narrator) frames a conventionalized story to the interests of an audience. In the Movie Drome the image was projected above onto a dome like a planetarium. In a dome projection the image will be larger than the viewing range of the audience meaning that the image is frameless and immersive. The live improvisation of the performance was uniquely different in VanDerBeek's and other artists working with immersion and multiple screens. Artist working in this tendency, questioning the form of cinema, present the image in a way that questions how and what we see bringing the fact of the image being an image forward. This feedback loop between the viewer and the image what Flusser talks about when how our relationship to the apparatus is one of play. He contends that this relationship one that places us in relationship to the other.

Another artist who questions the nature of the projected image in a fundamental way is Anthony McCall. Where Warhol created projected images questioning duration and VanDerBeek worked in what would become live cinema, McCall uses projection to create sculptural spaces that people interact with by moving through them. Beginning with *Dot Describing a Cone* in 1973 McCall has created works where the space between the projector and the screen is the event. In light sculptures a shape is drawn on the film/digital file which is projected in a space where mist has been added. The mist allows the evolving space in which the image is project to take on a sculptural aspect. The image itself stops becoming of interest while the space between, the space that the viewer navigates through becomes the work. We are aware of how the apparatus create the image, but it is not the focus of what we see. We are involved in a tangible interactive space that exists for us to interact with. It bears a physicality yet is just light and smoke. As we move through it we change what it is. We are interacting with light as it is moving through space now. It gives a sense of present time, but also as we move through this space with others the playfulness of the work brings us together. We act and interact upon them creating playful feedback loops recreating the work in each moment.

Feedback itself becomes the basis for a communication creating a face-to-face interaction that presents otherness to us and us to the Other [10]. This relationship maybe temporal and spatial, but it tends towards being a relationship in present time.

We interact in the present and for the present. Where the other tendency of placing images out into the world beyond confining institution treats time in a different way.

Artists who create site specific works tied to specific places bring tie our relationship with images and place together in a way brings a being-with in to the world. In the series *Writing on the Wall* Shimon Attie projected images of pre-war Jewish street life in Berlin back on the building where the images were taken. The images not only bring a past into present time, but they reinforce the history that has happened in between. It creates a corporeal to people who were forcibly eliminated from this space. It points to us and indicates our personal responsibility for the other as *that* person in *that* photograph. Seeing these images in this place brings the weight of history to us in a direct fashion. In its very nature the work is about our responsibility to Otherness. Here the message is not found in the image itself, but in the structure of the installation. Where the traditional image has a conventionalized form where the content is placed with in the image here this is reversed it is the unique form that carries the meaning. This shift of how content is presented is an indication of how media art works are centered on the relationship between the work and the viewer. The work is a collaboration between the images, the space and the viewer, each element is necessary for the piece to exist. This collaborative formulation is what we have found in technical images from photography onwards. The apparatus through which we create images, installations, etc. is one that operates though feedback in creation and display. This tends towards a conversational relationship the overturns traditional hierarchies of artist and viewer. It places us in a condition of being-with the work and the space of the work. Similar to this is Krzysztof Wodiczko's *Tijuana Projection* which entailed him collaborating with female maquiladora[1] workers to tell the story of their lives and working conditions in these border factories. The work was projected on to the façade of the Omnimax Theater in Tijuana Mexico in 2000. Prerecorded video and live testimonials from the collaborators were projected onto the spherical building. The live parts consisted of the face of a collaborator who was wearing a headset with a camera and microphone. They were present within the space of the performance along with the audience. In both the live and prerecorded videos, the women spoke of their living and working conditions, working conditions, sexual harassment at work and traumatic experiences within this border area caused by police brutality, the dislocation of families and domestic violence. The audience was presented the face of the Other in the Lévinasian sense. One was confronted with a face that the viewer could not thematize. It was *that* person in *that* moment, which was demanding us to acknowledge their presence and bear witness to their pain. The demand of the confrontation was for the viewer to take on their ethical responsibility for this person in their otherness. As they bore witness to their traumas they were showing the viewer the consequences of a demand for cheap goods. An ethical challenge was put forward in this work that was only possible because of the relationship to otherness that was inherent in the apparatus itself. The entire system, the projections, the headset, and the setting created a space where the self and Otherness

---

[1] A foreign owned factory operating on the Mexican side of the Mexico/US border. They assemble parts imported from the US and manufacture finished goods tariff and duty free to be exported back to the US. Workers are paid lower wages and worker's right and labor conditions do not meet the standards of their counterparts in the US.

were put into an intimate relationship. The other called out to being in its actuality and demanded a face-to-face that is our being-in-the-world [14].

In less dramatic and political terms the work of teamLab from Tokyo creates interactive digital works also creating a relationship of being-with the viewer. They have made large installations that immerse the viewer. Their practice is centered on the idea of creating a presence with otherness. On their website they have an essay titled *Changing the Relationships Among People: Making the Presence of Others a Positive Experience* [15]. They state an interest in creating works that place the view in relationship with others through the works created. They state their aim to be for these environments to have a positive influence on the viewer. That the situation of being-with others is one that doesn't create stress or conflict. Where Attie and Wodiczko emphasize the responsibility to the Other as a way of facing trauma, teamLab 's approach is to presenting works emphasizing the creating our relationship as not only positive, but also new. They move away from history and try have us look at our being-in-the-world as being recreated every day. "In this way, the search for new relationships between people may be able to go beyond art, potentially creating new relationships between cities and individuals, as well as new ways to bring peace among people" [15]. This is seen by the fact they have created works for children and for adults. A work like *Future World* at the Art Science Museum in Singapore has parts that are in the tradition of installations found in children's museums where kids interact with elements of the work in order to gain knowledge through experiential learning. In many of their works, or adults and children, they use immersion to breakdown the separation of the viewer from the work. Bring the viewer into direct relationship with the work. Through the work the viewer becomes present in space that they call Ultrasubjective Space. [15] teamLab's approach combines traditional Japanese thought and image making with Western ontology.

A last way of seeing how technical images are used to create a sense of presence of the Other as a being-in-the-world is the use of streaming or remote imaging. One of the earliest such works was Kit Galloway and Sherrie Rabinowitz' *Hole in Space* in 1980. The artists set up satellite transmissions in store front windows in New York and Los Angeles. A camera and a large screen were placed in both windows. The public standing outside the storefronts got to see a live transmission from the other place. The projections were life size so the viewers had the sensation of seeing real people and not just images on a TV screen. The transmission was live so people could interact with each other. The sensation was that everyone was experiencing the event in the same time, while two different spaces were being compressed into one. The work created a presence in present time that transcended physical space. People present in each city were able to communicate with each other and according to the artists people separated from each other were able to reunite through this work. Beyond just being able transverse time and space, this work brought the viewer into a personal relationship with Otherness by being face-to-face with people from the other side of the continent. The factuality of the face that is seen is central to this work. There is no metaphor in the image it is the real face of a real person in real time. The structure of the work creates the context which allows for a metaphorical meaning, but the event is beyond such meanings. Wolfgang Staehle's untitled work of 2001 is another significant work using the idea of remote presence. This work was intended to be an update to the idea of

Andy Warhol's *Empire*, in Staehle's care just a static shot of downtown Manhattan from the window of Postmasters' Gallery in the Chelsea neighbourhood of New York. It was meant to allow anyone who logged into a website to see this shot. During the installation the events of 11 September 2001 happened live before his camera. This turned the work from an homage to Warhol into a witness to an event. The events actually transformed the work as the camera took on the role that we normally assume of another person. It was the third party, not me and not the other that I interact with, but the trace that indicates an immanence that transcends our experience to a past that indicates an Other beyond signification and which we bare a responsibility to [11].

Selina Grüter and Michèle Graf's *Watch the Sunset* series of installations presented sunsets from various locations into their studio space in Zürich. Transmissions of sunsets were time shifted so that they occurred concurrently with the sunset in Zürich. This time shift brought the two locations into alignment so that the viewer felt that they were experiencing a simultaneous event making the two events one. What is experienced happens in real time. The remote sunset is not delayed but presented in its actual time. The viewer relates to a sense of unified temporality and spatiality. This bringing together two different moments to be experienced at the same time collapses our feeling of distance and remoteness bringing otherness to us as a face-to-face.

4 Conclusion

This essay comes from my theoretical work [16] on the relationship of photography, ethics and otherness found and my developing media practice. From these perspectives an historical as well as theoretical analysis was needed. Taking a media archaeological approach, the intent was to show how we have gotten to our current condition and possibly indicate where we will be going. The interlinking relationship between art practice and a theoretical world view is one where both influence the other simultaneously. Deleuze observed this in his books on cinema. He wrote about how post war cinema reflected and presented a new awareness time and memory. One where time is experienced as both a present and memory in whose unity a future comes into being. Where thought is more important than a reactive action. Cinema was the place where this is presented to us, where we are aware of these changes. For him cinema's importance is that it reflects what is happening in the world beyond the film [9]. But what was missing from his work was the place of technics in this relationship. He doesn't look at our relationship to technology as anything more than as instrumental. Cinema is the result of useful technologies that are not investigated in themselves. Technology is still a means to an end. Here we have looked at how the developments of theory and technology do not just reflect each other, but create and reinforce each other.

Since the invention of photography, the nature of how we relate to images has changed. We have moved from image that present a distant interpretation of the world to ones based on incorporating time and presence into them. These images have become a vehicle for embodying the relationship of the being to Otherness. It has presented the face of the other before us in its reality. We have seen that as we are presented with otherness it the experience of the other that becomes the main tool of understanding. We identify with the other in relation to us. We come to understand that a demand is made for us to take on a responsibility to the other. In some works, like Attie or Wodiczko's this has taken on a political aspect while with artist like teamLab or Galloway and Rabinowitz a spatialized presence completes the self in its recognition of being in relation to the other. As we develop a world where our relationship to technics, to how we live *in* and *with* technology becomes more central to how we experience life. We have come to understand that we live in relation to Otherness and that it completes us and that the technical images we create help us in this process.

References

1. Stiegler, B.: Technics and Time, 1–2 edn. Stanford University Press, Palo Alto (1998)
2. Duchamp, M., Sanouillet, M., Peterson, E.: Salt Seller; The Writings of Marcel Duchamp. Marchand du sel. Oxford University Press, Oxford (1973)
3. Belting, H.: Florence and Baghdad: Renaissance Art and Arab Science. Harvard University Press, Cambridge (2011)
4. Deleuze, G.: Dualism, monism and multiplicities. (Desire-Pleasure-Jouissance). Contretemps: Online J. Philos. **2**, 92–108 (2001)
5. Barthes, R., Heath, S.: Image, Music, Text. Hill and Wang, New York City (1977)
6. Zielinski, S.: Deep Time of the Media: Toward an Archaeology of Hearing and Seeing by Technical Means. The MIT Press, Cambridge (2006)
7. Flusser, V.: Towards a Philosophy of Photography. Reaktion, London (2000)
8. Deleuze, G.: Cinema 1: The Movement-Image. University of Minnesota Press, Minneapolis (1986)
9. Deleuze, G.: Cinema 2: The Time-Image. University of Minnesota Press, Minneapolis (1989)
10. Flusser, V.: Into the Universe of Technical Images. University of Minnesota Press, Minneapolis (2011)
11. Lévinas, E., Peperzak, A., Critchley, S., Bernasconi, S.: Basic Philosophical Writings. Indiana University Press, Bloomington (1996)
12. Barthes, R., Howard, R.: Camera Lucida: Reflections on Photography. Hill and Wang, New York City (1981)
13. Uroskie, A.V.: Between the Black Box and the White Cube: Expanded Cinema and Postwar Art. University of Chicago Press, Chicago (2014)
14. Lévinas, E.: Entre Nous: Thinking of the Other. Columbia University Press, New York City (1991)
15. teamLab homepage: https://www.teamlab.art/concept/Relationships/. Accessed 19 Jan 2020
16. Feinstein, K.: The Image That Doesn't Want to be Seen. Atropos Press, Dresden (2010)

Applying Holo360 Video and Image Super-Resolution Generative Adversarial Networks to Virtual Reality Immersion

Chia-Hui Feng[1,2($\boxtimes$)], Yu-Hsiu Hung[1], Chao-Kuang Yang[3],
Liang-Chi Chen[3], Wen-Cheng Hsu[3], and Shih-Hao Lin[3]

[1] Department of Industrial Design, National Cheng Kung University,
No. 1, University Road, Tainan, Taiwan R.O.C.
p38041075@gs.ncku.edu.tw
[2] Department of Creative Product Design,
Southern Taiwan University of Science and Technology, No. 1, Nan-Tai Street,
Yongkang District, Tainan, Taiwan R.O.C.
[3] Compute Software Technology, Acer Incorporated,
9F, 88, Sec. 1, Xintai 5th Rd. Xizhi, New Taipei City, Taiwan R.O.C.

Abstract. Super-resolution deep learning methods focus on image processing solutions and discussions in two-dimensional super-resolution image processing NOT for 360 equirectangular images. Therefore, the motivation of this research is to establish the deep learning network model Holo360 SRGAN and data set of 360 equirectangular images, and observe whether the sharpness and noise of Holo360 SRGAN compared with the original image reach the optical verification standard. The results of this study point out two significant points: 1) For a convolution training core neuron with the best model architecture of Holo360 SRGAN with 360 images 8 K (8192 × 4096 px), FOV: 360°, the expanded the convolution core neuron size as 5 × 5 to contains more learning features. And 2) Holo360 SRGAN image experiment results, 6 ROI optical analysis clarity increased by 27%, and sharpness increased by 42%. The experimental original image noise SNR is 28.2 dB, and the Holo360 SRGAN (×2) noise SNR is 36.8 dB, so it is increased by +8.6 dB, and the amount of image detail is also increased. Contributions enhance the super-resolution visual experience of equirectangular video or image.

Keywords: 360 equirectangular · Super resolution GAN · Virtual reality · Tensorlayer

1 Introduction

In recent years, in-depth studies of learning single-image super-resolution (SR) have produced impressive results. For converting low-resolution (LR) single images to high-resolution (HR), SR has shifted the focus away from classic computer vision. In the digital field, the resolution of an image is a description of the image's details. HR images are correlated with increases in imaging precision and detail. SR is the estimation of an HR image from an LR image [10].

© Springer Nature Switzerland AG 2020
M. Kurosu (Ed.): HCII 2020, LNCS 12181, pp. 569–584, 2020.
https://doi.org/10.1007/978-3-030-49059-1_42

Currently, generating images or videos from ordinary 2D images produces blurred results because of the influences of optical devices, such as the lens or aperture, and the unstable shooting of distant scenes. Problems associated with LR imaging are widely discussed in contemporary research. LR images affect visual perception capability and hamper identification. However, the current applications of SR are primarily topics relating to 2D images, such as the use of machine learning and HR solutions and the exploration of super-resolution convolutional neural network (SRCNN).

At present, SR is used to enhance the definition of images from long-distance shooting or image capturing in order to reduce the resolution blur and increase precision. HR technologies [11] employ various observation images to rebuild or restore facial recognition, satellite aerial image [14], digital media content, or remote monitoring for security or defense. These technologies can also use specific biological features from observations such as images of medical pathologies or biological features to enhance recognition precision [6, 12].

SR-related studies have focused on three major fields, namely conventional filtering, image-based training, and neural networks such as SRCNNs and super-resolution generative adversarial network (SRGANs). Irani and Peleg suggested an iterative algorithm for SR, which is applied to a single image without increasing the sampling rate, to reduce SR blur. Moreover, this approach results in translation, rotation, and perspective transformation, with multiple dynamic algorithms for an image and the division of the image into multiple areas. Within each area, several even motions can be used to further enhance resolution [9]. Shi et al. used a high-performance sub-pixel interpolation method to produce immediate single images and videos, with an emphasis on high-performance CNN computation featuring +0.15 dB for images and +0.39 dB for videos [13].

In 2016, SRCNN was used to explore different network structures and parameter changes, achieve a trade-off between performance and speed, extend the network structure to deal with three color channels at the same time, and demonstrate improved overall quality [4]. ProGanSR has exhibited continual progress in its system structure and training. It allows the network to sample images during the intermediate steps. The training process is structured according to learning difficulty during the training process. The network follows a total incremental method design [15].

This approach allows expansion to higher up-sampling factors ($8\times$), and it requires only 4.5 s to reach a quality of $8\times$ the original resolution; moreover, it can enhance the reconstruction quality for all sampling factors $5\times$ faster than the original speed.

The aforementioned SR studies have focused on the gradual increase in popularity of 360° camera devices used to capture images or videos for 2D imaging or 2D SRCNN computation. However, viewing the entirety of 360° images on a flat-screen remains difficult. Viewing the entire image requires a specific viewer or virtual reality (VR) device.

When the output reaches the computer, the resolution is as high as 4 or 6 K and is displayed using a 360° equirectangular mode with image contents in spherical panorama or cubic shapes. Imaging with a resolution of 16 K is similar to the resolution of the human eye. However, devices with a 16 K resolution are not currently available. The highest available resolution is approximately 8 K, which requires HR to react with high distance displayed by a head-mounted display (HMD) in a special image.

This study investigated the display of Holo360 images by applying SRGAN in an HMD. SRGAN technology was applied to Holo360 images and the training and inferences of relevant datasets were explored to enhance the VR display resolution. The 360° HR equirectangular image with an HMD was employed to view the Holo360 images. VR devices have three degrees of freedom (DOF), enabling Holo360 imaging to achieve higher SR sharpness and improved stereopsis effects.

The study investigated the probe and target practicing of Holo360 SRGAN VR projection and inferred the following three overall distributions:

(1) In this study, new in-depth learning methods were established for the Holo360 SRGAN and compared with the original SRGAN. Furthermore, optical verification was used to evaluate whether the sharpness and noise of Holo360 SRGAN achieved the required standard. This also provided suggestions for outcome comparison and the best model structure network when designing Holo360 SRGAN.
(2) The study proposed a generative adversarial network (GAN) for the SR Holo360 images displayed using an HMD. The network can directly project the LR Holo360 image into the HMD, and optimize the Holo360 image for more detail.
(3) Universal Windows Platform (UWP) was used to simulate the experiences in HMD; the imaging technology achieved fine quality and fast computation speed.

2 Literature Review

2.1 SR

SR was proposed by Gerchberg in 1974. A new iterative phase retrieval [5] achieves SR and enhances the resolution of data objects through reducing errors. Using a process of continuous section spectrum, SR can achieve a resolution enhancement for area objects. Image SR can be divided into three types: traditional filtering methods, training-based methods, and neural network approaches. The classic computer vision approaches to in-depth SR learning and GAN involve the reconstruction of HR images from multiple LR images or a single LR image. This approach is mostly used for satellite observation imaging and medical imaging, and it is based on in-depth learning. SR enables direct learning through the neural network of the corresponding functions for point to point LR resolution to SR image and display higher resolution [10].

2.2 GANs

In 2014, Goodfellow et al. proposed the GAN machine learning model, an in-depth learning model, which is one of the most promising algorithms in unsupervised learning. GANs use a small amount of real data to generate a large amount of training data. This is currently the most popular machine learning style for artificial intelligence.

The design concept of GANs comprises two neural networks: a data generator and a data discriminator. Training two competing neural networks is a compelling and powerful technique. The data generator learns to generate large quantities of data that are similar to the real data in order to trick the discriminator. The data discriminator continuously learns to enhance the discrimination of real data to counteract the fraud of the data generator. The data generator can generate data that is similar to the real data. The use of generated data can compensate for the lack of real images during training, and the data generator can complete the equivalent training. To deepen the breadth of training, simulating situations that the discriminator would not have encountered will improve the model's discrimination and learning speed. This would improve the accuracy of the model but can also produce high-quality training data, as well as more favorable effects for the model. In 2017, Ledig et al. conducted an SRGAN experiment for superior performance perception, which was optimized for new perceptual loss. They performed an extensive mean opinion score test with images from three public benchmark datasets. Reconstruction of $4\times$ SRGAN modules obtained higher fidelity. SRGAN became the most advanced technology, which can be applied to the realistic SR of magnified images [10].

2.3   Google SRGAN

For Google's SRGAN research, a large number of 2D image datasets were collected and deconstructed to enlarge the image four times. Thus, the Google datasets could be observed as standard 2D images rather than the processed 360° images. Random numbers were used to sample the image range, calculate the screenshot, repeat sampling action, and sample random numbers before the screenshot. For each iteration, 384×384 px sampling was used, followed by 384×384 px, to capture downwards for the 96×96 px sampling image.

Furthermore, 96×96 px and 384×384 px samples were continuously compared to verify the feasibility, and the data training image was maintained to be similar to the training image. The weights of the SRGAN modules were then recorded. Deconstructing the Google SRGAN reveals a 3×3 convolutional neural networks. This method yields a resolution of approximately 2 K and a field of view (FOV) of approximately 90°. This value correlates with the camera lens, with approximately 5.7 px per degree. The present study employed this method to calculate a 360° equirectangular PPD.

2.4   VR HMD

Ivan Sutherland created the first HMD. In 2015, Palmer Luckey initiated a Kickstarter fundraising for the Oculus Rift HMD, which was eventually acquired by Facebook and commercialized as Oculus. Consumer-oriented VR HMDs subsequently entered consumption markets. Furthermore, Microsoft developed the WMR HMD, which does not require an exterior positioning track system. This HMD's light-weight design lead to a breakthrough in immersion VR headset technology. VR HMDs' are compatible with independent to top-class workstation computers and can be directly connected to laptop computers to execute computations, watch Acer WebVR [3] online, or view 360° digital content on YouTube, among other functions.

Immersion VR indicates integration of the hardware technology of display headsets and VR software. The intuition of immersion is the understanding of space that allows users to watch virtual environments replacing their actual surroundings. Human brains can perceive the reconstruction of 3D environmental images. When the head turns, the HMDs' tracking activates the virtual visual angles to change the stereoscopic image. This enables the users to perceive the visual difference between stereopsis and motion parallax [1].

Immersion VR offers profound clues that other technologies fail to provide. A higher degree of immersion can deepen the spatial perception. The FOV in the headset refers to the widest scope of the image captured by the camera and lens. Larger FOV angles are associated with richer content. The vision can reach a maximum of 360° by 90°. The 360° by 90° FOV can display a range of 960 × 960 px. Wider FOV angles of the HMD lead to a stronger perception of the overall experience of immersion. Experience varies according to changes in FOV. Another value that affects HMD video is frames per second (FPS). FPS refers to the number of continuous images displayed per second in the displaying device. Most consumer 360° cameras provide 30 FPS, whereas professional 360° cameras provides ≥ 60 FPS. In a VR HMD experiment, this enables an improved steadiness in various FOV scenes.

2.5 Holo360 VR Images

The Holo360 images have two commonly used display methods in VR. One is a spherical 2D isometric projection called lat-long and the other is CUBEMAPs, through which the Holo360 image is disassembles into a hexahedron to form a virtual cube. The 3D immersion VR browses the content of the X, Y, and Z axes images in the headset from the Holo360 image content by using a three DOF vertical axis of yaw, pitch, and roll motions.

VR scenes with six DOF consist of front–back, up–down, and left–right exercise reactions along with perception input and output sense. This allows users to immerse themselves in the simulated world because the movement of their perceived surroundings is convincing. They will sense the bona fide perception which realizes the feelings in the simulated world.

When shooting with different types of 360° cameras, the resolution will determine how much visual information can be obtained. Image or video resolution refers to the number of pixels displayed in each dimension, usually indicated in width by height. HD (1920 × 1080 px), 4 K, and 8 K refer to the width and pixels of the image. The standard resolution of 4 K is 3840 × 2160 px. The estimated resolution of human eyes is approximately 16 K. At present, professional cameras provide up to 8 K images or videos. Content uploaded to YouTube has a maximal resolution of 8192 × 8192 px. The 360° images and video on YouTube are immersive VR environments, with a multitude of visual details. Background details that are distant from the camera lens frequently escape notice. This study explored Holo360 SRGAN resolution, which could optimize VR image quality, to improve the sharpness of displayed images through 360° SR.

2.6   Optical Sharpness Measurement

The modulation transfer function (MTF) characterizes system quality in terms of definition. The definition is illustrated as a bar graph of increasing spatial frequency, as illustrated in Fig. 1. The top of the rectangle is sharp with clear boundaries whereas the bottom is blurred. Figure 1 illustrates a black and white bar pattern provided by Imatest. The content captured by all cameras will be blurred to a certain extent. For a spatial frequency ν and a lower MTF, the texture of the scene at low frequencies will become blurred [8], as illustrated in Fig. 1.

Fig. 1. Bar pattern: original with lens degradation

Nyquist frequencies are cases in which one pixel is black and the other pixel is white, which means that one cycle occupies two pixels. Therefore, νNy = 0.5 cy/px, where the units cy/px represent the overall quality of the imaging system, regardless of screen size or resolution. In this study, the sharpness of images were compared at 1:1 (1 image pixel to 1 screen pixel). For the same content and different image sizes, comparison with digital standardization is more favorable.

One line-width according to the Nyquist frequency is one pixel. If the image has 2 K pixels in the vertical direction, then the Nyquist frequency is 2 K LWPH. ν [LWPH] = 2 Picture Height [px] × ν [cy/px]. LWPH and cy/px are both units of measurement for spatial frequency. The definition refers to the details or rendering accuracy that can be distinguished in the scene: Output (ν) = MTF (ν) × Input (ν). MTF50 was a crucial basis for the optical evaluation of Holo360 SRGAN in this study.

3   Methodology

3.1   Purpose of the Research Method

This study investigated Holo360 images and verified the SRGAN outcome by using SRGAN immersion VR. The effects on image resolution were assessed based on the training and inference of the Holo360 SRGAN dataset. Currently, no relevant studies have implemented SRGAN in 360° equirectangular and HMD designs. Therefore, the purpose of this study was to explore the Holo360 SRGAN SR module.

3.2   Research Structure

The study was divided into three phases. The first phase was 2D imaging and 360° equirectangular dataset training. The second phase was Holo360 SRGAN evaluation and testing as well as optical verification. The third phase was VR UWP software development and evaluation of VR HMD browsing of 360° images.

3.3   Experiment Equipment

Holo360 SRGAN VR images were used to perform GAN training, which required collocation with software and hardware equipment. The required hardware was mainly the computer to retrain the Holo360 SRGAN module for 360° images. SRGAN used Predator Helios 700 for calculation.

An Acer Holo360 camera was used to capture the required 360° equirectangular image, an Acer Swift 5 (SF514-54T) was used for software development, and an Ice Lake Core i7 plus 64Execution Units UHD was used for inference. TensorFlow SRGAN was used for training and the related capture and inference features of the Holo360 SRGAN. This process produced a 360° equirectangular SRGAN TensorFlow model, and a Windows UWP was developed to display images on the bridged Acer WMR OJO HMD, with the device resolution of 2880 × 1440 px, FOV of 100°, and a single-lens display of 1.4 K. The experimental results were verified using an Acer WMR OJO HMD, and the experimental equipment is displayed in Fig. 2.

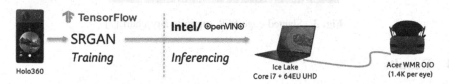

Fig. 2. Holo360 SRGAN experiment equipment

3.4   Experiment Procedure

The execution of this study required the Google Tensorlayer SRGAN program as the main base of 360° SRGAN improvements to extend the SR application. The Google Tensorlayer SR GAN program collected the 2D image dataset, executed the training, and used the fisheye spherical 360° equirectangular Image datasets to generate module differences and perform the extraction of general images and Holo360 image features, which were then used to assess the results of the GAN. The SRGAN module performs the GAN training for the 360° equirectangular image dataset, iteratively revises the model, reduces the feature in the model, expands the convolutional range, and adjusts the image multiplications, until the Holo360 SRGAN module can predict the display of high-quality feature image. Through these calculations, the 360° SRGAN module was trained to produce 360° images. Optics were used to verify and capture the regions of interest (ROIs) for further analysis.

This method mainly specifies a rectangular range, but one of the specific capture elements in the rectangular range closely follows this area as the focus of optical analysis [2]. The Holo360 camera was used to capture indoor and outdoor ROIs to analyze the pros and cons of the HR image. Because human visual inspection cannot be verified, sharpness measurement and Imatest related tools were used to perform these measurements [8]. According to the definition of visual observation, estimates an improved consistency with an MTF of 50%. An MTF of 50% can refer to 50% of its low frequency value (MTF50) or 50% of its peak value (MTF50P). This method compares the proportions of image detail that were lost. According to the aforementioned formula analysis, the optical lab measured the specific data of images. Sharpness and noise were compared for an equirectangular photograph taken using the Holo360 camera and verified by the ISO12233:2000 optical scale by measuring the standard degrees of sharpness, as illustrated in Fig. 3. The aforementioned process was the Holo360 image experiment protocol employed in this study.

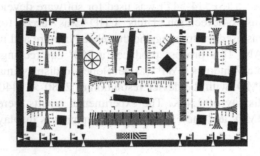

Fig. 3. Slanted-edge SFR supports any chart [7]

4   Results

The experimental module was constructed using Google Tensorlayer SRGAN in this study. The structure based on SR continued to Holo360 SRGAN application. Google Tensorlayer SRGAN technology enables the collection of a large number of equiangular rectangular images as a dataset for training. However, training datasets require a large number of normal images with an FOV of 90°. Because the 360° SRGAN Tensorlayer model requires a Holo360 image instead of normal images for module training, the following experiments were conducted to determine the appropriate model framework.

4.1   Experiment 1: Holo360 SRGAN Dataset Training

Holo360 SRGAN was directly applied 360° equirectangular image datasets. Collection of 360° equirectangular images and training were performed to extract features; this differed from the use of random numbers to extract normal 2D images. The 360° image files were recorded using a fisheye spherical lens, and the images had distorted features, contrary to normal images.

The sampled random numbers points were retained in the images to extend the RGB color values surrounding the sample. Surrounding values in normal image random number points differed from those in Holo360 images. Applying the imaging training results for ordinary images also resulted in 2D images, without the spherical panorama feature of 360° images. This outcome was entirely different, and compensating to complete the Holo360 image feature training remains unknown.

Training was conducted similarly with Holo360 images with a resolution of 2 K image (384 × 384 px, FOV of 360°, and approximately 1.4 px per degree); the resulting module did not differ from that generated using the original image at 5.7 px per degree. In this study, training produced unsatisfactory results both with and without PPD. The training was also unsuccessful when applying 4 K images to capture features at approximately 2.8 PPD.

Regarding the size scale, 4 K is smaller than 8 K. An 8 K image is too large for training because insufficient memory causes the overall calculating speed to slow down, which is why 4 K images were applied in training to enhance pixel quality (Table 1).

Table 1. Difference between SRGAN and 360 SRGAN Module PPD

SRGAN model	Image type	Image size	FOV	Pixel pre degreed
Google SRGAN	2D	384 × 384 px	90°	5.7
Holo360 SRGAN	360 equirectangular	384 × 384 px	360°	1.4

(1) **360° SR Training Image Simulation Test 1**

The deformation edges of the upper and lower side results in the 360° equirectangular training images were deleted. These calculations aimed to test image information following training. The outcome was unsatisfactory because the 360° fisheye feature was lacking.

(2) **360° SR Training Image Simulation Test 2**

The 360° equirectangular images was compressed to half the width to learn features. The images were squeezed to a very flat ratio to train the Holo360 spherical panorama feature; however, this also failed to produce a training image file dataset. After allowing the model to learn the 360° equirectangular feature, the outcome failed to achieve the required training effect. Subsequently, the image was resolution was increased to 16 K in the 360° equirectangular images, the noise was eliminated, and the size was reduced according to Holo360 by using the averaging to enlarge from 2× to 8 K to eliminate excessive noises. The minification process on an enlarged image reduced some noise. Training of these learned features produced rippling image features. Effective training was not achieved.

(3) **360° SR Training Image Simulation Test 3**

The 360° equirectangular images were deconstructed, thereby dewarping a 360° spherical panorama image into four 90° visual charts of the top, bottom, front, and back; the aim was to allow the dataset to learn the equirectangular features. This also failed to achieve the effect of 360° training.

(4) **360° SR Training Image Simulation Test 4**

In Tensorlayer SRGAN, the resolution of the ordinary images was approximately 2 K (FOV of 90°). Tensorlayer SRGAN randomly cropped the images to 384 × 384 px, and then reduced the cropped images to 96 × 96 px to train the model. The PPD used for training was 5.7 (96 × 2048/90 × 3840). The core size of the original convolutional configuration was 3 × 3.

The ordinary images for the SRGAN with a 90° FOV had the core size of the original convolutional configuration (i.e., 3 × 3). The ordinary images with 90° FOV had a visible overall form. This sampling was too limited. Images of partial scope did not contain an overall view of the image under Holo360 imaging. The 360° SRGAN Tensorlayer model used the initial value setting of a rectangular image dataset such as 360°, and the PPD was 1.4, which was insufficient for training.

Therefore, the 360° SRGAN Tensorlayer model collected 360° images with a resolution of 4 K and other rectangular images as datasets, with the PPD of 2.84 (96 × 4096/360 × 384), which was close to the original PPD of 5.7. Moreover, the convolutional range was increased to 5 × 5. When performing the convolutional process, a pixel point to referred to the surrounding 24 points. Holo360 images (FOV of 360°) expanded the extraction feature to display more results. Based on these results, the convolutional core of training network was modified from 3 × 3 to 5 × 5. The 360° SRGAN Tensorlayer model expanded the size of the convolutional core to 5 × 5. This change introduced more detail into the convolution for in-depth learning to improve the model effects.

Further expanding the convolutional core of the SRGAN to 9 × 9 and increasing the range of image calculations were required. However, the speed of computer operations was limited. Learning features resulted in an increase in speckles and warping noise on the image. This verification expanded the core instead of generating an improved module. The resulting convolutional core was 5 × 5, which was suitable for the 360v equirectangular SRGAN TensorFlow model.

4.2   Experiment 2: Holo360 SRGAN Image Experiment Effectiveness

For the indoor images recorded using the Holo360 camera, inference was executed before the training module pretraining with the aforementioned experiment. However, the indoor and outdoor optical tests followed this inference.

1. Experimental Test 1: Holo360 SRGAN indoor image test

The location of Experimental Test 1 was primarily indoors. The optical test results were compared with the original image and enlarged. To apply GIMP, cubic interpolation was used, and no sharpening effects were applied. As a result, the image appeared with vertical bands, washed-out regions, edge artifacts, and false data. Their existence affected the image calculation results, as displayed in Fig. 4. Optical verification of the SRGAN experimental image and comparing the result with the original image revealed sharpness increases of 21% (×2) and 45% (×4). Compared with the enlarged version, the MTF50 sharpness increased by 73.5% (×2) and 113% (×4). Compared with the original image, the enlarged 360° SRGAN image did not exhibit loss or gain in the signal-to-noise ratio (SNR). The enlarged 360° SRGAN image was softer than the original image, as summarized in Table 2.

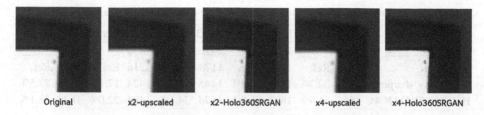

Original   x2-upscaled   x2-Holo360SRGAN   x4-upscaled   x4-Holo360SRGAN

Fig. 4. Experiment Test 1 indoor image ROI sampling and Holo360SRGAN verification results

Table 2. Experiment Test 1 Holo360SRGAN indoor optical analysis results

Results	Original	×2 upscaled	Holo360 SRGAN ×2	Δ	×4 upscaled	Holo360 SRGAN ×4	Δ
SNR-Gray [dB]	32.5	33.9	32.3	−1.6	33.9	31.7	−2.2
SNR-Black [dB]	16.1	17.9	16.6	−1.3	18.1	15.9	−2.2
MTF50 [LWPH]	1640	1141	1980	73.5%	1117	2379	113.0%
EdgeSize [Edges/PH]	1665	1090	2009	84.3%	1059	2160	104.0%

2. Experimental Test 2: Holo360 SRGAN indoor image test

The 360° SRGAN module revealed that the 360° images mostly satisfied the conditions of the Holo360 SRGAN. However, the effects of the small image area were not very favorable. If the small area required analysis and adjustment, Experimental Test 2 employed ROI sampling for analysis, as illustrated in Fig. 5. The original image and the enlarged (×4) image exhibited vertical distortion in the ROI sampling. Noise was identified in the selected area and some inaccuracies appeared in area edges. Image detail increased, but the borders still included mostly unclean areas. The average MTF50 sharpness of the four ROIs in the image for 360° SRGAN was 38.1%, as displayed in Table 3.

ROI1   ROI2   ROI3   ROI4

Fig. 5. Experiment Test 2 indoor image ROI sampling points

Table 3. Experiment Test 2 MTF50 results of 4 ROIs image

MTF50 [LWPH]	ROI1 (vert.)		ROI2 (hor.)		ROI3 (perp.)		ROI4 (perp.)		Average	
Original	1456		1544		1476		1456		1483	
GIMP 4x	1187	Ref.	1137	Ref.	1174	Ref.	1216	Ref.	1179	Ref.
GIMP 4x+ sharpen	1576	32.7%	1568	37.9%	1445	23.1%	1424	17.1%	1503	27.5%
Holo360 SRGAN 4x	1566	31.9%	1887	66.0%	1574	34.1%	1484	22.0%	1628	38.1%

In Experimental Test 2, the edge sizes were compared between the original image and its enlarged version (×4) to calculate the degree of sharpness. The edge size results of the four ROIs in the image displayed increased sharpness compared with the original image. The average increase in sharpness in the four ROIs was 47.34%, as reported in Table 4.

Table 4. Experiment Test 2 edge size results of 4 ROIs image

Edge size [#/PH]	ROI1 (vert.)		ROI2 (hor.)		ROI3 (perp.)		ROI4 (perp.)		Average	
Original	1390		1420		1626		1539		1494	
GIMP 4x	1125	Ref.	1071	Ref.	1196	Ref.	1186	Ref.	1144	Ref.
GIMP4x+ sharpen	1871	66.36%	1929	80.14%	2111	76.44%	2036	71.72%	1987	73.61%
Holo360 SRGAN 4x	1812	61.12%	1716	60.21%	1670	39.54%	1548	30.52%	1686	47.34%

In Experiment Test 2, the average result SNR of these four ROIs and the degrees of sharpness exhibited reduced noise at −2.0 on SNR grayscale and −2.6 on SNR black scale, as displayed in Table 5. Gray (dB) converted the image to grayscale, and Black (dB) converted the image to black and white. The signal-noise ratio was (×4).

Table 5. Experiment Test 2 noise ratio results of 4 ROI SNR signals

Image/index		4x (Holo360SRGAN)	Δ
SNR	Gray (dB)	39.8	−2.0
	Black (dB)	17.1	−2.6
Sharpness	MTF50 [LWPH]	1628	38.1%
	Edge size [Edges/PH]	1686	47.3%

3. Experimental Test 3: Holo360 SRGAN outdoor image test

In Experimental Test 3, an outdoor field test, six ROIs were selected for comparison with the original image, as illustrated in Fig. 6.

Fig. 6. Experiment Test 3 outdoor image 6ROI sampling points

The preliminary results of Experimental Test 3 indicated that the three problems of vertical deformation, speckles, and errors on the image were solved. This verification also exhibited higher sharpness. However, edge artifacts existed on the image and speckles on the screen were not resolved effectively, as illustrated in Fig. 7.

Original   Holo360 SRGAN x2   Holo360 SRGAN x2 +   Original   Holo360 SRGAN x2   Holo360 SRGAN x2 +
median filter (r=1)   median filter (r=1)

Fig. 7. Experiment Test 3 outdoor image results

The results of Experiment Test 3 are reported in Table 6. Compared with the original image, Experiment Test 3 resulted in an improvement in definition of 27%. With the addition of GIMP to improve sharpness, the definition was enhanced by 42%.

Table 6. Experiment Test 3 360 SRGAN 6 ROI's image qwerty test analysis results

MTF50			Average (6 ROI)		
x1	Original	cy/px	0.215		
		LWPH	880.0		
x2	GIMP	cy/px	0.096	−55%	
		LWPH	790.0	−10%	
	GIMP + Sharpen	cy/px	0.153	−29%	59%
		LWPH	1250.8	42%	58%
	Holo360 SRGAN	cy/px	0.137	−36%	42%
		LWPH	1120.8	27%	42%

The SNR of the original image was 28.2 dB, whereas the SNR of the Holo360 SRGAN image (×2) was 36.8 dB. Therefore, it increased by +8.6 dB, as summarized in Table 7. The image detail also increased, but defects in image edge and artifact errors were observed. Additionally, a media filter was applied with a value of r = 1 to reduce the speckles on the image and increased its smoothness.

Table 7. Experiment Test 3 Holo360 SRGAN 3 image qwerty test analysis results

Holo360 SRGAN (x2)		Experiment Test-3
Image Qwerty	Sharpness	27%
	Noise	+8.6 dB
Issues	Vertical bands	None
	Washed out regions	None
	Edge artifacts	Yes
	False data	None

4.3 Holo360 SRGAN UWP Viewer

UWP software was developed for Windows in this study. In HMD, this software can be used to view the Holo360 image or experiment videos. The UWP software connects the three DOF interaction of the spherical panorama 360° image at 2048 × 2048 px (FOV of 90°), processed from the WMR headset, to produce SR image immersion VR browsing.

5 Discussion

In SR, images and videos are produced from LR content, which is frequently needed in the digital calculation. In medical imaging, satellite imaging, and long-distance security imaging, the images may be too blurred or contain too much noise. Several in-depth learning models of SRCNNs have exhibited increasingly promising performances in rebuilding precision; thus, SR has been developed for single-image SR calculation.

Therefore, the overall contribution of this study was based on the results of the Holo360 SRGAN image feature training. Studies have demonstrated that in-depth training of a Holo360 SRGAN improved sharpness and noise to optical standards. For 360° images with a resolution of 8 K (8192 × 4096 px, FOV of 360°), a convolutional core of 5 × 5 was optimal for training the Holo360 SRGAN network. This core can contain more features in convolution used during deep learning, display the SR image in the Holo360 image optimization details in the HMD, and simulate the SR in the HMD on the UWP computer software to obtain clear Holo360 SRGAN image verification results.

6 Conclusion

The principal aims of this study were the convolutional training of the Holo360 SRGAN network, improving the basis to sustain SR applications, and initiating an increase in Holo360 image and video applications. Given the 360° SRGAN convolutional inference and Experimental Test 3, future research should employ the GIMP software to increase definition. A video processing mean filter could be added to the core program to calculate the average median filter, or media filters could soften high image sharpness to enhance the smoothing process. Screening yielded unnecessary noise and could increase image precision. The degrees of sharpness and noise would thus decrease, thereby smoothing the image.

These research results can provide a reference for 360° equirectangular and SRGAN applications as well as for SR-related research and product development on VR using 360° videos or images. Finally, the possible effects of research restrictions on the results are as follows: 1. UWP VR browser presentation used a spherical panorama without further exploration of a special type browsing presentation. 2. This study was technology-oriented and did not explore user testing and perception. 3. The browsing model of this study did not explore six DOF actual viewing perception. 4. Without eliminating zenith, nadir, or stitch lines, only the camera's software was used to solve the seam line problem.

Acknowledgement.   Many thanks to the supports by Acer Product R&D II, Optical RD Supervisor Sergio Cantero with optical verification technology and theoretical basis.

References

1. Bowman, D.A., McMahan, R.P.: Virtual reality: how much immersion is enough? Computer **40**(7), 36–43 (2007)
2. Brinkmann, R.: The Art and Science of Digital Compositing, p. 184. Morgan Kaufmann, Burlington (1999)
3. Acer WebVR Start Page. https://acerwebvr.github.io/. Accessed 6 Jan 2019
4. Dong, C., Loy, C.C., He, K., Tang, X.: Image super-resolution using deep convolutional networks. IEEE Trans. Pattern Anal. Mach. Intell. **38**(2), 295–307 (2016)
5. Gerchberg, R.W.: Super-resolution through error energy reduction. Opt. Acta: Int. J. Opt. **21**(9), 709–720 (1974)
6. Hayat, K.: Multimedia super-resolution via deep learning: a survey. Digit. Signal Process. **81**, 198–217 (2018)
7. Interactive Analysis of Resolution-Related Charts. http://www.imatest.com/docs/rescharts/. Accessed 25 Dec 2019
8. Measuring Sharpness. http://www.imatest.com/docs/sharpness/. Accessed 23 Dec 2019
9. Irani, M., Peleg, S.: CVGIP: Improving resolution by image registration. Graph. Models Image Process. **53**(3), 231–239 (1991)
10. Ledig, C., et al.: Photo-realistic single image super-resolution using a generative adversarial network. In: The IEEE Conference on Computer Vision and Pattern Recognition, pp. 4681–4690 (2017)
11. Milanfar, P.: Super-Resolution Imaging. CRC Press, Boca Raton (2011)

12. Nguyen, K., Fookes, C., Sridharan, S., Tistarelli, M., Nixon, M.: Super-resolution for biometrics: a comprehensive survey. Pattern Recogn. **78**, 23–42 (2018)
13. Shi, W., et al.: Real-time single image and video super-resolution using an efficient sub-pixel convolutional neural network. In: The IEEE Conference on Computer Vision and Pattern Recognition, pp. 1874–1883. IEEE (2016)
14. Thornton, M.W., Atkinson, P.M., Holland, D.A.: Sub-pixel mapping of rural land cover objects from fine spatial resolution satellite sensor imagery using super-resolution pixel-swapping. Int. J. Remote Sensing **27**(3), 473–491 (2006)
15. Wang, Y., Perazzi, F., McWilliams, B., Sorkine-Hornung, A., Sorkine-Hornung, O., Schroers, C.: A fully progressive approach to single-image super-resolution. In: The IEEE Conference on Computer Vision and Pattern Recognition, pp. 864–873 (2018)

Single Image Contrast Enhancement by Training the HDR Camera Data

Kenji Iwata[1]([✉]), Ryota Suzuki[1], Yue Qiu[2], and Yutaka Satoh[1,2]

[1] National Institute of Advanced Industrial Science and Technology (AIST),
Tsukuba, Japan
kenji.iwata@aist.go.jp
[2] Tsukuba University, Tsukuba, Japan

Abstract. For real-time user interaction such as telepresence, we propose an image processing approach for presenting natural images to users in the situation of brightness change. We use a high dynamic range camera for training the contrast enhancement method based on CNN. The advantage of the pro-posed approach is that a large number of multiple exposure images necessary for CNN training can be collected easily by taking some videos with the HDR camera in various environments. We collected HDR camera dataset for training while moving indoors and outdoors on foot about 10 min. The data are 500 images randomly extracted from the video sequence. We compared some types of training data. Even in our easily generated dataset, the generated images showed good results. This makes it possible to generate an image equivalent to the HDR camera with a low-cost standard camera.

Keywords: Single image contrast enhancement · High dynamic range camera · DC-GAN

1 Introduction

For real-time user interaction such as telepresence, we propose an image processing approach for presenting natural images to users in the situation of brightness change. Multiple exposure image fusion (MEF) [1] and single image contrast enhancement (SICE) [2] have been studied mainly in the field of digital photography. The field focuses on gradation, color vividness, and detail drawing. In particular, in order to maintain gradation, a dark scene that avoids saturation is often used.

On the other hand, when aiming at real-time image acquisition, such as telepresence, user interaction, and mobile robot, there can be a sudden change in brightness. For example, indoor scenes with external light or when moving indoors to/from outdoors. In order to cope with such a scene, an approach different from that of a digital photograph is required. Deep SICE [3] based on CNN has yielded good results, and can be adapted to our purpose by preparing training data. However, it is generally hard to collect a sufficient amount of training data, which are many images of multiple exposure in some scenes that the user wants to use.

In recent years, the development of CMOS technology [4] has made it possible to use high dynamic range (HDR) cameras. HDR cameras can acquire multiple exposure

© Springer Nature Switzerland AG 2020
M. Kurosu (Ed.): HCII 2020, LNCS 12181, pp. 585–595, 2020.
https://doi.org/10.1007/978-3-030-49059-1_43

images at once time, and real-time MEF is also possible. On the other hand, HDR cameras are expensive, so we would like to perform SICE using standard cameras. Therefore, it is possible to generate HDR images in various environments by training images acquired from the HDR camera with Deep SICE. The advantage of the proposed approach is that a large number of multiple exposure images necessary for Deep SICE training can be collected easily by taking some videos with the HDR camera. This makes it possible to generate an image equivalent to the HDR camera with a low-cost standard camera.

2 Related Works

Traditional methods of single image contrast enhancement (SICE) are based on histogram smoothing [2, 5]. These methods are fast and useful, but are not good at strong local brightness changes. Therefore, a method of coping with a local brightness change by using at a histogram for local region has been proposed [6].

Multiple exposure image fusion (MEF) generate high-contrast image from Multiple exposure images. MEF generally uses a method using tone mapping [1]. Local reproducibility and handling of moving objects were implemented [7].

On the other hand, an image generation method using a convolutional neural network (CNN) has been developed. For example, semantic segmentation [8], image conversion [9] and image style conversion [10], etc. Meanwhile, a SICE can be performed by training enhanced images to CNN [11]. An approach of learning the best enhanced image by human evaluation has been proposed [3].

3 Proposed Method

3.1 Architecture

Figure 1 gives an overview of the proposed approach. We use ViewPLUS Xviii [12] as the HDR camera. As input data, images of various 8-bit gradient are acquired from 18-bit gradient HDR data. One of these images is input to the neural network. The neural network is based on DCGAN [9]. Compared with the direct learning method [3], the detail drawing is inferior, but the convergence is fast. An image created from the multiple exposure image by the method of Mertens [1] or Ma [6] is referred to as ground truth. Training is performed by minimizing the composite value of structural similarity (SSIM) loss and Adversarial loss. SSIM is as follows.

$$\text{SSIM} = \frac{1}{\mu^2 \cdot \mu'^2} \sum_{x \in \Omega} [I(x) - I'(x)]^2, \tag{1}$$

where Ω is whole domain of image, I is input image, I' is output image, μ and μ' are averages of input image and output image, respectively. The value subtracted from 1 is used as loss function. With about 50 epoch training, an enhanced image can be generated.

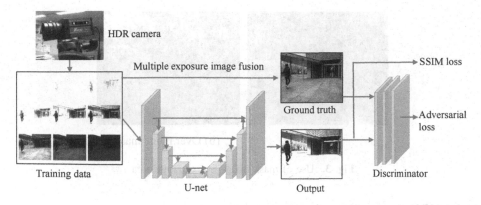

Fig. 1. Block diagram of the proposed approach.

3.2 Noise Removal in Overrange Area

Over-ranged areas such as over-exposure and under-exposure are filled with 0 or 255 in some color channel. In these areas, information that was in the original environment has been lost. Figure 2(a) shows an example with many overrange. Figure 2(b) shows the output of the method described in the previous section, when many of over-ranged images are included in the training data. Many block noises can be seen in the over-range region.

(a) Input   (b) w/o over range mask   (c) w/ over range mask

Fig. 2. Example of an overrange image and image generation results

Therefore, we took the following measures. First, a mask image of overrange areas is created using a fixed threshold value as shown in Fig. 3. Next, the ground truth image corresponding to the mask area is blurred by gaussian filter. The blurred image is used as a new ground truth image for training. With this measure, noise can be suppressed as shown in Fig. 2(c).

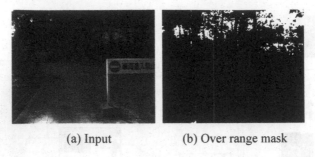

(a) Input   (b) Over range mask

Fig. 3. Use of mask image in overrange area

3.3 HDR Camera Dataset

We collected HDR camera dataset for training as shown in Fig. 4. While moving indoors and outdoors on foot, we recorded HDR video sequence with an HDR camera for about 10 min. This data includes a scene with a large difference in brightness, such as a corridor or a piloti with sun light enters. In addition, indoor data includes a dark scene without sun light.

Training data is 500 images randomly extracted from the video sequence. To obtain such data with a general camera, it is necessary to take multiple exposures at 500 locations. It is not desirable that there is a moving object or that there is camera shake. It is necessary to use a tripod to prevent camera shake, and to shoot at the moment when a subject such as people does not move. By using an HDR camera, data can be easily obtained without such restrictions.

Fig. 4. Examples of HDR camera dataset.

4   Experimental Results

4.1   Difference of Ground Truth Methods

Two types of MEF algorithms are verified for creating ground truth images. We compared Mertens [1] or Ma [6] to generate ground truth images as shown in Fig. 5. Column (a) is the input images. Column (c) and column (e) are ground truth images by Ma and Martens algorithms, respectively. Column (b) and column (d) are the output images of the neural networks that trained each ground truth. Neural networks are adapted to each MEF algorithm, because similar images are generated. Ma algorithm compresses the contrast and produces a stronger color.

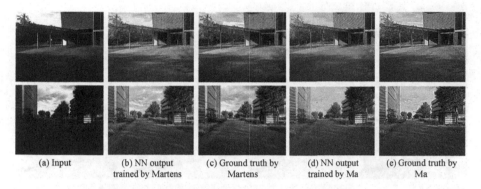

| (a) Input | (b) NN output
trained by Martens | (c) Ground truth by
Martens | (d) NN output
trained by Ma | (e) Ground truth by
Ma |

Fig. 5. Output results due to differences in ground truth. (Color figure online)

4.2   Experiments with Different Training Data

We compared three types of training data: Cai's dataset [3], HDR camera dataset, and both datasets. Figure 6 shows the generated images. Column (a) is the input images. Column (b), column (c) and column (d) are the output images of the neural networks that trained Cai's dataset, HDR camera dataset and both datasets, respectively. In column (b), it can be seen that the color has become lighter. This is thought to reflect the characteristics of the Cai's dataset. In column (c), even in our easily generated dataset, the generated images showed good results. However, some over-exposure is observed on the wall exposed to direct sunlight.

The generated images were evaluated using PSNR and FSIM [13]. PSNR is as follows.

$$PSNR = 10 \log_{10} \frac{255^2}{MSE} \tag{2}$$

$$MSE = \frac{1}{|\Omega|} \sum\nolimits_{x \in \Omega} [I(x) - I'(x)]^2 \tag{3}$$

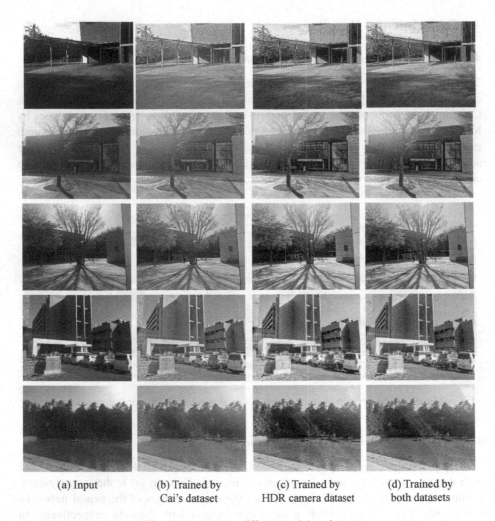

| (a) Input | (b) Trained by Cai's dataset | (c) Trained by HDR camera dataset | (d) Trained by both datasets |

Fig. 6. Results by different training dataset

The following equation is FSIM for color image.

$$\text{FSIM}_C = \frac{\sum_{x \in \Omega} S_L(x) \cdot [S_C(x)]^{\lambda} \cdot PC_m(x)}{\sum_{x \in \Omega} PC_m(x)}, \qquad (4)$$

where S_L is local similarity, PC_m is weight of importance, and S_C is chrominance similarity. Each detail is given in Ref. [13].

Table 1 shows the results. Each index indicates that higher numbers can generate images closer to ground truth images. The error distribution at this time is shown in Fig. 7. Evaluation data is acquired by the HDR camera that is not included in the

Table 1. Average PSNR (dB) and FSIM indices for quality evaluation.

Training dataset	PSNR	SSIM
Cai's dataset [1]	18.3 ± 1.6	0.832 ± 0.065
HDR camera dataset (proposed)	24.0 ± 2.2	0.872 ± 0.057
HDR camera dataset + Cai's dataset	24.3 ± 2.5	0.882 ± 0.056

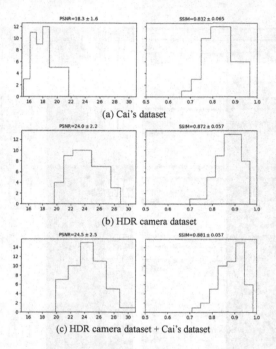

(a) Cai's dataset

(b) HDR camera dataset

(c) HDR camera dataset + Cai's dataset

Fig. 7. Error distribution of PSNR and FSIM.

training dataset. Each index is higher when using HDR dataset than when using Cai's dataset with different characteristics. The best results are obtained when both datasets are used for training.

4.3 Verification of Effects on Brightness Change

In this section, we will verify the output results for the brightness of the input image. Figure 8 shows results of two image in the HDR dataset. Thus, some images can be output regardless of the brightness of the input image. A single color was drawn on the overexposed area of the ground. Such an area does not have the information necessary for drawing, so this result is obtained. However, noise-free images could be generated by the overrange measures described in Sect. 3.2.

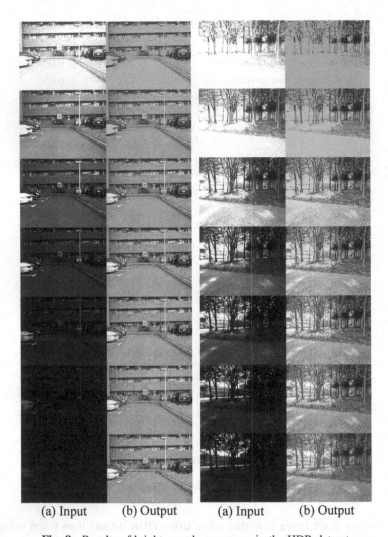

(a) Input   (b) Output   (a) Input   (b) Output

Fig. 8. Results of brightness change scene in the HDR dataset.

Figure 9 shows results of two photos in the Cai's dataset. The same output results are obtained regardless of brightness change. However, the drawing of the sky differs greatly depending on the saturation and shape. Since there were many cloudy scenes in the training data, it was difficult to draw the blue sky.

(a) Input   (b) Output   (c) Ground truth

Fig. 9. Results of brightness change scene in the Cai's dataset. (Color figure online)

4.4 Application Example with Spherical Camera

A spherical camera as shown in Fig. 10 is a practical application of proposed technology. In the upper row, dark areas such as trees are clear in the output image than in the input image. In the lower row, the interior is brightly depicted, and the outdoors is depicted without being overexposed.

(a) Input   (b) Output

Fig. 10. A result with spherical camera image.

5 Conclusion

We proposed an approach of single image contrast enhancement (SICE) by using DC-GAN-based network with training dataset captured by HDR camera. We evaluated some situation and three types of training data. Even in our easily generated dataset, the generated images showed good results. This makes it possible to generate an image equivalent to the HDR camera with a low-cost standard camera.

In future work, we consider how to compensate for areas where information was completely lost due to overrange.

References

1. Mertens, T., Kautz, J., Reeth, F.V.: Exposure fusion. In: Computer Graphics and Applications, pp. 382–390 (2007)
2. Arici, T., Dikbas, S., Altunbasak, Y.: A histogram modification framework and its application for image contrast enhancement. IEEE Trans. Image Process. **18**(9), 1921–1935 (2009)
3. Cai, J., Gu, S., Zhang, L.: Learning a deep single image contrast enhancer from multi-exposure images. IEEE Trans. Image Process. **27**(4), 2049–2062 (2018)
4. Seo, M., et al.: A low-noise high-dynamic-range 17-b 1.3-megapixel 30-fps CMOS image sensor with column-parallel two-stage folding-integration/cyclic ADC. IEEE Trans. Electron Devices **59**(12), 3396–3400 (2012)
5. Celik, T., Tjahjadi, T.: Contextual and variational contrast enhancement. IEEE Trans. Image Process. **20**(12), 3431–3441 (2011)
6. Yuan, L., Sun, J.: Automatic exposure correction of consumer photographs. In: Fitzgibbon, A., Lazebnik, S., Perona, P., Sato, Y., Schmid, C. (eds.) ECCV 2012. LNCS, vol. 7575, pp. 771–785. Springer, Heidelberg (2012). https://doi.org/10.1007/978-3-642-33765-9_55

7. Ma, K., Li, H., Yong, H., Wang, Z., Meng, D., Zhang, L.: Robust multi-exposure image fusion: a structural patch decomposition approach. IEEE Trans. Image Process. **26**(5), 2519–2532 (2017)
8. Ronneberger, O., Fischer, P., Brox, T.: U-Net: convolutional networks for biomedical image segmentation. In: Navab, N., Hornegger, J., Wells, W.M., Frangi, A.F. (eds.) MICCAI 2015. LNCS, vol. 9351, pp. 234–241. Springer, Cham (2015). https://doi.org/10.1007/978-3-319-24574-4_28
9. Isola, P., Zhu, J., Zhou, T., Efros, A.: Image-to-image translation with conditional adversarial networks. In: The IEEE Conference on Computer Vision and Pattern Recognition (2017)
10. Zhu, J., Park, T., Isola, P., Efros, A.: Unpaired image-to-image translation using cycle-consistent adversarial networks, pp. 2242–2251 (2017). https://doi.org/10.1109/iccv.2017.244
11. Shen, L., Yue, Z., Feng, F., Chen, Q., Liu, S., Ma, J.: MSR-net:Low-light Image Enhancement Using Deep Convolutional Network. arXiv:1711.02488. (2017)
12. http://www.viewplus.co.jp/
13. Zhang, L., Zhang, L., Mou, X., Zhang, D.: FSIM: A feature similarity index for image quality assessment. IEEE Trans. Image Process. **20**(8), 2378–2386 (2011)

Baguamarsh: An Immersive Narrative Visualization for Conveying Subjective Experience

Fei Jiang[1,2]([⊠]), Don Derek Haddad[2], and Joseph Paradiso[2]

[1] Shanghai Academy of Fine Arts, Shanghai, China
fred_jf@hotmail.com
[2] MIT Media Lab, Cambridge, USA

Abstract. As ubiquitous sensing becomes embedded in our everyday world, we can easily obtain multimodal sensor data from our physical surroundings. Objectivity is a core value in the visualization research community. However, personal experiences are characterized not only by objective facts, but by personal emotions. In this paper, we explore immersive data visualization for conveying personal subjective perception and experience by using multidimensional data and multimedia. We introduce a framework to describe narrative structures in immersive data visualization, and provide an example project Baguamarsh as a proof of theme-based creative methods for designing correlations between different information. We hope this study may offer outline opportunities for future research in narrative visualization.

Keywords: Virtual reality · Narrative visualization · Multidimentional data · Storytelling · Bagua · Book of Changes

1 Introduction

As ubiquitous sensing becomes embedded in our everyday world, we can easily obtain multimodal sensor data from our physical world, as personal health data, meteorological data, geographical data and etc. There are many approaches that have been designed to present date for users to communicate information clearly and efficiently. Data visualizations are commonly presented quantitatively, as statistical graphics, plots, charts and other tools [1]. Objectivity is a core value in the visualization research community [2]. However, personal experiences are characterized not only by objective facts, but by personal emotions [3]. How to convey personal subjective perception and experience by using multidimensional data becomes both an opportunity and a challenge in visualization field.

On the one hand, storytelling is an effective way of conveying information and enhancing understanding [4], as narrators can leverage personal information (data, photos, audio, etc.) and express their subjective ideas through narrative visualization. On the other hand, as VR headsets have become affordable for individuals, virtual reality becomes a user-friendly platform for reconstructing and representing digital information.

© Springer Nature Switzerland AG 2020
M. Kurosu (Ed.): HCII 2020, LNCS 12181, pp. 596–613, 2020.
https://doi.org/10.1007/978-3-030-49059-1_44

In this paper, our approach treats the data visualization as a narrative and uses virtual reality as a platform to convey a narrator's story. Firstly, we discuss related work on visualization research. Secondly, we introduce a framework to describe narrative structures in immersive data visualization. Finally, we provide an example project "Baguamarsh" as a proof of concept. Each of these aspects plays a great role in allowing the narrator to affect the observer emotionally and intellectually by conveying a rich, significant idea.

2 Related Work

2.1 Pre-research

Project "Moments" is a prototype system for saving and representing personal moments [5] and presents an overview of a whole process of creating an immersive data visualization, which provide a good reference value for this study.

A wireless sensor network (deployed at Tidmarsh Wildlife Sanctuary in southeastern Massachusetts) [6], and Chain-API (a RESTful service providing sensor data), provide a place instrumented with a dense senor network for field study and an open-data platform for collecting environmental data, hence provides an ideal setting for this project.

2.2 Subjectivity in Narrative Visualization

As narrative visualizations combine patterns of communicative and exploratory information visualization to convey intended stories [4], many communities have commented on the importance of narrative in data visualization [9]. But according to Tong et al. [7], comparing with the development in other fields, storytelling is a relatively new subject in visualization. On one hand, even storytelling has become a common topic of discussion in data visualization now, but most research commonly represents objective facts [7], and there is only a little research on personal storytelling [3]. On the other hand, there are some data artworks that express subjectivity as a design goal, but they do not describe specific techniques and methodologies for creating subjective representation [3].

2.3 Immersive Data Visualization

Virtual reality not only has been shown to lead to better discovery in domains whose primary dimensions are spatial [8], but also to enhance situation awareness [9] and media richness [10]. On one hand, according to Donalek et al., as virtual reality can maximize the intrinsic human pattern recognition skills [8], immersive data visualization provides more intuitive data understanding than traditional "desktop" visualization tools. On the other hand, the public has understood that virtual reality already portended a new medium for almost two decades [11], and we have seen much research on interactive experience, presence, immersion and interaction [12–17], but not many works that address immersive narrative visualization involve live sensor data.

3 Framework

We explore the use of immersive virtual reality platforms for narrative visualization to convey subjective experience. To achieve our goal, we introduce a theme-based framework (shown in Fig. 1) with which a user not only can convey personal subjective perception and experience by using multimedia and multidimensional data, but also can enhance multidimensional expression.

According to the commonly used pipeline for collecting data [3] and creating information visualizations [18], we inject a theme-based method in workflow to represent subjective personal narratives in an immersive environment. Firstly, a main theme chosen by a narrator is the selection criteria for collecting information (data, media, etc.). Secondly, according to the theme, the narrator can choose to simplify, classify, connect or reconstruct information materials. Thirdly, rhetorical strategy is used to map all content for representing annotation, user interface, presence and interactivity. Finally, perceptualization is integrated for building up an immersive and interactive environment.

4 Project Introduction

In this section, we present a project "Baguamarsh" that exemplifies the goals described in last section. This project takes the idea of the unity between heaven and man of the ancient Chinese philosophy I Ching (Book of Changes) [19], combines the Bagua (Eight Trigrams) of the I Ching with multidimensional data and multimedia, and uses an immersive interactive environment to present a novel form of narrative visualization. The main theme of this project is the "Unity between Heaven and Man", namely the harmony of nature and human. It systematically expounds the relationship between man and nature, that man must follow the laws of the universe, to respect and protect nature, and to have an insight into the truth that harmony can produce all things. According to the main theme, we designed this project under the form of a virtual reality environment by integrating personal data, environmental data and media materials.

An I Ching framework has been used in prior work to interpret and represent wearable sensor data for a quantified self application [20], but not to our knowledge for integrated personal and large-scale environments sensing.

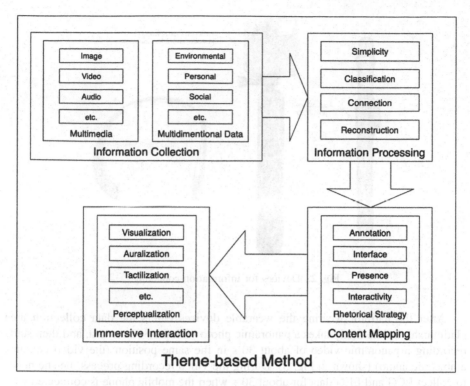

Fig. 1. Theme-based framework for constructing immersive narrative visualization

5 Information Collection and Processing

The data used for this project is divided into user data and environmental data. The user data is mainly from wearable devices, that is to say an Apple Watch 4 and a Muse BioHarness in this project. These two kinds of devices are separately responsible for collecting a narrator's ECG and EEG. Environmental data is mainly obtained in two ways: (1) a GoPro 360 camera is responsible for taking 360° panoramic photos and recording ambisonic audio from user environments (shown in Fig. 2), (2) Using the open data interface to obtain environmental data through time and GPS information encoded in the panoramic photo EXIF information.

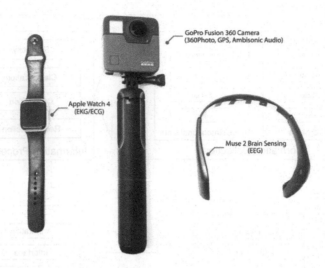

Fig. 2. Devices for information collecting

After the narrator wearing the wearable devices enters the data collection area (Tidmarsh), he/she firstly takes a panoramic photo with the 360 camera, and then starts recording a panoramic video of about 30 s in the same position (the video contains ambisonic audio) (shown in Fig. 3). During the video recording process, he/she needs to collect ECG and EEG data for about 30 s when the mobile phone is connected with the wearable device. The narrator may take advantage of the features of the 360° camera, as he/she doesn't need to focus or frame when shooting image material, so he/she can collect other data at the same time, which greatly shortens the information collection time. After actual operation, we find that the information collection process for one location usually takes no more than 2 min.

Fig. 3. Information collection in Tidmarsh

Information processing is mainly divided into three steps: information extraction, data expansion and data archiving (shown in Fig. 4). (1) Information extraction: mainly for the image materials captured by the 360° camera, which includes panoramic photos and panoramic videos. The panorama photo is a JPG image file, and each file contains EXIF information. We use a program written in Python to extract the time and GPS information from each photo for later use in data expansion. The extraction process for panoramic video file information is relatively time consuming. We import the panoramic video into the post-processing software Premiere before extracting the 4-channel ambisonic audio. In addition, we use a sound generation program written in Python to convert the ECG signals collected in the previous period (Fig. 4, top) into 30-s heartbeat sounds, which will be used in the later virtual reality interaction. (2) Data expansion: using the time and GPS information in the previous photos, we obtain the 24-h environmental information of the information collection day through an open data interface. The open data platforms used in this project include the following: Google Maps API, AccuWeather APIs, Chain API [21]. We use Python-written programs to get locations and elevations from the Google Map API, get temperatures and winds across the entire area from AccuWeather APIs, and get the pressure, relative humidity, visible light, intensity of infrared and ultraviolet light, soil temperature and humidity from the Chain API in the area where the user is located at Tidmarsh. We put all of this data together to generate a text file in JSON format. (3) Data archiving: We use the desktop program written by Unity to package panoramic photos, ambisonic audio and text files containing all metadata into an archive file, which is convenient for subsequent virtual reality program calls.

6 Content Mapping

The way we present content has the following characteristics: (1) Narrative visualization will be presented in the VR environment reconstructed from 360 panoramic photos, and users can switch between the real environment and special effects environment. (2) By combining the physical properties of the phenomena described by the data with commonly used visualization methods, we develop novel and user-friendly modes of presentation. (3) Eight Trigrams (see below) will persist across the entire visual representation, and the symbols corresponding to each kind of trigram will be adopted as the basic visual elements of the environmental data points, which also reflect the connection between data and trigrams on the micro level and make the observation more convenient, thereby improving annotation. (4) Most of the visualization objects in this project are time series datasets in the unit of scenes. All data points can not only display the visualization effects at different times and in different trigrams, but also reflect the relationship between personal data and environmental data, thereby abstracting a visual pattern of "Unity between Heaven and Man" to users.

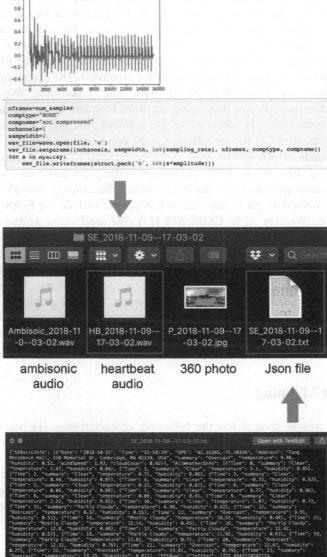

Fig. 4. Information processing

Eight Trigrams are the basic concept of the Book of Changes and can represent the dynamic and still states of all natural phenomena. Eight kinds of symbols used in the Eight Trigram correspond to eight phenomena in nature (Heaven, Earth, Water, Fire, Thunder, Wind, Mountain, Marsh), and their names are "Qian, Kun, Kan, Li, Zhen, Xun, Gen and Dui". Through the evolution of these eight natural phenomena, we speculate on the laws of man and nature in an attempt to achieve a world view of harmony between humanity and nature. The Eight Trigrams are divided into Earlier Eight Trigrams and Later Eight Trigrams. What is used in the project is the Later Eight Trigrams, which are said to have been made by Zhou Wenwang. In the Later Eight Trigrams, the Trigram Zhen is the starting point and it is due east. According to the clockwise direction order, there are in sequence: Trigram Xun–Southeast; Trigram Li —South; Trigram Kun–Southwest; Trigram Dui—West; Trigram Qian–Northwest; Trigram Kan—North; Trigram Gen–Northeast. The order of the Later Eight Trigrams are: one of Kan, two of Kun, three of Zhen, four of Xun, five of the center, six of Qian, seven of Dui, eight of Gen, and nine of Li. The ancients used to draw maps with south at the top and east in the left. We create a three-dimensional interactive menu based on graphics of Eight Trigrams and the shape of the Fengshui Bagua mirror for the interaction of the VR controller (shown in Fig. 5).

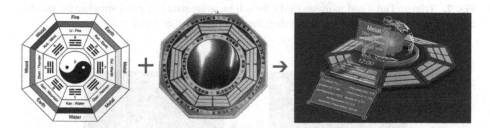

Fig. 5. Bagua menu

According to the eight phenomena described in the Bagua, we divide the acquired environmental data into eight categories that correspond to each of the Trigrams (shown in Fig. 14) in the menu: (1) Trigram Qian: atmospheric pressure (2) Trigram Dui: soil moisture (3) Trigram Li: UV index (4) Trigram Zhen: cloud cover (5) Trigram Xun: wind speed (6) Trigram Kan: humidity (7) Trigram Gen: elevation (8) Trigram Kun: soil temperature. Users can interact with the data space through the Bagua menu: the specific visualizations are as follows (Figs. 6, 7, 8, 9, 10, 11, 12 and 13):

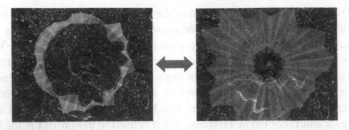

Fig. 6. Trigram Qian – atmospheric pressure (AP): the atmospheric pressure data is used to control the volume of a ring around an object. The higher the pressure, the larger its volume.

Fig. 7. Trigram Dui – soil moisture (SM): the soil moisture data is used to simulate the water on the ground. The greater the moisture value, the wider the line of water.

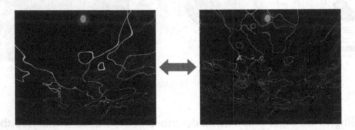

Fig. 8. Trigram Li – UV index (UV): the UV index represents twinkling lines in the sky. The higher the value, the high their density.

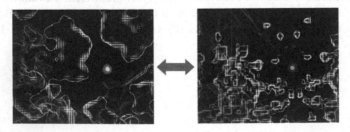

Fig. 9. Trigram Zhen – cloud cover (CC): the value of cloud cover is used to control the density of clouds in the sky. Cloud density increases with the value of cloud cover.

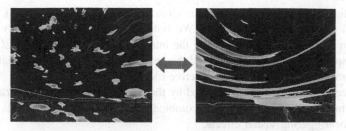

Fig. 10. Trigram Xun – wind speed (WS): wind data is used to control the rotational speed of visual elements. The higher its value, the faster the rotational speed.

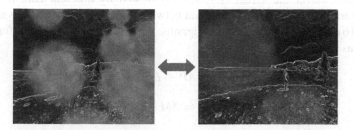

Fig. 11. Trigram Kan – humidity (Hu): humidity is used to control the density of visual elements. The larger the value, the higher the density.

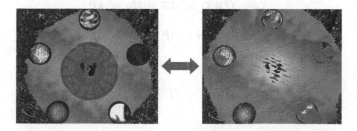

Fig. 12. Trigram Gen – elevation (El): elevation data controls height differences between water particles and other objects. The higher the value, the bigger the gap.

Fig. 13. Trigram Kun – soil temperature (ST): the soil temperature is used to control the color tone of ground material. The higher the temperature, the warmer the color.

According to the I Ching, Trigram Qian corresponds to the body's brain, and Trigram Li corresponds to the heart. We build the EEG and ECG into a dynamic model, then place them at the centre of the interactive menu. Both the EEG and ECG data are displayed as line graphs around the model, and all environment data is shown on the submenus attached to the interactive menu (shown in Fig. 5).

The green main menu can be rotated by the VR controller. Each Trigram contains different kinds of data and different combinations of the Five Elements which are designed for triggering visual effects.

Users can select the environmental data within 24 h of the day of the encounter through the menu selection. We map the elements represented by each trigram to the relationship between the five elements. We superimpose the elements corresponding to these attributes over the visual elements manifested by different data to reflect the process of mutual promotion and restraint between the five elements (shown in Fig. 15 and Fig. 16), reflected by the Eight Trigrams. The calculation formulas for each Trigram are as follows:

$$\text{Qian: } f(AP) = AP + EEG + El - UV \tag{1}$$

$$\text{Dui: } f(SM) = SM + ST - UV \tag{2}$$

$$\text{Li: } f(UV) = UV + ECG + CC + WS - Hu \tag{3}$$

$$\text{Zhen: } f(CC) = CC + Hu - SM \tag{4}$$

$$\text{Xun: } f(WS) = WS + Hu - AP \tag{5}$$

$$\text{Kan: } f(Hu) = Hu + AP + SM - ST - El \tag{6}$$

$$\text{Gen: } f(El) = El + UV - CC \tag{7}$$

$$\text{Kun: } f(ST) = ST + UV - WS \tag{8}$$

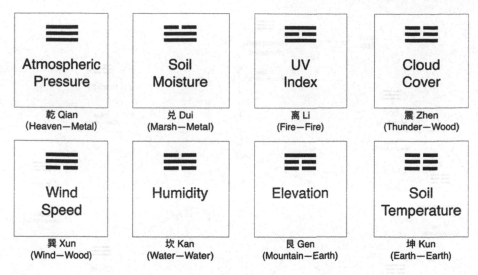

Fig. 14. Data mapping of eight Trigrams

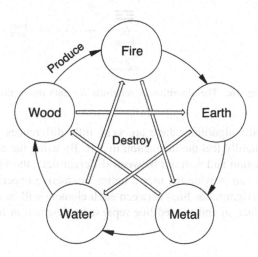

Fig. 15. The production and destruction relations in five elements

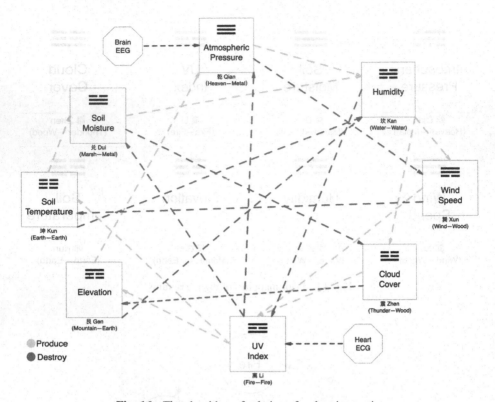

Fig. 16. The algorithm of relations for data interaction

Before we use the algorithm, there are very little differences between each time point, so users can hardly feel the interaction in VR. By using the calculation formulas of the mutual promotion and restraint between different data, the visual effect changes dramatically, which can provide the user a better interactive experience. When a user chooses a different Trigram, the lines between each element will be changed. The green line represents production and the red line represents destruction (shown in Fig. 16).

Fig. 17. Different options presents different hints (Color figure online)

7 Immersive Interaction

For highly immersive visualization purposes, a first-person view is appropriate (shown in Fig. 18). The observer will experience both visual and audio cues. This project is currently available as a prototype application for Oculus Go, which has a relatively high performance/price ratio on the market. This VR headset does not need to be connected to a computer, which makes a better user experience. In terms of software production, we use Unity3D to import the archive files that were previously packaged by the desktop program into the VR main program in batches, and generate an Android program that supports Oculus Go. Based on the characteristics of the device, we design a VR interactive mode according to the mode chosen in the menu.

When a user is in the VR environment, he/she can not only walk around, look around, hear 3D background sound, select scenes, and hide or move visual objects, but also can select different trigrams to explore different visualization and auralization results. For example, when a user chooses Trigram Li, it will begin to rain Trigrams (shown in Fig. 19). He/she can hear the sound of heartbeats and a UV Index data value is loaded for the interactive menu. The users can switch between the real environment and the data environment (shown in Fig. 21), or change the time to see what would happen to the environment then. He/she can even use the controller cursor to select a 3D object to change its appearance (shown in Fig. 20) based on the value of Trigram that he/she chose.

Fig. 18. First-person view

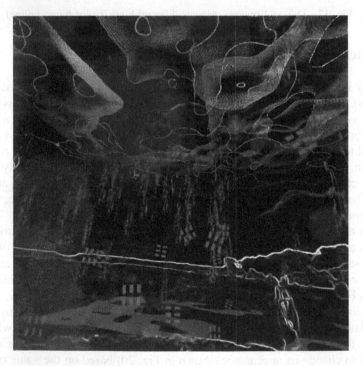

Fig. 19. Trigram rain for notification

Fig. 20. Change the appearance of a tree

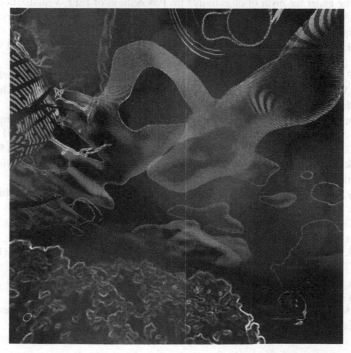

Fig. 21. Sky of data environment

8 Conclusion

In this paper, we introduced a framework and an ongoing project to describe how to design an immersive narrative visualization for conveying subjective experience. We describe the whole process of project Baguamarsh for deliberately expressing subjectivity during information collection, processing, interaction and presentation. These preliminary studies show us the first insights into the potential of immersive data visualization as a subjective storytelling platform and prompt a discussion for future research on conveying subjective experience in personal visual storytelling. More visuals and video from this project can be viewed at https://www.media.mit.edu/projects/baguamarsh/overview/.

Acknowledgments. This study is supported by The Responsive Environments Group at The MIT Media Lab. This group mainly explores how sensor networks augment and mediate human experience, interaction, and perception, while developing new sensing modalities and enabling technologies that create new forms of interactive experience and expression.

References

1. Friendly, M.: Milestones in the history of thematic cartography, statistical graphics, and data visualization (2008)
2. Jorgenson, L., Kritz, R., Mones-Hattal, B., Rogowitz, B., Fraccia, D.F.: Is visualization struggling under the myth of objectivity? In: Proceedings of IEEE Visualization (1995)
3. Thudt, A., Perin, C., Willett, W., Carpendale, S.: Subjectivity in personal storytelling with visualization. Inf. Design J. **23**(1), 48–64 (2017)
4. Segel, E., Heer, J.: Narrative visualization: telling stories with data. IEEE TVCG **16**(6), 1139–1148 (2010)
5. Jiang, F.: A prototype system for saving and representing personal moments. In: Marcus, A., Wang, W. (eds.) HCII 2019. LNCS, vol. 11585, pp. 314–322. Springer, Cham (2019). https://doi.org/10.1007/978-3-030-23538-3_24
6. Mayton, B., et al.: The networked sensory landscape: capturing and experiencing ecological change across scales. Presence Teleoper. Virtual Environ. **26**(2), 182–209 (2017)
7. Tong, C., et al.: Storytelling and visualization: an extended survey. Information **9**, 65 (2018)
8. Donalek, C., et al.: Immersive and collaborative data visualization using virtual reality platforms. In: 2014 IEEE International Conference on Big Data (2014)
9. Endsley, M.R.: Toward a theory of situation awareness in dynamic systems. Hum. Factors: J. Hum. Factors Ergon. Soc. **37**(1), 32–64 (1995)
10. Klein, G., Militello, L.: Some guidelines for conducting a cognitive task analysis. Adv. Hum. Perform. Cognit. Eng. Res. **1**, 161–199 (2001)
11. Bates, J.: Virtual reality, art, and entertainment. J. Teleoper. Virtual Environ. **1**(1), 133–138 (1991)
12. Jennett, C., et al.: Measuring and defining the experience of immersion in games. Int. J. Hum.-Comput. Stud. **66**, 641–661 (2008)
13. Usoh, M., Catena, E., Arman, S., Slater, M.: Using presence questionnaires in reality. Teleoper. Virtual Environ. **9**(5), 497–503 (2000)

14. Garau, M., Slater, M., Vinayagamoorthy, V., Brogni, A., Steed, A., Sasse, M.A.: The impact of avatar realism and eye gaze control on perceived quality of communication in a shared immersive virtual environment. In: Proceedings of the 2003 Conference on Human Factors in Computing Systems, CHI, Ft. Lauderdale, Florida, USA (2003)

15. Heidicker, P., Langbehn, E., Steinicke, F.: Influence of avatar appearance on presence in social VR. In: 2017 IEEE Symposium on 3D User Interfaces (3DUI). IEEE (2017)

16. Schubert, T., Friedmann, F., Regenbrecht, H.: The experience of presence: factor analytic insights. Teleoper. Virtual Environ. **10**(3), 266–281 (2001)

17. Witmer, B.G., Singer, M.J.: Measuring presence in virtual environments: a presence questionnaire. Teleoper. Virtual Environ. **7**(3), 225–240 (1998)

18. Card, M.: Readings in Information Visualization: Using Vision to Think. Morgan Kaufmann, Burlington (1999)

19. Wilhelm, H., Baynes, C.F., Jung, C.G.: The I Ching or Book of Changes. Princeton University Press, Princeton (1997)

20. Yano, K.: AI for taking on the challenges of an unpredictable era. Hitachi Rev. **65**, 35–39 (2016)

21. Russell, S., Paradiso, J.A.: Hypermedia APIs for sensor data: a pragmatic approach to the web of things. In: Proceedings of the 11th International Conference on Mobile and Ubiquitous Systems: Computing, Networking and Services (2014)

Information Visualization-Based Study on Interactive Design of Elderly Health Management Application

Yuzhao Liu[✉]

School of Design Arts and Media, Nanjing University of Science
and Technology, 200, Xiaolingwei Street, Nanjing 210094, Jiangsu, China
694333246@qq.com

Abstract. In the world, the growth of the elderly population is an inevitable trend of social development. The problem of aging affects all aspects of society. In the interface design, designers focus on how to meet the cognitive and behavioral needs of the elderly group, and match the developing design concept with the elderly industry. Based on the concept of information visualization, this paper introduces the operation mechanism of information visualization and then analyzes the relationship between information visualization and the interaction design of elderly health management application. And this article summarizes the functional requirements and design principles of elderly health management application. It is designed to help the elder to get information, process information and take action when using the information interactive interface, so as to obtain a better interactive experience.

Keywords: Information visualization · Interactive design · Elderly · Healthy management

1 Introduction

According to statistics from the United Nations, by 2050, the world's population will reach 9 to 10 billion, of which 2 billion will be over 60 years old and 1.5 billion will be over 65 years old. As the proportion of the elderly population increases, more and more countries will face problems caused by aging, such as the lack of labor, the lack of vitality in society, the weak creativity of the society, the heavy burden of old-age care in the whole society, etc. As the country with the largest number of elderly people, China is facing severe aging issues. In China, in order to cope with the social problems brought about by aging, the government strongly supports the development of the industry to care for the elder, and institutions such as universities and companies have done more and more in-depth research on the elderly.

With the rapid development of computer technology and communication technology, a lot of information has poured into people's lives. Every day, our brains need to process huge amounts of information about working, playing, socializing, and so on. A large amount of information can bring convenience to people's lives, but also will

© Springer Nature Switzerland AG 2020
M. Kurosu (Ed.): HCII 2020, LNCS 12181, pp. 614–624, 2020.
https://doi.org/10.1007/978-3-030-49059-1_45

bring a large cognitive load to everyone. Information visualization studies the visual presentation of large-scale information resources in order to help people understand and analyze information. Information visualization uses graphic technologies and methods to simplify the difficult-to-understand abstract data and structures into a visual expression and interaction. The application of information visualization in interactive interfaces helps designers to continuously optimize the interactive interface. In this way, the interactive interface can better match the user's psychological characteristics and operational methods, so that the user's cognitive efficiency of information is improved.

The elderly health management application combines medical management and computer technology to establish a high-quality health management system for the elderly, including functions such as health monitoring, disease prevention, and disease reminders. Intelligent equipments collect the physical health data of the elderly in real time, and transmit the data to the system. Users can open the app anytime to view physical health data. Based on the physical health of each elderly person, the application develops a detailed health plan for the elderly and will send health knowledge, health warnings and health trend reports to the elderly. In addition, the system will collect health data of the elderly, and then establish an integrated health management system for the elderly through various methods such as statistics, detection, and early warning. The application of health management for the elderly can prevent the occurrence and development of chronic and common diseases, reduce the risk of sudden illness, thereby improving the quality of patient life, reducing medical costs, and achieving comprehensive health management for the elderly. Taking blood pressure monitoring as an example, blood pressure is an important characteristic index for assessing the health status of the elderly, and is closely related to the daily habits and physical conditions of the elderly. The application can not only display the blood pressure data of the elderly in real time, but also predict the future blood pressure through the processing and analysis of the blood pressure data of the elderly for several consecutive days. In this way, the short-term prediction function of the physical health of the population can be realized, and abnormal blood pressure can be found in time. Thereby reducing the incidence of diseases caused by blood pressure. In general, health management plays a very important role in people's lives, especially for the elderly.

Elderly health management application is mainly aimed at the elderly who can take care of themselves. There are a large number of data and chart structures in the elderly health management application, which is not easy to understand. And older people are less likely to adapt to complex interactions. This article discusses how to design a simple interface and a clear way of interaction in elderly health management applications. This article classifies and defines the health information and interactive processes in the health management application for the elderly, and studies the development trend and expression of the health management interactive interface. From the user's perspective, by analyzing the behavioral characteristics of the elderly, find out the factors that affect the cognitive efficiency of the elderly. In combination with these factors, explore how to better present the required information in the design of the interface of the elderly health management application and improve the cognitive efficiency of the elderly. Combined with theoretical research, this article summarizes the design principles of the elderly health management application's interactive interface from the usability principle. Finally, this article gives guidance on the interaction interface of the elderly health management application from the theoretical knowledge and macroscopic aspect.

2 The Relationship Between Information Visualization and Elderly Health Management Application

Information visualization is to convert some boring text information, data information or some abstract relationships into intuitive graphics. This conversion makes it easier for viewers to understand, enhances people's awareness of these abstract information, and thus improves cognitive efficiency. Through the study of information visualization, the data information and graphic language in the interaction interface of the elderly health management application are classified and summarized, so as to explore the information cognition process of the elderly when using the app, and better present the interaction process Information. For the design of the interactive interface of the elderly health management application, information visualization not only focuses on the interaction mode of the interactive interface, but also focuses on the way of information presentation, such as screen size, fonts, graphics, colors, arrangement, and even the shape and arrangement of the keys, the multi-channel way of conveying information and so on. Based on information visualization, the interactive interface design of the elderly health management application can comprehensively consider the foreseeable use scenarios, and explore which design methods and expressions are used to better present the information. The purpose of the information visualization of the interactive interface design of the elderly health management application is to help the elder to better obtain information, process information and make actions when using the information interactive interface, so as to obtain a better interactive experience.

3 Information Visualization

3.1 Definition

The term information visualization was coined by Stuart K. Card, Jock D. Mackinlay, and George G. Robertson in 1989. With the rapid development of information and networks, the development of information and communication is required to develop into composite media, which brings a certain development space for the presentation of information. Information visualization is not limited to visual communication design. It has very close connections with many designs, such as product design, space design, and so on. By visually presenting abstract information, it strengthens human cognitive activities. Although the term information visualization only became popular at the end of the twentieth century, it has appeared in various maps, newspapers, books, news, magazines, and technical documents.

People receive information through perception and vision, and visualization is the process of establishing a mental model of something, thereby strengthening human cognitive activities. Therefore, information visualization is the process of receiving information and processing information based on human cognitive activities. People are not only the recipients of information, but also the creators of information. Information visualization has five characteristics: simple, clear, flow, wordless, and attractive.

3.2 Operation Mechanism

(1) Collection and Sampling of Data. Data is the foundation of information visualization design. Before information is converted into visual graphics, data collection and sampling are essential. Collect data according to the expressed information topics, and organize and analyze the collected content and data. It is important to extract and understand requirement information throughout the collection and sampling process. The more detailed and deeper the understanding of the original information, the richer and more accurate the final visualization process.

(2) Information Architecture. The process of information visualization is shown in Fig. 1. Collect raw information from the outside world, filter and process to form data. Through the analysis and research of the data, new information was formed and the new information was visually transformed. The user decodes and recognizes the information to implement the process of understanding the information. In short, it is the process of structural classification and information processing. The combination of information will help people explain the structure of the framework. The combination of information can be expressed through the time dimension, space dimension and form dimension. For example, people often need to query information such as historical events and query train schedules by time dimension. And people are used to organizing the information environment according to the development of time. The space dimension is related to where to get the information. Different forms of information such as sound, images, and text form a form dimension and are also a way to combine information. These information processing methods can also be understood as the classification of information. Separating the original data from the original information can express the information more effectively and clearly.

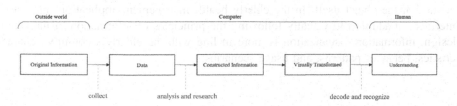

Fig. 1. The process of information visualization

(3) Visual Performance. The visual expression of information visualization is reflected in the final visual expression, displaying information through different fonts, graphics, colors, structures and dynamic effects. Arrange the overall picture according to the internal relationship of the information. As shown in the information visualization chart in Fig. 2, each information visualization chart has its fixed theme and main idea to be conveyed. Arrange the information structure of the screen according to the theme and main ideas. Use different sizes of text, different color blocks, and graphics to represent information.

Fig. 2. Information visualization chart

3.3   Characteristics of Information Visualization

The basic way of communication in people's lives is text and graphics. From birth, people use their feelings, imagination, emotions, and some form of conversation with the products and environment around them. The interface design of the health management application for the elderly is part of the human-computer interaction design, forming an overlapping relationship with most disciplines. Information visualization and interaction design are closely linked. Information visualization design solves the problem of information expression. Based on this, the elderly health management application interaction design provides a better way for users to interact with information.

American psychologist James Jerome Gibson believes that all the bearing characteristics of an object can be intuitive, and its information can be directly expressed in vision. For example, people judge how to open a door based on the shape of the door handle. The information transfer in interactive interface is shown in Fig. 3. An object serves multiple purposes. People will arrange their behavior according to the characteristics of the object itself. In the elderly health management application interactive interface, in addition to visually following the principles of information visualization design, information visualization is more in line with the elderly's cognitive characteristics, behavior patterns, and usage scenarios.

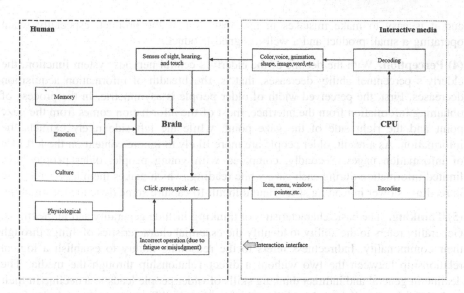

Fig. 3. Information transfer in interactive interface

4 Cognitive and Behavioral Analysis of the Elderly

(1) Vision Sense. As the visual organ, the eye is the most important part of the human perception system. It can make the most direct judgment and positioning of the received information, and plays a very important role in the transmission of information. However, as we age, the human visual organs begin to undergo degenerative changes. The vision of the elderly is reduced, and people's perception of graphics is reduced. They cannot accurately judge and grasp the relationship between them. At the same time, the elderly's color recognition ability has also decreased significantly, especially the distinction between adjacent colors has some difficulties. Vision loss also has a certain negative effect on the psychological activities of the elderly.

(2) Auditory Sense. The auditory organs also decline significantly with age, ears and auditory nerve cells gradually apoptosis, and sensitivity to sound decreases. Studies have found that at the same sound frequency, a 65-year-old needs 10 times the intensity of a 30-year-old's voice to perceive the same sound. This makes the elderly not only have a certain influence on the acquisition of information in daily life, but also their language expression and perception.

(3) Tactile Sense. In the process of information interface interaction, timely information feedback can help the elderly understand the role of interaction and feedback results. The tactile degradation of the elderly is mainly manifested by the aging of the body, the decline of various body functions, the slow metabolism and the reduction of epidermal cells, which makes the skin of the elderly not smooth, dry, and the hands and joints become stiff and rigid. The tactile sensation of the object is significantly reduced, and it is easy to make mistakes in the operation of the product, especially when operating a small product and a well-designed product.

(4) Perception. With the decline of the elderly's central nervous system function, the elderly's perceptual ability decreases, that is, the breadth of information acquisition decreases. First, the perceived width of older people is asymmetric. In the process of obtaining information from the interface, most of the information comes from the gaze point and the right side of the gaze point, while the left side rarely extracts the information. As a result, older people are more likely to ignore content on the left side of information pages. Secondly, compared with young people, older people have limited information during each gaze while reading, which makes them less perceptive in reading, slower in reading speed, and difficult to capture some dynamic information.

(5) Thinking. The basic characteristics of thinking include generality and indirectness. Generality refers to the ability to identify the essential characteristics of things through their commonality. Indirectness refers to the reasoning ability to establish a logical relationship between the two without a direct relationship through the media. The decline in general and indirect thinking skills of older people leads to a decline in their logical thinking and reasoning skills, which makes it difficult to distinguish the functions of interactive operations, predict the outcome of interactions, and understand and derive interactive interfaces with different hierarchical relationships.

(6) Memory. As people get older, memory decline is the most obvious feature. The study found that after 60 years of age, memory began to decline significantly. The main changes are slower memory and smaller range. Memory is reduced, but older people's memory decline is characterized by their deep memory of things before they begin to decline. They have weak memories of recent events, and sometimes they just do things and forget them when they turn around. The decline in memory makes it difficult for older people to accept new things. It often becomes a major obstacle for older people to learn new things, which makes them easy to fear when exposed to new things, instinctively resistant or extremely confident.

(7) Action. As people grow older, their physical fitness will decline, and they will face many physical problems as they age. First, the muscle strength of older people weakens, resulting in slow movements, which hinders rapid interaction. In addition, older people's joints are aging and cannot interact for long periods of time. Finally, the brain control ability of the elderly is reduced, most elderly people experience hand tremor, and some misoperation occurs due to hand tremor.

5 Functional Requirements of Elderly Health Management Application

Elderly health management application is an important data management platform for intelligent elderly care. The system uses information technology and artificial intelligence technology to provide effective solutions for the management and use of elderly health information. It also provides powerful help and support for the comprehensive functions of elderly care institutions and the formulation of policies by relevant government departments. Intelligent elderly health management system can well prevent problems that some elderly people cannot find and treat in time due to sudden illness. Data monitoring can timely understand the health status of the elderly and solve the problems caused by the elderly's untimely detection. Avoid causing unnecessary diseases and prevent accidents. Solve some social problems to a certain extent.

The functions of elderly health management application should include the following:

(1) Health file. When the customer registers, enter the relevant data of the customer into the system and generate health documents for the customer, including personal information, medical reports, health data information, drug information, recommended registration information, health plans, etc. Real-time update of customers' health files based on the health data collected from customers.

(2) Diagnostic report management. After the customer visits the doctor, the diagnostic report will be saved in the system. This allows customers to easily view diagnostic reports and update their health files at any time. When the client sees the doctor again, the doctor can view the client's previous diagnosis report as the basis for the diagnosis.

(3) Health data collection. The system defines health data collection index items in advance, and collects health data of service objects through health collection equipment. Each type of health data corresponds to a collection index entry. The attribute of the index entry is used as the evaluation criterion of the health data. Compare to determine the health of the collection.

(4) Health reminder. When health data changes significantly and health collection tends to be dangerous, alerts are sent to service objects and clients. It can help customers better manage their health and avoid missing the best treatment time.

(5) Health intervention. Develop a health management system and rehabilitation plan for the elderly in need. It can provide clients with rehabilitation training instruction videos, help clients with rehabilitation training and keep them healthy. Customers can set reminder time for training.

(6) Medication management. Centrally manage medications used by customers, such as reminding customers of medications, drug registrations and medication plans. Record each medication record, including any adverse reactions that may occur after the medication, and push it to the family doctor.

(7) Telemedicine. Clients can make remote appointments and referrals through this application and have access to online clinics. In this application, customers can contact their family doctor.

6 Interactive Interface Design Principles of Elderly Health Management Application

At present, although some research has been done on the design of the interface for the elderly at home and abroad, they are unilateral. Some existing information interaction interface designs on the market show a more serious polarization trend. A very feature-rich interface is very popular with most young people. However, this is inconsistent with the cognitive characteristics of the elderly, which will undoubtedly increase their difficulty of operation and cause them to lose self-confidence, and even face such products will have a sense of fear and rejection. The other is an information interaction interface designed for the elderly. The function is too simple and the form is complicated. It can only be used to satisfy some basic functions.

Based on information visualization, this article analyzes the cognitive and behavioral capabilities of the elderly, and summarizes the following design principles:

6.1   Multi-channel Perception

Vision is the most important way for older people to use information interaction interfaces. However, as the vision of the elderly generally declines, it is inevitable that there will be obstacles to perceiving information only in this way. Therefore, it is necessary to use it in combination with other sensing channels to prevent the elderly from encountering obstacles when using the information interaction interface. The perception of the elderly in the interaction process is a very important link. Therefore, in order to ensure the rationality of the design of the sensing system, the following points should be noted:

(1) icon. Icons are very important elements in interface design. They should be concise and clear, and include an appropriate amount of information when designing so that older users can easily perceive the information during the operation. Convenient for the brain to store information faster without being forgotten.

(2) language. Language is the most important form of information transmission, including graphic and text languages. When designing an interactive interface for older people, it's best to choose more graphic languages to convey information, because graphics contain much more information than text. It can reduce cognitive difficulties and memory load in the elderly when receiving information.

(3) color. Color design is an essential step in interface design. It is important to consider the correct use and matching of colors. Studies have shown that older people are less able to distinguish blue colors. Combining the visual characteristics of the elderly, the author believes that when designing the interface of the elderly, try to use contrasting colors instead of adjacent colors.

(4) Feedback. Adding some audible and tactile feedback to the interaction design can help older people understand the interaction to a certain extent, such as changing the color of buttons at the same time when pressing a key, vibration feedback and sound feedback.

(5) perception. The design should be simpler and allow older people more time to read the information. Place more frequently interacting icons and messages on the right side of the interface for easy reading.

6.2   Interface Interaction Design

Human use of any product is an interactive process. How users get the information they need from products and how products communicate known information to users all require designers to communicate information through interface design. This process is interaction design. This article gives some interface interaction design principles based on the behavioral characteristics of the elderly:

(1) Simple interface. Compared with exaggerated and complicated interface design, most seniors prefer a simple interface. The simple and generous background is used to highlight the main functions, eliminating unnecessary trouble caused by visual defects in the elderly during use.

(2) Consistency principle. For interactive interfaces with similar functions, the interface layout should be consistent. This reduces the operational difficulties of the elderly and promotes learning and memory.

(3) Information prompt function. Designers should pay attention to setting the information prompt function during the interface design process, for example, providing the next step help information in the first operation to reduce the user's storage burden.

(4) Real-time feedback. During the use of the user, the interface should feedback the status information of the user operation to the user in real time, so that the user can intuitively grasp the current status.

6.3   Structural Design

Structural design is the framework of the entire interactive interface, which determines its ease of use in the process. It mainly includes two parts: information architecture and information expression.

(1) Information Architecture. The so-called information architecture is a method for unified management of virtual information (such as images, text, and sound) in an interactive interface. The information architecture is based on sufficient data obtained from the survey, is user-centric, understands the needs of users, classifies the functions they need in a structured and systematic way, and prioritizes the most important or commonly used functions to display On the main interface. This is the principle of designing information architecture for ordinary users. Based on the analysis of the behavioral characteristics of the elderly, in the interaction design for the elderly, the memory characteristics of the elderly must be fully considered, and the trade-off between depth and width must be paid attention to. Too deep or too wide can increase memory stress in older people. Research shows that, to a certain extent, width takes precedence over depth. The author believes that in the design of the architecture, attention should be paid to the clarity and clarity of the architecture to avoid redundant architectures and to ensure the accuracy of the logic sequence. Ensure that each functional module can be accessed directly from the home page to reduce redundant operations.

(2) Information Expression. Information expression means that after completing the design of the information architecture, the designer displays the content in the information architecture in a form that the user can understand, such as language and symbols. Designers should try to use a non-proprietary name that matches the habits or familiarity of the target user when doing this part of the design. Allows users to quickly access interactive systems and easily, quickly, and accurately obtain the information they need.

7 Conclusion

As the number of older people continues to expand, the demand for products continues to grow. The research on the interaction interface design for the elderly has important practical significance. This article analyzes and sorts out the cognitive and behavioral characteristics of the elderly. This article actively explores the interface design for the elderly. However, in the course of the research, due to the constraints of various factors, the whole is still incomplete and is still in its infancy, and needs to be further improved. It is hoped to provide a reference for the research work on the interaction interface design for the elderly.

References

1. Angeli, D., Brahnam, S., Wallis, P.: Abuse: the darker side of human computer interaction. Paper presented at the Interact 2005, Rome, Italy (2005)
2. Sternberg, R.J.: Cognitive Psychology. China Light Industry Press, Beijing (2016)
3. Kunz, W.: Issues as elements of information systems, vol. **50**(35) 221–244(24) (1970)
4. Yi, J.S., Kang, Y.A., Stasko, J., et al.: Toward a deeper understanding of the role of interaction in information visualization. IEEE Trans. Vis. Comput. Graph. **13**(6), 1224–1231 (2007)
5. Masui, T., Tsukada, K., Siio, I.: Mousefield: a simple and versatile input device for ubiquitous computing. Ipsj J. **46**, 319–328 (2004)
6. Schuppler, B., Ernestus, M., Scharenborg, O., et al.: HMI interface design of engineering machinery based on MiniGUI. Constr. Mach. Technol. Manage. **39**(1), 96–109 (2008)

A Hashing Algorithm of Depth Image Matching for Liver Surgery

Satoshi Numata[✉], Masanao Koeda, Katsuhiko Onishi,
Kaoru Watanabe, and Hiroshi Noborio

Osaka Electro-Communication University, Shijonawate, Osaka 5750063, Japan
numata@osakac.ac.jp

Abstract. As we have been developing a liver surgical navigation system that uses a scanned 3D liver model of the patient, we have pointed the necessity of the efficient posture estimation from depth images to be matched with the posture of a virtual liver rendered on a computer. We have previously used the technique of calculating the sum of squared errors using whole pixels contained in the depth images, and have compared over nine images simultaneously using the technique for the posture estimation. However, it requires a massive number of calculation repetition and that could be a barrier to the real time navigation through the surgery. In this paper, we propose a new method for comparing depth images and estimating postures by hashing the depth images vertically and horizontally. The liver postures can be identified by calculating 25 dimensional integer hashed values with the accuracy around 90%. By combining the previous posture estimation techniques with this method, the efficiency of the navigation system should be increased for the practical use in the real time surgical environment.

Keywords: Liver surgery support · Navigation · Hashing

1 Introduction

Liver surgery requires a very precise treatment, because a liver contains several types of blood vessels such as arteries or veins inside its soft organ. Surgeons have often used X-ray imaging, computed tomography (CT) scanning, or magnetic resonance imaging (MRI) in two dimensional way, in which exact locations of vessels cannot be determined. In most of the cases, surgeons have to use projected data around the liver on two dimensional monitors during the surgery. Therefore, we are developing a liver surgical navigation system that helps surgeons to compare a liver STL data scanned from a patient with an operating liver in three dimensional way in real time. We have developed a system for liver surgery navigation by tracking knife positions and liver states using the STL liver model [1–4]. We have also examined its performance from the aspect of the algorithm [5], from the aspect of the inter-process communication cost [6], and from the aspect of the shape characteristics of the liver [7].

In this paper, we introduce a hashing algorithm to simplify the calculation of comparison between two depth images of a liver. Since the liver has a very unique shape, the shape can help us to identify the exact direction. Instead of comparing all

© Springer Nature Switzerland AG 2020
M. Kurosu (Ed.): HCII 2020, LNCS 12181, pp. 625–634, 2020.
https://doi.org/10.1007/978-3-030-49059-1_46

pixels in the images, we propose that just sampling a number of pixels might enough to compare the depth images of the liver. We examine that the hashing can be applied to the depth images from all direction, and verify that every hashing values can be different values that indicate unique postures of the liver.

2 Liver Surgical Navigation System

2.1 System Overview

The goal of our system is to track the liver deformation and navigate surgeons according to the paths previously prepared using the liver models scanned from patients, and to alert surgeons visually and audibly to be careful around the high risk areas with important vessels. Figure 1 shows the system image. This system uses one depth camera to get depth images of a liver, and a marker camera to track a position of a knife. Inside the system, OpenGL is rendering STL liver data from many directions to estimate the exact posture of the real liver.

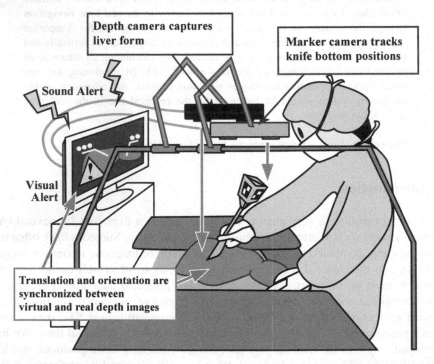

Fig. 1. System overview of the liver surgery navigation system.

This system receives a depth image of the real liver using a depth camera at certain intervals, and extrapolates its exact position and rotation to show the virtual liver on a screen overlapping on the real liver to navigate surgeons. To compare the depth image with the other depth image derived from rendered STL liver data on a computer, it is required to calculate how much those images are in the same condition. We have used the sum of squared errors to perform the calculation, but this method involves a large number of iteration for each pixel of those images, and that can be a barrier for the real time navigation of the liver surgery.

2.2 Liver Surgical Navigator

The liver surgical navigator shows the status of the virtual liver, whose translation and orientation are synchronized with the real liver via the liver posture estimator that is described next. It also shows the estimated knife position via the knife position estimator using the marker camera. Figure 2 shows the experimental implementation of the navigator.

We are currently trying to improve the efficiency and accuracy of the liver and knife posture estimation for better navigation using this system.

Fig. 2. The liver surgical navigator to check the liver status using STL data

2.3 Liver Posture Estimator

The liver posture estimator repeats comparing depth images from the depth camera and from the OpenGL rendering buffers to estimate the current liver posture. Both depth images from the depth camera and OpenGL are image-processed and converted to binary (black and white) images. Figure 3 shows how the real liver model (A), binary depth image of the liver(B) and the depth image rendered on the graphics memory using OpenGL (C).

Both binary converted depth images are expressed as OpenCV matrices in our system. There is a function that compares those OpenCV matrices in the liver posture estimator. By changing the implementation of the function, we can change the comparison algorithms, so that we can optimize the efficiency and accuracy of the liver posture estimation.

(a)   **(b)**   **(c)**

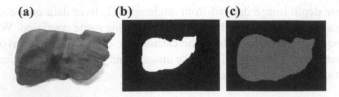

Fig. 3. Real liver model (A), a depth of real liver (B), and a depth of virtual liver (C)

Figure 4 shows the comparison between a depth image of a real liver and multiple depth images of virtual livers with several different rotations. By performing the depth image comparisons, one posture of the real liver is estimated.

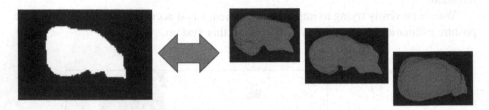

Fig. 4. Comparison between real depth image and virtual depth images

We have shown that the depth image of the liver has very characteristic shape [7]. The scores calculated by comparing binary images (with just black and white pixels) can beautifully tend to a specific rotation that enables tracking the liver posture shown as Fig. 5.

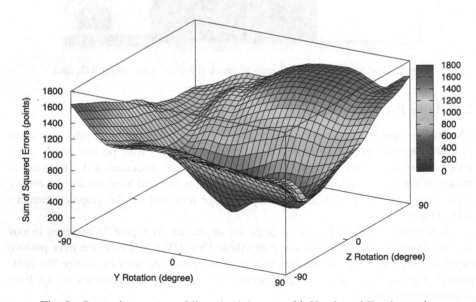

Fig. 5. Comparison scores of liver depth images with Y-axis and Z-axis rotations

2.4   Data Flow

The liver posture estimator periodically takes depth images from the depth camera, and compares the shape with Polyhedrons rendered on the memory for finding the exact location of the liver and its orientation. Figure 6 shows the data flow of the navigation system and how they are converted through the system.

The accuracy of the posture estimation is important for tracking liver state and displaying navigation information over the virtual liver. To improve the accuracy, both of the performance of depth image comparison and the performance of posture tracking are important to be investigated.

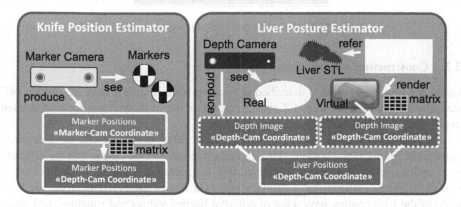

Fig. 6. Data flow of the navigation system

3   Hashing Algorithm for Posture Estimation

3.1   Basic Idea of Hashing

To calculate a set of the hashed value for a depth image of the rotated liver, we start from finding a contour of the depth image. Starting from the left edge and right edge, find x coordinates of the first column that includes at least one white pixel. Do the same thing from the top edge and bottom edge, find y coordinates of the first row that includes at lease one white pixel. This can find the contour - outline of the liver body, which is indicated by green lines in Fig. 7. The aspect ratio of the contour (0.69 in the case of Fig. 7) will be one of the hashing value and used later.

After the contour was found, we divide the horizontal and vertical edges of the contour equally. The blue lines in Fig. 7 shows the division. In the case of the figure, the division count is set 5, so the inside area of the contour are equally divided into 25 areas. Along the blue lines, left/right edges and top/bottom edges are detected. Those edges are marked as blue circles in the figure. The x and y coordinate values are normalized into the range [0, 1], and those values (and the aspect ratio of the contour) will be used to represent the rotation of the liver as a set of hashed values.

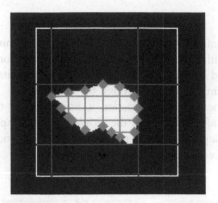

Fig. 7. Find contour and hashing the depth image

3.2 Constructing a Hash Table

Using the hashing algorithm described above, we have rotated a liver from 0 to 360° stepping 10° on each X, Y, and Z axes, to calculate the hashed values for each rotated depth images of the liver, shown as Fig. 8.

Of course, the same hashed values (hashed value collision) can be calculated sometimes for different rotations. This includes two cases. One case is that the different x, y, and z rotation degrees are combined into the identical rotation. The other case is that the different rotations have similar shapes (in binary image). Therefore, the hash table of the liver posture have a list of different hashed values and rotations, and chain rotations that have same hashed values (they are referred as siblings later in this paper) as linked lists. Figure 9 shows how the hash table is represented as a class in C++ programming language.

When the division is performed with the size of 3 × 3 to 8 × 8, the number of maximum siblings is around 36, and the average number of siblings is 2.

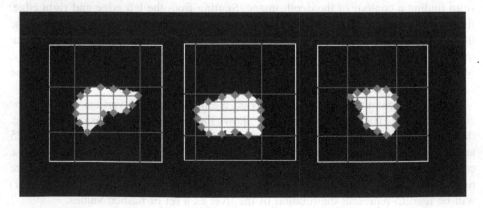

Fig. 8. Rotating a liver to create a hash table

```cpp
struct RotHash {
    cv::Vec3f    rotation;
    float        hash_values[(DIV_COUNT-1)*4+1];
    RotHash      *next;
};

struct RotHashTable {
    std::vector<RotHash *>    hashes;
};
```

Fig. 9. C++ code that represents a hash table of liver rotations

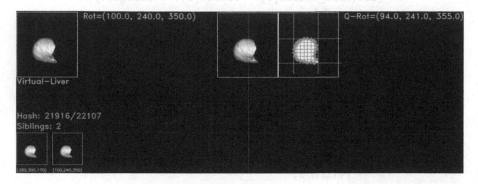

Fig. 10. Hash with two siblings

Figure 10 shows the case of a set of hashed values that have two siblings. Like this case, most of the hashed values have two siblings that indicate the same rotation with different x, y, and z axes values. Figure 11 shows the case of the maximum 36 siblings.

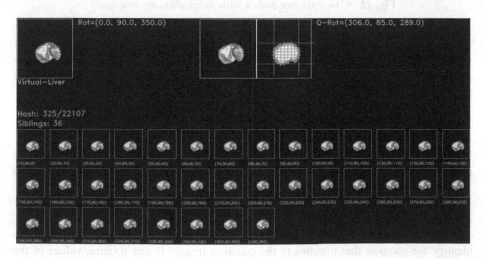

Fig. 11. Hash with many siblings

3.3   Identifying a Posture Using the Hash Table

The hash table now maps hash values to the specific rotations. Now we can calculate a set of hashed values using the hashing algorithm for a depth image, and look up the hash table for the same set of the hashed values to get a specific rotation.

However, considering noises and other environmental influences, we have to allow a certain amount of ambiguity when looking up the hash table. Therefore, the looking up is performed as shown in Fig. 12.

```cpp
bool RotHash::CheckHashValues(int values[], int ambiguity) const {
    for (int i = 0; i < (DIV_COUNT - 1) * 4 + 1; i++) {
        if (abs(hash_values[i] - values[i]) > ambiguity) {
            return false;
        }
    }
    return true;
}


int RotHashTable::FindHashIndex(int values[]) {
    for (int ambiguity = 0; ambiguity <= 10; ambiguity++) {
        for (int i = 0; i < list.size(); i++) {
            if (list[i]->CheckHashValues(values, ambiguity)) {
                return i;
            }
        }
    }
    return -1;
}
```

Fig. 12. C++ code that finds a hash index allowing ambiguity

We use an integer value changing from 0 to 10 that indicates the ambiguity, and the value is used for regarding a set of hashed values that is slightly different from the pre-calculated values. As we describe later, this achieves the accuracy of the hash table hit to approximately 90%.

3.4   Accuracy Test

To check how much the hashing technique can afford us the effective navigation, we performed the accuracy test using the hash table. We tried different division size from 3×3 to 9×9, and compared the accuracies.

At the beginning of the test, X-axis, Y-axis, and Z-axis rotation values are randomly generated from 0 to 359° each. We render the virtual liver on the OpenGL display, and get the depth image as a question image. Next, use the hash table to identify the rotation that matches to the question image. If any rotation values of the siblings is very close to the original question rotation, the system get one point as a score. We repeated this for 500 times for each division size settings. Figure 13 shows the result of the accuracy comparison.

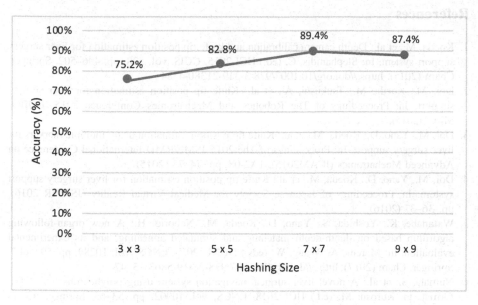

Fig. 13. Accuracy of posture estimation by hashing

From the division size of 3 × 3, the accuracy is not bad. The result of 7 × 7 and 9 × 9 shows that they are almost the maximum resolution of the hash table lookup. They indicate very high accuracy of the posture estimation just by looking up a set of simple hashed values. We can use this technique to increase the efficiency of the posture estimation system, and even if the look up failed in the case of 10.6% to 12.6%, we can get back to the conventional tracking techniques published in [6, 7].

4   Conclusion

In this paper, we proposed a new method to identify the rotation by using the hashed values. Though the same values can be calculated in some cases as siblings, we can manage those values using linked list. This technique does not require full pixel comparisons nor multiple virtual liver renderings. Instead, just looking up for a set of hashed values with a certain amount of ambiguity can instantly identify the rotation, thanks to the characteristic shape of the liver.

In the future, we would like to examine the efficiency of the whole system combining this technique with the conventional model tracking techniques.

Acknowledgement. This research was supported by Grants-in-Aid for Scientific Research (No. 26289069) from the Ministry of Education, Culture, Sports, Science and Technology (MEXT), Japan.

References

1. Koeda, M., et al.: Depth camera calibration and knife tip position estimation for liver surgery support system. In: Stephanidis, C. (ed.) HCI 2015. CCIS, vol. 528, pp. 496–502. Springer, Cham (2015). https://doi.org/10.1007/978-3-319-21380-4_84
2. Doi, M., Koeda, M., Tsukushi, A., et al.: Kinfe tip position estimation for liver surgery support. In: Proceedings of The Robotics and Mechatronics Conference 2015 (ROBO-MECH2015), 1A1-E01 (2015)
3. Doi, M., Yano, D., Koeda, M., et al.: Knife tip position estimation using multiple markers for liver surgery support. In: Proceedings of The 2015 JSME/RMD International Conference on Advanced Mechatronics (ICAM2015), 1A2-08, pp. 74–75 (2015)
4. Doi, M., Yano, D., Koeda, M., et al.: Knife tip position estimation for liver surgery support system. In: Proceedings of Japanese Society for Medical Virtual Reality (JSMVR 2016), pp. 36–37 (2016)
5. Watanabe, K., Yoshida, S., Yano, D., Koeda, M., Noborio, H.: A new organ-following algorithm based on depth-depth matching and simulated annealing, and its experimental evaluation. In: Marcus, A., Wang, W. (eds.) DUXU 2017. LNCS, vol. 10289, pp. 594–607. Springer, Cham (2017). https://doi.org/10.1007/978-3-319-58637-3_47
6. Numata, S., et al.: A novel liver surgical navigation system using polyhedrons with STL-format. In: Kurosu, M. (ed.) HCI 2018. LNCS, vol. 10902, pp. 53–63. Springer, Cham (2018). https://doi.org/10.1007/978-3-319-91244-8_5
7. Numata, S., Koeda, M., Onishi, K., Watanabe, K., Noborio, H.: Performance and accuracy analysis of 3D model tracking for liver surgery. In: Kurosu, M. (ed.) HCII 2019. LNCS, vol. 11567, pp. 524–533. Springer, Cham (2019). https://doi.org/10.1007/978-3-030-22643-5_41

Automatic Deformation Detection and Analysis Visualization of 3D Steel Structures in As-Built Point Clouds

Rogério Pinheiro de Souza[1]($\boxtimes$), César A. Sierra-Franco[2],
Paulo Ivson Netto Santos[2], Marina Polonia Rios[2],
Daniel Luiz de Mattos Nascimento[3], and Alberto Barbosa Raposo[1]

[1] Department of Informatics, Tecgraf Institute, Pontifical Catholic University of Rio de Janeiro (PUC-Rio), Gávea, Rio de Janeiro 22451-900, Brazil
`{rogerps,abraposo}@tecgraf.puc-rio.br`
[2] Tecgraf Institute, Pontifical Catholic University of Rio de Janeiro (PUC-Rio), Gávea, Rio de Janeiro 22451-900, Brazil
`{casfranco,psantos,marina.rios}@tecgraf.puc-rio.br`
[3] CERTI Foundation - Centro de Referências de Tecnologias Inovadoras, Florianópolis, Brazil
`dln@certi.org.br`

Abstract. The use of Building Information Modeling (BIM) is a growing reality in the civil industry. Merging 3D geometric information with engineering data, the BIM model combines geometry, spatial relationships, and other properties used at all stages of the building's life cycle. With the need to apply such methodology to existing buildings, researchers have focused on how to automatically generate or update such models from 3D point clouds provided by laser scanning sensors or photogrammetry methods. Most of this research has focused on the recognition of either planar (e.g., floor, walls) or cylindrical (e.g., piping) structures. Few works have dealt with the detection of steel structural elements, due to its particular shape, and only recently focused on detecting their geometric specifications. However, in these approaches, the point cloud of each structural element was manually separated from the point cloud of the entire building. This situation creates a challenge since the manual segmentation of a point cloud is a long and subjective process. In addition to geometric information, recent research has focused on automatically detecting anomalies in structures. Such information, incorporated into the BIM model, allows the structural element to be evaluated using structural analysis applications. The availability of the results of this analysis to BIM professionals is essential for the correct planning of possible interventions. Unfortunately, open-source BIM model visualization tools restrict their functionalities to design review and construction analysis. In this work, we propose an extension of a previous automated method to detect steel elements to identify and measure deformations and a visualization tool that shows the quality of an existing building's structural elements directly in the 3D point cloud. With the results of deformation detection, we compute the quality level of structural

© Springer Nature Switzerland AG 2020
M. Kurosu (Ed.): HCII 2020, LNCS 12181, pp. 635–654, 2020.
https://doi.org/10.1007/978-3-030-49059-1_47

elements and present it directly in the 3D view of the building, preserving its spatial context, with the use of colors and annotations.

Keywords: Visualization · BIM · Anomalies · Structural elements

1 Introduction

Building Information Modeling (BIM) is a methodology based on digital technologies developed in the Architecture, Engineering, Construction, Operation, and Maintenance (AECOM) industry [26]. Applied at all stages of the building's life cycle, it improves communication and decision making among stakeholders. Initially, BIM was employed to allow the realization of a project with more accurate estimates of time and cost. Later research has demonstrated several other advantages in its use, such as consistencies verification in the design phase, structural and energy analysis, and facility management, among others [15,62]. More recently, it has been used in maintenance, refurbishment, and deconstruction phases, especially in industrialized countries [51]. It is important, therefore, to maintain up-to-date BIM models of existing facilities.

A BIM model consists of a virtual representation of real buildings through semantically enriched and consistent digital models. Objects must contain geometric and non-geometric attributes with semantic (aggregation or contention), topological (spatial relationships), or functional information (e.g., cost and material amounts), allowing deeper analysis of the construction [65].

A popular method for the generation and updating the BIM model of an existing building is by using a 3D point cloud provided by laser scanning or photogrammetry methods. The 3D point cloud represents the current external geometry of the structure. This 3D point cloud is an unstructured set of points without any classification. It needs to be processed so that the building elements can be correctly identified. When done manually, this process is long, subjective, requires specialized people, and is prone to errors [32]. For these reasons, several research has focused on automating this process.

Early work explored the automatic generation of a 3D geometric model from the point cloud. Most of this research has focused on the recognition of either planar (e.g., floor, ceiling, walls) or cylindrical (e.g., piping) structures. Detection of structural steel elements, typically columns, and beams, remains a poorly researched area due to its particular shape and small dimensions of its components. Only recently, a few works have been able to detect some of their specifications (e.g., profile, web and flange dimensions). However, in these approaches, the point cloud of each structural element was manually separated from the point cloud of the entire building.

This gap motivates a study to propose a method to automatically detect the structural steel elements and its geometric features in a 3D point cloud without the need for previous segmentation. The basic idea of our approach was first presented in [56] where we combined a slice approach with image processing and a machine learning strategy. The proposed method shows excellent results

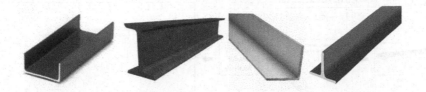

Fig. 1. Steel elements automatically detected by the proposed method. From left to right: C, I, L, and T-shapes.

in tests carried out in simulated scenarios, detecting with more than 94% of precision four types of steel structural shapes: C, I, L, and T-shapes (Fig. 1).

Moreover, steel structures present several types of anomalies over time, including deformation due to loads of hanging facilities (such as lamps, fire systems, ventilation ducts, air conditioning units, etc.) and corrosion due to the steel features and the action of the environment. In addition to geometric information, research has focused on detecting these types of anomalies automatically in steel structures using 3D point clouds and images [21, 41]. Such information, incorporated into the BIM model, allows the structural element to be evaluated using applications that perform structural analysis. The knowledge of the quality of the structural elements is of utmost importance to plan countermeasures necessary for structural integrity. The availability of this information to the responsible professionals is essential for the correct planning of possible interventions in the built environment. Visualization tools can play a key role in this situation highlighting the most compromised elements. Unfortunately, open-source BIM model visualization tools are restricted to present features and to provide functionalities for design review and construction analysis. Therefore, the existence of a visualization tool with InfoVis features [27] that highlights the severity level of the structural elements will allow the user a better understanding of its real situation.

These aspects motivate this study, which proposes a visualization system that presents the quality of building structural elements directly in the 3D point cloud. Using our proposed method to automatically detect the structural elements, we extend it to identify and measure some types of deformations. With this information, we compute the quality level of structural elements and present it to the user directly in the 3D view of the building. Using the annotations and color scheme features, the system presents the most compromised elements according to the severity level (Fig. 2). The visualization of the quantitative and qualitative information of the deformations together with their spatial context allows the responsible engineer a richer and more accurate analysis of the actual situation of the structure.

This work is organized as follows. Section 2 presents an overview of previous work related to detection of objects in point clouds and BIM visualization tools. Section 3 describes our proposed method. In Sect. 4.1 we detail our approach to assess anomalies and represent such results visually. Section 5 presents details of

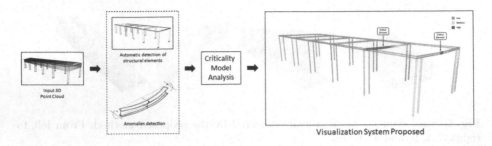

Fig. 2. Proposed visualization tool.

the implementation, the results obtained and a discussion about the effectiveness of our method. Finally, Sect. 6 summarizes the conclusions and suggestions for future work.

2   Related Work

A 3D point cloud is a set of points, represented by its X, Y, and Z coordinates, that represents the external geometry of existing structures. A common method to generate these datasets with high precision is LIDAR (Light Detection And Ranging), where sensors obtain the position of each point using reflected laser light. The steady evolution of this technology has produced more and more accurate devices over time [4,6]. The combination of LIDAR with other kinds of sensors allows adding more information to the captured dataset, such as colors and thermal information [31].

Laser scanning technology can be used in several applications, such as: generation of existing construction models [10,14], construction progress tracking [19,59], health monitoring of structures [49,53] and even in autonomous vehicles [29,44]. These demands have encouraged the research and development of several techniques to process 3D point cloud data. Over time, systematic reviews of techniques for generating existing building models from point clouds have also been devised [58,61,63]. Despite the evolution of existing solutions, the automatic detection of solid models from point clouds remains a major challenge. Therefore, human intervention is still necessary to generate a reliable BIM model.

According to Wang [63], the most popular detection approaches can be classified in 4 categories: (1) geometric shape descriptor, (2) hard-coded knowledge, (3) supervised learning, and (4) matching by alignment with existing BIM.

Geometric shape descriptor based approach is suitable when the CAD model of the object is available. Using local, semi-local and global descriptors previously calculated for CAD models in a database, a search for the target object is performed comparing with descriptors calculated for some points in the cloud [23,38].

Hard-coded knowledge-based approach uses a prior understanding of elements for object detection. In the first step, a point cloud segmentation is applied to divide the data into homogeneous regions with similar properties (normal, curvature, color, etc.). RANSAC (RANdom SAmple Consensus) [28,55], Hough Transform [18,33] or region growing methods [24,39,40] are common strategies used to detect planar or cylindrical regions. Common primitive types in buildings are planar (walls, ceilings and floors) and cylindrical surfaces (pipes). Using domain knowledge, research have been able to recognize elements specific to the BIM model (e.g., vertical planes can be classified as walls; holes can be classified as windows; cylinders as plumbing systems; etc.) [25,37,66,68].

Supervised learning-based approach uses machine learning methods to classify point cloud data in object categories. The classification process can be applied directly to the points, using features such as geometric properties and colors, or segments, after the application of some segmentation method. This approach has wide applicability and is able to handle objects with complex geometries, like light poles [34] and construction equipment [22]. However, the disadvantage of this approach is the necessity of a large labeled dataset to train the classifier properly. Recent research has used this approach with deep learning algorithms [52,64].

Matching by alignment with an existing BIM-based approach aligns point cloud data with a reference BIM model to recognize the scene objects. Using its geometric and semantic features, each point is matched to a model element. This approach is normally used to detect differences from what was defined in the design phase (as-designed) to what was really constructed (as-built/as-is) and to infer the semantic information for the new elements found [19,47].

Detection of steel structural elements, typically columns and beams, remains a poorly researched area. Most previous work focused on concrete structures such as bridge constructions [46,53,60]. Anil [12] investigated the influence of data acquisition methods and small dimensions of steel structural components as challenges to identify steel sections, using manual methods to measure the accuracy of the point cloud acquired. Cabaleiro et al. [20] proposed an automated method using Hough transform to detect flange and web lines of steel frame connections, but their thickness were not identified. [42,67] are the works that come closest to this objective, presenting methods to detect the steel section's shape type and its normative features (height, width, web and flange thickness). However, these require that the point cloud of the structural element to be manually segmented from the scene. In [56], Souza et al. present an approach that combines image processing and a machine learning strategy to detect steel structure elements in a 3D point cloud of existing buildings, without the need for previous segmentation.

In the field of analysis of deformed beams, early research focused on detecting only bending in beam's point cloud [30,43]. In [21], Cabaleiro et al. proposed an algorithm to compute bending and torsion from point cloud using a surface polynomial to fit points previously segmented as a flange. Jafari et al. [36] proposed a method for deformation tracking, comparing changes in element's point cloud over time.

In visualization field, the concept of BIM model, which allows the inclusion of any type of information useful to the building life cycle, creates many opportunities for different kinds of visualization research. According to Ivson et al. [35], the BIM domain still remains largely unexplored by this community. The authors found that about 90% of the visualization research in the BIM area until 2017 is concentrated in the design review and construction analysis phases. Operations phase, which includes stages such as asset management and facility maintenance, is still a poorly researched area. In this systematic review, only two works were cited for applying visualization to the use case denominated *damage assessment* [11,13]. However, in both, the research focused on the method of building analysis based on the BIM model and not on visualization of anomalies.

The current work aims to contribute with two research areas. First, extending the method proposed in [56] to detect deformations using the element point cloud. Second, presenting a tool to visualize quantitative and qualitative information of the detected deformations with the use of annotations and a color scheme applied directly to the 3D point cloud.

3   Proposed Method

In this section, we describe our method for detection of structural steel elements and deformations in a 3D point cloud (Fig. 3). The first seven steps compose the method proposed in [56] to automatically detect the structural steel elements and its geometric features in a 3D point cloud without the need for previous segmentation. In this work, we added the eighth step to compute deformations for each element detected. In the following subsections, we summarize the method to detect the structural elements and describe in detail the extension to compute some types of deformations.

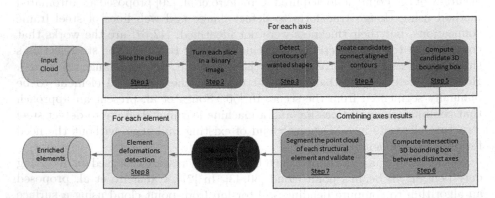

Fig. 3. Summary of the proposed method to automatic detection of steel elements and deformations in a point cloud.

3.1   Elements Detection

To detect structural steel elements and its geometric features in a 3D point cloud without the need for previous segmentation, [56] proposed a method that combines a slice approach with image processing and a machine learning strategy. The point cloud is divided into slices along the canonical axes to detect desired cross-section shapes. This work focus on the detection of C, I, L, and T-shapes; however, the method can be extended to other shapes as well. This method is split in seven steps:

Step 1: Division of the Point Cloud in Slices Along an Axis. In the first step, we divide the the the point cloud P into a set of slices $S = \{S_0, S_1, ..., S_n\}$, each one with a thickness equal to a predefined value Δs (except the last one, which may be smaller).

Step 2: Transforming a Slice into a Binary Image. In this step, we transform each slice S_i generated along the canonical axis A into a binary image I_i. Using a predefined value Δp for the pixel size in millimeters, we define a transformation to map each point in the slice from the cloud coordinate system to image coordinate system.

Step 3: Detection of Elements' Cross-Sections in Binary Images. The goal of this step is to detect geometric shapes that correspond to cross-sections of the wanted elements. This process is performed for each binary generated image. To achieve this, we create a hybrid method combining the results of two strategies, using image processing and machine learning techniques (Fig. 4).

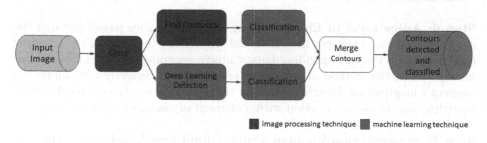

Fig. 4. Hybrid method to detect and classify elements' cross-sections.

In the first strategy, we apply the topological operator for edge contour detection created by [57] to obtain the contours of elements in an image. However, this technique was not be able to detect correctly the wanted structural elements when they were attached to larger elements such as walls and roofs. To solve this problem, we implemented a second strategy by training an object detection model based on deep learning techniques to detect the wanted shapes of cross-sections [54]. Despite solving the problem not solved by the first strategy, this strategy generates several false positives. Thence, we implemented a process to discard false positives contours reported by the object detection model, according to their classification and the number of connections with other elements in the image. We chose to use both strategies to take advantage of each technique, merging the valid contours found by each one.

In classification step, we used a machine learning strategy for contour classification [16]. We created a synthetic image dataset with cross-section contours for the four wanted shapes, with different dimensions and flange and web thickness, for training process. We also add to the dataset cross-sections to be detected as undesired shapes. This classification strategy allows us to extend the method to other shapes by just adding examples of the new desired shape in the training process.

Step 4: Contour Alignment and Element Candidate Generation. After the method detects all wanted cross-sections in all slices along a specific canonical axis, they are grouped as element candidates according to classification provided by the machine learning algorithm and the distance between the contours centers. It is important to emphasize that the cross-sections of a given group do not need to belong to neighboring slices. During the 3D scanning process, other objects may have obstructed the structural elements. Therefore, the point cloud may have discontinuous regions.

Step 5: Bounding Box Calculation and Final Element Definition. Using all of the cross-sections that form an element candidate, we compute its 3D bounding box. As the scanning process could generate an incomplete point cloud due to occlusions or even because the sensor cannot reach the entire surface of the object, we combine the candidates that have their 3D bounding boxes intersecting in a single element. After the end of all the necessary combinations, the method defines the resulting set as the set of structural elements in the scene.

Step 6: Adjustment of Element Length. When a slice passes through the connection of two elements in orthogonal directions, the process of detecting the contours in the corresponding binary image generates contours classified as invalid. Thus, the method identifies the cross-sections correctly only along the element's longitudinal direction. To solve this problem, we stretch the element's bounding box to the intersection with a element of another canonical axis.

Step 7: Segmentation Element Point Cloud and Validation. The goal of this final step is to segment each element's point cloud and validate it. Using its bounding box, this process is executed in two sub-steps. In the first sub-step, we filter the point cloud so that the point belongs to the element if it is inside the element's bounding box and over any of the contours found in step 3. In the second sub-step, we use a strategy proposed by [42] to infer the cross-section shape with higher accuracy. We used the kernel density estimation (KDE) to detect web and flanges through local maximum peaks of probability density shape (PDS). Hence, according to the number and local peaks, the element shape is re-evaluated. Elements re-classified as invalid are discarded.

3.2   Deformation Detection

Deformation is one of the most common types of anomalies found in steel structures due to loads of hanging facilities, such as lamps, fire systems, ventilation ducts, air conditioning units, etc. The traditional practice of detecting anomalies through visual inspections relies heavily on personal judgment, observation skills, and the experience of inspectors. Therefore, as already mentioned in the related work section (Sect. 2), several work have been proposing methods to automate the detection of anomalies. In this subsection, we describe how, using the information generated by the element detection method, we automatically check the existence of deformations in the detected elements.

The goal of this method extension is to detect two types of deformations: bending and torsion. According [17], bending characterizes the behavior of a slender structural element subjected to an external load applied perpendicularly to a longitudinal axis of the element (Fig. 5a). Torsion is the twisting of an object due to an applied torque (Fig. 5b).

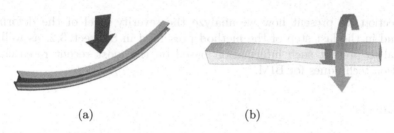

(a)   (b)

Fig. 5. (a) bending deformation; (b) torsion deformation   (figures taken from Wikipedia).

As mentioned in Sect. 3.1, the detection method slices the point cloud orthogonal to the longitudinal axis of the element. After detection, each slice contains a subset of the element's point cloud (Fig. 6a). For each slice, we compute the oriented bounding box of its points. Projecting this oriented bounding box on a plane orthogonal to the longitudinal axis of the element, we have an oriented rectangle. For this rectangle, we compute its center and the smallest angle between one side and the vertical direction (Fig. 6b).

We compute bending and torsion values relative to first slice (one of element's extreme). The bending of a slice, B_{S_i}, is computed as:

$$B_{S_i} = dist(center(ORect_{S_i}), center(ORect_{S_0}))   \tag{1}$$

where $ORect_{S_i}$ is oriented rectangle of slice i (Fig. 6b). The torsion of slice i, T_{S_i}, is computed as:

$$T_{S_i} = \alpha_i - \alpha_0   \tag{2}$$

where α_i is the smallest angle between one side of the oriented rectangle and the vertical direction (Fig. 6b). The values of bending and torsion calculated for

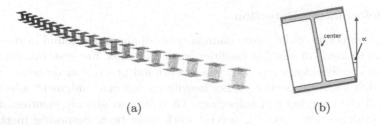

(a)   (b)

Fig. 6. (a) Point cloud of some slices of a detected element; (b) oriented rectangle generated by the projection of the oriented bounding box in the plane orthogonal to the longitudinal axis of the element.

each element slice will be used to analyze its severity level, as explained in the next section.

4   Deformation Analysis and Visualization

In this section we present how we analyze the severity level of the deformations found in the last step of the method presented in Subsect. 3.2, as well as a proposal to present such information based on the most recent research in visualization techniques for BIM.

4.1   Analysis

Deformation analysis of structural elements is a complex discipline. Several factors can be considered depending on the type of analysis that the engineer wants to perform. For example, some building codes state that in the analysis of the bending suffered by an element, factors such as its orientation and its function must be considered [1]. In this case, such factors define the severity level for bending as a function of a percentage of the element length.

Torsion may be critical to steel structural elements with open cross-section shapes (such as C, I, L and T-shapes). These profiles present flanges with free ending that are prone to buckling. The torsional displacements change the stresses distributions on the profile and may cause concentrations on such flanges that may buckle locally, changing the geometric properties of the element [48]. The presence of any torsional damage should be highlighted in the inspection results as a severe damage condition.

In this work, the focus is on how the visualization tool should present the result of the analysis. With the support of professionals specialized in steel structures, we decided to simplify the analysis criteria. For bending, we define the severity level according to a user-configurable percentage value of the element length. For example, the user could configure that 5% of the element length is an acceptable bending value and that above 10% the element is compromised. For torsion, we define the severity level according to user-configurable absolute values in degrees.

In this work, we compute the deformation values for each type of anomaly in each slice. Then, using these values, we associate each point from the slice to the same severity level.

4.2 Visualization

The proposed visualization system aims to present the severity level of anomalies found in structural elements directly in the 3D point cloud. The system discretizes the severity in categories to help the responsible engineer understand the qualitative information of the anomaly. Each category is previously associated with a color. The cloud points are colored according to the associated severity value, allowing the user to more accurately identify the compromised regions of the element.

To visually represent the severity level, the system requires that the user defines categories of severity. The following information must be set to each category:

- a name;
- a color;
- a continuous range of possible values for the type of anomaly analyzed;
- a flag to indicate if the structural element must be highlighted when it has parts associated with that category;
- a message to be presented when the structural element is highlighted.

The visualization techniques for information in BIM can be organized in two categories [35]:

- *The type of view*: spacial views (2D CAD, 3D CAD, point cloud, ...) or abstract views (charts);
- *How to display the information in each view*: according Munzner [50], information can be displayed using marks and channels. Marks represent graphical entities, like original geometry, annotations, icons, etc. Channels correspond to visual properties, like colors, transparency, texture, etc.

Based on these concepts, the proposed visualization system uses a 3D point cloud viewer as the type of view. With the collaboration of domain experts, we define the following marks and channels to display the information:

- *Legend*: presents in top-right corner the defined categories, with color and name associated;
- *Original geometry*: the points of the cloud are colored according to their severity level;
- *Color*: represents the point severity level according the categories defined and color associated;
- *Annotation*: indicate that a element has parts of category that must be highlighted.

As we mentioned in the Subsect. 4.1, all points of the same slice are associated with the same severity level. Therefore, all of them are associated with the same category and, consequently, to the same color. To smooth the color transition between neighboring slices with different categories, the color of a point is calculated using a weighted average between the colors associated with each category. The weight for each color is inversely proportional to the distance between the point and the center of its slice.

5   Validation

To validate the proposed methods and visualization system, we implemented them in C++, in a Windows 10 64-bit environment, using the Microsoft Visual Studio 2017 IDE. We used PCL (Point Cloud Library) [8] for point cloud manipulation and visualization resources to create the visualization tool. For image manipulation and classification tasks we use OpenCV (Open Source Computer Vision Library) [7]. We use the RetinaNet [45] architecture for the object detection module, implemented on Keras [5] library with Tensorflow [9] as backend. The machine used in testing has an Intel i7-7700 3.60 GHz processor, with 16 GB of RAM and an NVidia GeForce GTX 1050 Ti video card with 4 GB of dedicated memory.

Due to the unavailability in the literature of a point cloud database for the type of building to use in this work, we performed tests with point clouds generated by a virtual 3D scanning sensor from CAD models, adding Gaussian noise with mean 0.0 and standard deviation 0.0005. This algorithm closely reproduces the behavior of real-world laser scanners, simulating occlusions from other objects and sensor imprecision. To merge the clouds generated by the sensor, we used CloudCompare [3], subsampling the cloud with a precision of 1 mm. The value of Δs used in the step 1 described in Sect. 3.1 was set to 20 cm, as suggested in [19]. The value of Δp used in the step 2 described in Sect. 3.1 was set to 5 mm. We choose this value for it is the mean between the flange and web thickness found in the AISC catalog [2]. Figure 7 presents a model of shed used in test.

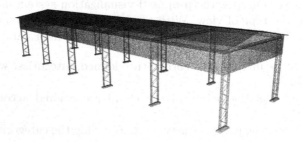

Fig. 7. Synthetic point cloud of a shed used in test

Table 1. Summary of the results applying the proposed method to detect deformations.

Element	Length (in meters)	Max. Bending Modeled (in meters)	Max. Bending Detected (in meters)	Max. Torsion Modeled (in degrees)	Max. Torsion Detected (in degrees)
Element 1	7.97	0.120	0.1174	15.0	14.876
Element 2	10.63	0.100	0.0999	10.0	9.869

Table 2. Deformation detection error for each element.

Element	Bending error	Torsion error
Element 1	2.16%	0.83%
Element 2	0.10%	1.31%

(a)   (b)

Fig. 8. Elements with bending and torsion added in shed model: (a) Element 1 and (b) Element 2.

To evaluate the extent of the method for detecting deformations, in the shed model, we added bending and torsion in two elements (Fig. 8). In Element 1 (Fig. 8a), we added a bend in the middle of its length and a torsion that increases linearly along its entire longitudinal axis. In Element 2 (Fig. 8b), we again added a bend in the middle of its length and a localized torsion also in the middle. Table 1 describes the features of each deformed element and the results obtained when applying the proposed method to detect deformations. Table 2 presents the precision error obtained.

Figure 9 presents the visualization of the deformation analysis for each deformed element in isolation. With the guidance of domain experts, for both types of deformations, we define 3 categories for severity level: *Low, Medium* and *High*. The respective colors associated are: *Green, Yellow* and *Red*, according to color scheme defined by ISO22324:2015 to indicate severity of hazards in public warnings. Table 3 presents the intervals used for each type of deformation. Only the category *High* was set to highlight the element.

Table 3. Limits used for each severity level for each type of deformation.

Deformation	Low	Medium	High
Bending (% of element length)	[0% .. 0.01%[	[0.01% .. 0.02%[	[0.02% .. ∞[
Torsion (in degrees)	[0 .. 4.0[	[4.0 .. 8.0[	[8.0 .. ∞[

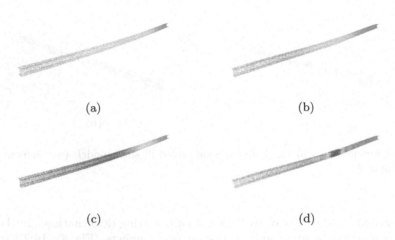

(a)   (b)

(c)   (d)

Fig. 9. Visualization of deformation analysis: (a) bending visualization of Element 1, (b) bending visualization of Element 2, (c) torsion visualization of Element 1, and (d) torsion visualization of Element 2.

Figure 10 presents the shed model in the proposed visualization system with the results for bending and torsion analysis. Note that, for torsion analysis, the tool highlights both elements with annotations due to the presence of parts with severity level categorized as *High*.

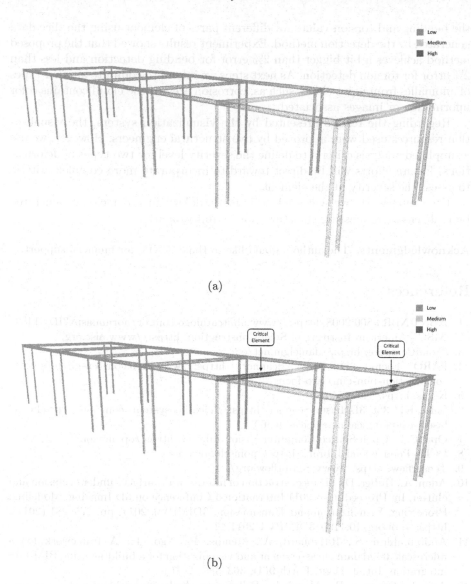

(a)

(b)

Fig. 10. Visualization of the analysis performed on the shed model in the proposed system: (a) bending analysis and (b) torsion analysis.

6   Conclusions and Future Works

In this paper, we presented a visualization system that presents the quality of building structural elements directly in the 3D point cloud. The anomaly type used to test was deformation, more specific bending and torsion. To compute this information, we extend the method to automate the detection of steel structural elements in point clouds of existing buildings presented in [56]. We compute the bending and torsion values for different parts of element using the slice data generated by the detection method. Experiment results showed that the proposed method achieves a bit bigger than 2% error for bending detection and less than 2% error for torsion detection. As next steps we intend to compute another types of anomalies from point cloud, such as, corrosion areas if the cloud contains color information or images associated.

Regarding the results presented by the visualization system, the visualization resources used were approved by two structural engineers. However, we use a simplified analysis criteria to define the severity level for two types of deformations. Future efforts will be direct toward to incorporate more complex criteria to assess the severity of the element.

For future work, we will apply this methodology in point clouds generated by real sensors in existing structures for its full validation.

Acknowledgments. The authors would like to thank CNPq for financial support.

References

1. ABNT NBR 8800:2008. https://www.abntcatalogo.com.br/norma.aspx?ID=1459/
2. AISC - American Institute of Steel Construction. https://www.aisc.org/
3. CloudCompare. http://danielgm.net/cc/
4. FARO Focus 3D Laser Scanner. https://www.faro.com/en-gb/products/construction-bim-cim/faro-focus/
5. Keras. https://keras.io/
6. Leica RTC360 3D Laser Scanner. https://leica-geosystems.com/en-sg/products/laser-scanners/scanners/leica-rtc360
7. OpenCV - Open Source Computer Vision Library. http://opencv.org/
8. PCL - Point Cloud Library. http://pointclouds.org/
9. Tensorflow. https://www.tensorflow.org/
10. Adan, A., Huber, D.: 3D reconstruction of interior wall surfaces under occlusion and clutter. In: Proceedings - 2011 International Conference on 3D Imaging, Modeling, Processing, Visualization and Transmission, 3DIMPVT 2011, pp. 275–281 (2011). https://doi.org/10.1109/3DIMPVT.2011.42
11. Amirebrahimi, S., Rajabifard, A., Mendis, P., Ngo, T.: A framework for a microscale flood damage assessment and visualization for a building using BIM-GIS integration. Int. J. Digit. Earth **9**(4), 363–386 (2016)
12. Anil, E., Sunnam, R., Akinci, B.: Full paper: challenges of identifying steel sections for the generation of as-is BIMs from laser scan data. Gerontechnology **11**(2) (2012). https://doi.org/10.4017/gt.2012.11.02.266.662
13. Anil, E.B., Akinci, B., Kurc, O., Garrett, J.H.: Building-information-modeling-based earthquake damage assessment for reinforced concrete walls. J. Comput. Civ. Eng. **30**(4), 04015076 (2016)
14. Barnea, S., Filin, S.: Segmentation of terrestrial laser scanning data using geometry and image information. ISPRS J. Photogramm. Remote Sens. **76**, 33–48 (2013). https://doi.org/10.1016/j.isprsjprs.2012.05.001
15. Becerik-Gerber, B., Jazizadeh, F., Li, N., Calis, G.: Application areas and data requirements for BIM-enabled facilities management. J. Constr. Eng. Manag. **138**(3), 431–442 (2012). https://doi.org/10.1061/(asce)co.1943-7862.0000433

16. Bishop, C.M.: Pattern Recognition and Machine Learning. Springer, New York (2006)
17. Boresi, A.P., Schmidt, R.J., Sidebottom, O.M., et al.: Advanced Mechanics of Materials, vol. 6. Wiley, New York (1985)
18. Borrmann, D., Elseberg, J., Lingemann, K., Nüchter, A.: The 3D hough transform for plane detection in point clouds: a review and a new accumulator design. 3D Res. **2**(2), 3 (2011). https://doi.org/10.1007/3DRes.02(2011)3
19. Bosché, F., Ahmed, M., Turkan, Y., Haas, C.T., Haas, R.: The value of integrating Scan-to-BIM and Scan-vs-BIM techniques for construction monitoring using laser scanning and BIM: the case of cylindrical MEP components. Autom. Constr. **49**, 201–213 (2015). https://doi.org/10.1016/j.autcon.2014.05.014
20. Cabaleiro, M., Riveiro, B., Arias, P., Caamaño, J.C., Vilán, J.A.: Automatic 3D modelling of metal frame connections from LiDAR data for structural engineering purposes. ISPRS J. Photogramm. Remote Sens. **96**, 47–56 (2014). https://doi.org/10.1016/j.isprsjprs.2014.07.006
21. Cabaleiro, M., Riveiro, B., Arias, P., Caamaño, J.: Algorithm for beam deformation modeling from LiDAR data. Measurement **76**, 20–31 (2015)
22. Chen, J., Fang, Y., Cho, Y.K.: Performance evaluation of 3D descriptors for object recognition in construction applications. Autom. Constr. **86**(May 2017), 44–52 (2018). https://doi.org/10.1016/j.autcon.2017.10.033
23. Czerniawski, T., Nahangi, M., Haas, C., Walbridge, S.: Pipe spool recognition in cluttered point clouds using a curvature-based shape descriptor. Autom. Constr. **71**(Part 2), 346–358 (2016). https://doi.org/10.1016/j.autcon.2016.08.011
24. Deschaud, J.-E., Goulette, F.: A fast and accurate plane detection algorithm for large noisy point clouds using filtered normals and voxel growing. In: 3DPVT, Paris, France (2010). https://hal-mines-paristech.archives-ouvertes.fr/hal-01097361
25. Dimitrov, A., Golparvar-Fard, M.: Segmentation of building point cloud models including detailed architectural/structural features and MEP systems. Autom. Constr. **51**(C), 32–45 (2015). https://doi.org/10.1016/j.autcon.2014.12.015
26. Eastman, C., Teicholz, P., Sacks, R., Liston, K.: BIM Handbook: A Guide to Building Information Modeling for Owners, Managers, Designers, Engineers and Contractors. Wiley, Hoboken (2011)
27. Fekete, J.D.: The infovis toolkit. In: IEEE Symposium on Information Visualization, pp. 167–174. IEEE (2004)
28. Fischler, M.A., Bolles, R.C.: Paradigm for model. Commun. ACM **24**(6), 381–395 (1981). https://doi.org/10.1145/358669.358692
29. Geiger, A., Lenz, P., Urtasun, R.: Are we ready for autonomous driving? the KITTI vision benchmark suite. In: Proceedings of the IEEE Computer Society Conference on Computer Vision and Pattern Recognition, pp. 3354–3361 (2012). https://doi.org/10.1109/CVPR.2012.6248074
30. Gordon, S.J., Lichti, D.D.: Modeling terrestrial laser scanner data for precise structural deformation measurement. J. Surv. Eng. **133**(2), 72–80 (2007)
31. Grilli, E., Menna, F., Remondino, F.: A review of point clouds segmentation and classification algorithms. Int. Arch. Photogramm. Remote Sens. Spat. Inf. Sci. - ISPRS Arch. **42**(23), 339–344 (2017). https://doi.org/10.5194/isprs-archives-XLII-2-W3-339-2017
32. Hajian, H., Becerik-Gerber, B.: A research outlook for real-time project information management by integrating advanced field data acquisition systems and building information modeling, pp. 83–94 (2009). https://doi.org/10.1061/41052(346)9
33. Hough, P.V.C.: Method and Means for Recognizing Complex Patterns. Google Patents (1962)

34. Huang, J., You, S.: Pole-like object detection and classification from urban point clouds. In: Proceedings - IEEE International Conference on Robotics and Automation 2015-June, pp. 3032–3038 (2015). https://doi.org/10.1109/ICRA.2015.7139615

35. Ivson, P., Moreira, A., Queiroz, F., Santos, W., Celes, W.: A systematic review of visualization in building information modeling. IEEE Trans. Vis. Comput. Graph. (2019). https://doi.org/10.1109/TVCG.2019.2907583

36. Jafari, B., Khaloo, A., Lattanzi, D.: Deformation tracking in 3D point clouds via statistical sampling of direct cloud-to-cloud distances. J. Nondestr. Eval. **36**(4), 65 (2017)

37. Jung, J., et al.: Productive modeling for development of as-built BIM of existing indoor structures. Autom. Constr. **42**, 68–77 (2014). https://doi.org/10.1016/j.autcon.2014.02.021

38. Kasaei, S.H., Tomé, A.M., Seabra Lopes, L., Oliveira, M.: GOOD: a global orthographic object descriptor for 3D object recognition and manipulation. Pattern Recogn. Lett. **83**, 312–320 (2016). https://doi.org/10.1016/j.patrec.2016.07.006

39. Khaloo, A., Lattanzi, D.: Robust normal estimation and region growing segmentation of infrastructure 3D point cloud models. Adv. Eng. Inform. **34**, 1–16 (2017). https://doi.org/10.1016/j.aei.2017.07.002

40. Klasing, K., Wollherr, D., Buss, M.: A clustering method for efficient segmentation of 3D laser data. In: Proceedings - IEEE International Conference on Robotics and Automation, pp. 4043–4048 (2008). https://doi.org/10.1109/ROBOT.2008.4543832

41. Koch, C., Georgieva, K., Kasireddy, V., Akinci, B., Fieguth, P.: A review on computer vision based defect detection and condition assessment of concrete and asphalt civil infrastructure. Adv. Eng. Inform. **29**(2), 196–210 (2015)

42. Laefer, D.F., Truong-Hong, L.: Toward automatic generation of 3D steel structures for building information modelling. Autom. Constr. **74**, 66–77 (2017). https://doi.org/10.1016/j.autcon.2016.11.011

43. Lee, H., Park, H.S.: Estimation of deformed shape of beam structure using 3D coordinate information from terrestrial laser scanning. Comput. Model. Eng. Sci. **29**(1), 29–44 (2008)

44. Levinson, J., et al.: Towards fully autonomous driving systems and algorithms, pp. 3–8 (2011). https://doi.org/10.1109/IVS.2011.5940562

45. Lin, T.Y., Goyal, P., Girshick, R., He, K., Dollár, P.: Focal loss for dense object detection. In: Proceedings of the IEEE International Conference on Computer Vision, pp. 2980–2988 (2017)

46. Lu, R., Brilakis, I., Middleton, C.R.: Detection of structural components in point clouds of existing RC bridges. Comput.-Aided Civ. Infrastruct. Eng. **34**(3), 191–212 (2019). https://doi.org/10.1111/mice.12407

47. Martinez, P., Ahmad, R., Al-Hussein, M.: A vision-based system for pre-inspection of steel frame manufacturing. Autom. Constr. **97**(June 2018), 151–163 (2019). https://doi.org/10.1016/j.autcon.2018.10.021

48. Martins, R.J.L.: Resistência à torção de perfis metálicos em forma de I ou H. Master's thesis, Faculdade de Ciências e Tecnologia, Universidade Nova de Lisboa, Portugal (2018)

49. Masciotta, M.G., Roque, J.C., Ramos, L.F., Lourenço, P.B.: A multidisciplinary approach to assess the health state of heritage structures: the case study of the Church of Monastery of Jerónimos in Lisbon. Constr. Build. Mater. **116**, 169–187 (2016). https://doi.org/10.1016/j.conbuildmat.2016.04.146

50. Munzner, T.: Visualization Analysis and Design. A K Peters/CRC Press, Natick (2014)
51. Penttila, H., Rajala, M., Freese, S.: Building information modelling of modern historic buildings. In: Predicting the Future, 25th eCAADe Konferansı, Frankfurt am Main, Germany, pp. 607–614 (2007)
52. Qi, C.R., Su, H., Mo, K., Guibas, L.J.: PointNet: deep learning on point sets for 3D classification and segmentation, December 2016
53. Riveiro, B., DeJong, M.J., Conde, B.: Automated processing of large point clouds for structural health monitoring of masonry arch bridges. Autom. Constr. **72**, 258–268 (2016). https://doi.org/10.1016/j.autcon.2016.02.009
54. Schmidhuber, J.: Deep learning in neural networks: an overview. Neural Netw. **61**, 85–117 (2015)
55. Schnabel, R., Wahl, R., Klein, R.: Efficient RANSAC for point-cloud shape detection. Comput. Graph. Forum **26**(2), 214–226 (2007). https://doi.org/10.1111/j.1467-8659.2007.01016.x
56. de Souza, R.P., Santos, P.I.N., Franco, C.A.S., Raposo, A.B.: Automatic detection of 3D steel structures in as-built point clouds. In: 2019 International Conference on Computing and Pattern Recognition (2019). https://doi.org/10.1145/3373509.3373565
57. Suzuki, S., Be, K.: Topological structural analysis of digitized binary images by border following. Comput. Vis. Graph. Image Process. **30**(1), 32–46 (1985). https://doi.org/10.1016/0734-189X(85)90016-7
58. Tang, P., Huber, D., Akinci, B., Lipman, R., Lytle, A.: Automatic reconstruction of as-built building information models from laser-scanned point clouds: a review of related techniques. Autom. Constr. **19**(7), 829–843 (2010). https://doi.org/10.1016/j.autcon.2010.06.007
59. Tuttas, S., Braun, A., Borrmann, A., Stilla, U.: Acquisition and consecutive registration of photogrammetric point clouds for construction progress monitoring using a 4D BIM. PFG – J. Photogramm. Remote Sens. Geoinf. Sci. **85**(1), 3–15 (2017). https://doi.org/10.1007/s41064-016-0002-z
60. Vo, A.V., Truong-Hong, L., Laefer, D.F., Bertolotto, M.: Octree-based region growing for point cloud segmentation. ISPRS J. Photogramm. Remote Sens. **104**(November 2017), 88–100 (2015). https://doi.org/10.1016/j.isprsjprs.2015.01.011
61. Volk, R., Stengel, J., Schultmann, F.: Building information modeling (BIM) for existing buildings - literature review and future needs. Autom. Constr. **38**, 109–127 (2014). https://doi.org/10.1016/j.autcon.2013.10.023
62. Walsh, S.B., Borello, D.J., Guldur, B., Hajjar, J.F.: Data processing of point clouds for object detection for structural engineering applications. Comput.-Aided Civ. Infrastruct. Eng. **28**(7), 495–508 (2013). https://doi.org/10.1111/mice.12016
63. Wang, Q., Kim, M.K.: Applications of 3D point cloud data in the construction industry: a fifteen-year review from 2004 to 2018. Adv. Eng. Inform. **39**(February), 306–319 (2019). https://doi.org/10.1016/j.aei.2019.02.007
64. Wang, Y., Shi, T., Yun, P., Tai, L., Liu, M.: PointSeg: Real-Time Semantic Segmentation Based on 3D LiDAR Point Cloud (2018)
65. Wong, J., Yang, J.: Research and application of Building Information Modelling (BIM) in the Architecture, Engineering and Construction (AEC) industry: a review and direction for future research. In: Proceedings of the 6th International Conference on Innovation in Architecture, Engineering & Construction (AEC), pp. 356–365. Loughborough University, UK, Pennsylvania State University (2010)

66. Xiong, X., Adan, A., Akinci, B., Huber, D.: Automatic creation of semantically rich 3D building models from laser scanner data. Autom. Constr. **31**, 325–337 (2013). https://doi.org/10.1016/j.autcon.2012.10.006
67. Yeung, J., Nahangi, M., Walbridge, S., Haas, C.: A preliminary investigation into automated identification of structural steel without a priori knowledge. In: ISARC. Proceedings of the International Symposium on Automation and Robotics in Construction, vol. 31, p. 1. IAARC Publications (2014)
68. Zolanvari, S.M., Laefer, D.F., Natanzi, A.S.: Three-dimensional building façade segmentation and opening area detection from point clouds. ISPRS J. Photogramm. Remote Sens. **143**, 134–149 (2018). https://doi.org/10.1016/j.isprsjprs.2018.04.004

Revisiting Visualization Task Taxonomies: Specifying Functions for the Data Transformations Stage

Ariane Moraes Bueno Rodrigues[(✉)] [ID], Gabriel Diniz Junqueira Barbosa[ID],
Raul de Araújo Lima[ID], Dieinison Jack Freire Braga[ID],
Hélio Côrtes Vieira Lopes[ID], and Simone Diniz Junqueira Barbosa[ID]

Departamento de Informatica, PUC-Rio, Gavea, Rio de Janeiro, Brazil
{arodrigues,rlima,dbraga,lopes,simone}@inf.puc-rio.br,
gabrieldjb@gmail.com

Abstract. Several visualization task taxonomies have been defined in the literature, taking into account several factors, such as the user's goals when analyzing a visual representation of data, the data characteristics, how they are mapped onto the visualization, to name a few. Some studies also use task taxonomies as a tool to evaluate the effectiveness of visual representations. Because each task taxonomy may have been created for a different purpose, we find that they often overlap, and the task definitions are often implicit or ambiguous. We have analyzed several visualization taxonomies, and realized they crosscut different stages of the visualization process. In this work, we focus on the data transformations stage and define a set of data functions related to the tasks in the studied taxonomies. We specify these functions to bring clarity and consistency, as well as to enable them to be used in different scenarios. This work is a first step toward a more comprehensive visualization ontology.

Keywords: Visualization data functions · Visualization tasks · Visualization process · Information visualization

1 Introduction

Several different visualization taxonomies have been proposed to try and guide the process of creating data visualizations [1,3,4,8,10,12,15–17,19]. Each has its own purpose, specificities, advantages and disadvantages. In this work, we propose a multi-stage functional approach to building visualizations and narrow the focus to define the data transformations functions as the first necessary step to support visualization tasks. Visualization tasks can be considered as different activities that the analyst can perform during the creation and interpretation of visualizations [14]. These activities consist of actions taken on specific targets, resulting in the final visualizations.

© Springer Nature Switzerland AG 2020
M. Kurosu (Ed.): HCII 2020, LNCS 12181, pp. 655–671, 2020.
https://doi.org/10.1007/978-3-030-49059-1_48

We analyzed several visualization taxonomies. Different taxonomies use slightly different definitions of visualization tasks, so we need to look deeper into the definitions and not rely on the labels. Based on our insights, we defined a set of data transformation functions, which can be used in different scenarios and to compose different visualization tasks. By specifying these functions, we tried to avoid some of the ambiguity present in existing taxonomies and to make it easier to implement them in executable code. The consideration of inputs and outputs allows us to distinguish between the resources used for each function and its results. Since inputs may vary, they allow us to create more general low-level tasks. Each function's output may even serve as an input to another function. Through the use of function outputs as inputs of other functions, multiple low-level tasks can be composed to fulfill higher-level tasks' needs. For example, we can define a 'find extremum' task as a composition of a 'sort' and a 'select_cases' function, where the output of the sorting function is used as the input for the selection function.

We set out to operationalize the visualization process as defined by Ware [18]. During our analysis of existing taxonomies, we noticed that some tasks seemed to span different stages of the visualization process. We then decided to separate these tasks into different functions at each stage of the visualization process, specifying the functions in such a way that we can use their output in later stages of the visualization building process.

In this paper, we focus on the data transformations stage of these visualization tasks. Data transformation involves selecting and manipulating the data for the visual mapping. This process comprises different functions, which we sought to identify in the taxonomies we analyzed. Some high-level tasks may not involve a data transformation component, acting on other stages of the visualization process.

In the following section, we introduce relevant works about visualization task taxonomies and Ware's visualization process. Section 3 presents our methodology, and in Sect. 4, we describe the data transformation functions identified. Section 5 describes the next steps of our research, namely defining functions related to the visual encoding and the visual and cognitive processing stages. In Sect. 6, we report the results of a preliminary evaluation of the expressiveness of our data functions. Finally, we present some concluding remarks in Sect. 7.

2   Related Work

In this section, we describe some research results that we find relevant to our work, namely: visualization task taxonomies (Sect. 2.1) and visualization process (Sect. 2.2).

2.1   Visualization Task Taxonomies

Several approaches attempt to classify the different intentions that an analyst may have when visualizing the data. These approaches are split in two fundamental ways in the literature: high-level tasks, which define conceptual tasks

[3,14] or general goals [7,15]; and low-level tasks, which identify specific goals [1,12] or analytical actions [6,19]. Although the researchers agree to name these classifications as visualization task taxonomies, they differ in some of their definitions. For example, while Wehrend and Lewis [19] call 'Identify' an *operator*, Sarikaya and Gleicher [13] call it an *analysis task*. For consistency, in this paper, we will call 'visualization tasks' the different activities (goals, tasks, functions, and actions) that the analyst can perform to extract accurate information from the visual representation of the data. We are also interested in task taxonomies in their most specific forms (*i.e.*, 'Retrieve Value' [1] instead of 'Overview' [15]). According to the authors, the taxonomies we analyzed were derived empirically, through surveys or by observing the tasks people do when interpreting and interacting with visualizations, either focused on specific questions or exploring data.

Wehrend and Lewis [19] defined a classification scheme for finding visualization techniques that are relevant to a given problem. The classification is a two-dimensional matrix with the objects (data attributes) of representation (*e.g.*, direction, shape, position) and the perceptual tasks or operations (representation objectives). It is a low-level, user-centric taxonomy that identifies the following perceptual tasks: locate, distinguish, categorize, cluster, distribution, rank, compare within and between relations, associate, and correlate.

Roth and Mattis [12] classified visualization problems and their solutions independently of the domain. They proposed a taxonomy that provides a list of different user information-seeking goals and visualization expressivity (*e.g.*, number of data records). They use two different characteristics to deal with these goals: display functions of data presentation and distribution functions of the data within the presentation. Their proposed classification is very similar to Wehrend and Lewis's and also low-level and user-centric, albeit more concise and focused on the automatic generation of visual representation. We analyzed the display functions of their taxonomy, which comprises the following tasks: accurate value lookup, comparison of values within relations, pairwise or n-wise comparison of relations, distributions of values, functional correlations among attributes, and indexing.

Zhou and Feiner [20] derived a visual taxonomy based on works that link high-level presentation intentions with low-level visual techniques. They mapped them onto two intents (inform and enable), called visual accomplishments, and several visual tasks, which are the visual implications. With this taxonomy, there are several ways a visual task can help achieve a presentation intent. For example, to achieve *correlate* task, one may have the intent 'enable-compute-sum' or 'enable-compute-differentiate'. The resulting taxonomy is as follows:

- associate: collocate, connect, unite, attach.
- categorize: mark-distribute.
- cluster: outline, individualize.
- compare: differentiate, intersect.
- correlate: plot, mark-compose.
- distinguish: mark-distribute, isolate.
- identify: name, portray, individualize, profile.

- locate: position, situate, pinpoint, outline.
- rank: time.
- background: background.
- emphasize: focus, isolate, reinforce.
- generalize: merge.
- reveal: expose, itemize, specify, separate.
- switch: switch.
- encode: label, symbolize, portray, tabulate, plot, structure, trace, map.

Amar et al. [1] defined low-level analysis tasks that an analyst may perform when working with data. They bring the 'aggregation function' concept that creates a numeric representation for a set of data cases (entities in the dataset). Their low-level tasks are: cluster, correlate, characterize distribution, retrieve value, sort, filter, compute derived value, find extremum, determine range, and find anomalies.

Valiati et al. [17] presented a taxonomy of specific tasks to guide the evaluation and design of multidimensional visualizations techniques. Their taxonomy integrates different levels of tasks, such as analytic, cognitive, and operational, resulting in a blend of high and low-level tasks. They organized the taxonomy in tasks and sub-tasks, as follows:

- identify: clusters, correlations, categories, properties, patterns, characteristics, thresholds, similarities/differences, dependencies/independencies, and uncertainties/variations.
- determine: mean, median, variance, standard deviation, amplitude, percentile, sum, proportions, differences, correlation coefficients, probabilities, and other statistics.
- compare: dimensions, items, data, values, clusters, properties, proportions, positions/locations, distances, and graphical primitives.
- infer: hypothesis, rules, trends, probabilities, and cause/effect.
- configure: normalizations, classification, filtering, zoom, dimensions, order derived attributes, and graphical primitives.
- locate: items, data, values, clusters, properties, positions/locations, distances, and graphical primitives.
- visualize: n dimensions, n items, data, and domain parameters/attribute information/metadata.

The tasks 'visualize' and 'configure' are intermediate-level tasks to support the other analytical ones.

Later studies became more specific, as is the case of Lee et al. [9]. They defined a list of graph visualization tasks with enough detail for it to be useful to designers who seek to improve their systems and to evaluators who try to compare graph visualization systems. By contrast, all tasks were composed of the primitive tasks described by Amar et al. [1], as well as two generic tasks (scan and set operation) and one graph-specific task (find adjacent nodes). The resulting taxonomy is low-level, user-centric, and representation-specific.

Chen et al. [4] explored tasks related to data, visualization, and user goal. They defined a taxonomy to categorize facts extracted from multidimensional data in a visual data analysis task. Facts are patterns, relationships, or anomalies extracted from data through analysis. They defined the following tasks: association, cluster, difference, distribution, rank, value/derived value, extreme, outliers, categories, trend, meta fact, and compound fact. Besides describing low-level tasks, this taxonomy has a different focus from the others, since it characterizes facts resulting from the analytical tasks. This is the closest taxonomy of ours since it also has a formal definition with the description of the essential attributes of the tasks.

Some researchers consider the use of more than one taxonomy, as is the case of VLAT [10]. To develop VLAT, a visualization literacy test, Lee et al. associated tasks from three different taxonomies. First, they combined a low-level taxonomy [1] with a facts-based one [4], and afterward discarded some of the *how* and *why* abstract tasks of [3] – the discarded tasks were related to manipulation and generation of new elements, and not reading and interpretation of visual representations of data. VLAT uses the following taxonomy for possible visualization data tasks: retrieve value, find extremum, determine range, characterize distribution, find anomalies, find clusters, find correlations/trends, and make comparisons. As the authors' goal was to use this taxonomy to formalize the literacy test, they do not describe the tasks. They only relate them with the different types of possible visualizations, the data that can be analyzed, and sample questions.

Choi et al. [5] conducted an exploratory study to investigate how people can interact with a concept-driven visualization interface. The taxonomy resulted from an exploratory study after users externalized their preconceived hypotheses and expectations when interacting with a visualization interface of data analysis. They defined three major model types the participants externalized: relationships, partial ordering, and predicted trends and values. The tasks in each model are:

- relationships: cause and effect, mediation, causal sequence, and correlation.
- partial ordering: direct manipulation, ranking.
- trends and values: values, trends.

They described each task based on their study findings in a quasi-formal way, by defining an expectation template related to each task. They codified slots for an independent template, which represents data attributes, geographies, time periods, event sequences, quantitative values and trends, and other qualifiers.

Schulz et al. [14] created a design space of visualizations tasks in an attempt to bring together the different aspects of task taxonomies. They described five dimensions for task analysis and user intentions:

- goal: the intent with which the task is pursued (exploratory analysis, confirmatory analysis, and presentation)
- means: the method for reaching the goal (navigation, [re-]organization, and relation)

- characteristics: the facets of the data that the task aims to reveal (low-level and high-level characteristics)
- target: which part of the data it is carried out (attribute relations like temporal or spatial and structural relations)
- cardinality: how many instances of the chosen target are considered by the task (single, multiple, and all)

In an effort to formalize their taxonomy, they defined a tuple with these dimensions. For example, for the task 'compare variable distributions', the notation is:

$$(confirmatory, search|compare|navigate, distributions,$$
$$attrib(attribute_1)|attrib(attribute_2), all)$$

We can note that there are significant overlaps among these different taxonomies. For example, some tasks may be re-written in terms of other tasks. Some flat task lists in certain taxonomies even contain tasks that should be in different levels of abstraction. These overlaps, inconsistencies, and ambiguities have motivated us to create a clear specification of visualization tasks.

2.2 Visualization Process

Transforming data into a visual representation is only one of the stages of the visualization process. Ware [18] defined visualization process as comprising four stages (Fig. 1):

1. *data collection and storage*
2. *data transformations*, transforming and/or reducing the data to a subset with the aspects to be visualized
3. mapping the selected data onto a visual representation, *i.e.*, *visual encoding*
4. *visual and cognitive processing* by the human perceiver, who will manipulate the view to explore the data

In the visual encoding stage, the mapping of the data onto a visual representation can be performed either by an algorithm, to produce the visualization, or by the user themselves, who can modify the mapping and highlight subsets, transforming the visualization.

The task taxonomies described in the previous section cannot be directly mapped onto the stages of the visualization process. For example, 'find extremum' [1] can be a visual and cognitive process (stage 4) if the data was preprocessed neatly (stage 3). This indicates that high-level visualization tasks can be decomposed into more specific actions at each stage of the visualization process.

3   Methodology

Inspired by Ware's visualization process, we aim to define functions for three stages involved in building visualizations (Fig. 2).

In the data transformations stage (1), data-related functions prepare the data for visual encoding. Different from Ware's process, we are not taking into consideration data collection and storage in this process. This stage is iterative, since multiple rounds of data transformation may be required for adjusting the data for the final visualization, according to the data characteristics. For instance, when trying to build a bar chart with too many categories to properly visualize them, those categories may then be grouped into higher-level categories so that they are better visualized. This function could then result in further con-

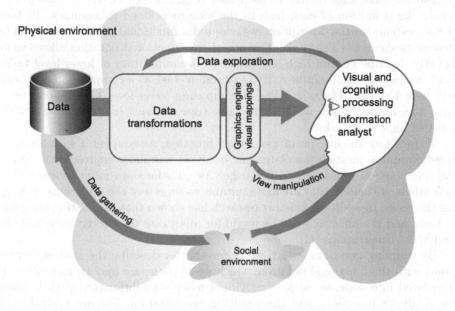

Fig. 1. The visualization process [18, p. 4]

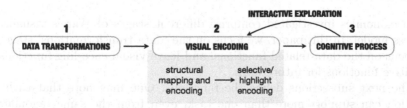

Fig. 2. The three stages we consider when defining visualizations.

siderations of the data characteristics, leading to further adjustments, thereby establishing an iterative process.

After the data are ready to visualize, we move on to the following steps in the visualization process: the visual encoding and the visual and cognitive processing. We unfolded Ware's visual encoding stage (2) in two steps: what to present (structural mapping) and what to call attention to (highlight encoding). The structural mapping and encoding involves setting the visual encodings for the relevant attributes (based on the visualization task) of all objects. When the task involves visually distinguishing a few selected objects, there is also a selective/highlight encoding step. In the third stage (3), after visual encoding, the cognitive process occurs, where the user can see and explore the visual representation and perform mental functions to gain insights.

Based on the investigated task taxonomies, we set out to detail the data transformations stage related to each task (Fig. 2, stage 1). We did so by analyzing the definition of each task in the aforementioned taxonomies. To keep the consistency in the description, we adopted a functional notation, inspired by that of Beshers and Feiner [2]. The use of the functional notation allows us to directly describe certain high-level tasks as a composition of lower-level tasks. For example, we can describe a 'find extremum' task as a composition of a 'sort' and 'select' tasks. The possibility of composing lower-level tasks allows us to have a more concise set, while at the same time allowing us to describe a wider array of high-level tasks.

To facilitate the interpretation of each function, we coupled it with a sample question and a question template. The question templates represent the gist of the functions, in quasi-natural language. As questions are more concrete than task labels, we believe they are more suitable to represent the intentions underlying the tasks. In addition, existing research has shown that associating questions to tasks and visualizations can be useful for analyzing the effectiveness and efficiency of visualizations [11].

By coupling questions, which we believe better describe the analyst's intentions, with the functional notation, which we hypothesize may be more directly translated into code, we seek to provide a more straightforward path between the analyst's intentions and the resulting visualization. Further evaluation is required to assess the adequacy of this approach.

4   Data Transformation Functions

The taxonomies investigated comprise different stages of Ware's visualization process model. In this paper, we focus on the 'data transformations' stage, *i.e.*, we focus on the data-related functions, and leave visual encoding functions and cognitive functions for future work.

The next subsections define the functions. One may note that each data function can support more than one task, even from the same taxonomy, as listed in the 'Related tasks' portion of each subsection. This means that the tasks may differ in terms of their visual encoding or visual and cognitive processing functions, but not in terms of the data transformation functions.

In this work, we have adopted the terminology objects, attributes, and values. Thinking of data in a table format, an object would be represented by a row, an attribute by a column, and a value by a cell. Note, however, that the terminology in different taxonomies differ. For instance, Amar et al. [1] calls objects *cases*, whereas Valiati et al. [17] calls them *items*. In our notation, uppercase letters denote sets (*e.g.*, O = objects; A = attributes; V = values) and lowercase letters denote elements of a set. We also use colors to facilitate the identification of the type of element, especially in the examples. For instance, O denotes a set of objects, and o denotes a single object.

4.1   Filter

The **filter** function returns a subset of objects of interest, given an input set of objects and a conditional expression on one or more attributes.

Specification: $filter($ O , conditions on A $) \rightarrow$ O' , $O' \subseteq O$

Related Tasks:

- filter [1]
- find anomalies [1]
- outliers [4]
- (configure) filtering [17]

Question Template: Which O satisfy boolean function(A , ...) ?

Sample Question: Which cities had over 500 homicides ?

4.2   Identify

The **identify** function returns a single object of interest, given an input set of objects and a conditional expression on one or more attributes which uniquely identify the object. It can be considered as a special case of *filter*.

Specification: $identify($ O , conditions on A $) \rightarrow$ o , $o \in O$

Related Tasks:

- identify [17,19,20]
- accurate value lookup [12]

Question Template: Which o has a = v ?

Sample Question: Which city has name São Paulo ?

4.3 Retrieve Values

The **_retrieve_values_** function returns the values of the given attributes of a specified set of objects.

Specification: $retrieve\_values(\boxed{O}, \boxed{A}) \rightarrow \{(\boxed{o_i}, \boxed{V_i})\}, \forall i\, o_i \in O, V_i = o_i.A$

Related Tasks:

- retrieve value [1]
- accurate value lookup [12]
- value [4]
- (locate) values [17]

Question Template: $\boxed{\text{What}}$ is the $\boxed{\text{attribute}}$ (value) of $\boxed{\text{object}}$?

Sample Question: $\boxed{\text{What}}$ is the $\boxed{\text{number of homicides}}$ of the $\boxed{\text{city of}}$ $\boxed{\text{São Paulo}}$?

4.4 Summarize

The **_summarize_** function returns a single value derived from applying a function to the set of values of a certain attribute of a set of objects.[1] Any function that receives an array of values and returns a single value may apply. Sample functions are: mean, median, min, among others. For functions that can be directly applied to the set of objects, such as *count*, the input attribute a is optional.

Specification: $summarize(\boxed{O}, \boxed{a}, \boxed{fn}, \dots) \rightarrow \boxed{v}, v = fn(O.a, \dots)$

Related Tasks:

- compute derived value [1]
- derived value [4]
- (configure) derived attributes [17]
- (determine) mean, median, variance etc [17]
- characterize distribution [1]
- distribution [4,19]

Question Template: $\boxed{\text{What}}$ is/was the $\boxed{\text{summarization fn}(\boxed{a})}$ of $\boxed{O}$?

Sample Question: $\boxed{\text{What}}$ was the $\boxed{\text{average}}$ $\boxed{\text{city}}$ $\boxed{\text{homicide rate}}$?

---

[1] In this and all other cases that may receive a function as input, the function may also receive additional input, depicted by the ellipsis.

4.5   Partition

The **partition** function splits a set of object into a partition of the set according to the values of one or more attributes, which will be used to describe each set.

Specification: $partition(\boxed{O}, \boxed{A}) \rightarrow \{(\boxed{O_i}, \boxed{V_i'})\}, \forall i O_i \subseteq O, V_i' = O_{i1}.A$

Related Tasks:

- cluster [1,4,19,20]
- (identify) clusters, (compare) clusters, (locate) clusters [17]

Question Template: $\boxed{\text{Which}}$ $\boxed{O}$ have each value of $\boxed{A}$?

Sample Question: $\boxed{\text{Which}}$ $\boxed{\text{cities}}$ are in each $\boxed{\text{state}}$?

4.6   Map

The **map** function returns a new attribute for O, whose values are the results of a given function applied to the value(s) of one or more original attributes of each object $o \in O$. This new attribute can then be used to partition O. Any function that receives one or more values and returns a single value may apply.

Specification: $map(\boxed{O}, \boxed{A}, \boxed{fn}, \dots) \rightarrow \boxed{a'}, \forall i \; o_i \in O, a_i' = fn(o_i.A, \dots)$

Related Tasks:

- compute derived value [1]
- derived value [4]
- (configure) derived attributes [17]

Question Template: $\boxed{\text{What}}$ are the values $V = \boxed{\text{function}(\boxed{A})}$ of $\boxed{O}$?

Sample Question: $\boxed{\text{What}}$ is the $\boxed{\text{number of violent crimes}}$ of each $\boxed{\text{city}}$, considering it as the $\boxed{\text{sum of} \boxed{\text{homicide and manslaughter}}}$?

4.7   S-Map

The **s-map** function applies a given function fn to each set of objects O_i in a set of sets of objects (typically returned by *partition*) and associates each set O_i to a single value returned by fn. Any function that receives one or more values and returns a single value may apply. For functions that can be directly applied to the set of objects, such as *count*, the input attributes A are optional.

Specification: $smap(\{(\boxed{O_i}, \_)\}, \boxed{A}, \boxed{fn}, \dots) \rightarrow \{(\boxed{O_i}, \boxed{v_i'})\}, \forall i, v_i' = fn(O_i, A, \dots)$

Related Tasks:

– characterize distribution [1]
– distribution [4, 19]
– distribution of values [12]

Question Template: What is the summarization fn(Partition) ?

Sample Question: What is the total number of homicides per city ?

4.8 Sort

The sort function returns a sequence of objects ordered according to a set of attributes in the specified directions.

Specification: $sort(\ O\ ,\ A\ ,\ Order\ ) \rightarrow \langle o_i \rangle$, where $|A| = |Order| \wedge \langle o_i \rangle$ is a sequence of all the objects $o_i \in O$ ordered in terms of each attribute $a_j \in A$, following the corresponding order $order_j \in \{ascending, descending\}$.

Related Tasks:

– sort [1]
– rank [4, 19, 20]
– indexing [12]
– (configure) dimensions order [17]

Question Template: How are O ordered by A?

Sample Question: How are cities ordered by violent crime rate ?

4.9 Find Extremum

The *find_extremum* function returns a sequence of k top or bottom objects, sorted on a given set of attributes A.

Specification: $find\_extremum(\ O\ ,\ A\ ,\ k\ ,\ Order\ ) =$
$select\_cases(sort(\ O\ ,\ A\ ,\ Order\ ), \langle 1, \ldots, k \rangle) \rightarrow \langle o_1, \ldots, o_k \rangle$.

Note that *find_extremum* uses a supporting function defined as:

$\qquad select\_cases(\ O\ ,\ Indices\ ) \rightarrow \langle o_i \rangle,\ \forall i \in Indices \wedge Indices \subseteq \{1, \ldots, |O|\}$,
i.e., *Indices* is a sequence of indices to O.

Related Tasks:

– find extremum [1]
– extreme [4]
– (identify) threshold [17]

Question Template: Which are the k O with the *direction* A?

Sample Question: Which are the 5 cities with the highest homicide rate ?

4.10   Categorize

The *categorize* function returns a partition of objects based on an attribute created through the application of some mapping function fn, which also returns a nominal or ordinal variable describing each set in the partition.

Specification: $categorize(\boxed{O}, \boxed{A}, \boxed{fn}, \ldots) = partition(\boxed{O}, map(\boxed{O}, \boxed{A}, \boxed{fn}, \ldots)) \rightarrow \{(\boxed{O_i}, \boxed{v_i'})\}$

Related Tasks:

- (identify) categories [17]
- categories [4]
- categorize [19, 20]

Question Template: Which $\boxed{O}$ are classified as $\boxed{A'} = \boxed{\text{function}(\boxed{A})}$?

Sample Question: Which $\boxed{\text{cities}}$ are $\boxed{\text{safe or unsafe}}$, as a $\boxed{\text{function of the}}$ $\boxed{\text{number of homicides}}$?

4.11   Composing Functions

Some tasks are related to a composition of functions. For instance, we have seen that *categorize* is a function of *map* and *partition*.

The data operations related to other tasks in the investigated taxonomies can be similarly mapped onto an application multiple functions, or multiple applications of a single function. For instance, *determine_range* [1] can be defined as a tuple of two *find_extremum* applications, with *min* and *max* parameters, respectively.

5   Next Stages: Visual Encoding and Visual and Cognitive Processing

As mentioned in the methodology section (Sect. 3), some tasks do not have a 1:1 correspondence with data transformation functions. Some tasks were not considered related to any functions in our model. In this section, we illustrate how a few tasks can be related to visual encoding functions and/or visual and cognitive processing functions.

Visual Encoding Functions. In terms of the visual encoding stage of the visualization process, we can outline two steps: structural encoding, and highlight encoding. Structural encoding is the process of selecting the type of visualization and mapping the different values into the structural slots of the selected visualization type. Highlight encoding is the process of selectively encoding a specific object's channel with one of its attribute values.

Examples of structural encoding include the mapping of objects to a column chart (vertical bar) format. This function could be described as follows:

$b1 = bar(O, a_{no}, a_q) \rightarrow vis(mark = bar, data = O, x = a_{no}, y = a_q)$, where a_{no} is a nominal or ordinal variable, a_q is a numeric (quantitative) variable

Examples of selective encoding include the mapping of specific object attributes to one of its channels, seeking to distinguish those objects from the others. This function could be described as follows:

$$distinguish(vis, O', a, channel)$$

For instance, $distinguish(b1, filter(O, u_q \geq 100), a_q, fillcolor = orange)$ changes to *orange* the *fillcolor* channel of all objects whose values of a_q are greater than or equal to 100.

Visual and Cognitive Processing Functions. Some taxonomies define tasks that rely heavily on cognitive processing, such as tasks for relating or comparing objects, including finding correlations and trends (*e.g.*, make comparisons [10]; association [4]; compare [12,19]; distinguish [19]; difference [4]; correlate [1,12, 19]; finding correlations/trends [10]; trend [4]; infer [17]). Assuming that the relevant attributes have been visually encoded, these tasks can be supported by the following function:

$$compare(O, A) \rightarrow \{(r_i(o_{ip_A}, o_{iq_A}), S_i)\} : \forall i, p, q, p \neq q \, \wedge \\ o_{ip} \in S_i \, \wedge \, o_{iq} \in S_i \, \wedge \, S_i \subseteq O$$

These tasks can be performed on the whole dataset, without necessarily applying specific data transformation functions.

6   Evaluating the Expressiveness of the Proposed Set of Data Transformation Functions

We evaluated the expressiveness of our functions by using a set of 76 empirically derived questions generated by multiple anonymous contributors using IMDb as domain. We eliminated 13 questions (17%), which did not directly refer to a visualization, such as 'Why did Sylvester Stallone get an Oscar for Rocky Balboa?' (as a side note, this question is not about a true fact). All remaining questions could be mapped onto our data transformation functions. Although we do claim that the proposed data transformation functions set is complete, the evaluation results show that it accounts for common user goals when using visualizations.

For each question in the study, we identified one or more data transformation functions involved in it. Figure 3 shows the frequency in which each function occurred in the study questions.

We found that the most frequent data transformation function related to the study questions was 'filter' (n = 24, 38.09%), followed by 'retrieve values'.

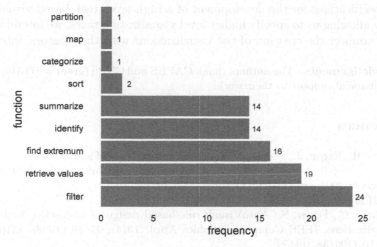

Fig. 3. Frequency of functions found in the study questions

These two functions also often appeared together for a single question. The three most frequent ones, including the 'identify' function, were all pertaining to the retrieval of some information, be it attribute values or objects. The least frequent functions were 'map', 'categorize', 'partition', and 'sort.' We hypothesize that this is due to their being more specific to low-level data functions that may not occur as frequently in questions, which tend to be broader in scope. Although the 'sort' function was not so frequent (n = 2, 3.17%), it was used indirectly, inside the much more frequent 'find extremum' function (n = 16, 25.39%).

7   Concluding Remarks

In this paper, we have specified data functions corresponding to the data transformations stage in Ware's visualization process [18]. We related each function to one or more tasks found in widespread task taxonomies [1,4,12,17,19,20] and provided a corresponding question template and examples to facilitate the usage of the functions. We defined these tasks using a functional notation so as to facilitate the composition of different low-level tasks into higher-level tasks.

A limitation of this work is to assume that a question template can be mapped onto a single data transformation function. Certain questions may combine different functions, requiring more advanced templates, or a way to compose our templates, to decompose them into our tasks. As future work, we plan to evaluate this assumption through an empirical study, and possibly extend our mappings between question templates and data transformation functions.

As future work, we intend to specify functions for both visual encoding and visual and cognitive processing. That way, we will be able to organize most of the visualization process space, as defined by Ware [18]. We also plan to later use these specifications for the development of a high-level, task-based visualization API. By allowing us to specify higher-level visualization tasks, we intend to more directly connect the creation of the visualizations with the creators' intent.

Acknowledgements. The authors thank CAPES and CNPq (grant #311316/2018-2) for the financial support to their work.

References

1. Amar, R., Eagan, J., Stasko, J.: Low-level components of analytic activity in information visualization. In: 2005 IEEE Symposium on Information Visualization. INFOVIS 2005, pp. 111–117, October 2005. https://doi.org/10.1109/INFVIS.2005. 1532136
2. Beshers, C., Feiner, S.: AutoVisual: rule-based design of interactive multivariate visualizations. IEEE Comput. Graphics Appl. **13**(4), 41–49 (1993). https://doi. org/10.1109/38.219450
3. Brehmer, M., Munzner, T.: A multi-level typology of abstract visualization tasks. IEEE Trans. Visual. Comput. Graphics **19**(12), 2376–2385 (2013). https://doi.org/ 10/f5h3q4
4. Chen, Y., Yang, J., Ribarsky, W.: Toward effective insight management in visual analytics systems. In: Proceedings of the 2009 IEEE Pacific Visualization Symposium. PACIFICVIS 2009, pp. 49–56. IEEE Computer Society, USA (2009). https:// doi.org/10.1109/PACIFICVIS.2009.4906837
5. Choi, I.K., Childers, T., Raveendranath, N.K., Mishra, S., Harris, K., Reda, K.: Concept-driven visual analytics: an exploratory study of model-and hypothesis-based reasoning with visualizations. In: Proceedings of the 2019 CHI Conference on Human Factors in Computing Systems, pp. 1–14 (2019)
6. Fujishiro, I., Ichikawa, Y., Furuhata, R., Takeshima, Y.: GADGET/IV: a taxonomic approach to semi-automatic design of information visualization applications using modular visualization environment. In: Proceedings of the IEEE Symposium on Information Visualization 2000. INFOVIS 2000, pp. 77–83. IEEE (2000)
7. Keller, P.R., Keller, M.M., Markel, S., Mallinckrodt, A.J., McKay, S.: Visual cues: practical data visualization. Comput. Phys. **8**(3), 297–298 (1994)
8. Lee, B., Plaisant, C., Parr, C.S., Fekete, J.D., Henry, N.: Task taxonomy for graph visualization. In: Proceedings of the 2006 AVI Workshop on BEyond Time and Errors Novel Evaluation Methods for Information Visualization - BELIV 2006, p. 1. ACM Press, Venice (2006). https://doi.org/10.1145/1168149.1168168
9. Lee, S., Kim, S., Hung, Y., Lam, H., Kang, Y., Yi, J.S.: How do people make sense of unfamiliar visualizations?: a grounded model of novice's information visualization sensemaking. IEEE Trans. Visual. Comput. Graphics **22**(1), 499–508 (2016). https://doi.org/10/gfw4vs
10. Lee, S., Kim, S., Kwon, B.C.: VLAT: development of a visualization literacy assessment test. IEEE Trans. Visual. Comput. Graphics **23**(1), 551–560 (2017). https:// doi.org/10/f92d38
11. Rodrigues, A.M.B., Barbosa, G.D.J., Lopes, H., Barbosa, S.D.J.: Comparing the effectiveness of visualizations of different data distributions. In: 2019 32nd SIBGRAPI Conference on Graphics, Patterns and Images (SIBGRAPI), pp. 84–91, October 2019. https://doi.org/10.1109/SIBGRAPI.2019.00020. ISSN 1530-1834

12. Roth, S.F., Mattis, J.: Data characterization for intelligent graphics presentation. In: Proceedings of the Conference on Human Factors in Computing Systems (SIGCHI 1990), pp. 193–200. ACM Press (1990)
13. Sarikaya, A., Gleicher, M.: Scatterplots: tasks, data, and designs. IEEE Trans. Visual. Comput. Graphics **24**(1), 402–412 (2018). https://doi.org/10/gcp79j
14. Schulz, H., Nocke, T., Heitzler, M., Schumann, H.: A design space of visualization tasks. IEEE Trans. Visual. Comput. Graphics **19**(12), 2366–2375 (2013). https://doi.org/10/f5h3mb
15. Shneiderman, B.: The eyes have it: a task by data type taxonomy for information visualizations. In: Proceedings 1996 IEEE Symposium on Visual Languages, pp. 336–343, September 1996. https://doi.org/10.1109/VL.1996.545307
16. Srinivasan, A., Stasko, J.: Natural language interfaces for data analysis with visualization: considering what has and could be asked. In: Proceedings of the Eurographics/IEEE VGTC Conference on Visualization: Short Papers. EuroVis 2017, pp. 55–59. Eurographics Association, Goslar, DEU (2017). https://doi.org/10.2312/eurovisshort.20171133
17. Valiati, E.R.A., Pimenta, M.S., Freitas, C.M.D.S.: A taxonomy of tasks for guiding the evaluation of multidimensional visualizations. In: Proceedings of the 2006 AVI Workshop on BEyond Time and Errors: Novel Evaluation Methods for Information Visualization. BELIV 2006, Venice, Italy, pp. 1–6. ACM, New York (2006). https://doi.org/10/ckfz4w
18. Ware, C.: Information Visualization: Perception for Design, 3rd edn. Morgan Kaufmann, Waltham (2012)
19. Wehrend, S., Lewis, C.: A problem-oriented classification of visualization techniques. In: 1990 Proceedings of the 1st Conference on Visualization. VIS 1990, pp. 139–143. IEEE Computer Society Press, Los Alamitos (1990). http://dl.acm.org/citation.cfm?id=949531.949553
20. Zhou, M.X., Feiner, S.K.: Automated visual presentation: from heterogeneous information to coherent visual discourse. J. Intell. Inf. Syst. **11**(3), 205–234 (1998). https://doi.org/10/d8f764

Semi-automatic Annotation of OCT Images for CNN Training

Sebastian Schleier$^{(\boxtimes)}$, Noah Stolz, Holger Langner, Rama Hasan,
Christian Roschke, and Marc Ritter

Professorship Media Informatics, University of Applied Sciences Mittweida,
Mittweida, Germany
{sebastian.schleier,noah.simon.stolz,holger.langner,rama.hasan,
christian.roschke,marc.ritter}@hs-mittweida.de

Abstract. Annotating image data is one of the most time-consuming parts of the training of machine learning algorithms. With this contribution, we are looking for a solution that decreases the time needed for annotating images of the human retina created by *Optical coherence tomography* (OCT). As a first step, we use a simple annotation tool to test whether the sorting of images by their predicted amount of parts that contain anomalies decreases the time needed for annotation without increasing the number of annotation mistakes. The predictions are made by a *convolutional neural network* (CNN) that was trained on a previously annotated image set. We investigated the annotation behaviour in two groups of five subjects each. The first group received the (OCT) images in the order of recording, the second group sorted by the number of predicted anomalies. We observed a significant increase in annotation speed in the subjects of the second group while the quality of annotation remained at least stable.

Keywords: Machine learning · Convolutional neural network · Annotation · Semi-automatic annotation · Feature prediction · Web app · Optical coherence tomography

1 Introduction

The human eye is a sensitive organ. Diseases such as *age-related macula degeneration* (AMD) affect a large part of the global population. Older people are particularly affected [10].

For the treatment of AMD, generally images taken using the *Optical coherence tomography* (OCT) method are used. Recently, machine learning algorithms such as *convolutional neural networks* (CNN) have made it possible to make automated predictions about various aspects of the scans [6].

For this purpose, however, it is necessary to annotate the existing image material, which leads to a high expenditure of time. Therefore, we investigate methods to shorten the time needed for annotation.

© Springer Nature Switzerland AG 2020
M. Kurosu (Ed.): HCII 2020, LNCS 12181, pp. 672–685, 2020.
https://doi.org/10.1007/978-3-030-49059-1_49

1.1   OCT-Scans

Optical coherence tomography (OCT) is a noninvasive method for creating images of biological tissue. To create the image, light is sent from several positions into the tissue along a lateral axis and the time it takes for their reflection to return is used to determine the internal shape of the tissue [16].

One of its most common uses are retinal scans, through which diseases like *retinal vein occlusion* (RVO) or *age-related macula degeneration* (AMD) are made visible, with one scan containing a stack of images. In this contribution, we use OCT scans of human retinas. The technology is however also being used in fields like cardiology and oncology [18].

OCT sets itself apart from other methods of imaging through a number of aspects. For one, the process of creating images takes very little time, which on one hand is important because human subjects generally have trouble keeping their position for extended periods of time, negatively affecting the image quality. On the other hand it allows for the creation of 3D scans which are made of numerous sequential 2D scans [8].

When anomalies in an OCT scan are mentioned in this work it occurs in reference to oedema or druses.

1.2   Convolutional Neural Network

A *convolutional neural network* is a type of supervised machine learning algorithm. These differ from regular algorithms in that their results are not clearly defined during their creation. Instead of creating and optimizing a solution, examples of valid results are used to train the algorithm to extract the patterns that define these results [14].

In general neural networks consist of several neurons or nodes organized in layers. Each node represents one feature that defines the given input. Every neural network includes one input and one output layer as well as any number of hidden layers between them [15].

A *convolutional neural network's* defining feature is the use of *convolution*, a type of linear operation, in one or more layers. *Convolution* is in most cases a lot more efficient compared to regular matrix operations. One of the main reasons for this is *sparse connectivity*, meaning that unlike with matrix operations, not every element of an input layer needs to interact with every element of the following output layer. This drastically reduces the necessary computation. Another such feature is *parameter sharing*. Instead of every connection having a unique weight which would only be used once in the operation, some or all connections between two layers can share the same weight. Both of these techniques can be effective due to the fact that when looking for features in an image, smaller parts of the image are often times subject to the same operations for example to find edges [5].

1.3 Annotation

Because neural networks are a type of supervised machine learning algorithm they have to be provided with data to train them and their effectiveness needs to be evaluated manually. For this purpose already labelled data is required. If for example an algorithm is supposed to classify images with or without cats, it needs to be provided with images that are labeled as *cat* and *not cat*. Once it has been trained with these images the algorithm classifies a different set of labeled images. The labels are then compared with the classes given by the algorithm and used to evaluate the algorithm. The process of labeling data is called *annotation*. Generally *annotation* has to be performed by a human since the algorithm needs to know what a human would want the data to be classified as. That is why *annotation* is one of the most important but also one of the most time consuming and expensive parts of supervised machine learning [2].

These endeavors are often also made more difficult by the fact that *annotation* can in a lot of cases not be performed by laymen. Even labeling something that is common knowledge can be difficult if there are domain specific requirements that need to be fulfilled. This leads to the need for training the annotators.

Before the process of annotating can be started, the annotator needs to ensure that several prerequisites are fulfilled. For one, a sufficient amount of data for both training and validating a model needs to be available. The quality of the used images also needs to be sufficient and consistent across a given sequence. Another important step is ensuring that the rules which the *annotation* should follow are clear and cover all the possible cases the annotator might encounter. These rules should also require as little interpretation as possible to reduce the variation among different annotators. Once the process of annotating the images begins the annotator needs to find a balance between accurate *annotation* and not using to much time for each individual image. One common issue is that depending on the domain, the amount of images with no need for *annotation* can make up a large portion of the image sequence and take up a lot of time just to be identified as not depicting any relevant data.

A possible approach for improving this process is using a neural network to learn from the *annotation* and make predictions about the given data. It might also be possible to give direct feedback to determine whether the current *annotation* improves or harms the quality of the models prediction ability.

1.4 Relevance

As stated above obtaining labelled data is a time consuming and expensive process. Therefore new approaches have to be found to alleviate or circumvent the problems related to this process.

Especially in fields like medicine there is usually a lack of qualified personal, while at the same time there is a high demand for machine learning techniques to help with various jobs in diagnosing patients. The German population has on average been getting older for a long time, and age related diseases like macula degeneration are becoming more and more common [13], meaning that time efficient methods of diagnosing and treating them are also becoming more relevant.

With the macula degeneration in particular an early diagnosis can help reduce the damage caused by the disease. It's treatment is also rather expensive so an automation of parts of the diagnosis process could help make it more affordable [12].

All of these aspects underline the importance of finding ways to move away from a purely manual way of annotating images and taking first steps toward automating the process to a degree where the required effort for creating a dataset of sufficient size and quality becomes more reasonable. To this end the sorting of images based on the predicted amount of relevant data is an opportunity to measure the effectiveness of an automated approach, which should, regardless of its success, provide a starting point for further research.

1.5   Toolchaining

In the process of creating this work several different tools came into use. For processing images *ImageJ* was used, a library widely used for working with images in an academic context. For this project the *Fiji* version was used, which comes preinstalled with several plugins for image analysis [11].

Furthermore the *Template Matching* and *Slice Alignment* plugins are used. The first plugin is used to find regions of an image matching a given source image. The second plugin's purpose is to take a series of images and align them by moving them so that the target region, marked by the user, is at the same position for all images [17].

Probably the most relevant tool is *ConvNetJS*, a JavaScript library for creating, training and evaluating neural networks, such as the above mentioned *convolutional neural network*, inside a browser, simplifying the process of getting the network up and running [7].

The annotation tool itself is developed for usage in browsers, so it uses mainly JavaScript for its business logic. To simplify the processes of training the CNN and predicting the images, the tool used for CNN training should use JavaScript as well.

1.6   State of the Art

Thanks to the increasing interest in machine learning in the last few years, the field of annotation and how to decrease the required effort has become the theme of many scientific works. This has created several tools for annotation that seek to improve the process using various approaches.

Via is a web-based tool for manual image and video annotation. It is useful in that it is a light weight tool that can be run in a browser requiring little time for deployment. Users can create annotations using rectangles, circles and polygons. It also provides options for face-tracking across frames [4].

Other tools try to automate the process of defining shapes to varying degrees. **ByLabel** is a boundary based semi automatic tool for annotating images which automatically detects edges inside an image. The human annotator then only needs to select the edges that define the outline of an object [9].

FreeLabel has user freehand tracing around the depicted objects to detect their shape, which is a fast and easy to learn process that requires little in the way of instructions [3].

With the **PolygonRNN++** tool images are annotated using polygons. The main factor here is that shapes are found in the image and a neural network decides which shape to select and draw a polygon around, before showing the polygon to the human annotator. The exact position of the polygon vertices is then adjusted using another neural network. If the human decides to adjust the polygon, that information is given back to the network and it is adjusted to make better predictions in the future [1].

The support these tools provide the human annotator varies from being almost completely manual to requiring minimal human input per image. To the best of our knowledge there have been no works focusing on using machine learning to automating the process across an image sequence. With this work we hope to provide a possible approach to further the progress in this field.

1.7   Concept Details

Before diving into the actual software, we want to describe the goal that we are aiming to reach. The annotation process as we hope to develop in this and future work consists of the following six steps.

Step 1: Loading images. The source can either be the local drive or a web server. The images are then stored on the web server together with the annotation data.

Step 2: Preprocessing of images. Possible methods can be quite simplistic, such as cropping a certain part of the image or shifting the color values to gain a unified brightness, but also more complex, such as aligning the images or identifying images that are not suitable for annotation.

Step 3: CNN-specific preprocessing of images. After generally processing the images, there are certain steps that can optionally be taken. It can be reasonable to split up the images into multiple *slices* or reduce the 3 channels of an RGB image that only describe greyscale values to one channel.

Step 4: Prediction of images. There are a lot of highly domain-specific aspects that could be predicted. Some of them are image-related, e.g. if the image shows a part of the retina, which is close to the macula. Some only describe a part of the image, e.g. a certain part contains an *anomaly* or errors created while taking the image.

Step 5: Annotation of images. In this step, the user has to use the given annotation tools to mark areas of great (if the area contains an important information) or low (if the area contains misleading errors or random noise) interest.

Step 6: Saving annotation data. The data that the user created needs to be saved so that it can easily be recombined with the images, that were used to create it.

Each step uses a number of parameters to fulfill the desired action. When setting up the process, these parameters have to be set to a specific value. Some values even have to be flexible for each step in order to modify them to fit the specific problems. The parameters for steps S1 and S6 are omitted from this work to focus on the parameters of the other steps.

The following enumeration shows some important parameters that need to be implemented. Thereby, *differs per OCT scan* means that a separate value must be determined for each OCT scan. *differs per OCT image* means that it is necessary to determine a specific value per image. Contrary, *constant across all OCT scans* means that it is crucial to keep the value constant through the whole process. Finally, *problem-specific* means that there ought to be a single value to keep constant while solving the problem.

S2 P1 **Align ROI**, *differs per OCT scan*. For aligning the images, a *region of interest* in one reference image has to be declared. The algorithm finds a similar region in the other images and shifts the pixels so that all similar regions have the same position within their image.

S2 P2 **Crop Rectangle**, *differs per OCT scan*. Cropping area can be chosen to make differently sized images align or to get rid of irrelevant parts around the actual scan image.

S2 P3 **Invert Image**, *differs per OCT scan*. The backgrounds of some OCT scans are bright, some are dark. Inverting some images to create consistent dataset can help with the CNN training.

S2 P4 **Drop Image**, *differs per OCT image*. Some images show the surface of the retina. These images are not suitable for training the same CNN and have to be omitted.

S3 P1 **Slice Rectangle**, *constant across all OCT scans*. Every image is divided into *slices* of equal size. *Slice* width and height ratio should be chosen so that it is equal to the original image, while the image width and height should be evenly dividable through the *slice* width and height respectively.

S3 P2 **Reduce Channels**, *constant across all OCT scans*. As every OCT image only contains greyscale values, the three RGB channels can be merged into one greyscale value.

S4 P1 **Predicted POI**, *constant across all OCT scans*. Slices that the CNN predicted to contain points of interest.

  a The **distance** towards the **macula** has a certain value.

  b The *slice* contains one or more **anomalies**.

  c The *slice* contains an **image error**.

  d The *slice* contains **random noise**.

  e The *slice* contains a **vessel**.

S4 P2 **CNN Structure**, *problem-specific*. For every aspect that has to be predicted, there is an optimal CNN structure. Partly, we can use the same CNN to predict multiple aspects, which probably makes the CNN more complex. The structure of a CNN consists of a number of layers, which each has a certain task.

S4 P3 **Training Parameters,** *problem-specific.*
   a **Solver:** Different variants of *stochastic gradient descent.*
   b **MinBatchSize:** The amount of data used for each step of updating the parameters of the network.
   c **MaxEpoch:** How often the training should run through the full dataset.
   d **LearningRate:** How strongly the parameters are adjusted during each training step.
S5 P1 **Annotation Tools,** *problem-specific.* The annotation software provides a certain amount of tools than can be used to annotate the given images.
   a **PixelAnnotation:** The tool allows annotating a single pixel.
   b **RectangleAnnotation:** The tool allows using a rectangle to label a certain area.
   c **CircularAnnotation:** The tool allows using a circle to label a certain area.
   d **PolygonAnnotation:** The tool allows using a polygon to label a certain area. The single corners have to be placed seperatly.
   e **PolygonAnnotationBezier:** A polygon as in d, but with curvy edges.
   f **AutoFill:** With the already annotated information as input, an algorithm annotates additional parts of the image.
   g **AutoEdge:** Lines that are used to specify the annotated part of the image are automatically transformed to match the edges found in the image.
   h **IncludeOtherImages:** If the annotated part in one image is similar in an adjacent image (or a maximum of n steps away), that part is annotated as well.

2   Implementation

The target of this contribution is to gain the desired insights of whether sorting images by predicted *anomalies* count improves the annotation speed. Therefore, we developed the two programs *Online Annotator* and *CNN Training*, which run separately on one web server. As described in this section, there are multiple interactions between these programs.

2.1   Image Preprocessing

The used OCT images are available in the PNG-Format with a size of 512×496 pixels. First, we used the *Slice Alignment* plugin for *Fiji* to align the retina in all OCT images. Afterwards, we cut this area out of the images to gain new images without any unnecessary information. These new images have a dimension of 512×180 pixels.

2.2   System Architecture

The system architecture consists of three main parts, as seen in Fig. 1. First the *online annotator* is used to create annotations for selected images. These annotations are stored in the *database*, making up the second part. Lastly, the *CNN training* uses the annotations inside the *database* to create a model for automatic annotations, which is also saved in the *database*. Lastly, the *online annotator* utilizes this model for automatic annotation.

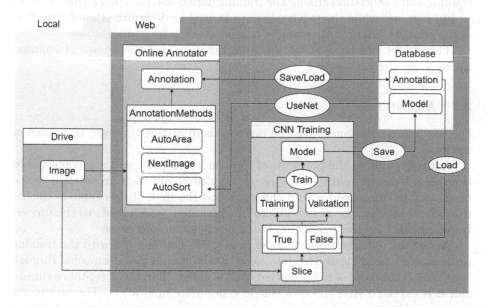

Fig. 1. The system is made up of one local part and three web-based parts, where the **Online Annotator** is used to annotate images, the **CNN Training** part uses these annotations to train a CNN and the **Database** stores the created annotation and model.

Before the user can start working, the necessary image or image sequence needs to be stored on the local drive. To start the annotation process the user opens a browser and visits the *online annotator* website, where the images to annotate need to be selected from the drive.

Two different annotation methods are provided to the user. **AutoArea** is the most basic method, where the user simply clicks on the pixel he wishes to annotate. Any surrounding pixels whose greyscale value is close enough to the first pixels value get marked as well. The other method, **AutoAnnotation**, uses a *convolutional neural network* to automatically annotate the image.

Once the user has finished annotating the images he can save the annotation, without the images, inside a database. It is also possible to load existing annotations from the database.

To train a model for automatic annotation the user needs to visits the *CNN Training* website. There the images that where annotated need to be loaded again. The images are then divided into slices of equal size. Using the annotations from the database the *slices* are assigned values of true, if they contain any annotation and false, if they do not. The *slices* are then randomly divided into a training and a validation group. The training data is used to train a *convolutional neural network*, while the validation data is used to determine the effectiveness of the training. The resulting model can be saved inside the database.

This model can be used for the *AutoAnnotation* of the *Online Annotator*, through the *UseNet* method.

2.3   Algorithms

For the purpose of annotating the images, there at this time are two different methods.

AutoArea takes the greyscale of the annotated pixel and a predetermined threshold. Next, any surrounding pixels are visited and their greyscale is multiplied with the distance between this pixel and the first. If this value is smaller than the threshold, the pixel will also be annotated, which leads to the process being repeated for the neighbours of the newly annotated pixel.

AutoSort uses the trained model from CNN Training. As with the training process, every image is divided into *slices*. Every *slice* is then forwarded through the CNN. If the score of the predicted class is higher than the acceptance threshold, it is expected that the *slice* should contain an annotation. The images are then sorted by the number of *slices* with expected annotations they contain and presented to the user in that order.

3   Evaluation

To gain first findings concerning the studied annotation methods, we examined the process that leads to fully annotated image material. For this, we use images from the TOPOs project[1]. They are made up of five OCT scans with a total of 165 OCT images. Each of these scans contains at least one *anomaly*. We used our toolchain, as described in Sect. 1.5 to get the desired images. Afterwards, we annotated the images manually, using the *AutoArea*- and the *NextImage*-annotation methods, as described in Sect. 2.3. The annotated images were used for training the CNN.

---

[1] https://topos.averbis.de/.

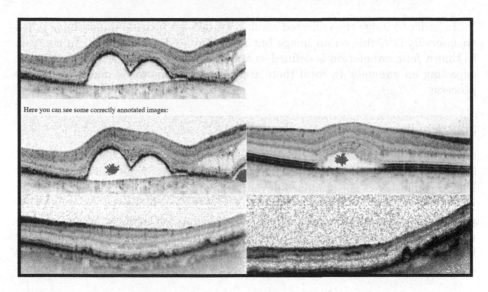

Fig. 2. The website *Online-Annotator* shows the currently annotated image at the top, an introduction and explanation text in the middle (omitted in the image) and four example images as a guidance for the annotator at the bottom.

3.1 Evaluation Setup

Our leading research question during this experiment was: Does sorting the images based on predicted number of *anomaly slices* reduce the time needed to annotate those images? To answer this we focused not only on how much time the annotating took but also on the quality, as in how often where *anomalies* missed and how often was something other then an *anomaly* annotated?

Ten subjects where divided into two equally large Groups. Every subject was given the task of annotating the same sequence of given images. Every Group uses *AutoArea* while Group 1 uses no additional method and Group 2 uses *AutoSort* to arrange the images in an order with those predicted to have the most *slices* to annotate first and those predicted to have the least last.

All subjects used a common laptop with an external mouse and the newest version of the Google Chrome browser. To annotate, they only needed the right and left arrow key and the left mouse button, meaning there was no need to alternate between different input devices.

The website (Fig. 2) used for the annotations shows the image currently being annotated. This is also the area, which the user clicks into to annotate the image. As the *AutoArea*-method is always in use, matching pixels in close proximity will also be annotated. The test subject can switch between images using the left and right arrow key. The time the subject takes to annotate each image begins counting once the subject navigates to that image and stops once they navigate to the next or the previous one.

In order to judge the collected results, we defined *missing annotations* when an *anomaly* is visible on an image but not annotated by a subject. In contrast to that a *false annotation* is defined as annotating a part of a picture that is not depicting an *anomaly*. In total there are 88 annotations to be made during the process.

3.2   Findings

On average the time needed to create the annotation across both Groups was 5:43. With the average time for deciding the annotations of one individual picture being around 1.8 s. The standard deviation is greater then the average time per picture with 2.0 s, the longest duration spent on one image being about 15 s while some picture were only looked at for 267 ms. Not annotating an *anomaly* was generally a lot more common (14.5 average) then annotating a part of the image that was not an *anomaly* (5.3 average). Table 1 shows a comparison of the average values of both Groups compared with those of each individual Group.

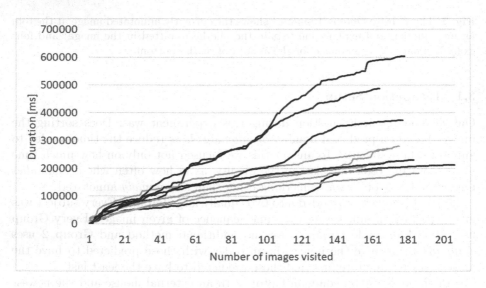

Fig. 3. The cumulative duration per image visited of each test subject. Blue lines indicate a participant of Group 1, orange lines indicate a participant of Group 2.

The data shows a much higher total duration for Group 1. This is due to most of Group 1's subjects spending a large amount of time on a few select images. However Group 1's median is still non the less almost double that of Group 2. The average number of *missing annotations* is about the same for both Groups, while the number of *false annotations* is less then half for Group 2. An overview for the time needed per image is shown in Fig. 3. The difference in the number of visited images is owed to the fact that it is possible to go forward and backward while annotating. So, not all subjects are necessarily at the same image after an

Table 1. The average values of both Groups together and separately. Group 1 annotated chronically sorted OCT images, Group 2 those sorted by amount of predicted anomalies.

Average values	All subjects	Group 1	Group 2
Total [min]	5:43	7:30	3:56
Mean per image [s]	1.8	2.2	1.3
Median per image [s]	1.0	1.3	0.8
Standard deviation [s]	2.0	2.5	1.5
Longest per image [s]	15.6	20.3	11.0
Shortest per image [ms]	266	225	308
Missing annotations	14.5	13.6	15.4
False annotations	5.3	7.6	3.0

equal amount of visited images. A steep curve means that the participant spent a lot of time on few images.

3.3 Discussion

Based on the findings of the experiment we can try to make several hypothesis regarding their cause. It should be noted that in this instance the experiment was conducted using a very small number of participants, for more robust results a larger sample size would be required.

The longer duration of Group 1 could originate from the fact that this Group's subjects needed a much longer time for images in the later part of the image set than Group 2's subjects. This could be caused by the possible speedup gained from the knowledge that there are only few remaining *anomalies* that need to be annotated. Therefore, the subjects can skip images with a high rate. Combined with the fact, that the count of *missing annotations* is not significantly increased, it seems plausible that the speedup comes with little to no costs in terms of accuracy.

The higher effectiveness of Group 2 could come from a higher level of concentration at the beginning of the annotation process. The more even distribution of *anomalies* in the unsorted image set of Group 1 necessitates a more sustained level of concentration than if most of the anomalies can be found in the earlier images of the image set.

Interestingly, the mean value of the shortest time per a single image is lower for Group 1 than for Group 2. We hypothesized the opposite, because it seemed plausible that the subjects of Group 2 can keep up a higher pace when annotating the last images.

Because the surroundings during the annotation process differed from subject to subject, it is possible that the duration per image is not perfectly accurate, the very high durations especially could come from small distractions. On the other hand, we eliminated all values that we perceived to be outliers, which decreased Group 1's mean duration significantly. Nonetheless, there could be values in the data that come from occasions, where the subject did not really focus on annotating.

4   Conclusion and Future Work

With this work, we started looking for strategies to enhance the annotation speed of human annotators by combining human intelligence with machine learning algorithms. We developed a toolchain that enables us to start looking at different aspects of the annotation process. We implemented a first machine learning algorithm and discovered, that by using machine learning supported annotation, the speed of annotation process can possibly be increased.

During our research we found multiple points of interest that might warrant a more thorough inspection in future work.

Image errors created while taking the picture could present a point of interest for annotation, in order to allow the rest of the process to ignore this particular area of the image or to maybe repair the error to a degree where it does not negatively effect the image.

It might also prove interesting to try and make predictions about images as soon as they are uploaded to reduce the time consuming steps currently needed to get to the prediction phase.

The possibility of training the model as more images are being annotated could also prove interesting. Furthermore giving the annotator feedback about the effect the new annotations are having on the quality of the current CNN model and it's predictions, might increase the effectiveness of the whole process even more, by allowing him to adjust insufficient annotations.

One important step in examining the relevance of this work would be a comparison to approaches that use raw data with only very basic annotations, that only note that something of interest is shown in the picture, not where it is exactly.

Since the possibility of labelling uploaded images with the predicted amount of *anomalies* is already implemented, it might be worth to try finding out what more can be made out of this label. For example, the amount of images that the annotator gets to see simultaneously can depend on the amount of predicted *anomalies*. If an image contains many predicted *anomalies*, no other image is shown parallel. But images that seem to contain no *anomalies* at all are visible at once.

Acknowledgement. We like to acknowledge that Prof. Dr. Andreas Stahl and the collaborators of the TOPOs project provided the OCT image data that was used in this study, as well as the ophthalmological background. TOPOs (*"Therapievorhersage durch Analyse von Patientendaten in der Ophthalmologie"*) is a collaborative project that is funded by BMBF (*"Bundesministerium für Bildung und Forschung"*, *"Federal Ministry of Education & Resarch"*) (FKZ: 13GW0170B) from March 2017 to January 2020.

The SMWK (*"Sächsisches Staatsministerium für Wissenschaft, Kultur und Tourismus"*) supported this work by funding the project *"Digitale Produkt- und*

Prozessinnovationen 2020", which contains a work package named *"Entwicklung und Implementierung eines begehbaren Auges zur computergestützten Annotation von Augenkrankheiten in der virtuellen Realität"*. This work describes findings that were made while working on this work package.

References

1. Acuna, D., Ling, H., Kar, A., Fidler, S.: Efficient interactive annotation of segmentation datasets with polygon-RNN++. In: Proceedings of the IEEE conference on Computer Vision and Pattern Recognition, pp. 859–868 (2018)
2. Culotta, A., McCallum, A.: Reducing labeling effort for structured prediction tasks. In: AAAI, vol. 5, pp. 746–751 (2005)
3. Dias, P.A., Shen, Z., Tabb, A., Medeiros, H.: Freelabel: a publicly available annotation tool based on freehand traces. In: 2019 IEEE Winter Conference on Applications of Computer Vision (WACV), pp. 21–30. IEEE (2019)
4. Dutta, A., Zisserman, A.: The via annotation software for images, audio and video. In: Proceedings of the 27th ACM International Conference on Multimedia, pp. 2276–2279 (2019)
5. Goodfellow, I., Bengio, Y., Courville, A.: Deep Learning. MIT Press, Cambridge (2016). http://www.deeplearningbook.org
6. Hasan, R., Langner, H., Ritter, M., Eibl, M.: Investigating the robustness of pretrained networks on OCT-dataset. In: Actual Problems of System and Software Engineering, November 2019
7. Karpathy, A.: Convnetjs. https://cs.stanford.edu/people/karpathy/convnetjs/index.html. Accessed 14 Feb 2020
8. Podoleanu, A.G.: Optical coherence tomography. J. Microscopy **247**(3), 209–219 (2012). https://doi.org/10.1111/j.1365-2818.2012.03619.x. https://onlinelibrary.wiley.com/doi/abs/10.1111/j.1365-2818.2012.03619.x
9. Qin, X., He, S., Zhang, Z., Dehghan, M., Jagersand, M.: ByLabel: a boundary based semi-automatic image annotation tool. In: 2018 IEEE Winter Conference on Applications of Computer Vision (WACV), pp. 1804–1813. IEEE (2018)
10. Resnikoff, S., et al.: Global data on visual impairment in the year 2002. Bull. World Health Organ. **82**(11), 844–851 (2004)
11. Schindelin, J., et al.: Fiji: an open-source platform for biological-image analysis. Nat. Methods **9**(7), 676–682 (2012)
12. Schmidt-Erfurth, U.M., et al.: Guidance for the treatment of neovascular age-related macular degeneration. Acta Ophthalmol. Scand. **85**(5), 486–494 (2007)
13. Schrader, W.F.: Altersbedingte makuladegeneration. Der Ophthalmol. **103**(9), 742–748 (2006)
14. Simeone, O.: A very brief introduction to machine learning with applications to communication systems. IEEE Trans. Cogn. Commun. Netw. **4**(4), 648–664 (2018)
15. Specht, D.F., et al.: A general regression neural network. IEEE Trans. Neural Netw. **2**(6), 568–576 (1991)
16. Swanson, E.A., et al.: In vivo retinal imaging by optical coherence tomography. Opt. Lett. **18**(21), 1864–6 (1993)
17. Tseng, Q., et al.: Spatial organization of the extracellular matrix regulates cell–cell junction positioning. Proc. Natl. Acad. Sci. (2012). https://doi.org/10.1073/pnas.1106377109. https://www.pnas.org/content/early/2012/01/09/1106377109
18. Zysk, A.M., Nguyen, F.T., Oldenburg, A.L., Marks, D.L., Boppart, S.A.: Optical coherence tomography: a review of clinical development from bench to bedside. J. Biomed. Opt. **12**(5), 051403 (2007)

The Impact of Increasing and Decreasing the Professionalism of News Webpage Aesthetics on the Perception of Bias in News Articles

Brendan Spillane[✉], Séamus Lawless, and Vincent Wade

ADAPT Centre, Trinity College Dublin, Dublin, Ireland
{brendan.spillane,seamus.lawless,vincent.wade}@adaptcentre.ie

This paper is dedicated to the memory of Professor Séamus "Shay" Lawless who died after fulfilling his dream of summiting Mount Everest on May 16th 2019.

Abstract. This paper reports further results from a large study examining the impact of the visual aesthetics of news websites on the perception of bias in news articles. It focuses on the characteristic of professionalism, which is of particular importance to mainstream news websites. Nine news articles were amended to create a range of biased content. They were then paired with webpages from nine popular news websites which underwent common cumulative distortions to degrade the professionalism of their aesthetics. Pre-tests confirmed the effectiveness of these processes. A crowdsourced experiment and ANOVA analysis ($N = 405$, $\alpha = 0.05$, ES $= 0.24$) demonstrated a negative correlation between the professionalism of the aesthetics and perceptions of bias. These effects were common across all nine news websites and news articles with different levels of bias.

Keywords: Bias · News webpage aesthetics · News website design

1 Introduction

Bias has been a factor in news since time immemorial. The production, dissemination, and consumption stages of the news cycle are rife with opportunities for its introduction and influence [85]. Bias in the dissemination of news on the Internet, is an increasingly important issue [74]. Despite this, there is a lack of research investigating its manifestation or effect. With the current focus on the veracity and quality of news, especially online, research is required to understand if the medium and method of its presentation may be exerting undue influence. One factor which has received little attention is the impact of the professionalism of the aesthetics of news webpages on the perception of bias in news articles. Professionalism is an important characteristic of successful mainstream news websites [54].

© Springer Nature Switzerland AG 2020
M. Kurosu (Ed.): HCII 2020, LNCS 12181, pp. 686–710, 2020.
https://doi.org/10.1007/978-3-030-49059-1_50

Understanding whether the visual presentation of news online impacts consumers perception of bias is important because of the unknown influence it may have on consumers and the long-term consequences for news agencies. Bias is considered a core dimension and measure of credibility. Credibility has been defined as a multi-dimensional construct [35], and/or as a perceptual variable [27]. Dimensions such as trustworthiness, expertise, bias, believability, accuracy, fairness, and depth of coverage have all regularly been used in studies to measure credibility. Which dimensions and their number depends on multiple factors including what is being assessed (source, message or medium), and the domain it is being measured in. Thus, dimensions such as *qualified* and *safe* are often used when measuring the credibility of healthcare websites, while *bias* and *accuracy* are more often relied on when measuring the credibility of news websites.

Fogg et al. have shown that the importance of bias as a dimension increases when users are judging news online [29]. Fico et al. have shown that an increase in perceived bias in a news article has a corresponding decrease in credibility of the news organization behind it [26]. Chiagouris et al. have also shown that credibility factors have a significant relationship to positive attitudes towards a news website [13]. Thus, an increase in perceived bias, reduces perceived credibility, which can negatively impact a user's attitude towards a news website and the news organization behind it, resulting in them turning to other sources of news.

2 Motivation

Historically, research into bias in the news can be visualized as a grid. On the x-axis are the various mediums of dissemination; Print, Radio, Television, and the Internet. On the y-axis are the three main stages of the news cycle; Production, Dissemination, and Consumption. While there is large overlap, most studies on bias in the news, whether on selection, partisan, agenda setting, coverage, or framing bias etc., fit within this grid. The few examples of research into bias in the dissemination of news online [103,104] are outweighed by the preponderance of studies investigating bias in the dissemination of news in print, radio, and television shown below.

Production: Studies include research proving news agencies purposely bias their news to match the opinions of their target audiences [36,79], the impact of advertisers on news agencies [2,20,45,91,93], the influence of editors, editorials, and policy [21,31,52,57,70,115], and individual journalistic biases [23,25,44,87, 89,97].

Dissemination: There is an extensive compendium of research on bias in the dissemination of news in print, radio, and television. A small sample of the research includes studies on bias in photographs in newspapers and news magazines [5,42,55,76,77], research into the overarching area of visual biases [38,43,56, 96], bias in news anchors' facial expressions [32,73,80,117], news anchor intonation and tone [41,78], presenters' non-verbal communication [3,69,114], television soundbites and image-bites [24,40], newspaper layout [8,99], newspaper coverage [9,10,17,58,59,64,84,92], newspaper headlines and lead stories [52,58,60,63,70, 98,105,106,108,110], and description or labelling bias [22,66–68].

Consumption: The impact of bias in the consumption stage of the news cycle has tended to focus on the impact on voting in elections [18,21,37,80], with several attempts proposed to mitigate its effects [81,85,86].

3   Related Work

This paper reports results from an experiment that investigates the impact of aesthetic *professionalism* on the perception of bias in news articles on mainstream news websites. It is the second experiment reported from a large multi-faceted study which investigated how design and visual aesthetics influence the perception of news. A previously reported experiment demonstrated a negative correlation between *visual quality* and perceived bias in news articles [104]. The distortions in that emulated lower quality news outlets such as tabloids, entertainment news websites, and content farms. The experiment reported in this paper is distinct from that work. It has a different research question, objectives, and separate hypotheses. For the most part, it uses different data to answer the hypotheses, though there are some crossover observations used in both experiments, e.g. the D0 controls are the same. The news articles that were inserted into the webpages and the procedure they underwent to add bias are also the same. As a result of the aligned though separate nature of these experiments, much of the experiment setup is the same. To avoid replication, brief synopses of certain experiment setup procedures are provided, with further detail available in [104].

3.1   Professionalism Versus Visual Quality

The results reported in [104] show that increasing and decreasing the *visual quality* of news webpages impacts the perception of bias in news articles is of limited relevance to mainstream news websites. The elements which impact *visual quality* such as loud, prominent, gaudy and cheap advertising and excessive calls to action, are typically only found on low quality, tabloid, entertainment news, or content farm news websites. The majority of mainstream news websites such as those used in this study do not include such elements. Thus, this study instead focuses on the characteristic of *professionalism* as it is more important to mainstream news agencies than *visual quality* [6,100,101,112]. In her work on the visual identity of mainstream and alternative news websites, Kenix argues that *"When something embodies professional characteristics, the audience assumes that there is a higher level of competence and specialized knowledge present"* [54].

3.2   The Impact of Visual Design and Aesthetics on Credibility

In their review of empirical literature investigating the impact of website design on initial impressions of trust, Karimov, Brengman and Van Hove present a conceptual framework based on the literature defining the three main dimensions of website design (visual design, social cue design, and content design) and several sub dimensions [53]. They define visual design, which we call aesthetics, as *"graphical and structural factors that give consumers a first impression"*. Lavie and Tractinsky identified *'classical'* and *'expressive'* as the main dimensions of website aesthetics [61]. Several studies have also shown that website aesthetics impact perceptions of credibility [15, 27, 51, 95, 102].

3.3 Bias - a Core Dimension and Measure of Credibility

The closest related work on the impact of aesthetics on bias is in the overarching domain of credibility, of which bias is a core dimension and measure. Credibility may be defined in terms of believability [30], its dimensions [35, 48], or as a perceptual variable [50, 83]. Being perceived as credible is of paramount importance to news organizations. Cassidy maintains that *"journalism is built on credibility"* [11]. Fogg et al. have also shown that bias is especially relied upon in judgements of credibility of online news [29]. Abdulla et al. also found that *"online news credibility... ...was built upon trustworthiness, timeliness, and bias factors"* [1].

3.4 Professionalism and Mainstream News Websites

Professionalism is one of the most important characteristics of mainstream news media. Vuontela roots her definitions of mainstream news in its professionalism with *"print, broadcast (television and radio), or online news items that are meant for mass communication and are published by professional media companies and/or journalists."* [111]. Leccese defines mainstream news websites as *"Web sites operated by mass media outlets that employ salaried staff and whose Web site is a supplement to its print editions, broadcasts, or syndicated news service"* [62]. As many news websites now exist without such traditional mediums of dissemination, this study adopts the definition of Deuze who maintains that mainstream news websites have two common characteristics, editorial content, and a minimal often moderated form of participatory communication. He further maintains: *"This type of news site cannot be said to differ - in its approach to journalistic storytelling, news values, relationships with audiences - fundamentally from journalism as it is practised in print or broadcasting media"* [19].

3.5 MTFS of Credibility Judgement and Underlying Theory

Unlike economics [109], or political communication [116], there are currently no general models or theories to explain how users form judgements of bias when consuming news on the Internet. Yet numerous texts exist demonstrating that the news we consume has an innate bias favouring the privileged while ignoring the needs of minorities [7, 14, 46]. News agencies have also been shown to bias their news in favour of the views of the segment of the market they are trying to attract [36, 79]. Consequently, the overarching domain of credibility was explored. Ten cognitive Models, Theories, Frameworks, and Schematics (MTFS) which explain how users form judgements of credibility online were identified [28,30,33,47,65,71,72,94,107,113]. Each of these provide a different arc of perspective on the same problem. Many highlight the iterative nature of the process, where users continuously notice different elements and make or refine their credibility judgements. Most of the MTFS do not solely focus on the content or message, but also highlight the importance of its presentation. Many, such as Sundar's MAIN model, maintain that visual cues in a webpage enable the user to make judgements heuristically [107]. Metzger and Flanagin go further and categorize three types of cues (site, message, and author), by which judgements of credibility are formed. Combined with characteristics of the receiver, they influence credibility evaluations online [72]. Hilligoss and Rieh also highlight the importance of three types of cues; content, peripheral source, and peripheral information objects [47].

Almost all of the MTFS rely in part on underlying theory provided by the Elaboration Likelihood Model (ELM) or the Heuristic Systematic Model (HSM) [12,88], two of the Dual-Process Models of Persuasion [34]. They generally contend that if the user is unmotivated, uninspired, or uncommitted, or if the task is unimportant, mundane or repetitive, the user will adopt the less cognitively demanding peripheral route or heuristic strategy from the ELM or HSM when judging information. This research was undertaken under the supposition that like credibility, judgements of perceived bias in online news, are at least partially judged heuristically and there would be a negative correlation between professionalism and bias.

4   Hypotheses

H1: H_0 Perceived bias will not be decreased due to an increase in the professionalism of the news webpage's aesthetics. This focuses on the impact of increasing the professionalism of news webpage's aesthetics on perceived bias.

H2: H_0 Perceived bias will not be increased due to a decrease in the professionalism of news webpage's aesthetics. This focuses on the impact of decreasing the professionalism of the webpage's aesthetics on perceived bias. It should be noted that this is not simply the opposite of H1.

H3: H_0 The impact of the professionalism of the aesthetics will be inconsistent, regardless of the level of bias in the article. This focuses on whether any potential impact of the primary hypotheses is dependent on the level of bias in a news article itself, rather than the webpage.

5   Experiment Design

A single webpage was selected from nine news websites and paired with one of nine news articles for the duration of the experiment. The text of each news article was modified before the experiment began and then remained unchanged. Each news article was inserted into the webpage's HTML replacing the existing article so that the website's CSS rendered it like an original. Each web-page/article combination was then subject to a series of common, cumulative distortions. After each distortion was applied (D6–D0), a static image was captured for use in the experiment. Four levels of degrading distortion (D4 to D1 below) were chosen as a balance between enough granularity and the natural break points provided by the underlying technologies which could be removed in stages.

- **D6:** An undistorted version of each webpage/article combination with their original name, branding, and logo.
- **D5:** Name, branding and logos replaced with the generic moniker NewsCom matching the original colour palette.
- **D4–D1:** Incrementally less aesthetically professional versions of D5.
- **D0:** The controls, plain text versions of each article to establish ground truth bias ratings.

6   Methodology

The experiment was set up as a 9×7 within subjects incomplete counterbal-anced measures design. Incomplete counterbalancing was achieved by arranging the webpage/article combinations and distortions (D0–D6) in a reduced form Latin square. Participants were randomly assigned to one of 9 diagonal paths through the Latin square that intersected with the 9×7 distorted webpage/article combinations, thus ensuring that each participant experienced each news webpage/article and each distortion once. To reduce carryover effects and task fatigue, once assigned to a path, the distorted webpage/article combinations the participant would encounter were displayed in random order. Two attention questions, to determine continued diligence to the task were also added to each path.

6.1   Creating a Range of Biased News Articles

Existing news articles on un-emotive topics were modified to create a range of biased content to test H3. This is described in detail in [104]. A pre-test bias rating task which showed that a range of biased content was successfully created.

6.2   Selection of Websites and Webpages and Their Pairing

The selection process for the websites[1] and individual webpages is described in detail in [104]. In summary, they were all English language news websites which fit Kenix's description of mainstream [54]. The individual webpages were the most recent from each website related to the article that would be inserted. It should be noted, that as explained in [104], it is incidental that e.g. the Guardian

---

[1] theguardian.com, telegraph.co.uk, independent.co.uk, economist.com, spectator. co.uk, newstatesman.com, aljazeera.com, bbc.com, and reuters.com.

Table 1. The main factors of professional design, the main underlying design or technical means of conveying it, and the action required to degrade it.

Aspect of (Un)Professionalism Conveyed to the User	Means of affordance	Degrading action
Overall design/colour scheme	Design, layout, images, colour schemes	Add issues with alignment and layout. Reduce the quality of the colour scheme
Technical quality of the website	HTML/CSS/JavaScript	Reduce or remove elements that convey technical ability
Design appropriateness, reserved, custom, unique or non-standard features or elements	Image quality, fonts, interactive features and widgets	Degrade quality of images, introduce basic or standard elements e.g. fonts or third party services
Money and/or technical ability in the organization behind the website	Technical ability	Introduce obvious technical issues
Credibility, focus on the news article	Size, prominence, quality of advertising	Increase amount and prominence of advertising
Excessive calls to action on the user	Sharing, signup, user interaction or other methods of connecting	Increase the amount or size of calls to action
Expertise's on the topic, history dealing with the subject	Information scent via links to supporting content	Remove or reduce supporting links

was considered highly biased or that the New Statesman was considered mostly unbiased. The bias ratings are due to the articles that were inserted into the webpages. It should also be noted that only the D6 distortions had branding applied. We simply use the website names for simplicity and descriptive purposes to describe the webpage/article combination rather than e.g. W1, W2 etc.

6.3   Distorting the Professionalism of the Aesthetics

The aim of the distortion process was to progressively and commonly degrade the professionalism of the aesthetics of each webpage in stages to ascertain if there was a corresponding increase in the perception of bias in the news articles they contain. An image of each distorted webpage/article combination was used in the experiment to negate browser support issues resulting from the distorted code and to prevent participants navigating away from the webpages.

In Kenix's work on the visual identity of news websites, she explores design principles and professionalism in detail [54]. She maintains that *"the overall design of a Web page itself can suggest an identity of sophistication, seriousness, and professionalism if it follows a structured, aligned construction."* [54]. This is conveyed through alignment, unity, balance, rhythm, and contrast among other factors. She argues that these elements can also be manipulated to convey a sense of *"unprofessionalism characterized by disorder, tension, a sense of chaos, and division"* [54]. With this knowledge, a review of the news websites used in this experiment and others was conducted by five experienced website designers, see Table 1. This focused on identifying the means by which professionalism is conveyed and the degrading action necessary to negatively impact it.

6.4   Creating and Applying the Distortions

Based on Kenix's work and the design review, a two-pronged approach was used to distort the webpage/article combinations. First, technical support for underlying technologies, which Sundar claims are the means of providing such affordances [107], was removed by deleting the underlying code. This contributed to a reduced visual aesthetic. Second, every image used in each webpage was degraded by reducing file size, bit rate, and DPI. The screenshot of each webpage/article combination taken after each stage of the distortion process was also similarly degraded. The distortion process is detailed in Table 2 and an example of the D5-D2 distortions for Al Jazeera are shown in Fig. 1. The decision to include seven levels of distortion was based on the following.

- **D6:** These were included to see if branding made a significant difference to participant bias ratings.
- **D5:** These formed the basis from which the cumulative process to reduce the professionalism of each webpage/article's aesthetic begun.
- **D4–D1:** The decision to incrementally reduce the level of professionalism over four levels was primarily based on the underlying support provided by W3C standards. During research into content preparation it was found that removing the underlying technological support for the W3C standards shown in Table 2 across all nine websites produced roughly equal incremental reductions in professional appearance.
- **D0:** These were included to establish a ground truth bias rating.

Table 2. Distortion stages and descriptions.

Distortion	Distortion descriptions
D6 branded	Visible comments in comment facilities removed so that the opinions expressed in such would not impact the experiment
D5 unbranded	Remove Logo, Name, and Branding
D4	Remove CSS 3 and CSS 4, Reduce the quality (DPI) of each image used in the website
D3	Remove all elements introduced in HTML 5.1 Further reduce the DPI of each image used in the website. Resize images to show stretching Remove all custom fonts Remove all JavaScript functionality
D2	Remove CSS 2/2.1 support Further reduce DPI of images and skew size
D1	Unlink all CSS files but keep HTML elements Further reduce DPI of images and skew size
D0 control	Remove all CSS/HTML except for the plain text, <p> and <h1> tags in the article

The distortion process was designed to be replicable and focus on removing and/or slowly breaking underlying technologies and reducing the quality of images and graphics. This would replicate the sense of disorder, tensions, chaos and division described by Kenix which contribute to an unprofessional appearance [54]. While colour schemes were raised several times during the review, no distortion was applied to this aspect due to reductions in quality being subjective and difficult to replicate. Depending on their construction and underlying technologies, there was some variation in the commonality of the degrading effect of each level of distortion. However, this could not be helped and the overall trend of increasingly unprofessional aesthetics from D4 to D1 was common overall.

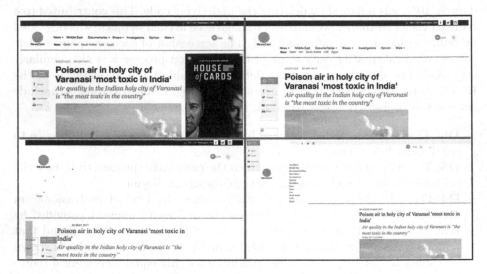

Fig. 1. (Top row) D5, D4, (bottom row) D3, and D2 distorted webpage/article combinations for the Al Jazeera webpage and its paired article.

6.5 Measuring the Success of the Distortion Process

To ensure that the distorted webpage/article combinations for each website reflected a range from professional to unprofessional, a pre-test evaluation was undertaken. Twelve participants were presented with the D5-D1 distorted webpage/article combinations from each website in random order, and were tasked with ranking them from most to least professional. D0 was not included as it is a plain text version of the news article, while the D6s were not included as they are just branded versions of the D5s. Cronbach's Alpha [16], showed a high level of consistency in the participants' ordering, see Table 3. Gower's Similarity Coefficient (GSC) [39], was used to calculate the similarity of the participants ordering of the five webpage/article combinations to the 'correct' or intended order. GSC is usually used for calculating distance for data with mixed variables. However, it has been shown to work for ordinal type data [4,49], and has even been extended for such [90]. GSC analysis showed a high level of similarity when then the Dissimilarity Threshold (DT) was set to 0.50, which allows for one or two differences in order and position. The GSC results show that overall, most pre-test participants arranged the five distorted webpage/article combinations for each website in roughly the correct order (D5 to D1).

Table 3. Cronbach's Alpha and Gower's similarity coefficient scores.

Website Assigned	Cronbach's Alpha	GSC DT: 0.95	GSC DT: 0.75	GSC DT: 0.50
Guardian	.948	3	5	12
Economist	.891	1	5	11
Al Jazeera	.961	4	8	12
Telegraph	.969	2	5	11
Spectator	.950	4	4	11
BBC	.893	1	3	12
Independent	.897	3	5	12
New Statesman	.848	2	9	12
Reuters	.979	4	4	9

6.6 Crowdsourcing, Statistical Power Analysis, and Validity

Participants were recruited through the Prolific Academic[2] marketplace and paid £1.25. Participants were over 18 with English as their first language. Participation was limited to the US to increase the homogeneity of the data and because the experiment assumptions were based on a US population. To ensure balance in age, the experiment was run in three iterations to collect data from different age groups, over four days in late August 2017. In total, 508 participants completed the experiment. 47 submissions were rejected for failing one or both attention questions. 32 were rejected for having missing or erroneous completion codes and/or for completing the experiment within 1–2 min, indicating automated bots at work. 10 were rejected due to the participants rating >4 webpage/distortion combinations as having 0 bias. 10 were rejected due to having missing data. The last 4 submissions were rejected to balance the dataset. Therefore, the final dataset consisted of 405 submissions, yielding 45 participant bias ratings for each distorted webpage/article combination. A post hoc statistical power analysis for ANOVA: fixed effects, special, main effects and interactions using G*Power revealed a >.95 Actual Power to detect a strong effect size of 0.24 with the 405 submissions. Four actions were taken to increase validity. These included instruction tasks, attention questions, comparative re-evaluation, and the selection of un-emotive content. These are described in more detail in [104].

[2] www.prolific.co.

6.7   Instructions, Definition of Bias, and VAS Rating Scale

During recruitment participants were informed that *"In this study, you will be asked to rate, from 0 to 100, how biased different online news articles are. 0 being unbiased and 100 being extremely biased."*. Bias was defined as *"Deliberate or accidental slant by the journalist, editor or publication to distort reality"*. These were reiterated during the instruction tasks. A Visual Analogue Scale (VAS) from 0–100 was used to measure bias. This was placed below each distorted webpage/article combination. Above each VAS was the instruction *"Please rate how Biased this News Article is. 0 being unbiased and 100 being extremely Biased"* The left and right of the VAS was anchored with 0 and 100 with the headings *"Unbiased"* and *"Biased"* respectively. Further detail on this is provided in [104].

7   Participant Profile

N = 405: Male 51.4%, Female 47.2%, Other 1.4%. Mean age 36.48. Participants were spread across 44 US states and Washington D.C. Education and Occupation revealed a highly educated, mostly professional sample with 57% having completed a four-year degree or higher. Internet usage was extremely high with the largest group, 31.11%, using the Internet for >8 hours per day. Participants regularly accessed news via. Radio: 25.43%, Television: 51.11%, Print: 25.68%, Internet: 95.56%, Social Media: 61.73%, Other: 0.74, and None: 0.74%.

8   Statistical Analysis

A 9 × 7, two-way repeated measures ANOVA was undertaken using the Bonferroni correction for multiple comparisons. An analysis of the studentized residuals for data points ± SD revealed no outliers. A Shapiro-Wilk test ($p > .05$) for normality on the studentized residuals revealed 40% was not normally distributed. However, the Shapiro-Wilk test is considered especially sensitive to deviations from normality on data sets >50. As this dataset has 405, a visual inspection of QQ plots was undertaken which showed that, of the 40%, half was not normally distributed. Due to the central limit theorem, when N ≥ 30, one-way ANOVAs can still provide valid results even when the distribution of the data is very non-normal. ANOVA are also considered fairly robust to deviations from normality. Mauchly's Test of Sphericity (MTS) ($p > .05$) indicated that the assumption of sphericity had been violated for the two-way interaction. Consequently, the Greenhouse-Geisser correction is reported rather than the Huynh-Feldt as epsilon (ϵ) was <0.75. The two-way ANOVA revealed no statistically significant two-way interaction between webpage/article combinations and distortions, $F(23.22, 1021.79) = .861$, $p = .655$. This was expected as the experiment was designed to measure the impact of distortions on each webpage/article combination.

8.1 Main Effects

The **main effects of webpage/article combinations** test showed a statistically significant difference $F(6.60, 290.28) = 80.38$, p <.0005. This was a likely due to slight variances in the level of effect of each distortion at each stage on each website. As the focus was on investigating the impact of distortions, further exploration via **simple main effects of webpage/article combinations** were not undertaken. The **main effects of distortions** test showed that there was a statistically significant difference $F(5.46, 240.42) = 12.24$, p < .0005. Thus, **simple main effects of distortions** are further explored in the next section.

8.2 Simple Main Effects of Distortions

While simple main effects of distortions would not usually be explored without a significant two-way ANOVA, the focus is comparing the distorted webpage/article combinations and the D0 controls to each other. In SPSS, simple main effects are undertaken by performing multiple one-way repeated measures ANOVAs. Alternatively, one could perform multiple paired samples t-tests, however the increased validity of the one-way ANOVA due to the option of the Bonferroni correction is preferred. The data assumptions required for two-way ANOVAs are also valid for one-way ANOVAs.

The **simple main effects of distortions** test revealed four significant results. Telegraph (D1–D6), Independent (D1–D6 and D0–D1), and the Spectator (D0–D1). Detailed results for these are presented below. As there were no significant results for the Guardian, Economist, New Statesman, Al Jazeera, BBC, or Reuters, their simple main effects of distortions are not shown below in detail. However, the Mean bias rating, Standard Deviation and Standard Error for each are shown in Table 4. The Means are also graphed in Fig. 2.

Telegraph: MTS (p > .05) was met for the one-way interaction, $X^2(2) = 9.632$, p = .974. Mean bias rating for distortions was significantly different for the Telegraph, $F(6, 264) = 4.294$, p < .0005, partial $\eta^2 = .089$. An analysis of the pairwise comparisons showed a decrease in perceived bias from D1, 59.44 ± 25.07 to D6, 41.00 ± 26.70 (95% CI 1.71 to 35.17), p = .019.

Independent: MTS (p > .05) was met for the one-way interaction, $X^2(2) = 26.595$, p = .148. Mean bias rating for distortions was significantly different for the Independent, $F(6, 264) = 3.328$, p = .004, partial $\eta^2 = .070$. An analysis of the pairwise comparisons showed a decrease in perceived bias from D1 44.62 ± 24.96 to D0 26.98 ± 24.16 (95% CI 2.66 to 32.62), p = .009. Pairwise analysis showed a second significant reduction in bias from D1 44.62 ± 24.96 to D6 27.84 ± 25.28 (95% CI 0.85 to 32.70), p = .031.

Spectator: MTS (p > .05) was met for the one-way interaction, $X^2(2) = 13.221$, p = .868. Mean bias rating for distortions was not significantly different for the Spectator, $F(6, 264) = 1.725$, p = .115, partial $\eta^2 = .038$. While no significant difference was revealed in the simple main effects, an analysis of the pairwise comparisons showed a significant decrease in perceived bias from D1 $53.04 \pm$

28.88 to D0 36.02 ± 26.99 (95% CI 0.054 to 33.991), p = .049. This is likely due to the different sensitivities of the two tests.

Table 4. Results of one-way repeated measures ANOVAs - simple main effects for distortions with the Bonferroni correction for multiple comparisons.

	D0 Control	D1	D2	D3	D4	D5 Original Unbranded	D6 Original Branded
	← H2 Comparison →	← H1 Comparison →					
Guardian	M 70.51 SD 29.07 SE 4.33	M 76.91 SD 19.22 SE 2.87	M 74.04 SD 21.46 SE 3.20	M 74.47 SD 21.34 SE 3.18	M 63.13 SD 31.64 SE 4.72	M 63.29 SD 27.75 SE 4.14	M 64.96 SD 27.37 SE 4.08
Telegraph	M 54.27 SD 27.91 SE 4.16	M 59.44 SD 25.07 SE 3.74	M 59.53 SD 24.10 SE 3.59	M 58.98 SD 27.83 SE 4.15	M 43.18 SD 28.28 SE 4.22	M 44.60 SD 30.07 SE 4.48	M 41.00 SD 26.70 SE 3.98
		F 4.294 p .019					F 4.294 p .019
Independent	M 26.98 SD 24.16 SE 3.60	M 44.62 SD 24.96 SE 3.72	M 35.33 SD 24.11 SE 3.59	M 38.84 SD 25.96 SE 3.87	M 30.04 SD 23.38 SE 3.49	M 30.40 SD 27.54 SE 4.11	M 27.84 SD 25.28 SE 3.77
	F 3.328 p .009	F 3.328 p .009					
		F 3.328 p .031					F 3.328 p .031
Economist	M 30.27 SD 27.53 SE 4.10	M 46.04 SD 29.72 SE 4.43	M 43.09 SD 30.47 SE 4.54	M 41.84 SD 28.14 SE 4.20	M 42.27 SD 32.74 SE 4.88	M 41.00 SD 26.96 SE 4.02	M 36.18 SD 28.10 SE 4.19
Spectator	M 36.02 SD 27.00 SE 4.02	M 53.04 SD 28.89 SE 4.31	M 50.33 SD 26.75 SE 3.99	M 46.36 SD 30.03 SE 4.48	M 48.22 SD 28.71 SE 4.28	M 41.80 SD 31.12 SE 4.64	M 45.73 SD 29.02 SE 4.33
	F 1.725 p .049	F 1.725 p .049					
New Statesman	M 20.02 SD 25.49 SE 3.80	M 31.73 SD 29.03 SE 4.33	M 31.11 SD 29.07 SE 4.33	M 28.00 SD 29.59 SE 4.41	M 32.36 SD 25.38 SE 3.78	M 19.47 SD 17.92 SE 2.67	M 23.56 SD 24.71 SE 3.68
Al Jazeera	M 42.78 SD 30.59 SE 4.56	M 54.20 SD 29.99 SE 4.47	M 52.09 SD 24.59 SE 3.67	M 50.58 SD 31.01 SE 4.62	M 40.51 SD 29.64 SE 4.42	M 47.87 SD 28.57 SE 4.26	M 45.29 SD 27.65 SE 4.12
BBC	M 31.87 SD 28.67 SE 4.27	M 41.51 SD 27.61 SE 4.12	M 37.09 SD 27.58 SE 4.11	M 37.13 SD 27.77 SE 3.39	M 41.87 SD 24.67 SE 3.68	M 26.53 SD 26.31 SE 3.92	M 32.78 SD 30.76 SE 4.59
Reuters	M 22.36 SD 25.02 SE 3.73	M 33.33 SD 27.71 SE 4.13	M 25.69 SD 25.86 SE 3.86	M 25.58 SD 28.18 SE 4.20	M 24.07 SD 22.56 SE 3.36	M 23.49 SD 25.27 SE 3.77	M 22.53 SD 26.60 SE 3.97

9   Results

H1: H_0 Perceived bias will not be decreased due to an increase in the professionalism of the news webpage's aesthetics.
H1: H_A Perceived bias will be decreased due to an increase in the professionalism of the news webpage's aesthetics.

The impact of increasingly professional aesthetics to reduce the perception of bias in news articles is evident in Table 4 and Fig. 2. While there were some slight

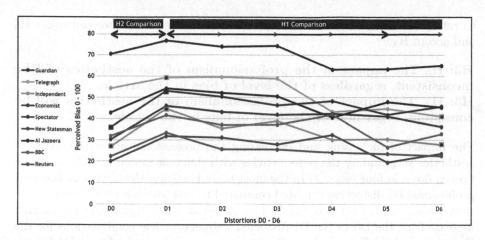

Fig. 2. Graph of the mean bias scores from Table 4 for the nine webpage/article combinations.

individual inconsistencies, overall the perception of bias decreased in each webpage/article combination by an average of: D1 to D2 (3.61%); D2 to D3 (0.73%); D3 to D4 (4.01%), and D4 to D5 (3.02%). Combined, this 11.37% decrease in perceived bias was virtually identical to the average 11.75% increase from D0 to D1. This effect is common across all nine webpage/article combinations and across articles with different levels of bias. This demonstrates that as the professionalism of the aesthetics of a news webpage increases, the perception of bias in the news article it contains decreases.

While there were no significant results between the D1 and D5, there is between the D1 and D6 distortions. D6 is simply a branded version of D5 with similar mean bias scores. It is also worth noting that if the D1 distortions were made more unprofessional, there would likely have been several significant results further proving the impact of professional aesthetics on decreasing the perception of bias. Therefore, based on these results we can reject H_0 and accept H_A.

H2: H_0 Perceived bias will not be increased due to a decrease in the professionalism of news webpage's aesthetics.
H2: H_A Perceived bias will be increased due to a decrease in the professionalism of news webpage's aesthetics.

As can be seen in Table 4 and Fig. 2, there is a marked difference in perceived bias ratings between the D0 ground truth controls and their respective least professional D1 versions. The average increase in perceived bias was 11.75%. This increase is both large and common. It was also significant in the Independent and the Spectator, see Table 4. This demonstrates that unprofessional webpage aesthetics surrounding a news article increases perceived bias when compared to ground truth versions of the same article. This effect is common across all nine news websites and news articles with different levels of bias. This is despite the participants being directed multiple times, including via two Instruction Tasks, to rate perceived bias in the news article only. Consequently, we can reject H_0 and accept H_A.

H3: H_0 The impact of the professionalism of the aesthetics will be inconsistent, regardless of the level of bias in the article.
H3: H_A The impact of the professionalism of the aesthetics will be consistent, regardless of the level of bias in the article.

The impact of increasing and decreasing the professionalism of the webpage aesthetics surrounding the news articles with different amounts of bias can be broken down in four ways. 1) In the most biased articles, the impact of the least professional D1 distortion is muted compared to articles with lower levels of perceived bias, see Table 4 and Fig. 2. This is visible when comparing the smaller increase from the D0 to the D1 distorted webpage/article combinations for the Guardian and the Telegraph, to the larger increases from the D0 to D1 for the other seven webpage/article combinations. This would suggest that it is harder to make an already highly biased article appear more biased by its aesthetics. 2) Conversely, it also appears that it is easier to make news articles with lower levels of bias appear more biased due to unprofessional aesthetics. This is evident in Fig. 2 where the webpage/article combinations with the least amount of bias registered the greatest increase from D0 to D1. This means that high-quality news organizations who try to disseminate unbiased news have the most to lose from the unprofessional presentation of news articles. 3) Worryingly for consumers, the results of the experiment demonstrate that aesthetically professional webpages have the greatest impact on reducing the perception of bias in the most biased news articles. This is visible in the large reduction in perceived bias for the Guardian and the Telegraph, and to a lesser extent Al Jazeera, from their D1s to their respective D5/D6s in comparison to the smaller reduction the other six webpage/article combinations received. 4) Notwithstanding the above, overall, the impact of increasing and decreasing the professionalism of the aesthetic of each webpage/article combination on the perception of bias in the news articles they contain, was largely consistent.

Based the results in Table 4 and Fig. 2, the overall impact of the level of professionalism of the aesthetics of a news webpage is largely consistent across news articles with different levels of bias. Although the impact of unprofessional aesthetics is muted and the impact of professional aesthetics is exaggerated on the most biased webpage/article combinations, overall the effect of each level of distortion was fairly consistent. This is most evident in the graph presented in Fig. 2. Consequently, it is possible to reject H_0 and accept H_A.

9.1 Implications for News Website Designers, Online Editors, and Journalists

With the current focus on the quality and veracity of news, especially online, news website designers, online editors, and journalists, need to be fully aware that any reduction in the professionalism of the aesthetics of news webpages, can increase the perception of bias in the news articles they contain. Although uncommon, some of the issues introduced in this experiment to reduce the professionalism of a news webpage's aesthetic can occasionally be seen in the webpages of high-quality news agencies. These issues can be introduced in six ways. 1) Poor design. 2) Sub-standard coding. This often manifests itself through lack of robustness to different types of content or screen widths. 3) Not checking newly posted content to confirm it does not break standard templates and conforms to style guidelines. 4) Poorly integrated third-party content or services. 5) Using miss sized or stretched images with low DPI. 6) Lack of maintenance.

Decreasing the professionalism of a webpage's visual aesthetic, and thus increasing the perception of bias in the news articles they contain, can have long term consequences. As Fico has previously demonstrated, as the perception of bias in a news article increases, the perception of the credibility of the news agency behind it decreases [26]. They are therefore likely to turn to one of the many alternative sources of news online.

9.2 Implications for Consumers

The core concern for news consumers is that biased news could be perceived as being less biased by presenting it in an aesthetically professional manner. Conversely, unbiased news articles could be considered more biased due to unprofessional aesthetics. News consumers need to be aware that the visual characteristics of a news website's design or webpage's aesthetic such as professionalism may influence their perception of the news they consume. While this study demonstrated the impact of professional aesthetics on the perception of bias, other visual characteristics of a news website's design or a webpage's aesthetic such as seriousness, trustworthiness, boldness, gaudiness, traditional, conservative etc., could be similarly affecting their perception of news articles.

10   Discussion

This research was undertaken under the supposition that news webpage's aesthetics impact the perception of bias within a news article. This was based on the knowledge that a website's design and individual structural features have previously been shown to impact perceived credibility. Bias is a core dimension and measure of credibility, especially when judging news online [29].

The credibility of a news website or news article is judged by a host of features, including message features such as judgements of information quality and argument quality which in turn are judged on balance, objectivity etc. Yet, a large proportion of empirical studies have focused on the means of presentation of information on judgements of credibility, especially online. Most of the ten MTFS explaining judgements of credibility online also highlight the importance of the visual presentation and heuristic evaluation of such. Eight out of the ten MTFS rely on the underlying theory provided by the ELM or HSM [12,88]. They maintain that users can form judgements of credibility by the peripheral route or heuristic strategy, which rely on visual cues.

This study has demonstrated that like credibility, perceived bias in news articles on the Internet is partially judged heuristically. This finding has long term ramifications for the domain. Historically, many studies into bias in the news have not focused on the content of the message, but on its means of dissemination. This includes visual analysis of political imagery, area or duration of coverage, or the influence of news anchors. However, despite this very little work has been done on the dissemination of news online. This research addresses this imbalance.

Another critical contribution absent from the body of knowledge is the lack of cognitive models explaining how judgements of bias are formed when consuming news online, similar to the ten MTFS of credibility judgement highlighted earlier. Such contributions are important as they form the theoretical underpinnings which subsequent empirical works can be based on. This is a definite lacuna in the literature. A future aim is to present such a model. A second aim is to understand the process leading to judgments of bias in news articles.

Traditionally the consumption of news was a definitive act. Watching the 6 o'clock or reading the morning paper. Consumers were limited in the news they were exposed to. Whether it was by the papers their local shop stocked and they selected each day or each week, or by the news which the editors and journalists covered [115], or their access to radio or television stations. News consumption was limited to local events or national events of importance which trickled down to available mediums and formats. In comparison, today's consumers are exposed to an almost unlimited range of local, national, and international news. While many local newspapers failed, they have been replaced by additional radio stations and television channels, many of which now offer always on, 24-h news, with headlines at 15-min intervals. Smartphones have also enabled access to an almost unlimited range of news from around the world, and because of push notifications, the user is alerted within minutes of an important event or a news story, often relating to a topic which they have expressed interest in previously. Consequently, many news consumers do not have the time to properly read and digest this constant stream of information. News is scanned, or headlines and notifications are perused and dismissed with impunity. Many news consumers visit news websites for minutes or less multiple times throughout the day to *"'snack' or 'graze' on the news"* [75,82]. This rapid consumption provides the consumer with a visual snapshot of what is important and how much it is being discussed. Due to time constraints and the ease of rapidly traversing though multiple articles quickly online, news consumers now regularly scan the news and individual articles to get a sense of how a subject is being treated. Thus, they heavily rely on rapid heuristic evaluation and are more reliant on the visual presentation. Consequently, further investigation is required to ascertain whether other news website design or aesthetics characteristics may be influencing the perception of the message within the news article.

11 Conclusion

Bias is one of the most destructive forces on the credibility of successful mainstream news websites. Increased perception of bias in a news article decreases the credibility of the news organisation behind it, resulting in consumers turning to alternative sources. News agencies and news website designers strive to convey a sense of professionalism in the design and aesthetic of their websites. Historically judgements of professionalism of a news organization were entwined with their reputation and the quality of the news output. However, with changing news consumption practices, news website design and aesthetics have become increasingly important. This study has demonstrated a negative correlation between the professionalism of the aesthetics of news webpages and the perception of bias in news articles. This effect was common across nine news websites and across news articles with different levels of bias. This study provides further evidence that like credibility, perceived bias in a news article online is at least partially judged visually or heuristically.

Acknowledgements. This research was conducted with the financial support of Science Foundation Ireland under Grant Agreement No. 13/RC/2106 at the ADAPT SFI Research Centre at Trinity College Dublin. The ADAPT SFI Centre for Digital Media Technology is funded by Science Foundation Ireland through the SFI Research Centres Programme and is co-funded under the European Regional Development Fund (ERDF) through Grant Number 13/RC/2106.

References

1. Abdulla, R.A., Garrison, B., Salwen, M., Driscoll, P., Casey, D.: The credibility of newspapers, television news, and online news. Artículo presentado en la Association for Education in Journalism and Mass Communication (2002). http://www.com.miami.edu/car/miamibeach1.pdf
2. An, S., Bergen, L.: Advertiser pressure on daily newspapers: a survey of advertising sales executives. J. Advert. **36**(2), 111–121 (2007). https://doi.org/10.2753/JOA0091-3367360208. Accessed 17 Mar 2018
3. Babad, E.: Preferential treatment in television interviewing: evidence from non-verbal behavior. Polit. Commun. **16**(3), 337–358 (1999). https://doi.org/10.1080/105846099198668. Accessed 22 May 2018
4. Bacher, J., Wenzig, K., Vogler, M.: SPSS two step cluster - a first evaluation **2004–2** (2004)
5. Barrett, A.W., Barrington, L.W.: Bias in newspaper photograph selection. Polit. Res. Q. **58**(4), 609–618 (2005). 00038. http://prq.sagepub.com/content/58/4/609.short
6. Beam, R.A.: Journalism professionalism as an organizational-level concept. Assoc. Educ. J. Mass Commun. **121**, 43 (1990)
7. Bernays, E.L.: Propaganda. Ig Publishing, New York (1928)
8. Bernstein, D.: Israel in the media: a guide to producing effective media critiques. The American Jewish Committie, June 2004. http://www.kintera.org/atf/cf/%7B42D75369-D582-4380-8395-D25925B85EAF%7D/Israel%20in%20the%20Media.pdf. Accessed 17 Mar 2018

9. Brandenburg, H.: Political bias in the Irish media: a quantitative study of campaign coverage during the 2002 general election. Irish Polit. Stud. **20**(3), 297–322 (2005). https://doi.org/10.1080/07907180500359350. Accessed 16 Feb 2018

10. Brandenburg, H.: Party strategy and media bias: a quantitative analysis of the 2005 UK election campaign. J. Election. Public Opin. Part. **16**(2), 157–178 (2006). https://doi.org/10.1080/13689880600716027. Accessed 15 Feb 2018

11. Cassidy, W.P.: Online news credibility: an examination of the perceptions of newspaper journalists. J. Comput.-Mediat. Commun. **12**(2), 478–498 (2007). https://doi.org/10.1111/j.1083-6101.2007.00334.x. https://academic.oup.com/jcmc/artic le/12/2/478/4583013

12. Chaiken, S.: Heuristic versus systematic information processing and the use of source versus message cues in persuasion. J. Pers. Soc. Psychol. **39**(5), 752–766 (1980). 03839. https://www.unc.edu/ fbaum/teaching/articles/jpsp-1980-Chaik en.pdf

13. Chiagouris, L., Long, M.M., Plank, R.E.: The consumption of online news: the relationship of attitudes toward the site and credibility. J. Internet Commer. **7**(4), 528–549 (2008)

14. Chomsky, N.: Media Control: The Spectacular Achievements of Propaganda. Open Media Series. Seven Stories Press, New York (2002)

15. Chung, C.J., Nam, Y., Stefanone, M.A.: Exploring online news credibility: the relative influence of traditional and technological factors. J. Comput.-Mediat. Commun. **17**(2), 171–186 (2012). https://doi.org/10.1111/j.1083-6101.2011.01565.x. Accessed 18 Aug 2012

16. Cronbach, L.J.: Coefficient alpha and the internal structure of tests. Psychometrika **16**(3), 297–334 (1951). https://doi.org/10.1007/BF02310555

17. D'Alessio, D., Allen, M.: Media bias in presidential elections: a meta-analysis. J. Commun. **50**(4), 133–156 (2000). https://doi.org/10.1111/j.1460-2466.2000.tb02866.x. Accessed 10 Feb 2018

18. DellaVigna, S., Kaplan, E.: The fox news effect: media bias and voting. Q. J. Econ. **122**(3), 1187–1234 (2007)

19. Deuze, M.: Online journalism: Modelling the first generation of news media on the world wide web. First Monday **6**(10) (2001)

20. Di Tella, R., Franceschelli, I.: Government advertising and media coverage of corruption scandals. Am. Econ. J. Appl. Econ. **3**(4), 119–151 (2011). http://www.jstor.org/stable/41288653. Accessed 16 Feb 2018

21. Druckman, J.N., Parkin, M.: The impact of media bias: how editorial slant affects voters. J. Polit. **67**(4), 1030–1049 (2005)

22. Earl, J., Martin, A., McCarthy, J.D., Soule, S.A.: The use of newspaper data in the study of collective action. Ann. Rev. Sociol. **30**, 65–80 (2004). 00546. http://www.jstor.org/stable/29737685

23. Ekström, M., Eriksson, G., Johansson, B., Wikström, P.: Biased interrogations? J. Stud. **14**(3), 423–439 (2013). https://doi.org/10.1080/1461670X.2012.689488. Accessed 18 Mar 2018

24. Esser, F.: Dimensions of political news cultures: sound bite and image bite news in France, Germany, Great Britain, and the United States. Int. J. Press/Polit. **13**(4), 401–428 (2008). https://doi.org/10.1177/1940161208323691. Accessed 17 Mar 2018

25. Fahmy, S., Johnson, T.J.: "how we performe": embedded journalists' attitudes and perceptions towards covering the Iraq war. J. Mass Commun. Q. **82**(2), 301–317 (2005). https://doi.org/10.1177/107769900508200205. Accessed 17 Feb 2018

26. Fico, F., Richardson, J.D., Edwards, S.M.: Influence of story structure on perceived story bias and news organization credibility. Mass Commun. Soc. **7**(3), 301–318 (2004). https://doi.org/10.1207/s15327825mcs0703_3

27. Flanagin, A.J., Metzger, M.J.: The role of site features, user attributes, and information verification behaviors on the perceived credibility of web-based information. New Media Soc. **9**(2), 319–342 (2007). https://doi.org/10.1177/1461444807075015. 00355. http://nms.sagepub.com/content/9/2/319

28. Fogg, B.J.: Prominence-interpretation theory: explaining how people assess credibility online. In: CHI EA 2003, pp. 722–723. ACM, New York (2003). https://doi.org/10.1145/765891.765951. https://doi.org/10.1145/765891.765951, 00233

29. Fogg, B.J., Soohoo, C., Danielson, D.R., Marable, L., Stanford, J., Tauber, E.R.: How do users evaluate the credibility of web sites?: A study with over 2,500 participants, pp. 1–15 (2003). http://dl.acm.org/citation.cfm?id=997097, 00420

30. Fogg, B.J., Tseng, H.: The elements of computer credibility. In: CHI 1999, pp. 80–87. ACM, New York (1999). https://doi.org/10.1145/302979.303001, 00613

31. Forward, R.: Editorial opinion and the Whitlam government. Politics **12**(1), 136–141 (1977). https://doi.org/10.1080/00323267708401596. Accessed 16 Feb 2018

32. Friedman, H.S., Mertz, T.I., DiMatteo, M.R.: Perceived bias in the facial expressions of television news broadcasters. J. Commun. **30**(4), 103–111 (1980). https://doi.org/10.1111/j.1460-2466.1980.tb02022.x. 00033

33. Fritch, J.W., Cromwell, R.L.: Evaluating internet resources: identity, affiliation, and cognitive authority in a networked world. J. Am. Soc. Inf. Sci. Technol. **52**(6), 499–507 (2001). https://doi.org/10.1002/asi.1081. http://onlinelibrary.wiley.com/doi/10.1002/asi.1081/abstract, 00158

34. Gawronski, B., Creighton, L.A.: Dual-process theories, pp. 282–312 (2013)

35. Gaziano, C., McGrath, K.: Measuring the concept of credibility. J. Q. **63**(3), 451–462 (1986)

36. Gentzkow, M., Shapiro, J.M.: What drives media slant? Evidence from U.S. daily newspapers. Econometrica **78**(1), 35–71 (2010). https://doi.org/10.3982/ECTA7195. https://doi.org/10.3982/ECTA7195/abstract, 00707

37. Gerber, A.S., Karlan, D., Bergan, D.: Does the media matter? A field experiment measuring the effect of newspapers on voting behavior and political opinions. Am. Econ. J.: Appl. Econ. **1**(2), 35–52 (2009)

38. Goodnow, T.: Visual bias in time's "the great divid": a semiotic analysis of Clinton and Obama photographs. Am. Behav. Sci. **54**(4), 406–416 (2010). https://doi.org/10.1177/0002764210381865. Accessed 21 Mar 2018

39. Gower, J.C.: A general coefficient of similarity and some of its properties. Biometrics **27**(4), 857–871 (1971). https://doi.org/10.2307/2528823. https://www.jstor.org/stable/2528823

40. Grabe, M.E., Bucy, E.P.: Image Bite Politics: News and the Visual Framing of Elections. Oxford University Press, Oxford (2009). google-Books-ID: ahISDAAAQBAJ

41. Green-Pedersen, C., Mortensen, P.B., Thesen, G.: The incumbency bonus revisited: causes and consequences of media dominance. Br. J. Polit. Sci. **47**(1), 131–148 (2017)

42. Greenwood, K.: Picturing presidents: a content analysis of photographs of presidents from the pictures of the year. Int. Commun. Assoc. 1–34 (2005)

43. Groeling, T.: Media bias by the numbers: challenges and opportunities in the empirical study of partisan news. Ann. Rev. Polit. Sci. **16**(1), 129–151 (2013). https://doi.org/10.1146/annurev-polisci-040811-115123. http://www.annualreviews.org/doi/abs/10.1146/annurev-polisci-040811-115123, 00017

44. Hackett, R.A.: A hierarchy of access: aspects of source bias in Canadian TV news. J. Q. **62**(2), 256–277 (1985). https://doi.org/10.1177/107769908506200205. Accessed 12 Mar 2018

45. Hays, R.G., Reisner, A.E.: Farm journalists and advertiser influence: pressures on ethical standards. J. Q. **68**(1–2), 172–178 (1991). https://doi.org/10.1177/107769909106800118. Accessed 18 Mar 2018

46. Herman, E.S., Chomsky, N.: Manufacturing Consent: The Political Economy of the Mass Media. Pantheon, New York, reprint edition, January 2002

47. Hilligoss, B., Rieh, S.Y.: Developing a unifying framework of credibility assessment: construct, heuristics, and interaction in context. Inf. Process. Manage. **44**, 1467–1484 (2008). http://rieh.people.si.umich.edu/papers/hilligossipm.pdf, 00258

48. Hovland, C.I., Janis, I.L., Kelley, H.H.: Communication and Persuasion: Psychological Studies of Opinion Change. Yale University Press, London (1953)

49. Hummel, M., Edelmann, D., Kopp-Schneider, A.: Clustering of samples and variables with mixed-type data. PLoS One **12**(11) (2017). https://doi.org/10.1371/journal.pone.0188274. https://www.ncbi.nlm.nih.gov/pmc/articles/PMC5705083/

50. Johnson, T.J., Kaye, B.K.: Cruising is believing?: comparing internet and traditional sources on media credibility measures. J. Mass Commun. Q. **75**(2), 325–340 (1998). 00552

51. Jung, W.S., Chung, M.Y., Rhee, E.S.: The effects of attractiveness and source expertise on online health sites. Health Commun. 1–10 (2017). pMID: 28569543. https://doi.org/10.1080/10410236.2017.1323364

52. Kahn, K.F., Kenney, P.J.: The slant of the news: how editorial endorsements influence campaign coverage and citizens' views of candidates. Am. Polit. Sci. Rev. **96**(2), 381–394 (2002). https://doi.org/10.1017/S0003055402000230. https://www.cambridge.org/core/journals/american-political-science-review/article/slant-of-the-news-how-editorial-endorsements-influence-campaign-coverage-and-citizens-views-of-candidates/71FB7C8336B7B12EB239802C09A37F4DOnline; accessed2018-03-18

53. Karimov, F.P., Brengman, M., Van Hove, L.: The effect of website design dimensions on initial trust: a synthesis of the empirical literature. J. Electron. Commerce Res. **12**(4) (2011)

54. Kenix, L.J.: A converging image? Commercialism and the visual identity of alternative and mainstream news websites. J. Stud. **14**(6), 835–856 (2013)

55. Kenney, K., Simpson, C.: Was coverage of the 1988 presidential race by Washington's two major dailies biased? J. Q. **70**(2), 345–355 (1993). https://doi.org/10.1177/107769909307000210. Accessed 14 Feb 2018

56. Kepplinger, H.M.: Visual biases in television campaign coverage. Commun. Res. **9**(3), 432–446 (1982). https://doi.org/10.1177/009365082009003005. Accessed 17 Mar 2018

57. Kerrick, J.S., Anderson, T.E., Swales, L.B.: Balance and the writer's attitude in news stories and editorials. J. Q. **41**(2), 207–215 (1964). https://doi.org/10.1177/107769906404100207. Accessed 12 Mar 2018

58. Kingsbury, S., Hart, H.: Measuring the ethics of American newspapers iii. Newspaper bias on congressional controversies. J. Bull. **10**(4), 323–342 (1933). https://doi.org/10.1177/107769903301000411. Accessed 12 Mar 2018

59. Klein, M.W., Maccoby, N.: Newspaper objectivity in the 1952 campaign. J. Bull. **31**(3), 285–296 (1954). https://doi.org/10.1177/107769905403100301. Accessed 14 Feb 2018

60. Kriesberg, M.: Soviet news in the "new york times". Public Opin. Q. **10**(4), 540–564 (1946). https://doi.org/10.1093/poq/10.4.540. https://academic.oup.com/poq/article/10/4/540/1861359. Accessed 12 Mar 2018
61. Lavie, T., Tractinsky, N.: Assessing dimensions of perceived visual aesthetics of web sites. Int. J. Hum. Comput. Stud. **60**(3), 269–298 (2004)
62. Leccese, M.: Online information sources of political blogs. J. Mass Commun. Q.; Thousand Oaks **86**(3), 578–593 (2009). https://search.proquest.com/docview/216940194/abstract/7ECF2800BBE4A4APQ/1
63. Lott, J.R., Hassett, K.A.: Is newspaper coverage of economic events politically biased? Public Choice **160**(1–2), 65–108 (2014). https://doi.org/10.1007/s11127-014-0171-5. Accessed 24 Apr 2018
64. Lowry, D.T.: Measures of network news bias in the 1972 presidential campaign. J. Broadcast. **18**, 387 (1973). http://heinonline.org/HOL/Page?handle=hein.journals/jbem18&id=389&div=&collection=journals, 00012
65. Lucassen, T., Muilwijk, R., Noordzij, M.L., Schraagen, J.M.: Topic familiarity and information skills in online credibility evaluation. J. Am. Soc. Inf. Sci. Technol. **64**(2), 254–264 (2013). https://doi.org/10.1002/asi.22743. http://onlinelibrary.wiley.com/doi/10.1002/asi.22743/abstract, 00025
66. McCarthy, J.D., McPhail, C.: The institutionalization of protest in the united states. In: Meyer, D.S., Tarrow, S. (eds.) The Social Movement Society: Contentious Politics for a New Century, pp. 83–110. Rowman and Littlefield Publishers (1997). Google-Books-ID: g0M3AgAAQBAJ
67. McCarthy, J.D., McPhail, C., Smith, J.: Images of protest: Dimensions of selection bias in media coverage of Washington demonstrations, 1982 and 1991. Am. Sociol. Rev. **61**(3), 478–499 (1996). https://doi.org/10.2307/2096360. http://www.jstor.org/stable/2096360?origin=crossref. Accessed 10 Apr 2018
68. McCarthy, J.D., McPhail, C., Smith, J., Crishock, L.: Electronic and print media representations of Washington D.C. demonstrations, 1982 and 1991. In: Rucht, D., Koopmans, R., Neidhardt, F. (eds.) Acts of Dissent: New Developments in the Study of Protest, pp. 113–130. Rowman and Littlefield, Lanham (1999). http://d-scholarship.pitt.edu/20703/. Accessed 22 Apr 2018
69. Meadors, J.D., Murray, C.B.: Measuring nonverbal bias through body language responses to stereotypes. J. Nonverbal Behav. **38**(2), 209–229 (2014). https://doi.org/10.1007/s10919-013-0172-y. Accessed 22 May 2018
70. Merron, J., Gaddy, G.D.: Editorial endorsements and news play: bias in coverage of ferraro's finances. J. Q. **63**(1), 127–137 (1986). https://doi.org/10.1177/107769908606300119. Accessed 15 Feb 2018
71. Metzger, M.J.: Making sense of credibility on the web: models for evaluating online information and recommendations for future research. J. Am. Soc. Inf. Sci. Technol. **58**(13), 2078–2091 (2007). https://doi.org/10.1002/asi.20672. https://doi.org/10.1002/asi.20672/abstract, 00506
72. Metzger, M.J., Flanagin, A.J.: Psychological approaches to credibility assessment online (2015). http://www.comm.ucsb.edu/faculty/flanagin/CV/MetzgerandFlanagin2015(HPCT).pdf, 00002
73. Miller, A., Coleman, R., Granberg, D.: Tv anchors, elections & bias: a longitudinal study of the facial expressions of Brokaw rather Jennings. Vis. Commun. Q. **14**(4), 244–257 (2007). https://doi.org/10.1080/15551390701730232. Accessed 20 Jan 2018
74. Mitchell, A., Simmons, K., Matsa, K.E., Silver, L.: People around world want unbiased news. Technical report, 1615 L St. NW, Suite 800 Washington, DC 20036 USA (2018). http://www.pewglobal.org/2018/01/11/. Accessed 08 Jan 2019

75. Molyneux, L.: Mobile news consumption: a habit of snacking. Digit. J. **6**(5), 634–650 (2018). https://doi.org/10.1080/21670811.2017.1334567
76. Moriarty, S.E., Garramone, G.M.: A study of newsmagazine photographs of the 1984 presidential campaign. J. Q. **63**(4), 728–734 (1986). https://doi.org/10.1177/107769908606300408. Accessed 13 Feb 2018
77. Moriarty, S.E., Popovich, M.N.: Newsmagazine visuals and the 1988 presidential election. J. Q. **68**(3), 371–380 (1991). https://doi.org/10.1177/107769909106800307. Accessed 21 Jan 2018
78. Moss, P.: Words, words, words: radio news discourses and how they work. Eur. J. Commun. **3**(2), 207–230 (1988). https://doi.org/10.1177/0267323188003002006. Accessed 24 Mar 2018
79. Mullainathan, S., Shleifer, A.: The market for news. Am. Econ. Rev. **95**(4), 1031–1053 (2005). http://www.jstor.org/stable/4132704. Accessed 13 Feb 2018
80. Mullen, B., et al.: Newcasters' facial expressions and voting behavior of viewers: can a smile elect a president? J. Pers. Soc. Psychol. **51**(2), 291 (1986)
81. Narwal, V., et al.: Automated assistants to identify and prompt action on visual news bias. arXiv:1702.06492 [cs], pp. 2796–2801 (2017). https://doi.org/10.1145/3027063.3053227, http://arxiv.org/abs/1702.06492
82. Nelson, J.L., Lei, R.F.: The effect of digital platforms on news audience behavior. Digit. J. **6**(5), 619–633 (2018). https://doi.org/10.1080/21670811.2017.1394202
83. Newhagen, J., Nass, C.: Differential criteria for evaluating credibility of newspapers and tv news. J. Q. **66**(2), 277–284 (1989)
84. Nokelainen, T., Kanniainen, J.: Coverage bias in business news: evidence and methodological implications. Manage. Res. Rev. **41**(4), 487–503 (2018). https://doi.org/10.1108/MRR-02-2017-0048. Accessed 27 Apr 2018
85. Park, S., Kang, S., Chung, S., Song, J.: NewsCube: delivering multiple aspects of news to mitigate media bias. In: CHI 2009, pp. 443–452. ACM, New York (2009). https://doi.org/10.1145/1518701.1518772, 00036
86. Park, S., Ko, M., Kim, J., Choi, H., Song, J.: Newscube2. 0: an exploratory design of a social news website for media bias mitigation (2011). http://nclab.kaist.ac.kr/papers/Conference/NC2.pdf, 00003
87. Patterson, T.E., Donsbagh, W.: News decisions: journalists as partisan actors. Polit. Commun. **13**(4), 455–468 (1996). https://doi.org/10.1080/10584609.1996.9963131. 00306
88. Petty, R.E., Cacioppo, J.T.: The elaboration likelihood model of persuasion. In: Petty, R.E., Cacioppo, J.T. (eds.) Communication and Persuasion. Springer Series in Social Psychology, pp. 1–24. Springer, New York (1986). https://doi.org/10.1007/978-1-4612-4964-1_1
89. Pfau, M., et al.: Embedding journalists in military combat units: impact on newspaper story frames and tone. J. Mass Commun. Q. **81**(1), 74–88 (2004). https://doi.org/10.1177/107769900408100106. Accessed 18 Mar 2018
90. Podani, J.: Extending Gower's general coefficient of similarity to ordinal characters. TAXON **48**(2), 331–340 (1999). https://doi.org/10.2307/1224438. https://onlinelibrary.wiley.com/doi/abs/10.2307/1224438
91. Price, C.J.: Interfering owners or meddling advertisers: how network television news correspondents feel about ownership and advertiser influence on news stories. J. Media Econ. **16**(3), 175–188 (2003). https://doi.org/10.1207/S15327736ME1603_3. Accessed 17 Mar 2018

92. Puglisi, R., Snyder, J.M.: Newspaper coverage of political scandals. J. Polit. **73**(3), 931–950 (2011). https://doi.org/10.1017/S0022381611000569. https://www.jour nals.uchicago.edu/doi/abs/10.1017/S0022381611000569. Accessed 18 May 2018

93. Reuter, J., Zitzewitz, E.: Do ads influence editors? Advertising and bias in the financial media. Q. J. Econ. **121**(1), 197–227 (2006). https://doi.org/10.1093/qje/121.1.197. https://academic.oup.com/qje/article/121/1/197/1849013. Accessed 21 Jan 2018

94. Rieh, S.Y.: Judgment of information quality and cognitive authority in the web. J. Am. Soc. Inf. Sci. Technol. **53**(2), 145–161 (2002). https://onlinelibrary.wiley.com/doi/full/10.1002/asi.10017, 00637

95. Robins, D., Holmes, J.: Aesthetics and credibility in web site design. Inf. Process. Manage. **44**(1), 386–399 (2008). https://doi.org/10.1016/j.ipm.2007.02.003. http://www.sciencedirect.com/science/article/pii/S0306457307000568, 00218

96. Robinson, C.: Visual press bias in a multi-party electoral context. Design and Democracy, p. 37 (2016), https://static1.squarespace.com/static/578aa0eac534a56f885f3d9b/t/579db422b8a79bb7da57671c/1469953062061/Visualforpublishing.pdf

97. Rucinski, D.: Personalized bias in news: the potency of the particular? Commun. Res. **19**(1), 91–108 (1992). https://doi.org/10.1177/009365092019001004. Accessed 12 Mar 2018

98. Sachsman, D.B.: A test of 'loading': new measure of bias. J. Q. **47**(4), 759–762 (1970). https://doi.org/10.1177/107769907004700415. http://journals.sagepub.com/doi/10.1177/107769907004700415. Accessed 12 Mar 2018

99. Schindler, J., Krämer, B., Müller, P.: Looking left or looking right? Effects of newspaper layout style on the perception of political news. Eur. J. Commun. **32**(4), 348–366 (2017). https://doi.org/10.1177/0267323117718463. Accessed 17 Mar 2018

100. Schudson, M., Anderson, C.: Objectivity, professionalism, and truth seeking in journalism, pp. 108–121. Routledge (2009)

101. Soloski, J.: News reporting and professionalism: Some constraints on the reporting of the news, vol. 11, pp. 207–228 (1989)

102. Spillane, B., Hoe, I., Brady, M., Wade, V., Lawless, S.: Tabloidization versus credibility: short term gain for long term pain. In: CHI Conference on Human Factors in Computing Systems (CHI 2020), 25–30 April 2020, Honolulu, HI, USA. ACM, April 2020. https://doi.org/10.1145/3313831.3376388

103. Spillane, B., Lawless, S., Wade, V.: Perception of bias: the impact of user characteristics, website design and technical features, WI 2017, pp. 227–236. ACM, New York (2017). https://doi.org/10.1145/3106426.3106474, Accessed 18 Sept 2017

104. Spillane, B., Lawless, S., Wade, V.: Increasing and decreasing perceived bias by distorting the quality of news website design. In: British HCI 2018, Belfast, Northern Ireland, p. 13, July 2018

105. Stempel-III, G.H.: The prestige press covers the 1960 presidential campaign. J. Q. **38**(2), 157–163 (1961). https://doi.org/10.1177/107769906103800201. Accessed 09 Mar 2018

106. Stoodley, B.H.: Bias in reporting the FCC investigation. Public Opin. Q. **24**(1), 92–98 (1960). https://doi.org/10.1086/266933. https://academic.oup.com/poq/article/24/1/92/1824637. Accessed 12 Mar 2018

107. Sundar, S.S.: The main model: a heuristic approach to understanding technology effects on credibility. Digital media, youth, and credibility, pp. 73–100 (2008). http://www.marketingsociale.net/download/modello_MAIN.pdf, 00327

108. Tannenbaum, P.H.: The effect of headlines on the interpretation of news stories. J. Bull. **30**(2), 189–197 (1953). https://doi.org/10.1177/107769905303000206. http://journals.sagepub.com/doi/10.1177/107769905303000206. Accessed 12 Mar 2018

109. Tversky, A., Kahneman, D.: Judgment under uncertainty: heuristics and biases. Science **185**(4157), 1124–1131 (1974). https://doi.org/10.1126/science.185.4157.1124. pMID: 17835457. http://science.sciencemag.org/content/185/4157/1124

110. Van Dijk, T.A.: New(s) Racism: a discourse analytical approach. Ethnic Minorit. Media **37**, 33–49 (2000). http://dare.uva.nl/search?metis.record.id=203737. Accessed 20 Apr 2018

111. Vuontela, S.: Women's hidden agency in the news coverage of the Tibetian riots. Nordlit, pp. 129–142, October 2012. https://doi.org/10.7557/13.2376. https://septentrio.uit.no/index.php/nordlit/article/view/2376

112. Waisbord, S.: Reinventing Professionalism: Journalism and News in Global Perspective. Wiley, Hoboken (2013)

113. Wathen, C.N., Burkell, J.: Believe it or not: factors influencing credibility on the web. J. Am. Soc. Inf. Sci. Technol. **53**(2), 134–144 (2002). http://onlinelibrary.wiley.com/doi/10.1002/asi.10016/full. Accessed 17 Jan 2013

114. Weisbuch, M., Pauker, K., Ambady, N.: The subtle transmission of race bias via televised nonverbal behavior. Science **326**(5960), 1711–1714 (2009). https://doi.org/10.1126/science.1178358. pMID: 20019288. http://science.sciencemag.org/content/326/5960/1711

115. White, D.M.: The "Gate Keeper": a case study in the selection of news. J. Bull. **27**(4), 383–390 (1950). https://doi.org/10.1177/107769905002700403. http://journals.sagepub.com/doi/10.1177/107769905002700403, Accessed 18 Mar 2018

116. Zaller, J.: A Theory of Media Politics: How the Interests of Politicians, Journalists, and Citizens Shape the News. University of Chicago Press (1999). Google-Books-ID: 9KmwXwAACAAJ

117. Zimmerman, J.: Media bias through facial expressions on local Las Vegas television news (2013)

Author Index

Printed in the United States
By Bookmasters